150 Best Jobs for a Secure Future

Part of JIST's Best Jobs® Series

Laurence Shatkin, Ph.D.

Also in JIST's *Best Jobs* Series

- ✳ *Best Jobs for the 21st Century*
- ✳ *150 Best Federal Jobs*
- ✳ *200 Best Jobs for College Graduates*
- ✳ *300 Best Jobs Without a Four-Year Degree*
- ✳ *200 Best Jobs Through Apprenticeships*
- ✳ *50 Best Jobs for Your Personality*
- ✳ *40 Best Fields for Your Career*

- ✳ *225 Best Jobs for Baby Boomers*
- ✳ *250 Best-Paying Jobs*
- ✳ *150 Best Jobs for Your Skills*
- ✳ *150 Best Jobs for a Better World*
- ✳ *200 Best Jobs for Introverts*
- ✳ *10 Best College Majors for Your Personality*
- ✳ *150 Best Low-Stress Jobs*

JIST Works
America's Career Publisher®

150 Best Jobs for a Secure Future

© 2012 by JIST Publishing

Published by JIST Works, an imprint of JIST Publishing
875 Montreal Way
St. Paul, MN 55102

Phone: 800-648-JIST   E-mail: info@jist.com   Website: www.jist.com

---

Some Other Books by Laurence Shatkin, Ph.D.

The Sequel	50 Best Jobs for Your Personality
150 Best Federal Jobs	250 Best-Paying Jobs

Quantity discounts are available for JIST products. Please call 800-648-JIST or visit www.jist.com for a free catalog and more information.

Visit www.jist.com for information on JIST, free job search tips, tables of contents, sample pages, and ordering information on our many products.

Acquisitions Editor: Susan Pines
Development Editor: Stephanie Koutek
Production Editor: Jeanne Clark
Cover and Interior Designer: Aleata Halbig
Cover Image © iStockphoto/Konstantin Yuganov. Used by permission.
Interior Layout: Aleata Halbig
Proofreader: Chuck Hutchinson
Indexer: Cheryl Ann Lenser

Printed in the United States of America

16 15 14 13 12 11   9 8 7 6 5 4 3 2 1

Library of Congresss Cataloging-in-Publication data is on file with the Library of Congress.

ISBN 978-1-59357-889-3

This Is a Big Book, but It Is Very Easy to Use

Are you tired of riding the economic roller coaster? Are you worried that you may become a disposable worker? This book can help your career avoid the ups and downs in the economy.

Every few years the United States economy goes into a slowdown. Experienced workers lose their jobs and young people leaving school have a hard time finding work.

But some jobs and career fields are considered secure because they meet needs that are not diminished even during hard times. These jobs and fields are the focus of this book.

Here you'll find lists of good jobs that are selected and ordered to emphasize those with the highest earnings and the highest demand for workers. Specialized lists arrange these jobs by the level of education or training required and by personality types. You can also see lists of metropolitan areas where the secure jobs are most densely clustered and skills that are most relevant to the secure jobs.

Every job and career field is described in detail in the book, so you can explore the jobs and fields that interest you the most. For the jobs, you'll learn the major work tasks, the important skills, educational programs, fastest-growing industries, and many other informative facts. For the career fields, you'll learn how the field is structured, the jobs with the largest workforces, how people prepare to enter the field, and the job outlook for the field, including trends that affect job security.

You'll also find tips about how to boost your security in your job—ideas that can help you get ahead in both good times and bad.

Using this book, you'll be surprised how quickly you'll get new ideas for careers that are good bets for an unsteady economy and can suit you in many other ways.

Some Things You Can Do with This Book

* Identify secure jobs that don't require you to get additional training or education, perhaps as options for retirement or a second career.

* Develop long-term career plans that may require additional training, education, or experience.

* Explore and select a training or educational program that relates to a career objective unlikely to be affected by economic downturns.

* Prepare for interviews by learning how to connect your work preferences to your career goal.

These are a few of the many ways you can use this book. I hope you find it as interesting to browse as I did to put together. I have tried to make it easy to use and as interesting as occupational information can be.

When you are done with this book, pass it along or tell someone else about it. I wish you well in your career and in your life.

Table of Contents

Summary of Major Sections

Introduction. A short overview to help you better understand and use the book. *Starts on page 1.*

Part I. Why Job Security Matters and How to Achieve It. Explains what a recession is, what makes a job secure, and strategies for keeping your job during hard times or bouncing back from job loss. Learn how to take advantage of well-known economic trends and ensure your job against unforeseen forces. These suggestions are useful for your career no matter what shape the economy is in. *Starts on page 23.*

Part II. Six Career Fields with Security. Describes six career fields that have consistently resisted the periodic ups and downs in the economy. You'll understand what kind of work goes on in each field, what kind of education or training is appropriate, how the earnings compare to those in other fields, and what economic trends are expected to shape the job outlook for the field. *Starts on page 31.*

Part III. The Best Jobs Lists: Jobs with Security. Very useful for exploring career options! Lists are arranged into easy-to-use groups. The first list presents, for each of six secure career fields, the best jobs overall. These jobs are selected to be mostly unaffected by economic downturns and be outstanding in terms of earnings, job growth, and job openings. Additional lists give, for each field, the 20 best-paying secure jobs, the 20 fastest-growing secure jobs, and the 20 secure jobs with the most openings. More-specialized lists follow, presenting jobs that have a high concentration of certain kinds of workers (for example, workers in certain age brackets, self-employed workers, or female workers) and lists with the jobs organized by level of education or training and by personality type. The column starting at right presents all the list titles. *Starts on page 67.*

Part IV. Descriptions of the Best Secure Jobs. Provides complete descriptions of the jobs that appear on the lists in Part III. Each description contains information on work tasks, skills, education and training required, earnings, projected growth, fastest-growing detailed career fields, job duties, related knowledge and courses, working conditions, and many other details. *Starts on page 137.*

Appendix. Definitions of Skills and Knowledge/Courses Referenced in This Book. Defines some of the terms used in the job descriptions. *Starts on page 393.*

Detailed Table of Contents

Introduction

Not everybody will want to read this introduction. You may want to skip this background information and go directly to Part II, which describes six secure career fields, or to Part III, which lists the best secure jobs.

But if you want to understand how (and why) I put this book together, where the information comes from, and what makes a job "secure" or "best," this introduction can answer many questions.

How This Book Can Help You in Both Good and Bad Economic Times

When you choose a career and prepare for it, you want some assurances that you will be able to find work in the career. You can improve your chances by focusing on careers that have a good job outlook. The U.S. Department of Labor projects the future demand for various occupations, and you can choose one that is expected to grow and take on many new workers. But keep in mind that these labor-market forecasts are like a Midwestern weather forecast that says the days will get warmer over the course of March. Yes, the weather will be warmer by March 31, but during those 31 days there will be cold spells, maybe even snowstorms.

The economy also has ups and downs. Despite the efforts of the wizards at the Federal Reserve Bank, the economy tends to experience a repeated sequence called the *business cycle*. During an upswing in the cycle, businesses invest in equipment, build up inventory, and—most important for your career decision—hire workers. As long as the economic outlook remains optimistic, businesses expect to gain greater productivity from their new equipment, sell their newly created inventory, and find work for their new employees. But eventually, for one economic reason or another, the outlook becomes gloomy. Businesses stop buying new equipment and may even shut down facilities, they slash prices and reduce their inventory, and they trim payroll expenses by laying off workers and not hiring replacements for those who leave.

Business cycles are not the only forces that can affect your job security. Certain long-term trends such as automation, the aging of the population, and increased global competition can make your job either more or less vulnerable to downsizing and shrinking job opportunities.

The good news is that some occupations and career fields are less sensitive than others to these swings of the business cycle. These occupations and career fields produce goods or perform services that are necessary no matter which way the economy is trending. They also are not threatened by long-term economic trends and may even benefit from them. This book focuses on those more-secure jobs and fields. Even though the economy is now on the upswing, you should consider that another recession is certain to arrive eventually. This book can help you identify jobs and fields that are more likely to weather future storms.

(This book uses the term "career fields" or "fields" instead of the more technical term "industries," because most people associate "industry" with smokestacks and manufacturing.)

People who are really savvy about their career development don't wait until the eve of a recession to think about job security. They consider it during all phases of the business cycle and may make career moves during boom times to position themselves better for a downturn. For example, if you're interested in engineering as a career, you might start out working in this book's 36th-ranked job in the Government field, Environmental Engineers. Unlike most other engineering jobs, this job is considered a good bet during hard times. You could gain experience in this occupation even when other engineers are being laid off. Then, when the economy improves, you may have acquired enough skills and knowledge to be ready for a job in engineering management—a less secure position, but perhaps worth the risk because of its higher pay (on average, about 50 percent higher). You might then try to move into another secure industry, such as Utilities, or acquire the skills needed to work in a more secure managerial specialization, such as human resources, to reduce the chances that your job will be threatened by the next economic downturn.

Here's an example that may convince you of the importance of choosing a secure field, not just a secure occupation. Let's say you were thinking of Accountants and Auditors as a career goal. In general, this occupation is more secure than most. But let's look at how this career fared recently in a notoriously insecure field, Construction of Buildings. Between 2007 and 2008, employment of Accountants and Auditors in the field rose a modest 3.6 percent. The following year, as the Great Recession set in, the bottom fell out: Employment dropped by 13.9 percent in 2009 and a further 14.1 percent in 2010. Meanwhile, in the Government field, employment of Accountants and Auditors gained only 0.5 percent between 2007 and 2008. But over the next two years, while jobs were vaporizing in Construction of Buildings, employment in Government stayed stable, gaining 0.2 percent one year and 0.8 percent the next.

If you were graduating college in 2007 with an accounting degree in your hand, you might have been tempted by the higher salary in the Construction of Buildings field—an average of $58,690, compared to $55,370 in Government. Furthermore, that year's increase in Construction of Buildings employment would have created job openings to add to the temptation. But you would have been much more likely to keep your job when recession struck if you had gone to work in Government instead.

You should understand that no job or field is completely secure. People sometimes lose their jobs for reasons that have nothing to do with the ups and downs of the economy. Even highly competent workers may be laid off because a business is suffering from mismanagement, a bad location, a natural disaster, or some other mishap. In fact, the overall trend for many years has been a slow erosion of job security for all workers. So don't consider the "secure future" in this book's title as a guarantee, and keep in mind that the "secure jobs" and "secure fields" referred to in this book are only *more secure than average.*

On the other hand, you can add to the security of any job by taking steps to be more visible and more irreplaceable in your organization and your career field. Part I of this book offers specific suggestions for doing this.

Where the Information Came From

The information I used in creating this book came from several government databases, especially those created by the U.S. Department of Labor:

❋ The Bureau of Labor Statistics (BLS) provided detailed economic data about the jobs and career fields. Figures on earnings, job growth, and job openings are reported under a classifying system called Standard Occupational Classification (SOC), which organizes the U.S. workforce into approximately 800 job titles. You'll find figures that provide averages (for example, earnings) for jobs within particular fields and for jobs with all employers. The lists in Part III are all based on SOC titles.

❋ The Spring 2010 issue of the *Occupational Outlook Quarterly (OOQ),* a BLS publication, provided the statements about "Other Considerations for Job Outlook." The *OOQ* is available on the Web at www.bls.gov/opub/ooq.

❋ To obtain additional information about occupations, I linked the SOC job titles to titles in the O*NET (Occupational Information Network) database, which is now the primary source of detailed information on occupations. The Labor Department updates the O*NET regularly, and I used the most recent version available: O*NET release 15.1. Data from the O*NET was the basis of the information about the personality types associated with jobs, as well as the important work tasks, skills, types of knowledge, and work conditions. Because the O*NET uses a slightly different set of job titles than SOC, I matched similar titles. In the Part IV job descriptions, some O*NET occupations are identified as "job specializations" within their related SOC occupation. In a few cases, O*NET data was not available about some topics for every occupation. Nevertheless, the information reported here is the most reliable data obtainable. Note, however, that the O*NET information topics apply to the occupation as a whole, not just to jobs within the particular fields covered by this book.

❋ Data on the demographic characteristics of workers came from the Current Population Survey (CPS), conducted by the U.S. Census Bureau. This includes the information about the proportion of workers in each job who are men and women or who are within various age brackets. The CPS also provided the basis for the statements about work hours, part-time workers, and union membership in the descriptions of career fields.

❋ Information about the level of education or training required for each occupation is taken mostly from a table on the website of the Office of Occupational Statistics and Employment Projections (www.bls.gov/emp/ep_table_111.htm). For recently emerged job specializations not included in that table, I relied on other sources of information, such as professional associations.

❋ I used the Classification of Instructional Programs, a system developed by the U.S. Department of Education, for the names of the education and training programs related to each job. I linked programs to jobs by following the crosswalk developed jointly by the BLS and the National Center for Education Statistics (NCES).

❋ Information about the career clusters and pathways linked to each occupation is based on materials developed for the U.S. Department of Education's Office of Vocational and Adult Education (OVAE).

As you can see, this information came from numerous databases housed in various government agencies. In its original database formats, the information would have been disjointed and sometimes confusing, so I did many things to connect related data and present it to you in a form that is easy to understand.

How the Best Jobs Were Selected

The Bureau of Labor Statistics, my main source of career information, provides projections of job growth and annual job openings for about 750 individual occupations. However, the BLS does not attempt to predict recessions or boom times when it makes these projections. Rather, the BLS bases its projections on the *average* growth and openings over a 10-year period (currently, the period from 2008 to 2018). Therefore, to choose secure jobs for this book, I could not rely simply on job-growth projections averaged out over a decade.

In addition, I wanted to focus this book on jobs in particular career *fields*. Occupation titles alone don't identify where the secure positions are. A worker in one career field may have a lot more job security than a worker in a different field, even though they share the same job title. As it does with occupations, the BLS projects growth of career fields over a 10-year period, but this also is an average and does not reveal which fields have the greatest security.

To identify the most secure occupations and fields, I followed this procedure:

1. To select the jobs that are likely to be least sensitive to economic downturns, I followed the ratings given by an article in the *Occupational Outlook Quarterly (OOQ)*, a BLS publication. It rates jobs on a scale from 0 to 3 for "economic sensitivity," which means how closely the jobs have, in the past, prospered or suffered along with the economy. For an additional check, I consulted the 2010–2011 edition of the *Occupational Outlook Handbook,* another BLS publication, focusing on the outlook statements given for the occupations. When necessary, I adjusted the sensitivity ratings for some jobs. Because many of the job titles in the *OOQ* article are very diverse collections of jobs—for example, Designers—I did not automatically assume that all the related specific titles deserve to share the same numerical rating for economic sensitivity. To determine separate ratings in these cases, I performed a statistical analysis comparing the historical ups and downs in the workforce size of occupations with the ups and downs in the national economy. For each job in these cases, I also considered the economic outlook projected between 2008 and 2018, because for some occupations the outlook is so good that even economic downturns are not a threat.

2. Next, I identified the career fields where the jobs rated 0 or 1 for economic sensitivity (that is, the most secure jobs) are concentrated. I checked further by consulting the *Career Guide to Industries*, 2010–2011 edition, a Web-only publication of the Bureau of Labor Statistics. (You can find the CGI at www.bls.gov/oco/cg.) The CGI covers 41 career fields and, among other topics, discusses factors affecting the employment outlook in each field. As a final check, I looked at data from the Department of Labor's Job Openings and Labor Turnover Survey (JOLTS). Specifically, for each career field, I looked at how the rate of layoffs and discharges over the past decade compared to the fluctuating rates in the economy as a whole. Taken together, this research suggested that I focus the book on six fields: Health Care, Government, Educational Services, Computer Systems Design, Utilities, and Repair and Maintenance. I prepared a separate list for each field, consisting of secure jobs with workforces of at least 1,000 workers in that field. Taken together, the lists included 302 unique job titles.

3. To determine which jobs are best (in economic terms) in each career field, I used the BLS as my source of field-specific data on earnings, projected job growth, and projected annual job openings for each secure occupation. For the last of these factors, job openings, I needed to develop my own formula for computing a rough estimate from BLS figures, as I explain later in this introduction.

4. In each field, I eliminated the jobs with field-specific annual median earnings lower than those of the lowest 25 percent of all wage-earners in that field. This cutoff level varied from a high of $49,050 in Computer Systems Design to a low of $21,840 in Repair and Maintenance, and a total of 31 unique jobs were eliminated. Although some of these jobs may employ many workers, even in recessions, their low pay makes them unlikely to be of interest to the readers of this book. Admittedly, some of the jobs that do appear in this book may be unappealing to you for other reasons, but I'll leave it to you to decide how you feel about other aspects of jobs. Three occupations in the Utilities field had to be removed because they were concentrated in the nuclear power industry, which has proved to be unstable. I also eliminated 15 occupations that cannot be considered best jobs because, in their career field, they are expected to create fewer than 50 job openings per year. Even if they are unaffected by recessions, these occupations offer little job opportunity. The list at this point included 256 unique jobs.

5. One factor that makes a job insecure is the possibility that it may be offshored—meaning that the work can readily be done by people in foreign countries. Four of the occupations on my lists at this point were identified as vulnerable to offshoring in the most recent edition of the *Occupational Outlook Handbook:* Purchasing Agents, Except Wholesale, Retail, and Farm Products; Computer Support Specialists; Electrical and Electronics Engineering Technicians; and Bookkeeping, Accounting, and Auditing Clerks. Some of these offshorable jobs have a very good employment outlook through 2018, but their long-term security is questionable, so they cannot be considered secure. The list now included 252 unique jobs, or 498 job-field combinations.

6. I ranked the collection of jobs assigned to each field three times, based on three economic criteria, all of them specific to the career fields: median annual earnings, projected growth through 2018, and number of job openings projected per year. I then added the three numerical rankings for each job to calculate its overall score within its field. Occupations that appeared in more than one field had different standings in their various fields because they had different field-specific figures and competed against different occupations. For example, Management Analysts ranked 8th among the 30 Computer Systems Design jobs but only 18th among the 30 Utilities jobs.

7. To emphasize jobs that tend to pay more, are likely to grow more rapidly, and have more job openings, I selected a subset of secure job titles with the best total overall scores for each career field. The number of titles I selected for each field reflects the size and level of security of the field's workforce: 30 titles each for the Computer Systems Design, Utilities, and Repair and Maintenance fields; 50 each for the Government and Educational Services fields; and 70 for the Health Care field. Some job titles appear on multiple lists, so the actual number of unique jobs is 150.

For example, the job in the Utilities field with the best combined score for earnings, growth, and number of job openings is Electrical and Electronics Repairers, Powerhouse, Substation, and Relay, so this job is listed first even though it is not the best-paying job (which is Chief Executives), the fastest-growing job (which is Computer Network Architects), or the job with the most openings (which is Network and Computer Systems Administrators).

Understand the Limits of the Data in This Book

In this book, I used the most reliable and up-to-date information available on earnings, projected growth, number of openings, and other topics. The earnings data came from the U.S. Department of Labor's Bureau of Labor Statistics. As you look at the figures, keep in mind that they are estimates. They give you a general idea about the number of workers employed, annual earnings, rate of job growth, and annual job openings.

Understand that a problem with such data is that it describes an average. Just as there is no precisely average person, there is no such thing as a statistically average example of a particular job, even within a single career field. I say this because data, while helpful, can also be misleading.

Take, for example, the yearly earnings information in this book. This is highly reliable data obtained from a very large U.S. working population sample by the Bureau of Labor Statistics. It reports the average annual pay received as of May 2010 by people in various job titles (actually, it is the median annual pay, which means that half earned more and half less). It is available for both workers in specific career fields and workers in all fields.

This sounds great, except that half of all people in the occupation earned less than that amount. For example, people who are new to the occupation or with only a few years of work experience often earn much less than the median amount.

Also keep in mind that the figures for job growth and number of openings are projections by labor economists—their best estimates of what we can expect between now and 2018. (The projections for job openings are particularly rough, as explained later in this introduction.) These projections are not guarantees. A catastrophic economic downturn, war, or technological breakthrough could change the actual outcome. The projections are also averages over a 10-year period. During economic slowdowns, you can expect job growth and openings to be lower, even for secure jobs; during recoveries, both will be higher. Political developments may change the outlook for jobs in government or in government-funded education or health care.

Finally, don't forget that the job market consists of both job openings and job *seekers*. The figures on job growth and openings don't tell you how many people will be competing with you to be hired. The Department of Labor does not publish figures on the supply of job candidates, so I can't provide a number that tells how much competition you can expect. Competition is an important issue that you should research for any tentative career goal. Each job description in Part III includes a brief statement about outlook that may include a comment about competition. You can find additional discussion in the *Occupational Outlook Handbook*. You also should speak to people who educate or train tomorrow's workers; they probably have a good idea of how many graduates find rewarding employment and how quickly. People in the workforce, especially in the career field that interests you, can provide insights into this issue. Use your critical thinking skills to evaluate what people tell you. For example, educators or trainers may be trying to recruit you, whereas people in the workforce may be trying to discourage you from competing. Get a variety of opinions to balance out possible biases.

So, in reviewing the information in this book, please understand the limitations of the data. You need to use common sense in career decision making as in most other things in life. I hope that, by using that approach, you find the information helpful and interesting.

The Data Complexities

If you are curious about details, the following section explains some of the complexities inherent in the sources of information I used and what I did to make sense of them. You don't need to know this to use the book, so jump to the section about "How This Book Is Organized" if you are bored with details.

As explained earlier, I selected the jobs on the basis of economic data specific to jobs in certain career fields. You'll find information on earnings, projected growth, and number of job openings for each job throughout this book.

Earnings

The employment security agency of each state gathers information on earnings for various jobs and forwards it to the U.S. Bureau of Labor Statistics. This information is organized in standardized ways by a BLS program called Occupational Employment Statistics (OES). To keep the earnings for the various jobs and regions comparable, the OES screens out certain types of earnings and includes others, so the OES earnings I use in this book represent straight-time gross pay exclusive of premium pay. More specifically, the OES earnings include the job's base rate; cost-of-living allowances; guaranteed pay; hazardous-duty pay; incentive pay, including commissions and production bonuses; on-call pay; and tips. They do not include back pay, jury duty pay, overtime pay, severance pay, shift differentials, nonproduction bonuses, or tuition reimbursements. The earnings of self-employed workers also are not included.

For each job described in Part IV, you'll find four facts related to earnings, all based on the OES survey:

❋ The Annual Earnings figures show the median earnings (half earn more, half earn less) for workers who hold the job in each field to which it is assigned in this book and for all workers who hold the job.

❋ The Earnings Growth Potential statement represents the gap between the 10th percentile and the median. This information answers the question, "If I compared the wages of the low earners to the median, how much of a pay difference (in percentage terms) would I find?" If the difference is large, the job has great potential for increasing your earnings as you gain experience and skills. If the difference is small, you probably will need to move on to another occupation to improve your earnings substantially. Because a percentage figure would be hard to interpret, I also provide an easy-to-understand verbal tag that expresses the Earnings Growth Potential: "very low" when the percentage is less than 25 percent, "low" for 25–35 percent, "medium" for 36–40 percent, "high" for 41–50 percent, and "very high" for any figure higher than 50 percent. You should understand that the Earnings Growth Potential statement applies to all workers in the occupations; the potential may be higher or lower for workers in the specific career fields covered by this book.

The median earnings for all workers in all occupations in all career fields were $33,840 in May 2010. However, workers in the six fields covered by this book tend to be paid better (on average) than those in all fields. The following table shows how the median earnings for *all* jobs in these fields compare to the median earnings for the jobs selected for this book:

| | Median Earnings | |
Career Field	All Jobs	Jobs in This Book
Computer Systems Design	$73,730	$85,867
Educational Services	$43,120	$58,732
Government	$45,710	$62,106
Health Care	$37,960	$60,578
Repair and Maintenance	$31,480	$36,744
Utilities	$60,770	$68,340

All of these figures are weighted averages, which means that jobs with larger workforces are given greater weight in the computations.

When I compute the average earnings of the 150 jobs *across* all six career fields (as I do for some of the Part III lists), I find only one-quarter of the jobs with earnings less than $39,876. The median earnings figure is $55,860. One-quarter of the jobs have earnings greater than $72,718.

Projected Growth and Number of Job Openings

This information comes from the Office of Occupational Statistics and Employment Projections, a program within the Bureau of Labor Statistics that develops information about projected trends in the nation's labor market for the next 10 years. As mentioned earlier, the most recent projections available cover the years 2008 to 2018. The projections are based on information about people moving into and out of occupations. The BLS uses data from various sources in projecting the growth and number of openings for each job title; some data comes from the Census Bureau's Current Population Survey and some comes from an OES survey. In making the projections, the BLS economists assume that there will be no major war, depression, or other economic upheaval. They do assume that recessions may occur, in keeping with the business cycles we have experienced for several decades, but because the projections cover 10 years, they are intended to provide an average of both the good times and the bad times.

Like the earnings figures in Part IV, the figures on projected growth are reported for each occupation both for workers in all fields and for those in the six fields covered by this book.

While salary figures are fairly straightforward, you may not know what to make of figures for job growth. For example, is a projected growth of 15 percent good or bad? Keep in mind that the average (mean) growth for all occupations in all career fields, as projected by the Bureau of Labor Statistics, is 10.1 percent. One-quarter of the SOC occupations have a growth projection of 0.3 percent or lower. Growth of 9.1 percent is the median, meaning that half of the occupations have more, half less. Only one-quarter of the occupations have growth projected at more than 15.4 percent. Here are the job-growth projections for all jobs in the six fields covered by this book and for the 150 best jobs in these fields:

	Job Growth 2008–2018	
Career Field	All Jobs	Jobs in This Book
Computer Systems Design	45.2%	53.4%
Educational Services	12.5%	16.2%
Government	7.1%	15.8%
Health Care	22.5%	19.6%
Repair and Maintenance	5.1%	7.2%
Utilities	–10.5%	–9.4%

You'll note that job growth for the best jobs is slightly lower than average in one field, Health Care. That's because this field includes several fast-growing occupations, such as Home Health Aides, that pay too little to be included in the book. You probably also wonder why I included the Utilities field in this book, with its negative figure for job growth even among the best jobs. Keep in mind that even occupations that are shrinking will continue to offer job openings, and in this field the jobs tend to be more secure than most.

I've computed job growth across the six career fields for the 150 best jobs, and I find only one-quarter of them with projected growth less than 10.3 percent. The median growth is 18.6 percent. One-quarter of the jobs have projected growth greater than 27.5 percent.

Unlike figures for earnings and job growth, BLS figures on job *openings* are not available for specific fields. The BLS projects only one figure for each occupation: the figure for openings in all career fields. If you sort these figures, you find that one-quarter of all SOC occupations are projected to have 610 or fewer annual job openings. The median is 1,800 job openings. Only one-quarter of the occupations have 5,010 or more projected job openings.

Although the BLS does not project openings for specific career fields, I was able to compute a rough estimate for the occupations in each of the six fields covered by this book. To explain the procedure that I followed, I'll use the Health Care field and the occupation Biomedical Engineers as an example:

1. First, I obtained the Department of Labor's estimate of the number of Biomedical Engineers employed in Health Care (1,810). I divided this by the number of Biomedical Engineers employed in *all* fields (16,050) to get a percentage for that one field's workforce—the "Health Care portion" of the people working as Biomedical Engineers. I multiplied this percentage (11.3 percent) by the number of job openings that the BLS projects for Biomedical Engineers in all fields (1,490) to get a preliminary estimate of the Health Care portion of these projected openings (168 jobs).

2. Second, I addressed the concern that job turnover in Health Care may be either faster or slower than in other fields, resulting in either more or fewer openings than the preliminary figure for the Health Care portion would indicate. Each month, the Job Openings and Labor Turnover Survey (JOLTS) by the Department of Labor measures the *job-opening rate* for major career fields—that is, the monthly number of jobs in the field expressed as a percentage of the total workforce. For Health Care and Social Assistance (which JOLTS lumps together) during the months from January 2001 to March 2011, this rate ranged from a low of 2.5 percent in June 2010 to a high of 6.1 percent in January 2001. The average monthly rate over those nine years was 3.9 percent. The monthly percent average for all career fields over that same time period was 2.7 percent. I divided 3.9 by 2.7 to get 1.5, the *job-opening ratio* for Health Care jobs compared to all jobs.

3. For Biomedical Engineers (and for all other secure jobs in the Health Care field), I multiplied the preliminary estimated Health Care portion of projected openings (168 in this example, from step 1) by this job-opening ratio (1.5, from step 2). The product, 252, was a somewhat better estimate of the Health Care job openings that can be expected for Biomedical Engineers. Because this estimate is still rough (turnover probably varies among occupations, even within the same career field), I rounded this figure to the nearest 10: 250.

Here are the figures for the average job openings projected for the six career fields covered by this book, both for *all* occupations in these fields and for the occupations selected for the book. I rounded the figures to the nearest thousand:

Career Field	Average Annual Job Openings 2008–2018	
	All Jobs	Jobs in This Book
Computer Systems Design	38,000	1,000
Educational Services	8,000	5,000
Government	10,000	4,000
Health Care	16,000	9,000
Repair and Maintenance	27,000	1,000
Utilities	18,000	1,000

You should not be surprised to find that in all six career fields, the occupations included in the book have lower-than-average figures for job openings. The relatively high pay and high job growth of these occupations make them a selective set. Each of these career fields includes occupations that have plentiful job openings but that pay too little or are growing too slowly to be included in the book. Notable examples are Home Health Aides in the Health Care field, with 55,000 job openings, and Teacher Assistants in the Educational Services field, with 41,000 job openings.

When I computed total projected job openings across the six career fields for the 150 best jobs, I found only one-quarter of the jobs with fewer than 420 openings. The median is 1,950 openings. One-quarter of the jobs had more than 6,120 openings.

Perhaps you're wondering why this book offers figures on both job growth *and* number of openings. Aren't these two ways of saying the same thing? Actually, you need to know both. Consider (again) the occupation Biomedical Engineers, which is projected to grow at the phenomenal rate of 69.2 percent in Health Care. There should be lots of opportunities in such a fast-growing job, right? Not exactly. This is a tiny occupation, with only about 1,800 workers in this career field. So although it is growing rapidly, it will not create many new jobs (about 250 per year). Now consider the Government job Postal Service Mail Sorters, Processors, and Processing Machine Operators. Because automation has taken over many tasks of this job, this occupation actually has a *negative* growth rate, with the alarming figure of –30.4 percent. Nevertheless, this is a very large occupation that employs more than 175,000 workers, so although it is shrinking, it is expected to take on more than 1,660 new workers each year as existing workers retire, die, or move on to other jobs. That's why I based my selection of the best jobs on both of these economic indicators and why you should pay attention to both when you scan the lists of best jobs.

How This Book Is Organized

The information in this book about best secure jobs and career fields moves from the general to the highly specific.

Part I: Why Job Security Matters and How to Achieve It

In Part I, I explain what factors, such as recessions, cause job insecurity, as well as the reasons some jobs and career fields are more secure than others. I offer several suggestions for how to make yourself essential to your employer and how to be a resilient worker who can bounce back from a layoff. These pointers can be helpful for improving your career prospects in boom times as well as in recessions.

Part II: Six Career Fields with Security

This part introduces the six career fields that are covered by this book. For each field, you'll find these information topics:

❋ What function the field serves

❋ How the field is organized

❋ Working conditions in the field

❋ How many people are employed in the field, including a list of the 20 occupations that account for the largest shares of the workforce

❋ How workers prepare to enter the field

❋ The outlook for the field, including the factors that cause jobs in the field to be higher than average in security

❈ Earnings in the field

❈ Sources of further information

This information can help you decide which field suits you best.

Part III: The Best Jobs Lists

For many people, the 68 lists in Part III are the book's most interesting feature. Here you can see the titles of jobs in each secure career field with high salaries, fast growth, and plentiful job openings. You can see which jobs are best in terms of each of these factors combined and considered separately. Additional lists highlight jobs with particular characteristics, such as a high percentage of female, male, or self-employed workers. Look in the Table of Contents for a complete list of lists. Although there are a lot of lists, they are not difficult to understand because they have clear titles and are organized into groupings of related lists.

Depending on your situation, some of the lists in Part III will interest you more than others. For example, if you are young, you may be interested in the secure jobs that employ high percentages of people age 16–24. Other lists show jobs within personality types, levels of education, or other ways that you might find helpful in exploring your career options.

Whatever your situation, I suggest you use the lists that make sense for you to help explore career options. Following are the names of each group of lists along with short comments on each group. You will find additional information in a brief introduction provided at the beginning of each group of lists in Part III.

Best Jobs Overall: Secure Jobs with the Highest Pay, Fastest Growth, and Most Openings

These lists are the ones that most people want to see first. For each career field, there is a list of the top occupation titles in order of their combined scores for earnings, growth, and number of job openings. (These economic statistics apply specifically to workers employed by the field in question.) Additional lists are extracted from the best jobs and present, for each field, the 20 jobs with the highest earnings, the 20 jobs projected to grow most rapidly, and the 20 jobs with the most openings.

Best Jobs Lists by Demographic

Like other books in the *Best Jobs* series, this one includes lists that show what sorts of jobs different types of people are most likely to have. For example, you can see which secure jobs have the highest percentage of men or young workers. I'm not saying that men or young people should consider these jobs over others based solely on this information, but it is interesting information to know.

In some cases, the lists can give you ideas for jobs to consider that you might otherwise overlook. For example, perhaps women should consider some jobs that traditionally have high percentages of men in them. Or older workers might consider some jobs typically held by young people. Although these aren't obvious ways of using these lists, the lists may give you some good ideas of jobs to consider. The lists may also help you identify jobs that work well for others in your situation—for example, jobs with plentiful opportunities for self-employment, if that's a work arrangement that appeals to you.

All lists in this section were created through a similar process. I began with the 150 unique best jobs and sorted these jobs by the primary criterion for each set of lists. For example, I sorted the jobs based on the percentage of workers age 16–24 from highest to lowest percentage and then selected the jobs with a high percentage (15 jobs with a percentage greater than 15). Then I sorted these jobs by their combined scores for earnings, growth rate, and number of openings. The lists show these three economic factors for each job. The economic figures I used are the averages for all the secure fields to which the job is linked. In a column immediately to the right of each occupation name, you can see abbreviations (such as U for Utilities) that indicate the names of these secure fields.

I used the same basic process to create all the lists in this section, and I formatted them all the same way. The lists are very interesting, and I hope you find them helpful.

Best Jobs Lists Based on Levels of Education, Training, and Experience

I created a separate list for each level of education and training as defined by the U.S. Department of Labor and I assigned job titles to the lists based on the education, training, and experience usually required for entry. Jobs within these lists are presented in order of their total combined scores for earnings, growth, and number of openings.

For each job, in addition to the economic information that guided the ordering, I show the career fields that were averaged into the economic figures. The lists include jobs in these groupings:

❈ Short-term on-the-job training

❈ Moderate-term on-the-job training

❈ Long-term on-the-job training

❈ Work experience in a related job

❈ Postsecondary vocational training

❈ Associate degree

❈ Bachelor's degree

❈ Work experience plus degree

❈ Master's degree

❈ Doctoral degree

❈ First professional degree

Best Jobs Lists Based on Personality Types

These lists organize the 150 unique best jobs into six personality types described in the introduction to the lists: Realistic, Investigative, Artistic, Social, Enterprising, and Conventional. In each of the six lists, the jobs are presented in order of their combined scores for earnings, growth, and number of openings, and the career fields for each job are identified.

Bonus Lists: Metropolitan Areas Where the Secure Fields Are Concentrated

Job opportunities in secure fields vary according to where you're located. These lists identify the 10 metropolitan areas that have the highest concentrations of jobs in each of the six secure fields.

Bonus Lists: Skills Concentrated in the Secure Fields

The six secure fields require different skills from workers. This set of lists shows, for each field, the 10 transferable skills that dominate the jobs associated with the field. An additional list shows the 10 dominant skills for the jobs in all six fields taken together.

Part IV: Descriptions of the Best Secure Jobs

This part contains descriptions of the 150 best jobs, using a format that is informative yet compact and easy to read. The descriptions contain statistics such as earnings and projected percent of growth and lists such as major skills and work conditions, as well as important work tasks and personality type. The jobs in this section are arranged in alphabetical order, so you can easily find a job that you've identified from Part III and that you want to learn more about.

As I explain earlier in this introduction, the job titles used in the list are based on the Standard Occupational Classification (SOC), but in Part IV the information is partly derived from the O*NET database. Sometimes the O*NET information is listed under "Job Specialization" headings that are subsumed under the SOC title used in the Part III lists.

Although I've tried to make the descriptions easy to understand, the sample that follows—with an explanation of each of its parts—may help you better understand and use the descriptions.

Here are some details on each of the major parts of the job descriptions you will find in Part IV:

❋ **Job Title:** This is the title for the job as defined by the Standard Occupational Classification (SOC) taxonomy.

❋ **Data Elements:** The information comes from various databases, mostly from the U.S. Department of Labor, as explained elsewhere in this introduction. For each job, you can see figures that apply both to workers in all career fields and to workers in the related secure fields. I use abbreviations (for example, G for Government) to indicate which field's workers the figure is based on. An asterisk (*) indicates the figures for workers in all fields.

❋ **Detailed Fields with Greatest Employment** and **Detailed Fields with Highest Growth (Projected Growth for This Job):** For the occupation being described, these fields employ the largest numbers of workers and have the highest growth projections. These detailed fields are more narrowly defined than the six fields used in this book (the one exception being the detailed field Computer Systems Design). For example, the detailed field State and Local Government is a subset of the book's Government field. (In Part II, under the heading "How the Field Is Organized," you can find descriptions of the detailed fields within each of the book's fields.) Many of the fields listed here, such as Management of Companies and Enterprises, are not subsets of the book's six secure fields. Therefore, you should not assume that all of the detailed fields are secure; in fact, some of them may be very insecure.

❋ **Summary Description and Tasks:** The boldfaced sentence provides a summary description of the occupation. It is followed by a listing of tasks generally performed by people who work in this job. This information comes from the O*NET database but, where necessary, has been edited to avoid exceeding 1,000 characters.

❋ **Considerations for Job Outlook:** This information, based on *Occupational Projections and Training Data*, explains some factors that are expected to affect opportunities for job seekers. Note that these comments apply to the period of time from 2008 to 2018 and apply to the occupation as a whole, not just to jobs in any one career field.

❋ **Personality Type:** The O*NET database assigns each job to a primary personality type and to as many as two secondary types. These job descriptions include the name of the related personality types as well as a brief definition of the primary type.

❋ **Career Clusters and Pathways:** This information cross-references the scheme of career clusters and pathways that was created by the U.S. Department of Education's Office of Vocational and Adult Education around 1999 and is now used by many states to organize career-oriented programs and career information. In identifying a career cluster and pathway for the job (sometimes more than one), I followed the assignments of the online O*NET database. Your state might assign this job to a different career pathway or even a different cluster.

❋ **Skills:** For each job, I included the skills whose level-of-performance scores exceeded the average for all jobs by the greatest amount and whose ratings on the importance scale were higher than very low. I included as many as six such skills for each job, and we ranked them by the extent to which their rating exceeds the average. You'll find a definition for each skill in the Appendix.

❋ **Education/Training Required:** Based mostly on information from the BLS, this phrase identifies the most common level of education or training that is required of workers entering the career. Understand that a higher level of preparation may sometimes be beneficial, either to make you more competitive against other job seekers or to allow you to enter the job at a more responsible and better-paying level. On the other hand, if the demand for workers is high, it sometimes may be possible for you to enter the career with a lower level of preparation.

❋ **Education/Training Program(s):** This part of the job description provides the name of the educational or training program(s) for the job. It will help you identify sources of formal or informal training for a job that interests you. To get this information, I adapted a crosswalk created by the National Center for O*NET Development to connect information in the Classification of Instructional Programs (CIP) to the O*NET job titles I used in this book. I made various changes to connect the O*NET job titles to the education or training programs related to them and also modified the names of some education and training programs so that they would be more easily understood. In eight cases, I abbreviated the listing of related programs for the sake of space; such entries end with "others."

* **Knowledge/Courses:** This entry can help you understand the most important knowledge areas that are required for a job and the types of courses or programs you will likely need to take to prepare for it. I used information in the O*NET database for this entry. For each job, I identified any knowledge area with a rating that was higher than the average rating for that knowledge area for all jobs; then I listed as many as six in descending order. You'll find a definition for each knowledge area in the Appendix.

* **Work Environment:** I included any work condition with a rating that exceeds the midpoint of the rating scale. The order does not indicate their frequency on the job. Consider whether you like these conditions and whether any of these conditions would make you uncomfortable. Keep in mind that when hazards are present (such as contaminants), protective equipment and procedures are provided to keep you safe.

Getting all the information I used in the job descriptions was not a simple process, and it is not always perfect. Even so, I used the best and most recent sources of data I could find, and I think that my efforts will be helpful to many people.

Job Title →

Training and Development Specialists

Data Elements →

- ❋ Annual Earnings: G $52,010, E $53,350, H $54,913, C $64,380, U $76,060, * $54,160
- ❋ Earnings Growth Potential: High (42.6%)
- ❋ Growth: U –7.9%, G 18.3%, H 25.6%, E 33.3%, C 54.3%, * 23.3%
- ❋ Annual Job Openings: U 120, C 490, E 600, G 680, H 1,400, * 10,710
- ❋ Self-Employed: 1.6%

Detailed Fields with Greatest Employment and Highest Growth →

Detailed Fields with Greatest Employment: State and Local Government (8.9%); Educational Services, Public and Private (7.7%); Administrative and Support Services (7.2%); Management of Companies and Enterprises (7.1%); Insurance Carriers and Related Activities (6.3%)

Detailed Fields with Highest Growth (Projected Growth for This Job): Internet Service Providers, Web Search Portals, and Data Processing Services (62.7%); Professional, Scientific, and Technical Services (60.4%); Lessors of Nonfinancial Intangible Assets (Except Copyrighted Works) (49.3%); Waste Management and Remediation Services (46.9%); Other Information Services (43.1%)

Considerations for Job Outlook →

Other Considerations for Job Outlook: Efforts to recruit and retain employees, the growing importance of employee training, and new legal standards are expected to increase employment of these workers. College graduates and those with certification should have the best opportunities.

Conduct training and development programs for employees. Keep up with developments in area of expertise by reading current journals, books and magazine articles. Present information, using a variety of instructional techniques and formats such as role playing, simulations, team exercises, group discussions, videos, and lectures. Schedule classes based on availability of classrooms, equipment, and instructors. Organize and develop, or obtain, training procedure manuals and guides and course materials such as handouts and visual materials. Offer specific training programs to help workers maintain or improve job skills. Monitor, evaluate, and record training activities and program effectiveness. Attend meetings and seminars to obtain information for use in training programs, or to inform management of training program status. Coordinate recruitment and placement of training program participants. Evaluate training materials prepared by instructors, such as outlines, text, and handouts.

← **Summary Descriptions and Tasks**

Education/Training Required: Work experience plus degree. **Education and Training Program:** Human Resources Development. **Knowledge/Courses:** Education and Training; Sociology and Anthropology; Sales and Marketing; Clerical; Personnel and Human Resources; Psychology.

← **Education/Training Required, Education/Training Programs, Knowledge/Courses**

Personality Type: Social-Artistic-Conventional. **Career Clusters:** 04 Business, Management, and Administration; 05 Education and Training. **Career Pathway:** 4.3 Human Resources. **Other Jobs in This Pathway:** Human Resources Specialists.

← **Personality Type, Career Clusters, and Career Pathways**

Skills: Operations Analysis; Learning Strategies; Science; Instructing; Systems Evaluation; Management of Material Resources; Writing; Management of Financial Resources.

← **Skills**

Work Environment: Indoors; sitting.

← **Work Environment**

Credits and Acknowledgments: While the author created this book, it is based on the work of many others. The occupational information is based on data obtained from the U.S. Department of Labor and the U.S. Census Bureau. These sources provide the most authoritative occupational information available. The job titles and their related descriptions are from the O*NET database, which was developed by researchers and developers under the direction of the U.S. Department of Labor. They, in turn, were assisted by thousands of employers who provided details on the nature of work in the many thousands of job samplings used in the database's development. I used the most recent version of the O*NET database, release 15.1. I appreciate and thank the staff of the U.S. Department of Labor for their efforts and expertise in providing such a rich source of data.

PART I

Why Job Security Matters and How to Achieve It

Nobody's job is 100 percent secure, but you can take steps to reduce your chances of being laid off in the event of an economic downturn and to increase your chances of bouncing back if you are laid off anyway. You can **add security to your career** by choosing the right career field and occupation, choosing the right job within that field and occupation, making yourself the indispensable employee within that job, and being resilient enough to be able to rebound from a job loss. The ideas in this part of the book can be valuable for your career no matter whether the economy is booming or stagnating.

The Age of the Jobless Recovery

I don't have to tell you that job security is important. But you may not realize *how* important job security has become in recent years or why this is so.

We now live in the age of the "jobless recovery." In the last half of the previous century, whenever America pulled out of a recession, the jobs came back quickly. Typically, employment surged back to pre-recession levels in a year or less. But we're seeing a different pattern in the 21st century. After the dot-com bubble burst in 2001, it took a full 39 months before employment recovered. The Great Recession that began in 2008 destroyed even more jobs, and this time even more time will pass before the American workforce regains the lost ground.

Yet, as I write this, the economy officially has recovered already. The stock market has rebounded; corporations are running up huge profits. So why are employers still reluctant to hire? Some employers are nervous about whether the uptick in the economy is going to last. They want to increase production to meet the increasing demands of buyers, but they don't want to be stuck with a large payroll if the economic recovery sputters. In addition, intense international competition encourages employers to look for ways to increase efficiency by using fewer workers.

Some employers are finding ways to automate various work tasks, and new technologies are constantly making this easier and cheaper to do. Some employers are finding ways to shift tasks from professionals to highly trained but lower-paid technicians or from clerical workers to interns. Others are offshoring jobs to low-wage workers in foreign countries, which becomes easier with each free-trade agreement that the United States signs. Thanks to the Internet and cheap telecommunications, even white-collar jobs can be exported. Many employers are economizing by hiring part-time or temporary workers (often without benefits) or by asking current employees to work longer hours. The more people are out of work, the easier it is for employers to find workers who will agree to these unattractive work arrangements.

This means that if you lose a job nowadays, you may have a hard time finding a new job or may have to settle for one with unappealing hours or pay—even though the economy may be growing.

Job Loss Has Long-Term Consequences

Here's another reason to be concerned about job loss: Nowadays the consequences are more severe than ever.

In a jobless recovery, people who are unemployed *stay* unemployed longer. Each week that you're out of work adds to the difficulty of finding another job. It's not just that employers assume that there must be something wrong with you because you've been idle so long. They also realize that you are losing skills while you're out of work. Most job-related skills are learned on the job, and you're not on the job. New technologies are being installed, new business models are being adopted, new partnerships are being forged, and new markets are opening, but you're not learning these new skills and opportunities.

Loss of skills can be a particular problem for older workers, who suffer (often unfairly) from a widespread perception that they are less likely than younger workers to have the latest skills. But young people who graduate from school into a tough job market face a similar problem: Those who don't land a job immediately after graduation also lose skills that they paid so dearly to acquire. Studies have shown that graduates who don't get hired quickly into their targeted career will experience lower earnings for many years. So, if you're still in school as you're deciding on your career goal, try to identify one that has a good job outlook even during economic downturns—the kinds of jobs that are included in this book.

Identify a Secure Career Field and Occupation

It used to be a common belief among economy-watchers that the best indicator of the current state of the economy is production of corrugated cardboard. Almost everything that businesses produce and that you buy is shipped in a cardboard box; when the economy cools down, cardboard is in less demand, and when the economy heats up, cardboard boxes are everywhere. It follows that when cardboard box–makers are out of work, many of the rest of us will soon be out of work. This idea is no longer as fashionable as it once was because an increasing amount of economic activity consists of services such as health care, education, information, and financial transactions, none of which is delivered in a box. Also, each year more goods we buy are imported from foreign countries and have been boxed overseas.

Although the cardboard box industry may not be the career field to watch, it is still true that employment in certain fields and occupations tends to go up and down in step with changes in the economy, whereas employment remains steady in certain other fields and occupations even during hard times. In this book, I concentrate on steady fields and occupations because they are where you have the most job security.

Some jobs have security because they provide goods or services that are essential to everyday life. For example, you'll find Power Plant Operators included in this book because in even the most dire economic times, people need electricity. Power consumption may diminish a bit as economic activity slows down, but almost all the operators at the power plant remain at work. Technology is unlikely to develop a useful substitute for electricity or to make human operators unnecessary at the power plant, and electricity can't be shipped here from China or India. The only long-term trend that might reduce the need for workers is if widely scattered solar panels (as opposed to solar power plants) became commonplace, and that seems unlikely to happen in the near future. The career field where you'll find these power plant workers—and about half a million others—is **Utilities.** Just as you expect electric power when you flick a switch, you expect flowing water when you turn on the faucet, bars on your cell phone wherever you go, and reliable delivery of your e-mail. The utilities field needs a steady supply of skilled technicians, managers, and support staff to maintain and improve these essential functions.

We have other basic needs besides utilities: learning (especially when we're young), staying healthy, and having some organization in our society. The career fields that provide these essential services are **Education, Health Care,** and **Government.** Some of the jobs in these fields are Elementary School Teachers; Physician Assistants; and Tax Examiners, Collectors, and Revenue Agents. (You know what they say about death and taxes.)

You can also find security in career fields that are growing so fast that employers have a steady need for American workers and can't replace them with machines or offshore workers. Health Care, our fastest-growing field, fits this description, but so does the highly specialized field of **Computer Systems Design.** Just think about the excitement that surrounded the arrival of smartphones and tablet computers and that will strike again when the next must-have gadget hits the market.

So the word "jobs" may appear prominently in the title of this book, but the book also focuses on career *fields* that have a secure future. And you should keep both in mind as you plan your career—or your next career move. If you skipped over the Introduction, go back to the first part and read about the effect of the recent recession on Accountants and Auditors. It's an example of how working in a stable field like Government can grant much more job security than working in an unstable field, even in the same occupation.

Limitations of Forecasts

All of this book's forecasts of secure jobs and industries are based on well-known economic trends, but economists know only what they know and tend to be unaware of what they don't know. One such unknown factor is a new technology that drastically changes the way people can do their jobs. For example, the invention of the phonograph severely reduced the number of jobs for musicians, musical instrument makers, and music teachers because live performance no longer was the only way to listen to music. On the other hand, the new technology also created jobs. Record companies formed, and for decades every downtown business district or shopping mall had at least one record store, providing jobs that didn't exist before Thomas Edison's invention. Now we're seeing a drastic loss of jobs in the music distribution business because the way we obtain music has changed again, this time the result of the Internet. The Internet will certainly destroy jobs in many fields, but it also will create many jobs.

The lesson to take away is that a recession is not the only economic event or trend that can threaten your job. Evolving technologies and other factors prevent me from being able to identify any particular job or career field that will *guarantee* you a lifetime of employment. Even natural disasters sometimes can have an impact. Careers in nuclear energy were starting to look more promising as this century began and power companies were seeking ways to move away from fossil fuels. Then the 2011 earthquake and tsunami in Japan caused a massive radiation leak from a nuclear plant, and suddenly atomic power became controversial again.

So understand that the jobs and fields that this book highlights are the ones that appear best suited for the economic trends that currently are well understood.

More important, *even if every job-related prediction in this book turns out to be inaccurate,* the following tips will be useful because they can help you hang onto a threatened job or shift to a new job with minimal disruption to your life.

Be the Irreplaceable Worker

Sometimes jobs are threatened by short-term or local events. For example, if you live in a town where the economy is dominated by a steel mill and the mill shuts down, your job may be threatened even if you are working as a dental hygienist, school bus driver, or librarian. One of the bonus lists in Part III shows the metropolitan areas where the secure jobs are most densely clustered, and moving to one of these areas may help you avoid a local downturn.

More commonly, jobs are threatened because a particular business gets into trouble even though the economy may be in good shape. Perhaps a manager makes some very bad decisions, a competitor captures a large market share, or an essential raw material suddenly jumps in price. Now the employer has to decide how to cut costs to stay in business, and the most obvious way is to get rid of some workers.

Even a prosperous business may need to lay off workers. Let's say the business is so successful that a larger company sees it as an excellent investment and acquires it. But now some of the jobs in the new subsidiary are redundant because the parent company already has staff to perform those business functions. The result: layoffs.

Whatever the reason for layoffs, you may be able to hang onto your job *if you're irreplaceable.* You need to be so vital to the business that it can't go on without you. Here are some techniques to be the irreplaceable worker:

❋ **Focus on the core mission of the business.** Many businesses diversify and serve several functions, but usually there's a central mission that makes money and determines whether the business will succeed or fail. Identify that central function and play a role in it. Identify the skills the business needs for future development of this function and acquire them.

❋ **Accept change.** Better yet, be a part of it. Keep abreast of new business methods, especially for handling communication and information, and find ways to use them in your work. The attitude "We've always done it this way" will not advance the organization's mission.

❋ **Be exceptionally productive.** This doesn't necessarily mean working longer hours. It's more important to find a task or role you can handle that goes beyond your job description. Here again, skills are important because they are the key to productivity. If you have any time and energy to spare, volunteer to take over a small task that unburdens your manager or a coworker; this both broadens your skill set and showcases your productivity. Don't catch yourself saying, "That's not my job."

❋ **Be visible.** In many businesses, the person whose office is next to the boss's tends to get the best performance appraisals. If you don't have that office, find ways to make your accomplishments known; don't wait for performance-appraisal season. For example, start an in-house Web page, newsletter, or bulletin board showcasing the project you're working on and soliciting suggestions from people outside the project. This will encourage them to buy into the project and make your efforts look not purely self-promotional. If you have a work-at-home arrangement, find reasons to show up at the office regularly or make lunch dates.

❋ **Acquire a mentor.** Find someone who really knows the business; be helpful; and ask a lot of very specific questions, including questions about how to improve your work. Give public credit to the mentor for the advice you get.

❋ **Be pleasant.** Be someone customers like to deal with. Find ways to say positive things about your coworkers and promote their accomplishments. Back-stabbing may seem like a way to get ahead, but it can hurt you in the long run. Abrasiveness or whining may make you stand out, but for the wrong reasons. If you really can't get along with some people in your work group, try to be transferred to one where you'll fit in better.

Be a Resilient Worker

For one reason or another, you may lose your job or get stuck in a dead-end job even while following the preceding tips. But your career can be (and probably will be) more than one job. So you can become more secure in your career, even if one job lets you down, by learning how to *be resilient,* able to bounce back quickly. Here's how:

❋ **Specialize and focus on a specific goal.** After a few years in an occupation or career field, find a niche that is not overcrowded and is related to your core skills; then acquire the specialized skills to excel in that role. In a tight job market, employers are more interested in someone with the perfect fit of skills than in a generalist. Your niche may be at the intersection of two very different skills; for example, you may be the chemist who is an ace computer programmer or the police officer who is an inspiring teacher.

❋ **Be visible beyond your workplace.** Join a professional organization, find something missing from its services, and put yourself in that key role. Start a blog or be active in commenting on a prominent blog; this is a readily available way to become known by people with connections in your industry. Become a brand; in the same way that Volvo is known as The Car that is Crashworthy and Wal-Mart is known as The Store with Low Prices, become known as The Person Who _____ [fill in the blank].

❋ **Keep your resume up to date.** Do more than list your current job title. Be sure to include a recent accomplishment so you don't look as though your career has been coasting. Make sure that your skills are easy to identify.

✳ **Keep your skills up to date.** The particular skills needed by your field and for your targeted role will vary, but the bonus lists of skills concentrated in the secure jobs in Part III may give you some ideas about the capabilities that will be most valued in the emerging economy.

✳ **Believe in yourself.** Every job you hold is just one scene in the drama that is your life. If one episode is going badly or ends suddenly, it doesn't have to turn the whole arc of your career into a tragedy. Instead, think of the setback as a plot complication or as an adventure.

When you rebound from a job loss, it may be into another job in the same occupation. If you can pursue that occupation in a more secure career field than you've been in previously, you may diminish your chances of a future layoff. For ideas about secure fields, turn the page and read the descriptions of six such fields.

On the other hand, you may decide to rebound by moving into a different occupation, one that's usually unaffected by economic downturns. If you're considering that strategy, turn to Part III and start scanning the lists of the best jobs in six secure career fields.

PART II

Six Career Fields with Security

This part of the book profiles six career fields that offer more job security than most. During economic downturns, these fields tend not to shed workers as much as other fields do, and the overall outlook for employment in these fields is good to excellent. Not every job in these fields is secure, so you'll want to look at the lists in Part III, where I identify the jobs that combine security with high economic rewards.

The following information about these fields is derived mainly from the U.S. Department of Labor, especially the *Career Guide to Industries,* a Web-only publication that is updated every two years with the latest outlook data. The Census Bureau is another source.

Note: In the tables that show the largest occupations in each career field, secure jobs are shown **in bold.** Some of these secure jobs were eliminated from the list of *best* jobs in their career field—for example, because of low earnings—but all of them are considered to be less sensitive to downturns in the economy than most occupations.

Computer Systems Design

Workers in this career field design computer and information systems, develop custom software programs, and manage computer facilities. They also may perform various other functions, such as software installation and disaster recovery. They generally work on a contract basis. They may assist an organization with a particular project or problem, such as setting up a secure website or establishing a marketplace online, or they may handle ongoing activities, such as management of an onsite data center or help desk.

This field is growing so rapidly that it offers many jobs with high security.

How the Field Is Organized

Custom programming establishments write, modify, test, and support software to meet the needs of a particular customer.

Systems design services firms plan and design computer systems that integrate computer hardware, software, and communications technologies.

Computer facilities management services usually are offered at the customer's site. Establishments offering these services provide onsite management and operation of the client's computer systems and facilities, as well as other services that support the facilities.

Establishments that provide *disaster recovery* services help organizations prepare for a major malfunction of their computer systems.

Recent Developments

The widespread use of the Internet and intranets has resulted in an increased focus on information security. To mitigate threats of viruses and identity theft, many organizations are employing the services of security consulting firms, which specialize in all aspects of information technology (IT) security.

Working Conditions

In 2008, workers in this field averaged 38.8 hours per week, compared with 33.6 for all fields combined. About 19 percent work 50 or more hours a week. Only about 6 percent of the workers in the field work part time.

Most workers in the Computer Systems Design field work in clean, quiet offices. Those in facilities management and maintenance may work in computer operations centers. Given the technology available today, however, more work can be done from remote locations using e-mail and the Internet.

Injuries in this field are rare, but those who work with computers for extended periods may experience musculoskeletal strain, eye problems, or repetitive motion injuries, such as carpal tunnel syndrome.

Employment

In 2008, there were about 1.5 million wage and salary jobs in the Computer Systems Design field. While the field has both large and small firms, the average establishment is relatively small; about 78 percent of establishments employed fewer than 5 workers in 2008. The majority of jobs, however, are found in establishments that employ 50 or more workers.

Compared with the rest of the economy, there are significantly fewer workers 45 years of age and older in this field. The workforce remains younger than most, with a large proportion of workers in the 25-to-44 age range. This reflects the field's explosive growth in employment in the 1980s and 1990s that provided opportunities to thousands of young workers who possessed the latest technological skills.

Largest Occupations in Computer Systems Design (Secure Jobs Bold)	
Job	Workforce in Computer Systems Design
1. **Software Developers, Applications**	175,160
2. Computer Programmers	141,180
3. **Computer Systems Analysts**	126,330
4. **Software Developers, Systems Software**	113,710
5. Computer Support Specialists	99,820
6. **Computer Network Architects**	53,480
7. **Network and Computer Systems Administrators**	50,500
8. Computer and Information Systems Managers	47,910
9. **Network Systems and Data Communications Analysts**	41,350
10. **Customer Service Representatives**	34,710
11. **Management Analysts**	33,930
12. **General and Operations Managers**	31,830
13. Sales Representatives, Services, All Other	30,960
14. Office Clerks, General	27,710
15. Sales Representatives, Wholesale and Manufacturing, Technical and Scientific Products	27,550
16. **Executive Secretaries and Executive Administrative Assistants**	24,320
17. **Computer Occupations, All Other**	23,830
18. **Database Administrators**	18,820
19. **Accountants and Auditors**	18,540
20. Business Operations Specialists, All Other	18,400

Education and Training

Occupations in the Computer Systems Design field require varying levels of education, but because of the high proportion of workers in professional occupations, the education level of workers in this field is higher than average. The level of education and type of training required depend on employers' needs, which often are affected by such aspects as local demand for workers, project timelines, and changes in technology and business conditions.

Outlook

The Computer Systems Design field grew dramatically throughout the 1990s as employment more than doubled. While growth has been decidedly slower since the turn of the century, this field is still projected to be one of the 10 fastest growing in the nation.

Employment change. Wage-and-salary employment is expected to grow 45 percent from 2008 to 2018, about 4 times as fast as the 11 percent growth projected for all industries combined. In addition, this field will add about 656,400 jobs over the decade. An increasing reliance on information technology will spur demand for Computer Systems Design. Organizations will continue to turn to firms in this field to maximize their return on investments in equipment and to help them satisfy their growing computing needs.

The most rapid growth will occur among network systems and data communications analysts. Other rapidly growing occupations include computer software engineers, database administrators, and network and computer system administrators. Business and financial operations occupations will also see rapid growth, because information technology has become a vital aspect of business.

Job prospects. Given the rate at which the Computer Systems Design field is expected to grow, job opportunities should be excellent for most workers. The best opportunities will be in computer specialist occupations, reflecting their growth and the continuing demand for the high-level skills that are needed to keep up with changes in technology. In addition, as individuals and organizations continue to conduct business electronically, the importance of maintaining system and network security will increase. Employment opportunities should be especially good for individuals involved in cyberspace security services, such as disaster recovery services, custom security programming, and security software installation services.

Job security. The rapid growth of this field is the chief factor that will contribute to high security in many occupations. Some offshoring of work will occur as universities in low-wage foreign countries such as India and China continue to produce graduates in computer science and engineering. However, the work that is offshored will mostly be routine coding and bug fixes to existing software. Research and development of new products and services will create more than enough jobs to employ skilled American workers who have advanced skills and are good at working collaboratively.

Earnings

Workers in the Computer Systems Design field generally command higher earnings than the national average. All production or nonsupervisory workers in the field averaged $1,313 a week in May 2010, significantly higher than the average of $749 for all private industry. This reflects the concentration of professionals and specialists, who often are highly compensated for their specialized skills or expertise.

Benefits and union membership. Workers generally receive standard benefits, including health insurance, paid vacation and sick leave, and pension plans. Unionization is rare in the Computer Systems Design field. In 2008, only 2 percent of all workers were union members or covered by union contracts, compared with an average of 14 percent of workers throughout all private industries.

Sources of Additional Information

Further information about computer careers is available from

❋ Association for Computing Machinery, 2 Penn Plaza, Suite 701, New York, NY 10121-0701. Internet: www.acm.org

❋ National Workforce Center for Emerging Technologies, 3000 Landerholm Circle SE, Bellevue, WA 98007. Internet: www.nwcet.org

❋ National Center for Women and Information Technology, University of Colorado, Campus Box 322, Boulder, CO 80309-0322. Internet: www.ncwit.org

❋ Institute of Electrical and Electronics Engineers Computer Society, Care of IEEE USA, 2001 L St. NW, Suite 700, Washington, DC 20036. Internet: www.computer.org

❋ University of Washington Computer Science and Engineering Department, AC101 Paul G. Allen Center, Box 352350, 185 Stevens Way, Seattle, WA 98195-2350. Internet: www.cs.washington.edu/WhyCSE

Educational Services

Education is an important part of life. The amount and type of education that individuals receive are a major influence on both the types of jobs they are able to hold and their earnings. Lifelong learning is important in acquiring new knowledge and upgrading one's skills, particularly in this age of rapid technological and economic changes. The Educational Services field includes a variety of institutions that offer academic education, career and technical instruction, and other education and training to millions of students each year.

Because education is such a vital need, this is a field with many secure jobs.

How the Field Is Organized

Because school attendance is compulsory until at least age 16 in all 50 states and the District of Columbia, *elementary, middle, and secondary schools* are the most numerous of all educational establishments. They provide academic instruction to students in kindergarten through grade 12 in a variety of settings, including public schools, parochial schools, boarding and other private schools, and military academies.

Postsecondary institutions—universities, colleges, professional schools, community or junior colleges, and career and technical institutes—provide education and training in both academic and technical subjects for high school graduates and other adults.

This field also includes institutions that provide training, consulting, and other support services to schools and students, such as curriculum development, student exchanges, and tutoring. Also included are schools or programs that offer nonacademic or self-enrichment classes, such as automobile driving and cooking instruction, among others.

Recent Developments

In an effort to promote innovation in public education, many local and state governments have authorized the creation of public charter schools, in the belief that, by presenting students and their parents with a greater range of instructional options, schools and students will be encouraged to strive for excellence.

Quality improvements also are being made to career and technical education at secondary and postsecondary schools. Academics are playing a more important role in career and technical curricula, and programs are being made relevant to the local job market.

Computer technology continues to affect the education field. Teachers use the Internet in classrooms, as well as to communicate with colleagues and parents; students use the Internet for research projects. Distance learning continues to expand.

Despite these improvements in quality, problems remain. High school completion rates remain low, particularly for minority students, and employers contend that numerous high school graduates still lack many of the math and communication skills needed in today's workplace. School budgets often are not sufficient to meet an institution's various goals, particularly in the inner cities, where aging facilities and chronic teacher shortages make educating children more difficult.

Working Conditions

Most elementary and secondary schools generally operate 10 months a year, but a small percentage operate year-round. In schools with a 10-month school year, summer sessions for special education or remedial students are common. In addition, education administrators, office and administrative support workers, and janitors and cleaners often work the entire year. Postsecondary institutions operate year-round but may have reduced offerings during summer months. Institutions that cater to adult students and those that offer educational support services such as tutoring may operate year-round as well. Night and weekend work is common for teachers of adult literacy and remedial and self-enrichment education, postsecondary teachers, and library workers in postsecondary institutions. Part-time work is common for this same group of teachers and for teacher assistants. Many teachers spend significant time outside of school preparing for class, doing administrative tasks, conducting research, writing articles and books, and pursuing advanced degrees.

Elementary and secondary school conditions often vary from town to town. Some schools in poorer neighborhoods may be run-down, have few supplies and equipment, and lack air conditioning. Other schools may be new and well equipped and maintained. Conditions at postsecondary institutions are generally very good. At all levels of education, seeing students develop and enjoy learning can be rewarding for teachers and other education workers. However, dealing with unmotivated students or those with social or behavioral problems can be stressful and require patience and understanding.

Employment

The Educational Services field was the second-largest career field in the economy in 2008, providing jobs for about 13.5 million wage and salary workers.

Largest Occupations in Educational Services (Secure Jobs Bold)

Job	Workforce in Educational Services
1. **Elementary School Teachers, Except Special Education**	1,520,080
2. **Teacher Assistants**	1,091,720
3. **Secondary School Teachers, Except Special and Career/Technical Education**	1,075,430
4. **Middle School Teachers, Except Special and Career/Technical Education**	652,500
5. **Teachers and Instructors, All Other**	509,660
6. **Janitors and Cleaners, Except Maids and Housekeeping Cleaners**	472,300
7. Office Clerks, General	391,560
8. **Secretaries and Administrative Assistants, Except Legal, Medical, and Executive**	379,440
9. **Bus Drivers, School or Special Client**	241,020
10. **Education Administrators, Elementary and Secondary School**	214,440
11. **Executive Secretaries and Executive Administrative Assistants**	210,930
12. **Special Education Teachers, Preschool, Kindergarten, and Elementary School**	210,560
13. **Educational, Guidance, School, and Vocational Counselors**	204,510
14. **Kindergarten Teachers, Except Special Education**	164,140
15. Combined Food Preparation and Serving Workers, Including Fast Food	160,080
16. **Childcare Workers**	147,650
17. **Special Education Teachers, Secondary School**	142,050
18. Coaches and Scouts	131,810
19. Cooks, Institution and Cafeteria	125,820
20. Education Administrators, Postsecondary	118,170

Education and Training

The Educational Services field employs some of the most highly educated workers in the labor force. About 64 percent of employees have at least a bachelor's degree, the degree required for nearly all professional occupations in the industry. Many professional occupations also require a master's degree or doctorate, particularly for jobs at postsecondary institutions or in administration.

Outlook

Greater numbers of children and adults enrolled in all types of schools will generate employment growth in this field. A large number of retirements will add additional job openings and create good job prospects for many of those seeking work in Educational Services.

Employment change. Wage and salary employment growth of 12 percent is expected in the Educational Services field over the 2008–2018 period, comparable to the 11 percent increase projected for all industries combined. Over the long term, the overall demand for workers in Educational Services will increase as a result of a growing emphasis on improving education and making it available not only to more children and young adults, but also to those currently employed and in need of improving their skills. Much of the demand for Educational Services is driven by growth in the population of students at each level. Low enrollment growth projections at the secondary school level are likely to limit growth somewhat, resulting in average growth for these teachers, However, enrollment growth is expected to be larger at the elementary (grades 1–5) and middle school (grades 6–8) levels, which will likely result in slightly higher employment growth for teachers at these levels. Reforms, such as universal preschool and all-day kindergarten, will require more preschool and kindergarten teachers.

Due to continued emphasis on the inclusion of disabled students in general education classrooms and an effort to reach students with problems at younger ages, special education teachers will experience relatively strong growth. School reforms calling for more individual attention to students will require additional teacher assistants, particularly to work with special education and English-as-a-second-language students.

Enrollments are expected to grow at a faster rate in postsecondary institutions as more high school graduates attend college and as more working adults return to school to enhance or update their skills. As a result, postsecondary teachers will experience growth that is faster than the field as a whole.

Despite expected increases in education expenditures over the next decade, budget constraints at all levels of government may place restrictions on Educational Services, particularly in light of the rapidly escalating costs associated with increased college enrollments, special education, construction of new schools, and other services.

Job prospects. In addition to job openings due to employment growth, retirements will create large numbers of job openings as a greater-than-average number of workers are over the age of 55 in nearly all the major occupations that make up the field—from janitors to education administrators.

School districts, particularly those in urban and rural areas, continue to report difficulties in recruiting qualified teachers, administrators, and support personnel. Fast-growing areas of the country—including several states and cities in the South and West—also report difficulty recruiting education workers, especially teachers. Retirements are expected to remain high over the 2008–2018 period, so the number of students graduating with education degrees may not be sufficient to meet this field's growing needs, making job opportunities for graduates in many education fields good to excellent. Currently, alternative licensing programs are helping to attract more people into teaching, especially those from other career paths, but opportunities should continue to be very good for highly qualified teachers, especially those in subject areas with the highest needs, such as math, science, and special education.

At the postsecondary level, increases in student enrollments and projected retirements of current faculty should contribute to a favorable job market for postsecondary teachers. However, candidates applying for tenured positions will continue to face keen competition as many colleges and universities rely on adjunct or part-time faculty and graduate students to make up a larger share of the total instructional staff than in the past.

Job security. The Great Recession had a delayed impact on public-sector jobs in the Educational Services field, partly because the federal stimulus plan provided funds to offset the loss of tax revenues that occurred as business activity slowed down. The field experienced 445,000 layoffs and discharges in 2009, but its rate of layoffs and discharges for that year was only 14.4 percent, considerably lower than the rate of 20.1 percent for workers in all nonfarm career fields. Because K–12 education is mandated by law, professional instructional jobs at this level will continue to have greater security than most careers. This is particularly true for specializations such as English as a second language, special education, math, and science.

Earnings

Wages of occupations concentrated in the Educational Services field—education administrators, teachers, counselors, and librarians—are higher than the average for all occupations, because workers tend to be older and have higher levels of educational attainment. Among teachers, earnings increase with higher educational attainment and more years of service. Full-time postsecondary teachers earn the most, followed by elementary, middle, and secondary school teachers. Most teachers are paid a salary, but part-time instructors in postsecondary institutions usually are paid a fixed amount per course. Educational Services employees who work the traditional school year can earn additional money during the summer in jobs related to, or outside of, education. Benefits generally are good, but, as in other industries, part-time workers often do not receive the same benefits that full-time workers do.

Benefits and union membership. About 38 percent of workers in the Educational Services field are union members or are covered by union contracts, compared with only 14 percent of workers in all industries combined. Unionization is more common in public elementary, middle, and secondary schools than in other school settings.

The American Federation of Teachers and the National Education Association are the largest unions representing teachers and other school personnel. In several states, unions representing teachers who work in public schools have recently experienced political pressure to make concessions on pensions, health-care benefits, and collective bargaining rights; it is not yet clear whether this trend will continue.

Sources of Additional Information

Information on unions and education-related issues can be obtained from the following organizations:

* American Federation of Teachers, 555 New Jersey Ave. NW, Washington, DC 20001. Internet: www.aft.org
* National Education Association, 1201 16th St. NW, Washington, DC 20036. Internet: www.nea.org

Information about early childhood education can be obtained from the following organizations:

* National Association for the Education of Young Children, 1313 L St. NW, Suite 500, Washington, DC 20005. Internet: www.naeyc.org
* Council for Professional Recognition, 2460 16th St. NW, Washington, DC 20009. Internet: www.cdacouncil.org

Government

The federal government's essential duties include defending the United States from foreign aggression, representing U.S. interests abroad, creating and enforcing national laws and regulations, and administering domestic programs and agencies. State and local governments provide their constituents with vital services that may not be available otherwise, such as transportation, public safety, health care, education, utilities, and courts. Many of these governmental services cannot easily be privatized and are needed no matter how the economy fluctuates.

How the Field Is Organized

As you probably learned in civics class, the three branches of the *federal government* are the legislative, judicial, and executive.

The legislative branch is responsible for forming and amending the legal structure of the nation. Its largest component, the Congress, employs only about 1 percent of federal workers, nearly all of whom work in the Washington, DC, area.

The judicial branch is responsible for interpreting the laws that are established by the legislative branch and employs about 2 percent of federal workers. Unlike the legislative branch, it has offices and employees dispersed throughout the country.

Of the three branches, the executive branch has the widest range of responsibilities. Consequently, it employed about 97 percent of all federal civilian employees (excluding Postal Service workers) in 2008. The executive branch is comprised of the Executive Office of the President, 15 executive Cabinet departments, and about 70 independent agencies.

In addition to the 50 state governments, there were about 87,500 local governments in 2007, according to the U.S. Census Bureau. *State and local governments* employ about 8.3 million workers, excluding education and hospitals, placing them among the largest employers in the economy. Seven out of 10 of these employees work for local governments, such as counties, cities, special districts, and towns. In addition, large numbers of state and local workers work in public education—a major part of the Educational Services industry, which is discussed elsewhere in Part II. Many state and local workers also work in public hospitals, which are included in the Health Care field, described elsewhere in Part II.

In many areas of the country, citizens are served by more than one local government unit. For example, most states have counties, which may contain various municipalities such as cities or towns, but which also often include unincorporated rural areas. Supplementing these forms of local government, special district government bodies are independent, limited-purpose governmental units that usually perform a single function or activity. For example, fire fighting and ambulance services often are provided by a special district.

Working Conditions

Hours. The vast majority of federal employees work full time; some work on flexible schedules that allow workers more control over their work schedules. Some agencies also offer telecommuting programs, which allow selected workers to perform some job duties at home or from regional centers.

At the state or local level, working conditions vary by occupation and, in some instances, by size and location of the jurisdiction.

Most professional, financial operations, and office and administrative support workers in state or local government work a standard 40-hour week in an office environment.

However, firefighters' hours are longer and vary more widely than those of most workers. Most police and detectives work 40 hours a week, with paid overtime when they testify in court or work on an investigation. Because police protection must be provided around the clock, some officers must work weekends, holidays, and nights. A number of other state and local government jobs also require weekend or night work. For example, split, weekend, and night shifts are common for water and other public utility workers.

Work environment. Because of the wide range of government jobs, working conditions vary considerably. Most government employees work in office buildings, hospitals, or laboratories, but a large number also can be found at border crossings, airports, shipyards, military bases, construction sites, national parks, and other settings. Work environments vary from clean and comfortable to hazardous and stressful, such as those experienced by law enforcement officers and air traffic controllers.

Some government workers spend much of their time away from the offices in which they are based. For example, inspectors and compliance officers often visit businesses and worksites to ensure that laws and regulations are obeyed.

In administrative positions, the nature of the work may lead to repetitive movement conditions, such as carpal tunnel syndrome.

Employment

In 2008, the federal government, excluding the Postal Service, employed about 2.0 million civilian workers. The federal government is the nation's single largest employer. Only 15 percent of federal employees worked in the vicinity of the nation's capital in 2008. In addition to federal employees working throughout the United States, about 35,000, which includes foreign nationals, are assigned overseas, mostly in embassies or defense installations.

State and local governments, excluding education and hospitals, employed about 8.3 million people in 2008. About 70 percent of these workers were employed in local government.

The Government field makes an effort to have a workforce as diverse as the nation's civilian labor force. Government serves as a model for all employers in abiding by equal employment opportunity legislation, which protects current and potential employees from discrimination based on race, color, religion, sex, national origin, disability, or age. Most governmental agencies also make a special effort to recruit and accommodate persons with disabilities.

Largest Occupations in Government (Secure Jobs Bold)

Job	Workforce in Government
1. **Police and Sheriff's Patrol Officers**	1,197,100
2. **Correctional Officers and Jailers**	591,890
3. **Firefighters**	581,020
4. Office Clerks, General	514,990
5. **Postal Service Mail Carriers**	343,340
6. Business Operations Specialists, All Other	329,520
7. **Secretaries and Administrative Assistants, Except Legal, Medical, and Executive**	273,100
8. **Maintenance and Repair Workers, General**	257,530
9. **Executive Secretaries and Administrative Assistants**	241,810
10. **Highway Maintenance Workers**	240,360
11. **Janitors and Cleaners, Except Maids and Housekeeping Cleaners**	222,810
12. Recreation Workers	208,660
13. **Bookkeeping, Accounting, and Auditing Clerks**	207,030
14. **Registered Nurses**	205,590
15. **Court, Municipal, and License Clerks**	201,530
16. **Compliance Officers**	192,230
17. Landscaping and Groundskeeping Workers	180,590
18. Postal Service Mail Sorters, Processors, and Processing Machine Operators	179,740
19. **Police, Fire, and Ambulance Dispatchers**	174,550
20. **Child, Family, and School Social Workers**	174,220

Education and Training

The educational and training requirements for jobs in the Government mirror those in the private sector for most major occupational groups. Many jobs in managerial or professional and related occupations, for example, require a four-year college degree. Some, such as engineers, physicians and surgeons, and biological and physical scientists, require a bachelor's or higher degree in a specific field of study. In addition, many occupations, such as registered nurses and engineering technicians, require at least two years of training after high school. Many additional jobs, such as those in office and administrative support, have more general requirements. Some have no formal educational requirement, while others require a high school diploma or some related experience.

Outlook

Government will continue to be a large employer. Many jobs will come open as workers retire over the next decade, although job prospects are expected to vary by occupation.

Employment change. Wage and salary employment in the federal government, apart from the Post Office, is expected to increase by 10 percent over the coming decade, which is close to the 11 percent growth rate for all industries combined. Staffing levels in federal government can be subject to change in the long run because of changes in public policies as legislated by Congress, which affect spending levels and hiring decisions for the various departments and agencies. In general, over the coming decade, domestic programs are likely to see an increase in employment.

While there will be growth in many occupations over the coming decade, demand will be especially strong for specialized workers in areas related to public health, information security, scientific research, law enforcement, and financial services.

At the state and local level, overall prospects are expected to be favorable, although job prospects vary by state and region. Wage and salary employment in state and local government is projected to increase 8 percent during the 2008–2018 period, slower than the 11 percent growth projected for all sectors of the economy combined.

Job growth will stem from the rising demand for services at the state and local levels, particularly demand for public safety and health services. Despite this demand, employment growth will continue to be dampened because budgets will be constrained by the rapidly increasing proportion of revenues devoted to the Medicaid program and by public resistance to tax increases. Outsourcing of government jobs to the private sector will also limit employment in state and local government. When economic times are good, many state and local governments increase spending on programs and employment.

Professional and service occupations accounted for over half of all jobs in state and local government. Most new jobs will stem from steady demand for community and social services; health services; and protective services, including law enforcement and fire fighting and prevention workers.

Employment of management, business, and financial occupations is projected to grow at about the same rate as overall employment in state and local government. Employment in office and administrative support occupations in state and local government is expected to remain close to current levels.

Job prospects. Job prospects in Government are expected to vary by occupation. Over the next decade, a significant number of workers are expected to retire, which will create a large number of job openings. This may create favorable prospects in certain occupations, but job seekers may face competition for positions in occupations with fewer retirements or for popular jobs that attract many applicants.

At the state and local level, job prospects vary by state and region. Prospects with managerial experience will have better opportunities, as a growing number of managers are expected to retire in the coming decade. Currently, some states and localities are being forced to reduce payrolls; however, as state and local budgets improve, new opportunities should arise.

Job security. Government used to be the most secure field to work in. Although this security has diminished somewhat, especially as budgets have become constrained, government is considered to be relatively stable because it is less susceptible than private industries to fluctuations in the economy. In fact, this perception causes competition for Government positions to increase during times of economic uncertainty.

Earnings

The majority of professional and administrative federal workers are paid under the General Schedule (GS). The General Schedule has 15 grades of pay for civilian white-collar and service workers and smaller within-grade step increases that occur based on length of service and quality of performance. In an effort to make federal pay more responsive to local labor market conditions, federal employees working in the continental United States receive locality pay.

For those in craft, repair, operator, and laborer jobs, the Federal Wage System (FWS) is used to determine worker pay. This schedule sets federal wages so that they are comparable with prevailing regional wage rates for similar types of jobs. As a result, wage rates paid under the FWS can vary significantly from one locality to another.

In state and local governments, earnings and wages vary by occupation, size of the state or locality, and region of the country. As in most industries, professionals and managers earn more than other workers.

Benefits and union membership. Benefits are an important part of employee compensation for Government workers. Many Government employees receive health and life insurance options that are partially subsidized. In addition, many Government workers participate in a retirement plan that may include a pension and an optional savings program similar to a 401(k) plan.

Government employees receive both vacation and sick leave. They also tend to get more holiday leave than workers in private industry. A little less than one-third of federal workers are unionized, but state and local workers have a relatively high rate of union membership.

Recently, some states have attempted to curb the ability of unions to negotiate on behalf of state workers. As of this writing, it is not yet clear whether this trend will continue, will slow down, or will be reversed.

Sources of Additional Information

Information on obtaining a position with the federal government is available from the Office of Personnel Management (OPM) through USAJOBS, the federal government's official employment information system. This resource for locating and applying for job opportunities can be accessed through the Internet at www.usajobs.opm.gov.

For advice on finding a job with the federal government and more information on the federal hiring process and employment system, contact

❋ Partnership for Public Service, 1100 New York Ave. NW, Suite 1090 East, Washington, DC 20005. Internet: www.ourpublicservice.org

❋ American Society for Public Administration, 1301 Pennsylvania Ave. NW, Suite 840, Washington, DC 20004. Internet: www.publicservicecareers.org

For more information on union membership for federal government employees, contact

❋ American Federation of Government Employees, 80 F St. NW, Washington, DC 20001. Internet: www.afge.org

Individuals interested in working for state or local government agencies should contact the appropriate agencies. City, county, and state personnel and human resources departments and local offices of state employment services have applications and additional information. Many states provide sites similar to the federal government's USAJOBS where you can locate and apply for state jobs; often you can access them through the website of your state's civil service commission.

For more information about careers in local government management, including local government management internship programs, contact

❋ International City/County Management Association, 777 North Capitol St. NE, Suite 500, Washington, DC 20002. Internet: www.icma.org

Health Care

Combining medical technology and the human touch, the Health Care field diagnoses, treats, and administers care around the clock, responding to the needs of millions of people—from newborns to the terminally ill. Because it meets a lifelong need and the demand for health care is increasing rapidly, this is one of the most secure career fields.

About 595,800 establishments make up the Health Care field; they vary greatly in terms of size, staffing patterns, and organizational structures. About 76 percent of Health Care establishments are offices of physicians, dentists, or other health practitioners. Although hospitals constitute only 1 percent of all Health Care establishments, they employ 35 percent of all workers.

The Health Care field includes establishments ranging from small-town private practices of physicians who employ only one medical assistant to busy inner-city hospitals that provide thousands of diverse jobs. In 2008, around 48 percent of nonhospital Health Care establishments employed fewer than 5 workers. In contrast, 72 percent of hospital employees were in establishments with more than 1,000 workers.

How the Field Is Organized

The Health Care field consists of the following segments:

Hospitals. Hospitals provide complete medical care, ranging from diagnostic services to surgery to continuous nursing care. Some hospitals specialize in treatment of the mentally ill, cancer patients, or children. Hospital-based care may be on an inpatient (overnight) or outpatient basis.

Nursing and residential care facilities. Nursing care facilities provide inpatient nursing, rehabilitation, and health-related personal care to those who need continuous nursing care but do not require hospital services. Other facilities, such as convalescent homes, help patients who need less assistance. Residential care facilities provide around-the-clock social and personal care to children, the elderly, and others who have limited ability to care for themselves.

Offices of physicians. About 36 percent of all Health Care establishments fall into this segment of the field. Physicians and surgeons practice privately or in groups of practitioners who have the same or different specialties.

Offices of dentists. About 20 percent of Health Care establishments are dentist's offices. Most employ only a few workers, who provide preventive, cosmetic, or emergency care.

Home health-care services. Skilled nursing or medical care is sometimes provided in the home, under a physician's supervision. Home health-care services are provided mainly to the elderly.

Offices of other health practitioners. This segment of the field includes the offices of chiropractors, optometrists, podiatrists, occupational and physical therapists, psychologists, audiologists, speech-language pathologists, dietitians, and other health practitioners.

Ambulatory health-care services. This segment includes outpatient care centers and medical and diagnostic laboratories. These establishments are diverse, including kidney dialysis centers; outpatient mental health and substance abuse centers; blood and organ banks; and medical labs that analyze blood, do diagnostic imaging, and perform other clinical tests.

Recent Developments

In the rapidly changing Health Care field, technological advances have made many new procedures and methods of diagnosis and treatment possible. In addition, advances in information technology have improved patient care and worker efficiency.

Cost containment also is shaping the Health Care field, as shown by the growing emphasis on providing services on an outpatient, ambulatory basis; limiting unnecessary or low-priority services; and stressing preventive care, which reduces the potential cost of undiagnosed, untreated medical conditions. Enrollment in managed care programs continues to grow.

Various health-care reforms are presently in the process of being adopted. These reforms may affect the number of people covered by some form of health insurance, the number of people being treated by health-care providers, and the number and type of health-care procedures that will be performed.

Working Conditions

In 2008, the incidence of occupational injury and illness in hospitals was higher than the average for the private field overall. Nursing care facilities had an even higher rate.

Health Care workers involved in direct patient care must take precautions to prevent back strain from lifting patients and equipment, to minimize exposure to radiation and caustic chemicals, and to guard against infectious diseases. Home care personnel and other Health Care workers who travel as part of their job are exposed to the possibility of being injured in highway accidents.

Employment

As one of the largest industries in 2008, Health Care provided 14.3 million jobs for wage and salary workers. About 40 percent were in hospitals, another 21 percent were in nursing and residential care facilities, and 16 percent were in offices of physicians.

Largest Occupations in Health Care (Secure Jobs Bold)	
Job	Workforce in Health Care
1. **Registered Nurses**	2,192,420
2. **Nursing Aides, Orderlies, and Attendants**	1,285,220
3. **Home Health Aides**	702,680
4. **Licensed Practical and Licensed Vocational Nurses**	619,120
5. **Physicians and Surgeons**	512,470
6. **Medical Assistants**	450,730
7. **Medical Secretaries**	437,310
8. **Receptionists and Information Clerks**	386,270
9. Office Clerks, General	298,290
10. **Dental Assistants**	282,800
11. **Maids and Housekeeping Cleaners**	257,850
12. **Personal Care Aides**	238,130
13. **Secretaries and Administrative Assistants, Except Legal, Medical, and Executive**	213,810
14. **Medical and Health Services Managers**	206,850
15. **Radiologic Technologists and Technicians**	201,280
16. **Billing and Posting Clerks and Machine Operators**	194,770
17. **First-Line Supervisors of Office and Administrative Support Workers**	190,880
18. **Dental Hygienists**	169,670
19. **Physical Therapists**	153,940
20. **Medical and Clinical Laboratory Technologists**	149,420

Each segment of the Health Care field provides a different mix of wage and salary health-related jobs.

Hospitals. Hospitals employ workers with all levels of education and training, thereby providing a wider variety of opportunities than is offered by other segments of the Health Care field. About 28 percent of hospital workers are registered nurses. Hospitals also employ many physicians and surgeons, therapists, and social workers. About 21 percent of hospital jobs are in a service occupation, such as nursing, psychiatric, and home health aides or building cleaning workers. Hospitals also employ large numbers of office and administrative support workers.

Nursing and residential care facilities. About 63 percent of nursing and residential care facility jobs are in service occupations, primarily nursing, psychiatric, and home health aides. Professional and administrative support occupations make up a much smaller percentage of employment in this segment, compared with other parts of the Health Care field.

Offices of physicians. Many of the jobs in offices of physicians are in professional and related occupations, primarily physicians, surgeons, and registered nurses. About 37 percent of all jobs, however, are in office and administrative support occupations, such as receptionists and information clerks.

Offices of dentists. Roughly 35 percent of all jobs in this segment are in service occupations, mostly dental assistants. The typical staffing pattern in dentists' offices consists of one dentist with a support staff of dental hygienists and dental assistants.

Home health-care services. About 59 percent of jobs in this segment are in service occupations, mostly home health aides and personal and home care aides. Nursing and therapist jobs also account for substantial shares of employment in this segment.

Offices of other health practitioners. About 42 percent of jobs in this segment of the field are professional and related occupations, including physical therapists, occupational therapists, dispensing opticians, and chiropractors. Health-care practitioners and technical occupations and office and administrative support occupations also accounted for a significant portion of all jobs—35 percent and 31 percent, respectively.

Ambulatory health-care services. Outpatient care centers employed high percentages of professional and related workers, such as counselors and registered nurses. Medical and diagnostic laboratories predominantly employ clinical laboratory and radiological technologists and technicians. Emergency medical technicians and paramedics are also employed in ambulatory services.

Education and Training

A wide variety of people with various educational backgrounds are necessary for the Health Care field to function. The Health Care field employs some highly educated occupations that often require many years of training beyond graduate school. However, most of the occupations in the Health Care field require less than four years of college.

Some Health Care establishments provide on-the-job or classroom training, as well as continuing education. Most Health Care workers who do not have postsecondary occupational training and work directly with patients will receive some on-the-job training. Hospitals are more likely than other facilities to have the resources and incentive to provide training programs and advancement opportunities to their employees.

Persons considering careers in Health Care should have a strong desire to help others, genuine concern for the welfare of patients and clients, and an ability to deal with people of diverse backgrounds in stressful situations. Many of the Health Care jobs that are regulated by state licensure require professional workers to complete continuing education at regular intervals to maintain valid licensure.

Outlook

Health Care will generate 3.2 million new wage and salary jobs between 2008 and 2018, more than any other field, largely in response to rapid growth in the elderly population. Ten of the 20 fastest-growing occupations are related to Health Care. Many job openings should arise in all Health Care employment settings as a result of employment growth and the need to replace workers who retire or leave their jobs for other reasons.

Employment change. Wage and salary employment in the Health Care field is projected to increase 22 percent through 2018, compared with 11 percent for all industries combined. Employment growth is expected to account for about 22 percent of all new wage and salary jobs in the field over the 2008–2018 period. Projected rates of employment growth for the various segments of the field range from 10 percent in hospitals, the largest and slowest-growing segment of the field, to 46 percent in the much smaller home health-care services segment.

Job prospects. Many job openings should arise in all employment settings as a result of employment growth and the need to replace workers who retire or leave their jobs for other reasons. Tougher immigration rules that are slowing the numbers of foreign Health Care workers entering the United States should make it easier to get a job in this field.

Occupations with the most replacement openings are usually large, with high turnover stemming from low pay and status, poor benefits, low training requirements, and a high proportion of young and part-time workers. Nursing aides, orderlies, and attendants and home health aides are among the occupations adding the most new jobs in this field between 2008 and 2018, about 592,200 combined. In contrast, occupations with relatively few replacement openings—such as physicians and surgeons—are characterized by high pay and status, lengthy training requirements, and a high proportion of full-time workers.

Health Care workers at all levels of education and training will continue to be in demand. In many cases, it may be easier for job seekers with health-specific training to obtain jobs and advance in their careers. Specialized clinical training is a requirement for many jobs in Health Care and is an asset even for many administrative jobs that do not specifically require it.

Job security. In the list of the 20 largest jobs in this field, only one is not considered secure. The rapid growth of this field is one important reason for its security. In addition, most of the jobs require in-person work by humans and therefore cannot be offshored or automated. Finally, the state of the economy has little effect on the demand for most health-care services. Patients may postpone some dental visits or elective surgery during hard times, but these services are exceptional.

Earnings

Average earnings of nonsupervisory workers in most Health Care segments are higher than the average for all private industry, with hospital workers earning considerably more than the average and those employed in nursing and residential care facilities and home health-care services earning less.

As in most industries, professionals and managers working in Health Care typically earn more than other workers in the field. Wages in individual Health Care occupations vary as widely as the duties, level of education and training, and amount of responsibility required by the occupation. Some establishments offer tuition reimbursement, paid training, child day-care services, and flexible work hours. Health Care establishments that must be staffed around the clock to care for patients and handle emergencies often pay premiums for overtime and weekend work, holidays, late shifts, and time spent on call.

Benefits and union membership. Health Care workers generally receive standard benefits, such as health insurance, paid vacation and sick leave, and pension plans. However, benefits can vary greatly by occupation and by employer.

Although some hospitals have unions, the Health Care field is not heavily unionized. In 2008, 17 percent of workers in hospitals were members of unions or covered by union contracts, while all other Health Care sectors had rates below the 14 percent average for all industries.

Sources of Additional Information

For additional information on specific health-related occupations, contact

❉ American Medical Association/Health Professions Career and Education Directory, 515 N. State St., Chicago, IL 60654. Internet: www.ama-assn.org/go/alliedhealth

For information on physician careers and applying to medical school, contact

❉ Association of American Medical Colleges, 2450 N St. NW, Washington, DC 20037. Internet: www.aamc.org/students

General information on health careers is available from

❋ Bureau of Health Professions, Room 8A-09, 5600 Fishers Lane, Rockville, MD 20857. Internet: http://bhpr.hrsa.gov/

For a list of accredited programs in allied health fields, contact

❋ Commission on Accreditation of Allied Health Education Programs, 1361 Park St., Clearwater, FL 33756. Internet: www.caahep.org

Repair and Maintenance

It's a fact of life that machines and electronic equipment sometimes break down and need to be restored to working order. Routine maintenance services, such as changing the oil in your automobile, often can prevent breakdowns and keep equipment running efficiently. This work provides the livelihood for workers in the Repair and Maintenance career field.

Some establishments in the Repair and Maintenance field primarily serve only businesses or only households. For example, businesses would be the primary clients for a company that services vending machines. A shoe repair business, on the other hand, would serve mainly households. Many Repair and Maintenance establishments serve both kinds of customers. For example, establishments repairing computers and consumer electronics products are two examples of such overlap.

How the Field Is Organized

Automotive repair and maintenance is the largest sector in this career field. The Department of Transportation estimates that about 140 million cars and 8 million motorcycles are registered in the United States. In addition to general automotive repair shops, this sector of the field includes specialized establishments that focus on exhaust systems, transmissions, the body and its paint, the interior, glass, oil change, and lubrication. Car washes are also included.

Many other establishments and workers are involved in *electronic and precision equipment repair and maintenance.* Some of them service consumer electronics products, such as television sets, video games, VCRs, stereo equipment, radios, and cameras. Others repair and maintain computers and other office machines, such as photocopiers. Some recycle printer cartridges. Communication devices, including fax machines, telephones, and public address systems, also require routine servicing and repairs. Some workers focus on specialized electronic equipment, such as laboratory instruments, medical equipment, or navigational instruments.

The mining, manufacturing, agriculture, and construction industries depend on repair and maintenance of many kinds of equipment. So do many other businesses that use electrical and mechanical equipment. This sector of the career field is known as *commercial and industrial machinery and equipment (except automotive and electronic) repair and maintenance.* It includes establishments that service electric motors, farm machinery, heavy construction machinery, forklifts, paper-making equipment, textile machinery, freezers, printing presses, food-processing machinery, and many other kinds of industrial and commercial equipment.

Other workers and establishments repair and maintain *personal and household goods.* For example, they service lawn and garden equipment, repair household appliances, reupholster furniture, and resole shoes.

A substantial amount of repair is done by establishments that also manufacture machinery, equipment, and other goods, but these establishments are considered to belong in the Manufacturing field. In addition, repair of transportation equipment is often provided by or based at transportation facilities, such as airports and seaports, and these activities are included in the Transportation and Warehousing field. Many workers who repair buildings, such as plumbers, electricians, painters, and roofers, are often involved in new construction; therefore, this work is considered to belong to the Construction field—one of the less secure career fields.

Recent Developments

In the trend toward miniaturization of electronic products, integrated circuitry has replaced many systems that consisted of replaceable components. In some cases, moving parts such as switches have been replaced by nonmoving electronic parts. These miniaturized systems tend to be more reliable, with less need for maintenance and repair. They often are cheaper to buy and more difficult to service because of their small size and the tight integration of components. As a result, it is often more economical to dispose of a malfunctioning product than to repair it. Rapid advances in technology, such as faster desktop computers and more powerful mobile phones, sometimes spur consumers and businesses to upgrade to new equipment rather than service existing devices.

With automobiles, however, the trend is in the opposite direction: In recent years, the average age of motor vehicles has increased. Although some components of vehicles are more reliable and less in need of service than in past years, the overall need for vehicle repair and maintenance continues to be steady.

Working Conditions

In 2008, workers in this field averaged 39.3 hours per week, compared with 33.6 for all fields combined. About 27 percent work 50 or more hours a week. Only about 1.3 percent work part time.

Because there is so much variation in the kinds of equipment that can be repaired or maintained, working conditions vary greatly. For example, many workers who service office equipment spend most of their time in clean, well-lighted, and comfortable offices, whereas workers who repair and maintain manufacturing equipment may work in settings that are noisy, dirty, damp, hot or cold, cramped, or at high elevation. Some workers spend part or all of their time at a repair facility rather than at the site where the equipment is used.

Workers may be exposed to noise, fumes, vibration, sharp objects, the possibility of electric shock, and other hazards, but they are trained to use appropriate safety equipment and procedures that minimize risks. In addition to safety gear, some workers wear uniforms, especially those who work for franchised service companies.

Employment

In 2008, there were about 1.2 million wage and salary jobs in the Repair and Maintenance field. While the field has both large and small firms, the average establishment is relatively small; about 53 percent of establishments employed fewer than 5 workers in 2007. Less than 1 percent of the jobs are found in establishments that employ 50 or more workers.

The average age of the workers in this field is about 46, amost 10 years higher than the average in most fields.

Largest Occupations in Repair and Maintenance (Secure Jobs Bold)	
Job	Workforce in Repair and Maintenance
1. **Automotive Service Technicians and Mechanics**	236,140
2. Cleaners of Vehicles and Equipment	127,270
3. **Automotive Body and Related Repairers**	99,240
4. First-Line Supervisors of Mechanics, Installers, and Repairers	49,640
5. Office Clerks, General	46,880
6. **Automotive and Watercraft Service Attendants**	36,130
7. **Industrial Machinery Mechanics**	27,500
8. Bus and Truck Mechanics and Diesel Engine Specialists	25,950

Largest Occupations in Repair and Maintenance (Secure Jobs Bold)

Job	Workforce in Repair and Maintenance
9. **Secretaries and Administrative Assistants, Except Legal, Medical, and Executive**	25,750
10. **Painters, Transportation Equipment**	24,680
11. Helpers—Installation, Maintenance, and Repair Workers	23,800
12. **General and Operations Managers**	22,640
13. **Welders, Cutters, Solderers, and Brazers**	20,060
14. **Computer, Automated Teller, and Office Machine Repairers**	17,730
15. **Automotive Glass Installers and Repairers**	15,540
16. Counter and Rental Clerks	14,880
17. Maintenance and Repair Workers, General	12,340
18. **Home Appliance Repairers**	12,070
19. Upholsterers	11,790
20. First-Line Supervisors of Helpers, Laborers, and Material Movers, Hand	11,530

Education and Training

Occupations in the Repair and Maintenance field require varying levels of education, but because so many of the occupations require only on-the-job training, the education level of workers in this field is lower than average. The level of education and type of training required depend largely on the nature of the technology the worker will be repairing or maintaining, although in some cases (such as servicing upholstery) it can take lengthy training to achieve skill doing low-tech repairs.

Sometimes workers service the same type of equipment with different levels of skill and, therefore, will have prepared differently. For example, some service technicians who work on cars perform only a limited set of routine tasks, such as changing the oil, and short-term on-the-job training would be sufficient preparation for them. Other technicians may need several years of training, perhaps in an apprenticeship, plus an additional few years of work experience to become fully qualified to perform complex and varied repairs on cars. Similarly, welding, soldering, and brazing workers can prepare for careers at various levels of skill.

Some industrial machinery mechanics enter the occupation through an apprenticeship program that typically lasts about four years. Apprenticeships can be sponsored by local union chapters, employers, or the state labor department. Training in these apprenticeships involves a combination of on-the-job training and classroom learning. Job seekers can apply for union apprenticeships, and qualified applicants may begin training in local training facilities and factories.

Industrial machinery mechanics usually need a year or more of formal education and training after high school to learn the growing range of mechanical and technical skills that they need. While mechanics used to specialize in one area, such as hydraulics or electronics, many factories now require every mechanic to have knowledge of electricity, electronics, hydraulics, and computer programming. As competition with foreign manufacturers heats up, higher and higher levels of skill are needed.

Technicians who have a general knowledge of repair and maintenance techniques can sometimes learn how to service specific makes and models of equipment through classes offered by manufacturers. Other highly focused classes are given by specialized industry associations. Through such a class, technicians may earn a certificate that documents their specialized skill. In some occupations, certification is also available to show mastery of a broad range of skills—for example, in automotive repair, where versatility can be an asset.

Outlook

Employment is expected to gain slightly over the next decade to keep the nation's motor vehicles and industrial equipment running longer than in the past.

Employment change. The Repair and Maintenance field is expected to experience a 5.1 percent increase in wage and salary employment from 2008–2018, compared with 11 percent growth projected for all career fields combined. Fastest growth will be in repairing and maintaining motor vehicles, electronic and precision equipment, and commercial and industrial machinery and equipment.

Job prospects. Job prospects should be favorable for skilled technicians but less good for managerial workers. Among the larger occupations, vehicle mechanics and repairers should have many opportunities. Industrial machinery mechanics are expected to be in demand in industries that are not offshored, such as energy and automotive manufacturing. Medical equipment repairers are presently few in number, but the occupation is expected to grow very rapidly.

Job security. The continuing need to maintain machinery, including motor vehicles, is the main reason for the security of many occupations in this field. Almost none of the work can be offshored, and very little can be automated. Decreasing costs and increased reliability of electronic products will shift greater security to jobs that involve mechanical products and equipment. However, service technicians will need skills with the electronic and computer components that increasingly are being integrated with mechanical equipment and that are used to diagnose problems.

Earnings

Production workers in the Repair and Maintenance field averaged $624 a week in May 2010, somewhat lower than the average of $749 in all private industry. Workers in a few specialized repair occupations had higher earnings; for example, medical appliance technicians averaged $813 a week.

Benefits and union membership. Workers generally receive standard benefits, including health insurance, paid vacation and sick leave, and pension plans. Unionization is uncommon in the Repair and Maintenance field. In 2008, less than 1 percent of all workers were union members or covered by union contracts, compared with an average of 14 percent of workers throughout all private industries.

Sources of Additional Information

For general information about a career as an automotive service technician, contact

⚜ Automotive Careers Today, 8400 Westpark Dr., MS #2, McLean, VA 22102. Internet: www.autocareerstoday.org

⚜ Automotive Service Association, P.O. Box 929, Bedford, TX 76095. Internet: www.asashop.org

For information about medical equipment technicians and a list of schools with related programs of study, contact

⚜ Association for the Advancement of Medical Instrumentation (AAMI), 1110 N. Glebe Rd., Suite 220, Arlington, VA 22201-4795. Internet: www.aami.org

For further information on apprenticeship programs, write to the Apprenticeship Council of your state's labor department or local firms that employ mechanics and repairers.

Utilities

The Utilities field includes companies that generate, transmit, and distribute electrical power; distribute natural gas; treat and distribute fresh water; and treat wastewater. The federal government and many state and local governments also provide electric, gas, water, and wastewater treatment services and employ a significant number of workers in similar jobs, but they are not included in the figures for this field.

The Utilities field is unique in that urban areas with many inhabitants generally have relatively few utility companies. Also unlike most industries, the Utilities field imports and exports only a small portion of its product. Because of the essential nature of the product and the relative lack of competition, this field has more security than most.

How the Field Is Organized

The Utilities field comprises three distinctly different sectors.

The *electric power generation, transmission, and distribution* segment generates slightly less than half of the nation's electrical energy from coal. The majority of the rest is produced by a combination of natural gas, nuclear energy, and hydroelectric generators. Renewable sources of electric power—including geothermal, wind, and solar energy—are expanding rapidly but make up only a small percentage of total generation. Deregulation—a major legislative trend at both the federal and state levels during the 1990s—has allowed local utility companies to buy power from companies that own generators and resell that energy to consumers.

The *natural gas distribution segment* transmits the gas through pressurized pipelines. Local distribution companies take natural gas from the pipeline; depressurize it; add odor to it; and deliver the gas to industrial, residential, and commercial customers.

The *water, sewage, and other systems segment* treats and distributes tap water for use by business and residential customers. It also operates sewer systems or plants that collect, treat, and dispose of waste from homes and industries.

The various segments of the Utilities field vary in the degree to which their workers are involved in production activities, administration and management, or research and development. Some segments, such as water supply, employ relatively few workers, mostly concentrated in production and plant operation. On the other hand, electric utilities generally operate larger plants using very expensive, high-technology equipment and thus employ more professional and technical personnel.

Recent Developments

Energy policy is one of the key issues facing policy makers today. Issues such as energy security, pollution, greenhouse gas emissions, and toxic waste disposal are debated regularly in Congress. In both 2005 and 2007, Congress promoted conservation by passing new energy legislation that created subsidies for clean technologies. The expansion of nuclear power also is a major topic of discussion, and several new plants have received building permits, although none have began construction. The fastest-growing segment of the electric power industry is renewable energy. While renewables only make up a relatively small piece of the nation's energy mix, both wind and solar energy are expanding rapidly, and the companies engaged in production and installation are hiring a significant number of new workers.

The natural gas industry also is evolving. While the share of natural gas being consumed by residential households and businesses has reached a near-term plateau, consumption by other sectors continue to increase. Meanwhile, new sources of natural gas in shale beds are being discovered and exploited, ensuring that gas will remain an important utility.

The water and sewage systems segment continues to face challenges. As urban areas continue to grow and demand greater amounts of water, sources of fresh water are being exhausted. At the same time, companies are having difficulty complying with federal and state water quality regulations. In many areas, aging infrastructure is a significant problem and will have to be replaced during the projection period.

All utilities continue to be affected by the anticipated baby boom retirements, which are expected to dramatically reduce the supply of domestic utility workers. As a result, the Utilities field is teaming up with universities, community colleges, and trade schools to train new workers and prepare the utility workforce of the future.

Working Conditions

Hours. Electricity, gas, and water are used continuously throughout each day. As a result, split, weekend, and night shifts are common for many utility workers. The average weekly hours worked for production workers in Utilities was 42.7 hours in 2008, compared with 33.2 hours for all trade, transportation, and utilities fields, and 33.6 hours for all private industries. At times, some employees must work overtime to accommodate peaks in demand and to repair damage caused by storms, cold weather, accidents, and other occurrences. The field employs relatively few part-time workers.

Work environment. The hazards of working with electricity, natural gas, treatment chemicals, and wastes can be substantial, but workers generally avoid them by following rigorous safety procedures. Protective gear such as rubber gloves and rubber sleeves, nonsparking maintenance equipment, and body suits with breathing devices designed to filter out any harmful fumes are mandatory for work in dangerous environments. Employees also undergo extensive training on working with hazardous materials and utility company safety measures.

Employment

Utilities had 559,500 wage and salary jobs in 2008. Electric power generation, transmission, and distribution provided about 404,700 jobs. The diversity of production processes in the Utilities field is reflected in the size of the establishments that make up the field. For example, the electric power and natural gas distribution sectors consist of relatively large plants. In 2008, electric power generation, transmission, and distribution plants employed an average of about 50 workers per establishment. On the other hand, the water, sewage, and other systems sector employed an average of only 8 workers per establishment.

Although many establishments are small, the majority of Utilities jobs were in establishments with 100 or more workers.

About 226,500 jobs—approximately 40 percent of all wage and salary jobs in the Utilities field—were in production or installation, maintenance, and repair occupations in 2008. About 21 percent of jobs were in office and administrative support occupations; 15 percent were in professional and related occupations; and 13 percent were in management, business, and financial occupations. The remaining jobs were in construction, transportation, sales, and service occupations.

Largest Occupations in Utilities (Secure Jobs Bold)

Job	Workforce in Utilities
1. **Electrical Power-Line Installers and Repairers**	54,480
2. Customer Service Representatives	29,460
3. **Power Plant Operators**	25,480
4. **Meter Readers, Utilities**	20,070
5. Control and Valve Installers and Repairers, Except Mechanical Door	18,670
6. **Electrical and Electronics Repairers, Powerhouse, Substation, and Relay**	18,210
7. First-Line Supervisors of Mechanics, Installers, and Repairers	15,570
8. **Electrical Engineers**	12,770
9. **Water and Wastewater Treatment Plant and System Operators**	12,490
10. First-Line Supervisors of Production and Operating Workers	11,060
11. **Maintenance and Repair Workers, General**	10,680
12. **General and Operations Managers**	9,950
13. **Industrial Machinery Mechanics**	9,270
14. **Executive Secretaries and Executive Administrative Assistants**	9,070
15. Electricians	8,570
16. Office Clerks, General	8,480
17. **First-Line Supervisors of Office and Administrative Support Workers**	8,420

Largest Occupations in Utilities (Secure Jobs Bold)	
Job	Workforce in Utilities
18. Plumbers, Pipefitters, and Steamfitters	8,320
19. Business Operations Specialists, All Other	8,080
20. **Accountants and Auditors**	7,540

Education and Training

Utilities provide career opportunities for persons with varying levels of experience and education. However, because the Utilities field consists of many different companies and products, skills developed in one segment of the field may not be transferable to other segments.

High school graduates qualify for many entry-level production jobs, although most new workers usually are required to undergo company training. In some cases, especially in the electric power industry, companies require higher standards for employment, such as a degree from a technical school, community college, or university.

Most office and administrative support workers are required to have a high school diploma and typically receive on-the-job training.

Most computer, engineering, and technician jobs require technical education after high school, although opportunities exist for persons with degrees ranging from an associate degree to a doctorate.

Managerial jobs generally require a four-year college degree, although a two-year technical degree may be sufficient, depending on the employee's level of experience.

Outlook

Employment in Utilities is expected to decline; nevertheless, many job openings will arise because large numbers of many workers in the field are approaching retirement age and will need to be replaced.

Employment change. Wage and salary employment in Utilities is expected to decline 11 percent between 2008 and 2018, compared with an increase of 11 percent for all industries combined. Projected employment change varies among the segments of the field. Although electric power and natural gas continue to be essential to everyday life, the increased size and efficiency of new power plants will lead to an overall decline in employment. The water, sewage, and other systems segment of the field, however, will continue to grow as the population of the country increases and urban areas expand.

Employment in the electric power generation, transmission, and distribution segment is expected to decline by about 15 percent over the 2008–2018 period. Although the demand for electricity continues to increase over time, deregulation has led to greater cost-cutting measures that will allow power generation companies to be profitable in a competitive marketplace. As older, less efficient plants are retired, they are being replaced with new plants that require fewer workers. Nevertheless, some segments within electric power generation are likely to increase employment, such as electric transmission and renewable energy. Should state and federal governments continue offering incentives to companies utilizing these technologies, employment should grow even more unimpeded.

The natural gas distribution industry is expected to decline 6 percent over the projections decade. Industry consolidation has significantly impacted this industry, a trend that is expected to continue. Use of newer, more automated equipment will result in fewer operators to monitor these systems.

Water and sewage systems services are projected to grow 13 percent, as water systems are expanding rapidly and as the industry has not yet experienced the efficiency gains seen among other utilities. Additionally, regulatory changes have benefited this industry. While most water systems remain locally operated and fairly small in scale, water quality standards for both drinking water and disposal of wastewater have been tightened for public health and environmental reasons, requiring more workers. Hiring freezes have been less common in water than in other parts of the field, and much of the water workforce is nearing retirement age.

Job prospects. Despite overall declining employment, job prospects for qualified applicants entering the Utilities field are expected to be excellent during the next 10 years. As of 2008, about 53 percent of the Utilities field workforce is age 45 or older. Many of these workers will either retire or prepare to retire within the next 10 years. Because on-the-job training is very intensive in many Utilities occupations, preparing a new workforce will be one of the field's highest priorities during the next decade.

In general, persons with college training in advanced technology will have the best opportunities in the Utilities field. Network systems and data communications analysts are expected to be among the fastest-growing occupations in the professional and related occupations group, as plants emphasize automation and productivity.

New and continuing energy policies also provide investment tax credits for research and development of renewable sources of energy and ways to improve the efficiency of equipment used in electric utilities. As a result, electric utilities will continue to increase the productivity of their plants and workers, resulting in a slowdown in new employment. This slowdown will lead to keen competition for some jobs in the field. However, at the same time, these new technologies will create jobs for highly skilled technical personnel with the education and experience to take advantage of these developments in electric utilities.

Job security. Utilities serve functions that are vital to everyday life, such as electric power, water supply, and wastewater treatment. Although demands for electric power vary somewhat in response to changes in business activity, these fluctuations rarely endanger workers' jobs.

However, increasing automation and outsourcing are likely to threaten the jobs of many office and administrative support workers, such as utilities meter readers and bookkeeping, accounting, and auditing clerks. Technologies including radio-transmitted meter reading and computerized billing procedures are expected to decrease employment. The most secure jobs will be in the technical and managerial occupations.

Earnings

Earnings in Utilities are generally higher than earnings in other industries. Earnings vary by segment within Utilities. Wages for production workers are higher on average in natural gas distribution and in electric power generation than in water, sewage, and other systems. The hourly earnings for production workers in Utilities averaged $29.84 in May 2010, compared with $15.13 in all private industry. This was due in part to more overtime and weekend work, as utility plant operations must be monitored 24 hours a day.

Benefits and union membership. Most full-time workers in the Utilities field receive substantial benefits in addition to their salaries or hourly wages. The Utilities field is heavily unionized. In 2008, about 30 percent of workers in Utilities were union members or covered by union contracts, more than double the proportion for all industries. Union contracts often give workers better job stability and ensure reliable wages and benefits.

Sources of Additional Information

Information on employment in electric power generation, transmission, and distribution is available from

❋ American Public Power Association, 1875 Connecticut Ave. NW, Washington, DC 20009. Internet: www.appanet.org

❋ Center for Energy Workforce Development, 701 Pennsylvania Ave. NW, Washington, DC 20004-2696. Internet: www.cewd.org

Information on employment in natural gas distribution is available from

❋ American Public Gas Association, 201 Massachusetts Ave. NE, Suite C-4, Washington, DC 20002. Internet: www.apga.org

Information on employment in water and sewage treatment is available from

❋ American Water Works Association, 6666 W. Quincy Ave., Denver, CO 80235. Internet: www.awwa.org

❋ Water Environment Federation, 601 Wythe St., Alexandria, VA 22314. Internet: www.wcf.org

PART III

The Best Jobs Lists—Jobs with Security

This part contains many interesting lists, and it's a good place for you to start using the book. Here are some suggestions for using the lists to explore career options that are likely to be less sensitive than most to economic slowdowns:

- ✺ The table of contents at the beginning of this book presents a complete listing of the list titles in this section. You can browse the lists or use the table of contents to find those that interest you most.

- ✺ I gave the lists clear titles, so most require little explanation. I provide comments for each group of lists.

- ✺ As you review the lists of jobs, one or more of the jobs may appeal to you enough that you want to seek additional information. As this happens, mark that job (or, if someone else will be using this book, write it on a separate sheet of paper) so that you can look up the description of the job in Part IV.

- ✺ Keep in mind that all jobs in these lists meet my basic criteria for being included in this book, as I explain in the introduction. All lists, therefore, contain jobs in the six secure fields, with emphasis on occupations that have high pay, high growth, or large numbers of openings. These last three economic measures are easily quantified and are often presented in lists of best jobs in the newspapers and other media. Although earnings, growth, and openings are important, you also should consider other factors in your career planning. Obviously, you are considering the chances of riding out a future recession in the job; that's why you're reading this book. Other examples of factors to consider are location, liking the people you work with, and having opportunities to be creative. Many other factors that may help define the ideal job for you are difficult or impossible to quantify and thus aren't used in this book, so you need to consider the importance of these issues yourself.

❋ All data used to create these lists comes from the U.S. Department of Labor and the Census Bureau. The earnings figures are based on the average annual pay received by full-time workers in the six secure career fields. Note that all these earnings figures represent averages, and actual pay rates can vary greatly by location, amount of previous work experience, and other factors.

Some Details on the Lists

The sources of the information I used in constructing these lists are presented in this book's introduction. Here are some additional details on how I created the lists:

❋ Some jobs have the same scores for one or more data elements. For example, in the category of fastest growing, two Health Care jobs—Compliance Officers and Physician Assistants—are expected to grow at the same rate, 41.3 percent. Therefore, I ordered these two jobs alphabetically, and their order has no other significance. Avoiding these ties was impossible, so understand simply that the difference of several positions on a list may not mean as much as it seems.

❋ Some job titles represent combinations of two or more closely related job specializations. For example, here in Part III you will find a job called Clinical, Counseling, and School Psychologists. The U.S. Department of Labor provides data on earnings, job growth, and job openings for this job title, so it is useful for the purposes of these lists. In Part IV, however, where you'll turn to find more detailed information about the jobs on these lists, you can find *separate* descriptions of the jobs Clinical Psychologists, Counseling Psychologists, and School Psychologists under the heading "Job Specializations." That level of detail is more appropriate for that section of the book.

Best Secure Jobs Overall: Jobs in Each Field with the Highest Pay, Fastest Growth, and Most Openings

The 24 lists that follow are the most important lists in this book. The first six lists present, for each of the six secure career fields, the jobs meeting the criteria for this book with the highest combined scores for pay, growth, and number of openings. These are very appealing lists because they represent secure jobs that have the very highest quantifiable measures from our labor market. The 150 unique jobs in the first set of lists are the basis for all the job lists in Part III and are described in detail in Part IV.

The three additional sets of lists each present, for each secure field, 20 jobs with the highest scores on each of three measures: annual earnings, projected percentage growth, and largest number of openings.

The Best Secure Jobs Overall in Each Field

Most people want to see this set of lists first. For each of six career fields, you can see the secure jobs with the highest overall combined ratings for earnings, projected growth, and number of openings. (The section in the introduction on "How the Best Secure Jobs Were Selected" explains in detail how I selected and sorted jobs to assemble this list.)

A look at one of these lists will clarify how I ordered the jobs. The Educational Services occupation with the best total score was Administrative Services Managers, so it tops the list. The occupation coming in at second place, Instructional Coordinators, offers considerably faster job growth than the top-ranked job, but its average earnings are $14,000 less per year and its expected job openings are slightly lower than those of Administrative Services Managers, so it had a lower total score. The other occupations follow in descending order based on their total scores. Many jobs had tied scores and were simply listed one after another, so often only very small or even no differences exist between the scores of jobs that are near each other on the list. All other job lists in this book (other than the bonus lists) use these jobs as their source list. You can find descriptions for each of these jobs in Part IV, beginning on page 137. If a job appeals to you, or if you're not sure what it is, find it alphabetically in the section of Part IV that covers the particular career field and read the job description.

The 30 Best Secure Computer Systems Design Jobs Overall

Job	Annual Earnings	Percent Growth	Annual Openings
1. Software Developers, Systems Software	$92,130	57.4%	6,120
2. Software Developers, Applications	$87,220	57.3%	10,300
3. Computer Network Architects	$77,190	95.6%	4,090
4. Network and Computer Systems Administrators	$74,230	71.7%	2,793
5. Database Administrators	$82,820	57.3%	960
6. Accountants and Auditors	$69,100	65.5%	990
7. Computer Systems Analysts	$80,830	40.2%	7,330
8. Management Analysts	$87,950	40.2%	1,930
9. Computer and Information Research Scientists	$96,590	43.0%	420
10. Industrial Engineers	$78,670	64.5%	200
11. General and Operations Managers	$137,170	28.7%	1,280

(continued)

(continued)

The 30 Best Secure Computer Systems Design Jobs Overall

Job	Annual Earnings	Percent Growth	Annual Openings
12. Human Resources Managers	$115,750	40.8%	140
13. Computer Occupations, All Other	$74,560	40.2%	1,150
14. Electronics Engineers, Except Computer	$92,460	40.2%	160
15. Employment, Recruitment, and Placement Specialists	$63,090	54.3%	630
16. Training and Development Specialists	$64,380	54.3%	490
17. Administrative Services Managers	$90,340	40.2%	160
18. Logisticians	$73,700	54.2%	230
19. Chief Executives	$166,400+	26.2%	270
20. Compliance Officers	$68,710	71.6%	100
21. Public Relations Specialists	$68,760	54.2%	230
22. Compensation, Benefits, and Job Analysis Specialists	$66,450	59.9%	150
23. Mechanical Engineers	$79,000	50.2%	90
24. Electrical Engineers	$86,030	40.2%	110
25. Graphic Designers	$50,640	40.3%	530
26. Operations Research Analysts	$78,620	30.4%	350
27. Budget Analysts	$77,630	40.2%	80
28. Technical Writers	$66,860	30.9%	430
29. First-Line Supervisors of Office and Administrative Support Workers	$56,140	40.1%	490
30. Industrial Engineering Technicians	$53,250	54.1%	80

The 50 Best Secure Educational Services Jobs Overall

Job	Annual Earnings	Percent Growth	Annual Openings
1. Administrative Services Managers	$74,970	19.3%	3,430
2. Instructional Coordinators	$60,450	27.6%	3,130
3. Computer Network Architects	$61,220	51.7%	670
4. Teachers, Postsecondary	$64,086	15.2%	39,780
5. Software Developers, Applications	$71,990	25.5%	370
6. Medical Scientists, Except Epidemiologists	$53,470	34.6%	1,320
7. Education Administrators, All Other	$72,330	31.7%	190
8. Special Education Teachers, Preschool, Kindergarten, and Elementary School	$52,650	18.5%	7,060
9. Training and Development Specialists	$53,350	33.3%	600

The 50 Best Secure Educational Services Jobs Overall

Job	Annual Earnings	Percent Growth	Annual Openings
10. General and Operations Managers	$88,880	11.3%	47,370
11. Human Resources Managers	$93,700	17.5%	270
12. Educational, Guidance, School, and Vocational Counselors	$55,860	14.0%	5,150
13. Management Analysts	$66,100	17.8%	410
14. Accountants and Auditors	$54,810	17.8%	1,250
15. Elementary School Teachers, Except Special Education	$51,690	15.8%	43,080
16. Social Scientists and Related Workers, All Other	$59,280	24.1%	270
17. Middle School Teachers, Except Special and Career/Technical Education	$51,980	15.4%	18,290
18. Education Administrators, Elementary and Secondary School	$87,020	8.7%	44,620
19. Employment, Recruitment, and Placement Specialists	$50,810	33.9%	420
20. Software Developers, Systems Software	$75,000	24.1%	110
21. Special Education Teachers, Secondary School	$54,900	13.3%	4,100
22. Self-Enrichment Education Teachers	$37,400	49.6%	3,720
23. Computer Systems Analysts	$63,990	13.8%	840
24. Physician Assistants	$80,890	23.1%	110
25. Physicians and Surgeons	$74,135	12.4%	700
26. Public Relations Specialists	$48,700	26.5%	970
27. Training and Development Managers	$83,430	27.3%	60
28. Compliance Officers	$54,250	35.3%	130
29. Kindergarten Teachers, Except Special Education	$49,790	15.4%	4,240
30. Registered Nurses	$57,210	12.3%	2,570
31. Compensation, Benefits, and Job Analysis Specialists	$53,390	23.6%	200
32. Biomedical Engineers	$59,010	68.1%	80
33. Police and Sheriff's Patrol Officers	$44,410	30.3%	430
34. Adult Basic and Secondary Education and Literacy Teachers and Instructors	$47,460	18.0%	1,410
35. Social and Community Service Managers	$62,690	18.2%	120
36. Chief Executives	$133,090	8.3%	830
37. Medical and Health Services Managers	$90,440	12.4%	140
38. First-Line Supervisors of Office and Administrative Support Workers	$48,860	14.1%	1,780
39. Clinical, Counseling, and School Psychologists	$67,660	10.4%	1,370
40. Education Administrators, Postsecondary	$83,560	2.0%	1,230
41. Operations Research Analysts	$53,220	24.4%	120
42. Athletic Trainers	$44,130	23.2%	330

(continued)

(continued)

The 50 Best Secure Educational Services Jobs Overall

Job	Annual Earnings	Percent Growth	Annual Openings
43. Customer Service Representatives	$30,070	44.7%	600
44. Sociologists	$68,860	23.1%	50
45. Network and Computer Systems Administrators	$59,230	11.5%	1,212
46. Biochemists and Biophysicists	$50,780	34.4%	100
47. Executive Secretaries and Executive Administrative Assistants	$42,380	13.4%	4,080
48. Teachers and Instructors, All Other	$29,070	18.0%	11,300
49. Computer Occupations, All Other	$60,300	12.0%	360
50. Interpreters and Translators	$39,010	19.7%	480

The 50 Best Secure Government Jobs Overall

Job	Annual Earnings	Percent Growth	Annual Openings
1. Social Scientists and Related Workers, All Other	$76,120	19.3%	860
2. Compliance Officers	$57,500	29.9%	4,730
3. Air Traffic Controllers	$111,880	10.8%	750
4. Registered Nurses	$67,930	13.9%	4,190
5. Detectives and Criminal Investigators	$68,630	16.8%	2,790
6. Financial Examiners	$80,090	41.5%	420
7. Computer Network Architects	$63,760	45.2%	720
8. Logisticians	$77,350	17.8%	750
9. Management Analysts	$74,880	8.4%	2,990
10. Biological Scientists, All Other	$70,330	18.9%	660
11. Accountants and Auditors	$60,030	16.9%	2,820
12. Budget Analysts	$67,570	19.7%	620
13. Claims Adjusters, Examiners, and Investigators	$64,880	17.2%	1,210
14. Software Developers, Applications	$73,640	19.3%	400
15. Writers and Authors	$70,020	9.3%	1,700
16. Computer and Information Research Scientists	$100,920	19.5%	180
17. First-Line Supervisors of Police and Detectives	$78,600	8.0%	3,530
18. Firefighters	$45,840	18.9%	10,000
19. Urban and Regional Planners	$61,920	14.0%	790
20. Probation Officers and Correctional Treatment Specialists	$47,700	19.2%	2,740
21. Public Relations Specialists	$57,690	18.8%	680
22. Electrical Power-Line Installers and Repairers	$57,900	27.4%	420

The 50 Best Secure Government Jobs Overall

Job	Annual Earnings	Percent Growth	Annual Openings
23. Operations Research Analysts	$71,110	17.5%	340
24. Administrative Services Managers	$77,220	7.9%	2,970
25. Compensation, Benefits, and Job Analysis Specialists	$57,970	18.7%	590
26. First-Line Supervisors of Fire Fighting and Prevention Workers	$68,560	8.2%	2,170
27. Political Scientists	$115,730	18.4%	130
28. Human Resources Specialists	$58,040	8.5%	2,330
29. Mechanical Engineers	$89,440	9.2%	270
30. Transportation Inspectors	$63,000	18.7%	340
31. Medical Scientists, Except Epidemiologists	$95,000	29.8%	80
32. Pharmacists	$107,500	8.5%	240
33. Paralegals and Legal Assistants	$51,630	18.7%	980
34. General and Operations Managers	$92,970	–2.5%	112,930
35. Physician Assistants	$85,170	18.8%	130
36. Environmental Engineers	$77,680	8.2%	580
37. Medical and Health Services Managers	$89,870	8.1%	530
38. Computer Occupations, All Other	$87,160	7.6%	1,840
39. Tax Examiners and Collectors, and Revenue Agents	$49,360	13.2%	2,340
40. Network and Computer Systems Administrators	$67,070	8.3%	522
41. Training and Development Specialists	$52,010	18.3%	680
42. Water and Wastewater Treatment Plant and System Operators	$40,820	18.9%	2560
43. Environmental Scientists and Specialists, Including Health	$60,570	8.2%	1390
44. Industrial Engineers	$88,950	21.0%	50
45. Police and Sheriff's Patrol Officers	$53,800	8.1%	14660
46. First-Line Supervisors of Correctional Officers	$56,080	8.2%	1,280
47. Industrial Machinery Mechanics	$53,000	24.6%	210
48. Clinical, Counseling, and School Psychologists	$68,970	8.4%	250
49. Instructional Coordinators	$63,210	8.2%	480
50. Police, Fire, and Ambulance Dispatchers	$35,880	18.6%	2,350

The 70 Best Secure Health Care Jobs Overall

Job	Annual Earnings	Percent Growth	Annual Openings
1. Physicians and Surgeons	$153,970	26.0%	29,480
2. Physical Therapists	$76,653	34.3%	9,640

(continued)

(continued)

The 70 Best Secure Health Care Jobs Overall

Job	Annual Earnings	Percent Growth	Annual Openings
3. Physician Assistants	$86,462	41.3%	5,530
4. Dental Hygienists	$68,460	36.6%	13,990
5. Optometrists	$95,066	35.0%	1,900
6. Occupational Therapists	$74,360	31.6%	4,910
7. Speech-Language Pathologists	$74,247	34.0%	2,470
8. Medical Scientists, Except Epidemiologists	$72,858	42.0%	1,400
9. Registered Nurses	$64,717	23.4%	127,890
10. Medical and Health Services Managers	$83,271	18.0%	7,700
11. Computer Network Architects	$69,789	65.1%	630
12. Network and Computer Systems Administrators	$65,616	46.3%	1,050
13. General and Operations Managers	$84,032	11.4%	188,340
14. Administrative Services Managers	$72,547	18.3%	6,160
15. Chiropractors	$67,182	31.3%	1,450
16. Physical Therapist Assistants	$49,717	34.7%	4,170
17. Computer Systems Analysts	$70,745	28.5%	1,040
18. Radiation Therapists	$74,625	27.0%	940
19. Dental Assistants	$33,381	36.7%	22,490
20. Healthcare Social Workers	$49,227	25.5%	7,640
21. Biomedical Engineers	$69,368	69.2%	250
22. Psychologists, All Other	$83,340	39.5%	190
23. First-Line Supervisors of Office and Administrative Support Workers	$47,329	23.8%	10,060
24. Audiologists	$68,403	35.3%	530
25. Occupational Therapy Assistants	$52,213	33.0%	1,470
26. Pharmacists	$110,597	14.0%	3,860
27. Software Developers, Applications	$78,233	28.4%	420
28. Licensed Practical and Licensed Vocational Nurses	$40,037	22.0%	47,420
29. Radiologic Technologists	$54,116	17.5%	9,300
30. Respiratory Therapists	$54,350	21.3%	5,450
31. Accountants and Auditors	$56,913	22.3%	2,860
32. Database Administrators	$67,736	49.8%	170
33. Clinical, Counseling, and School Psychologists	$66,728	18.9%	2,340
34. Compliance Officers	$58,844	41.3%	380
35. Surgical Technologists	$39,876	25.5%	6,460
36. Mental Health Counselors	$37,457	27.6%	5,720

The 70 Best Secure Health Care Jobs Overall

Job	Annual Earnings	Percent Growth	Annual Openings
37. Special Education Teachers, Preschool, Kindergarten, and Elementary School	$50,027	37.9%	850
38. Training and Development Specialists	$54,913	25.6%	1,400
39. Employment, Recruitment, and Placement Specialists	$50,133	26.4%	1,660
40. Medical Equipment Repairers	$46,974	39.3%	820
41. Mental Health and Substance Abuse Social Workers	$39,270	23.0%	6,660
42. Athletic Trainers	$40,625	51.6%	630
43. Cardiovascular Technologists and Technicians	$49,347	24.0%	2,680
44. Diagnostic Medical Sonographers	$64,305	18.3%	2,310
45. Public Relations Specialists	$48,719	29.2%	1,440
46. Compensation, Benefits, and Job Analysis Specialists	$52,505	33.7%	600
47. Medical Secretaries	$30,512	27.4%	25,630
48. Software Developers, Systems Software	$82,895	26.0%	100
49. Massage Therapists	$38,240	44.8%	710
50. Medical and Clinical Laboratory Technologists	$55,821	11.7%	6,740
51. Customer Service Representatives	$30,703	31.6%	5,610
52. Chief Executives	$150,575	7.3%	1,490
53. Executive Secretaries and Executive Administrative Assistants	$41,468	18.8%	5,610
54. Secretaries and Administrative Assistants, Except Legal, Medical, and Executive	$30,919	27.5%	6,480
55. Substance Abuse and Behavioral Disorder Counselors	$36,902	25.1%	3,780
56. Health Educators	$49,683	20.8%	1,950
57. Nuclear Medicine Technologists	$68,713	16.3%	940
58. Pharmacy Technicians	$32,518	25.3%	5,360
59. Billing and Posting Clerks	$32,289	19.8%	9,290
60. Medical Records and Health Information Technicians	$31,644	20.7%	8,570
61. First-Line Supervisors of Personal Service Workers	$35,205	24.3%	2,340
62. Child, Family, and School Social Workers	$36,820	17.7%	5,800
63. Interpreters and Translators	$40,511	31.0%	430
64. Medical and Clinical Laboratory Technicians	$36,057	16.5%	6,620
65. Operations Research Analysts	$59,671	25.1%	150
66. Physicists	$152,545	16.7%	70
67. Orthotists and Prosthetists	$53,331	30.1%	80
68. Rehabilitation Counselors	$31,182	23.2%	5,240
69. Interviewers, Except Eligibility and Loan	$29,557	20.3%	6,940
70. Human Resources Managers	$90,279	13.3%	220

The 30 Best Secure Repair and Maintenance Jobs Overall

Job	Annual Earnings	Percent Growth	Annual Openings
1. Industrial Machinery Mechanics	$40,140	19.1%	650
2. Medical Equipment Repairers	$43,630	28.0%	360
3. Painters, Transportation Equipment	$39,170	12.8%	730
4. Automotive Service Technicians and Mechanics	$33,040	11.0%	6,120
5. Accountants and Auditors	$57,400	8.6%	150
6. Electrical and Electronics Repairers, Commercial and Industrial Equipment	$45,110	8.5%	150
7. Automotive Body and Related Repairers	$37,730	4.0%	2,850
8. Customer Service Representatives	$30,020	14.7%	540
9. General and Operations Managers	$78,440	–5.6%	3,090
10. Executive Secretaries and Executive Administrative Assistants	$40,880	4.8%	240
11. First-Line Supervisors of Office and Administrative Support Workers	$47,150	4.6%	220
12. Electric Motor, Power Tool, and Related Repairers	$34,920	5.8%	340
13. Maintenance and Repair Workers, General	$33,480	5.6%	350
14. Welders, Cutters, Solderers, and Brazers	$34,450	2.6%	670
15. Telecommunications Equipment Installers and Repairers, Except Line Installers	$37,210	6.7%	110
16. Machinists	$38,160	3.2%	120
17. Automotive Glass Installers and Repairers	$32,950	2.3%	380
18. Computer, Automated Teller, and Office Machine Repairers	$35,860	0.0%	330
19. Home Appliance Repairers	$35,890	0.6%	230
20. Billing and Posting Clerks	$32,790	4.5%	120
21. Transportation Inspectors	$29,390	13.0%	50
22. Chief Executives	$138,890	–6.2%	60
23. Receptionists and Information Clerks	$22,980	5.3%	230
24. Team Assemblers	$27,590	6.5%	90
25. Secretaries and Administrative Assistants, Except Legal, Medical, and Executive	$25,930	–4.9%	510
26. Stock Clerks and Order Fillers	$27,330	4.1%	140
27. Motorboat Mechanics and Service Technicians	$35,420	–11.4%	100
28. Inspectors, Testers, Sorters, Samplers, and Weighers	$29,200	1.3%	100
29. Coin, Vending, and Amusement Machine Servicers and Repairers	$29,150	2.8%	50
30. Dispatchers, Except Police, Fire, and Ambulance	$31,680	–4.5%	50

The 30 Best Secure Utilities Jobs Overall

Job	Annual Earnings	Percent Growth	Annual Openings
1. Electrical and Electronics Repairers, Powerhouse, Substation, and Relay	$66,270	10.3%	410
2. Electrical Engineers	$84,290	−8.8%	250
3. Computer Network Architects	$76,940	15.8%	80
4. Power Plant Operators	$64,440	−2.7%	700
5. Power Distributors and Dispatchers	$68,010	−1.0%	200
6. Software Developers, Applications	$85,170	−5.7%	70
7. General and Operations Managers	$109,870	−20.5%	2,540
8. Network and Computer Systems Administrators	$74,180	−15.0%	2,793
9. Training and Development Specialists	$76,060	−7.9%	120
10. Accountants and Auditors	$67,120	−11.5%	230
11. Compliance Officers	$75,640	5.3%	60
12. Industrial Machinery Mechanics	$57,270	−0.6%	160
13. Administrative Services Managers	$93,590	−14.5%	60
14. Computer Systems Analysts	$83,190	−16.3%	190
15. First-Line Supervisors of Office and Administrative Support Workers	$62,320	−12.5%	220
16. Gas Plant Operators	$56,830	7.7%	110
17. Logisticians	$76,950	−6.5%	50
18. Management Analysts	$76,000	−15.4%	190
19. Industrial Engineers	$75,270	−3.1%	50
20. Maintenance and Repair Workers, General	$49,030	−8.8%	220
21. Environmental Scientists and Specialists, Including Health	$83,530	−13.5%	50
22. Industrial Production Managers	$103,160	−15.2%	50
23. Public Relations Specialists	$63,030	−6.5%	60
24. Chief Executives	$166,400+	−21.3%	60
25. Electrical Power-Line Installers and Repairers	$62,270	−18.0%	1,730
26. Executive Secretaries and Executive Administrative Assistants	$47,610	−13.7%	190
27. Welders, Cutters, Solderers, and Brazers	$61,640	−15.8%	70
28. Stationary Engineers and Boiler Operators	$58,050	−14.8%	50
29. Production, Planning, and Expediting Clerks	$53,380	−15.9%	70
30. Security Guards	$46,070	−16.6%	100

The 20 Best-Paying Secure Jobs

On the following lists you'll find, for each of the six secure career fields, the 20 best-paying secure jobs that met my criteria for this book. These lists are appealing, for obvious reasons.

It shouldn't be a big surprise to learn that most of the highest-paying jobs require advanced levels of education, training, or experience. For example, in the Educational Services field, a bachelor's degree or higher is needed for every one of the top 20 jobs. In fact, 14 of these top 20 Educational Services jobs require an *additional* degree or work experience beyond the bachelor's.

Keep in mind that the earnings reflect the national average for all workers in the career field and in the occupation. This is an important consideration because starting pay in the job is usually much less than the pay that workers can earn with several years of experience. Earnings also vary significantly by region of the country, so actual pay in your area could be substantially different.

The 20 Best-Paying Secure Computer Systems Design Jobs	
Job	Annual Earnings
1. Chief Executives	$166,400+
2. General and Operations Managers	$137,170
3. Human Resources Managers	$115,750
4. Computer and Information Research Scientists	$96,590
5. Electronics Engineers, Except Computer	$92,460
6. Software Developers, Systems Software	$92,130
7. Administrative Services Managers	$90,340
8. Management Analysts	$87,950
9. Software Developers, Applications	$87,220
10. Electrical Engineers	$86,030
11. Database Administrators	$82,820
12. Computer Systems Analysts	$80,830
13. Mechanical Engineers	$79,000
14. Industrial Engineers	$78,670
15. Operations Research Analysts	$78,620
16. Budget Analysts	$77,630
17. Computer Network Architects	$77,190
18. Computer Occupations, All Other	$74,560
19. Network and Computer Systems Administrators	$74,230
20. Logisticians	$73,700

The 20 Best-Paying Secure Educational Services Jobs

Job	Annual Earnings
1. Chief Executives	$133,090
2. Human Resources Managers	$93,700
3. Medical and Health Services Managers	$90,440
4. General and Operations Managers	$88,880
5. Education Administrators, Elementary and Secondary School	$87,020
6. Education Administrators, Postsecondary	$83,560
7. Training and Development Managers	$83,430
8. Physician Assistants	$80,890
9. Software Developers, Systems Software	$75,000
10. Administrative Services Managers	$74,970
11. Physicians and Surgeons	$74,135
12. Education Administrators, All Other	$72,330
13. Software Developers, Applications	$71,990
14. Sociologists	$68,860
15. Clinical, Counseling, and School Psychologists	$67,660
16. Management Analysts	$66,100
17. Teachers, Postsecondary	$64,086
18. Computer Systems Analysts	$63,990
19. Social and Community Service Managers	$62,690
20. Computer Network Architects	$61,220

The 20 Best-Paying Secure Government Jobs

Job	Annual Earnings
1. Political Scientists	$115,730
2. Air Traffic Controllers	$111,880
3. Pharmacists	$107,500
4. Computer and Information Research Scientists	$100,920
5. Medical Scientists, Except Epidemiologists	$95,000
6. General and Operations Managers	$92,970
7. Medical and Health Services Managers	$89,870
8. Mechanical Engineers	$89,440
9. Industrial Engineers	$88,950
10. Computer Occupations, All Other	$87,160
11. Physician Assistants	$85,170
12. Financial Examiners	$80,090

(continued)

(continued)

The 20 Best-Paying Secure Government Jobs

Job	Annual Earnings
13. First-Line Supervisors of Police and Detectives	$78,600
14. Environmental Engineers	$77,680
15. Logisticians	$77,350
16. Administrative Services Managers	$77,220
17. Social Scientists and Related Workers, All Other	$76,120
18. Management Analysts	$74,880
19. Software Developers, Applications	$73,640
20. Operations Research Analysts	$71,110

The 20 Best-Paying Secure Health Care Jobs

Job	Annual Earnings
1. Physicians and Surgeons	$153,970
2. Physicists	$152,545
3. Chief Executives	$150,575
4. Pharmacists	$110,597
5. Optometrists	$95,066
6. Human Resources Managers	$90,279
7. Physician Assistants	$86,462
8. General and Operations Managers	$84,032
9. Psychologists, All Other	$83,340
10. Medical and Health Services Managers	$83,271
11. Software Developers, Systems Software	$82,895
12. Software Developers, Applications	$78,233
13. Physical Therapists	$76,653
14. Radiation Therapists	$74,625
15. Occupational Therapists	$74,360
16. Speech-Language Pathologists	$74,247
17. Medical Scientists, Except Epidemiologists	$72,858
18. Administrative Services Managers	$72,547
19. Computer Systems Analysts	$70,745
20. Computer Network Architects	$69,789

The 20 Best-Paying Secure Repair and Maintenance Jobs

Job	Annual Earnings
1. Chief Executives	$138,890
2. General and Operations Managers	$78,440
3. Accountants and Auditors	$57,400
4. First-Line Supervisors of Office and Administrative Support Workers	$47,150
5. Electrical and Electronics Repairers, Commercial and Industrial Equipment	$45,110
6. Medical Equipment Repairers	$43,630
7. Executive Secretaries and Executive Administrative Assistants	$40,880
8. Industrial Machinery Mechanics	$40,140
9. Painters, Transportation Equipment	$39,170
10. Machinists	$38,160
11. Automotive Body and Related Repairers	$37,730
12. Telecommunications Equipment Installers and Repairers, Except Line Installers	$37,210
13. Home Appliance Repairers	$35,890
14. Computer, Automated Teller, and Office Machine Repairers	$35,860
15. Motorboat Mechanics and Service Technicians	$35,420
16. Electric Motor, Power Tool, and Related Repairers	$34,920
17. Welders, Cutters, Solderers, and Brazers	$34,450
18. Maintenance and Repair Workers, General	$33,480
19. Automotive Service Technicians and Mechanics	$33,040
20. Automotive Glass Installers and Repairers	$32,950

The 20 Best-Paying Secure Utilities Jobs

Job	Annual Earnings
1. Chief Executives	$166,400+
2. General and Operations Managers	$109,870
3. Industrial Production Managers	$103,160
4. Administrative Services Managers	$93,590
5. Software Developers, Applications	$85,170
6. Electrical Engineers	$84,290
7. Environmental Scientists and Specialists, Including Health	$83,530
8. Computer Systems Analysts	$83,190
9. Logisticians	$76,950
10. Computer Network Architects	$76,940

(continued)

(continued)

The 20 Best-Paying Secure Utilities Jobs

Job	Annual Earnings
11. Training and Development Specialists	$76,060
12. Management Analysts	$76,000
13. Compliance Officers	$75,640
14. Industrial Engineers	$75,270
15. Network and Computer Systems Administrators	$74,180
16. Power Distributors and Dispatchers	$68,010
17. Accountants and Auditors	$67,120
18. Electrical and Electronics Repairers, Powerhouse, Substation, and Relay	$66,270
19. Power Plant Operators	$64,440
20. Public Relations Specialists	$63,030

The 20 Fastest-Growing Secure Jobs

From the list of the 150 best secure jobs, this list shows the 20 jobs in each career field projected to have the highest percentage increase in the numbers of people employed through 2018. Note that these growth figures refer to jobs within the career field, not for the occupation as a whole.

In terms of required training and education, these lists are more diverse than the lists of highest-paying jobs. For example, the third-highest job on the Government list, Compliance Officers, requires only long-term on-the-job training.

The 20 Fastest-Growing Secure Computer Systems Design Jobs

Job	Job Growth
1. Computer Network Architects	95.6%
2. Network and Computer Systems Administrators	71.7%
3. Compliance Officers	71.6%
4. Accountants and Auditors	65.5%
5. Industrial Engineers	64.5%
6. Compensation, Benefits, and Job Analysis Specialists	59.9%
7. Software Developers, Systems Software	57.4%
8. Database Administrators	57.3%
9. Software Developers, Applications	57.3%
10. Employment, Recruitment, and Placement Specialists	54.3%
11. Training and Development Specialists	54.3%

The 20 Fastest-Growing Secure Computer Systems Design Jobs

Job	Job Growth
12. Logisticians	54.2%
13. Public Relations Specialists	54.2%
14. Industrial Engineering Technicians	54.1%
15. Mechanical Engineers	50.2%
16. Computer and Information Research Scientists	43.0%
17. Human Resources Managers	40.8%
18. Graphic Designers	40.3%
19. Computer Systems Analysts	40.2%
20. Management Analysts	40.2%

The 20 Fastest-Growing Secure Educational Services Jobs

Job	Job Growth
1. Biomedical Engineers	68.1%
2. Computer Network Architects	51.7%
3. Self-Enrichment Education Teachers	49.6%
4. Customer Service Representatives	44.7%
5. Compliance Officers	35.3%
6. Medical Scientists, Except Epidemiologists	34.6%
7. Biochemists and Biophysicists	34.4%
8. Employment, Recruitment, and Placement Specialists	33.9%
9. Training and Development Specialists	33.3%
10. Education Administrators, All Other	31.7%
11. Police and Sheriff's Patrol Officers	30.3%
12. Instructional Coordinators	27.6%
13. Training and Development Managers	27.3%
14. Public Relations Specialists	26.5%
15. Software Developers, Applications	25.5%
16. Operations Research Analysts	24.4%
17. Social Scientists and Related Workers, All Other	24.1%
18. Software Developers, Systems Software	24.1%
19. Compensation, Benefits, and Job Analysis Specialists	23.6%
20. Athletic Trainers	23.2%

The 20 Fastest-Growing Secure Government Jobs

Job	Job Growth
1. Computer Network Architects	45.2%
2. Financial Examiners	41.5%
3. Compliance Officers	29.9%
4. Medical Scientists, Except Epidemiologists	29.8%
5. Electrical Power-Line Installers and Repairers	27.4%
6. Industrial Machinery Mechanics	24.6%
7. Industrial Engineers	21.0%
8. Budget Analysts	19.7%
9. Computer and Information Research Scientists	19.5%
10. Social Scientists and Related Workers, All Other	19.3%
11. Software Developers, Applications	19.3%
12. Probation Officers and Correctional Treatment Specialists	19.2%
13. Biological Scientists, All Other	18.9%
14. Firefighters	18.9%
15. Water and Wastewater Treatment Plant and System Operators	18.9%
16. Physician Assistants	18.8%
17. Public Relations Specialists	18.8%
18. Compensation, Benefits, and Job Analysis Specialists	18.7%
19. Paralegals and Legal Assistants	18.7%
20. Transportation Inspectors	18.7%

The 20 Fastest-Growing Secure Health Care Jobs

Job	Job Growth
1. Biomedical Engineers	69.2%
2. Computer Network Architects	65.1%
3. Athletic Trainers	51.6%
4. Database Administrators	49.8%
5. Network and Computer Systems Administrators	46.3%
6. Massage Therapists	44.8%
7. Medical Scientists, Except Epidemiologists	42.0%
8. Compliance Officers	41.3%
9. Physician Assistants	41.3%
10. Psychologists, All Other	39.5%
11. Medical Equipment Repairers	39.3%
12. Special Education Teachers, Preschool, Kindergarten, and Elementary School	37.9%

The 20 Fastest-Growing Secure Health Care Jobs

Job	Job Growth
13. Dental Assistants	36.7%
14. Dental Hygienists	36.6%
15. Audiologists	35.3%
16. Optometrists	35.0%
17. Physical Therapist Assistants	34.7%
18. Physical Therapists	34.3%
19. Speech-Language Pathologists	34.0%
20. Compensation, Benefits, and Job Analysis Specialists	33.7%

The 20 Fastest-Growing Secure Repair and Maintenance Jobs

Job	Job Growth
1. Medical Equipment Repairers	28.0%
2. Industrial Machinery Mechanics	19.1%
3. Customer Service Representatives	14.7%
4. Transportation Inspectors	13.0%
5. Painters, Transportation Equipment	12.8%
6. Automotive Service Technicians and Mechanics	11.0%
7. Accountants and Auditors	8.6%
8. Electrical and Electronics Repairers, Commercial and Industrial Equipment	8.5%
9. Telecommunications Equipment Installers and Repairers, Except Line Installers	6.7%
10. Team Assemblers	6.5%
11. Electric Motor, Power Tool, and Related Repairers	5.8%
12. Maintenance and Repair Workers, General	5.6%
13. Receptionists and Information Clerks	5.3%
14. Executive Secretaries and Executive Administrative Assistants	4.8%
15. First-Line Supervisors of Office and Administrative Support Workers	4.6%
16. Billing and Posting Clerks	4.5%
17. Stock Clerks and Order Fillers	4.1%
18. Automotive Body and Related Repairers	4.0%
19. Machinists	3.2%
20. Coin, Vending, and Amusement Machine Servicers and Repairers	2.8%

The 20 Fastest-Growing Secure Utilities Jobs

Job	Job Growth
1. Computer Network Architects	15.8%
2. Electrical and Electronics Repairers, Powerhouse, Substation, and Relay	10.3%
3. Gas Plant Operators	7.7%
4. Compliance Officers	5.3%
5. Industrial Machinery Mechanics	–0.6%
6. Power Distributors and Dispatchers	–1.0%
7. Power Plant Operators	–2.7%
8. Industrial Engineers	–3.1%
9. Software Developers, Applications	–5.7%
10. Logisticians	–6.5%
11. Public Relations Specialists	–6.5%
12. Training and Development Specialists	–7.9%
13. Electrical Engineers	–8.8%
14. Maintenance and Repair Workers, General	–8.8%
15. Accountants and Auditors	–11.5%
16. First-Line Supervisors of Office and Administrative Support Workers	–12.5%
17. Environmental Scientists and Specialists, Including Health	–13.5%
18. Executive Secretaries and Executive Administrative Assistants	–13.7%
19. Administrative Services Managers	–14.5%
20. Stationary Engineers and Boiler Operators	–14.8%

The 20 Secure Jobs with the Most Openings

From the list of 150 best secure jobs, this list shows the 20 jobs in each field projected to have the largest number of job openings per year through 2018. Keep in mind that these figures for job openings are average yearly openings within the career field over a 10-year period. Although these jobs are considered not sensitive to economic fluctuations, the number of openings is likely to vary somewhat from year to year.

Jobs with many openings present several advantages that you may find attractive. Employment can be easier to obtain, particularly for those just entering the job market. These jobs may also offer more opportunities to move from one employer to another with relative ease. Although some of these jobs have average or below-average pay, some also pay quite well and can provide good long-term career opportunities. These lists are especially noteworthy because more of the jobs here than in the preceding sets of lists require only on-the-job training.

The 20 Secure Computer Systems Design Jobs with the Most Openings

Job	Annual Openings
1. Software Developers, Applications	10,300
2. Computer Systems Analysts	7,330
3. Software Developers, Systems Software	6,120
4. Computer Network Architects	4,090
5. Network and Computer Systems Administrators	2,793
6. Management Analysts	1,930
7. General and Operations Managers	1,280
8. Computer Occupations, All Other	1,150
9. Accountants and Auditors	990
10. Database Administrators	960
11. Employment, Recruitment, and Placement Specialists	630
12. Graphic Designers	530
13. First-Line Supervisors of Office and Administrative Support Workers	490
14. Training and Development Specialists	490
15. Technical Writers	430
16. Computer and Information Research Scientists	420
17. Operations Research Analysts	350
18. Chief Executives	270
19. Logisticians	230
20. Public Relations Specialists	230

The 20 Secure Educational Services Jobs with the Most Openings

Job	Annual Openings
1. General and Operations Managers	47,370
2. Education Administrators, Elementary and Secondary School	44,620
3. Elementary School Teachers, Except Special Education	43,080
4. Teachers, Postsecondary	39,780
5. Middle School Teachers, Except Special and Career/Technical Education	18,290
6. Teachers and Instructors, All Other	11,300
7. Special Education Teachers, Preschool, Kindergarten, and Elementary School	7,060
8. Educational, Guidance, School, and Vocational Counselors	5,150
9. Kindergarten Teachers, Except Special Education	4,240
10. Special Education Teachers, Secondary School	4,100
11. Executive Secretaries and Executive Administrative Assistants	4,080
12. Self-Enrichment Education Teachers	3,720

(continued)

(continued)

The 20 Secure Educational Services Jobs with the Most Openings

Job	Annual Openings
13. Administrative Services Managers	3,430
14. Instructional Coordinators	3,130
15. Registered Nurses	2,570
16. First-Line Supervisors of Office and Administrative Support Workers	1,780
17. Adult Basic and Secondary Education and Literacy Teachers and Instructors	1,410
18. Clinical, Counseling, and School Psychologists	1,370
19. Medical Scientists, Except Epidemiologists	1,320
20. Accountants and Auditors	1,250

The 20 Secure Government Jobs with the Most Openings

Job	Annual Openings
1. General and Operations Managers	112,930
2. Police and Sheriff's Patrol Officers	14,660
3. Firefighters	10,000
4. Compliance Officers	4,730
5. Registered Nurses	4,190
6. First-Line Supervisors of Police and Detectives	3,530
7. Management Analysts	2,990
8. Administrative Services Managers	2,970
9. Accountants and Auditors	2,820
10. Detectives and Criminal Investigators	2,790
11. Probation Officers and Correctional Treatment Specialists	2,740
12. Water and Wastewater Treatment Plant and System Operators	2,560
13. Police, Fire, and Ambulance Dispatchers	2,350
14. Tax Examiners and Collectors, and Revenue Agents	2,340
15. Human Resources Specialists	2,330
16. First-Line Supervisors of Fire Fighting and Prevention Workers	2,170
17. Computer Occupations, All Other	1,840
18. Writers and Authors	1,700
19. Environmental Scientists and Specialists, Including Health	1,390
20. First-Line Supervisors of Correctional Officers	1,280

The 20 Secure Health Care Jobs with the Most Openings

Job	Annual Openings
1. General and Operations Managers	188,340
2. Registered Nurses	127,890
3. Licensed Practical and Licensed Vocational Nurses	47,420
4. Physicians and Surgeons	29,480
5. Medical Secretaries	25,630
6. Dental Assistants	22,490
7. Dental Hygienists	13,990
8. First-Line Supervisors of Office and Administrative Support Workers	10,060
9. Physical Therapists	9,640
10. Radiologic Technologists	9,300
11. Billing and Posting Clerks	9,290
12. Medical Records and Health Information Technicians	8,570
13. Medical and Health Services Managers	7,700
14. Healthcare Social Workers	7,640
15. Interviewers, Except Eligibility and Loan	6,940
16. Medical and Clinical Laboratory Technologists	6,740
17. Mental Health and Substance Abuse Social Workers	6,660
18. Medical and Clinical Laboratory Technicians	6,620
19. Secretaries and Administrative Assistants, Except Legal, Medical, and Executive	6,480
20. Surgical Technologists	6,460

The 20 Secure Repair and Maintenance Jobs with the Most Openings

Job	Annual Openings
1. Automotive Service Technicians and Mechanics	6,120
2. General and Operations Managers	3,090
3. Automotive Body and Related Repairers	2,850
4. Painters, Transportation Equipment	730
5. Welders, Cutters, Solderers, and Brazers	670
6. Industrial Machinery Mechanics	650
7. Customer Service Representatives	540
8. Secretaries and Administrative Assistants, Except Legal, Medical, and Executive	510
9. Automotive Glass Installers and Repairers	380
10. Medical Equipment Repairers	360
11. Maintenance and Repair Workers, General	350

(continued)

(continued)

The 20 Secure Repair and Maintenance Jobs with the Most Openings

Job	Annual Openings
12. Electric Motor, Power Tool, and Related Repairers	340
13. Computer, Automated Teller, and Office Machine Repairers	330
14. Executive Secretaries and Executive Administrative Assistants	240
15. Home Appliance Repairers	230
16. Receptionists and Information Clerks	230
17. First-Line Supervisors of Office and Administrative Support Workers	220
18. Accountants and Auditors	150
19. Electrical and Electronics Repairers, Commercial and Industrial Equipment	150
20. Stock Clerks and Order Fillers	140

The 20 Secure Utilities Jobs with the Most Openings

Job	Annual Openings
1. Network and Computer Systems Administrators	2,793
2. General and Operations Managers	2,540
3. Electrical Power-Line Installers and Repairers	1,730
4. Power Plant Operators	700
5. Electrical and Electronics Repairers, Powerhouse, Substation, and Relay	410
6. Electrical Engineers	250
7. Accountants and Auditors	230
8. First-Line Supervisors of Office and Administrative Support Workers	220
9. Maintenance and Repair Workers, General	220
10. Power Distributors and Dispatchers	200
11. Computer Systems Analysts	190
12. Executive Secretaries and Executive Administrative Assistants	190
13. Management Analysts	190
14. Industrial Machinery Mechanics	160
15. Training and Development Specialists	120
16. Gas Plant Operators	110
17. Security Guards	100
18. Computer Network Architects	80
19. Software Developers, Applications	70
20. Welders, Cutters, Solderers, and Brazers	70

Best Secure Jobs Lists by Demographic

Different types of jobs attract different types of workers. It's interesting to consider which secure jobs have the highest percentage of men or young workers. I'm not saying that men or young people should consider these jobs over others based solely on this information, but it is useful information to know.

In some cases, the lists can give you ideas for jobs to consider that you might otherwise overlook. For example, perhaps women should consider some jobs that traditionally have high percentages of men in them. Or older workers might consider some jobs typically held by young people. Although these aren't obvious ways of using these lists, the lists may give you some good ideas about jobs to consider. The lists may also help you identify jobs that work well for others in your situation—for example, secure jobs with plentiful opportunities for self-employment, if that's the work arrangement you prefer.

All lists in this section were created through a similar process. I began with the 150 best jobs and sorted those jobs in order of the primary criterion for each set of lists. Whatever this primary criterion was—for example, percentage of self-employed workers—the figures I was able to obtain applied to workers in *all* career fields, not just to workers in the six secure career fields covered by this book. I eliminated jobs that scored low on the primary criterion and created an initial list of jobs ordered from highest to lowest percentage of the criterion. For example, when I sorted the 150 jobs based on the percentage of self-employed workers, I set the cutoff point at 10 percent and produced a list of 22 jobs, ranging from a high of 69.4 percent to a low of 11.7 percent. For other criteria, such as number of workers age 16–24 or female workers, I used other cutoff levels.

Next, I sorted this initial list of jobs with a high percentage of each type of worker, using the three economic criteria that this book focuses on: earnings, growth rate, and number of openings. The figures I used for these economic criteria were averages (for earnings and job growth) or totals (for job openings) specific to *all* the career fields to which the job is linked in this book. So, for example, the earnings figure for Transportation Inspectors is $59,003, which is the average of the earnings for these workers in Government ($63,000) and in Repair and Maintenance ($29,390). This average is weighted to reflect the large number of workers in Government—more than 10 times as many as in Repair and Maintenance. Similarly, the 18.2 percent job growth for Transportation Inspectors reflects an average in which the slow growth in Repair and Maintenance (13.0 percent) only slightly weighs down the faster growth in Government (18.7 percent). I used this same approach for averaging all the economic figures across the six secure career fields in all subsequent lists in Part III.

Based on these three economic rankings, I created a list of the best 25 jobs overall that are high in the particular demographic criterion. (In many cases, fewer than 25 jobs exceeded the cutoff level.) For each job, I use abbreviations to indicate which secure career fields the job is linked to in this book. For example, C = Computer Systems Design; G = Government.

Best Secure Jobs with a High Percentage of Self-Employed Workers

About 8 percent of all working people are self-employed. Although you may think of the self-employed as having similar jobs, they actually work in an enormous range of situations, fields, and work environments that you may not have considered.

Among the self-employed are people who own small or large businesses, as many dentists and funeral directors do; people working on a contract basis for one or more employers, as many editors do; people running home consulting or other businesses, as many personal financial advisors do; and people in many other situations. They may go to the same worksite every day, as commercial and industrial designers do; visit multiple employers during the course of a week, as many translators do; or do most of their work from home. Some work part time, others full time, some as a way to have fun, some so they can spend time with their kids or go to school.

The point is that there is an enormous range of situations, and one of them could make sense for you now or in the future.

The following list contains secure jobs in which more than 10 percent of workers in *all* career fields are self-employed.

Best Secure Jobs with the Highest Percentage of Self-Employed Workers

Job	Career Field(s)	Percent Self-Employed Workers
1. Writers and Authors	G	69.4%
2. Massage Therapists	H	57.2%
3. Chiropractors	H	44.5%
4. First-Line Supervisors of Personal Service Workers	H	37.8%
5. Clinical, Counseling, and School Psychologists	E, G, H	34.1%
6. Psychologists, All Other	H	32.8%
7. Home Appliance Repairers	R	26.8%
8. Graphic Designers	C	26.3%
9. Interpreters and Translators Educational Services	H	26.1%
10. Management Analysts	C, E, G, U	25.8%
11. Optometrists	H	24.6%
12. Chief Executives	C, E, H, R, U	21.6%
13. Teachers and Instructors, All Other	E	20.6%
14. Adult Basic and Secondary Education and Literacy Teachers and Instructors	E	20.4%
15. Computer, Automated Teller, and Office Machine Repairers	R	19.8%
16. Computer Network Architects	C, E, G, H, U	19.4%
17. Self-Enrichment Education Teachers	E	17.3%
18. Medical Equipment Repairers	H, R	16.4%
19. Automotive Service Technicians and Mechanics	R	15.9%
20. Automotive Body and Related Repairers	R	12.9%
21. Motorboat Mechanics and Service Technicians	R	12.8%
22. Physicians and Surgeons	E, H	11.7%

Where the following list gives earnings estimates, keep in mind that these figures are based on a survey that *doesn't include self-employed workers*. The median earnings for self-employed workers in these occupations may be significantly higher or lower.

C=Computer Systems Design, E=Educational Services, G=Government, H=Health Care, R=Repair and Maintenance, U=Utilities

Best Secure Jobs Overall Employing a High Percentage of Self-Employed Workers

Job	Career Field(s)	Percent Self-Employed Workers	Annual Earnings	Percent Growth	Annual Openings
1. Computer Network Architects	C, E, G, H, U	19.4%	$72,718	74.6%	6,190
2. Physicians and Surgeons	E, H	11.7%	$151,255	25.4%	30,180
3. Optometrists	H	24.6%	$95,066	35.0%	1,900
4. Management Analysts	C, E, G, U	25.8%	$77,399	15.1%	5,520
5. Self-Enrichment Education Teachers	E	17.3%	$37,400	49.6%	3,720
6. Chief Executives	C, E, H, R, U	21.6%	$144,850	8.8%	2,710
7. Clinical, Counseling, and School Psychologists	E, G, H	34.1%	$67,472	13.1%	3,960
8. Psychologists, All Other	H	32.8%	$83,340	41.4%	190
9. Chiropractors	H	44.5%	$67,182	31.3%	1,450
10. Graphic Designers	C	26.3%	$50,640	40.2%	530
11. Medical Equipment Repairers	H, R	16.4%	$45,663	35.1%	1,180
12. Massage Therapists	H	57.2%	$38,240	44.9%	710
13. Teachers and Instructors, All Other	E	20.6%	$29,070	18.0%	11,300
14. Adult Basic and Secondary Education and Literacy Teachers and Instructors	E	20.4%	$47,460	18.0%	1,410
15. Writers and Authors	G	69.4%	$70,020	9.7%	1,700
16. Interpreters and Translators	E, H	26.1%	$39,402	21.4%	910
17. Automotive Service Technicians and Mechanics	R	15.9%	$33,040	11.0%	6,120
18. Automotive Body and Related Repairers	R	12.9%	$37,730	4.0%	2,850
19. First-Line Supervisors of Personal Service Workers	H	37.8%	$35,205	14.0%	2,340
20. Home Appliance Repairers	R	26.8%	$35,890	0.6%	230
21. Computer, Automated Teller, and Office Machine Repairers	R	19.8%	$35,860	0.0%	330
22. Motorboat Mechanics and Service Technicians	R	12.8%	$35,420	–11.4%	100

C=Computer Systems Design, E=Educational Services, G=Government, H=Health Care, R=Repair and Maintenance, U=Utilities

Best Secure Jobs with a High Percentage of Urban or Rural Workers

Some people have a strong preference for an urban setting. They want to live and work in a locale with more energy and excitement, more access to the arts, more diversity, more really good restaurants, and better public transportation. On the other hand, some prefer the open spaces, closeness to nature, quiet, and inexpensive housing of rural locations. If you are strongly attracted to either setting, you'll be interested in the following lists.

I identified urban jobs as those for which 40 percent or more of the workforce is located in the 38 most populous metropolitan areas of the United States. These 38 metro areas—the most populous 10 percent of all U.S. metro areas, according to the Census Bureau—consist primarily of built-up communities, unlike smaller metro areas, which consist of a core city surrounded by a lot of countryside. In the following lists of urban jobs, you'll see a figure called the "urban ratio" for each job that represents the percentage of the total U.S. workforce for the job that is located in those 38 huge metro areas.

The Census Bureau also identifies 173 nonmetropolitan areas—areas that have no city of 50,000 people and a total population of less than 100,000. I identified rural jobs as those for which 15 percent or more of the total U.S. workforce is located in these nonmetropolitan areas. In the following lists of rural jobs, you'll see a figure called the "rural ratio" that represents the percentage of the total U.S. workforce for the job that is located in nonmetropolitan areas.

The "best-of" lists of both urban and rural jobs are ordered by the usual three economic measures: earnings, growth, and openings.

Best Secure Jobs with the Highest Percentage of Urban Workers

Job	Career Field(s)	Urban Ratio
1. Biomedical Engineers	E, H	56.0%
2. Medical Equipment Repairers	H, R	50.5%
3. Psychologists, All Other	H	47.9%
4. Training and Development Managers	E	46.2%
5. Nuclear Medicine Technologists	H	44.4%
6. Audiologists	H	42.6%
7. Chiropractors	H	42.3%
8. Occupational Therapy Assistants	H	42.0%
9. Athletic Trainers	E, H	41.6%
10. Sociologists	E	40.2%
11. Biological Scientists, All Other	G	40.1%

C=Computer Systems Design, E=Educational Services, G=Government, H=Health Care, R=Repair and Maintenance, U=Utilities

Best Secure Jobs Overall Employing a High Percentage of Urban Workers

Job	Career Field(s)	Urban Ratio	Annual Earnings	Percent Growth	Annual Openings
1. Biomedical Engineers	E, H	56.0%	$83,340	41.4%	190
2. Medical Equipment Repairers	H, R	50.5%	$67,182	31.3%	1,450
3. Psychologists, All Other	H	47.9%	$52,213	32.8%	1,470
4. Audiologists	H	42.6%	$42,310	37.1%	960
5. Nuclear Medicine Technologists	H	44.4%	$64,111	69.4%	330
6. Occupational Therapy Assistants	H	42.0%	$45,663	35.1%	1,180
7. Training and Development Managers	E	46.2%	$68,403	35.3%	530
8. Athletic Trainers	E, H	41.6%	$88,650	6.5%	780
9. Chiropractors	H	42.3%	$70,330	18.9%	660
10. Sociologists	E	40.2%	$68,713	16.3%	940
11. Biological Scientists, All Other	G	40.1%	$89,207	14.7%	140

Best Secure Jobs with the Highest Percentage of Rural Workers

Job	Career Field(s)	Rural Ratio
1. Water and Wastewater Treatment Plant and System Operators	G	28.1%
2. First-Line Supervisors of Correctional Officers	G	27.6%
3. Electrical Power-Line Installers and Repairers	G, U	26.0%
4. Police, Fire, and Ambulance Dispatchers	G	22.4%
5. Education Administrators, Elementary and Secondary School	E	18.2%
6. Industrial Production Managers	U	16.6%
7. Kindergarten Teachers, Except Special Education	E	16.2%
8. Welders, Cutters, Solderers, and Brazers	R, U	16.2%
9. Power Plant Operators	U	16.1%
10. Industrial Machinery Mechanics	G, R, U	16.0%
11. Special Education Teachers, Preschool, Kindergarten, and Elementary School	E, H	15.8%
12. Gas Plant Operators	U	15.1%

C=Computer Systems Design, E=Educational Services, G=Government, H=Health Care, R=Repair and Maintenance, U=Utilities

Best Secure Jobs Overall Employing a High Percentage of Rural Workers

Job	Career Field(s)	Rural Ratio	Annual Earnings	Percent Growth	Annual Openings
1. Education Administrators, Elementary and Secondary School	E	18.2%	$87,020	8.7%	44,620
2. Special Education Teachers, Preschool, Kindergarten, and Elementary School	E, H	15.8%	$52,611	18.9%	7,910
3. Water and Wastewater Treatment Plant and System Operators	G	28.1%	$40,820	18.9%	2,560
4. Kindergarten Teachers, Except Special Education	E	16.2%	$49,790	15.4%	4,240
5. First-Line Supervisors of Correctional Officers	G	27.6%	$56,080	8.2%	1,280
6. Police, Fire, and Ambulance Dispatchers	G	22.4%	$35,880	18.6%	2,350
7. Electrical Power-Line Installers and Repairers	G, U	26.0%	$61,339	–8.0%	2,150
8. Industrial Machinery Mechanics	G, R, U	16.0%	$46,736	16.7%	1,020
9. Power Plant Operators	U	16.1%	$64,440	–2.7%	700
10. Gas Plant Operators	U	15.1%	$56,830	7.7%	110
11. Industrial Production Managers	U	16.6%	$103,160	–15.4%	50
12. Welders, Cutters, Solderers, and Brazers	R, U	16.2%	$37,943	0.3%	740

Best Secure Jobs with the Highest Percentage of Workers Age 16–24

These jobs have higher percentages (more than 15 percent) of workers between the ages of 16 and 24. Young people are found in almost all jobs, but those with higher percentages of young people may present more opportunities for initial entry. On the other hand, jobs with a large showing of young people also tend to be economically sensitive, so it's no coincidence that the following lists are among the shortest in this section, with only 15 jobs.

C=Computer Systems Design, E=Educational Services, G=Government, H=Health Care, R=Repair and Maintenance, U=Utilities

Best Secure Jobs with the Highest Percentage of Workers Age 16–24

Job	Career Field(s)	Percent Age 16–24
1. Stock Clerks and Order Fillers	R	31.6%
2. Receptionists and Information Clerks	R	22.6%
3. Customer Service Representatives	E, H, R	21.6%
4. Physical Therapist Assistants	H	21.6%
5. Pharmacy Technicians	H	21.5%
6. Surgical Technologists	H	21.5%
7. Automotive Glass Installers and Repairers	R	20.9%
8. Coin, Vending, and Amusement Machine Servicers and Repairers	R	20.2%
9. Dental Assistants	H	17.6%
10. Motorboat Mechanics and Service Technicians	R	17.0%
11. Adult Basic and Secondary Education and Literacy Teachers and Instructors	E	16.7%
12. Self-Enrichment Education Teachers	E	16.7%
13. Teachers and Instructors, All Other	E	16.7%
14. Automotive Body and Related Repairers	R	15.5%
15. Security Guards	U	15.3%

Best Secure Jobs Overall with a High Percentage of Workers Age 16–24

Job	Career Field(s)	Percent Age 16–24	Annual Earnings	Percent Growth	Annual Openings
1. Physical Therapist Assistants	H	21.6%	$49,717	34.6%	4,170
2. Dental Assistants	H	17.6%	$33,381	36.7%	22,490
3. Surgical Technologists	H	21.5%	$39,876	25.5%	6,460
4. Self-Enrichment Education Teachers	E	16.7%	$37,400	49.6%	3,720
5. Adult Basic and Secondary Education and Literacy Teachers and Instructors	E	16.7%	$47,460	18.0%	1,410
6. Customer Service Representatives	E, H, R	21.6%	$30,532	32.0%	6,750
7. Pharmacy Technicians	H	21.5%	$32,518	25.3%	5,360
8. Teachers and Instructors, All Other	E	16.7%	$29,070	18.0%	11,300
9. Automotive Body and Related Repairers	R	15.5%	$37,730	4.0%	2,850

C=Computer Systems Design, E=Educational Services, G=Government, H=Health Care, R=Repair and Maintenance, U=Utilities

Best Secure Jobs Overall with a High Percentage of Workers Age 16–24

Job	Career Field(s)	Percent Age 16–24	Annual Earnings	Percent Growth	Annual Openings
10. Security Guards	U	15.3%	$46,070	–16.6%	100
11. Automotive Glass Installers and Repairers	R	20.9%	$32,950	2.3%	380
12. Motorboat Mechanics and Service Technicians	R	17.0%	$35,420	–11.4%	100
13. Receptionists and Information Clerks	R	22.6%	$22,980	5.3%	230
14. Stock Clerks and Order Fillers	R	31.6%	$27,330	4.1%	140
15. Coin, Vending, and Amusement Machine Servicers and Repairers	R	20.2%	$29,150	2.8%	50

Best Secure Jobs with a High Percentage of Workers Age 55 and Over

I created the following two lists by identifying the best secure jobs that employ more than 20 percent of workers age 55 and over.

You may be surprised to note that 72 of the best 150 jobs meet this cutoff, whereas only 8 employ the same percentage of people age 16–24. One reason is that I eliminated low-wage jobs as part of my process for selecting the 150 best secure jobs. This resulted in the removal of a lot of entry-level jobs with high concentrations of young people. Also, many of the secure jobs require advanced education or years of work experience—credentials that people younger than 25 are unlikely to have on their resumes. Finally, the process of job-shifting over the course of a working lifetime results in a kind of job-*sifting*: People tend to lose recession-sensitive jobs when economic downturns strike, and the jobs they find during those hard times tend to be available because they're secure. By the time these workers reach age 55 and have weathered several recessions, they are more likely to have settled into a secure occupation.

C=Computer Systems Design, E=Educational Services, G=Government, H=Health Care, R=Repair and Maintenance, U=Utilities

Best Secure Jobs with the Highest Percentage of Workers Age 55 and Over

Job	Career Field(s)	Percent Age 55 and Over
1. Clinical, Counseling, and School Psychologists	E, G, H	41.9%
2. Psychologists, All Other	H	41.9%
3. Chief Executives	C, E, H, R, U	35.5%
4. Physicists	H	33.8%
5. Urban and Regional Planners	G	33.8%
6. Management Analysts	C, E, G, U	32.3%
7. Education Administrators, All Other	E	32.2%
8. Education Administrators, Elementary and Secondary School	E	32.2%
9. Education Administrators, Postsecondary	E	32.2%
10. Administrative Services Managers	C, E, G, H, U	31.9%
11. Instructional Coordinators	E, G	31.9%
12. Writers and Authors	G	31.9%
13. Transportation Inspectors	G, R	31.3%
14. Social and Community Service Managers	E	30.8%
15. Optometrists	H	30.6%
16. Teachers, Postsecondary	E	30.1%
17. Medical Equipment Repairers	H, R	29.3%
18. Audiologists	H	28.7%
19. Medical and Health Services Managers	E, G, H	28.7%
20. Technical Writers	C	28.6%
21. Stationary Engineers and Boiler Operators	U	28.5%
22. Executive Secretaries and Executive Administrative Assistants	E, H, R, U	28.4%
23. Medical Secretaries	H	28.4%
24. Secretaries and Administrative Assistants, Except Legal, Medical, and Executive	H, R	28.4%
25. Occupational Therapy Assistants	H	26.8%
26. Tax Examiners and Collectors, and Revenue Agents	G	26.4%
27. Physicians and Surgeons	E, H	26.3%
28. Home Appliance Repairers	R	25.5%
29. Security Guards	U	25.3%
30. Interviewers, Except Eligibility and Loan	H	24.8%
31. Environmental Scientists and Specialists, Including Health	G, U	24.6%
32. Respiratory Therapists	H	24.6%
33. Educational, Guidance, School, and Vocational Counselors	E	24.4%

C=Computer Systems Design, E=Educational Services, G=Government, H=Health Care, R=Repair and Maintenance, U=Utilities

Best Secure Jobs with the Highest Percentage of Workers Age 55 and Over

Job	Career Field(s)	Percent Age 55 and Over
34. Electrical and Electronics Repairers, Commercial and Industrial Equipment	R	24.4%
35. Electrical and Electronics Repairers, Powerhouse, Substation, and Relay	U	24.4%
36. Mental Health Counselors	H	24.4%
37. Rehabilitation Counselors	H	24.4%
38. Substance Abuse and Behavioral Disorder Counselors	H	24.4%
39. Athletic Trainers	E, H	24.1%
40. Adult Basic and Secondary Education and Literacy Teachers and Instructors	E	24.1%
41. Self-Enrichment Education Teachers	E	24.1%
42. Teachers and Instructors, All Other	E	24.1%
43. First-Line Supervisors of Office and Administrative Support Workers	C, E, H, R, U	23.6%
44. Interpreters and Translators	E, H	23.6%
45. Elementary School Teachers, Except Special Education	E	23.4%
46. Medical and Clinical Laboratory Technicians	H	23.4%
47. Medical and Clinical Laboratory Technologists	H	23.4%
48. Middle School Teachers, Except Special and Career/Technical Education	E	23.4%
49. Motorboat Mechanics and Service Technicians	R	23.3%
50. Compliance Officers	C, E, G, H, U	23.2%
51. Pharmacists	G, H	23.2%
52. Receptionists and Information Clerks	R	23.2%
53. Registered Nurses	E, G, H	23.2%
54. Water and Wastewater Treatment Plant and System Operators	G	23.1%
55. Industrial Engineers	C, G, U	23.0%
56. Training and Development Managers	E	22.9%
57. Human Resources Managers	C, E, H	22.9%
58. Inspectors, Testers, Sorters, Samplers, and Weighers	R	22.8%
59. Licensed Practical and Licensed Vocational Nurses	H	22.7%
60. Industrial Engineering Technicians	C	22.5%
61. Special Education Teachers, Preschool, Kindergarten, and Elementary School	E, H	22.4%
62. Industrial Production Managers	U	22.1%
63. Machinists	R	22.1%
64. Industrial Machinery Mechanics	G, R, U	21.6%

(continued)

C=Computer Systems Design, E=Educational Services, G=Government, H=Health Care, R=Repair and Maintenance, U=Utilities

(continued)

Best Secure Jobs with the Highest Percentage of Workers Age 55 and Over

Job	Career Field(s)	Percent Age 55 and Over
65. Accountants and Auditors	C, E, G, H, R, U	21.2%
66. Production, Planning, and Expediting Clerks	U	21.2%
67. Telecommunications Equipment Installers and Repairers, Except Line Installers	R	20.9%
68. General and Operations Managers	C, E, G, H, R, U	20.8%
69. Child, Family, and School Social Workers	H	20.6%
70. Healthcare Social Workers	H	20.6%
71. Mental Health and Substance Abuse Social Workers	H	20.6%
72. Chiropractors	H	20.4%

Best Secure Jobs Overall with a High Percentage of Workers Age 55 and Over

Job	Career Field(s)	Percent Age 55 and Over	Annual Earnings	Percent Growth	Annual Openings
1. Physicians and Surgeons	E, H	26.3%	$151,255	25.4%	30,180
2. Registered Nurses	E, G, H	23.2%	$64,660	22.4%	134,650
3. Optometrists	H	30.6%	$95,066	35.0%	1,900
4. Medical and Health Services Managers	E, G, H	28.7%	$84,044	16.6%	8,370
5. Administrative Services Managers	C, E, G, H, U	31.9%	$75,820	15.2%	12,780
6. General and Operations Managers	C, E, G, H, R, U	20.8%	$95,208	5.8%	355,550
7. Accountants and Auditors	C, E, G, H, R, U	21.2%	$59,496	20.9%	8,300
8. Education Administrators, Elementary and Secondary School	E	32.2%	$87,020	8.7%	44,620
9. Chiropractors	H	20.4%	$67,182	31.3%	1,450
10. Compliance Officers	C, E, G, H, U	23.2%	$57,895	30.4%	5,400
11. Industrial Engineers	C, G, U	23.0%	$80,847	38.8%	300
12. Psychologists, All Other	H	41.9%	$83,340	41.4%	190
13. Teachers, Postsecondary	E	30.1%	$64,086	15.2%	39,780
14. Audiologists	H	28.7%	$68,403	35.3%	530

C=Computer Systems Design, E=Educational Services, G=Government, H=Health Care, R=Repair and Maintenance, U=Utilities

Best Secure Jobs Overall for Workers Age 55 and Over

Job	Career Field(s)	Percent Age 55 and Over	Annual Earnings	Percent Growth	Annual Openings
15. Licensed Practical and Licensed Vocational Nurses	H	22.7%	$40,037	21.9%	47,420
16. First-Line Supervisors of Office and Administrative Support Workers	C, E, H, R, U	23.6%	$48,437	20.6%	12,770
17. Instructional Coordinators	E, G	31.9%	$60,791	24.8%	3,610
18. Pharmacists	G, H	23.2%	$110,226	13.3%	4,100
19. Education Administrators, All Other	E	32.2%	$72,330	31.7%	190
20. Management Analysts	C, E, G, U	32.3%	$77,399	15.1%	5,520
21. Special Education Teachers, Preschool, Kindergarten, and Elementary School	E, H	22.4%	$52,611	18.9%	7,910
22. Technical Writers	C	28.6%	$66,860	30.9%	430
23. Respiratory Therapists	H	24.6%	$54,350	21.3%	5,450
24. Elementary School Teachers, Except Special Education	E	23.4%	$51,690	15.8%	43,080
25. Occupational Therapy Assistants	H	26.8%	$52,213	32.8%	1,470

Best Secure Jobs Employing a High Percentage of Women

To create the lists that follow, I sorted the 150 best secure jobs according to the percentages of women and men in the workforce, setting the cutoff level at 70 percent. Similar lists of the best jobs with high percentages of men and women are included in all the books in the *Best Jobs* series. It's important to understand that these lists aren't meant to restrict women or men from considering job options. Actually, my reasoning for including them is exactly the opposite: I hope the lists help people see possibilities that they might not otherwise have considered.

The fact is that jobs with high percentages of women or high percentages of men offer good opportunities for both men and women if they want to do one of these jobs. So I suggest that women browse the lists of jobs that employ high percentages of men and that men browse the lists of jobs with high percentages of women. There are jobs in both sets of lists that pay well, and women or men who are interested in them and who have or can obtain the necessary education and training should consider them.

C=Computer Systems Design, E=Educational Services, G=Government, H=Health Care, R=Repair and Maintenance, U=Utilities

It is interesting to compare the two sets of secure jobs—those with the highest percentage of men and those with the highest percentage of women—in terms of the economic measures that we use to rank these lists. Sadly, the male-dominated jobs in the six secure career fields have higher average earnings than the female-dominated jobs: $65,115 compared to $51,287. On the other hand, the female-dominated jobs are expected to grow faster: an average of 20.9 percent compared to 18.3 percent. That's largely because female-dominated jobs are clustered in the booming Health Care and Educational Services fields.

Best Secure Jobs Employing the Highest Percentage of Women

Job	Career Field(s)	Percent Women
1. Kindergarten Teachers, Except Special Education	E	98.4%
2. Speech-Language Pathologists	H	97.7%
3. Executive Secretaries and Executive Administrative Assistants	E, H, R, U	96.8%
4. Medical Secretaries	H	96.8%
5. Secretaries and Administrative Assistants, Except Legal, Medical, and Executive	H, R	96.8%
6. Dental Assistants	H	96.7%
7. Dental Hygienists	H	96.1%
8. Receptionists and Information Clerks	R	92.4%
9. Licensed Practical and Licensed Vocational Nurses	H	91.4%
10. Registered Nurses	E, G, H	90.7%
11. Billing and Posting Clerks	H, R	89.6%
12. Athletic Trainers	E, H	88.9%
13. Medical Records and Health Information Technicians	H	88.4%
14. Paralegals and Legal Assistants	G	86.7%
15. Special Education Teachers, Preschool, Kindergarten, and Elementary School	E, H	85.0%
16. Special Education Teachers, Secondary School	E	85.0%
17. Interviewers, Except Eligibility and Loan	H	84.4%
18. Occupational Therapists	H	81.7%
19. Child, Family, and School Social Workers	H	81.5%
20. Healthcare Social Workers	H	81.5%
21. Mental Health and Substance Abuse Social Workers	H	81.5%
22. Elementary School Teachers, Except Special Education	E	81.3%
23. Middle School Teachers, Except Special and Career/Technical Education	E	81.3%
24. Physical Therapist Assistants	H	78.6%

C=Computer Systems Design, E=Educational Services, G=Government, H=Health Care, R=Repair and Maintenance, U=Utilities

Best Secure Jobs Employing the Highest Percentage of Women

Job	Career Field(s)	Percent Women
25. Audiologists	H	77.8%
26. Occupational Therapy Assistants	H	77.8%
27. Pharmacy Technicians	H	77.6%
28. Surgical Technologists	H	77.6%
29. Instructional Coordinators	E, G	77.4%
30. Massage Therapists	H	77.1%
31. Tax Examiners and Collectors, and Revenue Agents	G	72.2%
32. Medical and Clinical Laboratory Technicians	H	71.9%
33. Medical and Clinical Laboratory Technologists	H	71.9%
34. Cardiovascular Technologists and Technicians	H	71.1%
35. Diagnostic Medical Sonographers	H	71.1%
36. Nuclear Medicine Technologists	H	71.1%
37. Radiologic Technologists	H	71.1%

Best Secure Jobs Overall Employing a High Percentage of Women

Job	Career Field(s)	Percent Women	Annual Earnings	Percent Growth	Annual Openings
1. Dental Hygienists	H	96.1%	$68,460	36.6%	13,990
2. Registered Nurses	E, G, H	90.7%	$64,660	22.4%	134,650
3. Occupational Therapists	H	81.7%	$74,360	30.7%	4,910
4. Speech-Language Pathologists	H	97.7%	$74,247	34.0%	2,470
5. Dental Assistants	H	96.7%	$33,381	36.7%	22,490
6. Licensed Practical and Licensed Vocational Nurses	H	91.4%	$40,037	21.9%	47,420
7. Audiologists	H	77.8%	$68,403	35.3%	530
8. Elementary School Teachers, Except Special Education	E	81.3%	$51,690	15.8%	43,080
9. Instructional Coordinators	E, G	77.4%	$60,791	24.8%	3,610
10. Medical Secretaries	H	96.8%	$30,512	27.4%	25,630
11. Physical Therapist Assistants	H	78.6%	$49,717	34.6%	4,170
12. Radiologic Technologists	H	71.1%	$54,116	17.5%	9,300

(continued)

C=Computer Systems Design, E=Educational Services, G=Government, H=Health Care, R=Repair and Maintenance, U=Utilities

(continued)

Best Secure Jobs Overall Employing a High Percentage of Women

Job	Career Field(s)	Percent Women	Annual Earnings	Percent Growth	Annual Openings
13. Special Education Teachers, Preschool, Kindergarten, and Elementary School	E, H	85.0%	$52,611	18.9%	7,910
14. Middle School Teachers, Except Special and Career/Technical Education	E	81.3%	$51,980	15.4%	18,290
15. Occupational Therapy Assistants	H	77.8%	$52,213	32.8%	1,470
16. Healthcare Social Workers	H	81.5%	$49,227	20.2%	7,640
17. Surgical Technologists	H	77.6%	$39,876	25.5%	6,460
18. Athletic Trainers	E, H	88.9%	$42,309	37.1%	960
19. Mental Health and Substance Abuse Social Workers	H	81.5%	$39,270	22.3%	6,660
20. Secretaries and Administrative Assistants, Except Legal, Medical, and Executive	H, R	96.8%	$30,367	25.6%	6,990
21. Medical and Clinical Laboratory Technologists	H	71.9%	$55,821	11.7%	6,740
22. Cardiovascular Technologists and Technicians	H	71.1%	$49,347	24.1%	2,680
23. Diagnostic Medical Sonographers	H	71.1%	$64,305	18.3%	2,310
24. Billing and Posting Clerks	H, R	89.6%	$32,296	19.5%	9,410
25. Massage Therapists	H	77.1%	$38,240	44.9%	710

Best Secure Jobs Employing a High Percentage of Men

If you haven't already read the intro to the previous pair of lists, "Best Secure Jobs Employing a High Percentage of Women," consider doing so. Much of the content there applies to the following pair of lists as well.

I didn't include these lists with the assumption that men should consider only jobs with high percentages of men or that women should consider only jobs with high percentages of women. Instead, these lists are here because I think they are interesting and perhaps helpful in considering nontraditional career options.

C=Computer Systems Design, E=Educational Services, G=Government, H=Health Care, R=Repair and Maintenance, U=Utilities

In the jobs on the following lists, more than 70 percent of the workers are men, but increasing numbers of women are entering many of these jobs. Note that some of the jobs listed as having 100 percent men probably include a few women but have such a small total workforce that the sample queried by the Census Department's Current Population Survey did not include any female workers.

Best Secure Jobs Employing the Highest Percentage of Men

Job	Career Field(s)	Percent Men
1. Automotive Glass Installers and Repairers	R	100.0%
2. Electric Motor, Power Tool, and Related Repairers	R	100.0%
3. Electrical and Electronics Repairers, Commercial and Industrial Equipment	R	100.0%
4. Electrical and Electronics Repairers, Powerhouse, Substation, and Relay	U	100.0%
5. Automotive Service Technicians and Mechanics	R	98.4%
6. Electrical Power-Line Installers and Repairers	G, U	98.4%
7. Automotive Body and Related Repairers	R	97.9%
8. Stationary Engineers and Boiler Operators	U	97.9%
9. Gas Plant Operators	U	97.5%
10. Maintenance and Repair Workers, General	R, U	97.3%
11. Industrial Machinery Mechanics	G, R, U	97.0%
12. Motorboat Mechanics and Service Technicians	R	97.0%
13. Home Appliance Repairers	R	96.8%
14. Welders, Cutters, Solderers, and Brazers	R, U	95.9%
15. Firefighters	G	95.5%
16. Mechanical Engineers	C, G	95.0%
17. Power Distributors and Dispatchers	U	94.7%
18. Power Plant Operators	U	94.7%
19. Machinists	R	93.8%
20. Water and Wastewater Treatment Plant and System Operators	G	93.0%
21. First-Line Supervisors of Fire Fighting and Prevention Workers	G	92.3%
22. Telecommunications Equipment Installers and Repairers, Except Line Installers	R	92.2%
23. Transportation Inspectors	G, R	91.5%
24. Electrical Engineers	C, U	91.3%
25. Electronics Engineers, Except Computer	C	91.3%
26. Painters, Transportation Equipment	R	91.0%

(continued)

C=Computer Systems Design, E=Educational Services, G=Government, H=Health Care, R=Repair and Maintenance, U=Utilities

(continued)

Best Secure Jobs Employing the Highest Percentage of Men

Job	Career Field(s)	Percent Men
27. Medical Equipment Repairers	H, R	89.4%
28. Biomedical Engineers	E, H	88.2%
29. First-Line Supervisors of Police and Detectives	G	88.0%
30. Industrial Production Managers	U	85.7%
31. Police and Sheriff's Patrol Officers	E, G	85.4%
32. Computer, Automated Teller, and Office Machine Repairers	R	84.4%
33. Industrial Engineering Technicians	C	83.0%
34. Industrial Engineers	C, G, U	82.1%
35. Coin, Vending, and Amusement Machine Servicers and Repairers	R	81.8%
36. Software Developers, Applications	C, E, G, H, U	78.7%
37. Software Developers, Systems Software	C, E, H	78.7%
38. Network and Computer Systems Administrators	C, E, G, H, U	78.4%
39. Computer Network Architects	C, E, G, H, U	77.5%
40. Security Guards	U	76.8%
41. Air Traffic Controllers	G	76.7%
42. Chief Executives	C, E, H, R, U	75.9%
43. Physicists	H	75.0%
44. Detectives and Criminal Investigators	G	74.4%
45. Computer and Information Research Scientists	C, G	72.2%
46. Computer Systems Analysts	C, E, H, U	72.2%
47. First-Line Supervisors of Correctional Officers	G	72.2%
48. General and Operations Managers	C, E, G, H, R, U	71.4%
49. Computer Occupations, All Other	C, E, G	71.0%
50. Environmental Scientists and Specialists, Including Health	G, U	70.4%

Best Secure Jobs Overall Employing a High Percentage of Men

Job	Career Field(s)	Percent Men	Annual Earnings	Percent Growth	Annual Openings
1. Software Developers, Applications	C, E, G, H, U	78.7%	$85,027	51.5%	11,560
2. Software Developers, Systems Software	C, E, H	78.7%	$91,505	55.9%	6,330

C=Computer Systems Design, E=Educational Services, G=Government, H=Health Care, R=Repair and Maintenance, U=Utilities

150 Best Jobs for a Secure Future © JIST Works

Best Secure Jobs Overall Employing a High Percentage of Men

Job	Career Field(s)	Percent Men	Annual Earnings	Percent Growth	Annual Openings
3. Computer Network Architects	C, E, G, H, U	77.5%	$72,718	74.6%	6,190
4. Computer Systems Analysts	C, E, H, U	72.2%	$77,742	33.2%	9,400
5. Network and Computer Systems Administrators	C, E, G, H, U	78.4%	$67,527	40.4%	8,370
6. Chief Executives	C, E, H, R, U	75.9%	$144,850	8.8%	2,710
7. General and Operations Managers	C, E, G, H, R, U	71.4%	$95,208	5.8%	355,550
8. Computer Occupations, All Other	C, E, G	71.0%	$81,888	15.5%	3,350
9. Computer and Information Research Scientists	C, G	72.2%	$98,704	32.2%	600
10. Detectives and Criminal Investigators	G	74.4%	$68,630	16.8%	2,790
11. Air Traffic Controllers	G	76.7%	$111,880	10.7%	750
12. Firefighters	G	95.5%	$45,840	18.9%	10,000
13. Electronics Engineers, Except Computer	C	91.3%	$92,460	40.4%	160
14. First-Line Supervisors of Police and Detectives	G	88.0%	$78,600	8.0%	3,530
15. Industrial Engineers	C, G, U	82.1%	$80,847	38.8%	300
16. Police and Sheriff's Patrol Officers	E, G	85.4%	$53,563	8.7%	15,090
17. Biomedical Engineers	E, H	88.2%	$64,111	69.4%	330
18. Mechanical Engineers	C, G	95.0%	$88,401	15.1%	360
19. First-Line Supervisors of Fire Fighting and Prevention Workers	G	92.3%	$68,560	8.2%	2,170
20. Medical Equipment Repairers	H, R	89.4%	$45,663	35.1%	1,180
21. Physicists	H	75.0%	$152,545	16.7%	70
22. Water and Wastewater Treatment Plant and System Operators	G	93.0%	$40,820	18.9%	2,560
23. Industrial Machinery Mechanics	G, R, U	97.0%	$46,736	16.7%	1,020
24. Transportation Inspectors	G, R	91.5%	$59,003	18.2%	390
25. Electrical and Electronics Repairers, Powerhouse, Substation, and Relay	U	100.0%	$66,270	10.3%	410

C=Computer Systems Design, E=Educational Services, G=Government, H=Health Care, R=Repair and Maintenance, U=Utilities

Best Secure Jobs Sorted by Education or Training Required

The lists in this section organize the 150 best secure jobs into groups based on the education or training typically required for entry. For each of the education levels, I provide one list that includes all the best secure jobs that fit into it and that ranks them by their total combined score for field-specific earnings, growth, and number of openings.

Some jobs appear on more than one list because of the differing requirements of job specializations. For example, you will find the job Customer Service Representatives on two lists because it includes a broadly defined occupation that people can enter by getting moderate-term on-the-job training and also includes a specialization, Patient Representatives, for which a bachelor's degree is the most common preparation.

These lists can help you identify a secure job with higher earnings or upward mobility but with a similar level of education to the job you now hold. This information can help you leverage your present skills and experience into jobs that might provide better long-term career opportunities.

You can also use these lists to explore possible job options if you were to get additional training, education, or work experience. For example, you can use these lists to identify secure occupations that offer high potential and then look into the education or training required to get the jobs that interest you most.

The lists can also help you when you plan your education. For example, you might be thinking about a job that involves technology in some way, but you aren't sure exactly what kind of work you want to do. The lists show that Technical Writers need a bachelor's degree plus work experience and earn $66,860 in the Computer Systems Design field, while Nuclear Medicine Technologists need only an associate degree but earn an average of $68,713 in the Health Care field. If you want higher earnings without lengthy training and are willing to be flexible about your intended career field, this information might make a difference in your choice.

The Education Levels

The U.S. Department of Labor defines the training and education levels used in this set of lists as follows:

❋ **Short-term on-the-job training:** It is possible to work in these occupations and achieve an average level of performance within a few days or weeks through on-the-job training.

❊ **Moderate-term on-the-job training:** Occupations requiring this type of training can be performed adequately after a 1- to 12-month period of combined on-the-job and informal training. Typically, untrained workers observe experienced workers performing tasks and are gradually moved into progressively more difficult assignments.

❊ **Long-term on-the-job training:** This training requires more than 12 months of on-the-job training or combined work experience and formal classroom instruction. This includes occupations that use formal apprenticeships for training workers that may take up to 4 years. It also includes intensive occupation-specific, employer-sponsored training, such as police academies. Furthermore, it includes occupations that require natural talent that must be developed over many years.

❊ **Work experience in a related occupation:** This type of job requires experience in a related occupation. For example, police detectives are selected based on their experience as police patrol officers.

❊ **Postsecondary vocational training:** This requirement can vary from training that involves a few months to usually less than one year. In a few instances, as many as four years of training may be required.

❊ **Associate degree:** This degree usually requires two years of full-time academic work beyond high school.

❊ **Bachelor's degree:** This degree requires approximately four to five years of full-time academic work beyond high school.

❊ **Work experience plus degree:** Many jobs in this category are management-related and require some experience in a related nonmanagerial position. Others require completion of a specific formal training program.

❊ **Master's degree:** Completion of a master's degree usually requires one to two years of full-time study beyond the bachelor's degree.

❊ **Doctoral degree:** This degree normally requires two or more years of full-time academic work beyond the bachelor's degree.

❊ **First professional degree:** This type of degree normally requires a minimum of two years of education beyond the bachelor's degree and frequently requires three years.

Another Warning About the Data

I warned you in the Introduction to use caution in interpreting the data in this book, and I want to do it again here. The occupational data I use is the most accurate available anywhere, but it has its limitations. The education or training requirements for entry into a job are those typically required as a minimum, but some people working in those jobs may have considerably more or different credentials. For example, although a bachelor's degree is considered the usual requirement for Medical and Health Services Managers, more than one-third of the people working in this occupation have no less formal education than that. On the other hand, Compliance Officers usually need to complete only long-term on-the-job training, but more than half of these workers have a bachelor's degree or higher.

You also need to be cautious about assuming that more education or training always leads to higher income. It is true that people with jobs that require long-term on-the-job training typically earn more than people with jobs that require short-term on-the-job training. (For the jobs in this book, the average annual difference is $22,694.) However, some people with short-term on-the-job training earn more than the average for the highest-paying occupations listed in this book. Furthermore, some people with long-term on-the-job training earn much less than the average shown in this book—this is particularly true of people just beginning in these careers.

So as you browse the following lists, please use them as a way to be encouraged rather than discouraged. Education and training are very important for success in the labor market of the future, but so are ability, drive, initiative, and—yes—luck.

Having said this, I encourage you to get as much education and training as you can. Continuous learning is one of single most important factors in job security. You used to be able to get your schooling and then close the schoolbooks forever, but this isn't a good attitude to have now. You will probably need to continue learning new things throughout your working life. This can be done by going back to school, which is a good thing for many people. But other workers may learn through workshops, adult education programs, certification programs, employer training, professional conferences, Internet training, or reading related books and magazines. Upgrading your computer skills—and other technical skills—is particularly important in our rapidly changing workplace, and you avoid doing so at your peril.

Best Secure Jobs Requiring Short-Term On-the-Job Training

Job	Career Field(s)	Annual Earnings	Percent Growth	Annual Openings
1. Interviewers, Except Eligibility and Loan	H	$29,557	20.3%	6,940
2. Teachers and Instructors, All Other	E	$29,070	18.0%	11,300
3. Receptionists and Information Clerks	R	$22,980	5.3%	230
4. Security Guards	U	$46,070	−16.6%	100
5. Stock Clerks and Order Fillers	R	$27,330	4.1%	140

C=Computer Systems Design, E=Educational Services, G=Government, H=Health Care, R=Repair and Maintenance, U=Utilities

Best Secure Jobs Requiring Moderate-Term On-the-Job Training

Job	Career Field(s)	Annual Earnings	Percent Growth	Annual Openings
1. Dental Assistants	H	$33,381	36.7%	22,490
2. Medical Secretaries	H	$30,512	27.4%	25,630
3. Billing and Posting Clerks	H, R	$32,296	19.5%	9,410
4. Customer Service Representatives	E, H, R	$30,532	32.0%	6,750
5. Pharmacy Technicians	H	$32,518	25.3%	5,360
6. Police, Fire, and Ambulance Dispatchers	G	$35,880	18.6%	2,350
7. Painters, Transportation Equipment	R	$39,170	12.8%	730
8. Secretaries and Administrative Assistants, Except Legal, Medical, and Executive	H, R	$30,367	25.6%	6,990
9. Maintenance and Repair Workers, General	R, U	$41,101	−1.1%	570
10. Production, Planning, and Expediting Clerks	U	$53,380	−15.9%	70
11. Inspectors, Testers, Sorters, Samplers, and Weighers	R	$29,200	1.3%	100
12. Dispatchers, Except Police, Fire, and Ambulance	R	$31,680	−4.5%	50
13. Team Assemblers	R	$27,590	6.5%	90
14. Coin, Vending, and Amusement Machine Servicers and Repairers	R	$29,150	2.8%	50

Best Secure Jobs Requiring Long-Term On-the-Job Training

Job	Career Field(s)	Annual Earnings	Percent Growth	Annual Openings
1. Compliance Officers	C, E, G, H, U	$57,895	30.4%	5,400
2. Claims Adjusters, Examiners, and Investigators	G	$64,880	19.5%	1,210
3. Firefighters	G	$45,840	18.9%	10,000
4. Air Traffic Controllers	G	$111,880	10.7%	750
5. Police and Sheriff's Patrol Officers	E, G	$53,563	8.7%	15,090
6. Water and Wastewater Treatment Plant and System Operators	G	$40,820	18.9%	2,560
7. Industrial Machinery Mechanics	G, R, U	$46,736	16.7%	1,020
8. Interpreters and Translators	E, H	$39,402	21.4%	910
9. Electrical Power-Line Installers and Repairers	G, U	$61,339	−8.0%	2,150

(continued)

C=Computer Systems Design, E=Educational Services, G=Government, H=Health Care, R=Repair and Maintenance, U=Utilities

(continued)

Best Secure Jobs Requiring Long-Term On-the-Job Training

Job	Career Field(s)	Annual Earnings	Percent Growth	Annual Openings
10. Automotive Body and Related Repairers	R	$37,730	4.0%	2,850
11. Power Distributors and Dispatchers	U	$68,010	−1.0%	200
12. Power Plant Operators	U	$64,440	−2.7%	700
13. Gas Plant Operators	U	$56,830	7.7%	110
14. Machinists	R	$38,160	3.2%	120
15. Automotive Glass Installers and Repairers	R	$32,950	2.3%	380
16. Home Appliance Repairers	R	$35,890	0.6%	230
17. Stationary Engineers and Boiler Operators	U	$58,050	−14.8%	50
18. Motorboat Mechanics and Service Technicians	R	$35,420	−11.4%	100

Best Secure Jobs Requiring Work Experience in a Related Occupation

Job	Career Field(s)	Annual Earnings	Percent Growth	Annual Openings
1. Compliance Officers	C, E, G, H, U	$57,895	30.4%	5,400
2. Teachers, Postsecondary	E	$64,086	15.2%	39,780
3. Computer Occupations, All Other	C, E, G	$81,888	15.5%	3,350
4. First-Line Supervisors of Office and Administrative Support Workers	C, E, H, R, U	$48,437	20.6%	12,770
5. Detectives and Criminal Investigators	G	$68,630	16.8%	2,790
6. Self-Enrichment Education Teachers	E	$37,400	49.6%	3,720
7. First-Line Supervisors of Police and Detectives	G	$78,600	8.0%	3,530
8. Executive Secretaries and Executive Administrative Assistants	E, H, R, U	$42,187	14.2%	10,120
9. Transportation Inspectors	G, R	$59,003	18.2%	390
10. First-Line Supervisors of Fire Fighting and Prevention Workers	G	$68,560	8.2%	2,170
11. Industrial Production Managers	U	$103,160	−15.4%	50
12. First-Line Supervisors of Correctional Officers	G	$56,080	8.2%	1,280
13. First-Line Supervisors of Personal Service Workers	H	$35,205	14.0%	2,340

C=Computer Systems Design, E=Educational Services, G=Government, H=Health Care, R=Repair and Maintenance, U=Utilities

Best Secure Jobs Requiring Postsecondary Vocational Training

Job	Career Field(s)	Annual Earnings	Percent Growth	Annual Openings
1. Licensed Practical and Licensed Vocational Nurses	H	$40,037	21.9%	47,420
2. Computer Occupations, All Other	C, E, G	$81,888	15.5%	3,350
3. Surgical Technologists	H	$39,876	25.5%	6,460
4. Massage Therapists	H	$38,240	44.9%	710
5. Electrical and Electronics Repairers, Powerhouse, Substation, and Relay	U	$66,270	10.3%	410
6. Automotive Service Technicians and Mechanics	R	$33,040	11.0%	6,120
7. Electrical and Electronics Repairers, Commercial and Industrial Equipment	R	$45,110	8.5%	150
8. Welders, Cutters, Solderers, and Brazers	R, U	$37,943	0.3%	740
9. Electric Motor, Power Tool, and Related Repairers	R	$34,920	5.8%	340
10. Telecommunications Equipment Installers and Repairers, Except Line Installers	R	$37,210	6.7%	110
11. Computer, Automated Teller, and Office Machine Repairers	R	$35,860	0.0%	330

Best Secure Jobs Requiring an Associate Degree

Job	Career Field(s)	Annual Earnings	Percent Growth	Annual Openings
1. Dental Hygienists	H	$68,460	36.6%	13,990
2. Registered Nurses	E, G, H	$64,660	22.4%	134,650
3. Radiation Therapists	H	$74,625	27.0%	940
4. Respiratory Therapists	H	$54,350	21.3%	5,450
5. Physical Therapist Assistants	H	$49,717	34.6%	4,170
6. Radiologic Technologists	H	$54,116	17.5%	9,300
7. Computer Occupations, All Other	C, E, G	$81,888	15.5%	3,350
8. Diagnostic Medical Sonographers	H	$64,305	18.3%	2,310
9. Industrial Engineering Technicians	C	$53,250	54.0%	80
10. Occupational Therapy Assistants	H	$52,213	32.8%	1,470
11. Medical and Clinical Laboratory Technologists	H	$55,821	11.7%	6,740
12. Cardiovascular Technologists and Technicians	H	$49,347	24.1%	2,680
13. Medical Equipment Repairers	H, R	$45,663	35.1%	1,180

(continued)

C=Computer Systems Design, E=Educational Services, G=Government, H=Health Care, R=Repair and Maintenance, U=Utilities

(continued)

Best Secure Jobs Requiring an Associate Degree

Job	Career Field(s)	Annual Earnings	Percent Growth	Annual Openings
14. Medical Records and Health Information Technicians	H	$31,644	20.7%	8,570
15. Nuclear Medicine Technologists	H	$68,713	16.3%	940
16. Medical and Clinical Laboratory Technicians	H	$36,057	16.5%	6,620
17. Paralegals and Legal Assistants	G	$51,630	18.2%	980

Best Secure Jobs Requiring a Bachelor's Degree

Job	Career Field(s)	Annual Earnings	Percent Growth	Annual Openings
1. Software Developers, Applications	C, E, G, H, U	$85,027	51.5%	11,560
2. Software Developers, Systems Software	C, E, H	$91,505	55.9%	6,330
3. Computer Network Architects	C, E, G, H, U	$72,718	74.6%	6,190
4. Computer Systems Analysts	C, E, H, U	$77,742	33.2%	9,400
5. Network and Computer Systems Administrators	C, E, G, H, U	$67,527	40.4%	8,370
6. Database Administrators	C, H	$80,094	56.2%	1,130
7. Electronics Engineers, Except Computer	C	$92,460	40.4%	160
8. Financial Examiners	G	$80,090	41.4%	420
9. Accountants and Auditors	C, E, G, H, R, U	$59,496	20.9%	8,300
10. Industrial Engineers	C, G, U	$80,847	38.8%	300
11. Teachers, Postsecondary	E	$64,086	15.2%	39,780
12. Biomedical Engineers	E, H	$64,111	69.4%	330
13. Human Resources Specialists	C, E, G, H	$55,562	25.5%	5,040
14. Computer Occupations, All Other	C, E, G	$81,888	15.5%	3,350
15. Instructional Coordinators	E, G	$60,791	24.8%	3,610
16. Logisticians	C, G, U	$76,838	21.3%	1,030
17. Elementary School Teachers, Except Special Education	E	$51,690	15.8%	43,080
18. Customer Service Representatives	E, H, R	$30,532	32.0%	6,750
19. Special Education Teachers, Preschool, Kindergarten, and Elementary School	E, H	$52,611	18.9%	7,910
20. Technical Writers	C	$66,860	30.9%	430

C=Computer Systems Design, E=Educational Services, G=Government, H=Health Care, R=Repair and Maintenance, U=Utilities

Best Secure Jobs Requiring a Bachelor's Degree

Job	Career Field(s)	Annual Earnings	Percent Growth	Annual Openings
21. Compensation, Benefits, and Job Analysis Specialists	C, E, G, H	$56,518	26.0%	1,540
22. Education Administrators, All Other	E	$72,330	31.7%	190
23. Middle School Teachers, Except Special and Career/Technical Education	E	$51,980	15.4%	18,290
24. Budget Analysts	C, G	$68,100	22.4%	700
25. Public Relations Specialists	C, E, G, H, U	$52,970	24.8%	3,380
26. Healthcare Social Workers	H	$49,227	20.2%	7,640
27. Graphic Designers	C	$50,640	40.2%	530
28. Substance Abuse and Behavioral Disorder Counselors	H	$36,902	26.1%	3,780
29. Mechanical Engineers	C, G	$88,401	15.1%	360
30. Medical and Clinical Laboratory Technologists	H	$55,821	11.7%	6,740
31. Teachers and Instructors, All Other	E	$29,070	18.0%	11,300
32. Athletic Trainers	E, H	$42,309	37.1%	960
33. Writers and Authors	G	$70,020	9.7%	1,700
34. Special Education Teachers, Secondary School	E	$54,900	13.3%	4,100
35. Electrical Engineers	C, U	$84,616	1.3%	360
36. Health Educators	H	$49,683	19.7%	1,950
37. Kindergarten Teachers, Except Special Education	E	$49,790	15.4%	4,240
38. Environmental Engineers	G	$77,680	8.1%	580
39. Tax Examiners and Collectors, and Revenue Agents	G	$49,360	19.5%	2,340
40. Orthotists and Prosthetists	H	$53,331	30.0%	80
41. Probation Officers and Correctional Treatment Specialists	G	$47,700	19.2%	2,740
42. Industrial Production Managers	U	$103,160	–15.4%	50
43. Social and Community Service Managers	E	$62,690	18.3%	120
44. Child, Family, and School Social Workers	H	$36,820	13.2%	5,800
45. Adult Basic and Secondary Education and Literacy Teachers and Instructors	E	$47,460	18.0%	1,410

C=Computer Systems Design, E=Educational Services, G=Government, H=Health Care, R=Repair and Maintenance, U=Utilities

Best Secure Jobs Requiring Work Experience Plus Degree

Job	Career Field(s)	Annual Earnings	Percent Growth	Annual Openings
1. Medical and Health Services Managers	E, G, H	$84,044	16.6%	8,370
2. General and Operations Managers	C, E, G, H, R, U	$95,208	5.8%	355,550
3. Education Administrators, Elementary and Secondary School	E	$87,020	8.7%	44,620
4. Human Resources Managers	C, E, H	$95,254	17.1%	630
5. Chief Executives	C, E, H, R, U	$144,850	8.8%	2,710
6. Administrative Services Managers	C, E, G, H, U	$75,820	15.2%	12,780
7. Computer Occupations, All Other	C, E, G	$81,888	15.5%	3,350
8. Training and Development Managers	E	$83,430	27.5%	60
9. Management Analysts	C, E, G, U	$77,399	15.1%	5,520
10. Training and Development Specialists	C, E, G, H, U	$56,120	26.8%	3,290
11. Education Administrators, All Other	E	$72,330	31.7%	190
12. Detectives and Criminal Investigators	G	$68,630	16.8%	2,790
13. Education Administrators, Postsecondary	E	$83,560	2.0%	1,230

Best Secure Jobs Requiring a Master's Degree

Job	Career Field(s)	Annual Earnings	Percent Growth	Annual Openings
1. Physician Assistants	E, G, H	$86,264	39.6%	5,770
2. Physical Therapists	H	$76,653	34.2%	9,640
3. Computer Systems Analysts	C, E, H, U	$77,742	33.2%	9,400
4. Psychologists, All Other	H	$83,340	41.4%	190
5. Occupational Therapists	H	$74,360	30.7%	4,910
6. Speech-Language Pathologists	H	$74,247	34.0%	2,470
7. Registered Nurses	E, G, H	$64,660	22.4%	134,650
8. Mental Health Counselors	H	$37,457	28.6%	5,720
9. Instructional Coordinators	E, G	$60,791	24.8%	3,610
10. Mental Health and Substance Abuse Social Workers	H	$39,270	22.3%	6,660
11. Operations Research Analysts	C, E, G, H	$70,302	23.8%	960
12. Political Scientists	G	$115,730	18.4%	130
13. Social Scientists and Related Workers, All Other	E, G	$73,932	20.5%	1,130

C=Computer Systems Design, E=Educational Services, G=Government, H=Health Care, R=Repair and Maintenance, U=Utilities

Best Secure Jobs Requiring a Master's Degree

Job	Career Field(s)	Annual Earnings	Percent Growth	Annual Openings
14. Educational, Guidance, School, and Vocational Counselors	E	$55,860	14.0%	5,150
15. Sociologists	E	$68,860	23.1%	50
16. Rehabilitation Counselors	H	$31,182	11.6%	5,240
17. Urban and Regional Planners	G	$61,920	14.0%	790
18. Environmental Scientists and Specialists, Including Health	G, U	$61,445	7.6%	1,440

Best Secure Jobs Requiring a Doctoral Degree

Job	Career Field(s)	Annual Earnings	Percent Growth	Annual Openings
1. Psychologists, All Other	H	$83,340	41.4%	190
2. Computer and Information Research Scientists	C, G	$98,704	32.2%	600
3. Medical Scientists, Except Epidemiologists	E, G, H	$64,407	36.9%	2,800
4. Audiologists	H	$68,403	35.3%	530
5. Biological Scientists, All Other	G	$70,330	18.9%	660
6. Clinical, Counseling, and School Psychologists	E, G, H	$67,472	13.1%	3,960
7. Physicists	H	$152,545	16.7%	70
8. Teachers, Postsecondary	E	$64,086	15.2%	39,780
9. Biochemists and Biophysicists	E	$50,780	34.4%	100

Best Secure Jobs Requiring a First Professional Degree

Job	Career Field(s)	Annual Earnings	Percent Growth	Annual Openings
1. Physicians and Surgeons	E, H	$151,255	25.4%	30,180
2. Optometrists	H	$95,066	35.0%	1,900
3. Pharmacists	G, H	$110,226	13.3%	4,100
4. Teachers, Postsecondary	E	$64,086	15.2%	39,780
5. Chiropractors	H	$67,182	31.3%	1,450

C=Computer Systems Design, E=Educational Services, G=Government, H=Health Care, R=Repair and Maintenance, U=Utilities

Best Secure Jobs Sorted by Personality Types

These lists organize 148 of the 150 best secure jobs into groups matching six personality types. (The O*NET database, which was my source for personality information about the best jobs, provided no personality ratings for Education Administrators, All Other, or for Teachers and Instructors, All Other.) Within each personality type, I ranked the secure jobs based on each one's total combined score for field-specific earnings, growth, and annual job openings.

The personality types are Realistic, Investigative, Artistic, Social, Enterprising, and Conventional. This system was developed by Dr. John Holland and is used in the *Self-Directed Search (SDS)* and other career assessment inventories and information systems. If you have used one of these career inventories or systems, the lists will help you identify jobs that most closely match these personality types. Even if you have not used one of these systems, the concept of personality types and the jobs that are related to them can help you identify jobs that suit the type of person you are.

Like the set of lists based on educational and training requirements, this set assigns some of the jobs to more than one list in order to match the differing characteristics of job specializations. For example, you will find the job Clinical, Counseling, and School Psychologists on two lists because it is linked to the specializations School Psychologists and Clinical Psychologists (both Investigative) and Counseling Psychologists (Social). In addition, you should be aware that these lists are based on the primary personality type that describes the job, but most jobs also are linked to one or two secondary personality types. The job descriptions in Part IV indicate all significant personality types. Consider reviewing the jobs for more than one personality type so you don't overlook possible jobs that would interest you.

You'll notice that the list of Artistic jobs is considerably shorter than any of the others. Jobs in the arts tend to be less secure and are poorly represented in the six secure fields that are the focus of this book.

Descriptions of the Six Personality Types

Following are brief descriptions for each of the six personality types used in the lists. Select the two or three descriptions that most closely describe you and then use the lists to identify jobs that best fit these personality types.

❋ **Realistic:** These occupations frequently involve work activities that include practical, hands-on problems and solutions. They often deal with plants; animals; and real-world materials such as wood, tools, and machinery. Many of the occupations require working outside and don't involve a lot of paperwork or working closely with others.

❋ **Investigative:** These occupations frequently involve working with ideas and require an extensive amount of thinking. These occupations can involve searching for facts and figuring out problems mentally.

❋ **Artistic:** These occupations frequently involve working with forms, designs, and patterns. They often require self-expression, and the work can be done without following a clear set of rules.

❋ **Social:** These occupations frequently involve working with, communicating with, and teaching people. These occupations often involve helping or providing service to others.

❋ **Enterprising:** These occupations frequently involve starting up and carrying out projects. These occupations can involve leading people and making many decisions. They sometimes require risk taking and often deal with business.

❋ **Conventional:** These occupations frequently involve following set procedures and routines. These occupations can include working with data and details more than with ideas. Usually there is a clear line of authority to follow.

Best Secure Jobs for People with a Realistic Personality Type

Job	Career Field(s)	Annual Earnings	Percent Growth	Annual Openings
1. Electronics Engineers, Except Computer	C	$92,460	40.4%	160
2. Surgical Technologists	H	$39,876	25.5%	6,460
3. Security Guards	U	$46,070	−16.6%	100
4. Motorboat Mechanics and Service Technicians	R	$35,420	−11.4%	100
5. Automotive Service Technicians and Mechanics	R	$33,040	11.0%	6,120
6. Automotive Glass Installers and Repairers	R	$32,950	2.3%	380
7. Medical and Clinical Laboratory Technologists	H	$55,821	11.7%	6,740
8. Medical and Clinical Laboratory Technicians	H	$36,057	16.5%	6,620
9. Automotive Body and Related Repairers	R	$37,730	4.0%	2,850
10. Home Appliance Repairers	R	$35,890	0.6%	230
11. Radiologic Technologists	H	$54,116	17.5%	9,300
12. Industrial Machinery Mechanics	G, R, U	$46,736	16.7%	1,020
13. Electrical and Electronics Repairers, Powerhouse, Substation, and Relay	U	$66,270	10.3%	410
14. Electrical and Electronics Repairers, Commercial and Industrial Equipment	R	$45,110	8.5%	150

(continued)

C=Computer Systems Design, E=Educational Services, G=Government, H=Health Care, R=Repair and Maintenance, U=Utilities

(continued)

Best Secure Jobs for People with a Realistic Personality Type

Job	Career Field(s)	Annual Earnings	Percent Growth	Annual Openings
15. Electric Motor, Power Tool, and Related Repairers	R	$34,920	5.8%	340
16. Telecommunications Equipment Installers and Repairers, Except Line Installers	R	$37,210	6.7%	110
17. Computer, Automated Teller, and Office Machine Repairers	R	$35,860	0.0%	330
18. Stock Clerks and Order Fillers	R	$27,330	4.1%	140
19. Police and Sheriff's Patrol Officers	E, G	$53,563	8.7%	15,090
20. Cardiovascular Technologists and Technicians	H	$49,347	24.1%	2,680
21. Welders, Cutters, Solderers, and Brazers	R, U	$37,943	0.3%	740
22. Transportation Inspectors	G, R	$59,003	18.2%	390
23. Painters, Transportation Equipment	R	$39,170	12.8%	730
24. Gas Plant Operators	U	$56,830	7.7%	110
25. Water and Wastewater Treatment Plant and System Operators	G	$40,820	18.9%	2,560
26. Stationary Engineers and Boiler Operators	U	$58,050	−14.8%	50
27. Power Distributors and Dispatchers	U	$68,010	−1.0%	200
28. Firefighters	G	$45,840	18.9%	10,000
29. Machinists	R	$38,160	3.2%	120
30. Team Assemblers	R	$27,590	6.5%	90
31. Coin, Vending, and Amusement Machine Servicers and Repairers	R	$29,150	2.8%	50
32. Maintenance and Repair Workers, General	R, U	$41,101	−1.1%	570
33. Medical Equipment Repairers Health Care	R	$45,663	35.1%	1,180
34. Physician Assistants	E, G, H	$86,264	39.6%	5,770
35. Electrical Power-Line Installers and Repairers	G, U	$61,339	−8.0%	2,150
36. Power Plant Operators	U	$64,440	−2.7%	700

Best Secure Jobs for People with an Investigative Personality Type

Job	Career Field(s)	Annual Earnings	Percent Growth	Annual Openings
1. Biological Scientists, All Other	G	$70,330	18.9%	660
2. Industrial Engineering Technicians	C	$53,250	54.0%	80
3. Medical Scientists, Except Epidemiologists	E, G, H	$64,407	36.9%	2,800

C=Computer Systems Design, E=Educational Services, G=Government, H=Health Care, R=Repair and Maintenance, U=Utilities

Best Secure Jobs for People with an Investigative Personality Type

Job	Career Field(s)	Annual Earnings	Percent Growth	Annual Openings
4. Physicists	H	$152,545	16.7%	70
5. Medical and Clinical Laboratory Technologists	H	$55,821	11.7%	6,740
6. Physicians and Surgeons	E, H	$151,255	25.4%	30,180
7. Audiologists	H	$68,403	35.3%	530
8. Environmental Scientists and Specialists, Including Health	G, U	$61,445	7.6%	1,440
9. Sociologists	E	$68,860	23.1%	50
10. Psychologists, All Other	H	$83,340	41.4%	190
11. Biochemists and Biophysicists	E	$50,780	34.4%	100
12. Optometrists	H	$95,066	35.0%	1,900
13. Urban and Regional Planners	G	$61,920	14.0%	790
14. Political Scientists	G	$115,730	18.4%	130
15. Social Scientists and Related Workers, All Other	E, G	$73,932	20.5%	1,130
16. Clinical, Counseling, and School Psychologists	E, G, H	$67,472	13.1%	3,960
17. Operations Research Analysts	C, E, G, H	$70,302	23.8%	960
18. Software Developers, Systems Software	C, E, H	$91,505	55.9%	6,330
19. Computer Network Architects	C, E, G, H, U	$72,718	74.6%	6,190
20. Software Developers, Applications	C, E, G, H, U	$85,027	51.5%	11,560
21. Computer Systems Analysts	C, E, H, U	$77,742	33.2%	9,400
22. Pharmacists	G, H	$110,226	13.3%	4,100
23. Computer and Information Research Scientists	C, G	$98,704	32.2%	600
24. Computer Occupations, All Other	C, E, G	$81,888	15.5%	3,350
25. Management Analysts	C, E, G, U	$77,399	15.1%	5,520
26. Nuclear Medicine Technologists	H	$68,713	16.3%	940
27. Logisticians	C, G, U	$76,838	21.3%	1,030
28. Diagnostic Medical Sonographers	H	$64,305	18.3%	2,310
29. Compliance Officers	C, E, G, H, U	$57,895	30.4%	5,400
30. Biomedical Engineers	E, H	$64,111	69.4%	330
31. Electrical Engineers	C, U	$84,616	1.3%	360
32. Electronics Engineers, Except Computer	C	$92,460	40.4%	160
33. Environmental Engineers	G	$77,680	8.1%	580
34. Industrial Engineers	C, G, U	$80,847	38.8%	300
35. Mechanical Engineers	C, G	$88,401	15.1%	360
36. Network and Computer Systems Administrators	C, E, G, H, U	$67,527	40.4%	8,370

C=Computer Systems Design, E=Educational Services, G=Government, H=Health Care, R=Repair and Maintenance, U=Utilities

Best Secure Jobs for People with an Artistic Personality Type

Job	Career Field(s)	Annual Earnings	Percent Growth	Annual Openings
1. Graphic Designers	C	$50,640	40.2%	530
2. Technical Writers	C	$66,860	30.9%	430
3. Interpreters and Translators	E, H	$39,402	21.4%	910
4. Writers and Authors	G	$70,020	9.7%	1,700

Best Secure Jobs for People with a Social Personality Type

Job	Career Field(s)	Annual Earnings	Percent Growth	Annual Openings
1. Compliance Officers	C, E, G, H, U	$57,895	30.4%	5,400
2. Training and Development Specialists	C, E, G, H, U	$56,120	26.8%	3,290
3. Computer Systems Analysts	C, E, H, U	$77,742	33.2%	9,400
4. Teachers, Postsecondary	E	$64,086	15.2%	39,780
5. Special Education Teachers, Preschool, Kindergarten, and Elementary School	E, H	$52,611	18.9%	7,910
6. Chiropractors	H	$67,182	31.3%	1,450
7. Mental Health Counselors	H	$37,457	28.6%	5,720
8. Rehabilitation Counselors	H	$31,182	11.6%	5,240
9. Child, Family, and School Social Workers	H	$36,820	13.2%	5,800
10. Healthcare Social Workers	H	$49,227	20.2%	7,640
11. Mental Health and Substance Abuse Social Workers	H	$39,270	22.3%	6,660
12. Massage Therapists	H	$38,240	44.9%	710
13. Probation Officers and Correctional Treatment Specialists	G	$47,700	19.2%	2,740
14. Occupational Therapists	H	$74,360	30.7%	4,910
15. Kindergarten Teachers, Except Special Education	E	$49,790	15.4%	4,240
16. Elementary School Teachers, Except Special Education	E	$51,690	15.8%	43,080
17. Middle School Teachers, Except Special and Career/Technical Education	E	$51,980	15.4%	18,290
18. Special Education Teachers, Secondary School	E	$54,900	13.3%	4,100
19. Adult Basic and Secondary Education and Literacy Teachers and Instructors	E	$47,460	18.0%	1,410

C=Computer Systems Design, E=Educational Services, G=Government, H=Health Care, R=Repair and Maintenance, U=Utilities

Best Secure Jobs for People with a Social Personality Type

Job	Career Field(s)	Annual Earnings	Percent Growth	Annual Openings
20. Self-Enrichment Education Teachers	E	$37,400	49.6%	3,720
21. Health Educators	H	$49,683	19.7%	1,950
22. Registered Nurses	E, G, H	$64,660	22.4%	134,650
23. Physician Assistants	E, G, H	$86,264	39.6%	5,770
24. Physical Therapist Assistants	H	$49,717	34.6%	4,170
25. Instructional Coordinators	E, G	$60,791	24.8%	3,610
26. Occupational Therapy Assistants	H	$52,213	32.8%	1,470
27. Athletic Trainers	E, H	$42,309	37.1%	960
28. Orthotists and Prosthetists	H	$53,331	30.0%	80
29. Educational, Guidance, School, and Vocational Counselors	E	$55,860	14.0%	5,150
30. Dental Hygienists	H	$68,460	36.6%	13,990
31. Substance Abuse and Behavioral Disorder Counselors	H	$36,902	26.1%	3,780
32. Speech-Language Pathologists	H	$74,247	34.0%	2,470
33. Clinical, Counseling, and School Psychologists	E, G, H	$67,472	13.1%	3,960
34. Respiratory Therapists	H	$54,350	21.3%	5,450
35. Radiation Therapists	H	$74,625	27.0%	940
36. Physical Therapists	H	$76,653	34.2%	9,640
37. Customer Service Representatives	E, H, R	$30,532	32.0%	6,750
38. Licensed Practical and Licensed Vocational Nurses	H	$40,037	21.9%	47,420

Best Secure Jobs for People with an Enterprising Personality Type

Job	Career Field(s)	Annual Earnings	Percent Growth	Annual Openings
1. Customer Service Representatives	E, H, R	$30,532	32.0%	6,750
2. Human Resources Managers	C, E, H	$95,254	17.1%	630
3. First-Line Supervisors of Office and Administrative Support Workers	C, E, H, R, U	$48,437	20.6%	12,770
4. Detectives and Criminal Investigators	G	$68,630	16.8%	2,790
5. First-Line Supervisors of Fire Fighting and Prevention Workers	G	$68,560	8.2%	2,170

(continued)

C=Computer Systems Design, E=Educational Services, G=Government, H=Health Care, R=Repair and Maintenance, U=Utilities

(continued)

Best Secure Jobs for People with an Enterprising Personality Type

Job	Career Field(s)	Annual Earnings	Percent Growth	Annual Openings
6. First-Line Supervisors of Police and Detectives	G	$78,600	8.0%	3,530
7. First-Line Supervisors of Correctional Officers	G	$56,080	8.2%	1,280
8. Registered Nurses	E, G, H	$64,660	22.4%	134,650
9. Chief Executives	C, E, H, R, U	$144,850	8.8%	2,710
10. Writers and Authors	G	$70,020	9.7%	1,700
11. Public Relations Specialists	C, E, G, H, U	$52,970	24.8%	3,380
12. Police and Sheriff's Patrol Officers	E, G	$53,563	8.7%	15,090
13. Human Resources Specialists	C, E, G, H	$55,562	25.5%	5,040
14. First-Line Supervisors of Personal Service Workers	H	$35,205	14.0%	2,340
15. Education Administrators, Postsecondary	E	$83,560	2.0%	1,230
16. Training and Development Managers	E	$83,430	27.5%	60
17. Medical and Health Services Managers	E, G, H	$84,044	16.6%	8,370
18. Social and Community Service Managers	E	$62,690	18.3%	120
19. Education Administrators, Elementary and Secondary School	E	$87,020	8.7%	44,620
20. Logisticians	C, G, U	$76,838	21.3%	1,030
21. Administrative Services Managers	C, E, G, H, U	$75,820	15.2%	12,780
22. General and Operations Managers	C, E, G, H, R, U	$95,208	5.8%	355,550
23. Financial Examiners	G	$80,090	41.4%	420
24. Air Traffic Controllers	G	$111,880	10.7%	750
25. Industrial Production Managers	U	$103,160	−15.4%	50

Best Secure Jobs for People with a Conventional Personality Type

Job	Career Field(s)	Annual Earnings	Percent Growth	Annual Openings
1. Budget Analysts	C, G	$68,100	22.4%	700
2. Secretaries and Administrative Assistants, Except Legal, Medical, and Executive	H, R	$30,367	25.6%	6,990
3. Logisticians	C, G, U	$76,838	21.3%	1,030
4. Computer Occupations, All Other	C, E, G	$81,888	15.5%	3,350
5. Database Administrators	C, H	$80,094	56.2%	1,130
6. Police, Fire, and Ambulance Dispatchers	G	$35,880	18.6%	2,350
7. Medical Secretaries	H	$30,512	27.4%	25,630

C=Computer Systems Design, E=Educational Services, G=Government, H=Health Care, R=Repair and Maintenance, U=Utilities

Best Secure Jobs for People with a Conventional Personality Type

Job	Career Field(s)	Annual Earnings	Percent Growth	Annual Openings
8. Accountants and Auditors	C, E, G, H, R, U	$59,496	20.9%	8,300
9. Executive Secretaries and Executive Administrative Assistants	E, H, R, U	$42,187	14.2%	10,120
10. Tax Examiners and Collectors, and Revenue Agents	G	$49,360	19.5%	2,340
11. Interviewers, Except Eligibility and Loan	H	$29,557	20.3%	6,940
12. Compensation, Benefits, and Job Analysis Specialists	C, E, G, H	$56,518	26.0%	1,540
13. Billing and Posting Clerks	H, R	$32,296	19.5%	9,410
14. Claims Adjusters, Examiners, and Investigators	G	$64,880	19.5%	1,210
15. Detectives and Criminal Investigators	G	$68,630	16.8%	2,790
16. Dental Assistants	H	$33,381	36.7%	22,490
17. Medical Records and Health Information Technicians	H	$31,644	20.7%	8,570
18. Pharmacy Technicians	H	$32,518	25.3%	5,360
19. Receptionists and Information Clerks	R	$22,980	5.3%	230
20. Inspectors, Testers, Sorters, Samplers, and Weighers	R	$29,200	1.3%	100
21. Stock Clerks and Order Fillers	R	$27,330	4.1%	140
22. Paralegals and Legal Assistants	G	$51,630	18.2%	980
23. Production, Planning, and Expediting Clerks	U	$53,380	−15.9%	70
24. Dispatchers, Except Police, Fire, and Ambulance	R	$31,680	−4.5%	50
25. Compliance Officers	C, E, G, H, U	$57,895	30.4%	5,400

C=Computer Systems Design, E=Educational Services, G=Government, H=Health Care, R=Repair and Maintenance, U=Utilities

Bonus Lists: Metropolitan Areas Where the Secure Career Fields Are Concentrated

If you read Part I of this book, you know that you can improve your chances of staying employed during recessions by choosing not just the right occupation, but also the right location. The following lists can help you make these additional choices. To create the lists, I ranked metropolitan areas to identify those with the greatest concentrations of secure jobs in each of the six career fields. In the following lists, the degree of concentration is expressed as the percentage of the total workforce of the metro area that is employed in the secure jobs that this book links to each career field.

Metro Area	Percentage of Workers in Computer Systems Design Jobs
1. San Jose–Sunnyvale–Santa Clara, CA	17.4%
2. Washington-Arlington-Alexandria, DC-VA-MD-WV	16.5%
3. Huntsville, AL	15.2%
4. Boulder, CO	12.8%
5. Warner Robins, GA	12.6%
6. Tallahassee, FL	12.5%
7. Trenton-Ewing, NJ	11.7%
8. Austin–Round Rock, TX	11.4%
9. Denver-Aurora, CO	11.2%
10. San Francisco–Oakland–Fremont, CA	11.1%

Top 10 Metropolitan Areas Where Computer Systems Design Jobs Are Concentrated

Top 10 Metropolitan Areas Where Educational Services Jobs Are Concentrated

Metro Area	Percentage of Workers in Educational Services Jobs
1. Washington-Arlington-Alexandria, DC-VA-MD-WV	21.8%
2. Durham, NC	21.7%
3. San Jose–Sunnyvale–Santa Clara, CA	20.8%
4. Trenton-Ewing, NJ	19.8%
5. Boston-Cambridge-Quincy, MA-NH	19.2%
6. Atlanta–Sandy Springs–Marietta, GA	19.1%
7. Colorado Springs, CO	18.6%
8. Baltimore-Towson, MD	18.3%
9. Tallahassee, FL	18.2%
10. Sacramento–Arden-Arcade–Roseville, CA	18.1%

Top 10 Metropolitan Areas Where Government Jobs Are Concentrated

Metro Area	Percentage of Workers in Government Jobs
1. Washington-Arlington-Alexandria, DC-VA-MD-WV	16.3%
2. Tallahassee, FL	14.9%
3. Durham, NC	14.6%
4. Trenton-Ewing, NJ	13.9%
5. San Jose–Sunnyvale–Santa Clara, CA	13.9%
6. Olympia, WA	13.8%
7. Boulder, CO	13.8%
8. Baltimore-Towson, MD	13.2%
9. Rochester, MN	12.8%
10. Huntsville, AL	12.6%

Top 10 Metropolitan Areas Where Health Care Jobs Are Concentrated

Metro Area	Percentage of Workers in Health Care Jobs
1. Rochester, MN	26.0%
2. Durham, NC	25.4%
3. Boston-Cambridge-Quincy, MA-NH	22.9%
4. Boulder, CO	22.7%
5. San Jose–Sunnyvale–Santa Clara, CA	22.3%
6. Colorado Springs, CO	22.1%
7. Springfield, IL	22.0%
8. Washington-Arlington-Alexandria, DC-VA-MD-WV	22.0%
9. Jackson, MS	21.6%
10. Worcester, MA-CT	21.6%

Top 10 Metropolitan Areas Where Repair and Maintenance Jobs Are Concentrated

Metro Area	Percentage of Workers in Repair and Maintenance Jobs
1. Elkhart-Goshen, IN	20.8%
2. Spartanburg, SC	19.1%
3. Greenville-Mauldin-Easley, SC	18.4%
4. Rocky Mount, NC	18.3%
5. Tulsa, OK	18.2%
6. Montgomery, AL	18.0%
7. Dalton, GA	17.8%
8. Anniston-Oxford, AL	17.2%
9. Nashville-Davidson–Murfreesboro, TN	17.1%
10. Elizabethtown, KY	17.0%

Top 10 Metropolitan Areas Where Utilities Jobs Are Concentrated

Metro Area	Percentage of Workers in Utilities Jobs
1. Washington-Arlington-Alexandria, DC-VA-MD-WV	16.1%
2. San Jose–Sunnyvale–Santa Clara, CA	15.0%
3. Tallahassee, FL	14.7%
4. Huntsville, AL	13.5%
5. Atlanta–Sandy Springs–Marietta, GA	13.1%
6. Boulder, CO	12.7%
7. Trenton-Ewing, NJ	12.7%
8. Austin–Round Rock, TX	12.6%
9. San Francisco–Oakland–Fremont, CA	12.5%
10. Denver-Aurora, CO	12.4%

Bonus Lists: Top Skills for the Secure Career Fields

Part I of this book emphasizes the importance of developing your skills as a way of making your job secure. Some skills are highly specific to a particular job, such as mastery of a specialized software application. But other skills are transferable from many jobs to many others; they are especially valuable because they can be useful in a wide variety of work situations.

The O*NET database identifies the transferable skills for each occupation, and you can see the top skills for any of the 150 secure jobs by looking at the job descriptions in Part IV. However, I thought it would be especially useful to regard the jobs in each secure career field *as a group* and find the top 10 skills for each field. Because these 10 skills are associated with secure jobs that have good economic rewards, they may be the most valuable skills of all. You can find the definitions of all the O*NET skills in the Appendix.

The final list shows the top 10 skills for *all 150* secure jobs taken as a group.

To determine the top skills for the career fields, I computed an average score based on the O*NET ratings for level of skill required for the related jobs. I then weighted these scores, using the size of the workforces of the secure jobs.

The Top 10 Skills for the Computer Systems Design Field

Skill
1. Reading Comprehension
2. Critical Thinking
3. Systems Evaluation
4. Active Listening
5. Judgment and Decision Making
6. Complex Problem Solving
7. Monitoring
8. Active Learning
9. Speaking
10. Systems Analysis

The Top 10 Skills for the Educational Services Field

Skill
1. Reading Comprehension
2. Writing
3. Learning Strategies
4. Speaking
5. Active Listening
6. Monitoring
7. Critical Thinking
8. Instructing
9. Active Learning
10. Social Perceptiveness

The Top 10 Skills for the Government Field

Skill
1. Critical Thinking
2. Reading Comprehension
3. Active Listening
4. Speaking
5. Monitoring
6. Social Perceptiveness
7. Judgment and Decision Making
8. Writing
9. Coordination
10. Complex Problem Solving

The Top 10 Skills for the Health Care Field

Skill
1. Reading Comprehension
2. Active Listening
3. Social Perceptiveness
4. Speaking
5. Critical Thinking
6. Monitoring
7. Service Orientation
8. Writing
9. Coordination
10. Active Learning

The Top 10 Skills for the Repair and Maintenance Field

Skill
1. Critical Thinking
2. Active Listening
3. Monitoring
4. Complex Problem Solving
5. Reading Comprehension
6. Operation Monitoring
7. Judgment and Decision Making
8. Coordination
9. Repairing
10. Speaking

The Top 10 Skills for the Utilities Field

Skill
1. Reading Comprehension
2. Critical Thinking
3. Monitoring
4. Active Listening
5. Coordination
6. Complex Problem Solving
7. Judgment and Decision Making
8. Speaking
9. Active Learning
10. Time Management

The Top 10 Skills for the 150 Best Secure Jobs

Skill
1. Reading Comprehension
2. Active Listening
3. Critical Thinking
4. Speaking
5. Monitoring
6. Writing
7. Social Perceptiveness
8. Active Learning
9. Judgment and Decision Making
10. Coordination

PART IV

Descriptions of the Best Secure Jobs

This part provides descriptions for all the jobs included in one or more of the lists in Part III. The book's introduction gives more details on how to use and interpret the job descriptions, but here is some additional information:

* Job descriptions are organized alphabetically by job title. This approach allows you to find a description quickly if you know its title from one of the lists in Part III.

* Each job description begins with key economic figures for the job, such as the earnings and job growth. I include figures that are specific to workers in the secure field to which the job is linked (indicated by an abbreviation, such as H for Health Care) and figures that apply to workers in all fields (indicated by an asterisk). The figures for the specific fields are arranged in ascending order.

* In some cases, job titles are linked to one or more job specializations. For example, if you look for the job title Automotive Service Technicians and Mechanics, you will also find descriptions of the job specializations Automotive Master Mechanics and Automotive Specialty Technicians.

* Consider the job descriptions in this section as a first step in career exploration. When you find a job that interests you, turn to other online and print resources for further exploration.

* Part III features many interesting lists that will help you identify job titles to explore in more detail. If you have not browsed the lists in Part III, consider spending some time there. The lists are interesting and will help you identify job titles you can find described in the material that follows. If you are using this section to browse for interesting options, I suggest that you begin with the Table of Contents. The job titles and job specializations in Part IV are also listed in the Index.

Accountants and Auditors

- ❀ Annual Earnings: E $54,810, H $56,913, R $57,400, G $60,030, U $67,120, C $69,100, * $61,690

- ❀ Earnings Growth Potential: Medium (36.9%)

- ❀ Growth: U –11.5%, R 8.6%, G 16.9%, E 17.8%, H 22.3%, C 65.5%, * 21.6%

- ❀ Annual Job Openings: R 150, U 230, C 990, E 1,250, G 2,820, H 2,860, * 49,750

- ❀ Self-Employed: 8.1%

Detailed Fields with Greatest Employment: State and Local Government (7.0%); Management of Companies and Enterprises (6.0%); Professional, Scientific, and Technical Services (33.0%); Administrative and Support Services (3.9%); Educational Services, Public and Private (3.7%)

Detailed Fields with Highest Growth (Projected Growth for This Job): Internet Service Providers, Web Search Portals, and Data Processing Services (53.5%); Lessors of Nonfinancial Intangible Assets (Except Copyrighted Works) (39.4%); Professional, Scientific, and Technical Services (38.1%); Other Information Services (34.7%); Waste Management and Remediation Services (33.3%)

Other Considerations for Job Outlook: An increase in the number of businesses, a more stringent regulatory environment, and increased corporate accountability are expected to drive job growth for accountants and auditors. Opportunities should be favorable; job seekers with professional certification, especially a CPA, should have the best prospects.

Job Specialization: Accountants

Analyze financial information and prepare financial reports to determine or maintain record of assets, liabilities, profit and loss, tax liability, or other financial activities within an organization. Prepare, examine, or analyze accounting records, financial statements, or other financial reports to assess accuracy, completeness, and conformance to reporting and procedural standards. Compute taxes owed and prepare tax returns, ensuring compliance with payment, reporting, or other tax requirements. Analyze business operations, trends, costs, revenues, financial commitments, and obligations to project future revenues and expenses or to provide advice. Report to management regarding the finances of establishment. Establish tables of accounts and assign entries to proper accounts. Develop, maintain, and analyze budgets, preparing periodic reports that compare budgeted costs to actual costs. Develop, implement, modify, and document recordkeeping and accounting systems, making use of current computer technology. Prepare forms and manuals for accounting and bookkeeping personnel and direct their work activities.

Education/Training Required: Bachelor's degree. **Education and Training Programs:** Accounting; Accounting and Business/Management; Accounting and Computer Science; Accounting and Finance; Auditing; Taxation. **Knowledge/Courses:** Economics and Accounting; Clerical Practices; Mathematics; Computers and Electronics; Personnel and Human Resources; Administration and Management.

Personality Type: Conventional-Enterprising. **Career Cluster:** 04 Business, Management, and Administration. **Career Pathway:** 4.2 Business, Financial Management, and Accounting. **Other Jobs in This Pathway:** Auditors; Billing and Posting Clerks; Billing, Cost, and Rate Clerks; Bookkeeping, Accounting, and Auditing Clerks; Brokerage Clerks; Brownfield Redevelopment Specialists and Site Managers; Budget Analysts; Compliance

---

*C=Computer Systems Design, E=Educational Services, G=Government, H=Health Care, R=Repair and Maintenance, U=Utilities, *=All Fields*

Managers; Credit Analysts; Financial Analysts; Financial Managers, Branch or Department; Investment Fund Managers; Logistics Managers; Loss Prevention Managers; Managers, All Other; Natural Sciences Managers; Payroll and Timekeeping Clerks; Regulatory Affairs Managers; Security Managers; Statement Clerks; Supply Chain Managers; Tax Preparers; Treasurers and Controllers; Wind Energy Operations Managers; Wind Energy Project Managers; others.

Skills: Operations Analysis; Mathematics; Systems Analysis; Management of Financial Resources; Systems Evaluation; Critical Thinking; Judgment and Decision Making; Negotiation.

Work Environment: Indoors; sitting; repetitive motions.

Job Specialization: Auditors

Examine and analyze accounting records to determine financial status of establishment and prepare financial reports concerning operating procedures. Collect and analyze data to detect deficient controls; duplicated effort; extravagance; fraud; or noncompliance with laws, regulations, and management policies. Prepare detailed reports on audit findings. Supervise auditing of establishments and determine scope of investigation required. Report to management about asset utilization and audit results and recommend changes in operations and financial activities. Inspect account books and accounting systems for efficiency, effectiveness, and use of accepted accounting procedures to record transactions. Examine records and interview workers to ensure recording of transactions and compliance with laws and regulations. Examine and evaluate financial and information systems, recommending controls to ensure system reliability and data integrity. Review data

about material assets, net worth, liabilities, capital stock, surplus, income, and expenditures. Confer with company officials about financial and regulatory matters.

Education/Training Required: Bachelor's degree. **Education and Training Programs:** Accounting; Accounting and Business/Management; Accounting and Computer Science; Accounting and Finance; Auditing; Taxation. **Knowledge/Courses:** Economics and Accounting; Administration and Management; Personnel and Human Resources; Law and Government; Computers and Electronics; Mathematics.

Personality Type: Conventional-Enterprising-Investigative. **Career Cluster:** 04 Business, Management, and Administration. **Career Pathway:** 4.2 Business, Financial Management, and Accounting. **Other Jobs in This Pathway:** Accountants; Billing and Posting Clerks; Billing, Cost, and Rate Clerks; Bookkeeping, Accounting, and Auditing Clerks; Brokerage Clerks; Brownfield Redevelopment Specialists and Site Managers; Budget Analysts; Compliance Managers; Credit Analysts; Financial Analysts; Financial Managers, Branch or Department; Investment Fund Managers; Logistics Managers; Loss Prevention Managers; Managers, All Other; Natural Sciences Managers; Payroll and Timekeeping Clerks; Regulatory Affairs Managers; Security Managers; Statement Clerks; Supply Chain Managers; Tax Preparers; Treasurers and Controllers; Wind Energy Operations Managers; Wind Energy Project Managers; others.

Skills: Systems Evaluation; Systems Analysis; Management of Financial Resources; Mathematics; Programming; Writing; Operations Analysis; Management of Personnel Resources.

Work Environment: Indoors; sitting.

Adult Basic and Secondary Education and Literacy Teachers and Instructors

- ❋ Annual Earnings: E $47,460, * $46,530
- ❋ Earnings Growth Potential: High (41.8%)
- ❋ Growth: E 18.0%, * 15.1%
- ❋ Annual Job Openings: E 1,410, * 2,920
- ❋ Self-Employed: 20.4%

Detailed Fields with Greatest Employment: Educational Services, Public and Private (82.3%); Social Assistance (8.1%); Religious, Grantmaking, Civic, Professional, and Similar Organizations (1.3%); Administrative and Support Services (0.9%); Nursing and Residential Care Facilities (0.8%)

Detailed Fields with Highest Growth (Projected Growth for This Job): Administrative and Support Services (32.4%); Social Assistance (20.8%); Educational Services, Public and Private (18.0%); Religious, Grantmaking, Civic, Professional, and Similar Organizations (13.9%); Private Households; Primary and Secondary Jobs (11.1%)

Other Considerations for Job Outlook: As the need for educated workers increases, so will the need for teachers to instruct them. In addition, there should be employment growth for teachers to help immigrants and others improve their English language skills. Opportunities should be favorable.

Teach or instruct out-of-school youths and adults in remedial education classes, preparatory classes for the General Educational Development test, literacy, or English as a Second Language. Teaching may or may not take place in a traditional educational institution. Adapt teaching methods and instructional materials to meet students' varying needs, abilities, and interests.

Observe and evaluate students' work to determine progress and make suggestions for improvement. Instruct students individually and in groups, using various teaching methods such as lectures, discussions, and demonstrations. Plan and conduct activities for a balanced program of instruction, demonstration, and work time that provides students with opportunities to observe, question, and investigate. Maintain accurate and complete student records as required by laws or administrative policies. Prepare materials and classrooms for class activities. Establish clear objectives for all lessons, units, and projects and communicate those objectives to students. Conduct classes, workshops, and demonstrations to teach principles, techniques, or methods in subjects such as basic English language skills, life skills, and workforce entry skills.

Education/Training Required: Bachelor's degree. **Education and Training Programs:** Adult and Continuing Education and Teaching; Adult Literacy Tutor/Instructor Training; Bilingual and Multilingual Education; Multicultural Education; Teaching English as a Second or Foreign Language/ESL Language Instructor. **Knowledge/Courses:** English Language; History and Archeology; Education and Training; Sociology and Anthropology; Geography; Foreign Language.

Personality Type: Social-Artistic-Enterprising. **Career Cluster:** 05 Education and Training. **Career Pathway:** 5.3 Teaching/Training. **Other Jobs in This Pathway:** Athletes and Sports Competitors; Audio-Visual and Multimedia Collections Specialists; Career/Technical Education Teachers, Middle School; Career/Technical Education Teachers, Secondary School; Chemists; Coaches and Scouts; Dietitians and Nutritionists; Elementary School Teachers, Except Special Education; Fitness Trainers and Aerobics Instructors; Historians; Instructional Coordinators; Instructional Designers and Technologists; Interpreters and

*C=Computer Systems Design, E=Educational Services, G=Government, H=Health Care, R=Repair and Maintenance, U=Utilities, *=All Fields*

Translators; Kindergarten Teachers, Except Special Education; Librarians; Middle School Teachers, Except Special and Career/Technical Education; Physicists; Preschool Teachers, Except Special Education; Recreation Workers; Secondary School Teachers, Except Special and Career/Technical Education; Self-Enrichment Education Teachers; Teacher Assistants; Teachers and Instructors, All Other; Tutors.

Skills: Learning Strategies; Instructing; Writing; Reading Comprehension; Persuasion; Time Management; Social Perceptiveness; Negotiation.

Work Environment: Indoors; standing.

Air Traffic Controllers

- ❀ Annual Earnings: G $111,880, * $108,040
- ❀ Earnings Growth Potential: High (49.6%)
- ❀ Growth: G 10.8%, * 13.1%
- ❀ Annual Job Openings: G 750, * 1,230
- ❀ Self-Employed: 0.0%

Detailed Fields with Greatest Employment: Federal Government (88.2%); Support Activities for Transportation (5.3%); Air Transportation (2.3%); Administrative and Support Services (1.3%)

Detailed Fields with Highest Growth (Projected Growth for This Job): Administrative and Support Services (35.3%); Support Activities for Transportation (32.9%); Air Transportation (16.7%); Federal Government (10.7%)

Other Considerations for Job Outlook: More controllers are expected to be needed to handle increasing air traffic. Competition for admission to the FAA Academy—the usual first step in employment as an air traffic controller—is expected to remain keen.

Control air traffic on and within vicinity of airport and movement of air traffic between altitude sectors and control centers according to established procedures and policies. Authorize, regulate, and control commercial airline flights according to government or company regulations to expedite and ensure flight safety. Control air traffic on and within vicinity of airport and movement of air traffic between altitude sectors and control centers according to established procedures and policies. Authorize, regulate, and control commercial airline flights according to government or company regulations to expedite and ensure flight safety.

Education/Training Required: Long-term on-the-job training. **Education and Training Program:** Air Traffic Controller Training. **Knowledge/Courses:** Transportation; Geography; Telecommunications; Public Safety and Security; Physics; Education and Training.

Personality Type: Enterprising-Conventional. **Career Cluster:** 16 Transportation, Distribution, and Logistics. **Career Pathway:** 16.1 Transportation Operations. **Other Jobs in This Pathway:** Airline Pilots, Copilots, and Flight Engineers; Automotive and Watercraft Service Attendants; Automotive Master Mechanics; Bus Drivers, School or Special Client; Bus Drivers, Transit and Intercity; Commercial Pilots; Crane and Tower Operators; First-Line Supervisors of Helpers, Laborers, and Material Movers, Hand; First-Line Supervisors of Transportation and Material-Moving Machine and Vehicle Operators; Freight and Cargo Inspectors; Heavy and Tractor-Trailer Truck Drivers; Laborers and Freight, Stock, and Material Movers, Hand; Light Truck or Delivery Services Drivers; Mates—Ship, Boat, and Barge; Motor Vehicle Operators, All Other; Operating Engineers and Other Construction Equipment Operators; Parking Lot Attendants; Pilots, Ship; Railroad

Conductors and Yardmasters; Sailors and Marine Oilers; Ship and Boat Captains; Storage and Distribution Managers; Taxi Drivers and Chauffeurs; Transportation Managers; Transportation Workers, All Other; others.

Skills: Complex Problem Solving; Operation Monitoring; Judgment and Decision Making; Operations Analysis; Monitoring; Coordination; Systems Analysis; Systems Evaluation.

Work Environment: Indoors; sitting; using hands; repetitive motions; noise.

Athletic Trainers

- ❊ Annual Earnings: H $40,625, E $44,130, * $41,600
- ❊ Earnings Growth Potential: Medium (38.1%)
- ❊ Growth: E 23.2%, H 51.6%, * 36.9%
- ❊ Annual Job Openings: E 330, H 630, * 1,150
- ❊ Self-Employed: 0.7%

Detailed Fields with Greatest Employment: Performing Arts, Spectator Sports, and Related Industries (4.7%); Educational Services, Public and Private (39.3%); Ambulatory Health Care Services (20.2%); Hospitals, Public and Private (17.1%); Amusement, Gambling, and Recreation Industries (14.8%)

Detailed Fields with Highest Growth (Projected Growth for This Job): Ambulatory Health Care Services (76.8%); Amusement, Gambling, and Recreation Industries (36.9%); Performing Arts, Spectator Sports, and Related Industries (35.5%); Religious, Grantmaking, Civic, Professional, and Similar Organizations (30.8%); Educational Services, Public and Private (23.2%)

Other Considerations for Job Outlook: Employment growth is expected to be concentrated in the health-care industry, as athletic training is increasingly used to prevent illness and injury. Job prospects for athletic trainers should also be good in high schools. Keen competition is expected for positions with professional and college sports teams.

Evaluate, advise, and treat athletes to assist recovery from injury, avoid injury, or maintain peak physical fitness. Conduct an initial assessment of an athlete's injury or illness to provide emergency or continued care and to determine whether he or she should be referred to physicians for definitive diagnosis and treatment. Care for athletic injuries, using physical therapy equipment, techniques, and medication. Evaluate athletes' readiness to play and provide participation clearances when necessary and warranted. Apply protective or injury-preventive devices such as tape, bandages, or braces to body parts such as ankles, fingers, or wrists. Assess and report the progress of recovering athletes to coaches and physicians. Collaborate with physicians to develop and implement comprehensive rehabilitation programs for athletic injuries. Advise athletes on the proper use of equipment. Plan and implement comprehensive athletic injury and illness prevention programs. Develop training programs and routines designed to improve athletic performance.

Education/Training Required: Bachelor's degree. **Education and Training Program:** Athletic Training/Trainer. **Knowledge/Courses:** Medicine and Dentistry; Therapy and Counseling; Biology; Psychology; Customer and Personal Service; Clerical.

Personality Type: Social-Realistic-Investigative. **Career Cluster:** 08 Health Science. **Career Pathway:** 8.2 Diagnostics Services. **Other Jobs in This Pathway:** Ambulance Drivers and Attendants, Except Emergency Medical Technicians; Anesthesiologist Assistants; Cardiovascular Technologists and Technicians; Cytogenetic Technologists; Cytotechnologists; Diagnostic Medical Sonographers;

---

*C=Computer Systems Design, E=Educational Services, G=Government, H=Health Care, R=Repair and Maintenance, U=Utilities, *=All Fields*

Emergency Medical Technicians and Paramedics; Endoscopy Technicians; Health Diagnosing and Treating Practitioners, All Other; Health Technologists and Technicians, All Other; Healthcare Practitioners and Technical Workers, All Other; Histotechnologists and Histologic Technicians; Medical and Clinical Laboratory Technicians; Medical and Clinical Laboratory Technologists; Medical and Health Services Managers; Medical Assistants; Medical Equipment Preparers; Neurodiagnostic Technologists; Ophthalmic Laboratory Technicians; Physical Scientists, All Other; Physician Assistants; Radiologic Technicians; Radiologic Technologists; Surgical Technologists; Veterinary Assistants and Laboratory Animal Caretakers; others.

Skills: Learning Strategies; Quality Control Analysis; Service Orientation; Instructing; Social Perceptiveness; Science; Monitoring; Systems Evaluation.

Work Environment: More often indoors than outdoors; standing; using hands; exposed to disease or infections.

Audiologists

- ❋ Annual Earnings: H $68,403, * $66,660
- ❋ Earnings Growth Potential: Medium (36.1%)
- ❋ Growth: H 35.3%, * 25.0%
- ❋ Annual Job Openings: H 530, * 580
- ❋ Self-Employed: 1.3%

Detailed Fields with Greatest Employment: Ambulatory Health Care Services (51.1%); State and Local Government (2.6%); Health and Personal Care Stores (17.0%); Educational Services, Public and Private (14.3%); Hospitals, Public and Private (12.4%)

Detailed Fields with Highest Growth (Projected Growth for This Job): Social Assistance (44.4%); Ambulatory Health Care Services (41.1%); Educational Services, Public and Private (14.4%); Hospitals, Public and Private (11.5%); State and Local Government, Excluding Education and Hospitals (9.1%)

Other Considerations for Job Outlook: Employment of audiologists is expected to grow as the population ages and more care is needed for the elderly, who often have problems with hearing and balance. Job prospects should be favorable for job seekers who have a doctorate in audiology.

Assess and treat persons with hearing and related disorders. May fit hearing aids and provide auditory training. May perform research related to hearing problems. Examine and clean patients' ear canals. Educate and supervise audiology students and health-care personnel. Develop and supervise hearing screening programs. Counsel and instruct patients and their families in techniques to improve hearing and communication related to hearing loss. Evaluate hearing and balance disorders to determine diagnoses and courses of treatment. Program and monitor cochlear implants to fit the needs of patients. Participate in conferences or training to update or share knowledge of new hearing or balance disorder treatment methods or technologies. Conduct or direct research on hearing or balance topics and report findings to help in the development of procedures, technology, or treatments. Plan and conduct treatment programs for patients' hearing or balance problems, consulting with educators, physicians, nurses, psychologists, speech-language pathologists, and other health-care personnel as necessary.

Education/Training Required: Doctoral degree. **Education and Training Programs:** Audiology/Audiologist; Audiology/Audiologist and

Speech-Language Pathology/Pathologist; Communication Disorders Sciences and Services, Other; Communication Disorders, General; Communication Sciences and Disorders, General. **Knowledge/Courses:** Therapy and Counseling; Medicine and Dentistry; Sales and Marketing; Psychology; Biology; Sociology and Anthropology.

Personality Type: Investigative-Social. **Career Cluster:** 08 Health Science. **Career Pathway:** 8.1 Therapeutic Services. **Other Jobs in This Pathway:** Clinical Psychologists; Community and Social Service Specialists, All Other; Counseling Psychologists; Dental Assistants; Dental Hygienists; Dentists, General; Health Technologists and Technicians, All Other; Healthcare Support Workers, All Other; Home Health Aides; Licensed Practical and Licensed Vocational Nurses; Low Vision Therapists, Orientation and Mobility Specialists, and Vision Rehabilitation Therapists; Massage Therapists; Medical and Clinical Laboratory Technicians; Medical and Health Services Managers; Medical Scientists, Except Epidemiologists; Medical Secretaries; Occupational Therapists; Pharmacists; Pharmacy Technicians; Radiologic Technologists; School Psychologists; Social and Human Service Assistants; Speech-Language Pathologists; Speech-Language Pathology Assistants; Substance Abuse and Behavioral Disorder Counselors; others.

Skills: Science; Repairing; Equipment Selection; Reading Comprehension; Technology Design; Troubleshooting; Learning Strategies; Active Learning.

Work Environment: Indoors; sitting; using hands; exposed to disease or infections.

Automotive Body and Related Repairers

- ❋ Annual Earnings: R $37,730, * $38,130
- ❋ Earnings Growth Potential: Medium (39.7%)
- ❋ Growth: R 4.0%, * 0.5%
- ❋ Annual Job Openings: R 2,850, * 4,380
- ❋ Self-Employed: 12.9%

Detailed Fields with Greatest Employment: Repair and Maintenance (68.5%); Motor Vehicle and Parts Dealers (23.1%); Merchant Wholesalers, Durable Goods (2.4%); Transportation Equipment Manufacturing (1.2%); Truck Transportation (0.7%)

Detailed Fields with Highest Growth (Projected Growth for This Job): Wholesale Electronic Markets and Agents and Brokers (24.1%); Administrative and Support Services (20.0%); Support Activities for Transportation (15.6%); Specialty Trade Contractors (14.3%); Educational Services, Public and Private (12.5%)

Other Considerations for Job Outlook: As vehicle components become more technologically advanced and expensive, the trend for vehicles to be declared a total loss following a collision is expected to result in fewer repairs and, thus, minimal employment growth for these workers. But many job openings are expected to occur as existing workers leave the occupation permanently. Job seekers with formal training should have the best prospects.

Repair and refinish automotive vehicle bodies and straighten vehicle frames. File, grind, sand, and smooth filled or repaired surfaces, using power tools and hand tools. Sand body areas to be painted and cover bumpers, windows, and

*C=Computer Systems Design, E=Educational Services, G=Government, H=Health Care, R=Repair and Maintenance, U=Utilities, *=All Fields*

trim with masking tape or paper to protect them from the paint. Follow supervisors' instructions as to which parts to restore or replace and how much time a job should take. Remove damaged sections of vehicles, using metal-cutting guns, air grinders, and wrenches, and install replacement parts, using wrenches or welding equipment. Cut and tape plastic separating film to outside repair areas to avoid damaging surrounding surfaces during repair procedure and remove tape and wash surfaces after repairs are complete. Prime and paint repaired surfaces, using paint spray guns and motorized sanders. Inspect repaired vehicles for dimensional accuracy and test-drive them to ensure proper alignment and handling. Mix polyester resins and hardeners to be used in restoring damaged areas.

Education/Training Required: Long-term on-the-job training. **Education and Training Program:** Autobody/Collision and Repair Technology/Technician. **Knowledge/Courses:** Mechanical Devices; Chemistry; Production and Processing; Engineering and Technology.

Personality Type: Realistic. **Career Cluster:** 16 Transportation, Distribution, and Logistics. **Career Pathway:** 16.4 Facility and Mobile Equipment Maintenance. **Other Jobs in This Pathway:** Aircraft Mechanics and Service Technicians; Aircraft Structure, Surfaces, Rigging, and Systems Assemblers; Automotive Glass Installers and Repairers; Automotive Master Mechanics; Automotive Specialty Technicians; Bicycle Repairers; Bus and Truck Mechanics and Diesel Engine Specialists; Cleaners of Vehicles and Equipment; Electrical and Electronics Installers and Repairers, Transportation Equipment; Electronic Equipment Installers and Repairers, Motor Vehicles; Engine and Other Machine Assemblers; Gem and Diamond Workers; Installation, Maintenance, and Repair Workers, All Other; Motorboat Mechanics and Service Technicians; Motorcycle Mechanics; Outdoor

Power Equipment and Other Small Engine Mechanics; Painters, Transportation Equipment.

Skills: Repairing; Equipment Selection; Installation; Equipment Maintenance; Operation and Control; Troubleshooting; Quality Control Analysis; Operation Monitoring.

Work Environment: Standing; walking and running; kneeling, crouching, stooping, or crawling; using hands; bending or twisting the body; noise; contaminants; cramped work space; hazardous conditions; hazardous equipment; minor burns, cuts, bites, or stings.

Automotive Glass Installers and Repairers

- ❋ Annual Earnings: R $32,950, * $33,160
- ❋ Earnings Growth Potential: Medium (37.7%)
- ❋ Growth: R 2.3%, * 1.8%
- ❋ Annual Job Openings: R 380, * 440
- ❋ Self-Employed: 7.5%

Detailed Fields with Greatest Employment: Repair and Maintenance (86.0%); Motor Vehicle and Parts Dealers (5.9%); Specialty Trade Contractors (2.2%); Building Material and Garden Equipment and Supplies Dealers (1.9%); Transportation Equipment Manufacturing (1.2%)

Detailed Fields with Highest Growth (Projected Growth for This Job): Administrative and Support Services (14.3%); Specialty Trade Contractors (7.5%); Rental and Leasing Services (5.9%); Building Material and Garden Equipment and Supplies Dealers (2.9%); Repair and Maintenance (2.3%)

Other Considerations for Job Outlook: As vehicle components become more technologically advanced and expensive, the trend for vehicles to be declared a total loss following a collision is expected to result in fewer repairs and, thus, minimal employment growth for these workers. But many job openings are expected to occur as existing workers leave the occupation permanently. Job seekers with formal training should have the best prospects.

Replace or repair broken windshields and window glass in motor vehicles. Remove all dirt, foreign matter, and loose glass from damaged areas; then apply primer along windshield or window edges and allow it to dry. Install replacement glass in vehicles after old glass has been removed and all necessary preparations have been made. Allow all glass parts installed with urethane ample time to cure, taking temperature and humidity into account. Prime all scratches on pinch welds with primer and allow primed scratches to dry. Obtain windshields or windows for specific automobile makes and models from stock and examine them for defects before installation. Apply a bead of urethane around the perimeter of each pinch weld and dress the remaining urethane on the pinch welds so that it is of uniform level and thickness all the way around. Check for moisture or contamination in damaged areas, dry out any moisture before making repairs, and keep damaged areas dry until repairs are complete.

Education/Training Required: Long-term on-the-job training. **Education and Training Program:** Autobody/Collision and Repair Technology/Technician. **Knowledge/Courses:** Mechanical Devices; Production and Processing; Customer and Personal Service; Administration and Management; Sales and Marketing; Transportation.

Personality Type: Realistic-Conventional-Enterprising. **Career Cluster:** 16 Transportation, Distribution, and Logistics. **Career Pathway:** 16.4 Facility and Mobile Equipment Maintenance. **Other Jobs in This Pathway:** Aircraft Mechanics and Service Technicians; Aircraft Structure,

Surfaces, Rigging, and Systems Assemblers; Automotive Body and Related Repairers; Automotive Master Mechanics; Automotive Specialty Technicians; Bicycle Repairers; Bus and Truck Mechanics and Diesel Engine Specialists; Cleaners of Vehicles and Equipment; Electrical and Electronics Installers and Repairers, Transportation Equipment; Electronic Equipment Installers and Repairers, Motor Vehicles; Engine and Other Machine Assemblers; Gem and Diamond Workers; Installation, Maintenance, and Repair Workers, All Other; Motorboat Mechanics and Service Technicians; Motorcycle Mechanics; Outdoor Power Equipment and Other Small Engine Mechanics; Painters, Transportation Equipment.

Skills: Installation; Repairing; Equipment Selection; Equipment Maintenance; Operation and Control; Troubleshooting; Quality Control Analysis; Management of Material Resources.

Work Environment: Outdoors; standing; using hands; bending or twisting the body; repetitive motions; noise; very hot or cold; bright or inadequate lighting; contaminants; cramped work space; hazardous equipment; minor burns, cuts, bites, or stings.

Automotive Service Technicians and Mechanics

* Annual Earnings: R $33,040, * $35,790
* Earnings Growth Potential: High (43.6%)
* Growth: R 11.0%, * 4.7%
* Annual Job Openings: R 6,120, * 18,170
* Self-Employed: 15.9%

Detailed Fields with Greatest Employment: Motor Vehicle and Parts Dealers (41.8%); State and Local Government (4.2%); Repair and Maintenance (36.8%); Gasoline Stations (3.4%); Merchant Wholesalers, Durable Goods (2.2%)

*C=Computer Systems Design, E=Educational Services, G=Government, H=Health Care, R=Repair and Maintenance, U=Utilities, *=All Fields*

Detailed Fields with Highest Growth (Projected Growth for This Job): Professional, Scientific, and Technical Services (35.3%); Waste Management and Remediation Services (26.5%); Wholesale Electronic Markets and Agents and Brokers (26.2%); Specialty Trade Contractors (23.8%); Social Assistance (22.2%)

Other Considerations for Job Outlook: Consolidation in the automobile dealer industry, a significant employer of technicians, is expected to limit growth in this occupation. But some opportunities are expected because of the need to service the growing number of vehicles in the United States. Job seekers who complete formal training should have good prospects.

Job Specialization: Automotive Master Mechanics

Repair automobiles, trucks, buses, and other vehicles. Master mechanics repair virtually any part on the vehicle or specialize in the transmission system. Examine vehicles to determine extent of damage or malfunctions. Test-drive vehicles and test components and systems, using equipment such as infrared engine analyzers, compression gauges, and computerized diagnostic devices. Repair, reline, replace, and adjust brakes. Review work orders and discuss work with supervisors. Follow checklists to ensure all important parts are examined, including belts, hoses, steering systems, spark plugs, brake and fuel systems, wheel bearings, and other potentially troublesome areas. Plan work procedures, using charts, technical manuals, and experience. Test and adjust repaired systems to meet manufacturers' performance specifications. Confer with customers to obtain descriptions of vehicle problems and to discuss work to be performed and future repair requirements. Perform routine and scheduled maintenance services such as oil changes, lubrications, and tune-ups. Disassemble units and inspect parts for wear, using micrometers, calipers, and gauges.

Education/Training Required: Postsecondary vocational training. **Education and Training Programs:** Alternative Fuel Vehicle Technology/Technician; Autobody/Collision and Repair Technology/Technician; Automobile/Automotive Mechanics Technology/Technician; Automotive Engineering Technology/Technician; Medium/Heavy Vehicle and Truck Technology/Technician; Vehicle Emissions Inspection and Maintenance Technology/Technician. **Knowledge/Courses:** Mechanical Devices; Engineering and Technology; Physics; Design; Chemistry; Computers and Electronics.

Personality Type: Realistic-Investigative. **Career Cluster:** 16 Transportation, Distribution, and Logistics. **Career Pathways:** 16.1 Transportation Operations; 16.4 Facility and Mobile Equipment Maintenance. **Other Jobs in These Pathways:** Aircraft Mechanics and Service Technicians; Aircraft Structure, Surfaces, Rigging, and Systems Assemblers; Airline Pilots, Copilots, and Flight Engineers; Automotive and Watercraft Service Attendants; Automotive Body and Related Repairers; Automotive Specialty Technicians; Bus and Truck Mechanics and Diesel Engine Specialists; Bus Drivers, School or Special Client; Bus Drivers, Transit and Intercity; Cleaners of Vehicles and Equipment; Crane and Tower Operators; First-Line Supervisors of Helpers, Laborers, and Material Movers, Hand; First-Line Supervisors of Transportation and Material-Moving Machine and Vehicle Operators; Gem and Diamond Workers; Heavy and Tractor-Trailer Truck Drivers; Installation, Maintenance, and Repair Workers, All Other; Laborers and Freight, Stock, and Material Movers, Hand; Light Truck or Delivery Services Drivers; Motor Vehicle Operators, All Other; Operating Engineers and Other Construction Equipment Operators; Painters, Transportation Equipment; Parking Lot Attendants; Storage and Distribution Managers; Taxi Drivers and Chauffeurs; Transportation Managers; others.

Skills: Repairing; Equipment Maintenance; Installation; Troubleshooting; Equipment Selection; Operation and Control; Quality Control Analysis; Operation Monitoring.

Work Environment: Standing; using hands; bending or twisting the body; repetitive motions; noise; very hot or cold; bright or inadequate lighting; contaminants; cramped work space; hazardous conditions; hazardous equipment; minor burns, cuts, bites, or stings.

Job Specialization: Automotive Specialty Technicians

Repair only one system or component on a vehicle, such as brakes, suspension, or radiator. Examine vehicles, compile estimates of repair costs, and secure customers' approval to perform repairs. Repair, overhaul, and adjust automobile brake systems. Use electronic test equipment to locate and correct malfunctions in fuel, ignition, and emissions control systems. Repair and replace defective ball joint suspensions, brake shoes, and wheel bearings. Inspect and test new vehicles for damage; then record findings so that necessary repairs can be made. Test electronic computer components in automobiles to ensure that they are working properly. Tune automobile engines to ensure proper and efficient functioning. Install and repair air conditioners and service components such as compressors, condensers, and controls. Repair, replace, and adjust defective carburetor parts and gasoline filters. Remove and replace defective mufflers and tailpipes. Repair and replace automobile leaf springs. Rebuild, repair, and test automotive fuel injection units.

Education/Training Required: Postsecondary vocational training. **Education and Training Programs:** Alternative Fuel Vehicle Technology/Technician; Autobody/Collision and Repair Technology/Technician; Automobile/Automotive Mechanics Technology/Technician; Automotive Engineering Technology/Technician; Medium/Heavy Vehicle and Truck Technology/Technician; Vehicle Emissions Inspection and Maintenance Technology/Technician. **Knowledge/Courses:** Mechanical Devices; Physics; Engineering and Technology; Customer and Personal Service; Sales and Marketing; Administration and Management.

Personality Type: Realistic-Investigative-Conventional. **Career Clusters:** 13 Manufacturing; 16 Transportation, Distribution, and Logistics. **Career Pathways:** 13.3 Maintenance, Installation, and Repair; 16.4 Facility and Mobile Equipment Maintenance. **Other Jobs in These Pathways:** Aircraft Mechanics and Service Technicians; Automotive Body and Related Repairers; Automotive Master Mechanics; Biological Technicians; Bus and Truck Mechanics and Diesel Engine Specialists; Civil Engineering Technicians; Cleaners of Vehicles and Equipment; Computer, Automated Teller, and Office Machine Repairers; Electrical and Electronic Equipment Assemblers; Electrical and Electronics Repairers, Commercial and Industrial Equipment; Electrical Engineering Technicians; Electrical Engineering Technologists; Electromechanical Engineering Technologists; Electronics Engineering Technicians; Electronics Engineering Technologists; Engineering Technicians, Except Drafters, All Other; Fuel Cell Technicians; Helpers—Installation, Maintenance, and Repair Workers; Industrial Engineering Technologists; Industrial Machinery Mechanics; Installation, Maintenance, and Repair Workers, All Other; Manufacturing Engineering Technologists; Mobile Heavy Equipment Mechanics, Except Engines; Telecommunications Line Installers and Repairers; Tire Repairers and Changers; others.

Skills: Repairing; Equipment Maintenance; Troubleshooting; Operation and Control; Equipment Selection; Installation; Quality Control Analysis; Operation Monitoring.

C=Computer Systems Design, E=Educational Services, G=Government, H=Health Care, R=Repair and Maintenance, U=Utilities, *=All Fields

Work Environment: Standing; walking and running; kneeling, crouching, stooping, or crawling; using hands; bending or twisting the body; repetitive motions; noise; very hot or cold; bright or inadequate lighting; contaminants; cramped work space; hazardous conditions; hazardous equipment; minor burns, cuts, bites, or stings.

Billing and Posting Clerks

- ❋ Annual Earnings: H $32,289, R $32,790, * $32,170
- ❋ Earnings Growth Potential: Low (30.8%)
- ❋ Growth: R 4.5%, H 19.8%, * 15.3%
- ❋ Annual Job Openings: R 120, H 9,290, * 16,760
- ❋ Self-Employed: 1.7%

Detailed Fields with Greatest Employment: Hospitals, Public and Private (8.9%); Administrative and Support Services (5.1%); Management of Companies and Enterprises (4.3%); Merchant Wholesalers, Durable Goods (3.8%); Insurance Carriers and Related Activities (3.1%)

Detailed Fields with Highest Growth (Projected Growth for This Job): Internet Service Providers, Web Search Portals, and Data Processing Services (48.6%); Professional, Scientific, and Technical Services (40.8%); Wholesale Electronic Markets and Agents and Brokers (28.2%); Waste Management and Remediation Services (27.9%); Administrative and Support Services (25.5%)

Other Considerations for Job Outlook: Employment growth is projected to stem from an increasing number of transactions, especially in the rapidly growing health-care industry. Prospects should be good.

Compile, compute, and record billing, accounting, statistical, and other numerical data for billing purposes. Prepare billing invoices for services rendered or for delivery or shipment of goods. No task data available.

Education/Training Required: Moderate-term on-the-job training. **Education and Training Program:** Accounting Technology/Technician and Bookkeeping. **Knowledge/Courses:** No data available.

Personality Type: No data available. **Career Cluster:** 04 Business, Management, and Administration. **Career Pathway:** 4.2 Business, Financial Management, and Accounting. **Other Jobs in This Pathway:** Accountants; Auditors; Billing, Cost, and Rate Clerks; Bookkeeping, Accounting, and Auditing Clerks; Brokerage Clerks; Brownfield Redevelopment Specialists and Site Managers; Budget Analysts; Compliance Managers; Credit Analysts; Financial Analysts; Financial Managers, Branch or Department; Investment Fund Managers; Logistics Managers; Loss Prevention Managers; Managers, All Other; Natural Sciences Managers; Payroll and Timekeeping Clerks; Regulatory Affairs Managers; Security Managers; Statement Clerks; Supply Chain Managers; Tax Preparers; Treasurers and Controllers; Wind Energy Operations Managers; Wind Energy Project Managers; others.

Skills: No data available.

Work Environment: No data available.

Job Specialization: Billing, Cost, and Rate Clerks

Compile data, compute fees and charges, and prepare invoices for billing purposes. Duties include computing costs and calculating rates for goods, services, and shipment of goods; posting data; and keeping other relevant records. May involve use of computer or typewriter, calculator, and adding and bookkeeping machines. Verify accuracy of billing data and revise any errors. Operate typing, adding, calculating, and billing machines. Prepare itemized statements, bills, or invoices and record amounts due for items purchased or services rendered. Review documents such as purchase orders, sales tickets, charge slips, or hospital records to compute fees and charges due. Perform bookkeeping work, including posting data and keeping other records concerning costs of goods and services and the shipment of goods. Keep records of invoices and support documents. Resolve discrepancies in accounting records. Type billing documents, shipping labels, credit memorandums, and credit forms, using typewriters or computers. Contact customers to obtain or relay account information. Compute credit terms, discounts, shipment charges, and rates for goods and services to complete billing documents. Answer mail and telephone inquiries regarding rates, routing, and procedures.

Education/Training Required: Moderate-term on-the-job training. **Education and Training Program:** Accounting Technology/Technician and Bookkeeping. **Knowledge/Courses:** Clerical Practices; Economics and Accounting; Computers and Electronics.

Personality Type: Conventional-Enterprising. **Career Cluster:** 04 Business, Management, and Administration. **Career Pathway:** 4.2 Business, Financial Management, and Accounting. **Other Jobs in This Pathway:** Accountants; Auditors; Billing and Posting Clerks; Bookkeeping, Accounting, and Auditing Clerks; Brokerage Clerks; Brownfield Redevelopment Specialists and Site Managers; Budget Analysts; Compliance Managers; Credit Analysts; Financial Analysts; Financial Managers, Branch or Department; Investment Fund Managers; Logistics Managers; Loss Prevention Managers; Managers, All Other; Natural Sciences Managers; Payroll and Timekeeping Clerks; Regulatory Affairs Managers; Security Managers; Statement Clerks; Supply Chain Managers; Tax Preparers; Treasurers and Controllers; Wind Energy Operations Managers; Wind Energy Project Managers; others.

Skills: Programming; Mathematics; Active Listening; Service Orientation.

Work Environment: Indoors; sitting.

Job Specialization: Statement Clerks

Prepare and distribute bank statements to customers, answer inquiries, and reconcile discrepancies in records and accounts. Encode and cancel checks, using bank machines. Take orders for imprinted checks. Compare previously prepared bank statements with canceled checks and reconcile discrepancies. Verify signatures and required information on checks. Post stop-payment notices to prevent payment of protested checks. Maintain files of canceled checks and customers' signatures. Match statements with batches of canceled checks by account numbers. Weigh envelopes containing statements to determine correct postage and affix postage, using stamps or metering equipment. Load machines with statements, cancelled checks, and envelopes to prepare statements for distribution to customers or stuff envelopes by hand. Retrieve checks returned to customers in error, adjusting customer accounts and answering inquiries about errors as necessary. Route statements for mailing or over-the-counter delivery to customers. Monitor equipment to ensure proper operation.

Education/Training Required: Moderate-term on-the-job training. **Education and Training Program:** Accounting Technology/Technician and Bookkeeping. **Knowledge/Courses:** Economics and Accounting; Clerical Practices; Administration and Management.

Personality Type: Conventional-Enterprising-Social. **Career Cluster:** 04 Business, Management, and Administration. **Career Pathway:** 4.2 Business, Financial Management, and Accounting. **Other Jobs**

C=Computer Systems Design, E=Educational Services, G=Government, H=Health Care, R=Repair and Maintenance, U=Utilities, *=All Fields

in This Pathway: Accountants; Auditors; Billing and Posting Clerks; Billing, Cost, and Rate Clerks; Bookkeeping, Accounting, and Auditing Clerks; Brokerage Clerks; Brownfield Redevelopment Specialists and Site Managers; Budget Analysts; Compliance Managers; Credit Analysts; Financial Analysts; Financial Managers, Branch or Department; Investment Fund Managers; Logistics Managers; Loss Prevention Managers; Managers, All Other; Natural Sciences Managers; Payroll and Timekeeping Clerks; Regulatory Affairs Managers; Security Managers; Supply Chain Managers; Tax Preparers; Treasurers and Controllers; Wind Energy Operations Managers; Wind Energy Project Managers; others.

Skills: Programming.

Work Environment: Indoors; sitting; repetitive motions.

Biochemists and Biophysicists

- ❋ Annual Earnings: E $50,780, * $79,390
- ❋ Earnings Growth Potential: High (45.8%)
- ❋ Growth: E 34.4%, * 37.4%
- ❋ Annual Job Openings: E 100, * 1,620
- ❋ Self-Employed: 2.7%

Detailed Fields with Greatest Employment: Educational Services, Public and Private (8.6%); Professional, Scientific, and Technical Services (48.6%); Chemical Manufacturing (31.6%); Computer and Electronic Product Manufacturing (2.7%); Hospitals, Public and Private (2.0%)

Detailed Fields with Highest Growth (Projected Growth for This Job): Ambulatory Health Care Services (59.7%); Professional, Scientific, and Technical Services (51.7%); Merchant Wholesalers, Nondurable Goods (44.0%); Educational Services, Public and Private (34.7%); Hospitals, Public and Private (29.1%)

Other Considerations for Job Outlook: Biotechnological research and development should continue to drive job growth. Doctoral degree holders are expected to face competition for research positions in academia.

Study the chemical composition and physical principles of living cells and organisms and their electrical and mechanical energy and related phenomena. May conduct research in order to further understanding of the complex chemical combinations and reactions involved in metabolism, reproduction, growth, and heredity. May determine the effects of foods, drugs, serums, hormones, and other substances on tissues and vital processes of living organisms. Design and perform experiments with equipment such as lasers, accelerators, and mass spectrometers. Analyze brain functions, such as learning, thinking, and memory, and analyze the dynamics of seeing and hearing. Share research findings by writing scientific articles and by making presentations at scientific conferences. Develop and test new drugs and medications intended for commercial distribution. Develop methods to process, store, and use foods, drugs, and chemical compounds. Develop new methods to study the mechanisms of biological processes. Examine the molecular and chemical aspects of immune system functioning. Investigate the nature, composition, and expression of genes and research how genetic engineering can impact these processes. Determine the three-dimensional structure of biological macromolecules. Prepare reports and recommendations based upon research outcomes. Design and build laboratory equipment needed for special research projects.

Education/Training Required: Doctoral degree. **Education and Training Programs:** Biochemistry; Biochemistry and Molecular Biology; Biophysics; Cell/Cellular Biology and Anatomical Sciences, Other; Molecular Biochemistry; Molecular Biophysics; Soil Chemistry and Physics; Soil Microbiology. **Knowledge/Courses:** Biology; Chemistry; Physics; Engineering and Technology; Medicine and Dentistry; Mechanical.

Personality Type: Investigative-Artistic-Realistic. **Career Clusters:** 01 Agriculture, Food, and Natural Resources; 15 Science, Technology, Engineering, and Mathematics. **Career Pathways:** 1.2 Plant Systems; 15.2 Science and Mathematics. **Other Jobs in These Pathways:** Architectural and Engineering Managers; Biofuels/Biodiesel Technology and Product Development Managers; Bioinformatics Scientists; Biological Scientists, All Other; Biologists; Chemists; Clinical Research Coordinators; Community and Social Service Specialists, All Other; Dietitians and Nutritionists; Education, Training, and Library Workers, All Other; First-Line Supervisors of Landscaping, Lawn Service, and Groundskeeping Workers; First-Line Supervisors of Retail Sales Workers; Floral Designers; Geneticists; Geoscientists, Except Hydrologists and Geographers; Landscaping and Groundskeeping Workers; Medical Scientists, Except Epidemiologists; Natural Sciences Managers; Operations Research Analysts; Precision Agriculture Technicians; Retail Salespersons; Social Scientists and Related Workers, All Other; Transportation Planners; Tree Trimmers and Pruners; Water Resource Specialists; others.

Skills: Science; Programming; Active Learning; Technology Design; Mathematics; Learning Strategies; Reading Comprehension; Writing.

Work Environment: Indoors; sitting; using hands; exposed to disease or infections.

Biological Scientists, All Other

- ❈ Annual Earnings: G $70,330, * $68,220
- ❈ Earnings Growth Potential: High (43.2%)
- ❈ Growth: G 18.9%, * 18.8%
- ❈ Annual Job Openings: G 660, * 1,610
- ❈ Self-Employed: 2.5%

Detailed Fields with Greatest Employment: Federal Government (58.2%); State and Local Government (3.9%); Chemical Manufacturing (2.7%); Hospitals, Public and Private (2.5%); Educational Services, Public and Private (13.9%)

Detailed Fields with Highest Growth (Projected Growth for This Job): Professional, Scientific, and Technical Services (33.7%); Ambulatory Health Care Services (31.1%); Museums, Historical Sites, and Similar Institutions (25.0%); Administrative and Support Services (21.7%); Federal Government (19.6%)

Other Considerations for Job Outlook: Biotechnological research and development should continue to drive job growth. Doctoral degree holders are expected to face competition for research positions in academia.

This occupation includes all biological scientists not listed separately. No task data available.

Education/Training Required: Doctoral degree. **Education and Training Program:** Biological and Biomedical Sciences, Other. **Knowledge/Courses:** No data available.

Personality Type: No data available. **Career Clusters:** 08 Health Science; 15 Science, Technology, Engineering, and Mathematics. **Career Pathways:** 8.5 Biotechnology Research and Development; 15.2 Science and Mathematics. **Other Jobs in These Pathways:** Architectural and

*C=Computer Systems Design, E=Educational Services, G=Government, H=Health Care, R=Repair and Maintenance, U=Utilities, *=All Fields*

150 Best Jobs for a Secure Future © JIST Works

153

Engineering Managers; Biochemists and Biophysicists; Biofuels/Biodiesel Technology and Product Development Managers; Bioinformatics Scientists; Biologists; Biostatisticians; Chemists; Clinical Data Managers; Clinical Research Coordinators; Community and Social Service Specialists, All Other; Dietitians and Nutritionists; Education, Training, and Library Workers, All Other; Geneticists; Geoscientists, Except Hydrologists and Geographers; Medical Scientists, Except Epidemiologists; Molecular and Cellular Biologists; Natural Sciences Managers; Operations Research Analysts; Pharmacists; Physical Scientists, All Other; Social Scientists and Related Workers, All Other; Statisticians; Survey Researchers; Transportation Planners; Water Resource Specialists; others.

Skills: No data available.

Work Environment: No data available.

Job Specialization: Bioinformatics Scientists

Conduct research using bioinformatics theory and methods in areas such as pharmaceuticals, medical technology, biotechnology, computational biology, proteomics, computer information science, biology and medical informatics. May design databases and develop algorithms for processing and analyzing genomic information or other biological information. Recommend new systems and processes to improve operations. Keep abreast of new biochemistries, instrumentation, or software by reading scientific literature and attending professional conferences. Confer with departments such as marketing, business development, and operations to coordinate product development or improvement. Collaborate with software developers in the development and modification of commercial bioinformatics software. Test new and updated bioinformatics tools and software. Provide statistical and computational tools for biologically based activities such as genetic analysis, measurement of gene expression, and gene function determination. Prepare summary statistics of information regarding human genomes. Instruct others in the selection and use of bioinformatics tools. Improve user interfaces to bioinformatics software and databases.

Education/Training Required: Doctoral degree. **Education and Training Program:** Bioinformatics. **Knowledge/Courses:** No data available.

Personality Type: Investigative-Conventional-Realistic. **Career Clusters:** 11 Information Technology; 15 Science, Technology, Engineering, and Mathematics. **Career Pathways:** 11.4 Programming and Software Development; 15.2 Science and Mathematics. **Other Jobs in These Pathways:** Architectural and Engineering Managers; Biochemists and Biophysicists; Biofuels/Biodiesel Technology and Product Development Managers; Biological Scientists, All Other; Biologists; Biostatisticians; Chemists; Clinical Data Managers; Clinical Research Coordinators; Community and Social Service Specialists, All Other; Computer Hardware Engineers; Dietitians and Nutritionists; Education, Training, and Library Workers, All Other; Geneticists; Geoscientists, Except Hydrologists and Geographers; Medical Scientists, Except Epidemiologists; Molecular and Cellular Biologists; Natural Sciences Managers; Operations Research Analysts; Physical Scientists, All Other; Social Scientists and Related Workers, All Other; Statisticians; Survey Researchers; Transportation Planners; Water Resource Specialists; others.

Skills: No data available.

Work Environment: No data available.

Job Specialization: Geneticists

Research and study the inheritance of traits at the molecular, organism, or population level. May evaluate or treat patients with genetic disorders. Write grants and papers or attend fundraising events to seek research funds. Verify that cytogenetic, molecular genetic, and related equipment and instrumentation is maintained in working condition to ensure accuracy and quality of experimental results. Plan curatorial programs for species collections that include acquisition, distribution, maintenance, or regeneration. Participate in the development of endangered species breeding programs or species survival plans. Maintain laboratory safety programs and train personnel in laboratory safety techniques. Instruct medical students, graduate students, or others in methods or procedures for diagnosis and management of genetic disorders. Evaluate, diagnose, or treat genetic diseases. Design and maintain genetics computer databases. Confer with information technology specialists to develop computer applications for genetic data analysis.

Education/Training Required: Doctoral degree. **Education and Training Programs:** Animal Genetics; Genetics, General; Genetics, Other; Genome Sciences/Genomics; Human/Medical Genetics; Microbial and Eukaryotic Genetics; Molecular Genetics; Plant Genetics. **Knowledge/Courses:** Biology; Chemistry; Medicine and Dentistry; Education and Training; English Language; Mathematics.

Personality Type: Investigative-Artistic-Realistic. **Career Clusters:** 01 Agriculture, Food, and Natural Resources; 15 Science, Technology, Engineering, and Mathematics. **Career Pathways:** 1.2 Plant Systems; 1.3 Animal Systems; 15.2 Science and Mathematics. **Other Jobs in These Pathways:** Animal Trainers; Architectural and Engineering Managers; Biofuels/Biodiesel Technology and Product Development Managers; Biologists; Chemists; Clinical Research Coordinators; Community and Social Service Specialists, All Other; Dietitians and Nutritionists; Education, Training, and Library Workers, All Other; First-Line Supervisors of Landscaping, Lawn Service, and Groundskeeping Workers; First-Line Supervisors of Retail Sales Workers; Floral Designers; Geoscientists, Except Hydrologists and Geographers; Landscaping and Groundskeeping Workers; Medical Scientists, Except Epidemiologists; Natural Sciences Managers; Nonfarm Animal Caretakers; Operations Research Analysts; Precision Agriculture Technicians; Retail Salespersons; Social Scientists and Related Workers, All Other; Transportation Planners; Tree Trimmers and Pruners; Veterinarians; Water Resource Specialists; others.

Skills: Science; Mathematics; Writing; Reading Comprehension; Learning Strategies; Systems Analysis; Instructing; Management of Material Resources.

Work Environment: Indoors; sitting; using hands.

Job Specialization: Molecular and Cellular Biologists

Research and study cellular molecules and organelles to understand cell function and organization. Verify that all financial, physical, and human resources assigned to research or development projects are used as planned. Participate in all levels of bio-product development, including proposing new products, performing market analyses, designing and performing experiments, and collaborating with operations and quality control teams during product launches. Evaluate new supplies and equipment to ensure operability in specific laboratory settings. Develop guidelines for procedures such as the management of viruses. Coordinate molecular or cellular research activities with scientists specializing in other fields. Confer with vendors to evaluate new equipment or reagents or to discuss the

C=Computer Systems Design, E=Educational Services, G=Government, H=Health Care, R=Repair and Maintenance, U=Utilities, *=All Fields

150 Best Jobs for a Secure Future © JIST Works

155

customization of product lines to meet user requirements. Supervise technical personnel and postdoctoral research fellows. Prepare reports, manuscripts, and meeting presentations.

Education/Training Required: Doctoral degree. **Education and Training Program:** Cell/Cellular Biology and Histology. **Knowledge/Courses:** Biology; Chemistry; English Language; Medicine and Dentistry; Computers and Electronics; Mathematics.

Personality Type: Investigative-Realistic-Artistic. **Career Cluster:** 15 Science, Technology, Engineering, and Mathematics. **Career Pathway:** 15.2 Science and Mathematics. **Other Jobs in This Pathway:** Architectural and Engineering Managers; Biochemists and Biophysicists; Biofuels/Biodiesel Technology and Product Development Managers; Bioinformatics Scientists; Biological Scientists, All Other; Biologists; Biostatisticians; Chemists; Clinical Data Managers; Clinical Research Coordinators; Community and Social Service Specialists, All Other; Dietitians and Nutritionists; Education, Training, and Library Workers, All Other; Geneticists; Geoscientists, Except Hydrologists and Geographers; Medical Scientists, Except Epidemiologists; Natural Sciences Managers; Operations Research Analysts; Physical Scientists, All Other; Social Scientists and Related Workers, All Other; Statisticians; Survey Researchers; Transportation Planners; Water Resource Specialists; Zoologists and Wildlife Biologists; others.

Skills: Science; Programming; Reading Comprehension; Active Learning; Mathematics; Management of Financial Resources; Writing; Learning Strategies.

Work Environment: Indoors; sitting; using hands; hazardous conditions.

Biomedical Engineers

- ❀ Annual Earnings: E $59,010, H $69,368, * $81,540
- ❀ Earnings Growth Potential: Medium (39.1%)
- ❀ Growth: E 68.1%, H 69.2%, * 72.0%
- ❀ Annual Job Openings: E 80, H 250, * 1,490
- ❀ Self-Employed: 3.3%

Detailed Fields with Greatest Employment: Computer and Electronic Product Manufacturing (8.8%); Educational Services, Public and Private (7.5%); Merchant Wholesalers, Durable Goods (3.4%); Miscellaneous Manufacturing (23.5%); Professional, Scientific, and Technical Services (23.0%)

Detailed Fields with Highest Growth (Projected Growth for This Job): Merchant Wholesalers, Nondurable Goods (100.0%); Administrative and Support Services (100.0%); Ambulatory Health Care Services (100.0%); Professional, Scientific, and Technical Services (91.9%); Miscellaneous Manufacturing (75.8%)

Other Considerations for Job Outlook: Biomedical engineers are expected to have employment growth of 72 percent from 2008–2018, much faster than the average for all occupations. The aging of the population and a growing focus on health issues will drive demand for better medical devices and equipment designed by biomedical engineers. Along with the demand for more sophisticated medical equipment and procedures, an increased concern for cost-effectiveness will boost demand for biomedical engineers, particularly in pharmaceutical manufacturing and related industries. Because of the growing interest in this field, the number of degrees granted in biomedical engineering has increased greatly. Many biomedical engineers, particularly those employed in research laboratories, need a graduate degree.

Apply knowledge of engineering, biology, and biomechanical principles to the design, development, and evaluation of biological and health systems and products, such as artificial organs, prostheses, instrumentation, medical information systems, and health management and care delivery systems. Evaluate the safety, efficiency, and effectiveness of biomedical equipment. Install, adjust, maintain, and/or repair biomedical equipment. Advise hospital administrators on the planning, acquisition, and use of medical equipment. Advise and assist in the application of instrumentation in clinical environments. Develop models or computer simulations of human bio-behavioral systems in order to obtain data for measuring or controlling life processes. Research new materials to be used for products such as implanted artificial organs. Design and develop medical diagnostic and clinical instrumentation, equipment, and procedures, utilizing the principles of engineering and bio-behavioral sciences. Conduct research, along with life scientists, chemists, and medical scientists, on the engineering aspects of the biological systems of humans and animals. Teach biomedical engineering or disseminate knowledge about field through writing or consulting.

Education/Training Required: Bachelor's degree. **Education and Training Program:** Bioengineering and Biomedical Engineering. **Knowledge/Courses:** Biology; Engineering and Technology; Physics; Design; Medicine and Dentistry; Chemistry.

Personality Type: Investigative-Realistic. **Career Cluster:** 15 Science, Technology, Engineering, and Mathematics. **Career Pathway:** 15.1 Engineering and Technology. **Other Jobs in This Pathway:**

Architectural and Engineering Managers; Automotive Engineers; Biochemical Engineers; Biofuels/Biodiesel Technology and Product Development Managers; Civil Engineers; Cost Estimators; Electrical Engineers; Electronics Engineers, Except Computer; Energy Engineers; Engineers, All Other; Fuel Cell Engineers; Human Factors Engineers and Ergonomists; Industrial Engineers; Manufacturing Engineers; Mechanical Engineers; Mechatronics Engineers; Microsystems Engineers; Nanosystems Engineers; Photonics Engineers; Radio Frequency Identification Device Specialists; Robotics Engineers; Solar Energy Systems Engineers; Transportation Engineers; Validation Engineers; Wind Energy Engineers; others.

Skills: Science; Technology Design; Programming; Installation; Operations Analysis; Mathematics; Troubleshooting; Equipment Selection.

Work Environment: Indoors; sitting.

Budget Analysts

- ✵ Annual Earnings: G $67,570, C $77,630, * $68,200
- ✵ Earnings Growth Potential: Low (34.2%)
- ✵ Growth: G 19.7%, C 40.2%, * 15.1%
- ✵ Annual Job Openings: C 80, G 620, * 2,230
- ✵ Self-Employed: 0.0%

Detailed Fields with Greatest Employment: Management of Companies and Enterprises (6.7%); Transportation Equipment Manufacturing (6.5%); Computer and Electronic Product Manufacturing (2.6%); Insurance Carriers and Related Activities (2.5%); Federal Government (18.6%)

Detailed Fields with Highest Growth (Projected Growth for This Job): Professional, Scientific, and

B

*C=Computer Systems Design, E=Educational Services, G=Government, H=Health Care, R=Repair and Maintenance, U=Utilities, *=All Fields*

Technical Services (42.9%); Wholesale Electronic Markets and Agents and Brokers (33.3%); Waste Management and Remediation Services (33.3%); Ambulatory Health Care Services (33.3%); Other Information Services (32.6%)

Other Considerations for Job Outlook: Projected employment growth will be driven by the continued demand for financial analysis in both the public and private sectors. Job seekers with a master's degree should have the best prospects.

Examine budget estimates for completeness, accuracy, and conformance with procedures and regulations. Analyze budgeting and accounting reports for the purpose of maintaining expenditure controls. Direct the preparation of regular and special budget reports. Consult with managers to ensure that budget adjustments are made in accordance with program changes. Match appropriations for specific programs with appropriations for broader programs, including items for emergency funds. Provide advice and technical assistance with cost analysis, fiscal allocation, and budget preparation. Summarize budgets and submit recommendations for the approval or disapproval of funds requests. Seek new ways to improve efficiency and increase profits. Review operating budgets to analyze trends affecting budget needs. Perform cost-benefit analyses to compare operating programs, review financial requests, or explore alternative financing methods. Interpret budget directives and establish policies for carrying out directives. Compile and analyze accounting records and other data to determine the financial resources required to implement a program.

Education/Training Required: Bachelor's degree. **Education and Training Programs:** Accounting; Finance, General. **Knowledge/Courses:** Economics and Accounting; Clerical Practices; Administration and Management; Mathematics; Personnel and Human Resources; Law and Government.

Personality Type: Conventional-Enterprising-Investigative. **Career Clusters:** 04 Business, Management, and Administration; 06 Finance. **Career Pathways:** 4.2 Business, Financial Management, and Accounting; 6.1 Financial and Investment Planning. **Other Jobs in These Pathways:** Accountants; Auditors; Billing and Posting Clerks; Billing, Cost, and Rate Clerks; Bookkeeping, Accounting, and Auditing Clerks; Brownfield Redevelopment Specialists and Site Managers; Compliance Managers; Financial Analysts; Financial Managers, Branch or Department; Investment Fund Managers; Loss Prevention Managers; Managers, All Other; Payroll and Timekeeping Clerks; Personal Financial Advisors; Regulatory Affairs Managers; Sales Agents, Financial Services; Sales Agents, Securities and Commodities; Securities and Commodities Traders; Securities, Commodities, and Financial Services Sales Agents; Security Managers; Statement Clerks; Supply Chain Managers; Treasurers and Controllers; Wind Energy Operations Managers; Wind Energy Project Managers; others.

Skills: Management of Financial Resources; Operations Analysis; Systems Analysis; Mathematics; Management of Material Resources; Systems Evaluation; Judgment and Decision Making; Active Learning.

Work Environment: Indoors; sitting; repetitive motions.

Cardiovascular Technologists and Technicians

- ❋ Annual Earnings: H $49,347, * $49,410
- ❋ Earnings Growth Potential: High (46.1%)
- ❋ Growth: H 24.0%, * 24.1%
- ❋ Annual Job Openings: H 2,680, * 1,910
- ❋ Self-Employed: 0.8%

Detailed Fields with Greatest Employment: Hospitals, Public and Private (77.2%); Ambulatory Health Care Services (19.9%); Educational Services, Public and Private (1.4%); Administrative and Support Services (0.9%); Professional, Scientific, and Technical Services (0.1%)

Detailed Fields with Highest Growth (Projected Growth for This Job): Ambulatory Health Care Services (45.4%); Administrative and Support Services (34.9%); Professional, Scientific, and Technical Services (28.6%); Educational Services, Public and Private (22.4%); Hospitals, Public and Private (18.5%)

Other Considerations for Job Outlook: An aging population and the continued prevalence of heart disease will drive employment growth for cardiovascular technologists and technicians. Prospects should be the best for job seekers who have multiple credentials.

Conduct tests on pulmonary or cardiovascular systems of patients for diagnostic purposes. May conduct or assist in electrocardiograms, cardiac catheterizations, pulmonary-functions, lung capacity, and similar tests. Monitor patients' blood pressures and heart rates, using electrocardiogram (EKG) equipment during diagnostic and therapeutic procedures to notify physicians if something appears wrong. Explain testing procedures to patients to obtain cooperation and reduce anxiety. Observe gauges, recorders, and video screens of data analysis systems during imaging of cardiovascular systems. Monitor patients' comfort and safety during tests, alerting physicians to abnormalities or changes in patient responses. Obtain and record patients' identities, medical histories, or test results. Attach electrodes to patients' chests, arms, and legs; connect electrodes to leads from electrocardiogram (EKG) machines; and operate EKG machines to obtain readings. Adjust equipment and controls according to physicians' orders or established protocol. Prepare and position patients for testing. Check, test, and maintain cardiology equipment, making minor repairs when necessary, to ensure proper operation.

Education/Training Required: Associate degree. **Education and Training Programs:** Cardiopulmonary Technology/Technologist; Cardiovascular Technology/Technologist; Electrocardiograph Technology/Technician; Perfusion Technology/Perfusionist. **Knowledge/Courses:** Medicine and Dentistry; Biology; Psychology; Customer and Personal Service; Sociology and Anthropology; Chemistry.

Personality Type: Realistic-Investigative-Social. **Career Cluster:** 08 Health Science. **Career Pathway:** 8.2 Diagnostics Services. **Other Jobs in This Pathway:** Ambulance Drivers and Attendants, Except Emergency Medical Technicians; Anesthesiologist Assistants; Cytogenetic Technologists; Cytotechnologists; Diagnostic Medical Sonographers; Emergency Medical Technicians and Paramedics; Endoscopy Technicians; Health Diagnosing and Treating Practitioners, All Other; Health Technologists and Technicians, All Other; Healthcare Practitioners and Technical Workers, All Other; Histotechnologists and Histologic Technicians; Medical and Clinical Laboratory Technicians; Medical and Clinical Laboratory Technologists; Medical and Health Services Managers; Medical Assistants; Medical Equipment Preparers; Neurodiagnostic Technologists; Nuclear Medicine Technologists; Ophthalmic Laboratory Technicians; Physical Scientists, All Other; Physician Assistants; Radiologic Technicians; Radiologic Technologists; Surgical Technologists; Veterinary Assistants and Laboratory Animal Caretakers; others.

Skills: Science; Equipment Maintenance; Operation and Control; Repairing; Operation Monitoring; Service Orientation; Equipment Selection; Troubleshooting.

C=Computer Systems Design, E=Educational Services, G=Government, H=Health Care, R=Repair and Maintenance, U=Utilities, *=All Fields

Work Environment: Indoors; standing; walking and running; using hands; repetitive motions; exposed to radiation; exposed to disease or infections.

Chief Executives

❋ Annual Earnings: E $133,090, R $138,890, H $150,575, C $166,400+, U $166,400+, * $165,080

❋ Earnings Growth Potential: Very High (54.5%)

❋ Growth: U –21.3%, R –6.2%, H 7.3%, E 8.3%, C 26.2%, * –1.4%

❋ Annual Job Openings: R 60, U 60, C 270, E 830, H 1,490, * 11,250

❋ Self-Employed: 21.6%

Detailed Fields with Greatest Employment: Professional, Scientific, and Technical Services (9.7%); Educational Services, Public and Private (8.3%); Management of Companies and Enterprises (7.0%); Administrative and Support Services (4.5%); Merchant Wholesalers, Durable Goods (3.5%)

Detailed Fields with Highest Growth (Projected Growth for This Job): Internet Service Providers, Web Search Portals, and Data Processing Services (33.6%); Professional, Scientific, and Technical Services (23.5%); Lessors of Nonfinancial Intangible Assets (Except Copyrighted Works) (23.1%); Other Information Services (16.7%); Ambulatory Health Care Services (16.2%)

Other Considerations for Job Outlook: The number of top executives is expected to remain steady, but employment may be adversely affected by consolidation and mergers. Keen competition is expected.

Determine and formulate policies and provide the overall direction of companies or private- and public-sector organizations within the guidelines set up by a board of directors or similar governing body. Plan, direct, or coordinate operational activities at the highest level of management with the help of subordinate executives and staff managers. Direct and coordinate an organization's financial and budget activities in order to fund operations, maximize investments, and increase efficiency. Confer with board members, organization officials, and staff members to discuss issues, coordinate activities, and resolve problems. Analyze operations to evaluate performance of a company and its staff in meeting objectives and to determine areas of potential cost reduction, program improvement, or policy change. Direct, plan, and implement policies, objectives, and activities of organizations or businesses in order to ensure continuing operations, to maximize returns on investments, and to increase productivity. Prepare budgets for approval, including those for funding and implementation of programs. Direct and coordinate activities of businesses or departments concerned with production, pricing, sales, and/or distribution of products.

Education/Training Required: Work experience plus degree. **Education and Training Programs:** Business Administration and Management, General; Business/Commerce, General; Entrepreneurship/Entrepreneurial Studies; International Business/Trade/Commerce; International Relations and Affairs; Public Administration; Public Administration and Social Service Professions, Other; Public Policy Analysis, General; Transportation/Mobility Management. **Knowledge/Courses:** Economics and Accounting; Administration and Management; Sales and Marketing; Personnel and Human Resources; Law and Government; Medicine and Dentistry.

Personality Type: Enterprising-Conventional. **Career Clusters:** 04 Business, Management, and Administration; 07 Government and Public

Administration; 10 Human Services; 16 Transportation, Distribution, and Logistics. **Career Pathways:** 4.1 Management; 7.1 Governance; 7.3 Foreign Service; 7.6 Regulation; 10.3 Family and Community Services; 16.2 Logistics, Planning, and Management Services. **Other Jobs in These Pathways:** Brownfield Redevelopment Specialists and Site Managers; Business Continuity Planners; Business Operations Specialists, All Other; Chief Sustainability Officers; Childcare Workers; Compliance Managers; Construction Managers; Customs Brokers; Energy Auditors; First-Line Supervisors of Office and Administrative Support Workers; General and Operations Managers; Investment Fund Managers; Loss Prevention Managers; Management Analysts; Managers, All Other; Nannies; Personal Care Aides; Regulatory Affairs Managers; Sales Managers; Security Management Specialists; Security Managers; Supply Chain Managers; Sustainability Specialists; Wind Energy Operations Managers; Wind Energy Project Managers; others.

Skills: Management of Financial Resources; Management of Material Resources; Management of Personnel Resources; Systems Evaluation; Systems Analysis; Judgment and Decision Making; Persuasion; Monitoring.

Work Environment: Indoors; sitting.

Job Specialization: Chief Sustainability Officers

Communicate and coordinate with management, shareholders, customers, and employees to address sustainability issues. Enact or oversee a corporate sustainability strategy. Identify educational, training, or other development opportunities for sustainability employees or volunteers. Identify and evaluate pilot projects or programs to enhance the sustainability research agenda. Conduct sustainability- or environment-related risk assessments. Create and maintain sustainability program documents, such as schedules and budgets. Write project proposals, grant applications, or other documents to pursue funding for environmental initiatives. Supervise employees or volunteers working on sustainability projects. Write and distribute financial or environmental impact reports. Review sustainability program objectives, progress, or status to ensure compliance with policies, standards, regulations, or laws. Formulate or implement sustainability campaign or marketing strategies. Research environmental sustainability issues, concerns, or stakeholder interests.

Education/Training Required: Work experience plus degree. **Education and Training Programs:** Business Administration and Management, General; Business/Commerce, General; Entrepreneurship/Entrepreneurial Studies; International Business/Trade/Commerce; International Relations and Affairs; Public Administration; Public Administration and Social Service Professions, Other; Public Policy Analysis, General; Transportation/Mobility Management. **Knowledge/Courses:** No data available.

Personality Type: No data available. **Career Clusters:** 04 Business, Management, and Administration; 07 Government and Public Administration; 16 Transportation, Distribution, and Logistics. **Career Pathways:** 4.1 Management; 7.1 Governance; 16.2 Logistics, Planning, and Management Services. **Other Jobs in These Pathways:** Administrative Services Managers; Brownfield Redevelopment Specialists and Site Managers; Business Continuity Planners; Business Operations Specialists, All Other; Chief Executives; Compliance Managers; Computer and Information Systems Managers; Construction Managers; Customs Brokers; Energy Auditors; First-Line Supervisors of Office and Administrative Support Workers; General and Operations Managers; Investment Fund Managers; Loss Prevention Managers; Management Analysts; Managers, All Other; Public Relations Specialists;

*C=Computer Systems Design, E=Educational Services, G=Government, H=Health Care, R=Repair and Maintenance, U=Utilities, *=All Fields*

Regulatory Affairs Managers; Sales Managers; Security Management Specialists; Security Managers; Supply Chain Managers; Sustainability Specialists; Wind Energy Operations Managers; Wind Energy Project Managers; others.

Skills: No data available.

Work Environment: No data available.

Child, Family, and School Social Workers

- ❋ Annual Earnings: H $36,820, * $40,210
- ❋ Earnings Growth Potential: Low (34.9%)
- ❋ Growth: H 17.7%, * 12.3%
- ❋ Annual Job Openings: H 5,800, * 10,960
- ❋ Self-Employed: 2.2%

Detailed Fields with Greatest Employment: Nursing and Residential Care Facilities (5.4%); State and Local Government (42.8%); Religious, Grantmaking, Civic, Professional, and Similar Organizations (4.7%); Ambulatory Health Care Services (3.4%); Social Assistance (27.1%)

Detailed Fields with Highest Growth (Projected Growth for This Job): Professional, Scientific, and Technical Services (27.5%); Administrative and Support Services (24.7%); Ambulatory Health Care Services (20.5%); Social Assistance (19.4%); Real Estate (15.0%)

Other Considerations for Job Outlook: The rapidly increasing elderly population is expected to spur demand for social services. Job prospects should be favorable because of the need to replace the many workers who are leaving the occupation permanently.

Provide social services and assistance to improve the social and psychological functioning of children and their families and to maximize the family well-being and the academic functioning of children. May assist single parents, arrange adoptions, and find foster homes for abandoned or abused children. In schools, they address such problems as teenage pregnancy, misbehavior, and truancy. May also advise teachers on how to deal with problem children. Interview clients individually, in families, or in groups, assessing their situations, capabilities, and problems, to determine what services are required to meet their needs. Counsel individuals, groups, families, or communities regarding issues including mental health, poverty, unemployment, substance abuse, physical abuse, rehabilitation, social adjustment, child care, or medical care. Maintain case history records and prepare reports. Counsel students whose behavior, school progress, or mental or physical impairment indicate a need for assistance, diagnosing students' problems and arranging for needed services. Consult with parents, teachers, and other school personnel to determine causes of problems such as truancy and misbehavior and to implement solutions. Counsel parents with child-rearing problems, interviewing the child and family to determine whether further action is required.

Education/Training Required: Bachelor's degree. **Education and Training Programs:** Juvenile Corrections; Social Work; Youth Services/Administration. **Knowledge/Courses:** Therapy and Counseling; Psychology; Philosophy and Theology; Sociology and Anthropology; Law and Government; Customer and Personal Service.

Personality Type: Social-Enterprising. **Career Clusters:** 10 Human Services; 12 Law, Public Safety, Corrections, and Security. **Career Pathways:** 10.3 Family and Community Services; 12.1 Correction Services. **Other Jobs in These Pathways:** Chief Executives; Childcare Workers; City and Regional Planning Aides; Counselors, All Other; Eligibility Interviewers, Government Programs; Farm and Home Management Advisors; First-Line Supervisors of Correctional Officers;

First-Line Supervisors of Police and Detectives; Legislators; Managers, All Other; Marriage and Family Therapists; Nannies; Personal Care Aides; Probation Officers and Correctional Treatment Specialists; Protective Service Workers, All Other; Security Guards; Social and Community Service Managers; Social Science Research Assistants; Social Scientists and Related Workers, All Other; Social Workers, All Other; Sociologists; Supply Chain Managers.

Skills: Operations Analysis; Science; Social Perceptiveness; Service Orientation; Negotiation; Active Listening; Persuasion; Speaking.

Work Environment: Indoors; sitting.

Chiropractors

- ❋ Annual Earnings: H $67,182, * $67,200
- ❋ Earnings Growth Potential: Very High (52.0%)
- ❋ Growth: H 31.3%, * 19.5%
- ❋ Annual Job Openings: H 1,450, * 1,820
- ❋ Self-Employed: 44.5%

Detailed Fields with Greatest Employment: Ambulatory Health Care Services (96.4%); Hospitals, Public and Private (2.2%)

Detailed Fields with Highest Growth (Projected Growth for This Job): Ambulatory Health Care Services (31.8%); Hospitals, Public and Private (11.9%)

Other Considerations for Job Outlook: Projected growth stems from increasing consumer demand for alternative health care. Job prospects for new chiropractors are expected to be good, especially for those who enter a multidisciplined practice.

Adjust spinal column and other articulations of the body to correct abnormalities of the human body believed to be caused by interference with the nervous system. Examine patients to determine nature and extent of disorders. Manipulate spines or other involved areas. May utilize supplementary measures such as exercise, rest, water, light, heat, and nutritional therapy. Diagnose health problems by reviewing patients' health and medical histories; questioning, observing, and examining patients; and interpreting X-rays. Maintain accurate case histories of patients. Evaluate the functioning of the neuromusculoskeletal system and the spine, using systems of chiropractic diagnosis. Perform a series of manual adjustments to spines, or other articulations of the body, to correct musculoskeletal systems. Obtain and record patients' medical histories. Advise patients about recommended courses of treatment. Consult with and refer patients to appropriate health practitioners when necessary. Analyze X-rays to locate the sources of patients' difficulties and to rule out fractures or diseases as sources of problems. Counsel patients about nutrition, exercise, sleeping habits, stress management, and other matters. Arrange for diagnostic X-rays to be taken. Suggest and apply the use of supports such as straps, tapes, bandages, and braces if necessary.

Education/Training Required: First professional degree. **Education and Training Program:** Chiropractic (DC). **Knowledge/Courses:** Medicine and Dentistry; Therapy and Counseling; Biology; Psychology; Personnel and Human Resources; Sales and Marketing.

Personality Type: Social-Investigative-Realistic. **Career Cluster:** 08 Health Science. **Career Pathway:** 8.1 Therapeutic Services. **Other Jobs in This Pathway:** Clinical Psychologists; Community and Social Service Specialists, All Other; Counseling Psychologists; Dental Assistants; Dental Hygienists; Dentists, General; Health Technologists and Technicians, All Other; Healthcare Support Workers, All Other; Home Health Aides; Licensed

C

*C=Computer Systems Design, E=Educational Services, G=Government, H=Health Care, R=Repair and Maintenance, U=Utilities, *=All Fields*

150 Best Jobs for a Secure Future © JIST Works

163

Practical and Licensed Vocational Nurses; Low Vision Therapists, Orientation and Mobility Specialists, and Vision Rehabilitation Therapists; Massage Therapists; Medical and Clinical Laboratory Technicians; Medical and Health Services Managers; Medical Scientists, Except Epidemiologists; Medical Secretaries; Occupational Therapists; Pharmacists; Pharmacy Technicians; Radiologic Technologists; School Psychologists; Social and Human Service Assistants; Speech-Language Pathologists; Speech-Language Pathology Assistants; Substance Abuse and Behavioral Disorder Counselors; others.

Skills: Science; Service Orientation; Management of Financial Resources; Operations Analysis; Writing; Reading Comprehension; Systems Evaluation; Time Management.

Work Environment: Indoors; standing; using hands; bending or twisting the body; repetitive motions; exposed to disease or infections.

Clinical, Counseling, and School Psychologists

- ❋ Annual Earnings: H $66,728, E $67,660, G $68,970, * $66,810
- ❋ Earnings Growth Potential: High (41.6%)
- ❋ Growth: G 8.4%, E 10.4%, H 18.9%, * 11.1%
- ❋ Annual Job Openings: G 250, E 1,370, H 2,340, * 5,990
- ❋ Self-Employed: 34.1%

Detailed Fields with Greatest Employment: Hospitals, Public and Private (9.5%); State and Local Government (9.4%); Social Assistance (8.2%); Educational Services, Public and Private (47.0%); Nursing and Residential Care Facilities (3.4%)

Detailed Fields with Highest Growth (Projected Growth for This Job): Professional, Scientific, and Technical Services (32.7%); Ambulatory Health Care Services (27.2%); Administrative and Support Services (26.8%); Social Assistance (21.3%); Religious, Grantmaking, Civic, Professional, and Similar Organizations (16.7%)

Other Considerations for Job Outlook: Employment growth is expected due to increased emphasis on mental health in a variety of specializations, including school counseling, depression, and substance abuse. Job seekers with a doctoral degree should have the best opportunities.

Job Specialization: Clinical Psychologists

Diagnose or evaluate mental and emotional disorders of individuals through observation, interview, and psychological tests and formulate and administer programs of treatment. Identify psychological, emotional, or behavioral issues and diagnose disorders, using information obtained from interviews, tests, records, and reference materials. Develop and implement individual treatment plans, specifying type, frequency, intensity, and duration of therapy. Interact with clients to assist them in gaining insight, defining goals, and planning action to achieve effective personal, social, educational, and vocational development and adjustment. Discuss the treatment of problems with clients. Utilize a variety of treatment methods such as psychotherapy, hypnosis, behavior modification, stress reduction therapy, psychodrama, and play therapy. Counsel individuals and groups regarding problems such as stress, substance abuse, and family situations to modify behavior or to improve personal, social, and vocational adjustment. Write reports on clients and maintain required paperwork.

Education/Training Required: Doctoral degree. **Education and Training Programs:** Psychoanalysis and Psychotherapy; Psychology, General. **Knowledge/Courses:** Therapy and Counseling; Psychology; Sociology and Anthropology; Philosophy and Theology; Customer and Personal Service; Medicine and Dentistry.

Personality Type: Investigative-Social-Artistic. **Career Clusters:** 08 Health Science; 10 Human Services. **Career Pathways:** 8.1 Therapeutic Services; 8.3 Health Informatics; 10.2 Counseling and Mental Health Services. **Other Jobs in These Pathways:** Clergy; Counseling Psychologists; Dental Assistants; Dental Hygienists; Engineers, All Other; Executive Secretaries and Executive Administrative Assistants; First-Line Supervisors of Office and Administrative Support Workers; Healthcare Support Workers, All Other; Home Health Aides; Licensed Practical and Licensed Vocational Nurses; Medical and Clinical Laboratory Technicians; Medical and Health Services Managers; Medical Assistants; Medical Records and Health Information Technicians; Medical Secretaries; Pharmacists; Pharmacy Technicians; Physical Therapists; Public Relations Specialists; Radiologic Technologists; Receptionists and Information Clerks; Recreation Workers; School Psychologists; Social and Human Service Assistants; Speech-Language Pathology Assistants; others.

Skills: Science; Social Perceptiveness; Active Listening; Operations Analysis; Learning Strategies; Speaking; Reading Comprehension; Service Orientation.

Work Environment: Indoors; sitting.

Job Specialization: Counseling Psychologists

Assess and evaluate individuals' problems through the use of case history, interview, and observation and provide individual or group counseling services to assist individuals in achieving more effective personal, social, educational, and vocational development and adjustment. Collect information about individuals or clients, using interviews, case histories, observational techniques, and other assessment methods. Counsel individuals, groups, or families to help them understand problems, define goals, and develop realistic action plans. Develop therapeutic and treatment plans based on clients' interests, abilities, and needs. Consult with other professionals to discuss therapies, treatments, counseling resources, or techniques and to share occupational information. Analyze data such as interview notes, test results, and reference manuals in order to identify symptoms and to diagnose the nature of clients' problems. Advise clients on how they could be helped by counseling. Evaluate the results of counseling methods to determine the reliability and validity of treatments. Provide consulting services to schools, social service agencies, and businesses. Refer clients to specialists or to other institutions for noncounseling treatment of problems.

Education/Training Required: Doctoral degree. **Education and Training Programs:** Psychoanalysis and Psychotherapy; Psychology, General. **Knowledge/Courses:** Therapy and Counseling; Philosophy and Theology; Sociology and Anthropology; Psychology; English Language; Customer and Personal Service.

Personality Type: Social-Investigative-Artistic. **Career Clusters:** 08 Health Science; 10 Human Services. **Career Pathways:** 8.1 Therapeutic Services; 10.2 Counseling and Mental Health Services. **Other Jobs in These Pathways:** Clergy; Clinical Psychologists; Community and Social Service Specialists, All Other; Dental Assistants; Dental Hygienists; Dentists, General; Healthcare Social Workers; Healthcare Support Workers, All Other; Home Health Aides; Licensed Practical and Licensed Vocational Nurses; Massage Therapists; Medical and Clinical Laboratory Technicians; Medical and

C

*C=Computer Systems Design, E=Educational Services, G=Government, H=Health Care, R=Repair and Maintenance, U=Utilities, *=All Fields*

150 Best Jobs for a Secure Future © JIST Works — 165

Health Services Managers; Medical Scientists, Except Epidemiologists; Medical Secretaries; Mental Health and Substance Abuse Social Workers; Mental Health Counselors; Pharmacists; Pharmacy Technicians; Radiologic Technologists; Recreation Workers; School Psychologists; Social and Human Service Assistants; Speech-Language Pathologists; Speech-Language Pathology Assistants; others.

Skills: Social Perceptiveness; Science; Negotiation; Active Listening; Operations Analysis; Service Orientation; Learning Strategies; Speaking.

Work Environment: Indoors; sitting.

Job Specialization: School Psychologists

Investigate processes of learning and teaching and develop psychological principles and techniques applicable to educational problems. Compile and interpret students' test results, along with information from teachers and parents, to diagnose conditions and to help assess eligibility for special services. Report any pertinent information to the proper authorities in cases of child endangerment, neglect, or abuse. Assess an individual child's needs, limitations, and potential, using observation, review of school records, and consultation with parents and school personnel. Select, administer, and score psychological tests. Provide consultation to parents, teachers, administrators, and others on topics such as learning styles and behavior modification techniques. Promote an understanding of child development and its relationship to learning and behavior. Collaborate with other educational professionals to develop teaching strategies and school programs. Counsel children and families to help solve conflicts and problems in learning and adjustment.

Education/Training Required: Doctoral degree. **Education and Training Programs:** Psychoanalysis and Psychotherapy; Psychology, General. **Knowledge/Courses:** Therapy and Counseling; Psychology; Sociology and Anthropology; Education and Training; Foreign Language; Mathematics.

Personality Type: Investigative-Social. **Career Clusters:** 08 Health Science; 10 Human Services. **Career Pathways:** 8.1 Therapeutic Services; 10.2 Counseling and Mental Health Services. **Other Jobs in These Pathways:** Clergy; Clinical Psychologists; Community and Social Service Specialists, All Other; Counseling Psychologists; Dental Assistants; Dental Hygienists; Dentists, General; Healthcare Social Workers; Healthcare Support Workers, All Other; Home Health Aides; Licensed Practical and Licensed Vocational Nurses; Massage Therapists; Medical and Clinical Laboratory Technicians; Medical and Health Services Managers; Medical Scientists, Except Epidemiologists; Medical Secretaries; Mental Health and Substance Abuse Social Workers; Mental Health Counselors; Pharmacists; Pharmacy Technicians; Radiologic Technologists; Recreation Workers; Social and Human Service Assistants; Speech-Language Pathologists; Speech-Language Pathology Assistants; others.

Skills: Social Perceptiveness; Learning Strategies; Writing; Judgment and Decision Making; Reading Comprehension; Negotiation; Active Listening; Systems Evaluation.

Work Environment: Indoors; sitting.

Coin, Vending, and Amusement Machine Servicers and Repairers

* Annual Earnings: R $29,150, * $30,490
* Earnings Growth Potential: Medium (36.7%)
* Growth: R 2.8%, * 7.0%
* Annual Job Openings: R 50, * 1,770
* Self-Employed: 7.7%

Detailed Fields with Greatest Employment: Merchant Wholesalers, Nondurable Goods (9.6%); Beverage and Tobacco Product Manufacturing

(6.6%); Accommodation, Including Hotels and Motels (4.6%); Nonstore Retailers (32.9%); Food Services and Drinking Places (3.6%)

Detailed Fields with Highest Growth (Projected Growth for This Job): Professional, Scientific, and Technical Services (38.1%); Miscellaneous Manufacturing (27.0%); Warehousing and Storage (20.0%); Administrative and Support Services (16.0%); Specialty Trade Contractors (15.8%)

Other Considerations for Job Outlook: Although the number of vending and slot machines is expected to rise, these machines are becoming easier to maintain and repair. There will be fewer video arcade machines as people play more of these games at home. Job opportunities should be excellent for repairers with training in electronics who are willing to travel and to work irregular hours.

Install, service, adjust, or repair coin, vending, or amusement machines, including video games, jukeboxes, pinball machines, or slot machines. Clean and oil machine parts. Replace malfunctioning parts, such as worn magnetic heads on automatic teller machine (ATM) card readers. Adjust and repair coin, vending, or amusement machines and meters and replace defective mechanical and electrical parts, using hand tools, soldering irons, and diagrams. Collect coins and bills from machines, prepare invoices, and settle accounts with concessionaires. Disassemble and assemble machines according to specifications, using hand and power tools. Fill machines with products, ingredients, money, and other supplies. Inspect machines and meters to determine causes of malfunctions and fix minor problems such as jammed bills or stuck products. Install machines, making the necessary water and electrical connections in compliance with codes. Make service calls to maintain and repair machines. Adjust machine pressure gauges and thermostats. Test machines to determine proper functioning.

Education/Training Required: Moderate-term on-the-job training. **Education and Training Programs:** Business Machine Repair; Computer Installation and Repair Technology/Technician; Electrical/Electronics Maintenance and Repair Technology, Other. **Knowledge/Courses:** Food Production; Mechanical Devices; Mathematics; Public Safety and Security; Customer and Personal Service; Building and Construction.

Personality Type: Realistic-Conventional. **Career Cluster:** 02 Architecture and Construction. **Career Pathway:** 2.3 Maintenance/Operations. **Other Jobs in This Pathway:** Heating and Air Conditioning Mechanics and Installers; Home Appliance Repairers; Refrigeration Mechanics and Installers; Security and Fire Alarm Systems Installers.

Skills: Repairing; Equipment Maintenance; Installation; Troubleshooting; Operation and Control; Equipment Selection; Operation Monitoring; Quality Control Analysis.

Work Environment: More often indoors than outdoors; standing; walking and running; using hands; bending or twisting the body; repetitive motions; noise; very hot or cold; bright or inadequate lighting; minor burns, cuts, bites, or stings.

Compensation, Benefits, and Job Analysis Specialists

* Annual Earnings: H $52,505, E $53,390, G $57,970, C $66,450, * $57,000

* Earnings Growth Potential: Medium (37.4%)

* Growth: G 18.7%, E 23.6%, H 33.7%, C 59.9%, * 23.6%

* Annual Job Openings: C 150, E 200, G 590, H 600, * 6,050

* Self-Employed: 1.6%

*C=Computer Systems Design, E=Educational Services, G=Government, H=Health Care, R=Repair and Maintenance, U=Utilities, *=All Fields*

Detailed Fields with Greatest Employment: Insurance Carriers and Related Activities (7.9%); Educational Services, Public and Private (4.8%); Religious, Grantmaking, Civic, Professional, and Similar Organizations (4.5%); Administrative and Support Services (4.1%); Credit Intermediation and Related Activities (3.8%)

Detailed Fields with Highest Growth (Projected Growth for This Job): Internet Service Providers, Web Search Portals, and Data Processing Services (70.3%); Professional, Scientific, and Technical Services (62.1%); Ambulatory Health Care Services (50.3%); General Merchandise Stores (45.3%); Other Information Services (43.8%)

Other Considerations for Job Outlook: Efforts to recruit and retain employees, the growing importance of employee training, and new legal standards are expected to increase employment of these workers. College graduates and those with certification should have the best opportunities.

Conduct programs of compensation and benefits and job analysis for employer. May specialize in specific areas, such as position classification and pension programs. Evaluate job positions, determining classification, exempt or nonexempt status, and salary. Ensure company compliance with federal and state laws, including reporting requirements. Advise managers and employees on state and federal employment regulations, collective agreements, benefit and compensation policies, personnel procedures, and classification programs. Plan, develop, evaluate, improve, and communicate methods and techniques for selecting, promoting, compensating, evaluating, and training workers. Provide advice on the resolution of classification and salary complaints. Prepare occupational classifications, job descriptions, and salary scales. Assist in preparing and maintaining personnel records and handbooks. Prepare reports, such as organization and flow charts and career path reports, to summarize job analysis and evaluation

and compensation analysis information. Administer employee insurance, pension, and savings plans, working with insurance brokers and plan carriers.

Education/Training Required: Bachelor's degree. **Education and Training Program:** Human Resources Management/Personnel Administration, General. **Knowledge/Courses:** Personnel and Human Resources; Economics and Accounting; Law and Government; Administration and Management; English Language; Mathematics.

Personality Type: Conventional-Enterprising. **Career Cluster:** 04 Business, Management, and Administration. **Career Pathway:** 4.3 Human Resources. **Other Jobs in This Pathway:** Human Resources Specialists.

Skills: Operations Analysis; Science; Systems Analysis; Mathematics; Programming; Systems Evaluation; Management of Financial Resources; Learning Strategies.

Work Environment: Indoors; sitting.

Compliance Officers

- ❋ Annual Earnings: E $54,250, G $57,500, H $58,844, C $68,710, U $75,640, * $58,720
- ❋ Earnings Growth Potential: High (41.2%)
- ❋ Growth: U 5.3%, G 29.9%, E 35.3%, H 41.3%, C 71.6%, * 31.0%
- ❋ Annual Job Openings: U 60, C 100, E 130, H 380, G 4,730, * 10,850
- ❋ Self-Employed: 1.4%

Detailed Fields with Greatest Employment: Federal Government (41.2%); Professional, Scientific, and Technical Services (4.9%); Insurance Carriers and Related Activities (4.3%); Credit Intermediation and Related Activities (3.7%); Management of Companies and Enterprises (3.0%)

Detailed Fields with Highest Growth (Projected Growth for This Job): Internet Service Providers, Web Search Portals, and Data Processing Services (78.9%); Professional, Scientific, and Technical Services (71.5%); Waste Management and Remediation Services (61.1%); Lessors of Nonfinancial Intangible Assets (Except Copyrighted Works) (61.0%); Broadcasting (Except Internet) (57.1%)

Other Considerations for Job Outlook: Much-faster-than-average employment growth is projected.

Examine, evaluate, and investigate eligibility for or conformity with laws and regulations governing contract compliance of licenses and permits and other compliance and enforcement inspection activities not classified elsewhere. No task data available.

Education/Training Required: Long-term on-the-job training. **Education and Training Program:** Business Administration and Management, General. **Knowledge/Courses:** No data available.

Personality Type: No data available. **Career Cluster:** 12 Law, Public Safety, Corrections, and Security. **Career Pathway:** 12.6 Inspection Services. **Other Jobs in This Pathway:** Coroners; Environmental Compliance Inspectors; Equal Opportunity Representatives and Officers; Government Property Inspectors and Investigators; Licensing Examiners and Inspectors; Regulatory Affairs Specialists.

Skills: No data available.

Work Environment: No data available.

Job Specialization: Coroners

Direct activities such as autopsies, pathological and toxicological analyses, and inquests relating to the investigation of deaths occurring within a legal jurisdiction to determine cause of death or to fix responsibility for accidental, violent, or unexplained deaths. Perform medico-legal examinations and autopsies, conducting preliminary examinations of the body in order to identify victims, to locate signs of trauma, and to identify factors that would indicate time of death. Inquire into the cause, manner, and circumstances of human deaths and establish the identities of deceased persons. Direct activities of workers who conduct autopsies, perform pathological and toxicological analyses, and prepare documents for permanent records. Complete death certificates, including the assignment of a cause and manner of death. Observe and record the positions and conditions of bodies and of related evidence. Collect and document any pertinent medical history information. Observe, record, and preserve any objects or personal property related to deaths, including objects such as medication containers and suicide notes. Complete reports and forms required to finalize cases.

Education/Training Required: Work experience in a related occupation. **Education and Training Program:** Public Administration. **Knowledge/Courses:** Medicine and Dentistry; Biology; Psychology; Therapy and Counseling; Chemistry; Law and Government.

Personality Type: Investigative-Realistic-Conventional. **Career Cluster:** 12 Law, Public Safety, Corrections, and Security. **Career Pathway:** 12.6 Inspection Services. **Other Jobs in This Pathway:** Compliance Officers; Environmental Compliance Inspectors; Equal Opportunity Representatives and Officers; Government Property Inspectors and Investigators; Licensing Examiners and Inspectors; Regulatory Affairs Specialists.

Skills: Science; Social Perceptiveness; Speaking; Critical Thinking; Writing; Management of Personnel Resources; Learning Strategies; Instructing.

Work Environment: More often indoors than outdoors; sitting; using hands; contaminants; exposed to disease or infections; hazardous equipment.

---

*C=Computer Systems Design, E=Educational Services, G=Government, H=Health Care, R=Repair and Maintenance, U=Utilities, *=All Fields*

Job Specialization: Environmental Compliance Inspectors

Inspect and investigate sources of pollution to protect the public and environment and ensure conformance with federal, state, and local regulations and ordinances. Determine the nature of code violations and actions to be taken and issue written notices of violation; participate in enforcement hearings as necessary. Examine permits, licenses, applications, and records to ensure compliance with licensing requirements. Prepare, organize, and maintain inspection records. Interview individuals to determine the nature of suspected violations and to obtain evidence of violations. Prepare written, oral, tabular, and graphic reports summarizing requirements and regulations, including enforcement and chain of custody documentation. Monitor follow-up actions in cases where violations were found and review compliance monitoring reports. Investigate complaints and suspected violations regarding illegal dumping, pollution, pesticides, product quality, or labeling laws. Inspect waste pretreatment, treatment, and disposal facilities and systems for conformance to federal, state, or local regulations.

Education/Training Required: Long-term on-the-job training. **Education and Training Program:** Natural Resources Management and Policy, Other. **Knowledge/Courses:** Biology; Law and Government; Chemistry; Geography; Physics; Engineering and Technology.

Personality Type: Conventional-Investigative-Realistic. **Career Clusters:** 07 Government and Public Administration; 12 Law, Public Safety, Corrections, and Security; 16 Transportation, Distribution, and Logistics. **Career Pathways:** 7.6 Regulation; 12.6 Inspection Services; 16.6 Health, Safety, and Environmental Management. **Other Jobs in These Pathways:** Chief Executives; Compliance Officers; Coroners; Environmental Engineers; Environmental Science and Protection Technicians, Including Health; Environmental Scientists and Specialists, Including Health; Equal Opportunity Representatives and Officers; Government Property Inspectors and Investigators; Health and Safety Engineers, Except Mining Safety Engineers and Inspectors; Licensing Examiners and Inspectors; Regulatory Affairs Managers; Regulatory Affairs Specialists.

Skills: Quality Control Analysis; Science; Programming; Troubleshooting; Mathematics; Reading Comprehension; Writing; Systems Evaluation.

Work Environment: More often indoors than outdoors; sitting; contaminants.

Job Specialization: Equal Opportunity Representatives and Officers

Monitor and evaluate compliance with equal opportunity laws, guidelines, and policies to ensure that employment practices and contracting arrangements give equal opportunity without regard to race, religion, color, national origin, sex, age, or disability. Investigate employment practices and alleged violations of laws to document and correct discriminatory factors. Interpret civil rights laws and equal opportunity regulations for individuals and employers. Study equal opportunity complaints to clarify issues. Meet with persons involved in equal opportunity complaints to verify case information and to arbitrate and settle disputes. Coordinate, monitor, and revise complaint procedures to ensure timely processing and review of complaints. Prepare reports of selection, survey, and other statistics and recommendations for corrective action. Conduct surveys and evaluate findings to determine whether systematic discrimination exists. Develop guidelines for nondiscriminatory employment practices and monitor their implementation and impact.

Review company contracts to determine actions required to meet governmental equal opportunity provisions.

Education/Training Required: Long-term on-the-job training. **Education and Training Program:** Public Administration and Social Service Professions, Other. **Knowledge/Courses:** Law and Government; Personnel and Human Resources; Clerical Practices; English Language; Customer and Personal Service; Administration and Management.

Personality Type: Social-Enterprising-Conventional. **Career Cluster:** 12 Law, Public Safety, Corrections, and Security. **Career Pathway:** 12.6 Inspection Services. **Other Jobs in This Pathway:** Compliance Officers; Coroners; Environmental Compliance Inspectors; Government Property Inspectors and Investigators; Licensing Examiners and Inspectors; Regulatory Affairs Specialists.

Skills: Persuasion; Reading Comprehension; Active Listening; Programming; Active Learning; Negotiation; Writing; Systems Evaluation.

Work Environment: Indoors; sitting; repetitive motions.

Job Specialization: Government Property Inspectors and Investigators

Investigate or inspect government property to ensure compliance with contract agreements and government regulations. Prepare correspondence, reports of inspections or investigations, and recommendations for action. Inspect government-owned equipment and materials in the possession of private contractors to ensure compliance with contracts and regulations and to prevent misuse. Examine records, reports, and documents to establish facts and detect discrepancies. Inspect manufactured or processed products to ensure compliance with contract specifications and legal requirements.

Locate and interview plaintiffs, witnesses, or representatives of business or government to gather facts relevant to inspections or alleged violations. Recommend legal or administrative action to protect government property. Submit samples of products to government laboratories for testing as required. Coordinate with and assist law enforcement agencies in matters of mutual concern. Testify in court or at administrative proceedings concerning findings of investigations. Collect, identify, evaluate, and preserve case evidence.

Education/Training Required: Long-term on-the-job training. **Education and Training Program:** Building/Home/Construction Inspection/Inspector. **Knowledge/Courses:** Building and Construction; Engineering and Technology; Public Safety and Security; Mechanical Devices; Transportation; Computers and Electronics.

Personality Type: Conventional-Enterprising-Realistic. **Career Cluster:** 12 Law, Public Safety, Corrections, and Security. **Career Pathway:** 12.6 Inspection Services. **Other Jobs in This Pathway:** Compliance Officers; Coroners; Environmental Compliance Inspectors; Equal Opportunity Representatives and Officers; Licensing Examiners and Inspectors; Regulatory Affairs Specialists.

Skills: Quality Control Analysis; Programming; Persuasion; Operation and Control; Systems Evaluation; Writing; Speaking; Judgment and Decision Making.

Work Environment: More often outdoors than indoors; sitting; noise; very hot or cold; contaminants.

Job Specialization: Licensing Examiners and Inspectors

Examine, evaluate, and investigate eligibility for, conformity with, or liability under licenses

C

*C=Computer Systems Design, E=Educational Services, G=Government, H=Health Care, R=Repair and Maintenance, U=Utilities, *=All Fields*

or permits. Issue licenses to individuals meeting standards. Evaluate applications, records, and documents in order to gather information about eligibility or liability issues. Administer oral, written, road, or flight tests to license applicants. Score tests and observe equipment operation and control in order to rate ability of applicants. Advise licensees and other individuals or groups concerning licensing, permit, or passport regulations. Warn violators of infractions or penalties. Prepare reports of activities, evaluations, recommendations, and decisions. Prepare correspondence to inform concerned parties of licensing decisions and of appeals processes. Confer with and interview officials, technical or professional specialists, and applicants in order to obtain information or to clarify facts relevant to licensing decisions. Report law or regulation violations to appropriate boards and agencies.

Education/Training Required: Long-term on-the-job training. **Education and Training Program:** Public Administration and Social Service Professions, Other. **Knowledge/Courses:** Clerical Practices; Customer and Personal Service; Law and Government; Foreign Language; Psychology; Public Safety and Security.

Personality Type: Conventional-Enterprising. **Career Cluster:** 12 Law, Public Safety, Corrections, and Security. **Career Pathway:** 12.6 Inspection Services. **Other Jobs in This Pathway:** Compliance Officers; Coroners; Environmental Compliance Inspectors; Equal Opportunity Representatives and Officers; Government Property Inspectors and Investigators; Regulatory Affairs Specialists.

Skills: Quality Control Analysis; Judgment and Decision Making; Social Perceptiveness; Speaking; Operation Monitoring; Service Orientation; Systems Evaluation; Reading Comprehension.

Work Environment: More often indoors than outdoors; sitting; using hands; repetitive motions; contaminants.

Job Specialization: Regulatory Affairs Specialists

Coordinate and document internal regulatory processes, such as internal audits, inspections, license renewals, or registrations. May compile and prepare materials for submission to regulatory agencies. Coordinate, prepare, or review regulatory submissions for domestic or international projects. Provide technical review of data or reports that will be incorporated into regulatory submissions to assure scientific rigor, accuracy, and clarity of presentation. Review product promotional materials, labeling, batch records, specification sheets, or test methods for compliance with applicable regulations and policies. Maintain current knowledge base of existing and emerging regulations, standards, or guidance documents. Interpret regulatory rules or rule changes and ensure that they are communicated through corporate policies and procedures. Advise project teams on subjects such as premarket regulatory requirements, export and labeling requirements, and clinical study compliance issues. Determine the types of regulatory submissions or internal documentation that are required in situations such as proposed device changes and labeling changes.

Education/Training Required: Work experience in a related occupation. **Education and Training Program:** Business Administration and Management, General. **Knowledge/Courses:** Law and Government; Biology; Medicine and Dentistry; Clerical Practices; English Language; Chemistry.

Personality Type: Conventional-Enterprising. **Career Cluster:** 12 Law, Public Safety, Corrections, and Security. **Career Pathway:** 12.6

Inspection Services. **Other Jobs in This Pathway:** Compliance Officers; Coroners; Environmental Compliance Inspectors; Equal Opportunity Representatives and Officers; Government Property Inspectors and Investigators; Licensing Examiners and Inspectors.

Skills: Systems Analysis; Systems Evaluation; Judgment and Decision Making; Persuasion; Writing; Speaking; Coordination; Reading Comprehension.

Work Environment: Indoors; sitting.

Computer and Information Research Scientists

- ❋ Annual Earnings: C $96,590, G $100,920, * $100,660
- ❋ Earnings Growth Potential: High (42.7%)
- ❋ Growth: G 19.5%, C 43.0%, * 24.2%
- ❋ Annual Job Openings: G 180, C 420, * 1,320
- ❋ Self-Employed: 4.6%

Detailed Fields with Greatest Employment: Educational Services, Public and Private (7.1%); Professional, Scientific, and Technical Services (44.4%); Merchant Wholesalers, Durable Goods (4.1%); Federal Government (20.8%); Computer and Electronic Product Manufacturing (2.9%)

Detailed Fields with Highest Growth (Projected Growth for This Job): Professional, Scientific, and Technical Services (35.9%); Publishing Industries (Except Internet) (28.1%); Other Information Services (25.0%); Federal Government (19.5%); Administrative and Support Services (16.7%)

Other Considerations for Job Outlook: Employment is expected to increase because of high demand for sophisticated technological research. Job prospects should be excellent.

Conduct research into fundamental computer and information science as theorists, designers, or inventors. Solve or develop solutions to problems in the field of computer hardware and software. Analyze problems to develop solutions involving computer hardware and software. Assign or schedule tasks in order to meet work priorities and goals. Evaluate project plans and proposals to assess feasibility issues. Apply theoretical expertise and innovation to create or apply new technology, such as adapting principles for applying computers to new uses. Consult with users, management, vendors, and technicians to determine computing needs and system requirements. Meet with managers, vendors, and others to solicit cooperation and resolve problems. Conduct logical analyses of business, scientific, engineering, and other technical problems, formulating mathematical models of problems for solution by computers. Develop and interpret organizational goals, policies, and procedures. Participate in staffing decisions and direct training of subordinates. Develop performance standards and evaluate work in light of established standards. Design computers and the software that runs them.

Education/Training Required: Doctoral degree. **Education and Training Programs:** Computer Graphics; Computer Science; Computer Software and Media Applications, Other; Computer Systems Networking and Telecommunications; Data Modeling/Warehousing and Database Administration; Modeling, Virtual Environments and Simulation; Web Page, Digital/Multimedia, and Information Resources Design. **Knowledge/Courses:** Computers and Electronics; Telecommunications; Engineering and Technology; Mathematics; Design; Education and Training.

---

*C=Computer Systems Design, E=Educational Services, G=Government, H=Health Care, R=Repair and Maintenance, U=Utilities, *=All Fields*

Personality Type: Investigative-Realistic-Conventional. **Career Cluster:** 11 Information Technology. **Career Pathways:** 8.3 Health Informatics; 11.1 Network Systems; 11.2 Information Support Services; 11.3 Interactive Media; 11.4 Programming and Software Development. **Other Jobs in These Pathways:** Architectural and Engineering Managers; Clinical Psychologists; Computer and Information Systems Managers; Computer Hardware Engineers; Computer Operators; Editors; Engineers, All Other; Executive Secretaries and Executive Administrative Assistants; First-Line Supervisors of Office and Administrative Support Workers; Graphic Designers; Health Educators; Medical and Health Services Managers; Medical Assistants; Medical Records and Health Information Technicians; Medical Secretaries; Medical Transcriptionists; Mental Health Counselors; Multimedia Artists and Animators; Physical Therapists; Psychiatric Aides; Public Relations Specialists; Receptionists and Information Clerks; Rehabilitation Counselors; Remote Sensing Technicians; Substance Abuse and Behavioral Disorder Counselors; others.

Skills: Programming; Technology Design; Systems Evaluation; Management of Financial Resources; Mathematics; Systems Analysis; Operations Analysis; Science.

Work Environment: Indoors; sitting; using hands; repetitive motions.

Computer Network Architects

* Annual Earnings: E $61,220, G $63,760, H $69,789, U $76,940, C $77,190, * $75,660
* Earnings Growth Potential: High (42.9%)
* Growth: U 15.8%, G 45.2%, E 51.7%, H 65.1%, C 95.6%, * 53.4%
* Annual Job Openings: U 80, H 630, E 670, G 720, C 4,090, * 20,830
* Self-Employed: 19.4%

Detailed Fields with Greatest Employment: Management of Companies and Enterprises (7.2%); State and Local Government (6.1%); Administrative and Support Services (5.5%); Educational Services, Public and Private (5.4%); Insurance Carriers and Related Activities (4.1%)

Detailed Fields with Highest Growth (Projected Growth for This Job): Internet Service Providers, Web Search Portals, and Data Processing Services (106.0%); Professional, Scientific, and Technical Services (93.3%); Lessors of Nonfinancial Intangible Assets (Except Copyrighted Works) (87.5%); Ambulatory Health Care Services (79.1%); Other Information Services (73.6%)

Other Considerations for Job Outlook: Employment of these workers should grow as organizations increasingly use network technologies. Job prospects are expected to be excellent.

Design and implement computer and information networks, such as local area networks (LAN), wide area networks (WAN), intranets, extranets, and other data communications networks. Perform network modeling, analysis, and planning. May also design network and computer security measures. May research and recommend network and data communications hardware and software. Adjust network sizes to meet volume or capacity demands. Communicate with customers, sales staff, or marketing staff to determine customer needs. Communicate with system users to ensure accounts are set up properly or to diagnose and solve operational problems. Coordinate installation of new equipment. Coordinate network operations, maintenance, repairs, or upgrades. Coordinate network or design activities with designers of associated networks. Design, build, or operate equipment configuration prototypes, including network hardware, software, servers, or server operation systems. Design, organize, and deliver product awareness, skills transfer, or product education sessions for staff or suppliers. Determine specific network hardware or software requirements, such as platforms, interfaces, bandwidths, or routine schemas. Develop and implement solutions for network problems. Develop and write procedures for installation, use, or troubleshooting of communications hardware or software.

Education/Training Required: Bachelor's degree. **Education and Training Program:** Computer Systems Networking and Telecommunications. **Knowledge/Courses:** Telecommunications; Computers and Electronics; Design; Engineering and Technology; Communications and Media; Clerical.

Personality Type: Investigative-Conventional-Realistic. **Career Cluster:** 11 Information Technology. **Career Pathway:** 11.4 Programming and Software Development. **Other Jobs in This Pathway:** Architectural and Engineering Managers; Bioinformatics Scientists; Computer Hardware Engineers; Computer Numerically Controlled Machine Tool Programmers, Metal and Plastic.

Skills: Programming; Technology Design; Equipment Selection; Operations Analysis; Equipment Maintenance; Quality Control Analysis; Troubleshooting; Repairing.

Work Environment: Indoors; sitting.

Job Specialization: Telecommunications Engineering Specialists

Design or configure voice, video, and data communications systems. Supervise installation and post-installation service and maintenance. Keep abreast of changes in industry practices and emerging telecommunications technology by reviewing current literature, talking with colleagues, participating in educational programs, attending meetings or workshops, or participating in professional organizations or conferences. Estimate costs for system or component implementation and operation. Develop, maintain, or implement telecommunications disaster recovery plans to ensure business continuity. Test and evaluate hardware and software to determine efficiency, reliability, or compatibility with existing systems. Supervise maintenance of telecommunications equipment. Review and evaluate requests from engineers, managers, and technicians for system modifications. Provide user support by diagnosing network and device problems and implementing technical or procedural solutions. Prepare system activity and performance reports.

Education/Training Required: Bachelor's degree. **Education and Training Program:** Computer Systems Networking and Telecommunications. **Knowledge/Courses:** No data available.

Personality Type: No data available. **Career Clusters:** 11 Information Technology; 15 Science, Technology, Engineering, and Mathematics. **Career Pathway:** 11.4 Programming and Software Development. **Other Jobs in This Pathway:** Architectural and Engineering Managers; Bioinformatics Scientists; Computer Hardware Engineers; Computer Numerically Controlled Machine Tool Programmers, Metal and Plastic.

Skills: No data available.

Work Environment: No data available.

*C=Computer Systems Design, E=Educational Services, G=Government, H=Health Care, R=Repair and Maintenance, U=Utilities, *=All Fields*

Computer Occupations, All Other

- ❋ Annual Earnings: E $60,300, C $74,560, G $87,160, * $79,240
- ❋ Earnings Growth Potential: High (47.4%)
- ❋ Growth: G 7.6%, E 12.0%, C 40.2%, * 13.1%
- ❋ Annual Job Openings: E 360, C 1,150, G 1,840, * 7,260
- ❋ Self-Employed: 3.9%

Detailed Fields with Greatest Employment: Management of Companies and Enterprises (7.3%); Educational Services, Public and Private (7.0%); Federal Government (33.4%); Publishing Industries (Except Internet) (3.8%); Administrative and Support Services (3.5%)

Detailed Fields with Highest Growth (Projected Growth for This Job): Internet Service Providers, Web Search Portals, and Data Processing Services (48.7%); Personal and Laundry Services (40.0%); Professional, Scientific, and Technical Services (37.8%); Waste Management and Remediation Services (35.7%); Ambulatory Health Care Services (33.0%)

Other Considerations for Job Outlook: Employment of these workers should grow as organizations increasingly use network technologies and collect and organize data. Job prospects are expected to be excellent.

This occupation includes all computer occupations not listed separately. No task data available.

Education/Training Required: No data available. **Education and Training Program:** Computer and Information Sciences and Support Services, Other. **Knowledge/Courses:** No data available.

Personality Type: No data available. **Career Cluster:** 11 Information Technology. **Career Pathways:** 11.2 Information Support Services; 11.3 Interactive Media; 11.4 Programming and Software Development. **Other Jobs in These Pathways:** Architectural and Engineering Managers; Bioinformatics Scientists; Computer and Information Systems Managers; Computer Hardware Engineers; Computer Numerically Controlled Machine Tool Programmers, Metal and Plastic; Computer Operators; Remote Sensing Scientists and Technologists; Remote Sensing Technicians.

Skills: No data available.

Work Environment: No data available.

Job Specialization: Business Intelligence Analysts

Produce financial and market intelligence by querying data repositories and generating periodic reports. Devise methods for identifying data patterns and trends in available information sources. Provide technical support for existing reports, dashboards, or other tools. Maintain library of model documents, templates, or other reusable knowledge assets. Identify or monitor current and potential customers, using business intelligence tools. Create or review technical design documentation to ensure the accurate development of reporting solutions. Communicate with customers, competitors, suppliers, professional organizations, or others to stay abreast of industry or business trends. Maintain or update business intelligence tools, databases, dashboards, systems, or methods. Manage timely flow of business intelligence information to users. Identify and analyze industry or geographic trends with business strategy implications.

Document specifications for business intelligence or information technology (IT) reports, dashboards, or other outputs. Disseminate information regarding tools, reports, or metadata enhancements.

Education/Training Required: Work experience plus degree. **Education and Training Program:** Computer and Information Sciences and Support Services, Other. **Knowledge/Courses:** No data available.

Personality Type: No data available. **Career Cluster:** 04 Business, Management, and Administration. **Career Pathway:** 11.2 Information Support Services. **Other Jobs in This Pathway:** Computer and Information Systems Managers; Computer Numerically Controlled Machine Tool Programmers, Metal and Plastic; Computer Operators; Remote Sensing Scientists and Technologists; Remote Sensing Technicians.

Skills: No data available.

Work Environment: No data available.

Job Specialization: Computer Systems Engineers/Architects

Design and develop solutions to complex applications problems, system administration issues, or network concerns. Perform systems management and integration functions. Communicate with staff or clients to understand specific system requirements. Provide advice on project costs, design concepts, or design changes. Document design specifications, installation instructions, and other system-related information. Verify stability, interoperability, portability, security, or scalability of system architecture. Collaborate with engineers or software developers to select appropriate design solutions or ensure the compatibility of system components. Evaluate current or emerging technologies to consider factors such as cost, portability, compatibility, or usability. Provide technical guidance or support for the development or troubleshooting of systems. Identify system data, hardware, or software components required to meet user needs. Provide guidelines for implementing secure systems to customers or installation teams. Monitor system operation to detect potential problems. Direct the analysis, development, and operation of complete computer systems.

Education/Training Required: Bachelor's degree. **Education and Training Programs:** Computer Engineering, General; Data Modeling/Warehousing and Database Administration. **Knowledge/Courses:** Computers and Electronics; Engineering and Technology; Telecommunications; Design; Mathematics; Sales and Marketing.

Personality Type: Investigative-Realistic-Conventional. **Career Cluster:** 11 Information Technology. **Career Pathway:** 11.4 Programming and Software Development. **Other Jobs in This Pathway:** Architectural and Engineering Managers; Bioinformatics Scientists; Computer Hardware Engineers; Computer Numerically Controlled Machine Tool Programmers, Metal and Plastic.

Skills: Programming; Operations Analysis; Science; Systems Evaluation; Quality Control Analysis; Management of Financial Resources; Equipment Maintenance; Equipment Selection.

Work Environment: Indoors; sitting; repetitive motions.

Job Specialization: Data Warehousing Specialists

Design, model, or implement corporate data warehousing activities. Program and configure warehouses of database information and provide support to warehouse users. Test software systems or applications for software enhancements

*C=Computer Systems Design, E=Educational Services, G=Government, H=Health Care, R=Repair and Maintenance, U=Utilities, *=All Fields*

150 Best Jobs for a Secure Future © JIST Works

177

or new products. Review designs, codes, test plans, or documentation to ensure quality. Provide or coordinate troubleshooting support for data warehouses. Prepare functional or technical documentation for data warehouses. Write new programs or modify existing programs to meet customer requirements, using current programming languages and technologies. Verify the structure, accuracy, or quality of warehouse data. Select methods, techniques, or criteria for data warehousing evaluative procedures. Perform system analysis, data analysis, or programming, using a variety of computer languages and procedures. Map data between source systems, data warehouses, and data marts. Implement business rules via stored procedures, middleware, or other technologies. Develop and implement data extraction procedures from other systems, such as administration, billing, or claims.

Education/Training Required: Bachelor's degree. **Education and Training Program:** Data Modeling/Warehousing and Database Administration. **Knowledge/Courses:** No data available.

Personality Type: No data available. **Career Cluster:** 11 Information Technology. **Career Pathway:** 11.2 Information Support Services. **Other Jobs in This Pathway:** Computer and Information Systems Managers; Computer Numerically Controlled Machine Tool Programmers, Metal and Plastic; Computer Operators; Remote Sensing Scientists and Technologists; Remote Sensing Technicians.

Skills: No data available.

Work Environment: No data available.

Job Specialization: Database Architects

Design strategies for enterprise database systems and set standards for operations, programming, and security. Design and construct large relational databases. Integrate new systems with existing warehouse structure and refine system performance and functionality. Test changes to database applications or systems. Provide technical support to junior staff or clients. Set up database clusters, backup, or recovery processes. Identify, evaluate, and recommend hardware or software technologies to achieve desired database performance. Plan and install upgrades of database management system software to enhance database performance. Monitor and report systems resource consumption trends to assure production systems meet availability requirements and hardware enhancements are scheduled appropriately. Identify and correct deviations from database development standards. Document and communicate database schemas, using accepted notations. Develop or maintain archived procedures, procedural codes, or queries for applications. Develop load-balancing processes to eliminate downtime for backup processes. Develop data models for applications, metadata tables, views, or related database structures.

Education/Training Required: Bachelor's degree. **Education and Training Program:** Data Modeling/Warehousing and Database Administration. **Knowledge/Courses:** No data available.

Personality Type: No data available. **Career Cluster:** 11 Information Technology. **Career Pathway:** 11.4 Programming and Software Development. **Other Jobs in This Pathway:** Architectural and Engineering Managers; Bioinformatics Scientists; Computer Hardware Engineers; Computer Numerically Controlled Machine Tool Programmers, Metal and Plastic.

Skills: No data available.

Work Environment: No data available.

Job Specialization: Document Management Specialists

Implement and administer enterprise-wide document management procedures for the capture, storage, retrieval, sharing, and destruction of electronic records and documents. Keep abreast of developments in document management by reviewing current literature, talking with colleagues, participating in educational programs, attending meetings or workshops, or participating in professional organizations or conferences. Monitor regulatory activity to maintain compliance with records and document management laws. Write, review, or execute plans for testing new or established document management systems. Search electronic sources, such as databases or repositories, or manual sources for information. Retrieve electronic assets from repository for distribution to users, collecting and returning to repository if necessary. Propose recommendations for improving content management system capabilities. Prepare support documentation and training materials for end users of document management systems. Prepare and record changes to official documents and confirm changes with legal and compliance management staff.

Education/Training Required: Associate degree. **Education and Training Program:** Computer and Information Sciences and Support Services, Other. **Knowledge/Courses:** No data available.

Personality Type: No data available. **Career Cluster:** 11 Information Technology. **Career Pathway:** 11.2 Information Support Services. **Other Jobs in This Pathway:** Computer and Information Systems Managers; Computer Numerically Controlled Machine Tool Programmers, Metal and Plastic; Computer Operators; Remote Sensing Scientists and Technologists; Remote Sensing Technicians.

Skills: No data available.

Work Environment: No data available.

Job Specialization: Geographic Information Systems Technicians

Assist scientists, technologists, and related professionals in building, maintaining, modifying, and using Geographic Information Systems (GIS) databases. May also perform some custom application development and provide user support. Recommend procedures and equipment or software upgrades to increase data accessibility or ease of use. Provide technical support to users or clients regarding the maintenance, development, or operation of Geographic Information Systems (GIS) databases, equipment, or applications. Read current literature, talk with colleagues, continue education, or participate in professional organizations or conferences to keep abreast of developments in Geographic Information Systems (GIS) technology, equipment, or systems. Confer with users to analyze, configure, or troubleshoot applications. Select cartographic elements needed for effective presentation of information. Transfer or rescale information from original photographs onto maps or other photographs. Review existing or incoming data for currency, accuracy, usefulness, quality, or completeness of documentation. Interpret aerial or ortho photographs.

Education/Training Required: Associate degree. **Education and Training Program:** Geographic Information Science and Cartography. **Knowledge/Courses:** No data available.

Personality Type: Investigative-Realistic-Conventional. **Career Cluster:** 11 Information Technology. **Career Pathway:** 11.4 Programming and Software Development. **Other Jobs in This Pathway:** Architectural and Engineering Managers; Bioinformatics Scientists; Computer Hardware Engineers;

---

*C=Computer Systems Design, E=Educational Services, G=Government, H=Health Care, R=Repair and Maintenance, U=Utilities, *=All Fields*

Computer Numerically Controlled Machine Tool Programmers, Metal and Plastic.

Skills: No data available.

Work Environment: No data available.

Job Specialization: Geospatial Information Scientists and Technologists

Research and develop geospatial technologies. May produce databases, perform applications programming, or coordinate projects. May specialize in areas such as agriculture, mining, health care, retail trade, urban planning, or military intelligence. Perform integrated and computerized Geographic Information Systems (GIS) analyses to address scientific problems. Develop specialized computer software routines, Internet-based GIS databases or business applications to customize geographic information. Provide technical support for computer-based GIS mapping software. Create visual representations of geospatial data using complex procedures such as analytical modeling, three-dimensional renderings, and plot creation. Perform computer programming, data analysis, or software development for GIS applications, including the maintenance of existing systems or research and development for future enhancements. Assist users in formulating GIS requirements or understanding the implications of alternatives.

Education/Training Required: Bachelor's degree. **Education and Training Program:** Geographic Information Science and Cartography. **Knowledge/Courses:** Geography; Computers and Electronics; Design; Engineering and Technology; Mathematics; Education and Training.

Personality Type: Investigative-Realistic-Conventional. **Career Cluster:** 11 Information Technology. **Career Pathway:** 11.4 Programming and Software

Development. **Other Jobs in This Pathway:** Architectural and Engineering Managers; Bioinformatics Scientists; Computer Hardware Engineers; Computer Numerically Controlled Machine Tool Programmers, Metal and Plastic.

Skills: Science; Programming; Operations Analysis; Systems Evaluation; Systems Analysis; Technology Design; Mathematics; Reading Comprehension.

Work Environment: Indoors; sitting; using hands; repetitive motions.

Job Specialization: Information Technology Project Managers

Plan, initiate, and manage information technology (IT) projects. Lead and guide the work of technical staff. Serve as liaison between business and technical aspects of projects. Plan project stages and assess business implications for each stage. Monitor progress to assure deadlines, standards, and cost targets are met. Perform risk assessments to develop response strategies. Submit project deliverables, ensuring adherence to quality standards. Monitor the performance of project team members, providing and documenting performance feedback. Confer with project personnel to identify and resolve problems. Assess current or future customer needs and priorities through communicating directly with customers, conducting surveys, or other methods. Schedule and facilitate meetings related to information technology projects. Monitor or track project milestones and deliverables. Negotiate with project stakeholders or suppliers to obtain resources or materials. Initiate, review, or approve modifications to project plans. Identify, review, or select vendors or consultants to meet project needs. Establish and execute a project communication plan. Identify need for initial or supplemental project resources. Direct or coordinate activities of project personnel.

Education/Training Required: Work experience in a related occupation. **Education and Training Program:** Information Technology Project Management. **Knowledge/Courses:** No data available.

Personality Type: No data available. **Career Clusters:** 04 Business, Management, and Administration; 11 Information Technology. **Career Pathway:** 11.4 Programming and Software Development. **Other Jobs in This Pathway:** Architectural and Engineering Managers; Bioinformatics Scientists; Computer Hardware Engineers; Computer Numerically Controlled Machine Tool Programmers, Metal and Plastic.

Skills: No data available.

Work Environment: No data available.

Job Specialization: Search Marketing Strategists

Employ search marketing tactics to increase visibility and engagement with content, products, or services in Internet-enabled devices or interfaces. Examine search query behaviors on general or specialty search engines or other Internet-based content. Analyze research, data, or technology to understand user intent and measure outcomes for ongoing optimization. Keep abreast of government regulations and emerging web technology to ensure regulatory compliance by reviewing current literature, talking with colleagues, participating in educational programs, attending meetings or workshops, or participate in professional organizations or conferences. Resolve product availability problems in collaboration with customer service staff. Implement online customer service processes to ensure positive and consistent user experiences. Identify, evaluate, or procure hardware or software for implementing online marketing campaigns. Identify methods for interfacing web application

technologies with enterprise resource planning or other system software. Define product requirements based on market research analysis in collaboration with design and engineering staff. Assist in the evaluation and negotiation of contracts with vendors and online partners. Propose online or multiple-sales-channel campaigns to marketing executives.

Education/Training Required: Bachelor's degree. **Education and Training Program:** Web Page, Digital/Multimedia, and Information Resources Design. **Knowledge/Courses:** No data available.

Personality Type: No data available. **Career Clusters:** 11 Information Technology; 14 Marketing, Sales, and Service. **Career Pathway:** 14.2 Professional Sales and Marketing. **Other Jobs in This Pathway:** Cashiers; Counter and Rental Clerks; Door-To-Door Sales Workers, News and Street Vendors, and Related Workers; Driver/Sales Workers; Energy Brokers; First-Line Supervisors of Non-Retail Sales Workers; First-Line Supervisors of Retail Sales Workers; Hotel, Motel, and Resort Desk Clerks; Marketing Managers; Marking Clerks; Online Merchants; Order Fillers, Wholesale and Retail Sales; Parts Salespersons; Property, Real Estate, and Community Association Managers; Real Estate Sales Agents; Reservation and Transportation Ticket Agents and Travel Clerks; Retail Salespersons; Sales and Related Workers, All Other; Sales Representatives, Services, All Other; Sales Representatives, Wholesale and Manufacturing, Except Technical and Scientific Products; Sales Representatives, Wholesale and Manufacturing, Technical and Scientific Products; Solar Sales Representatives and Assessors; Stock Clerks—Stockroom, Warehouse, or Storage Yard; Stock Clerks, Sales Floor; Telemarketers; others.

Skills: No data available.

Work Environment: No data available.

*C=Computer Systems Design, E=Educational Services, G=Government, H=Health Care, R=Repair and Maintenance, U=Utilities, *=All Fields*

Job Specialization: Software Quality Assurance Engineers and Testers

Develop and execute software test plans in order to identify software problems and their causes. Design test plans, scenarios, scripts, or procedures. Test system modifications to prepare for implementation. Develop testing programs that address areas such as database impacts, software scenarios, regression testing, negative testing, error or bug retests, or usability. Document software defects, using a bug tracking system, and report defects to software developers. Identify, analyze, and document problems with program function, output, online screen, or content. Monitor bug resolution efforts and track successes. Create or maintain databases of known test defects. Plan test schedules or strategies in accordance with project scope or delivery dates. Participate in product design reviews to provide input on functional requirements, product designs, schedules, or potential problems. Review software documentation to ensure technical accuracy, compliance, or completeness, or to mitigate risks. Document test procedures to ensure replicability and compliance with standards.

Education/Training Required: Bachelor's degree. **Education and Training Program:** Computer Engineering, General. **Knowledge/Courses:** Computers and Electronics; Engineering and Technology; Design; English Language; Mathematics; Clerical.

Personality Type: Investigative-Conventional-Realistic. **Career Cluster:** 11 Information Technology. **Career Pathway:** 11.4 Programming and Software Development. **Other Jobs in This Pathway:** Architectural and Engineering Managers; Bioinformatics Scientists; Computer Hardware Engineers; Computer Numerically Controlled Machine Tool Programmers, Metal and Plastic.

Skills: Programming; Installation; Technology Design; Operations Analysis; Troubleshooting; Science; Quality Control Analysis; Systems Evaluation.

Work Environment: Indoors; sitting; using hands; repetitive motions.

Job Specialization: Video Game Designers

Design core features of video games. Specify innovative game and role-play mechanics, storylines, and character biographies. Create and maintain design documentation. Guide and collaborate with production staff to produce games as designed. Review or evaluate competitive products, film, music, television, and other art forms to generate new game design ideas. Provide test specifications to quality assurance staff. Keep abreast of game design technology and techniques, industry trends, or audience interests, reactions, and needs by reviewing current literature, talking with colleagues, participating in educational programs, attending meetings or workshops, or participating in professional organizations or conferences. Create gameplay test plans for internal and external test groups. Provide feedback to designers and other colleagues regarding game design features. Balance and adjust gameplay experiences to ensure the critical and commercial success of the product. Write or supervise the writing of game text and dialogue. Solicit, obtain, and integrate feedback from design and technical staff into original game design. Provide feedback to production staff regarding technical game qualities or adherence to original design.

Education/Training Required: Postsecondary vocational training. **Education and Training Program:** Game and Interactive Media Design. **Knowledge/Courses:** No data available.

Personality Type: No data available. **Career Clusters:** 03 Arts, Audio/Video Technology, and Communications; 11 Information Technology. **Career Pathway:** 11.4 Programming and Software Development. **Other Jobs in This Pathway:** Architectural and Engineering Managers; Bioinformatics Scientists; Computer Hardware Engineers; Computer Numerically Controlled Machine Tool Programmers, Metal and Plastic.

Skills: No data available.

Work Environment: No data available.

Job Specialization: Web Administrators

Manage Web environment design, deployment, development, and maintenance activities. Perform testing and quality assurance of websites and Web applications. Back up or modify applications and related data to provide for disaster recovery. Determine sources of Web page or server problems and take action to correct such problems. Review or update Web page content or links in a timely manner, using appropriate tools. Monitor systems for intrusions or denial of service attacks, and report security breaches to appropriate personnel. Implement website security measures, such as firewalls or message encryption. Administer Internet/intranet infrastructure, including components such as Web, file transfer protocol (FTP), news, and mail servers. Collaborate with development teams to discuss, analyze, or resolve usability issues. Test backup or recovery plans regularly and resolve any problems. Monitor Web developments through continuing education, reading, or participation in professional conferences, workshops, or groups. Implement updates, upgrades, and patches in a timely manner to limit loss of service.

Education/Training Required: Bachelor's degree. **Education and Training Programs:** Computer and Information Systems Security/Information Assurance; Network and System Administration/Administrator; System, Networking, and LAN/WAN Management/Manager; Web/Multimedia Management and Webmaster Training. **Knowledge/Courses:** Computers and Electronics; Telecommunications; Design; Communications and Media; Sales and Marketing; Clerical.

Personality Type: Conventional-Enterprising-Investigative. **Career Cluster:** 11 Information Technology. **Career Pathway:** 11.4 Programming and Software Development. **Other Jobs in This Pathway:** Architectural and Engineering Managers; Bioinformatics Scientists; Computer Hardware Engineers; Computer Numerically Controlled Machine Tool Programmers, Metal and Plastic.

Skills: Programming; Operations Analysis; Troubleshooting; Science; Technology Design; Quality Control Analysis; Installation; Systems Evaluation.

Work Environment: Indoors; sitting; using hands; repetitive motions.

Computer Systems Analysts

* Annual Earnings: E $63,990, H $70,745, C $80,830, U $83,190, * $77,740
* Earnings Growth Potential: Medium (37.8%)
* Growth: U –16.3%, E 13.8%, H 28.5%, C 40.2%, * 20.3%
* Annual Job Openings: U 190, E 840, H 1,040, C 7,330, * 22,280
* Self-Employed: 5.7%

Detailed Fields with Greatest Employment: Management of Companies and Enterprises (7.6%); Insurance Carriers and Related Activities (7.2%); Educational Services, Public and Private (5.4%); Merchant Wholesalers, Durable Goods

*C=Computer Systems Design, E=Educational Services, G=Government, H=Health Care, R=Repair and Maintenance, U=Utilities, *=All Fields*

(4.6%); Credit Intermediation and Related Activities (4.1%)

Detailed Fields with Highest Growth (Projected Growth for This Job): Internet Service Providers, Web Search Portals, and Data Processing Services (66.1%); Professional, Scientific, and Technical Services (41.3%); Lessors of Nonfinancial Intangible Assets (Except Copyrighted Works) (35.0%); Waste Management and Remediation Services (33.3%); Ambulatory Health Care Services (31.4%)

Other Considerations for Job Outlook: Employment growth is projected as organizations continue to adopt the most efficient technologies and as the need for information security grows. Job prospects should be excellent.

Analyze science, engineering, business, and all other data-processing problems for application to electronic data-processing systems. Analyze user requirements, procedures, and problems to automate or improve existing systems and review computer system capabilities, workflow, and scheduling limitations. May analyze or recommend commercially available software. May supervise computer programmers. Provide staff and users with assistance solving computer related problems, such as malfunctions and program problems. Test, maintain, and monitor computer programs and systems, including coordinating the installation of computer programs and systems. Use object-oriented programming languages, as well as client and server applications development processes and multimedia and Internet technology. Confer with clients regarding the nature of the information processing or computation needs a computer program is to address. Coordinate and link the computer systems within an organization to increase compatibility and so information can be shared. Consult with management to ensure agreement on system principles. Expand or modify system to serve new purposes or improve work flow. Interview or survey workers, observe job performance, or perform the job to determine what information is processed and how it is processed. Determine computer software or hardware needed to set up or alter system.

Education/Training Required: Bachelor's degree. **Education and Training Programs:** Computer Systems Analysis/Analyst; Information Science/Studies. **Knowledge/Courses:** Computers and Electronics; Engineering and Technology; Mathematics; Clerical Practices; Telecommunications; English Language.

Personality Type: Investigative-Conventional-Realistic. **Career Cluster:** 11 Information Technology. **Career Pathways:** 11.2 Information Support Services; 11.3 Interactive Media; 11.4 Programming and Software Development. **Other Jobs in These Pathways:** Architectural and Engineering Managers; Bioinformatics Scientists; Computer and Information Systems Managers; Computer Hardware Engineers; Computer Numerically Controlled Machine Tool Programmers, Metal and Plastic; Computer Operators; Remote Sensing Scientists and Technologists; Remote Sensing Technicians.

Skills: Programming; Technology Design; Troubleshooting; Quality Control Analysis; Systems Evaluation; Operations Analysis; Systems Analysis; Mathematics.

Work Environment: Indoors; sitting; using hands; repetitive motions; noise.

Job Specialization: Informatics Nurse Specialists

Apply knowledge of nursing and informatics to assist in the design, development, and ongoing modification of computerized health-care

systems. May educate staff and assist in problem solving to promote the implementation of the health-care system. Design, develop, select, test, implement, and evaluate new or modified informatics solutions, data structures, and decision-support mechanisms to support patients, health-care professionals, and their information management and human-computer and human-technology interactions within health-care contexts. Disseminate information about nursing informatics science and practice to the profession, other health-care professions, nursing students, and the public. Translate nursing practice information between nurses and systems engineers, analysts, or designers using object-oriented models or other techniques. Plan, install, repair, or troubleshoot telehealth technology applications or systems in homes. Use informatics science to design or implement health information technology applications to resolve clinical or health-care administrative problems. Develop, implement, or evaluate health information technology applications, tools, processes, or structures to assist nurses with data management.

Education/Training Required: Master's degree. **Education and Training Programs:** Computer Systems Analysis/Analyst; Information Science/Studies. **Knowledge/Courses:** Medicine and Dentistry; Sociology and Anthropology; Education and Training; Engineering and Technology; Computers and Electronics; Clerical.

Personality Type: Social-Investigative. **Career Clusters:** 08 Health Science; 11 Information Technology. **Career Pathway:** 8.1 Therapeutic Services. **Other Jobs in This Pathway:** Clinical Psychologists; Community and Social Service Specialists, All Other; Counseling Psychologists; Dental Assistants; Dental Hygienists; Dentists, General; Health Technologists and Technicians, All Other; Healthcare Support Workers, All Other; Home Health Aides; Licensed Practical and Licensed Vocational Nurses; Low Vision Therapists, Orientation and Mobility Specialists, and Vision Rehabilitation Therapists; Massage Therapists; Medical and Clinical Laboratory Technicians; Medical and Health Services Managers; Medical Scientists, Except Epidemiologists; Medical Secretaries; Occupational Therapists; Pharmacists; Pharmacy Technicians; Radiologic Technologists; School Psychologists; Social and Human Service Assistants; Speech-Language Pathologists; Speech-Language Pathology Assistants; Substance Abuse and Behavioral Disorder Counselors; others.

Skills: Programming; Technology Design; Science; Systems Evaluation; Systems Analysis; Operations Analysis; Equipment Selection; Active Learning.

Work Environment: Indoors; sitting; using hands; repetitive motions.

Computer, Automated Teller, and Office Machine Repairers

- ❋ Annual Earnings: R $35,860, * $37,280
- ❋ Earnings Growth Potential: Medium (39.4%)
- ❋ Growth: R 0.0%, * –4.4%
- ❋ Annual Job Openings: R 330, * 2,630
- ❋ Self-Employed: 19.8%

Detailed Fields with Greatest Employment: Miscellaneous Store Retailers (7.6%); Merchant Wholesalers, Durable Goods (32.9%); Administrative and Support Services (3.7%); Wholesale Electronic Markets and Agents and Brokers (2.7%); Educational Services, Public and Private (2.6%)

Detailed Fields with Highest Growth (Projected Growth for This Job): Internet Service

*C=Computer Systems Design, E=Educational Services, G=Government, H=Health Care, R=Repair and Maintenance, U=Utilities, *=All Fields*

Providers, Web Search Portals, and Data Processing Services (42.2%); Ambulatory Health Care Services (40.0%); Professional, Scientific, and Technical Services (33.6%); Religious, Grantmaking, Civic, Professional, and Similar Organizations (20.0%); Wholesale Electronic Markets and Agents and Brokers (19.3%)

Other Considerations for Job Outlook: Projected employment growth will be constrained by the use of labor-saving technology. Job prospects are expected to be limited. Job seekers with certification, formal training, knowledge of electronics, and repair experience should have the best prospects.

Repair, maintain, or install computers, word-processing systems, automated teller machines, and electronic office machines such as duplicating and fax machines. Converse with customers in order to determine details of equipment problems. Reassemble machines after making repairs or replacing parts. Travel to customers' stores or offices to service machines or to provide emergency repair service. Reinstall software programs or adjust settings on existing software in order to fix machine malfunctions. Advise customers concerning equipment operation, maintenance, and programming. Assemble machines according to specifications, using hand tools, power tools, and measuring devices. Test new systems in order to ensure that they are in working order. Operate machines in order to test functioning of parts and mechanisms. Maintain records of equipment maintenance work and repairs. Install and configure new equipment, including operating software and peripheral equipment. Maintain parts inventories and order any additional parts needed for repairs. Update existing equipment, performing tasks such as installing updated circuit boards or additional memory.

Education/Training Required: Postsecondary vocational training. **Education and Training**

Programs: Business Machine Repair; Computer Installation and Repair Technology/Technician. **Knowledge/Courses:** Computers and Electronics; Telecommunications; Mechanical Devices; Customer and Personal Service; Engineering and Technology; Sales and Marketing.

Personality Type: Realistic-Conventional-Investigative. **Career Cluster:** 13 Manufacturing. **Career Pathway:** 13.3 Maintenance, Installation, and Repair. **Other Jobs in This Pathway:** Aircraft Mechanics and Service Technicians; Automotive Specialty Technicians; Biological Technicians; Civil Engineering Technicians; Electrical and Electronic Equipment Assemblers; Electrical and Electronics Repairers, Commercial and Industrial Equipment; Electrical Engineering Technicians; Electrical Engineering Technologists; Electromechanical Engineering Technologists; Electronics Engineering Technicians; Electronics Engineering Technologists; Engineering Technicians, Except Drafters, All Other; Fuel Cell Technicians; Helpers—Installation, Maintenance, and Repair Workers; Industrial Engineering Technologists; Industrial Machinery Mechanics; Installation, Maintenance, and Repair Workers, All Other; Manufacturing Engineering Technologists; Manufacturing Production Technicians; Mapping Technicians; Mechanical Engineering Technologists; Mobile Heavy Equipment Mechanics, Except Engines; Nanotechnology Engineering Technicians; Telecommunications Line Installers and Repairers; Tire Repairers and Changers; others.

Skills: Repairing; Installation; Equipment Maintenance; Troubleshooting; Equipment Selection; Operation and Control; Technology Design; Operation Monitoring.

Work Environment: Indoors; sitting; using hands; repetitive motions.

Customer Service Representatives

* ❋ Annual Earnings: R $30,020, E $30,070, H $30,703, * $30,460
* ❋ Earnings Growth Potential: Low (35.8%)
* ❋ Growth: R 14.7%, H 31.6%, E 44.7%, * 17.7%
* ❋ Annual Job Openings: R 540, E 600, H 5,610, * 110,840
* ❋ Self-Employed: 0.4%

Detailed Fields with Greatest Employment: Credit Intermediation and Related Activities (9.1%); Telecommunications (5.9%); Professional, Scientific, and Technical Services (5.2%); Merchant Wholesalers, Durable Goods (4.6%); Management of Companies and Enterprises (3.4%)

Detailed Fields with Highest Growth (Projected Growth for This Job): Internet Service Providers, Web Search Portals, and Data Processing Services (63.4%); Professional, Scientific, and Technical Services (50.3%); Lessors of Nonfinancial Intangible Assets (Except Copyrighted Works) (48.8%); Educational Services, Public and Private (44.7%); Other Information Services (43.1%)

Other Considerations for Job Outlook: Businesses are expected to place increasing emphasis on customer relations, resulting in increased employment for these workers. Prospects are expected to be good, particularly for job seekers who are fluent in more than one language.

Interact with customers to provide information in response to inquiries about products and services and to handle and resolve complaints. Confer with customers by telephone or in person to provide information about products and services, to take orders or cancel accounts, or to obtain details of complaints. Keep records of customer interactions and transactions, recording details of inquiries, complaints, and comments, as well as actions taken. Resolve customers' service or billing complaints by performing activities such as exchanging merchandise, refunding money, and adjusting bills. Check to ensure that appropriate changes were made to resolve customers' problems. Contact customers to respond to inquiries or to notify them of claim investigation results and any planned adjustments. Refer unresolved customer grievances to designated departments for further investigation. Determine charges for services requested, collect deposits or payments, or arrange for billing. Complete contract forms, prepare change of address records, and issue service discontinuance orders, using computers.

Education/Training Required: Moderate-term on-the-job training. **Education and Training Programs:** Customer Service Support/Call Center/Teleservice Operation; Receptionist Training. **Knowledge/Courses:** Clerical Practices; Customer and Personal Service; English Language.

Personality Type: Enterprising-Social-Conventional. **Career Cluster:** 04 Business, Management, and Administration. **Career Pathway:** 4.6 Administrative and Information Support. **Other Jobs in This Pathway:** Couriers and Messengers; Court Clerks; Court, Municipal, and License Clerks; Data Entry Keyers; Dispatchers, Except Police, Fire, and Ambulance; Executive Secretaries and Executive Administrative Assistants; File Clerks; Human Resources Assistants, Except Payroll and Timekeeping; Information and Record Clerks, All Other; Insurance Claims Clerks; Insurance Policy Processing Clerks; Interviewers, Except Eligibility and Loan; License Clerks; Mail Clerks and Mail Machine Operators, Except Postal Service; Office and Administrative Support Workers, All Other; Office Clerks, General; Order Clerks;

---

*C=Computer Systems Design, E=Educational Services, G=Government, H=Health Care, R=Repair and Maintenance, U=Utilities, *=All Fields*

Patient Representatives; Postal Service Mail Carriers; Postal Service Mail Sorters, Processors, and Processing Machine Operators; Receptionists and Information Clerks; Secretaries and Administrative Assistants, Except Legal, Medical, and Executive; Shipping, Receiving, and Traffic Clerks; Switchboard Operators, Including Answering Service; Word Processors and Typists; others.

Skills: Service Orientation; Persuasion; Negotiation; Active Listening; Speaking; Reading Comprehension; Programming.

Work Environment: Indoors; sitting; using hands; repetitive motions; noise.

Job Specialization: Patient Representatives

Assist patients in obtaining services, understanding policies and making health-care decisions. Explain policies, procedures, or services to patients using medical or administrative knowledge. Coordinate communication between patients, family members, medical staff, administrative staff, or regulatory agencies. Investigate and direct patient inquiries or complaints to appropriate medical staff members and follow up to ensure satisfactory resolution. Interview patients or their representatives to identify problems relating to care. Refer patients to appropriate health-care services or resources. Analyze patients' abilities to pay to determine charges on a sliding scale. Collect and report data on topics such as patient encounters and inter-institutional problems, making recommendations for change when appropriate. Develop and distribute newsletters, brochures, or other printed materials to share information with patients or medical staff. Teach patients to use home health-care equipment.

Education/Training Required: Bachelor's degree. **Education and Training Programs:** Customer Service Support/Call Center/Teleservice Operation; Receptionist Training. **Knowledge/ Courses:** No data available.

Personality Type: Social-Enterprising. **Career Cluster:** 04 Business, Management, and Administration. **Career Pathway:** 4.6 Administrative and Information Support. **Other Jobs in This Pathway:** Couriers and Messengers; Court Clerks; Court, Municipal, and License Clerks; Customer Service Representatives; Data Entry Keyers; Dispatchers, Except Police, Fire, and Ambulance; Executive Secretaries and Executive Administrative Assistants; File Clerks; Human Resources Assistants, Except Payroll and Timekeeping; Information and Record Clerks, All Other; Insurance Claims Clerks; Insurance Policy Processing Clerks; Interviewers, Except Eligibility and Loan; License Clerks; Mail Clerks and Mail Machine Operators, Except Postal Service; Office and Administrative Support Workers, All Other; Office Clerks, General; Order Clerks; Postal Service Mail Carriers; Postal Service Mail Sorters, Processors, and Processing Machine Operators; Receptionists and Information Clerks; Secretaries and Administrative Assistants, Except Legal, Medical, and Executive; Shipping, Receiving, and Traffic Clerks; Switchboard Operators, Including Answering Service; Word Processors and Typists; others.

Skills: No data available.

Work Environment: No data available.

Database Administrators

- ❋ Annual Earnings: H $67,736, C $82,820, * $73,490
- ❋ Earnings Growth Potential: High (43.4%)
- ❋ Growth: H 49.8%, C 57.3%, * 20.3%
- ❋ Annual Job Openings: H 170, C 960, * 4,440
- ❋ Self-Employed: 0.6%

Detailed Fields with Greatest Employment: Educational Services, Public and Private (8.7%);

Management of Companies and Enterprises (7.1%); Administrative and Support Services (5.1%); Insurance Carriers and Related Activities (5.0%); Merchant Wholesalers, Durable Goods (5.0%)

Detailed Fields with Highest Growth (Projected Growth for This Job): Hospitals, Public and Private (55.8%); Internet Service Providers, Web Search Portals, and Data Processing Services (51.1%); Professional, Scientific, and Technical Services (50.5%); Ambulatory Health Care Services (34.2%); Specialty Trade Contractors (33.3%)

Other Considerations for Job Outlook: Employment of these workers should grow as organizations increasingly collect and organize data. Job prospects are expected to be excellent.

Coordinate changes to computer databases; test and implement the databases, applying knowledge of database management systems. May plan, coordinate, and implement security measures to safeguard computer databases. Develop standards and guidelines to guide the use and acquisition of software and to protect vulnerable information. Modify existing databases and database management systems or direct programmers and analysts to make changes. Test programs or databases, correct errors, and make necessary modifications. Plan, coordinate, and implement security measures to safeguard information in computer files against accidental or unauthorized damage, modification, or disclosure. Approve, schedule, plan, and supervise the installation and testing of new products and improvements to computer systems such as the installation of new databases. Train users and answer questions. Establish and calculate optimum values for database parameters, using manuals and calculator. Specify users and user access levels for each segment of database. Develop data model describing data elements and

how they are used, following procedures and using pen, template, or computer software.

Education/Training Required: Bachelor's degree. **Education and Training Program:** Data Modeling/Warehousing and Database Administration. **Knowledge/Courses:** Computers and Electronics; Telecommunications; Clerical Practices; Communications and Media; Engineering and Technology; Mathematics.

Personality Type: Conventional-Investigative. **Career Cluster:** 11 Information Technology. **Career Pathways:** 4.4 Business Analysis; 11.2 Information Support Services; 11.4 Programming and Software Development. **Other Jobs in These Pathways:** Architectural and Engineering Managers; Bioinformatics Scientists; Computer and Information Systems Managers; Computer Hardware Engineers; Computer Numerically Controlled Machine Tool Programmers, Metal and Plastic; Computer Operators; Natural Sciences Managers; Operations Research Analysts; Remote Sensing Scientists and Technologists; Remote Sensing Technicians.

Skills: Programming; Technology Design; Troubleshooting; Systems Evaluation; Management of Financial Resources; Operations Analysis; Systems Analysis; Mathematics.

Work Environment: Indoors; sitting; using hands; repetitive motions; noise.

Dental Assistants

- ❋ Annual Earnings: H $33,381, * $33,470
- ❋ Earnings Growth Potential: Low (32.2%)
- ❋ Growth: H 36.7%, * 35.7%
- ❋ Annual Job Openings: H 22,490, * 16,100
- ❋ Self-Employed: 0.0%

*C=Computer Systems Design, E=Educational Services, G=Government, H=Health Care, R=Repair and Maintenance, U=Utilities, *=All Fields*

Detailed Fields with Greatest Employment: Ambulatory Health Care Services (95.1%); Federal Government (1.2%); Educational Services, Public and Private (1.0%); State and Local Government (0.9%); Administrative and Support Services (0.8%)

Detailed Fields with Highest Growth (Projected Growth for This Job): Professional, Scientific, and Technical Services (78.6%); Ambulatory Health Care Services (36.9%); Administrative and Support Services (23.5%); Miscellaneous Manufacturing (16.7%); Social Assistance (16.7%)

Other Considerations for Job Outlook: An aging population and increased emphasis on preventative dental care will create more demand for dental services, and dentists are expected to hire more assistants to perform routine tasks. Job prospects should be excellent.

Assist dentist, set up patient and equipment, and keep records. Prepare patient, sterilize and disinfect instruments, set up instrument trays, prepare materials, and assist dentist during dental procedures. Expose dental diagnostic X-rays. Record treatment information in patient records. Take and record medical and dental histories and vital signs of patients. Provide postoperative instructions prescribed by dentist. Assist dentist in management of medical and dental emergencies. Pour, trim, and polish study casts. Instruct patients in oral hygiene and plaque control programs. Make preliminary impressions for study casts and occlusal registrations for mounting study casts. Clean and polish removable appliances. Clean teeth, using dental instruments. Apply protective coating of fluoride to teeth. Fabricate temporary restorations and custom impressions from preliminary impressions. Schedule appointments, prepare bills, and receive payment for dental services; complete insurance forms; and maintain records, manually or using computer.

Education/Training Required: Moderate-term on-the-job training. **Education and Training Program:** Dental Assisting/Assistant. **Knowledge/Courses:** Medicine and Dentistry; Customer and Personal Service; Psychology; Sales and Marketing.

Personality Type: Conventional-Realistic-Social. **Career Cluster:** 08 Health Science. **Career Pathway:** 8.1 Therapeutic Services. **Other Jobs in This Pathway:** Clinical Psychologists; Community and Social Service Specialists, All Other; Counseling Psychologists; Dental Hygienists; Dentists, General; Health Technologists and Technicians, All Other; Healthcare Support Workers, All Other; Home Health Aides; Licensed Practical and Licensed Vocational Nurses; Low Vision Therapists, Orientation and Mobility Specialists, and Vision Rehabilitation Therapists; Massage Therapists; Medical and Clinical Laboratory Technicians; Medical and Health Services Managers; Medical Scientists, Except Epidemiologists; Medical Secretaries; Occupational Therapists; Ophthalmic Medical Technologists; Pharmacists; Pharmacy Technicians; Radiologic Technologists; School Psychologists; Social and Human Service Assistants; Speech-Language Pathologists; Speech-Language Pathology Assistants; Substance Abuse and Behavioral Disorder Counselors; others.

Skills: Repairing; Equipment Maintenance; Operation Monitoring; Equipment Selection; Service Orientation; Science; Operation and Control; Quality Control Analysis.

Work Environment: Indoors; standing; walking and running; using hands; bending or twisting the body; repetitive motions; contaminants; exposed to radiation; exposed to disease or infections; hazardous conditions.

Dental Hygienists

- ❋ Annual Earnings: H $68,460, * $68,250
- ❋ Earnings Growth Potential: Low (34.1%)
- ❋ Growth: H 36.6%, * 36.1%
- ❋ Annual Job Openings: H 13,990, * 9,840
- ❋ Self-Employed: 0.1%

Detailed Fields with Greatest Employment: Ambulatory Health Care Services (97.2%); Administrative and Support Services (1.1%); State and Local Government (0.5%); Educational Services, Public and Private (0.4%); Hospitals, Public and Private (0.4%)

Detailed Fields with Highest Growth (Projected Growth for This Job): Professional, Scientific, and Technical Services (84.2%); Ambulatory Health Care Services (36.8%); Social Assistance (22.2%); Administrative and Support Services (22.0%); Nursing and Residential Care Facilities (20.0%)

Other Considerations for Job Outlook: An increase in the number of older people and a growing emphasis on preventative dental care are expected to create jobs. To meet increased demand, dental hygienists will perform some services previously done by dentists. Job prospects should be favorable but will vary by geographic location.

Clean teeth and examine oral areas, head, and neck for signs of oral disease. May educate patients on oral hygiene, take and develop X-rays, or apply fluoride or sealants. Clean calcareous deposits, accretions, and stains from teeth and beneath margins of gums, using dental instruments. Feel and visually examine gums for sores and signs of disease. Chart conditions of decay and disease for diagnosis and treatment by dentist. Feel lymph nodes under patient's chin to detect swelling or tenderness that could indicate presence of oral cancer. Apply fluorides and other cavity-preventing agents to arrest dental decay. Examine gums, using probes, to locate periodontal recessed gums and signs of gum disease. Expose and develop X-ray film. Provide clinical services and health education to improve and maintain oral health of schoolchildren. Remove excess cement from coronal surfaces of teeth. Make impressions for study casts. Place, carve, and finish amalgam restorations. Administer local anesthetic agents. Conduct dental health clinics for community groups to augment services of dentist. Remove sutures and dressings.

Education/Training Required: Associate degree. **Education and Training Program:** Dental Hygiene/Hygienist. **Knowledge/Courses:** Medicine and Dentistry; Psychology; Therapy and Counseling; Chemistry; Biology; Sales and Marketing.

Personality Type: Social-Realistic-Conventional. **Career Cluster:** 08 Health Science. **Career Pathway:** 8.1 Therapeutic Services. **Other Jobs in This Pathway:** Clinical Psychologists; Community and Social Service Specialists, All Other; Counseling Psychologists; Dental Assistants; Dentists, General; Health Technologists and Technicians, All Other; Healthcare Support Workers, All Other; Home Health Aides; Licensed Practical and Licensed Vocational Nurses; Low Vision Therapists, Orientation and Mobility Specialists, and Vision Rehabilitation Therapists; Massage Therapists; Medical and Clinical Laboratory Technicians; Medical and Health Services Managers; Medical Scientists, Except Epidemiologists; Medical Secretaries; Occupational Therapists; Ophthalmic Medical Technologists; Pharmacists; Pharmacy Technicians; Radiologic Technologists; School Psychologists; Social and Human Service Assistants; Speech-Language Pathologists; Speech-Language Pathology Assistants; Substance Abuse and Behavioral Disorder Counselors; others.

D

*C=Computer Systems Design, E=Educational Services, G=Government, H=Health Care, R=Repair and Maintenance, U=Utilities, *=All Fields*

Skills: Science; Troubleshooting; Service Orientation; Writing; Instructing; Coordination; Operation Monitoring; Active Learning.

Work Environment: Indoors; sitting; using hands; bending or twisting the body; repetitive motions; noise; contaminants; exposed to radiation; exposed to disease or infections.

Detectives and Criminal Investigators

* Annual Earnings: G $68,630, * $68,820
* Earnings Growth Potential: High (43.5%)
* Growth: G 16.8%, * 16.6%
* Annual Job Openings: G 2,790, * 4,160
* Self-Employed: 1.1%

Detailed Fields with Greatest Employment: State and Local Government (60.1%); Federal Government (39.7%); Educational Services, Public and Private (0.3%)

Detailed Fields with Highest Growth (Projected Growth for This Job): Federal Government (29.8%); Educational Services, Public and Private (10.3%); State and Local Government, Excluding Education and Hospitals (8.2%)

Other Considerations for Job Outlook: Population growth is the main source of demand for police services. Overall, opportunities in local police departments should be favorable for qualified applicants.

Job Specialization: Criminal Investigators and Special Agents

Investigate alleged or suspected criminal violations of federal, state, or local laws to determine if evidence is sufficient to recommend prosecution. Record evidence and documents, using equipment such as cameras and photocopy machines. Obtain and verify evidence by interviewing and observing suspects and witnesses or by analyzing records. Examine records to locate links in chains of evidence or information. Prepare reports that detail investigation findings. Determine scope, timing, and direction of investigations. Collaborate with other offices and agencies to exchange information and coordinate activities. Testify before grand juries concerning criminal activity investigations. Analyze evidence in laboratories or in the field. Investigate organized crime, public corruption, financial crime, copyright infringement, civil rights violations, bank robbery, extortion, kidnapping, and other violations of federal or state statutes. Identify case issues and evidence needed, based on analysis of charges, complaints, or allegations of law violations. Obtain and use search and arrest warrants. Serve subpoenas or other official papers.

Education/Training Required: Work experience in a related occupation. **Education and Training Programs:** Criminal Justice/Police Science; Criminalistics and Criminal Science. **Knowledge/Courses:** Law and Government; Psychology; Geography; Public Safety and Security; Clerical Practices; Telecommunications.

Personality Type: Enterprising-Investigative. **Career Cluster:** 12 Law, Public Safety, Corrections, and Security. **Career Pathway:** 12.4 Law Enforcement Services. **Other Jobs in This Pathway:** Bailiffs; Correctional Officers and Jailers; First-Line Supervisors of Police and Detectives; Forensic Science Technicians; Immigration and Customs Inspectors; Intelligence Analysts; Police Detectives; Police Identification and Records Officers; Police Patrol Officers; Remote Sensing Scientists and Technologists; Sheriffs and Deputy Sheriffs.

Skills: Science; Persuasion; Negotiation; Active Listening; Speaking; Critical Thinking; Operation and Control; Writing.

Work Environment: More often outdoors than indoors; standing; noise; very hot or cold.

Job Specialization: Immigration and Customs Inspectors

Investigate and inspect persons, common carriers, goods, and merchandise arriving in or departing from the United States or moving between states to detect violations of immigration and customs laws and regulations. Examine immigration applications, visas, and passports and interview persons to determine eligibility for admission, residence, and travel in U.S. Detain persons found to be in violation of customs or immigration laws and arrange for legal action such as deportation. Locate and seize contraband or undeclared merchandise and vehicles, aircraft, or boats that contain such merchandise. Interpret and explain laws and regulations to travelers, prospective immigrants, shippers, and manufacturers. Inspect cargo, baggage, and personal articles entering or leaving U.S. for compliance with revenue laws and U.S. Customs Service regulations. Record and report job-related activities, findings, transactions, violations, discrepancies, and decisions. Institute civil and criminal prosecutions and cooperate with other law enforcement agencies in the investigation and prosecution of those in violation of immigration or customs laws. Testify regarding decisions at immigration appeals or in federal court.

Education/Training Required: Work experience in a related occupation. **Education and Training Programs:** Criminal Justice/Police Science; Criminalistics and Criminal Science. **Knowledge/Courses:** Public Safety and Security; Law and Government; Foreign Language; Geography; Customer and Personal Service; Philosophy and Theology.

Personality Type: Conventional-Enterprising-Realistic. **Career Cluster:** 12 Law, Public Safety,

Corrections, and Security. **Career Pathway:** 12.4 Law Enforcement Services. **Other Jobs in This Pathway:** Bailiffs; Correctional Officers and Jailers; Criminal Investigators and Special Agents; First-Line Supervisors of Police and Detectives; Forensic Science Technicians; Intelligence Analysts; Police Detectives; Police Identification and Records Officers; Police Patrol Officers; Remote Sensing Scientists and Technologists; Sheriffs and Deputy Sheriffs.

Skills: Active Listening; Persuasion; Negotiation; Operation and Control; Speaking; Social Perceptiveness; Time Management; Judgment and Decision Making.

Work Environment: More often outdoors than indoors; more often sitting than standing; using hands; repetitive motions; noise; very hot or cold; bright or inadequate lighting; contaminants; cramped work space; exposed to radiation; hazardous equipment.

Job Specialization: Intelligence Analysts

Gather, analyze, and evaluate information from a variety of sources, such as law enforcement databases, surveillance, intelligence networks, and Geographic Information Systems. Use data to anticipate and prevent organized crime activities, such as terrorism. Predict future gang, organized crime, or terrorist activity, using analyses of intelligence data. Study activities relating to narcotics, money laundering, gangs, auto theft rings, terrorism, or other national security threats. Design, use, or maintain databases and software applications, such as Geographic Information Systems (GIS) mapping and artificial intelligence tools. Establish criminal profiles to aid in connecting criminal organizations with their members. Evaluate records of communications, such as telephone calls, to plot activity and determine the size and location of criminal groups and members.

C=Computer Systems Design, E=Educational Services, G=Government, H=Health Care, R=Repair and Maintenance, U=Utilities, *=All Fields

Gather and evaluate information, using tools such as aerial photographs, radar equipment, or sensitive radio equipment. Gather intelligence information by field observation, confidential information sources, or public records. Gather, analyze, correlate, or evaluate information from a variety of resources, such as law enforcement databases.

Education/Training Required: Work experience plus degree. **Education and Training Programs:** Criminal Justice/Police Science; Criminalistics and Criminal Science. **Knowledge/Courses:** No data available.

Personality Type: No data available. **Career Cluster:** 12 Law, Public Safety, Corrections, and Security. **Career Pathway:** 12.4 Law Enforcement Services. **Other Jobs in This Pathway:** Bailiffs; Correctional Officers and Jailers; Criminal Investigators and Special Agents; First-Line Supervisors of Police and Detectives; Forensic Science Technicians; Immigration and Customs Inspectors; Police Detectives; Police Identification and Records Officers; Police Patrol Officers; Remote Sensing Scientists and Technologists; Sheriffs and Deputy Sheriffs.

Skills: No data available.

Work Environment: No data available.

Job Specialization: Police Detectives

Conduct investigations to prevent crimes or solve criminal cases. Provide testimony as witnesses in court. Secure deceased bodies and obtain evidence from them, preventing bystanders from tampering with bodies prior to medical examiners' arrival. Examine crime scenes to obtain clues and evidence such as loose hairs, fibers, clothing, or weapons. Obtain evidence from suspects. Record progress of investigations, maintain informational files on suspects, and submit reports to commanding officers or magistrates to authorize warrants. Check victims for signs of life such as breathing and pulse. Prepare charges or responses to charges, or information for court cases, according to formalized procedures. Obtain facts or statements from complainants, witnesses, and accused persons and record interviews, using recording devices. Prepare and serve search and arrest warrants. Note, mark, and photograph locations of objects found such as footprints, tire tracks, bullets, and bloodstains, and take measurements of each scene.

Education/Training Required: Work experience in a related occupation. **Education and Training Programs:** Criminal Justice/Police Science; Criminalistics and Criminal Science. **Knowledge/Courses:** Public Safety and Security; Law and Government; Psychology; Therapy and Counseling; Customer and Personal Service; Philosophy and Theology.

Personality Type: Enterprising-Investigative. **Career Cluster:** 12 Law, Public Safety, Corrections, and Security. **Career Pathway:** 12.4 Law Enforcement Services. **Other Jobs in This Pathway:** Bailiffs; Correctional Officers and Jailers; Criminal Investigators and Special Agents; First-Line Supervisors of Police and Detectives; Forensic Science Technicians; Immigration and Customs Inspectors; Intelligence Analysts; Police Identification and Records Officers; Police Patrol Officers; Remote Sensing Scientists and Technologists; Sheriffs and Deputy Sheriffs.

Skills: Science; Negotiation; Operation and Control; Social Perceptiveness; Operation Monitoring; Service Orientation; Active Learning; Systems Analysis.

Work Environment: More often outdoors than indoors; sitting; noise; very hot or cold; contaminants; exposed to disease or infections.

Job Specialization: Police Identification and Records Officers

Collect evidence at crime scene, classify and identify fingerprints, and photograph evidence

for use in criminal and civil cases. Photograph crime or accident scenes for evidence records. Analyze and process evidence at crime scenes and in the laboratory, wearing protective equipment and using powders and chemicals. Look for trace evidence, such as fingerprints, hairs, fibers, or shoe impressions, using alternative light sources when necessary. Dust selected areas of crime scene and lift latent fingerprints, adhering to proper preservation procedures. Testify in court and present evidence. Package, store, and retrieve evidence. Serve as technical advisor and coordinate with other law enforcement workers to exchange information on crime scene collection activities. Perform emergency work during off-hours. Submit evidence to supervisors. Process film and prints from crime or accident scenes. Identify, classify, and file fingerprints, using systems such as the Henry Classification system.

Education/Training Required: Work experience in a related occupation. **Education and Training Programs:** Criminal Justice/Police Science; Criminalistics and Criminal Science. **Knowledge/ Courses:** Public Safety and Security; Law and Government; Chemistry; Customer and Personal Service; Clerical Practices; Telecommunications.

Personality Type: Conventional-Realistic-Investigative. **Career Cluster:** 12 Law, Public Safety, Corrections, and Security. **Career Pathway:** 12.4 Law Enforcement Services. **Other Jobs in This Pathway:** Bailiffs; Correctional Officers and Jailers; Criminal Investigators and Special Agents; First-Line Supervisors of Police and Detectives; Forensic Science Technicians; Immigration and Customs Inspectors; Intelligence Analysts; Police Detectives; Police Patrol Officers; Remote Sensing Scientists and Technologists; Sheriffs and Deputy Sheriffs.

Skills: Operation and Control; Speaking; Operation Monitoring; Negotiation; Critical Thinking; Active Listening; Persuasion; Technology Design.

Work Environment: Indoors; sitting; using hands; noise; contaminants; exposed to disease or infections; hazardous conditions.

Diagnostic Medical Sonographers

- ❋ Annual Earnings: H $64,305, * $64,380
- ❋ Earnings Growth Potential: Low (30.3%)
- ❋ Growth: H 18.3%, * 18.3%
- ❋ Annual Job Openings: H 2,310, * 1,650
- ❋ Self-Employed: 0.8%

Detailed Fields with Greatest Employment: Hospitals, Public and Private (59.9%); Ambulatory Health Care Services (36.9%); Educational Services, Public and Private (1.5%); Administrative and Support Services (0.8%); Professional, Scientific, and Technical Services (0.2%)

Detailed Fields with Highest Growth (Projected Growth for This Job): Professional, Scientific, and Technical Services (81.8%); Ambulatory Health Care Services (35.6%); Administrative and Support Services (24.4%); Educational Services, Public and Private (14.5%); Hospitals, Public and Private (7.7%)

Other Considerations for Job Outlook: The aging population's need for safe and cost-effective diagnostic imaging treatment is expected to spur employment growth. Prospects should be good for job seekers who have multiple professional credentials.

Produce ultrasonic recordings of internal organs for use by physicians. Provide sonograms and oral or written summaries of technical findings to physicians for use in medical diagnosis. Decide which images to include, looking for differences between healthy and pathological areas. Operate ultrasound equipment to produce and record images of the motion, shape, and composition

C=Computer Systems Design, E=Educational Services, G=Government, H=Health Care, R=Repair and Maintenance, U=Utilities, *=All Fields

150 Best Jobs for a Secure Future © JIST Works

195

of blood, organs, tissues, and bodily masses such as fluid accumulations. Select appropriate equipment settings and adjust patient positions to obtain the best sites and angles. Observe screens during scans to ensure that images produced are satisfactory for diagnostic purposes, making adjustments to equipment as required. Prepare patients for exams by explaining procedures, transferring them to ultrasound tables, scrubbing skin and applying gel, and positioning them properly. Observe and care for patients throughout examinations to ensure their safety and comfort. Obtain and record accurate patient histories, including prior test results and information from physical examinations.

Education/Training Required: Associate degree. **Education and Training Programs:** Allied Health Diagnostic, Intervention, and Treatment Professions, Other; Diagnostic Medical Sonography/Sonographer and Ultrasound Technician Training. **Knowledge/Courses:** Medicine and Dentistry; Physics; Biology; Customer and Personal Service; Psychology; Clerical.

Personality Type: Investigative-Social-Realistic. **Career Cluster:** 08 Health Science. **Career Pathways:** 8.1 Therapeutic Services; 8.2 Diagnostics Services. **Other Jobs in These Pathways:** Clinical Psychologists; Counseling Psychologists; Cytogenetic Technologists; Cytotechnologists; Dental Assistants; Dental Hygienists; Dentists, General; Emergency Medical Technicians and Paramedics; Endoscopy Technicians; Healthcare Support Workers, All Other; Histotechnologists and Histologic Technicians; Home Health Aides; Licensed Practical and Licensed Vocational Nurses; Massage Therapists; Medical and Clinical Laboratory Technicians; Medical and Clinical Laboratory Technologists; Medical and Health Services Managers; Medical Assistants; Medical Secretaries; Pharmacists; Pharmacy Technicians; Radiologic Technologists; School Psychologists; Social

and Human Service Assistants; Speech-Language Pathology Assistants; others.

Skills: Science; Equipment Maintenance; Equipment Selection; Repairing; Operation and Control; Troubleshooting; Operation Monitoring; Quality Control Analysis.

Work Environment: Indoors; more often sitting than standing; using hands; bending or twisting the body; repetitive motions; contaminants; exposed to disease or infections.

Dispatchers, Except Police, Fire, and Ambulance

- ❋ Annual Earnings: R $31,680, * $34,560
- ❋ Earnings Growth Potential: Medium (39.1%)
- ❋ Growth: R –4.5%, * –2.6%
- ❋ Annual Job Openings: R 50, * 4,030
- ❋ Self-Employed: 2.0%

Detailed Fields with Greatest Employment: Administrative and Support Services (8.6%); Transit and Ground Passenger Transportation (8.1%); Specialty Trade Contractors (7.9%); Support Activities for Transportation (7.5%); State and Local Government (7.4%)

Detailed Fields with Highest Growth (Projected Growth for This Job): Professional, Scientific, and Technical Services (48.5%); Wholesale Electronic Markets and Agents and Brokers (15.8%); Specialty Trade Contractors (15.2%); Waste Management and Remediation Services (14.9%); Social Assistance (11.5%)

Other Considerations for Job Outlook: Increasing worker productivity is expected to cause a decline in employment, but this decline may be offset, somewhat, by population growth. Opportunities should be favorable.

Schedule and dispatch workers, work crews, equipment, or service vehicles for conveyance of materials, freight, or passengers or for normal installation, service, or emergency repairs rendered outside the place of business. Duties may include using radio, telephone, or computer to transmit assignments and compiling statistics and reports on work progress. Schedule and dispatch workers, work crews, equipment, or service vehicles to appropriate locations according to customer requests, specifications, or needs, using radios or telephones. Arrange for necessary repairs to restore service and schedules. Relay work orders, messages, and information to or from work crews, supervisors, and field inspectors, using telephones or two-way radios. Confer with customers or supervising personnel to address questions, problems, and requests for service or equipment. Prepare daily work and run schedules. Receive or prepare work orders. Oversee all communications within specifically assigned territories. Monitor personnel or equipment locations and utilization to coordinate service and schedules. Record and maintain files and records of customer requests, work or services performed, charges, expenses, inventory, and other dispatch information.

Education/Training Required: Moderate-term on-the-job training. **Education and Training Programs:** No related CIP programs; this job is learned through moderate-term on-the-job training. **Knowledge/Courses:** Transportation; Geography; Customer and Personal Service; Sales and Marketing; Administration and Management; Public Safety and Security.

Personality Type: Conventional-Realistic-Enterprising. **Career Cluster:** 04 Business, Management, and Administration. **Career Pathway:** 4.6 Administrative and Information Support. **Other Jobs in This Pathway:** Couriers and Messengers; Court Clerks; Court, Municipal, and License Clerks; Customer Service Representatives; Data

Entry Keyers; Executive Secretaries and Executive Administrative Assistants; File Clerks; Human Resources Assistants, Except Payroll and Timekeeping; Information and Record Clerks, All Other; Insurance Claims Clerks; Insurance Policy Processing Clerks; Interviewers, Except Eligibility and Loan; License Clerks; Mail Clerks and Mail Machine Operators, Except Postal Service; Office and Administrative Support Workers, All Other; Office Clerks, General; Order Clerks; Patient Representatives; Postal Service Mail Carriers; Postal Service Mail Sorters, Processors, and Processing Machine Operators; Receptionists and Information Clerks; Secretaries and Administrative Assistants, Except Legal, Medical, and Executive; Shipping, Receiving, and Traffic Clerks; Switchboard Operators, Including Answering Service; Word Processors and Typists; others.

Skills: Negotiation; Persuasion; Coordination; Active Listening; Speaking; Time Management; Service Orientation; Social Perceptiveness.

Work Environment: Indoors; sitting; repetitive motions; contaminants.

Education Administrators, All Other

- ❋ Annual Earnings: E $72,330, * $75,690
- ❋ Earnings Growth Potential: High (44.6%)
- ❋ Growth: E 31.7%, * 23.9%
- ❋ Annual Job Openings: E 190, * 1,690
- ❋ Self-Employed: 4.4%

Detailed Fields with Greatest Employment: Educational Services, Public and Private (66.4%); Religious, Grantmaking, Civic, Professional, and Similar Organizations (3.6%); Social Assistance (2.8%); Hospitals, Public and Private (2.2%); Federal Government (13.8%)

*C=Computer Systems Design, E=Educational Services, G=Government, H=Health Care, R=Repair and Maintenance, U=Utilities, *=All Fields*

Detailed Fields with Highest Growth (Projected Growth for This Job): Ambulatory Health Care Services (37.5%); Educational Services, Public and Private (31.7%); Administrative and Support Services (27.3%); Professional, Scientific, and Technical Services (26.3%); Museums, Historical Sites, and Similar Institutions (25.0%)

Other Considerations for Job Outlook: Increasing student enrollments are expected to drive employment growth for these workers. Prospects are expected to be good.

This occupation includes all education administrators not listed separately. No task data available.

Education/Training Required: Work experience plus degree. **Education and Training Program:** Adult and Continuing Education Administration. **Knowledge/Courses:** No data available.

Personality Type: No data available. **Career Cluster:** 05 Education and Training. **Career Pathway:** 5.1 Administration and Administrative Support. **Other Jobs in This Pathway:** Coaches and Scouts; Distance Learning Coordinators; Education Administrators, Elementary and Secondary School; Education Administrators, Postsecondary; Education Administrators, Preschool and Childcare Center/Program; Fitness and Wellness Coordinators; Fitness Trainers and Aerobics Instructors; Instructional Coordinators; Instructional Designers and Technologists; Umpires, Referees, and Other Sports Officials.

Skills: No data available.

Work Environment: No data available.

Job Specialization: Distance Learning Coordinators

Coordinate day-to-day operations of distance learning programs and schedule courses. Write and submit grant applications or proposals to secure funding for distance learning programs. Review distance learning content to ensure compliance with copyright, licensing, or other requirements. Conduct inventories of distance learning equipment, summarizing equipment usage data. Communicate technical or marketing information about distance learning via podcasts, webinars, and other technologies. Train instructors and distance learning staff in the use or support of distance learning applications, such as course management software. Troubleshoot and resolve problems with distance learning equipment or applications. Supervise distance learning support staff. Purchase equipment or services in accordance with distance learning plans and budget constraints. Select, direct, and monitor the work of vendors that provide products or services for distance learning programs. Prepare and manage distance learning program budgets.

Education/Training Required: Work experience plus degree. **Education and Training Program:** Adult and Continuing Education Administration. **Knowledge/Courses:** No data available.

Personality Type: No data available. **Career Cluster:** 05 Education and Training. **Career Pathway:** 5.1 Administration and Administrative Support. **Other Jobs in This Pathway:** Coaches and Scouts; Education Administrators, All Other; Education Administrators, Elementary and Secondary School; Education Administrators, Postsecondary; Education Administrators, Preschool and Childcare Center/Program; Fitness and Wellness Coordinators; Fitness Trainers and Aerobics Instructors; Instructional Coordinators; Instructional Designers and Technologists; Umpires, Referees, and Other Sports Officials.

Skills: No data available.

Work Environment: No data available.

Job Specialization: Fitness and Wellness Coordinators

Manage fitness and wellness programs and services. Direct and train staff of health educators, fitness instructors, or recreation workers. Track attendance, participation, or performance data related to wellness events. Provide individual support or counseling in general wellness or nutrition. Maintain or arrange for maintenance of fitness equipment and facilities. Develop marketing campaigns to promote a healthy lifestyle or participation in fitness and wellness programs. Conduct surveys to determine interest in, or satisfaction with, wellness and fitness programs, events, or services. Teach fitness classes to improve strength, flexibility, cardiovascular conditioning, or general fitness of participants. Select and supervise contractors, such as event hosts or health, fitness, and wellness practitioners. Respond to customer, public, or media requests for information about wellness programs and services. Recommend or approve new program or service offerings to promote wellness and fitness, produce revenues, and minimize costs. Prepare and implement budgets and strategic, operational, purchasing, and maintenance plans.

Education/Training Required: Bachelor's degree. **Education and Training Program:** Sport and Fitness Administration/Management. **Knowledge/Courses:** No data available.

Personality Type: No data available. **Career Cluster:** 05 Education and Training. **Career Pathway:** 5.1 Administration and Administrative Support. **Other Jobs in This Pathway:** Coaches and Scouts; Distance Learning Coordinators; Education Administrators, All Other; Education Administrators, Elementary and Secondary School; Education Administrators, Postsecondary; Education Administrators, Preschool and Childcare Center/Program; Fitness Trainers and Aerobics Instructors; Instructional Coordinators; Instructional Designers and Technologists; Umpires, Referees, and Other Sports Officials.

Skills: No data available.

Work Environment: No data available.

Education Administrators, Elementary and Secondary School

* Annual Earnings: E $87,020, * $86,970
* Earnings Growth Potential: Low (33.0%)
* Growth: E 8.7%, * 8.6%
* Annual Job Openings: E 44,620, * 8,880
* Self-Employed: 4.7%

Detailed Fields with Greatest Employment: Educational Services, Public and Private (97.6%); Religious, Grantmaking, Civic, Professional, and Similar Organizations (1.0%); State and Local Government (0.9%); Social Assistance (0.2%); Nursing and Residential Care Facilities (0.1%)

Detailed Fields with Highest Growth (Projected Growth for This Job): Professional, Scientific, and Technical Services (75.0%); Social Assistance (15.1%); Religious, Grantmaking, Civic, Professional, and Similar Organizations (13.9%); Nursing and Residential Care Facilities (12.5%); State and Local Government, Excluding Education and Hospitals (8.7%)

Other Considerations for Job Outlook: Increasing student enrollments are expected to drive employment growth for these workers. Prospects are expected to be good.

Plan, direct, or coordinate the academic, clerical, or auxiliary activities of public or private elementary or secondary-level schools. Review

*C=Computer Systems Design, E=Educational Services, G=Government, H=Health Care, R=Repair and Maintenance, U=Utilities, *=All Fields*

and approve new programs or recommend modifications to existing programs, submitting program proposals for school board approval as necessary. Prepare, maintain, or oversee the preparation and maintenance of attendance, activity, planning, or personnel reports and records. Confer with parents and staff to discuss educational activities, policies, and student behavioral or learning problems. Prepare and submit budget requests and recommendations or grant proposals to solicit program funding. Direct and coordinate school maintenance services and the use of school facilities. Counsel and provide guidance to students regarding personal, academic, vocational, or behavioral issues. Organize and direct committees of specialists, volunteers, and staff to provide technical and advisory assistance for programs. Teach classes or courses to students. Advocate for new schools to be built or for existing facilities to be repaired or remodeled.

Education/Training Required: Work experience plus degree. **Education and Training Programs:** Educational Administration and Supervision, Other; Educational Leadership and Administration, General; Educational, Instructional, and Curriculum Supervision; Elementary and Middle School Administration/Principalship; Secondary School Administration/Principalship. **Knowledge/Courses:** Therapy and Counseling; Education and Training; Philosophy and Theology; Sociology and Anthropology; Personnel and Human Resources; History and Archeology.

Personality Type: Enterprising-Social-Conventional. **Career Cluster:** 05 Education and Training. **Career Pathway:** 5.1 Administration and Administrative Support. **Other Jobs in This Pathway:** Coaches and Scouts; Distance Learning Coordinators; Education Administrators, All Other; Education Administrators, Postsecondary; Education Administrators, Preschool and Childcare Center/Program; Fitness and Wellness Coordinators; Fitness Trainers and Aerobics Instructors; Instructional Coordinators; Instructional Designers and Technologists; Umpires, Referees, and Other Sports Officials.

Skills: Management of Financial Resources; Management of Material Resources; Learning Strategies; Management of Personnel Resources; Systems Evaluation; Systems Analysis; Persuasion; Negotiation.

Work Environment: Indoors; sitting; noise.

Education Administrators, Postsecondary

- ✳ Annual Earnings: E $83,560, * $83,710
- ✳ Earnings Growth Potential: High (43.7%)
- ✳ Growth: E 2.0%, * 2.3%
- ✳ Annual Job Openings: E 1,230, * 4,010
- ✳ Self-Employed: 3.9%

Detailed Fields with Greatest Employment: Educational Services, Public and Private (98.7%); Hospitals, Public and Private (0.3%); Administrative and Support Services (0.2%); Management of Companies and Enterprises (0.2%); Religious, Grantmaking, Civic, Professional, and Similar Organizations (0.2%)

Detailed Fields with Highest Growth (Projected Growth for This Job): Administrative and Support Services (16.7%); Religious, Grantmaking, Civic, Professional, and Similar Organizations (11.5%); Hospitals, Public and Private (7.7%); Management of Companies and Enterprises (5.0%); Educational Services, Public and Private (2.0%)

Other Considerations for Job Outlook: Increasing student enrollments are expected to drive employment growth for these workers. Prospects are expected to be good.

Plan, direct, or coordinate research, instructional, student administration and services, and other educational activities at postsecondary institutions, including universities, colleges, and junior and community colleges. Recruit, hire, train, and terminate departmental personnel. Plan, administer, and control budgets; maintain financial records; and produce financial reports. Represent institutions at community and campus events, in meetings with other institution personnel, and during accreditation processes. Participate in faculty and college committee activities. Provide assistance to faculty and staff in duties such as teaching classes, conducting orientation programs, issuing transcripts, and scheduling events. Establish operational policies and procedures and make any necessary modifications, based on analysis of operations, demographics, and other research information. Confer with other academic staff to explain and formulate admission requirements and course credit policies. Appoint individuals to faculty positions and evaluate their performance. Direct activities of administrative departments such as admissions, registration, and career services.

Education/Training Required: Work experience plus degree. **Education and Training Programs:** Community College Education; Educational Administration and Supervision, Other; Educational Leadership and Administration, General; Educational, Instructional, and Curriculum Supervision; Higher Education/Higher Education Administration. **Knowledge/Courses:** Therapy and Counseling; Sociology and Anthropology; Psychology; Personnel and Human Resources; Education and Training; Philosophy and Theology.

Personality Type: Enterprising-Conventional-Social. **Career Cluster:** 05 Education and Training. **Career Pathway:** 5.1 Administration and Administrative Support. **Other Jobs in This Pathway:** Coaches and Scouts; Distance Learning

Coordinators; Education Administrators, All Other; Education Administrators, Elementary and Secondary School; Education Administrators, Preschool and Childcare Center/Program; Fitness and Wellness Coordinators; Fitness Trainers and Aerobics Instructors; Instructional Coordinators; Instructional Designers and Technologists; Umpires, Referees, and Other Sports Officials.

Skills: Management of Material Resources; Management of Financial Resources; Management of Personnel Resources; Negotiation; Systems Evaluation; Systems Analysis; Instructing; Time Management.

Work Environment: Indoors; sitting.

Educational, Guidance, School, and Vocational Counselors

- ✸ Annual Earnings: E $55,860, * $53,380
- ✸ Earnings Growth Potential: Medium (40.7%)
- ✸ Growth: E 14.0%, * 14.0%
- ✸ Annual Job Openings: E 5,150, * 9,440
- ✸ Self-Employed: 5.8%

Detailed Fields with Greatest Employment: Educational Services, Public and Private (78.7%); State and Local Government (4.0%); Nursing and Residential Care Facilities (2.2%); Social Assistance (10.8%); Administrative and Support Services (1.2%)

Detailed Fields with Highest Growth (Projected Growth for This Job): Professional, Scientific, and Technical Services (33.3%); Administrative and Support Services (23.9%); Social Assistance (22.2%); Ambulatory Health Care Services (18.9%); Miscellaneous Store Retailers (14.3%)

Other Considerations for Job Outlook: Increasing demand for services provided by counselors

---

*C=Computer Systems Design, E=Educational Services, G=Government, H=Health Care, R=Repair and Maintenance, U=Utilities, *=All Fields*

E

is expected to result in employment growth. But growth will vary by specialty and will be faster for mental health, substance abuse and behavioral disorder, and rehabilitation counselors than for counselors of other specialties. Opportunities should be favorable, particularly in rural areas.

Counsel individuals and provide group educational and vocational guidance services. Counsel students regarding educational issues such as course and program selection, class scheduling, school adjustment, truancy, study habits, and career planning. Counsel individuals to help them understand and overcome personal, social, or behavioral problems affecting their educational or vocational situations. Maintain accurate and complete student records as required by laws, district policies, and administrative regulations. Confer with parents or guardians, teachers, other counselors, and administrators to resolve students' behavioral, academic, and other problems. Provide crisis intervention to students when difficult situations occur at schools. Identify cases involving domestic abuse or other family problems affecting students' development. Meet with parents and guardians to discuss their children's progress and to determine their priorities for their children and their resource needs.

Education/Training Required: Master's degree. **Education and Training Programs:** College Student Counseling and Personnel Services; Counselor Education/School Counseling and Guidance Services. **Knowledge/Courses:** Therapy and Counseling; Psychology; Sociology and Anthropology; Education and Training; Philosophy and Theology; Clerical.

Personality Type: Social. **Career Cluster:** 05 Education and Training. **Career Pathway:** 5.2 Professional Support Services. **Other Jobs in This Pathway:** Librarians; Library Assistants, Clerical Practices; Library Technicians.

Skills: Social Perceptiveness; Service Orientation; Learning Strategies; Writing; Systems Evaluation; Active Listening; Systems Analysis; Persuasion.

Work Environment: Indoors; sitting.

Electric Motor, Power Tool, and Related Repairers

- ❋ Annual Earnings: R $34,920, * $36,170
- ❋ Earnings Growth Potential: Medium (40.1%)
- ❋ Growth: R 5.8%, * 5.1%
- ❋ Annual Job Openings: R 340, * 940
- ❋ Self-Employed: 2.1%

Detailed Fields with Greatest Employment: Building Material and Garden Equipment and Supplies Dealers (5.0%); Repair and Maintenance (34.4%); Amusement, Gambling, and Recreation Industries (3.0%); Electrical Equipment, Appliance, and Component Manufacturing (3.0%); Merchant Wholesalers, Durable Goods (27.6%)

Detailed Fields with Highest Growth (Projected Growth for This Job): Wholesale Electronic Markets and Agents and Brokers (31.8%); Administrative and Support Services (26.3%); Amusement, Gambling, and Recreation Industries (11.4%); Warehousing and Storage (11.1%); Mining (Except Oil and Gas) (9.1%)

Other Considerations for Job Outlook: Employment growth for these workers is expected to be limited as improvements in the quality of electrical and electronic equipment result in less need for repairs. The best prospects are expected for job seekers who have certification, an associate degree, and relevant experience.

Repair, maintain, or install electric motors, wiring, or switches. Measure velocity, horsepower, revolutions per minute (rpm), amperage, circuitry, and voltage of units or parts to diagnose problems, using ammeters, voltmeters, wattmeters, and other testing devices. Record repairs required, parts used, and labor time. Reassemble repaired electric motors to specified requirements and ratings, using hand tools and electrical meters. Maintain stocks of parts. Use hand tools and power tools to repair and rebuild defective mechanical parts in electric motors, generators, and related equipment. Rewire electrical systems and repair or replace electrical accessories. Inspect electrical connections, wiring, relays, charging resistance boxes, and storage batteries, following wiring diagrams. Read service guides to find information needed to perform repairs. Inspect and test equipment to locate damage or worn parts and diagnose malfunctions or read work orders or schematic drawings to determine required repairs.

Education/Training Required: Postsecondary vocational training. **Education and Training Program:** Electrical/Electronics Equipment Installation and Repair, General. **Knowledge/Courses:** Mechanical Devices; Engineering and Technology; Design; Production and Processing.

Personality Type: Realistic-Conventional. **Career Cluster:** 13 Manufacturing. **Career Pathway:** 13.3 Maintenance, Installation, and Repair. **Other Jobs in This Pathway:** Aircraft Mechanics and Service Technicians; Automotive Specialty Technicians; Biological Technicians; Civil Engineering Technicians; Computer, Automated Teller, and Office Machine Repairers; Electrical and Electronic Equipment Assemblers; Electrical and Electronics Repairers, Commercial and Industrial Equipment; Electrical Engineering Technicians; Electrical Engineering Technologists; Electromechanical Engineering Technologists; Electronics Engineering Technicians; Electronics Engineering Technologists; Engineering Technicians, Except Drafters, All Other; Fuel Cell Technicians; Helpers—Installation, Maintenance, and

Repair Workers; Industrial Engineering Technologists; Industrial Machinery Mechanics; Installation, Maintenance, and Repair Workers, All Other; Manufacturing Engineering Technologists; Manufacturing Production Technicians; Mapping Technicians; Mechanical Engineering Technologists; Mobile Heavy Equipment Mechanics, Except Engines; Telecommunications Line Installers and Repairers; Tire Repairers and Changers; others.

Skills: Repairing; Equipment Maintenance; Installation; Troubleshooting; Equipment Selection; Quality Control Analysis; Operation and Control; Operation Monitoring.

Work Environment: Outdoors; standing; walking and running; using hands; bending or twisting the body; noise; very hot or cold; bright or inadequate lighting; contaminants; cramped work space; hazardous conditions; hazardous equipment; minor burns, cuts, bites, or stings.

Electrical and Electronics Repairers, Commercial and Industrial Equipment

- ❋ Annual Earnings: R $45,110, * $51,820
- ❋ Earnings Growth Potential: Medium (37.2%)
- ❋ Growth: R 8.5%, * 3.8%
- ❋ Annual Job Openings: R 150, * 1,640
- ❋ Self-Employed: 0.0%

Detailed Fields with Greatest Employment: Specialty Trade Contractors (9.3%); Repair and Maintenance (8.2%); Chemical Manufacturing (5.3%); Telecommunications (4.7%); Machinery Manufacturing (3.3%)

Detailed Fields with Highest Growth (Projected Growth for This Job): Professional, Scientific, and

*C=Computer Systems Design, E=Educational Services, G=Government, H=Health Care, R=Repair and Maintenance, U=Utilities, *=All Fields*

E

Technical Services (32.1%); Specialty Trade Contractors (31.1%); Wholesale Electronic Markets and Agents and Brokers (30.7%); Administrative and Support Services (28.6%); Miscellaneous Manufacturing (20.8%)

Other Considerations for Job Outlook: Employment growth for these workers is expected to be limited as improvements in the quality of electrical and electronic equipment result in less need for repairs. The best prospects are expected for job seekers who have certification, an associate degree, and relevant experience.

Repair, test, adjust, or install electronic equipment, such as industrial controls, transmitters, and antennas. Perform scheduled preventive maintenance tasks, such as checking, cleaning, and repairing equipment, to detect and prevent problems. Examine work orders and converse with equipment operators to detect equipment problems and to ascertain whether mechanical or human errors contributed to the problems. Operate equipment to demonstrate proper use and to analyze malfunctions. Set up and test industrial equipment to ensure that it functions properly. Test faulty equipment to diagnose malfunctions, using test equipment and software and applying knowledge of the functional operation of electronic units and systems. Repair and adjust equipment, machines, and defective components, replacing worn parts such as gaskets and seals in watertight electrical equipment. Calibrate testing instruments and installed or repaired equipment to prescribed specifications. Advise management regarding customer satisfaction, product performance, and suggestions for product improvements.

Education/Training Required: Postsecondary vocational training. **Education and Training Programs:** Computer Installation and Repair Technology/Technician; Industrial Electronics Technology/Technician. **Knowledge/Courses:** Mechanical Devices; Computers and Electronics; Engineering and Technology; Design; Telecommunications; Physics.

Personality Type: Realistic-Investigative-Conventional. **Career Cluster:** 13 Manufacturing. **Career Pathway:** 13.3 Maintenance, Installation, and Repair. **Other Jobs in This Pathway:** Aircraft Mechanics and Service Technicians; Automotive Specialty Technicians; Biological Technicians; Civil Engineering Technicians; Computer, Automated Teller, and Office Machine Repairers; Electrical and Electronic Equipment Assemblers; Electrical Engineering Technicians; Electrical Engineering Technologists; Electromechanical Engineering Technologists; Electronics Engineering Technicians; Electronics Engineering Technologists; Engineering Technicians, Except Drafters, All Other; Fuel Cell Technicians; Helpers—Installation, Maintenance, and Repair Workers; Industrial Engineering Technologists; Industrial Machinery Mechanics; Installation, Maintenance, and Repair Workers, All Other; Manufacturing Engineering Technologists; Manufacturing Production Technicians; Mapping Technicians; Mechanical Engineering Technologists; Mobile Heavy Equipment Mechanics, Except Engines; Nanotechnology Engineering Technicians; Telecommunications Line Installers and Repairers; Tire Repairers and Changers; others.

Skills: Installation; Repairing; Equipment Maintenance; Equipment Selection; Troubleshooting; Quality Control Analysis; Technology Design; Operation Monitoring.

Work Environment: More often indoors than outdoors; standing; using hands; noise; very hot or cold; contaminants; cramped work space; hazardous conditions; hazardous equipment; minor burns, cuts, bites, or stings.

Electrical and Electronics Repairers, Powerhouse, Substation, and Relay

- ❋ Annual Earnings: U $66,270, * $65,230
- ❋ Earnings Growth Potential: Low (30.9%)
- ❋ Growth: U 10.3%, * 11.5%
- ❋ Annual Job Openings: U 410, * 670
- ❋ Self-Employed: 0.0%

Detailed Fields with Greatest Employment: Utilities (77.8%); State and Local Government (10.6%); Repair and Maintenance (1.4%); Merchant Wholesalers, Durable Goods (1.2%); Telecommunications (0.6%)

Detailed Fields with Highest Growth (Projected Growth for This Job): State and Local Government, Excluding Education and Hospitals (20.2%); Repair and Maintenance (15.6%); Educational Services, Public and Private (14.3%); Utilities (10.3%); Merchant Wholesalers, Durable Goods (6.9%)

Other Considerations for Job Outlook: Employment growth for these workers is expected to be limited as improvements in the quality of electrical and electronic equipment result in less need for repairs. The best prospects are expected for job seekers who have certification, an associate degree, and relevant experience.

Inspect, test, repair, or maintain electrical equipment in generating stations, substations, and in-service relays. Construct, test, maintain, and repair substation relay and control systems. Inspect and test equipment and circuits to identify malfunctions or defects, using wiring diagrams and testing devices such as ohmmeters, voltmeters, or ammeters. Consult manuals, schematics, wiring diagrams, and engineering personnel to troubleshoot and solve equipment problems and to determine optimum equipment functioning. Notify facility personnel of equipment shutdowns. Open and close switches to isolate defective relays; then perform adjustments or repairs. Prepare and maintain records detailing tests, repairs, and maintenance. Analyze test data to diagnose malfunctions, to determine performance characteristics of systems, and to evaluate effects of system modifications. Test insulators and bushings of equipment by inducing voltage across insulation, testing current, and calculating insulation loss. Repair, replace, and clean equipment and components such as circuit breakers, brushes, and commutators.

Education/Training Required: Postsecondary vocational training. **Education and Training Programs:** Electrical and Power Transmission Installers, Other; Mechanic and Repair Technologies/Technicians, Other. **Knowledge/Courses:** Mechanical Devices; Design; Telecommunications; Building and Construction; Physics; Public Safety and Security.

Personality Type: Realistic-Conventional. **Career Cluster:** 13 Manufacturing. **Career Pathway:** 13.3 Maintenance, Installation, and Repair. **Other Jobs in This Pathway:** Aircraft Mechanics and Service Technicians; Automotive Specialty Technicians; Biological Technicians; Civil Engineering Technicians; Computer, Automated Teller, and Office Machine Repairers; Electrical and Electronic Equipment Assemblers; Electrical and Electronics Repairers, Commercial and Industrial Equipment; Electrical Engineering Technicians; Electrical Engineering Technologists; Electromechanical Engineering Technologists; Electronics Engineering Technicians; Electronics Engineering Technologists; Engineering Technicians, Except Drafters, All Other; Fuel Cell Technicians; Helpers—Installation, Maintenance, and Repair Workers; Industrial Engineering Technologists; Industrial Machinery Mechanics; Installation,

*C=Computer Systems Design, E=Educational Services, G=Government, H=Health Care, R=Repair and Maintenance, U=Utilities, *=All Fields*

150 Best Jobs for a Secure Future © JIST Works

205

Maintenance, and Repair Workers, All Other; Manufacturing Engineering Technologists; Manufacturing Production Technicians; Mapping Technicians; Mechanical Engineering Technologists; Mobile Heavy Equipment Mechanics, Except Engines; Telecommunications Line Installers and Repairers; Tire Repairers and Changers; others.

Skills: Equipment Maintenance; Repairing; Troubleshooting; Operation and Control; Quality Control Analysis; Science; Operation Monitoring; Equipment Selection.

Work Environment: More often outdoors than indoors; standing; using hands; noise; very hot or cold; bright or inadequate lighting; contaminants; hazardous conditions; hazardous equipment; minor burns, cuts, bites, or stings.

Electrical Engineers

* Annual Earnings: U $84,290, C $86,030, * $84,540
* Earnings Growth Potential: Medium (36.1%)
* Growth: U –8.8%, C 40.2%, * 1.7%
* Annual Job Openings: C 110, U 250, * 3,890
* Self-Employed: 1.6%

Detailed Fields with Greatest Employment: Utilities (8.2%); Machinery Manufacturing (6.0%); Transportation Equipment Manufacturing (4.0%); Professional, Scientific, and Technical Services (32.5%); Electrical Equipment, Appliance, and Component Manufacturing (3.9%)

Detailed Fields with Highest Growth (Projected Growth for This Job): Internet Service Providers, Web Search Portals, and Data Processing Services (52.9%); Waste Management and Remediation Services (44.4%); Support Activities for Transportation (33.3%); Wholesale Electronic Markets and

Agents and Brokers (28.8%); Publishing Industries (Except Internet) (25.6%)

Other Considerations for Job Outlook: Electrical engineers are expected to have employment growth of 2 percent from 2008–2018. Although strong demand for electrical devices—including electric power generators, wireless phone transmitters, high-density batteries, and navigation systems—should spur job growth, international competition and the use of engineering services performed in other countries will limit employment growth. Electrical engineers working in firms providing engineering expertise and design services to manufacturers should have better job prospects.

Design, develop, test, or supervise the manufacturing and installation of electrical equipment, components, or systems for commercial, industrial, military, or scientific use. Confer with engineers, customers, and others to discuss existing or potential engineering projects and products. Design, implement, maintain, and improve electrical instruments, equipment, facilities, components, products, and systems for commercial, industrial, and domestic purposes. Operate computer-assisted engineering and design software and equipment to perform engineering tasks. Direct and coordinate manufacturing, construction, installation, maintenance, support, documentation, and testing activities to ensure compliance with specifications, codes, and customer requirements. Perform detailed calculations to compute and establish manufacturing, construction, and installation standards and specifications. Inspect completed installations and observe operations to ensure conformance to design and equipment specifications and compliance with operational and safety standards.

Education/Training Required: Bachelor's degree. **Education and Training Program:** Electrical and Electronics Engineering. **Knowledge/ Courses:** Design; Engineering and Technology;

Physics; Computers and Electronics; Mechanical Devices; Mathematics.

Personality Type: Investigative-Realistic. **Career Cluster:** 15 Science, Technology, Engineering, and Mathematics. **Career Pathway:** 15.1 Engineering and Technology. **Other Jobs in This Pathway:** Architectural and Engineering Managers; Automotive Engineers; Biochemical Engineers; Biofuels/Biodiesel Technology and Product Development Managers; Civil Engineers; Cost Estimators; Education, Training, and Library Workers, All Other; Electronics Engineers, Except Computer; Energy Engineers; Engineers, All Other; Fuel Cell Engineers; Human Factors Engineers and Ergonomists; Industrial Engineers; Manufacturing Engineers; Mechanical Engineers; Mechatronics Engineers; Microsystems Engineers; Nanosystems Engineers; Photonics Engineers; Radio Frequency Identification Device Specialists; Robotics Engineers; Solar Energy Systems Engineers; Transportation Engineers; Validation Engineers; Wind Energy Engineers; others.

Skills: Science; Troubleshooting; Repairing; Operations Analysis; Mathematics; Equipment Maintenance; Operation Monitoring; Technology Design.

Work Environment: Indoors; sitting; noise.

Electrical Power-Line Installers and Repairers

- ❋ Annual Earnings: G $57,900, U $62,270, * $58,030
- ❋ Earnings Growth Potential: High (42.0%)
- ❋ Growth: U –18.0%, G 27.4%, * 4.5%
- ❋ Annual Job Openings: G 420, U 1,730, * 4,550
- ❋ Self-Employed: 1.4%

Detailed Fields with Greatest Employment: Specialty Trade Contractors (6.0%); Utilities (48.5%); Heavy and Civil Engineering Construction (27.8%); State and Local Government (12.2%); Management of Companies and Enterprises (1.7%)

Detailed Fields with Highest Growth (Projected Growth for This Job): Specialty Trade Contractors (37.8%); State and Local Government, Excluding Education and Hospitals (29.8%); Heavy and Civil Engineering Construction (25.6%); Administrative and Support Services (21.2%); Educational Services, Public and Private (10.0%)

Other Considerations for Job Outlook: Slow decline in employment is projected.

Install or repair cables or wires used in electrical power or distribution systems. May erect poles and light- or heavy-duty transmission towers. Adhere to safety practices and procedures, such as checking equipment regularly and erecting barriers around work areas. Open switches or attach grounding devices to remove electrical hazards from disturbed or fallen lines or to facilitate repairs. Climb poles or use truck-mounted buckets to access equipment. Place insulating or fireproofing materials over conductors and joints. Install, maintain, and repair electrical distribution and transmission systems, including conduits; cables; wires; and related equipment such as transformers, circuit breakers, and switches. Identify defective sectionalizing devices, circuit breakers, fuses, voltage regulators, transformers, switches, relays, or wiring, using wiring diagrams and electrical-testing instruments. Drive vehicles equipped with tools and materials to job sites. Coordinate work assignment preparation and completion with other workers.

Education/Training Required: Long-term on-the-job training. **Education and Training Programs:** Electrical and Power Transmission Installation/

*C=Computer Systems Design, E=Educational Services, G=Government, H=Health Care, R=Repair and Maintenance, U=Utilities, *=All Fields*

150 Best Jobs for a Secure Future © JIST Works

207

Installer, General; Electrical and Power Transmission Installers, Other; Lineworker. **Knowledge/Courses:** Building and Construction; Mechanical Devices; Customer and Personal Service; Engineering and Technology; Transportation; Design.

Personality Type: Realistic-Investigative-Conventional. **Career Cluster:** 02 Architecture and Construction. **Career Pathway:** 2.2 Construction. **Other Jobs in This Pathway:** Brickmasons and Blockmasons; Cement Masons and Concrete Finishers; Construction and Building Inspectors; Construction Carpenters; Construction Laborers; Construction Managers; Cost Estimators; Drywall and Ceiling Tile Installers; Electricians; Engineering Technicians, Except Drafters, All Other; Excavating and Loading Machine and Dragline Operators; First-Line Supervisors of Construction Trades and Extraction Workers; Heating and Air Conditioning Mechanics and Installers; Helpers—Carpenters; Helpers—Electricians; Helpers—Pipelayers, Plumbers, Pipefitters, and Steamfitters; Highway Maintenance Workers; Operating Engineers and Other Construction Equipment Operators; Painters, Construction and Maintenance; Pipe Fitters and Steamfitters; Plumbers; Refrigeration Mechanics and Installers; Roofers; Rough Carpenters; Solar Energy Installation Managers; others.

Skills: Repairing; Troubleshooting; Equipment Maintenance; Operation and Control; Quality Control Analysis; Operation Monitoring; Installation; Equipment Selection.

Work Environment: Outdoors; standing; walking and running; using hands; bending or twisting the body; repetitive motions; noise; very hot or cold; bright or inadequate lighting; contaminants; cramped work space; high places; hazardous conditions; hazardous equipment; minor burns, cuts, bites, or stings.

Electronics Engineers, Except Computer

* ❋ Annual Earnings: C $92,460, * $90,170
* ❋ Earnings Growth Potential: Low (35.8%)
* ❋ Growth: C 40.2%, * 0.3%
* ❋ Annual Job Openings: C 160, * 3,340
* ❋ Self-Employed: 1.6%

Detailed Fields with Greatest Employment: Merchant Wholesalers, Durable Goods (6.3%); Transportation Equipment Manufacturing (3.4%); Computer and Electronic Product Manufacturing (25.1%); Management of Companies and Enterprises (2.9%); Professional, Scientific, and Technical Services (18.7%)

Detailed Fields with Highest Growth (Projected Growth for This Job): Internet Service Providers, Web Search Portals, and Data Processing Services (47.4%); Specialty Trade Contractors (36.0%); Professional, Scientific, and Technical Services (28.7%); Wholesale Electronic Markets and Agents and Brokers (28.4%); Publishing Industries (Except Internet) (24.0%)

Other Considerations for Job Outlook: Electronics engineers, except computer, are expected to experience little to no employment change from 2008–2018. Although rising demand for electronic goods—including communications equipment, defense-related equipment, medical electronics, and consumer products—should continue to increase demand for electronics engineers, foreign competition in electronic products development and the use of engineering services performed in other countries will limit employment growth. Growth is expected to be fastest in service-providing industries—particularly in firms that provide engineering and design services.

Research, design, develop, and test electronic components and systems for commercial, industrial, military, or scientific use, utilizing knowledge of electronic theory and materials properties. Design electronic circuits and components for use in fields such as telecommunications, aerospace guidance and propulsion control, acoustics, or instruments and controls. Design electronic components, software, products, or systems for commercial, industrial, medical, military, or scientific applications. Provide technical support and instruction to staff or customers regarding equipment standards, assisting with specific, difficult in-service engineering. Operate computer-assisted engineering and design software and equipment to perform engineering tasks. Analyze system requirements, capacity, cost, and customer needs to determine feasibility of project and develop system plan. Confer with engineers, customers, vendors, or others to discuss existing and potential engineering projects or products. Review and evaluate work of others inside and outside the organization to ensure effectiveness, technical adequacy, and compatibility in the resolution of complex engineering problems. Determine material and equipment needs and order supplies.

Education/Training Required: Bachelor's degree. **Education and Training Program:** Electrical and Electronics Engineering. **Knowledge/Courses:** Design; Engineering and Technology; Physics; Computers and Electronics; Mathematics; Production and Processing.

Personality Type: Investigative-Realistic. **Career Cluster:** 15 Science, Technology, Engineering, and Mathematics. **Career Pathway:** 15.1 Engineering and Technology. **Other Jobs in This Pathway:** Architectural and Engineering Managers; Automotive Engineers; Biochemical Engineers; Biofuels/Biodiesel Technology and Product Development Managers; Civil Engineers; Cost Estimators; Education,

Training, and Library Workers, All Other; Electrical Engineers; Energy Engineers; Engineers, All Other; Fuel Cell Engineers; Human Factors Engineers and Ergonomists; Industrial Engineers; Manufacturing Engineers; Mechanical Engineers; Mechatronics Engineers; Microsystems Engineers; Nanosystems Engineers; Photonics Engineers; Radio Frequency Identification Device Specialists; Robotics Engineers; Solar Energy Systems Engineers; Transportation Engineers; Validation Engineers; Wind Energy Engineers; others.

Skills: Programming; Repairing; Technology Design; Equipment Selection; Equipment Maintenance; Troubleshooting; Operation and Control; Quality Control Analysis.

Work Environment: Indoors; sitting; using hands.

Job Specialization: Radio Frequency Identification Device Specialists

Design and implement radio frequency identification device (RFID) systems used to track shipments or goods. Verify compliance of developed applications with architectural standards and established practices. Read current literature, attend meetings or conferences, or talk with colleagues to stay abreast of industry research about new technologies. Provide technical support for radio frequency identification device (RFID) technology. Perform systems analysis or programming of radio frequency identification device (RFID) technology. Document equipment or process details of radio frequency identification device (RFID) technology. Train users in details of system operation. Analyze radio frequency identification device (RFID)-related supply chain data. Test tags or labels to ensure readability. Test radio frequency identification device (RFID) software to ensure proper functioning. Select appropriate radio frequency identification device (RFID) tags and determine placement locations.

E

*C=Computer Systems Design, E=Educational Services, G=Government, H=Health Care, R=Repair and Maintenance, U=Utilities, *=All Fields*

Education/Training Required: Bachelor's degree. **Education and Training Program:** Electrical and Electronics Engineering. **Knowledge/Courses:** No data available.

Personality Type: Realistic-Investigative-Conventional. **Career Cluster:** 15 Science, Technology, Engineering, and Mathematics. **Career Pathway:** 15.1 Engineering and Technology. **Other Jobs in This Pathway:** Architectural and Engineering Managers; Automotive Engineers; Biochemical Engineers; Biofuels/Biodiesel Technology and Product Development Managers; Civil Engineers; Cost Estimators; Education, Training, and Library Workers, All Other; Electrical Engineers; Electronics Engineers, Except Computer; Energy Engineers; Engineers, All Other; Fuel Cell Engineers; Human Factors Engineers and Ergonomists; Industrial Engineers; Manufacturing Engineers; Mechanical Engineers; Mechatronics Engineers; Microsystems Engineers; Nanosystems Engineers; Photonics Engineers; Robotics Engineers; Solar Energy Systems Engineers; Transportation Engineers; Validation Engineers; Wind Energy Engineers; others.

Skills: No data available.

Work Environment: No data available.

Elementary School Teachers, Except Special Education

- ❀ Annual Earnings: E $51,690, * $51,660
- ❀ Earnings Growth Potential: Low (33.4%)
- ❀ Growth: E 15.8%, * 15.8%
- ❀ Annual Job Openings: E 43,080, * 59,650
- ❀ Self-Employed: 0.0%

Detailed Fields with Greatest Employment: Educational Services, Public and Private (98.1%);

Religious, Grantmaking, Civic, Professional, and Similar Organizations (1.1%); Administrative and Support Services (0.5%); Social Assistance (0.1%); Hospitals, Public and Private (0.0%)

Detailed Fields with Highest Growth (Projected Growth for This Job): Administrative and Support Services (16.1%); Educational Services, Public and Private (15.8%); Religious, Grantmaking, Civic, Professional, and Similar Organizations (11.9%); Social Assistance (6.3%); Hospitals, Public and Private (0.0%)

Other Considerations for Job Outlook: Enrollment from 2008–2018 is expected to grow more slowly than in recent years. Prospects are usually better in urban and rural areas, for bilingual teachers, and for math and science teachers.

Teach pupils in public or private schools at the elementary level basic academic, social, and other formative skills. Establish and enforce rules for behavior and procedures for maintaining order among the students for whom they are responsible. Observe and evaluate students' performance, behavior, social development, and physical health. Prepare materials and classrooms for class activities. Adapt teaching methods and instructional materials to meet students' varying needs and interests. Plan and conduct activities for a balanced program of instruction, demonstration, and work time that provides students with opportunities to observe, question, and investigate. Instruct students individually and in groups, using various teaching methods such as lectures, discussions, and demonstrations. Establish clear objectives for all lessons, units, and projects and communicate those objectives to students. Assign and grade classwork and homework. Read books to entire classes or small groups. Prepare, administer, and grade tests and assignments in order to evaluate students' progress.

Education/Training Required: Bachelor's degree. **Education and Training Programs:** Elementary Education and Teaching; Teacher Education, Multiple Levels. **Knowledge/Courses:** History and Archeology; Geography; Philosophy and Theology; Sociology and Anthropology; Therapy and Counseling; Fine Arts.

Personality Type: Social-Artistic-Conventional. **Career Cluster:** 05 Education and Training. **Career Pathway:** 5.3 Teaching/Training. **Other Jobs in This Pathway:** Adult Basic and Secondary Education and Literacy Teachers and Instructors; Athletes and Sports Competitors; Audio-Visual and Multimedia Collections Specialists; Career/Technical Education Teachers, Middle School; Career/Technical Education Teachers, Secondary School; Chemists; Coaches and Scouts; Dietitians and Nutritionists; Fitness Trainers and Aerobics Instructors; Historians; Instructional Coordinators; Instructional Designers and Technologists; Interpreters and Translators; Kindergarten Teachers, Except Special Education; Librarians; Middle School Teachers, Except Special and Career/Technical Education; Physicists; Preschool Teachers, Except Special Education; Recreation Workers; Secondary School Teachers, Except Special and Career/Technical Education; Self-Enrichment Education Teachers; Teacher Assistants; Teachers and Instructors, All Other; Tutors.

Skills: Learning Strategies; Social Perceptiveness; Monitoring; Systems Evaluation; Service Orientation; Writing; Systems Analysis; Instructing.

Work Environment: Indoors; standing; noise.

Environmental Engineers

❋ Annual Earnings: G $77,680, * $78,740
❋ Earnings Growth Potential: Medium (37.8%)
❋ Growth: G 8.2%, * 30.6%
❋ Annual Job Openings: G 580, * 2,790
❋ Self-Employed: 0.6%

Detailed Fields with Greatest Employment: Federal Government (7.6%); Professional, Scientific, and Technical Services (51.5%); Waste Management and Remediation Services (4.4%); State and Local Government (23.4%); Management of Companies and Enterprises (1.8%)

Detailed Fields with Highest Growth (Projected Growth for This Job): Professional, Scientific, and Technical Services (53.2%); Wholesale Electronic Markets and Agents and Brokers (40.0%); Waste Management and Remediation Services (29.5%); Administrative and Support Services (24.4%); Hospitals, Public and Private (16.7%)

Other Considerations for Job Outlook: Environmental engineers are expected to have employment growth of 31 percent from 2008–2018, much faster than the average for all occupations. More environmental engineers will be needed to help companies comply with environmental regulations and to develop methods of cleaning up environmental hazards. A shift in emphasis toward preventing problems rather than controlling those which already exist, as well as increasing public health concerns resulting from population growth, also are expected to spur demand for environmental engineers. Because of this employment growth, job opportunities should be favorable.

Design, plan, or perform engineering duties in the prevention, control, and remediation of environmental health hazards, using various engineering disciplines. Work may include waste

---

*C=Computer Systems Design, E=Educational Services, G=Government, H=Health Care, R=Repair and Maintenance, U=Utilities, *=All Fields*

treatment, site remediation, or pollution control technology. Collaborate with environmental scientists, planners, hazardous waste technicians, engineers, and other specialists and experts in law and business to address environmental problems. Inspect industrial and municipal facilities and programs to evaluate operational effectiveness and ensure compliance with environmental regulations. Prepare, review, and update environmental investigation and recommendation reports. Design and supervise the development of systems processes or equipment for control, management, or remediation of water, air, or soil quality. Provide environmental engineering assistance in network analysis, regulatory analysis, and planning or reviewing database development. Obtain, update, and maintain plans, permits, and standard operating procedures. Provide technical-level support for environmental remediation and litigation projects, including remediation system design and determination of regulatory applicability. Monitor progress of environmental improvement programs.

Education/Training Required: Bachelor's degree. **Education and Training Program:** Environmental/Environmental Health Engineering. **Knowledge/Courses:** Engineering and Technology; Physics; Design; Chemistry; Building and Construction; Biology.

Personality Type: Investigative-Realistic-Conventional. **Career Clusters:** 15 Science, Technology, Engineering, and Mathematics; 16 Transportation, Distribution, and Logistics. **Career Pathways:** 15.1 Engineering and Technology; 16.6 Health, Safety, and Environmental Management. **Other Jobs in These Pathways:** Architectural and Engineering Managers; Automotive Engineers; Biochemical Engineers; Biofuels/Biodiesel Technology and Product Development Managers; Civil Engineers; Cost Estimators; Electrical Engineers; Electronics Engineers, Except Computer; Energy Engineers; Engineers,

All Other; Environmental Compliance Inspectors; Fuel Cell Engineers; Human Factors Engineers and Ergonomists; Industrial Engineers; Manufacturing Engineers; Mechanical Engineers; Mechatronics Engineers; Microsystems Engineers; Nanosystems Engineers; Photonics Engineers; Robotics Engineers; Solar Energy Systems Engineers; Transportation Engineers; Validation Engineers; Wind Energy Engineers; others.

Skills: Mathematics; Science; Systems Analysis; Management of Financial Resources; Operations Analysis; Programming; Quality Control Analysis; Systems Evaluation.

Work Environment: More often indoors than outdoors; sitting; using hands; noise; contaminants.

Job Specialization: Water/Wastewater Engineers

Design or oversee projects involving provision of fresh water, disposal of wastewater and sewage, or prevention of flood-related damage. Prepare environmental documentation for water resources, regulatory program compliance, data management and analysis, and fieldwork. Perform hydraulic modeling and pipeline design. Write technical reports or publications related to water resources development or water use efficiency. Review and critique proposals, plans, or designs related to water and wastewater treatment systems. Provide technical support on water resource or treatment issues to government agencies. Provide technical direction or supervision to junior engineers, engineering or computer-aided design (CAD) technicians, or other technical personnel. Identify design alternatives for the development of new water resources. Develop plans for new water resources or water efficiency programs. Design or select equipment for use in wastewater processing to ensure compliance with government standards. Conduct water quality studies to identify and characterize water pollutant sources. Perform mathematical modeling of underground or surface water resources, such as floodplains, ocean coastlines, streams, rivers, and wetlands.

Education/Training Required: Bachelor's degree. **Education and Training Program:** Environmental/Environmental Health Engineering. **Knowledge/Courses:** No data available.

Personality Type: No data available. **Career Cluster:** 15 Science, Technology, Engineering, and Mathematics. **Career Pathway:** 15.1 Engineering and Technology. **Other Jobs in This Pathway:** Architectural and Engineering Managers; Automotive Engineers; Biochemical Engineers; Biofuels/Biodiesel Technology and Product Development Managers; Civil Engineers; Cost Estimators; Electrical Engineers; Electronics Engineers, Except Computer; Energy Engineers; Engineers, All Other; Fuel Cell Engineers; Human Factors Engineers and Ergonomists; Industrial Engineers; Manufacturing Engineers; Mechanical Engineers; Mechatronics Engineers; Microsystems Engineers; Nanosystems Engineers; Photonics Engineers; Radio Frequency Identification Device Specialists; Robotics Engineers; Solar Energy Systems Engineers; Transportation Engineers; Validation Engineers; Wind Energy Engineers; others.

Skills: No data available.

Work Environment: No data available.

Environmental Scientists and Specialists, Including Health

- ❋ Annual Earnings: G $60,570, U $83,530, * $61,700
- ❋ Earnings Growth Potential: Medium (38.7%)
- ❋ Growth: U –13.5%, G 8.2%, * 27.9%
- ❋ Annual Job Openings: U 50, G 1,390, * 4,840
- ❋ Self-Employed: 2.4%

Detailed Fields with Greatest Employment: Federal Government (7.3%); Professional, Scientific, and Technical Services (42.5%); Educational Services, Public and Private (4.4%); State and Local Government (38.0%); Utilities (1.2%)

Detailed Fields with Highest Growth (Projected Growth for This Job): Professional, Scientific, and Technical Services (55.0%); Waste Management and Remediation Services (31.5%); Social Assistance (30.0%); Administrative and Support Services (25.7%); Religious, Grantmaking, Civic, Professional, and Similar Organizations (12.9%)

Other Considerations for Job Outlook: A growing population and increased awareness of environmental concerns are expected to increase employment of environmental scientists. These workers should have good job prospects, particularly in state and local governments.

Conduct research or perform investigation for the purpose of identifying, abating, or eliminating sources of pollutants or hazards that affect either the environment or the health of the population. Using knowledge of various scientific disciplines, may collect, synthesize, study, report, and take action based on data derived from measurements or observations of air,

E

*C=Computer Systems Design, E=Educational Services, G=Government, H=Health Care, R=Repair and Maintenance, U=Utilities, *=All Fields*

150 Best Jobs for a Secure Future © JIST Works

213

food, soil, water, and other sources. Collect, synthesize, analyze, manage, and report environmental data such as pollution emission measurements, atmospheric monitoring measurements, meteorological and mineralogical information, and soil or water samples. Analyze data to determine validity, quality, and scientific significance, and to interpret correlations between human activities and environmental effects. Communicate scientific and technical information to the public, organizations, or internal audiences through oral briefings, written documents, workshops, conferences, training sessions, or public hearings. Provide scientific and technical guidance, support, coordination, and oversight to governmental agencies, environmental programs, industry, or the public. Process and review environmental permits, licenses, and related materials. Review and implement environmental technical standards, guidelines, policies, and formal regulations that meet all appropriate requirements.

Education/Training Required: Master's degree. **Education and Training Programs:** Environmental Science; Environmental Studies. **Knowledge/Courses:** Biology; Geography; Chemistry; Physics; Law and Government; Engineering and Technology.

Personality Type: Investigative-Realistic-Conventional. **Career Clusters:** 01 Agriculture, Food, and Natural Resources; 16 Transportation, Distribution, and Logistics. **Career Pathways:** 1.5 Natural Resources Systems; 16.6 Health, Safety, and Environmental Management. **Other Jobs in These Pathways:** Climate Change Analysts; Conveyor Operators and Tenders; Derrick Operators, Oil and Gas; Engineering Technicians, Except Drafters, All Other; Environmental Compliance Inspectors; Environmental Engineers; Environmental Restoration Planners; Environmental Science and Protection Technicians, Including Health; Fishers and Related Fishing Workers; Forest and Conservation Technicians; Health and Safety Engineers, Except Mining Safety Engineers and Inspectors; Helpers—Extraction Workers; Industrial Ecologists; Industrial Truck and Tractor Operators; Logging Equipment Operators; Mechanical Engineering Technicians; Park Naturalists; Range Managers; Recreation Workers; Refuse and Recyclable Material Collectors; Rotary Drill Operators, Oil and Gas; Service Unit Operators, Oil, Gas, and Mining; Soil and Water Conservationists; Wellhead Pumpers; Zoologists and Wildlife Biologists; others.

Skills: Science; Programming; Mathematics; Reading Comprehension; Operations Analysis; Writing; Systems Analysis; Complex Problem Solving.

Work Environment: More often indoors than outdoors; sitting; noise.

Job Specialization: Climate Change Analysts

Research and analyze policy developments related to climate change. Make climate-related recommendations for actions such as legislation, awareness campaigns, or fundraising approaches. Write reports or academic papers to communicate findings of climate-related studies. Promote initiatives to mitigate climate change with government or environmental groups. Present climate-related information at public interest, governmental, or other meetings. Present and defend proposals for climate change research projects. Prepare grant applications to obtain funding for programs related to climate change, environmental management, or sustainability. Gather and review climate-related studies from government agencies, research laboratories, and other organizations. Develop, or contribute to the development of, educational or outreach programs on the environment or climate change. Review existing policies or legislation to identify environmental impacts.

Provide analytical support for policy briefs related to renewable energy, energy efficiency, or climate change.

Education/Training Required: Master's degree. **Education and Training Programs:** Environmental Science; Environmental Studies. **Knowledge/Courses:** No data available.

Personality Type: No data available. **Career Cluster:** 01 Agriculture, Food, and Natural Resources. **Career Pathway:** 1.5 Natural Resources Systems. **Other Jobs in This Pathway:** Conveyor Operators and Tenders; Derrick Operators, Oil and Gas; Engineering Technicians, Except Drafters, All Other; Environmental Economists; Environmental Restoration Planners; Environmental Science and Protection Technicians, Including Health; Environmental Scientists and Specialists, Including Health; Fishers and Related Fishing Workers; Forest and Conservation Technicians; Geological Sample Test Technicians; Geophysical Data Technicians; Helpers—Extraction Workers; Industrial Ecologists; Industrial Truck and Tractor Operators; Logging Equipment Operators; Mechanical Engineering Technicians; Park Naturalists; Range Managers; Recreation Workers; Refuse and Recyclable Material Collectors; Rotary Drill Operators, Oil and Gas; Service Unit Operators, Oil, Gas, and Mining; Soil and Water Conservationists; Wellhead Pumpers; Zoologists and Wildlife Biologists; others.

Skills: No data available.

Work Environment: No data available.

Job Specialization: Environmental Restoration Planners

Collaborate with field and biology staff to oversee the implementation of restoration projects and to develop new products. Process and synthesize complex scientific data into practical strategies for restoration, monitoring or management. Notify regulatory or permitting agencies of deviations from implemented remediation plans. Develop environmental restoration project schedules and budgets. Develop and communicate recommendations for landowners to maintain or restore environmental conditions. Create diagrams to communicate environmental remediation planning using Geographic Information Systems (GIS), computer-aided design (CAD), or other mapping or diagramming software. Apply for permits required for the implementation of environmental remediation projects. Review existing environmental remediation designs. Supervise and provide technical guidance, training, or assistance to employees working in the field to restore habitats. Provide technical direction on environmental planning to energy engineers, biologists, geologists, or other professionals working to develop restoration plans or strategies.

Education/Training Required: Master's degree. **Education and Training Programs:** Environmental Science; Environmental Studies. **Knowledge/Courses:** No data available.

Personality Type: No data available. **Career Cluster:** 01 Agriculture, Food, and Natural Resources. **Career Pathway:** 1.5 Natural Resources Systems. **Other Jobs in This Pathway:** Climate Change Analysts; Conveyor Operators and Tenders; Derrick Operators, Oil and Gas; Engineering Technicians, Except Drafters, All Other; Environmental Economists; Environmental Science and Protection Technicians, Including Health; Environmental Scientists and Specialists, Including Health; Fishers and Related Fishing Workers; Forest and Conservation Technicians; Geological Sample Test Technicians; Geophysical Data Technicians; Helpers—Extraction Workers; Industrial Ecologists; Industrial Truck and Tractor Operators; Logging Equipment Operators; Mechanical Engineering Technicians; Park Naturalists; Range Managers; Recreation Workers; Refuse

C=Computer Systems Design, E=Educational Services, G=Government, H=Health Care, R=Repair and Maintenance, U=Utilities, *=All Fields

and Recyclable Material Collectors; Rotary Drill Operators, Oil and Gas; Service Unit Operators, Oil, Gas, and Mining; Soil and Water Conservationists; Wellhead Pumpers; Zoologists and Wildlife Biologists; others.

Skills: No data available.

Work Environment: No data available.

Job Specialization: Industrial Ecologists

Study or investigate industrial production and natural ecosystems to achieve high production, sustainable resources, and environmental safety or protection. May apply principles and activities of natural ecosystems to develop models for industrial systems. Write ecological reports and other technical documents for publication in the research literature or in industrial or government reports. Recommend methods to protect the environment or minimize environmental damage. Investigate accidents affecting the environment to assess ecological impact. Investigate the adaptability of various animal and plant species to changed environmental conditions. Review industrial practices, such as the methods and materials used in construction or production, to identify potential liabilities and environmental hazards. Research sources of pollution to determine environmental impact or to develop methods of pollution abatement or control. Provide industrial managers with technical materials on environmental issues, regulatory guidelines, or compliance actions. Plan or conduct studies of the ecological implications of historic or projected changes in industrial processes or development.

Education/Training Required: Master's degree. **Education and Training Programs:** Environmental Science; Environmental Studies. **Knowledge/Courses:** No data available.

Personality Type: No data available. **Career Cluster:** 01 Agriculture, Food, and Natural Resources.

Career Pathway: 1.5 Natural Resources Systems. **Other Jobs in This Pathway:** Climate Change Analysts; Conveyor Operators and Tenders; Derrick Operators, Oil and Gas; Engineering Technicians, Except Drafters, All Other; Environmental Economists; Environmental Restoration Planners; Environmental Science and Protection Technicians, Including Health; Environmental Scientists and Specialists, Including Health; Fishers and Related Fishing Workers; Forest and Conservation Technicians; Geological Sample Test Technicians; Geophysical Data Technicians; Helpers—Extraction Workers; Industrial Truck and Tractor Operators; Logging Equipment Operators; Mechanical Engineering Technicians; Park Naturalists; Range Managers; Recreation Workers; Refuse and Recyclable Material Collectors; Rotary Drill Operators, Oil and Gas; Service Unit Operators, Oil, Gas, and Mining; Soil and Water Conservationists; Wellhead Pumpers; Zoologists and Wildlife Biologists; others.

Skills: No data available.

Work Environment: No data available.

Executive Secretaries and Executive Administrative Assistants

- ✸ Annual Earnings: R $40,880, H $41,468, E $42,380, U $47,610, * $43,520
- ✸ Earnings Growth Potential: Low (34.0%)
- ✸ Growth: U –13.7%, R 4.8%, E 13.4%, H 18.8%, * 12.8%
- ✸ Annual Job Openings: U 190, R 240, E 4,080, H 5,610, * 41,920
- ✸ Self-Employed: 1.3%

Detailed Fields with Greatest Employment: State and Local Government (9.6%); Administrative and Support Services (6.7%); Religious,

Grantmaking, Civic, Professional, and Similar Organizations (5.7%); Management of Companies and Enterprises (3.9%); Ambulatory Health Care Services (3.6%)

Detailed Fields with Highest Growth (Projected Growth for This Job): Management, Scientific, and Technical Consulting Services (85.5%); Offices of Physical, Occupational and Speech Therapists, and Audiologists (58.0%); Data Processing, Hosting, and Related Services (48.4%); Internet Service Providers, Web Search Portals, and Data Processing Services (48.4%); Specialized Design Services (46.4%)

Other Considerations for Job Outlook: Projected employment growth varies by occupational specialty. Faster than average growth is expected for medical secretaries and legal secretaries; average growth for executive secretaries and administrative assistants; and slower than average growth for secretaries other than legal, medical, or executive, who account for most of the workers in these specialties. Many opportunities are expected.

Provide high-level administrative support by conducting research; preparing statistical reports; handling information requests; and performing clerical functions such as preparing correspondence, receiving visitors, arranging conference calls, and scheduling meetings. May also train and supervise lower-level clerical staff. Manage and maintain executives' schedules. Prepare invoices, reports, memos, letters, financial statements, and other documents, using word-processing, spreadsheet, database, or presentation software. Open, sort, and distribute incoming correspondence, including faxes and e-mail. Read and analyze incoming memos, submissions, and reports to determine their significance and plan their distribution. File and retrieve corporate documents, records, and reports. Greet visitors and determine whether they should be given access to specific individuals. Prepare responses to correspondence containing routine inquiries. Perform general office duties such as ordering supplies, maintaining records management systems, and performing basic bookkeeping work. Prepare agendas and make arrangements for committee, board, and other meetings. Make travel arrangements for executives.

Education/Training Required: Work experience in a related occupation. **Education and Training Programs:** Administrative Assistant and Secretarial Science, General; Executive Assistant/Executive Secretary Training; Medical Administrative/Executive Assistant and Medical Secretary Training. **Knowledge/Courses:** Clerical Practices; Personnel and Human Resources.

Personality Type: Conventional-Enterprising. **Career Clusters:** 04 Business, Management, and Administration; 08 Health Science. **Career Pathways:** 4.6 Administrative and Information Support; 8.3 Health Informatics. **Other Jobs in These Pathways:** Customer Service Representatives; Data Entry Keyers; Dispatchers, Except Police, Fire, and Ambulance; Engineers, All Other; File Clerks; First-Line Supervisors of Office and Administrative Support Workers; Information and Record Clerks, All Other; Insurance Claims Clerks; Insurance Policy Processing Clerks; Interviewers, Except Eligibility and Loan; Medical and Health Services Managers; Medical Assistants; Medical Records and Health Information Technicians; Medical Secretaries; Office and Administrative Support Workers, All Other; Office Clerks, General; Order Clerks; Patient Representatives; Physical Therapists; Postal Service Mail Carriers; Postal Service Mail Sorters, Processors, and Processing Machine Operators; Public Relations Specialists; Receptionists and Information Clerks; Secretaries and Administrative Assistants, Except Legal, Medical, and Executive; Shipping, Receiving, and Traffic Clerks; others.

*C=Computer Systems Design, E=Educational Services, G=Government, H=Health Care, R=Repair and Maintenance, U=Utilities, *=All Fields*

Skills: Service Orientation; Programming; Active Listening; Writing; Speaking; Time Management; Reading Comprehension; Monitoring.

Work Environment: Indoors; sitting; repetitive motions; noise.

Financial Examiners

- ❋ Annual Earnings: G $80,090, * $74,940
- ❋ Earnings Growth Potential: High (42.4%)
- ❋ Growth: G 41.5%, * 41.2%
- ❋ Annual Job Openings: G 420, * 1,600
- ❋ Self-Employed: 0.0%

Detailed Fields with Greatest Employment: Management of Companies and Enterprises (6.2%); Insurance Carriers and Related Activities (6.0%); Monetary Authorities–Central Bank (4.6%); Professional, Scientific, and Technical Services (4.5%); Federal Government (22.4%)

Detailed Fields with Highest Growth (Projected Growth for This Job): Internet Service Providers, Web Search Portals, and Data Processing Services (100.0%); Professional, Scientific, and Technical Services (72.7%); Administrative and Support Services (58.8%); Funds, Trusts, and Other Financial Vehicles (50.0%); Religious, Grantmaking, Civic, Professional, and Similar Organizations (50.0%)

Other Considerations for Job Outlook: Much faster than average employment growth is projected.

Enforce or ensure compliance with laws and regulations governing financial and securities institutions and financial and real estate transactions. May examine, verify correctness of, or establish authenticity of records. Investigate activities of institutions in order to enforce laws and regulations and to ensure legality of transactions and operations or financial solvency. Review and analyze new, proposed, or revised laws, regulations, policies, and procedures in order to interpret their meaning and determine their impact. Plan, supervise, and review work of assigned subordinates. Recommend actions to ensure compliance with laws and regulations or to protect solvency of institutions. Examine the minutes of meetings of directors, stockholders, and committees in order to investigate the specific authority extended at various levels of management. Prepare reports, exhibits, and other supporting schedules that detail an institution's safety and soundness, compliance with laws and regulations, and recommended solutions to questionable financial conditions. Review balance sheets, operating income and expense accounts, and loan documentation in order to confirm institution assets and liabilities.

Education/Training Required: Bachelor's degree. **Education and Training Programs:** Accounting; Taxation. **Knowledge/Courses:** Economics and Accounting; Law and Government; Clerical Practices; Mathematics; English Language; Administration and Management.

Personality Type: Enterprising-Conventional. **Career Clusters:** 04 Business, Management, and Administration; 07 Government and Public Administration. **Career Pathways:** 4.2 Business, Financial Management, and Accounting; 7.5 Revenue and Taxation. **Other Jobs in These Pathways:** Accountants; Auditors; Billing and Posting Clerks; Billing, Cost, and Rate Clerks; Bookkeeping, Accounting, and Auditing Clerks; Brokerage Clerks; Brownfield Redevelopment Specialists and Site Managers; Compliance Managers; Credit Analysts; Financial Analysts; Financial Managers, Branch or Department; Investment Fund Managers; Logistics Managers; Loss Prevention Managers; Managers, All Other; Payroll and Timekeeping Clerks; Regulatory Affairs Managers; Security

Managers; Statement Clerks; Supply Chain Managers; Tax Examiners and Collectors, and Revenue Agents; Tax Preparers; Treasurers and Controllers; Wind Energy Operations Managers; Wind Energy Project Managers; others.

Skills: Management of Personnel Resources; Systems Evaluation; Active Learning; Learning Strategies; Systems Analysis; Mathematics; Programming; Writing.

Work Environment: Indoors; sitting.

Firefighters

- ❋ Annual Earnings: G $45,840, * $45,250
- ❋ Earnings Growth Potential: High (49.1%)
- ❋ Growth: G 18.9%, * 18.5%
- ❋ Annual Job Openings: G 10,000, * 15,280
- ❋ Self-Employed: 0.2%

Detailed Fields with Greatest Employment: State and Local Government (93.3%); Federal Government (3.1%); Educational Services, Public and Private (0.1%); Professional, Scientific, and Technical Services (0.1%); Transportation Equipment Manufacturing (0.1%).

Detailed Fields with Highest Growth (Projected Growth for This Job): Support Activities for Transportation (30.0%); Professional, Scientific, and Technical Services (28.9%); Federal Government (19.1%); State and Local Government, Excluding Education and Hospitals (18.9%); Religious, Grantmaking, Civic, Professional, and Similar Organizations (16.7%).

Other Considerations for Job Outlook: Most job growth will stem from the conversion of volunteer firefighting positions into paid positions. Job seekers are expected to face keen competition. Those who have completed some firefighter education at a community college and have EMT or paramedic certification should have the best prospects.

Job Specialization: Forest Firefighters

Control and suppress fires in forests or vacant public land. Maintain contact with fire dispatchers at all times to notify them of the need for additional firefighters and supplies or to detail any difficulties encountered. Rescue fire victims and administer emergency medical aid. Collaborate with other firefighters as a member of a firefighting crew. Patrol burned areas after fires to locate and eliminate hot spots that may restart fires. Extinguish flames and embers to suppress fires, using shovels or engine- or hand-driven water or chemical pumps. Fell trees, cut and clear brush, and dig trenches to create firelines, using axes, chain saws, or shovels. Maintain knowledge of current firefighting practices by participating in drills and by attending seminars, conventions, and conferences. Operate pumps connected to high-pressure hoses. Participate in physical training to maintain high levels of physical fitness. Establish water supplies, connect hoses, and direct water onto fires. Maintain fire equipment and firehouse living quarters.

Education/Training Required: Long-term on-the-job training. **Education and Training Programs:** Fire Protection, Other; Fire Science/Firefighting. **Knowledge/Courses:** Geography; Building and Construction; Telecommunications; Public Safety and Security; Mechanical Devices; Customer and Personal Service.

Personality Type: Realistic-Social. **Career Cluster:** 12 Law, Public Safety, Corrections, and Security. **Career Pathways:** 12.2 Emergency and Fire Management Services; 12.3 Security and Protective Services. **Other Jobs in These Pathways:** Animal Control Workers; Correctional Officers and Jailers; Crossing Guards; Fire Inspectors; Fire

---

*C=Computer Systems Design, E=Educational Services, G=Government, H=Health Care, R=Repair and Maintenance, U=Utilities, *=All Fields*

Investigators; First-Line Supervisors of Protective Service Workers, All Other; Forest Fire Fighting and Prevention Supervisors; Forest Fire Inspectors and Prevention Specialists; Gaming Surveillance Officers and Gaming Investigators; Lifeguards, Ski Patrol, and Other Recreational Protective Service Workers; Municipal Fire Fighting and Prevention Supervisors; Municipal Firefighters; Parking Enforcement Workers; Police, Fire, and Ambulance Dispatchers; Private Detectives and Investigators; Retail Loss Prevention Specialists; Security Guards; Sheriffs and Deputy Sheriffs; Transit and Railroad Police.

Skills: Repairing; Equipment Maintenance; Equipment Selection; Operation and Control; Troubleshooting; Quality Control Analysis; Operation Monitoring; Coordination.

Work Environment: Outdoors; standing; walking and running; using hands; bending or twisting the body; repetitive motions; noise; very hot or cold; bright or inadequate lighting; contaminants; hazardous conditions; hazardous equipment; minor burns, cuts, bites, or stings.

Job Specialization: Municipal Firefighters

Control and extinguish municipal fires, protect life and property, and conduct rescue efforts. Administer first aid and cardiopulmonary resuscitation to injured persons. Rescue victims from burning buildings and accident sites. Search burning buildings to locate fire victims. Drive and operate firefighting vehicles and equipment. Move toward the source of a fire, using knowledge of types of fires, construction design, building materials, and physical layout of properties. Dress with equipment such as fire-resistant clothing and breathing apparatus. Position and climb ladders to gain access to upper levels of buildings or to rescue individuals from burning structures. Take action to contain hazardous chemicals that might catch fire, leak, or spill. Assess fires and situations and report conditions to superiors to receive instructions, using two-way radios. Respond to fire alarms and other calls for assistance, such as automobile and industrial accidents. Operate pumps connected to high-pressure hoses.

Education/Training Required: Long-term on-the-job training. **Education and Training Programs:** Fire Protection, Other; Fire Science/Firefighting. **Knowledge/Courses:** Building and Construction; Public Safety and Security; Mechanical Devices; Customer and Personal Service; Physics; Geography.

Personality Type: Realistic-Social-Enterprising. **Career Cluster:** 12 Law, Public Safety, Corrections, and Security. **Career Pathway:** 12.2 Emergency and Fire Management Services. **Other Jobs in This Pathway:** Correctional Officers and Jailers; Fire Inspectors; Fire Investigators; Forest Fire Fighting and Prevention Supervisors; Forest Fire Inspectors and Prevention Specialists; Forest Firefighters; Municipal Fire Fighting and Prevention Supervisors.

Skills: Equipment Maintenance; Repairing; Troubleshooting; Operation and Control; Equipment Selection; Science; Operation Monitoring; Quality Control Analysis.

Work Environment: More often outdoors than indoors; standing; using hands; noise; very hot or cold; bright or inadequate lighting; contaminants; cramped work space; exposed to disease or infections; hazardous conditions; hazardous equipment; minor burns, cuts, bites, or stings.

First-Line Supervisors of Correctional Officers

* ❊ Annual Earnings: G $56,080, * $55,910
* ❊ Earnings Growth Potential: Medium (37.9%)
* ❊ Growth: G 8.2%, * 8.5%
* ❊ Annual Job Openings: G 1,280, * 1,940
* ❊ Self-Employed: 0.0%

Detailed Fields with Greatest Employment: State and Local Government (93.4%); Federal Government (3.4%); Administrative and Support Services (2.9%); Nursing and Residential Care Facilities (0.2%)

Detailed Fields with Highest Growth (Projected Growth for This Job): Administrative and Support Services (17.9%); Nursing and Residential Care Facilities (11.9%); State and Local Government (8.2%); Federal Government (7.5%)

Other Considerations for Job Outlook: Employment growth is expected to stem from population increases and a corresponding rise in the prison population. Favorable job opportunities are expected.

Supervise and coordinate activities of correctional officers and jailers. Take, receive, and check periodic inmate counts. Maintain order, discipline, and security within assigned areas in accordance with relevant rules, regulations, policies, and laws. Respond to emergencies such as escapes. Maintain knowledge of, comply with, and enforce all institutional policies, rules, procedures, and regulations. Supervise and direct the work of correctional officers to ensure the safe custody, discipline, and welfare of inmates. Restrain, secure, and control offenders, using chemical agents, firearms, and other weapons of force as necessary. Supervise and perform searches of inmates and their quarters to locate contraband items. Monitor behavior of subordinates to ensure alert, courteous, and professional behavior toward inmates, parolees, fellow employees, visitors, and the public. Complete administrative paperwork and supervise the preparation and maintenance of records, forms, and reports. Instruct employees and provide on-the-job training.

Education/Training Required: Work experience in a related occupation. **Education and Training Programs:** Corrections; Corrections Administration. **Knowledge/Courses:** Public Safety and Security; Psychology; Therapy and Counseling; Personnel and Human Resources; Clerical Practices; Law and Government.

Personality Type: Enterprising-Conventional-Realistic. **Career Cluster:** 12 Law, Public Safety, Corrections, and Security. **Career Pathway:** 12.1 Correction Services. **Other Jobs in This Pathway:** Child, Family, and School Social Workers; First-Line Supervisors of Police and Detectives; Protective Service Workers, All Other; Security Guards.

Skills: Management of Personnel Resources; Negotiation; Persuasion; Time Management; Social Perceptiveness; Coordination; Systems Evaluation; Learning Strategies.

Work Environment: More often indoors than outdoors; more often sitting than standing; walking and running; using hands; noise; very hot or cold; bright or inadequate lighting; contaminants; exposed to disease or infections.

---

*C=Computer Systems Design, E=Educational Services, G=Government, H=Health Care, R=Repair and Maintenance, U=Utilities, *=All Fields*

First-Line Supervisors of Fire Fighting and Prevention Workers

* ❋ Annual Earnings: G $68,560, * $68,240
* ❋ Earnings Growth Potential: Medium (39.3%)
* ❋ Growth: G 8.2%, * 8.2%
* ❋ Annual Job Openings: G 2,170, * 3,250
* ❋ Self-Employed: 0.0%

Detailed Fields with Greatest Employment: State and Local Government (97.7%); Administrative and Support Services (1.3%); Federal Government (0.4%); Educational Services, Public and Private (0.1%); Fabricated Metal Product Manufacturing (0.1%)

Detailed Fields with Highest Growth (Projected Growth for This Job): Educational Services, Public and Private (16.7%); Federal Government (9.5%); State and Local Government, Excluding Education and Hospitals (8.2%); Administrative and Support Services (7.1%); Fabricated Metal Product Manufacturing (0.0%)

Other Considerations for Job Outlook: Most job growth will stem from the conversion of volunteer firefighting positions into paid positions. Job seekers are expected to face keen competition. Those who have completed some firefighter education at a community college and have EMT or paramedic certification should have the best prospects.

Job Specialization: Forest Fire Fighting and Prevention Supervisors

Supervise firefighters who control and suppress fires in forests or vacant public land. Communicate fire details to superiors, subordinates, and interagency dispatch centers, using two-way radios. Serve as working leader of an engine, hand, helicopter, or prescribed fire crew of three or more firefighters. Maintain fire suppression equipment in good condition, checking equipment periodically to ensure that it is ready for use. Evaluate size, location, and condition of forest fires in order to request and dispatch crews and position equipment so fires can be contained safely and effectively. Operate wildland fire engines and hoselays. Direct and supervise prescribed burn projects and prepare post-burn reports analyzing burn conditions and results. Monitor prescribed burns to ensure that they are conducted safely and effectively. Identify staff training and development needs to ensure that appropriate training can be arranged. Maintain knowledge of forest fire laws and fire prevention techniques and tactics. Recommend equipment modifications or new equipment purchases.

Education/Training Required: Work experience in a related occupation. **Education and Training Programs:** Fire Prevention and Safety Technology/Technician; Fire Services Administration. **Knowledge/Courses:** Public Safety and Security; Building and Construction; Mechanical Devices; Customer and Personal Service; Personnel and Human Resources; Transportation.

Personality Type: Enterprising-Realistic-Conventional. **Career Cluster:** 12 Law, Public Safety, Corrections, and Security. **Career Pathway:** 12.2 Emergency and Fire Management Services. **Other Jobs in This Pathway:** Correctional Officers and Jailers; Fire Inspectors; Fire Investigators; Forest Fire Inspectors and Prevention Specialists; Forest Firefighters; Municipal Fire Fighting and Prevention Supervisors; Municipal Firefighters.

Skills: Operations Analysis; Equipment Maintenance; Operation and Control; Management of Personnel Resources; Coordination; Operation Monitoring; Monitoring; Equipment Selection.

Work Environment: Outdoors; standing; walking and running; using hands; noise; very hot or cold; bright or inadequate lighting; contaminants; cramped work space; hazardous equipment; minor burns, cuts, bites, or stings.

Job Specialization: Municipal Fire Fighting and Prevention Supervisors

Supervise firefighters who control and extinguish municipal fires, protect life and property, and conduct rescue efforts. Assign firefighters to jobs at strategic locations to facilitate rescue of persons and maximize application of extinguishing agents. Provide emergency medical services as required and perform light to heavy rescue functions at emergencies. Assess nature and extent of fire, condition of building, danger to adjacent buildings, and water supply status to determine crew or company requirements. Instruct and drill fire department personnel in assigned duties, including firefighting, medical care, hazardous materials response, fire prevention, and related subjects. Evaluate the performance of assigned firefighting personnel. Direct the training of firefighters, assigning of instructors to training classes, and providing of supervisors with reports on training progress and status. Prepare activity reports listing fire call locations, actions taken, fire types and probable causes, damage estimates, and situation dispositions. Maintain required maps and records.

Education/Training Required: Work experience in a related occupation. **Education and Training Programs:** Fire Prevention and Safety Technology/Technician; Fire Services Administration. **Knowledge/Courses:** Building and Construction; Public Safety and Security; Medicine and Dentistry; Mechanical Devices; Chemistry; Personnel and Human Resources.

Personality Type: Enterprising-Realistic-Social. **Career Cluster:** 12 Law, Public Safety, Corrections, and Security. **Career Pathway:** 12.2 Emergency and Fire Management Services. **Other Jobs in This Pathway:** Correctional Officers and Jailers; Fire Inspectors; Fire Investigators; Forest Fire Fighting and Prevention Supervisors; Forest Fire Inspectors and Prevention Specialists; Forest Firefighters; Municipal Firefighters.

Skills: Operation and Control; Science; Equipment Selection; Repairing; Equipment Maintenance; Quality Control Analysis; Management of Personnel Resources; Systems Analysis.

Work Environment: More often outdoors than indoors; standing; using hands; noise; very hot or cold; bright or inadequate lighting; contaminants; cramped work space; exposed to disease or infections; high places; hazardous conditions; hazardous equipment; minor burns, cuts, bites, or stings.

First-Line Supervisors of Office and Administrative Support Workers

- ❋ Annual Earnings: R $47,150, H $47,329, E $48,860, C $56,140, U $62,320, * $47,460
- ❋ Earnings Growth Potential: Medium (39.2%)
- ❋ Growth: U –12.5%, R 4.6%, E 14.1%, H 23.8%, C 40.1%, * 11.0%
- ❋ Annual Job Openings: R 220, U 220, C 490, E 1,780, H 10,060, * 48,900
- ❋ Self-Employed: 1.4%

Detailed Fields with Greatest Employment: Ambulatory Health Care Services (9.2%); State and Local Government (7.3%); Professional, Scientific, and Technical Services (6.9%); Administrative and Support Services (5.8%); General Merchandise Stores (5.6%)

---

*C=Computer Systems Design, E=Educational Services, G=Government, H=Health Care, R=Repair and Maintenance, U=Utilities, *=All Fields*

Detailed Fields with Highest Growth (Projected Growth for This Job): Internet Service Providers, Web Search Portals, and Data Processing Services (48.4%); Lessors of Nonfinancial Intangible Assets (Except Copyrighted Works) (34.6%); Professional, Scientific, and Technical Services (33.5%); Ambulatory Health Care Services (30.4%); Other Information Services (29.9%)

Other Considerations for Job Outlook: Employment growth is expected to be tempered by technological advances that increase the productivity of—and thus decrease the need for—these workers and the workers they supervise. Keen competition is expected.

Supervise and coordinate the activities of clerical and administrative support workers. Resolve customer complaints and answer customers' questions regarding policies and procedures. Supervise the work of office, administrative, or customer service employees to ensure adherence to quality standards, deadlines, and proper procedures, correcting errors or problems. Provide employees with guidance in handling difficult or complex problems and in resolving escalated complaints or disputes. Implement corporate and departmental policies, procedures, and service standards in conjunction with management. Discuss job performance problems with employees to identify causes and issues and to work on resolving problems. Train and instruct employees in job duties and company policies or arrange for training to be provided. Evaluate employees' job performance and conformance to regulations and recommend appropriate personnel action. Recruit, interview, and select employees.

Education/Training Required: Work experience in a related occupation. **Education and Training Programs:** Agricultural Business Technology; Customer Service Management; Medical Staff Services Technology/Technician; Medical/Health Management and Clinical Assistant/Specialist Training; Office Management and Supervision. **Knowledge/Courses:** Clerical Practices; Economics and Accounting; Administration and Management; Personnel and Human Resources; Customer and Personal Service; Education and Training.

Personality Type: Enterprising-Conventional-Social. **Career Clusters:** 01 Agriculture, Food, and Natural Resources; 04 Business, Management, and Administration; 08 Health Science. **Career Pathways:** 1.1 Food Products and Processing Systems; 4.1 Management; 8.3 Health Informatics. **Other Jobs in These Pathways:** Brownfield Redevelopment Specialists and Site Managers; Business Continuity Planners; Business Operations Specialists, All Other; Chief Executives; Chief Sustainability Officers; Compliance Managers; Construction Managers; Customs Brokers; Energy Auditors; Executive Secretaries and Executive Administrative Assistants; General and Operations Managers; Investment Fund Managers; Loss Prevention Managers; Management Analysts; Managers, All Other; Medical Assistants; Medical Secretaries; Receptionists and Information Clerks; Regulatory Affairs Managers; Security Management Specialists; Security Managers; Supply Chain Managers; Sustainability Specialists; Wind Energy Operations Managers; Wind Energy Project Managers; others.

Skills: Management of Financial Resources; Management of Material Resources; Negotiation; Monitoring; Learning Strategies; Management of Personnel Resources; Persuasion; Time Management.

Work Environment: Indoors; sitting; noise.

First-Line Supervisors of Personal Service Workers

* ❋ Annual Earnings: H $35,205, * $35,290
* ❋ Earnings Growth Potential: Medium (37.9%)
* ❋ Growth: H 24.3%, * 15.4%
* ❋ Annual Job Openings: H 2,340, * 9,080
* ❋ Self-Employed: 37.8%

Detailed Fields with Greatest Employment: Nursing and Residential Care Facilities (9.7%); Religious, Grantmaking, Civic, Professional, and Similar Organizations (6.4%); Educational Services, Public and Private (4.4%); Motion Picture, Video, and Sound Recording Industries (3.8%); Accommodation, Including Hotels and Motels (3.1%)

Detailed Fields with Highest Growth (Projected Growth for This Job): Professional, Scientific, and Technical Services (45.7%); Ambulatory Health Care Services (44.9%); Support Activities for Transportation (32.8%); Social Assistance (32.1%); Personal and Laundry Services (29.6%)

Other Considerations for Job Outlook: Faster than average employment growth is projected.

Supervise and coordinate activities of personal service workers such as flight attendants, hairdressers, or caddies. Requisition necessary supplies, equipment, and services. Inform workers about interests and special needs of specific groups. Participate in continuing education to stay abreast of industry trends and developments. Meet with managers and other supervisors to stay informed of changes affecting operations. Collaborate with staff members to plan and develop programs of events, schedules of activities, or menus. Train workers in proper operational procedures and functions, and explain company policies. Furnish customers with information on events and activities. Resolve customer complaints regarding worker performance and services rendered. Analyze and record personnel and operational data, and write related activity reports. Observe and evaluate workers' appearance and performance to ensure quality service and compliance with specifications. Inspect work areas and operating equipment to ensure conformance to established standards in areas such as cleanliness and maintenance.

Education/Training Required: Work experience in a related occupation. **Education and Training Program:** Business, Management, Marketing, and Related Support Services, Other. **Knowledge/Courses:** Psychology; Therapy and Counseling; Education and Training; Philosophy and Theology; Public Safety and Security; Medicine and Dentistry.

Personality Type: Enterprising-Conventional-Social. **Career Cluster:** 04 Business, Management, and Administration. **Career Pathway:** 4.1 Management. **Other Jobs in This Pathway:** Brownfield Redevelopment Specialists and Site Managers; Business Continuity Planners; Business Operations Specialists, All Other; Chief Executives; Chief Sustainability Officers; Compliance Managers; Computer and Information Systems Managers; Construction Managers; Customs Brokers; Energy Auditors; First-Line Supervisors of Office and Administrative Support Workers; General and Operations Managers; Investment Fund Managers; Loss Prevention Managers; Management Analysts; Managers, All Other; Public Relations Specialists; Regulatory Affairs Managers; Sales Managers; Security Management Specialists; Security Managers; Supply Chain Managers; Sustainability Specialists; Wind Energy Operations Managers; Wind Energy Project Managers; others.

Skills: Management of Personnel Resources; Time Management; Management of Financial Resources; Operation Monitoring; Negotiation;

*C=Computer Systems Design, E=Educational Services, G=Government, H=Health Care, R=Repair and Maintenance, U=Utilities, *=All Fields*

150 Best Jobs for a Secure Future © JIST Works ⸻ 225

Management of Material Resources; Service Orientation; Systems Evaluation.

Work Environment: Indoors; standing; walking and running; using hands; noise; contaminants.

Job Specialization: Spa Managers

Plan, direct, or coordinate activities of a spa facility. Coordinate programs, schedule and direct staff, and oversee financial activities. Inform staff of job responsibilities, performance expectations, client service standards, or corporate policies and guidelines. Plan or direct spa services and programs. Train staff in the use or sale of products, programs, or activities. Assess employee performance and suggest ways to improve work. Check spa equipment to ensure proper functioning. Coordinate facility schedules to maximize usage and efficiency. Develop staff service or retail goals and guide staff in goal achievement. Establish spa budgets and financial goals. Inventory products and order new supplies. Monitor operations to ensure compliance with applicable health, safety, or hygiene standards. Perform accounting duties, such as recording daily cash flow, preparing bank deposits, or generating financial statements. Recruit, interview, or hire employees. Respond to customer inquiries or complaints. Schedule staff or supervise scheduling. Verify staff credentials, such as educational and certification requirements.

Education/Training Required: Work experience in a related occupation. **Education and Training Program:** Resort Management. **Knowledge/ Courses:** No data available.

Personality Type: Enterprising-Conventional-Social. **Career Cluster:** 04 Business, Management, and Administration. **Career Pathway:** 4.1 Management. **Other Jobs in This Pathway:** Brownfield Redevelopment Specialists and Site Managers; Business Continuity Planners; Business Operations Specialists, All Other; Chief Executives; Chief Sustainability Officers; Compliance Managers; Computer and Information Systems Managers; Construction Managers; Customs Brokers; Energy Auditors; First-Line Supervisors of Office and Administrative Support Workers; General and Operations Managers; Investment Fund Managers; Loss Prevention Managers; Management Analysts; Managers, All Other; Public Relations Specialists; Regulatory Affairs Managers; Sales Managers; Security Management Specialists; Security Managers; Supply Chain Managers; Sustainability Specialists; Wind Energy Operations Managers; Wind Energy Project Managers; others.

Skills: No data available.

Work Environment: No data available.

First-Line Supervisors of Police and Detectives

- ❋ Annual Earnings: G $78,600, * $78,260
- ❋ Earnings Growth Potential: Medium (40.4%)
- ❋ Growth: G 8.0%, * 8.1%
- ❋ Annual Job Openings: G 3,530, * 5,050
- ❋ Self-Employed: 0.0%

Detailed Fields with Greatest Employment: State and Local Government (90.1%); Federal Government (7.3%); Educational Services, Public and Private (2.6%); Hospitals, Public and Private (0.1%);

Detailed Fields with Highest Growth (Projected Growth for This Job): Hospitals, Public and Private (16.7%); Educational Services, Public and Private (11.6%); State and Local Government, Excluding Education and Hospitals (8.1%); Federal Government (6.9%)

Other Considerations for Job Outlook: Population growth is the main source of demand for police services. Overall, opportunities in local police departments should be favorable for qualified applicants.

Supervise and coordinate activities of members of police force. Supervise and coordinate the investigation of criminal cases, offering guidance and expertise to investigators, and ensuring that procedures are conducted in accordance with laws and regulations. Maintain logs; prepare reports; and direct the preparation, handling, and maintenance of departmental records. Explain police operations to subordinates to assist them in performing their job duties. Cooperate with court personnel and officials from other law enforcement agencies and testify in court as necessary. Review contents of written orders to ensure adherence to legal requirements. Investigate and resolve personnel problems within organization and charges of misconduct against staff. Direct collection, preparation, and handling of evidence and personal property of prisoners. Inform personnel of changes in regulations and policies, implications of new or amended laws, and new techniques of police work. Train staff in proper police work procedures.

Education/Training Required: Work experience in a related occupation. **Education and Training Programs:** Corrections; Criminal Justice/Law Enforcement Administration; Criminal Justice/Safety Studies. **Knowledge/Courses:** Public Safety and Security; Law and Government; Psychology; Sociology and Anthropology; Therapy and Counseling; Personnel and Human Resources.

Personality Type: Enterprising-Social-Conventional. **Career Cluster:** 12 Law, Public Safety, Corrections, and Security. **Career Pathways:** 12.1 Correction Services; 12.4 Law Enforcement Services. **Other Jobs in These Pathways:** Bailiffs; Child, Family, and School Social Workers; Correctional Officers and Jailers; Criminal Investigators and Special Agents; First-Line Supervisors of Correctional Officers; Forensic Science Technicians; Immigration and Customs Inspectors; Intelligence Analysts; Police Detectives; Police Identification and Records Officers; Police Patrol Officers; Protective Service Workers, All Other; Remote Sensing Scientists and Technologists; Security Guards; Sheriffs and Deputy Sheriffs.

Skills: Management of Financial Resources; Management of Personnel Resources; Persuasion; Management of Material Resources; Monitoring; Learning Strategies; Time Management; Instructing.

Work Environment: More often indoors than outdoors; sitting; noise; very hot or cold; bright or inadequate lighting; contaminants; hazardous equipment.

Gas Plant Operators

- ❋ Annual Earnings: U $56,830, * $57,200
- ❋ Earnings Growth Potential: Low (32.2%)
- ❋ Growth: U 7.7%, * –4.2%
- ❋ Annual Job Openings: U 110, * 340
- ❋ Self-Employed: 0.7%

Detailed Fields with Greatest Employment: Utilities (40.4%); Pipeline Transportation (26.7%); State and Local Government (2.6%); Oil and Gas Extraction (13.6%); Chemical Manufacturing (11.0%)

Detailed Fields with Highest Growth (Projected Growth for This Job): Utilities (7.7%); State and Local Government, Excluding Education and Hospitals (7.7%); Management of Companies and Enterprises (6.3%); Pipeline Transportation (–3.8%); Merchant Wholesalers, Nondurable Goods (–12.5%)

Other Considerations for Job Outlook: Slow decline in employment is projected.

*C=Computer Systems Design, E=Educational Services, G=Government, H=Health Care, R=Repair and Maintenance, U=Utilities, *=All Fields*

150 Best Jobs for a Secure Future © *JIST Works* — 227

Distribute or process gas for utility companies and others by controlling compressors to maintain specified pressures on main pipelines. Determine causes of abnormal pressure variances and make corrective recommendations such as installation of pipes to relieve overloading. Distribute or process gas for utility companies or industrial plants, using panel boards, control boards, and semi-automatic equipment. Start and shut down plant equipment. Test gas, chemicals, and air during processing to assess factors such as purity and moisture content and to detect quality problems or gas or chemical leaks. Adjust temperature, pressure, vacuum, level, flow rate, and transfer of gas to maintain processes at required levels or to correct problems. Change charts in recording meters. Calculate gas ratios to detect deviations from specifications, using testing apparatus. Clean, maintain, and repair equipment, using hand tools, or request that repair and maintenance work be performed. Collaborate with other operators to solve unit problems.

Education/Training Required: Long-term on-the-job training. **Education and Training Program:** Mechanic and Repair Technologies/Technicians, Other. **Knowledge/Courses:** Mechanical Devices; Physics; Building and Construction; Public Safety and Security; Chemistry; Engineering and Technology.

Personality Type: Realistic-Conventional. **Career Cluster:** 13 Manufacturing. **Career Pathway:** 13.1 Production. **Other Jobs in This Pathway:** Assemblers and Fabricators, All Other; Cabinetmakers and Bench Carpenters; Coating, Painting, and Spraying Machine Setters, Operators, and Tenders; Computer-Controlled Machine Tool Operators, Metal and Plastic; Cost Estimators; Cutting, Punching, and Press Machine Setters, Operators, and Tenders, Metal and Plastic; First-Line Supervisors of Mechanics, Installers, and Repairers; First-Line Supervisors of Production and Operating Workers; Geothermal Technicians; Helpers— Production Workers; Machine Feeders and Off-bearers; Machinists; Mixing and Blending Machine Setters, Operators, and Tenders; Molding, Coremaking, and Casting Machine Setters, Operators, and Tenders, Metal and Plastic; Packaging and Filling Machine Operators and Tenders; Packers and Packagers, Hand; Paper Goods Machine Setters, Operators, and Tenders; Production Workers, All Other; Recycling and Reclamation Workers; Recycling Coordinators; Sheet Metal Workers; Solderers and Brazers; Structural Metal Fabricators and Fitters; Team Assemblers; Welders, Cutters, and Welder Fitters; others.

Skills: Operation Monitoring; Operation and Control; Repairing; Equipment Maintenance; Troubleshooting; Equipment Selection; Quality Control Analysis; Technology Design.

Work Environment: More often outdoors than indoors; sitting; using hands; noise; very hot or cold; contaminants; cramped work space; hazardous conditions; hazardous equipment; minor burns, cuts, bites, or stings.

General and Operations Managers

- ❀ Annual Earnings: R $78,440, H $84,032, E $88,880, G $92,970, U $109,870, C $137,170, * $94,400
- ❀ Earnings Growth Potential: High (49.9%)
- ❀ Growth: U –20.5%, R –5.6%, G –2.5%, E 11.3%, H 11.4%, C 28.7%, * –0.1%
- ❀ Annual Job Openings: C 1,280, U 2,540, R 3,090, E 47,370, G 112,930, H 188,340, * 50,220
- ❀ Self-Employed: 0.9%

Detailed Fields with Greatest Employment: Professional, Scientific, and Technical Services (9.2%);

Administrative and Support Services (6.2%); Merchant Wholesalers, Durable Goods (4.6%); Specialty Trade Contractors (4.2%); Management of Companies and Enterprises (3.9%)

Detailed Fields with Highest Growth (Projected Growth for This Job): Internet Service Providers, Web Search Portals, and Data Processing Services (36.0%); Professional, Scientific, and Technical Services (23.9%); Lessors of Nonfinancial Intangible Assets (Except Copyrighted Works) (20.4%); Ambulatory Health Care Services (18.9%); Other Information Services (15.6%)

Other Considerations for Job Outlook: The number of top executives is expected to remain steady, but employment may be adversely affected by consolidation and mergers. Keen competition is expected.

Plan, direct, or coordinate the operations of companies or public- and private-sector organizations. Duties and responsibilities include formulating policies, managing daily operations, and planning the use of materials and human resources, but are too diverse and general in nature to be classified in any one functional area of management or administration, such as personnel, purchasing, or administrative services. Includes owners and managers who head small business establishments whose duties are primarily managerial. Oversee activities directly related to making products or providing services. Direct and coordinate activities of businesses or departments concerned with the production, pricing, sales, or distribution of products. Review financial statements, sales and activity reports, and other performance data to measure productivity and goal achievement and to determine areas needing cost reduction and program improvement. Manage staff, preparing work schedules and assigning specific duties. Direct and coordinate organization's financial and budget activities to fund operations, maximize investments and increase efficiency. Establish and implement departmental policies, goals, objectives, and procedures, conferring with board members, organization officials, and staff members as necessary. Determine staffing requirements and interview, hire, and train new employees, or oversee those personnel processes.

Education/Training Required: Work experience plus degree. **Education and Training Programs:** Business Administration and Management, General; Entrepreneurship/Entrepreneurial Studies; International Business/Trade/Commerce; Public Administration. **Knowledge/Courses:** Economics and Accounting; Personnel and Human Resources; Administration and Management; Sales and Marketing; Clerical Practices; Building and Construction.

Personality Type: Enterprising-Conventional-Social. **Career Clusters:** 04 Business, Management, and Administration; 07 Government and Public Administration. **Career Pathways:** 4.1 Management; 7.1 Governance. **Other Jobs in These Pathways:** Administrative Services Managers; Brownfield Redevelopment Specialists and Site Managers; Business Continuity Planners; Business Operations Specialists, All Other; Chief Executives; Chief Sustainability Officers; Compliance Managers; Computer and Information Systems Managers; Construction Managers; Customs Brokers; Energy Auditors; First-Line Supervisors of Office and Administrative Support Workers; Investment Fund Managers; Loss Prevention Managers; Management Analysts; Managers, All Other; Public Relations Specialists; Regulatory Affairs Managers; Sales Managers; Security Management Specialists; Security Managers; Supply Chain Managers; Sustainability Specialists; Wind Energy Operations Managers; Wind Energy Project Managers; others.

Skills: Management of Material Resources; Management of Financial Resources; Operations

G

C=Computer Systems Design, E=Educational Services, G=Government, H=Health Care, R=Repair and Maintenance, U=Utilities, *=All Fields

150 Best Jobs for a Secure Future © JIST Works 229

Analysis; Management of Personnel Resources; Negotiation; Systems Analysis; Coordination; Systems Evaluation.

Work Environment: Indoors; more often sitting than standing; noise.

Graphic Designers

- ❋ Annual Earnings: C $50,640, * $43,500
- ❋ Earnings Growth Potential: Medium (39.8%)
- ❋ Growth: C 40.3%, * 12.9%
- ❋ Annual Job Openings: C 530, * 12,480
- ❋ Self-Employed: 26.3%

Detailed Fields with Greatest Employment: Printing and Related Support Activities (8.4%); Professional, Scientific, and Technical Services (37.1%); Miscellaneous Manufacturing (3.6%); Administrative and Support Services (3.3%); Educational Services, Public and Private (2.9%)

Detailed Fields with Highest Growth (Projected Growth for This Job): Internet Service Providers, Web Search Portals, and Data Processing Services (45.7%); Lessors of Nonfinancial Intangible Assets (Except Copyrighted Works) (38.5%); Professional, Scientific, and Technical Services (37.2%); Ambulatory Health Care Services (32.0%); Other Information Services (30.6%)

Other Considerations for Job Outlook: Advertising firms that specialize in digital and interactive designs are expected to drive growth, but declines in print publishing will temper this growth. Competition is expected to be keen.

Design or create graphics to meet specific commercial or promotional needs such as packaging, displays, or logos. May use a variety of media to achieve artistic or decorative effects. Create designs, concepts, and sample layouts based on knowledge of layout principles and esthetic design concepts. Determine size and arrangement of illustrative material and copy; and select style and size of type. Confer with clients to discuss and determine layout designs. Develop graphics and layouts for product illustrations, company logos, and Internet websites. Review final layouts and suggest improvements as needed. Prepare illustrations or rough sketches of material, discussing them with clients or supervisors and making necessary changes. Use computer software to generate new images. Key information into computer equipment to create layouts for client or supervisor. Maintain archive of images, photos, or previous work products. Prepare notes and instructions for workers who assemble and prepare final layouts for printing. Draw and print charts, graphs, illustrations, and other artwork, using computer.

Education/Training Required: Bachelor's degree. **Education and Training Programs:** Agricultural Communication/Journalism; Commercial and Advertising Art; Computer Graphics; Design and Visual Communications, General; Graphic Design; Industrial and Product Design; Web Page, Digital/Multimedia and Information Resources Design. **Knowledge/Courses:** Fine Arts; Design; Communications and Media; Sales and Marketing; Sociology and Anthropology; Computers and Electronics.

Personality Type: Artistic-Realistic-Enterprising. **Career Clusters:** 01 Agriculture, Food, and Natural Resources; 03 Arts, Audio/Video Technology, and Communications; 11 Information Technology. **Career Pathways:** 1.7 Agribusiness Systems; 3.1 Audio and Video Technology and Film; 3.3 Visual Arts; 11.1 Network Systems. **Other Jobs in These Pathways:** Agents and Business Managers of Artists, Performers, and Athletes; Art Directors; Artists and Related Workers, All Other; Audio and Video Equipment Technicians; Broadcast

Technicians; Camera Operators, Television, Video, and Motion Picture; Choreographers; Commercial and Industrial Designers; Computer and Information Systems Managers; Craft Artists; Dancers; Designers, All Other; Farm and Home Management Advisors; Fashion Designers; Film and Video Editors; Fine Artists, Including Painters, Sculptors, and Illustrators; Interior Designers; Managers, All Other; Media and Communication Equipment Workers, All Other; Media and Communication Workers, All Other; Multimedia Artists and Animators; Painting, Coating, and Decorating Workers; Photographers; Reporters and Correspondents; Technical Directors/Managers; others.

Skills: Operations Analysis; Technology Design; Negotiation; Management of Financial Resources; Time Management; Complex Problem Solving; Reading Comprehension; Writing.

Work Environment: Indoors; sitting; using hands; repetitive motions.

Health Educators

- ❋ Annual Earnings: H $49,683, * $45,830
- ❋ Earnings Growth Potential: High (41.7%)
- ❋ Growth: H 20.8%, * 18.2%
- ❋ Annual Job Openings: H 1,950, * 2,600
- ❋ Self-Employed: 0.3%

Detailed Fields with Greatest Employment: Educational Services, Public and Private (9.2%); Nursing and Residential Care Facilities (2.9%); Professional, Scientific, and Technical Services (2.4%); Hospitals, Public and Private (18.8%); Social Assistance (15.0%)

Detailed Fields with Highest Growth (Projected Growth for This Job): Professional, Scientific, and Technical Services (41.5%); Ambulatory Health Care Services (35.8%); Administrative and Support Services (24.0%); Educational Services, Public and Private (23.9%); Social Assistance (23.4%)

Other Considerations for Job Outlook: As health-care costs rise, insurance companies, businesses, and governments are expected to hire health educators to teach the public how to avoid and detect illnesses. Opportunities should be favorable, especially for those who have gained experience through volunteer work or internships.

Promote, maintain, and improve individual and community health by assisting individuals and communities to adopt healthy behaviors. Collect and analyze data to identify community needs prior to planning, implementing, monitoring, and evaluating programs designed to encourage healthy lifestyles, policies, and environments. May also serve as a resource to assist individuals, other professionals, or the community and may administer fiscal resources for health education programs. Document activities, recording information such as the numbers of applications completed, presentations conducted, and persons assisted. Develop and present health education and promotion programs such as training workshops, conferences, and school or community presentations. Develop and maintain cooperative working relationships with agencies and organizations interested in public health care. Prepare and distribute health education materials, including reports; bulletins; and visual aids such as films, videotapes, photographs, and posters. Develop operational plans and policies necessary to achieve health education objectives and services. Collaborate with health specialists and civic groups to determine community health needs and the availability of services and to develop goals for meeting needs. Maintain databases, mailing lists, telephone networks, and other information to facilitate the functioning of health education programs.

---

*C=Computer Systems Design, E=Educational Services, G=Government, H=Health Care, R=Repair and Maintenance, U=Utilities, *=All Fields*

Education/Training Required: Bachelor's degree. **Education and Training Programs:** Community Health Services/Liaison/Counseling; Health Communication; International Public Health/International Health; Maternal and Child Health; Public Health Education and Promotion. **Knowledge/Courses:** Sociology and Anthropology; Customer and Personal Service; Education and Training; Personnel and Human Resources; Therapy and Counseling; Psychology.

Personality Type: Social-Enterprising. **Career Clusters:** 08 Health Science; 10 Human Services. **Career Pathways:** 8.3 Health Informatics; 10.2 Counseling and Mental Health Services. **Other Jobs in These Pathways:** Clergy; Clinical Psychologists; Counseling Psychologists; Directors, Religious Activities and Education; Editors; Engineers, All Other; Executive Secretaries and Executive Administrative Assistants; First-Line Supervisors of Office and Administrative Support Workers; Healthcare Social Workers; Medical and Health Services Managers; Medical Assistants; Medical Records and Health Information Technicians; Medical Secretaries; Medical Transcriptionists; Mental Health and Substance Abuse Social Workers; Mental Health Counselors; Physical Therapists; Psychiatric Aides; Psychiatric Technicians; Public Relations Specialists; Receptionists and Information Clerks; Recreation Workers; Rehabilitation Counselors; School Psychologists; Substance Abuse and Behavioral Disorder Counselors; others.

Skills: Operations Analysis; Science; Writing; Learning Strategies; Speaking; Persuasion; Social Perceptiveness; Service Orientation.

Work Environment: Indoors; sitting; using hands; exposed to disease or infections.

Healthcare Social Workers

- ❋ Annual Earnings: H $49,227, * $47,230
- ❋ Earnings Growth Potential: Medium (37.6%)
- ❋ Growth: H 25.5%, * 22.4%
- ❋ Annual Job Openings: H 7,640, * 6,590
- ❋ Self-Employed: 2.2%

Detailed Fields with Greatest Employment: Hospitals, Public and Private (35.0%); Religious, Grantmaking, Civic, Professional, and Similar Organizations (3.1%); Ambulatory Health Care Services (18.7%); Nursing and Residential Care Facilities (13.9%); Social Assistance (13.7%)

Detailed Fields with Highest Growth (Projected Growth for This Job): Professional, Scientific, and Technical Services (56.9%); Social Assistance (52.0%); Ambulatory Health Care Services (41.6%); Administrative and Support Services (25.0%); Nursing and Residential Care Facilities (22.1%)

Other Considerations for Job Outlook: The rapidly increasing elderly population is expected to spur demand for social services. Job prospects should be favorable because of the need to replace the many workers who are leaving the occupation permanently.

Provide persons, families, or vulnerable populations with the psychosocial support needed to cope with chronic, acute, or terminal illnesses such as Alzheimer's, cancer, or AIDS. Services include advising family caregivers, providing patient education and counseling, and making necessary referrals for other social services. Advocate for clients or patients to resolve crises. Collaborate with other professionals to evaluate patients' medical or physical condition and to assess client needs. Refer patients, clients, or families to community resources to assist in recovery from mental or physical illnesses and to provide access to services such as financial assistance, legal aid, housing, job placement, or education. Counsel clients and patients in individual and group sessions to help them overcome dependencies, recover from illnesses, and adjust to life. Use consultation data and social work experience to plan and coordinate client or patient care and rehabilitation, following through to ensure service efficacy. Plan discharge from care facility to home or other care facility. Organize support groups or counsel family members to assist them in understanding, dealing with, and supporting clients or patients. Modify treatment plans to comply with changes in clients' statuses.

Education/Training Required: Bachelor's degree. **Education and Training Program:** Clinical/Medical Social Work. **Knowledge/Courses:** Therapy and Counseling; Sociology and Anthropology; Psychology; Philosophy and Theology; Customer and Personal Service; Medicine and Dentistry.

Personality Type: Social-Investigative. **Career Cluster:** 10 Human Services. **Career Pathway:** 10.2 Counseling and Mental Health Services. **Other Jobs in This Pathway:** Clergy; Clinical Psychologists; Counseling Psychologists; Counselors, All Other; Directors, Religious Activities and Education; Epidemiologists; Health Educators; Marriage and Family Therapists; Mental Health and Substance Abuse Social Workers; Mental Health Counselors; Music Directors; Psychologists, All Other; Recreation Workers; Religious Workers, All Other; School Psychologists; Substance Abuse and Behavioral Disorder Counselors.

Skills: Social Perceptiveness; Science; Operations Analysis; Service Orientation; Learning Strategies; Active Listening; Writing; Systems Evaluation.

Work Environment: Indoors; sitting; noise; exposed to disease or infections.

Home Appliance Repairers

- ❀ Annual Earnings: R $35,890, * $34,730
- ❀ Earnings Growth Potential: High (41.3%)
- ❀ Growth: R 0.6%, * 2.2%
- ❀ Annual Job Openings: R 230, * 870
- ❀ Self-Employed: 26.8%

Detailed Fields with Greatest Employment: Merchant Wholesalers, Durable Goods (4.4%); Repair and Maintenance (33.3%); Electronics and Appliance Stores (33.1%); Personal and Laundry Services (3.4%); Utilities (3.3%)

Detailed Fields with Highest Growth (Projected Growth for This Job): Wholesale Electronic Markets and Agents and Brokers (29.4%); Specialty Trade Contractors (22.5%); Administrative and Support Services (18.2%); Warehousing and Storage (15.5%); Miscellaneous Store Retailers (15.2%)

Other Considerations for Job Outlook: Smaller, inexpensive appliances are increasingly replaced rather than repaired, resulting in minimal projected job growth for repairers to service major appliances. Excellent job prospects are expected, however. Opportunities should be best in metropolitan areas and for job seekers who have formal training.

Repair, adjust, or install all types of electric or gas household appliances, such as refrigerators, washers, dryers, and ovens. Clean, lubricate, and touch up minor defects on newly installed or repaired appliances. Observe and test operation of appliances following installation and make any initial installation adjustments that are necessary. Level refrigerators, adjust doors, and connect water lines to water pipes for ice makers and water dispensers, using hand tools. Level washing machines and connect hoses to water pipes, using hand tools.

---

*C=Computer Systems Design, E=Educational Services, G=Government, H=Health Care, R=Repair and Maintenance, U=Utilities, *=All Fields*

Maintain stocks of parts used in on-site installation, maintenance, and repair of appliances. Instruct customers regarding operation and care of appliances and provide information such as emergency service numbers. Provide repair cost estimates and recommend whether appliance repair or replacement is a better choice. Conserve, recover, and recycle refrigerants used in cooling systems. Contact supervisors or offices to receive repair assignments. Install gas pipes and water lines to connect appliances to existing gas lines or plumbing.

Education/Training Required: Long-term on-the-job training. **Education and Training Programs:** Appliance Installation and Repair Technology/Technician; Electrical/Electronics Equipment Installation and Repair, General; Home Furnishings and Equipment Installer Training. **Knowledge/Courses:** Sales and Marketing; Mechanical Devices; Customer and Personal Service; Physics; Economics and Accounting; Engineering and Technology.

Personality Type: Realistic-Conventional-Investigative. **Career Cluster:** 02 Architecture and Construction. **Career Pathway:** 2.3 Maintenance/Operations. **Other Jobs in This Pathway:** Coin, Vending, and Amusement Machine Servicers and Repairers; Heating and Air Conditioning Mechanics and Installers; Refrigeration Mechanics and Installers; Security and Fire Alarm Systems Installers.

Skills: Repairing; Equipment Maintenance; Troubleshooting; Installation; Quality Control Analysis; Equipment Selection; Operation and Control; Operation Monitoring.

Work Environment: Indoors; standing; kneeling; crouching, stooping, or crawling; using hands; bending or twisting the body; contaminants; cramped work space; minor burns, cuts, bites, or stings.

Human Resources Specialists

- ❀ Annual Earnings: H $50,133, E $50,810, G $58,040, C $63,090, * $52,690
- ❀ Earnings Growth Potential: High (44.9%)
- ❀ Growth: G 8.5%, H 26.4%, E 33.9%, C 54.3%, * 27.9%
- ❀ Annual Job Openings: E 420, C 630, H 1,660, G 2,330, * 11,230
- ❀ Self-Employed: 1.6%

Detailed Fields with Greatest Employment: State and Local Government (9.2%); Educational Services, Public and Private (5.2%); Social Assistance (5.2%); Administrative and Support Services (40.8%); Management of Companies and Enterprises (4.5%)

Detailed Fields with Highest Growth (Projected Growth for This Job): Internet Service Providers, Web Search Portals, and Data Processing Services (62.5%); Professional, Scientific, and Technical Services (45.6%); Wholesale Electronic Markets and Agents and Brokers (43.8%); Other Information Services (42.9%); Specialty Trade Contractors (40.0%)

Other Considerations for Job Outlook: Efforts to recruit and retain employees, the growing importance of employee training, and new legal standards are expected to increase employment of these workers. College graduates and those with certification should have the best opportunities.

Recruit and place workers. Address employee relations issues, such as harassment allegations, work complaints, or other employee concerns. Analyze employment-related data and prepare required reports. Conduct exit interviews and ensure that necessary employment termination paperwork is completed. Conduct reference or background checks on job applicants. Confer with management to develop or implement personnel policies or procedures. Contact job applicants to inform them of the status of their applications. Develop or implement recruiting strategies to meet current or anticipated staffing needs. Hire employees and process hiring-related paperwork. Inform job applicants of details such as duties and responsibilities, compensation, benefits, schedules, working conditions, or promotion opportunities. Interpret and explain human resources policies, procedures, laws, standards, or regulations. Interview job applicants to obtain information on work history, training, education, or job skills.

Education/Training Required: Bachelor's degree. **Education and Training Programs:** Human Resources Management/Personnel Administration, General; Labor and Industrial Relations. **Knowledge/Courses:** Personnel and Human Resources; Sales and Marketing; Clerical Practices; Law and Government; Customer and Personal Service; Communications and Media.

Personality Type: Enterprising-Social-Conventional. **Career Cluster:** 04 Business, Management, and Administration. **Career Pathway:** 4.3 Human Resources. **Other Jobs in This Pathway:** Business Teachers, Postsecondary; Compensation, Benefits, and Job Analysis Specialists; Employment, Recruitment, and Placement Specialists; Labor Relations Specialists; Training and Development Specialists.

Skills: Science; Service Orientation; Social Perceptiveness; Speaking; Operations Analysis; Management of Personnel Resources; Writing; Active Listening.

Work Environment: Indoors; sitting; repetitive motions.

Industrial Engineering Technicians

- ❋ Annual Earnings: C $53,250, * $48,210
- ❋ Earnings Growth Potential: Low (34.5%)
- ❋ Growth: C 54.1%, * 6.6%
- ❋ Annual Job Openings: C 80, * 1,850
- ❋ Self-Employed: 0.7%

Detailed Fields with Greatest Employment: Professional, Scientific, and Technical Services (9.3%); Machinery Manufacturing (8.1%); Chemical Manufacturing (5.0%); Administrative and Support Services (4.4%); Fabricated Metal Product Manufacturing (3.9%)

Detailed Fields with Highest Growth (Projected Growth for This Job): Internet Service Providers, Web Search Portals, and Data Processing Services (62.9%); Waste Management and Remediation Services (50.0%); Professional, Scientific, and Technical Services (45.8%); Wholesale Electronic Markets and Agents and Brokers (38.1%); Support Activities for Transportation (37.5%)

Other Considerations for Job Outlook: Labor-saving efficiencies and the automation of many engineering support activities will limit the need for new engineering technicians. In general, opportunities should be best for job seekers who have an associate degree or other postsecondary training in engineering technology.

Apply engineering theory and principles to problems of industrial layout or manufacturing production, usually under the direction of engineering staff. May study and record time, motion, method, and speed involved in performance of production, maintenance, clerical, and other worker operations for such purposes as establishing standard production rates

---

C=Computer Systems Design, E=Educational Services, G=Government, H=Health Care, R=Repair and Maintenance, U=Utilities, *=All Fields

or improving efficiency. Recommend revision to methods of operation, material handling, equipment layout, or other changes to increase production or improve standards. Study time, motion, methods, and speed involved in maintenance, production, and other operations to establish standard production rate and improve efficiency. Interpret engineering drawings, schematic diagrams, or formulas and confer with management or engineering staff to determine quality and reliability standards. Recommend modifications to existing quality or production standards to achieve optimum quality within limits of equipment capability. Aid in planning work assignments in accordance with worker performance, machine capacity, production schedules, and anticipated delays. Observe workers using equipment to verify that equipment is being operated and maintained according to quality assurance standards. Observe workers operating equipment or performing tasks to determine time involved and fatigue rate, using timing devices.

Education/Training Required: Associate degree. **Education and Training Programs:** Engineering/Industrial Management; Industrial Production Technologies/Technicians, Other; Industrial Technology/Technician; Manufacturing Engineering Technology/Technician. **Knowledge/Courses:** Production and Processing; Engineering and Technology; Design; Clerical Practices; Mathematics; Mechanical.

Personality Type: Investigative-Realistic-Conventional. **Career Clusters:** 13 Manufacturing; 15 Science, Technology, Engineering, and Mathematics. **Career Pathways:** 13.3 Maintenance, Installation, and Repair; 15.1 Engineering and Technology. **Other Jobs in These Pathways:** Architectural and Engineering Managers; Automotive Engineers; Automotive Specialty Technicians; Biochemical Engineers; Biofuels/Biodiesel Technology and Product Development Managers; Civil Engineers; Cost Estimators; Electrical and Electronic Equipment

Assemblers; Energy Engineers; Engineers, All Other; Fuel Cell Engineers; Human Factors Engineers and Ergonomists; Industrial Engineers; Industrial Machinery Mechanics; Manufacturing Engineers; Mechanical Engineers; Mechatronics Engineers; Microsystems Engineers; Nanosystems Engineers; Photonics Engineers; Robotics Engineers; Solar Energy Systems Engineers; Transportation Engineers; Validation Engineers; Wind Energy Engineers; others.

Skills: Technology Design; Mathematics; Systems Evaluation; Monitoring; Programming; Systems Analysis; Quality Control Analysis; Judgment and Decision Making.

Work Environment: Indoors; standing; walking and running; noise; contaminants; hazardous equipment.

Industrial Engineers

- ❋ Annual Earnings: U $75,270, C $78,670, G $88,950, * $76,100
- ❋ Earnings Growth Potential: Low (34.7%)
- ❋ Growth: U –3.1%, G 21.0%, C 64.5%, * 14.2%
- ❋ Annual Job Openings: G 50, U 50, C 200, * 8,540
- ❋ Self-Employed: 0.7%

Detailed Fields with Greatest Employment: Machinery Manufacturing (7.6%); Fabricated Metal Product Manufacturing (6.0%); Management of Companies and Enterprises (4.7%); Chemical Manufacturing (4.0%); Plastics and Rubber Products Manufacturing (3.9%)

Detailed Fields with Highest Growth (Projected Growth for This Job): Internet Service Providers, Web Search Portals, and Data Processing Services (74.5%); Professional, Scientific, and Technical Services (58.1%); Waste Management and Remediation Services (53.6%); Support Activities for Transportation (47.1%); Wholesale Electronic Markets and Agents and Brokers (46.5%)

Other Considerations for Job Outlook: Industrial engineers are expected to have employment growth of 14 percent from 2008–2018, faster than the average for all occupations. As firms look for new ways to reduce costs and raise productivity, they increasingly will turn to industrial engineers to develop more efficient processes and reduce costs, delays, and waste. This focus should lead to job growth for these engineers, even in some manufacturing industries with declining employment overall. Because their work is similar to that done in management occupations, many industrial engineers leave the occupation to become managers. Numerous openings will be created by the need to replace industrial engineers who transfer to other occupations or leave the labor force.

Design, develop, test, and evaluate integrated systems for managing industrial production processes, including human work factors, quality control, inventory control, logistics and material flow, cost analysis, and production coordination. Analyze statistical data and product specifications to determine standards and establish quality and reliability objectives of finished product. Develop manufacturing methods, labor utilization standards, and cost analysis systems to promote efficient staff and facility utilization. Recommend methods for improving utilization of personnel, material, and utilities. Plan and establish sequence of operations to fabricate and assemble parts or products and to promote efficient utilization. Apply statistical methods and perform mathematical calculations to determine manufacturing processes, staff requirements, and production standards. Coordinate quality control objectives and activities to resolve production problems, maximize product reliability, and minimize cost. Confer with vendors, staff, and management personnel regarding purchases, procedures, product specifications, manufacturing capabilities, and project status.

Education/Training Required: Bachelor's degree. **Education and Training Program:** Industrial Engineering. **Knowledge/Courses:** Engineering and Technology; Design; Production and Processing; Mechanical Practices; Physics; Mathematics.

Personality Type: Investigative-Conventional-Enterprising. **Career Cluster:** 15 Science, Technology, Engineering, and Mathematics. **Career Pathway:** 15.1 Engineering and Technology. **Other Jobs in This Pathway:** Architectural and Engineering Managers; Automotive Engineers; Biochemical Engineers; Biofuels/Biodiesel Technology and Product Development Managers; Civil Engineers; Cost Estimators; Education, Training, and Library Workers, All Other; Electrical Engineers; Electronics Engineers, Except Computer; Energy Engineers; Engineers, All Other; Fuel Cell Engineers; Human Factors Engineers and Ergonomists; Manufacturing Engineers; Mechanical Engineers; Mechatronics Engineers; Microsystems Engineers; Nanosystems Engineers; Photonics Engineers; Radio Frequency Identification Device Specialists; Robotics Engineers; Solar Energy Systems Engineers; Transportation Engineers; Validation Engineers; Wind Energy Engineers; others.

Skills: Management of Material Resources; Management of Financial Resources; Mathematics; Systems Evaluation; Systems Analysis; Reading Comprehension; Complex Problem Solving; Technology Design.

Work Environment: Indoors; sitting; noise; contaminants; hazardous equipment.

---

*C=Computer Systems Design, E=Educational Services, G=Government, H=Health Care, R=Repair and Maintenance, U=Utilities, *=All Fields*

Job Specialization: Human Factors Engineers and Ergonomists

Design objects, facilities, and environments to optimize human well-being and overall system performance, applying theory, principles, and data regarding the relationship between humans and respective technology. Investigate and analyze characteristics of human behavior and performance as it relates to the use of technology. Write, review, or comment on documents such as proposals, test plans, and procedures. Train users in task techniques or ergonomic principles. Review health, safety, accident, or worker compensation records to evaluate safety program effectiveness or to identify jobs with high incidents of injury. Provide human factors technical expertise on topics such as advanced user-interface technology development and the role of human users in automated or autonomous subsystems in advanced vehicle systems. Investigate theoretical or conceptual issues, such as the human design considerations of lunar landers or habitats. Estimate time and resource requirements for ergonomic or human factors research or development projects. Conduct interviews or surveys of users or customers to collect information on topics such as requirements, needs, fatigue, ergonomics, and interface.

Education/Training Required: Bachelor's degree. **Education and Training Program:** Industrial Engineering. **Knowledge/Courses:** No data available.

Personality Type: No data available. **Career Cluster:** 15 Science, Technology, Engineering, and Mathematics. **Career Pathway:** 15.1 Engineering and Technology. **Other Jobs in This Pathway:** Architectural and Engineering Managers; Automotive Engineers; Biochemical Engineers; Biofuels/Biodiesel Technology and Product Development Managers; Civil Engineers; Cost Estimators; Education, Training, and Library Workers, All Other; Electrical Engineers; Electronics Engineers, Except Computer; Energy Engineers; Engineers, All Other; Fuel Cell Engineers; Industrial Engineers; Manufacturing Engineers; Mechanical Engineers; Mechatronics Engineers; Microsystems Engineers; Nanosystems Engineers; Photonics Engineers; Radio Frequency Identification Device Specialists; Robotics Engineers; Solar Energy Systems Engineers; Transportation Engineers; Validation Engineers; Wind Energy Engineers; others.

Skills: No data available.

Work Environment: No data available.

Industrial Machinery Mechanics

- ❋ Annual Earnings: R $40,140, G $53,000, U $57,270, * $45,420
- ❋ Earnings Growth Potential: Low (34.2%)
- ❋ Growth: U –0.6%, R 19.1%, G 24.6%, * 7.3%
- ❋ Annual Job Openings: U 160, G 210, R 650, * 6,240
- ❋ Self-Employed: 2.2%

Detailed Fields with Greatest Employment: Repair and Maintenance (9.8%); Merchant Wholesalers, Durable Goods (8.7%); Chemical Manufacturing (6.7%); Transportation Equipment Manufacturing (5.6%); Machinery Manufacturing (5.2%)

Detailed Fields with Highest Growth (Projected Growth for This Job): Waste Management and Remediation Services (51.4%); Professional, Scientific, and Technical Services (44.3%); Miscellaneous Manufacturing (39.0%); Administrative and Support Services (37.5%); Construction of Buildings (35.3%)

Other Considerations for Job Outlook: The increasing reliance on machinery in manufacturing is expected to lead to employment growth for these maintenance and installation workers. Favorable job prospects are expected.

Repair, install, adjust, or maintain industrial production and processing machinery or refinery and pipeline distribution systems. Disassemble machinery and equipment to remove parts and make repairs. Repair and replace broken or malfunctioning components of machinery and equipment. Repair and maintain the operating condition of industrial production and processing machinery and equipment. Examine parts for defects such as breakage and excessive wear. Reassemble equipment after completion of inspections, testing, or repairs. Observe and test the operation of machinery and equipment to diagnose malfunctions, using voltmeters and other testing devices. Operate newly repaired machinery and equipment to verify the adequacy of repairs. Clean, lubricate, and adjust parts, equipment, and machinery. Analyze test results, machine error messages, and information obtained from operators to diagnose equipment problems. Record repairs and maintenance performed. Study blueprints and manufacturers' manuals to determine correct installation and operation of machinery.

Education/Training Required: Long-term on-the-job training. **Education and Training Programs:** Heavy/Industrial Equipment Maintenance Technologies, Other; Industrial Mechanics and Maintenance Technology. **Knowledge/Courses:** Mechanical Practices; Engineering and Technology; Building and Construction; Design; Chemistry; Physics.

Personality Type: Realistic-Investigative-Conventional. **Career Cluster:** 13 Manufacturing. **Career Pathway:** 13.3 Maintenance, Installation, and Repair. **Other Jobs in This Pathway:** Aircraft Mechanics and Service Technicians; Automotive Specialty Technicians; Biological Technicians; Civil Engineering Technicians; Computer, Automated Teller, and Office Machine Repairers; Electrical and Electronic Equipment Assemblers; Electrical and Electronics Repairers, Commercial and Industrial Equipment; Electrical Engineering Technicians; Electrical Engineering Technologists; Electromechanical Engineering Technologists; Electronics Engineering Technicians; Electronics Engineering Technologists; Engineering Technicians, Except Drafters, All Other; Fuel Cell Technicians; Helpers—Installation, Maintenance, and Repair Workers; Industrial Engineering Technologists; Installation, Maintenance, and Repair Workers, All Other; Manufacturing Engineering Technologists; Manufacturing Production Technicians; Mapping Technicians; Mechanical Engineering Technologists; Mobile Heavy Equipment Mechanics, Except Engines; Nanotechnology Engineering Technicians; Telecommunications Line Installers and Repairers; Tire Repairers and Changers; others.

Skills: Repairing; Equipment Maintenance; Troubleshooting; Installation; Operation Monitoring; Equipment Selection; Operation and Control; Quality Control Analysis.

Work Environment: Standing; walking and running; kneeling, crouching, stooping, or crawling; using hands; bending or twisting the body; repetitive motions; noise; very hot or cold; contaminants; cramped work space; high places; hazardous conditions; hazardous equipment; minor burns, cuts, bites, or stings.

C=Computer Systems Design, E=Educational Services, G=Government, H=Health Care, R=Repair and Maintenance, U=Utilities, *=All Fields

Industrial Production Managers

- ❋ Annual Earnings: U $103,160, * $87,160
- ❋ Earnings Growth Potential: Medium (39.6%)
- ❋ Growth: U –15.2%, * –7.7%
- ❋ Annual Job Openings: U 50, * 5,470
- ❋ Self-Employed: 1.3%

Detailed Fields with Greatest Employment: Transportation Equipment Manufacturing (8.6%); Chemical Manufacturing (7.9%); Computer and Electronic Product Manufacturing (7.4%); Machinery Manufacturing (7.4%); Food Manufacturing (6.6%)

Detailed Fields with Highest Growth (Projected Growth for This Job): Internet Service Providers, Web Search Portals, and Data Processing Services (43.8%); Waste Management and Remediation Services (29.3%); Professional, Scientific, and Technical Services (29.0%); Wholesale Electronic Markets and Agents and Brokers (22.9%); Miscellaneous Manufacturing (19.8%)

Other Considerations for Job Outlook: Moderate decline. Increased domestic labor productivity and rising imports are expected to reduce the need for these managers. Job seekers who have experience in production occupations—along with a degree in industrial engineering, management, or business administration—should have the best job prospects.

Plan, direct, or coordinate the work activities and resources necessary for manufacturing products in accordance with specifications for cost, quality, and quantity. Direct and coordinate production, processing, distribution, and marketing activities of industrial organization. Review processing schedules and production orders to make decisions concerning inventory requirements, staffing requirements, work procedures, and duty assignments, considering budgetary limitations and time constraints. Review operations and confer with technical or administrative staff to resolve production or processing problems. Develop and implement production tracking and quality control systems, analyzing reports on production, quality control, maintenance, and other aspects of operations to detect problems. Hire, train, evaluate, and discharge staff, and resolve personnel grievances. Set and monitor product standards, examining samples of raw products or directing testing during processing, to ensure finished products are of prescribed quality. Prepare and maintain production reports and personnel records.

Education/Training Required: Work experience in a related occupation. **Education and Training Programs:** Business Administration and Management, General; Business/Commerce, General; Operations Management and Supervision. **Knowledge/Courses:** Production and Processing; Mechanical Practices; Administration and Management; Design; Personnel and Human Resources; Engineering and Technology.

Personality Type: Enterprising-Conventional. **Career Cluster:** 04 Business, Management, and Administration. **Career Pathway:** 4.1 Management. **Other Jobs in This Pathway:** Brownfield Redevelopment Specialists and Site Managers; Business Continuity Planners; Business Operations Specialists, All Other; Chief Executives; Chief Sustainability Officers; Compliance Managers; Computer and Information Systems Managers; Construction Managers; Customs Brokers; Energy Auditors; First-Line Supervisors of Office and Administrative Support Workers; General and Operations Managers; Investment Fund Managers; Loss Prevention Managers; Management Analysts; Managers, All Other; Public Relations Specialists; Regulatory Affairs Managers; Sales Managers; Security Management

Specialists; Security Managers; Supply Chain Managers; Sustainability Specialists; Wind Energy Operations Managers; Wind Energy Project Managers; others.

Skills: Management of Financial Resources; Management of Material Resources; Management of Personnel Resources; Monitoring; Systems Analysis; Operation Monitoring; Judgment and Decision Making; Systems Evaluation.

Work Environment: Indoors; standing; walking and running; noise; very hot or cold; contaminants; hazardous equipment; minor burns, cuts, bites, or stings.

Job Specialization: Biofuels Production Managers

Manage operations at biofuel power-generation facilities. Collect and process information on plant performance, diagnose problems, and design corrective procedures. Provide training to subordinate or new employees to improve biofuels plant safety or increase the production of biofuels. Provide direction to employees to ensure compliance with biofuels plant safety, environmental, or operational standards and regulations. Monitor transportation and storage of flammable or other potentially dangerous feedstocks or products to ensure adherence to safety guidelines. Draw samples of biofuels products or secondary byproducts for quality control testing. Confer with technical and supervisory personnel to report or resolve conditions affecting biofuels plant safety, operational efficiency, and product quality. Supervise production employees in the manufacturing of biofuels, such as biodiesel or ethanol. Shut down and restart biofuels plant or equipment in emergency situations or for equipment maintenance, repairs, or replacements.

Education/Training Required: Work experience in a related occupation. **Education and Training Programs:** Business Administration and Management,

General; Business/Commerce, General; Operations Management and Supervision. **Knowledge/Courses:** No data available.

Personality Type: No data available. **Career Cluster:** 04 Business, Management, and Administration. **Career Pathway:** 4.1 Management. **Other Jobs in This Pathway:** Brownfield Redevelopment Specialists and Site Managers; Business Continuity Planners; Business Operations Specialists, All Other; Chief Executives; Chief Sustainability Officers; Compliance Managers; Computer and Information Systems Managers; Construction Managers; Customs Brokers; Energy Auditors; First-Line Supervisors of Office and Administrative Support Workers; General and Operations Managers; Investment Fund Managers; Loss Prevention Managers; Management Analysts; Managers, All Other; Public Relations Specialists; Regulatory Affairs Managers; Sales Managers; Security Management Specialists; Security Managers; Supply Chain Managers; Sustainability Specialists; Wind Energy Operations Managers; Wind Energy Project Managers; others.

Skills: No data available.

Work Environment: No data available.

Job Specialization: Biomass Power Plant Managers

Manage operations at biomass power-generation facilities. Direct work activities at plant, including supervision of operations and maintenance staff. Test, maintain, or repair electrical power distribution machinery or equipment, using hand tools, power tools, and testing devices. Manage parts and supply inventories for biomass plants. Monitor and operate communications systems, such as mobile radios. Compile and record operational data on forms or in log books. Adjust equipment controls to generate specified amounts of electrical power. Supervise operations

*C=Computer Systems Design, E=Educational Services, G=Government, H=Health Care, R=Repair and Maintenance, U=Utilities, *=All Fields*

150 Best Jobs for a Secure Future © JIST Works

241

or maintenance employees in the production of power from biomass such as wood, coal, paper sludge, or other waste or refuse. Shut down and restart biomass power plants or equipment in emergency situations or for equipment maintenance, repairs, or replacements. Review logs, datasheets, or reports to ensure adequate production levels and safe production environments or to identify abnormalities with power production equipment or processes. Review biomass operations performance specifications to ensure compliance with regulatory requirements.

Education/Training Required: Work experience in a related occupation. **Education and Training Programs:** Business Administration and Management, General; Business/Commerce, General; Operations Management and Supervision. **Knowledge/Courses:** No data available.

Personality Type: No data available. **Career Cluster:** 04 Business, Management, and Administration. **Career Pathway:** 4.1 Management. **Other Jobs in This Pathway:** Brownfield Redevelopment Specialists and Site Managers; Business Continuity Planners; Business Operations Specialists, All Other; Chief Executives; Chief Sustainability Officers; Compliance Managers; Computer and Information Systems Managers; Construction Managers; Customs Brokers; Energy Auditors; First-Line Supervisors of Office and Administrative Support Workers; General and Operations Managers; Investment Fund Managers; Loss Prevention Managers; Management Analysts; Managers, All Other; Public Relations Specialists; Regulatory Affairs Managers; Sales Managers; Security Management Specialists; Security Managers; Supply Chain Managers; Sustainability Specialists; Wind Energy Operations Managers; Wind Energy Project Managers; others.

Skills: No data available.

Work Environment: No data available.

Job Specialization: Geothermal Production Managers

Manage operations at geothermal power-generation facilities. Maintain and monitor geothermal plant equipment for efficient and safe plant operations. Conduct well field site assessments. Select and implement corrosion control or mitigation systems for geothermal plants. Communicate geothermal plant conditions to employees. Troubleshoot and make minor repairs to geothermal plant instrumentation or electrical systems. Record, review, or maintain daily logs, reports, maintenance, and other records associated with geothermal operations. Prepare environmental permit applications or compliance reports. Obtain permits for constructing, upgrading, or operating geothermal power plants. Perform or direct the performance of preventative maintenance on geothermal plant equipment. Negotiate interconnection agreements with other utilities. Monitor geothermal operations, using programmable logic controllers. Identify opportunities to improve plant electrical equipment, controls, or process control methodologies. Identify and evaluate equipment, procedural, or conditional inefficiencies involving geothermal plant systems.

Education/Training Required: Work experience in a related occupation. **Education and Training Programs:** Business Administration and Management, General; Business/Commerce, General; Operations Management and Supervision. **Knowledge/Courses:** No data available.

Personality Type: No data available. **Career Cluster:** 04 Business, Management, and Administration. **Career Pathway:** 4.1 Management. **Other Jobs in This Pathway:** Brownfield Redevelopment Specialists and Site Managers; Business Continuity Planners; Business Operations Specialists, All Other; Chief Executives; Chief Sustainability Officers; Compliance Managers; Computer and Information Systems Managers; Construction Managers; Customs Brokers; Energy Auditors; First-Line Supervisors of Office and Administrative Support Workers; General and Operations Managers; Investment Fund Managers; Loss Prevention Managers; Management Analysts; Managers, All Other; Public Relations Specialists; Regulatory Affairs Managers; Sales Managers; Security Management Specialists; Security Managers; Supply Chain Managers; Sustainability Specialists; Wind Energy Operations Managers; Wind Energy Project Managers; others.

Skills: No data available.

Work Environment: No data available.

Job Specialization: Hydroelectric Production Managers

Manage operations at hydroelectric power-generation facilities. Maintain and monitor hydroelectric plant equipment for efficient and safe plant operations. Develop or implement policy evaluation procedures for hydroelectric generation activities. Provide technical direction in the erection and commissioning of hydroelectric equipment and supporting electrical or mechanical systems. Develop and implement projects to improve efficiency, economy, or effectiveness of hydroelectric plant operations. Supervise hydropower plant equipment installations, upgrades, or maintenance. Respond to problems related to ratepayers, water users, power users, government agencies, educational institutions, and other private and public power resource interests. Plan or manage hydroelectric plant upgrades. Plan and coordinate hydroelectric production operations to meet customer requirements. Perform or direct preventive or corrective containment and cleanup to protect the environment. Operate energized high- and low-voltage hydroelectric power transmission system substations according to procedures and safety requirements.

Education/Training Required: Work experience in a related occupation. **Education and Training Programs:** Business Administration and Management, General; Business/Commerce, General; Operations Management and Supervision. **Knowledge/Courses:** No data available.

Personality Type: No data available. **Career Cluster:** 04 Business, Management, and Administration. **Career Pathway:** 4.1 Management. **Other Jobs in This Pathway:** Brownfield Redevelopment Specialists and Site Managers; Business Continuity Planners; Business Operations Specialists, All Other; Chief Executives; Chief Sustainability Officers; Compliance Managers; Computer and Information Systems Managers; Construction Managers; Customs Brokers; Energy Auditors; First-Line Supervisors of Office and Administrative Support Workers; General and Operations Managers; Investment Fund Managers; Loss Prevention Managers; Management Analysts; Managers, All Other; Public Relations Specialists; Regulatory Affairs Managers; Sales Managers; Security Management Specialists; Security Managers; Supply Chain Managers; Sustainability Specialists; Wind Energy Operations Managers; Wind Energy Project Managers; others.

Skills: No data available.

Work Environment: No data available.

Job Specialization: Methane/Landfill Gas Collection System Operators

Direct daily operations, maintenance, or repair of landfill gas projects, including maintenance of daily logs, determination of service priorities, and compliance with reporting requirements. Track volume and weight of landfill waste. Recommend or implement practices to reduce turnaround time for trucks in and out of landfill site. Prepare reports on landfill operations and gas collection system productivity or efficiency. Diagnose

*C=Computer Systems Design, E=Educational Services, G=Government, H=Health Care, R=Repair and Maintenance, U=Utilities, *=All Fields*

150 Best Jobs for a Secure Future © JIST Works

243

or troubleshoot gas collection equipment and programmable logic controller (PLC) systems. Coordinate the repair, overhaul, or routine maintenance of diesel engines used in landfill operations. Read meters, gauges, or automatic recording devices at specified intervals to verify gas collection systems operating conditions. Supervise landfill, well field, and other subordinate employees. Prepare and manage landfill gas collection system budgets. Prepare soil reports as required by regulatory or permitting agencies. Oversee landfill gas collection system construction, maintenance, and repair activities. Optimize gas collection landfill operational costs and productivity consistent with safety and environmental rules and regulations.

Education/Training Required: Work experience in a related occupation. **Education and Training Programs:** Business Administration and Management, General; Business/Commerce, General; Operations Management and Supervision. **Knowledge/Courses:** No data available.

Personality Type: No data available. **Career Cluster:** 04 Business, Management, and Administration. **Career Pathway:** 4.1 Management. **Other Jobs in This Pathway:** Brownfield Redevelopment Specialists and Site Managers; Business Continuity Planners; Business Operations Specialists, All Other; Chief Executives; Chief Sustainability Officers; Compliance Managers; Computer and Information Systems Managers; Construction Managers; Customs Brokers; Energy Auditors; First-Line Supervisors of Office and Administrative Support Workers; General and Operations Managers; Investment Fund Managers; Loss Prevention Managers; Management Analysts; Managers, All Other; Public Relations Specialists; Regulatory Affairs Managers; Sales Managers; Security Management Specialists; Security Managers; Supply Chain Managers; Sustainability Specialists; Wind Energy Operations Managers; Wind Energy Project Managers; others.

Skills: No data available.

Work Environment: No data available.

Job Specialization: Quality Control Systems Managers

Plan, direct, or coordinate quality assurance programs. Formulate quality control policies and control quality of laboratory and production efforts. Stop production if serious product defects are present. Review and approve quality plans submitted by contractors. Review statistical studies, technological advances, or regulatory standards and trends to stay abreast of issues in the field of quality control. Generate and maintain quality control operating budgets. Evaluate new testing and sampling methodologies or technologies to determine usefulness. Coordinate the selection and implementation of quality control equipment such as inspection gauges. Collect and analyze production samples to evaluate quality. Audit and inspect subcontractor facilities including external laboratories. Verify that raw materials, purchased parts or components, in-process samples, and finished products meet established testing and inspection standards. Review quality documentation necessary for regulatory submissions and inspections. Review and update standard operating procedures or quality assurance manuals.

Education/Training Required: Bachelor's degree. **Education and Training Programs:** Business Administration and Management, General; Business/Commerce, General; Operations Management and Supervision. **Knowledge/Courses:** No data available.

Personality Type: Enterprising-Conventional-Realistic. **Career Cluster:** 04 Business, Management, and Administration. **Career Pathway:** 4.1 Management. **Other Jobs in This Pathway:** Brownfield Redevelopment Specialists and Site Managers; Business Continuity Planners; Business

Operations Specialists, All Other; Chief Executives; Chief Sustainability Officers; Compliance Managers; Computer and Information Systems Managers; Construction Managers; Customs Brokers; Energy Auditors; First-Line Supervisors of Office and Administrative Support Workers; General and Operations Managers; Investment Fund Managers; Loss Prevention Managers; Management Analysts; Managers, All Other; Public Relations Specialists; Regulatory Affairs Managers; Sales Managers; Security Management Specialists; Security Managers; Supply Chain Managers; Sustainability Specialists; Wind Energy Operations Managers; Wind Energy Project Managers; others.

Skills: No data available.

Work Environment: No data available.

Inspectors, Testers, Sorters, Samplers, and Weighers

- ❋ Annual Earnings: R $29,200, * $33,030
- ❋ Earnings Growth Potential: Medium (39.0%)
- ❋ Growth: R 1.3%, * –3.6%
- ❋ Annual Job Openings: R 100, * 7,790
- ❋ Self-Employed: 1.3%

Detailed Fields with Greatest Employment: Administrative and Support Services (8.3%); Fabricated Metal Product Manufacturing (8.1%); Computer and Electronic Product Manufacturing (7.2%); Professional, Scientific, and Technical Services (6.6%); Food Manufacturing (5.9%)

Detailed Fields with Highest Growth (Projected Growth for This Job): Internet Service Providers, Web Search Portals, and Data Processing Services (44.9%); Professional, Scientific, and Technical Services (34.3%); Wholesale Electronic Markets and Agents and Brokers (24.7%); Waste

Management and Remediation Services (22.5%); Administrative and Support Services (21.0%)

Other Considerations for Job Outlook: Automated inspection equipment and a redistribution of some quality control duties from inspectors to production workers are expected to contribute to employment declines in these occupations. Job opportunities should be better for workers who have experience.

Inspect, test, sort, sample, or weigh non-agricultural raw materials or processed, machined, fabricated, or assembled parts or products for defects, wear, and deviations from specifications. May use precision measuring instruments and complex test equipment. Discard or reject products, materials, and equipment not meeting specifications. Analyze and interpret blueprints, data, manuals, and other materials to determine specifications, inspection and testing procedures, adjustment and certification methods, formulas, and measuring instruments required. Inspect, test, or measure materials, products, installations, and work for conformance to specifications. Notify supervisors and other personnel of production problems and assist in identifying and correcting these problems. Discuss inspection results with those responsible for products and recommend necessary corrective actions. Record inspection or test data, such as weights, temperatures, grades, or moisture content, and quantities inspected or graded. Mark items with details such as grade and acceptance or rejection status. Observe and monitor production operations and equipment to ensure conformance to specifications and make or order necessary process or assembly adjustments.

Education/Training Required: Moderate-term on-the-job training. **Education and Training Program:** Quality Control Technology/Technician. **Knowledge/Courses:** Production and Processing.

*C=Computer Systems Design, E=Educational Services, G=Government, H=Health Care, R=Repair and Maintenance, U=Utilities, *=All Fields*

Personality Type: Conventional-Realistic. **Career Cluster:** 13 Manufacturing. **Career Pathway:** 13.4 Quality Assurance. **Other Jobs in This Pathway:** Environmental Engineering Technicians; Occupational Health and Safety Specialists.

Skills: Quality Control Analysis; Operation and Control; Operation Monitoring; Troubleshooting; Operations Analysis; Science.

Work Environment: Standing; using hands; repetitive motions; noise.

Instructional Coordinators

- ❋ Annual Earnings: E $60,450, G $63,210, * $58,830
- ❋ Earnings Growth Potential: High (43.1%)
- ❋ Growth: G 8.2%, E 27.6%, * 23.2%
- ❋ Annual Job Openings: G 480, E 3,130, * 6,060
- ❋ Self-Employed: 2.9%

Detailed Fields with Greatest Employment: Educational Services, Public and Private (72.1%); Social Assistance (6.1%); Religious, Grantmaking, Civic, Professional, and Similar Organizations (2.6%); State and Local Government (10.1%); Federal Government (1.9%)

Detailed Fields with Highest Growth (Projected Growth for This Job): Professional, Scientific, and Technical Services (41.1%); Other Information Services (33.3%); Ambulatory Health Care Services (30.4%); Educational Services, Public and Private (27.6%); Administrative and Support Services (24.3%)

Other Considerations for Job Outlook: Continued efforts to improve educational standards are expected to result in more new jobs for these workers. Opportunities should be best for job seekers who train teachers to use classroom technology and who have experience in reading, mathematics, and science.

Develop instructional material, coordinate educational content, and incorporate current technology in specialized fields that provide guidelines to educators and instructors for developing curricula and conducting courses. Conduct or participate in workshops, committees, and conferences designed to promote the intellectual, social, and physical welfare of students. Plan and conduct teacher training programs and conferences dealing with new classroom procedures, instructional materials and equipment, and teaching aids. Advise teaching and administrative staff in curriculum development, use of materials and equipment, and implementation of state and federal programs and procedures. Recommend, order, or authorize purchase of instructional materials, supplies, equipment, and visual aids designed to meet student educational needs and district standards. Interpret and enforce provisions of state education codes and rules and regulations of state education boards. Confer with members of educational committees and advisory groups to obtain knowledge of subject areas and to relate curriculum materials to specific subjects, individual student needs, and occupational areas.

Education/Training Required: Master's degree. **Education and Training Programs:** Curriculum and Instruction; Educational/Instructional Technology. **Knowledge/Courses:** Education and Training; Therapy and Counseling; Philosophy and Theology; Sociology and Anthropology; Personnel and Human Resources; Psychology.

Personality Type: Social-Investigative-Enterprising. **Career Cluster:** 05 Education and Training. **Career Pathways:** 5.1 Administration and Administrative Support; 5.3 Teaching/Training. **Other Jobs in These Pathways:** Adult Basic and Secondary Education and Literacy Teachers and Instructors; Career/Technical Education Teachers, Secondary School; Chemists; Coaches and Scouts;

Dietitians and Nutritionists; Distance Learning Coordinators; Education Administrators, All Other; Education Administrators, Elementary and Secondary School; Education Administrators, Postsecondary; Education Administrators, Preschool and Childcare Center/Program; Elementary School Teachers, Except Special Education; Fitness and Wellness Coordinators; Fitness Trainers and Aerobics Instructors; Instructional Designers and Technologists; Interpreters and Translators; Kindergarten Teachers, Except Special Education; Librarians; Middle School Teachers, Except Special and Career/Technical Education; Preschool Teachers, Except Special Education; Recreation Workers; Secondary School Teachers, Except Special and Career/Technical Education; Self-Enrichment Education Teachers; Teacher Assistants; Teachers and Instructors, All Other; Tutors; others.

Skills: Learning Strategies; Systems Evaluation; Instructing; Management of Material Resources; Negotiation; Writing; Management of Personnel Resources; Systems Analysis.

Work Environment: Indoors; standing.

Job Specialization: Instructional Designers and Technologists

Develop instructional materials and products and assist in the technology-based redesign of courses. Assist faculty in learning about, becoming proficient in, and applying instructional technology. Observe and provide feedback on instructional techniques, presentation methods, or instructional aids. Edit instructional materials, such as books, simulation exercises, lesson plans, instructor guides, and tests. Develop measurement tools to evaluate the effectiveness of instruction or training interventions. Develop instructional materials, such as lesson plans, handouts, or examinations. Define instructional, learning, or performance objectives. Assess effectiveness and efficiency of instruction according to ease of instructional technology use and student learning, knowledge transfer, and satisfaction. Analyze performance data to determine effectiveness of instructional systems, courses, or instructional materials. Research and evaluate emerging instructional technologies or methods.

Education/Training Required: Bachelor's degree. **Education and Training Programs:** Curriculum and Instruction; Educational/Instructional Technology. **Knowledge/Courses:** No data available.

Personality Type: No data available. **Career Cluster:** 05 Education and Training. **Career Pathways:** 5.1 Administration and Administrative Support; 5.3 Teaching/Training. **Other Jobs in These Pathways:** Adult Basic and Secondary Education and Literacy Teachers and Instructors; Career/Technical Education Teachers, Secondary School; Chemists; Coaches and Scouts; Dietitians and Nutritionists; Distance Learning Coordinators; Education Administrators, All Other; Education Administrators, Elementary and Secondary School; Education Administrators, Postsecondary; Education Administrators, Preschool and Childcare Center/Program; Elementary School Teachers, Except Special Education; Fitness and Wellness Coordinators; Fitness Trainers and Aerobics Instructors; Instructional Coordinators; Interpreters and Translators; Kindergarten Teachers, Except Special Education; Librarians; Middle School Teachers, Except Special and Career/Technical Education; Preschool Teachers, Except Special Education; Recreation Workers; Secondary School Teachers, Except Special and Career/Technical Education; Self-Enrichment Education Teachers; Teacher Assistants; Teachers and Instructors, All Other; Tutors; others.

Skills: No data available.

Work Environment: No data available.

---

*C=Computer Systems Design, E=Educational Services, G=Government, H=Health Care, R=Repair and Maintenance, U=Utilities, *=All Fields*

Interpreters and Translators

- ❋ Annual Earnings: E $39,010, H $40,511, * $43,300
- ❋ Earnings Growth Potential: High (47.0%)
- ❋ Growth: E 19.7%, H 31.0%, * 22.2%
- ❋ Annual Job Openings: H 430, E 480, * 2,340
- ❋ Self-Employed: 26.1%

Detailed Fields with Greatest Employment: Hospitals, Public and Private (8.5%); Social Assistance (5.5%); Educational Services, Public and Private (38.0%); Professional, Scientific, and Technical Services (23.4%); Ambulatory Health Care Services (2.7%)

Detailed Fields with Highest Growth (Projected Growth for This Job): Management, Scientific, and Technical Consulting Services (102.4%); Services for the Elderly and Persons with Disabilities (73.6%); Outpatient Care Centers (61.7%); Ambulatory Health Care Services (54.0%); Offices of Physicians (48.2%)

Other Considerations for Job Outlook: Globalization and large increases in the number of nonnative English speakers in the United States are expected to lead to employment increases for these workers. Job prospects vary by specialty and language.

Translate or interpret written, oral, or sign language text into another language for others. Follow ethical codes that protect the confidentiality of information. Identify and resolve conflicts related to the meanings of words, concepts, practices, or behaviors. Proofread, edit, and revise translated materials. Translate messages simultaneously or consecutively into specified languages orally or by using hand signs, maintaining message content, context, and style as much as possible. Check translations of technical terms and terminology to ensure that they are accurate and remain consistent throughout translation revisions. Read written materials such as legal documents, scientific works, or news reports and rewrite material into specified languages. Refer to reference materials such as dictionaries, lexicons, encyclopedias, and computerized terminology banks as needed to ensure translation accuracy. Compile terminology and information to be used in translations, including technical terms such as those for legal or medical material.

Education/Training Required: Long-term on-the-job training. **Education and Training Programs:** American Sign Language (ASL); Ancient Near Eastern and Biblical Languages, Literatures, and Linguistics; Ancient/Classical Greek Language and Literature; Arabic Language and Literature; Celtic Languages, Literatures, and Linguistics; Chinese Language and Literature; Classics and Classical Languages, Literatures, and Linguistics, General; East Asian Languages, Literatures, and Linguistics, Other; Education/Teaching of Individuals with Hearing Impairments, Including Deafness; Foreign Languages and Literatures, General; Foreign Languages, Literatures, and Linguistics, Other; French Language and Literature; German Language and Literature; Germanic Languages, Literatures, and Linguistics, Other; Hebrew Language and Literature; Hindi Language and Literature; Italian Language and Literature; Japanese Language and Literature; Language Interpretation and Translation; Latin Language and Literature; Linguistics; Middle/Near Eastern and Semitic Languages, Literatures, and Linguistics, Other; others. **Knowledge/Courses:** Foreign Language; English Language; Geography; Sociology and Anthropology; Communications and Media; Computers and Electronics.

Personality Type: Artistic-Social. **Career Clusters:** 05 Education and Training; 10 Human Services. **Career Pathways:** 5.3 Teaching/Training; 10.5 Consumer Services Career. **Other Jobs in These Pathways:** Adult Basic and Secondary Education and Literacy Teachers and Instructors; Athletes and Sports Competitors; Career/Technical Education Teachers, Middle School; Career/Technical Education Teachers, Secondary School; Chemists; Coaches and Scouts; Dietitians and Nutritionists; Elementary School Teachers, Except Special Education; First-Line Supervisors of Retail Sales Workers; Fitness Trainers and Aerobics Instructors; Instructional Coordinators; Instructional Designers and Technologists; Kindergarten Teachers, Except Special Education; Librarians; Middle School Teachers, Except Special and Career/Technical Education; Physicists; Preschool Teachers, Except Special Education; Public Relations Specialists; Recreation Workers; Sales Managers; Secondary School Teachers, Except Special and Career/Technical Education; Self-Enrichment Education Teachers; Teacher Assistants; Teachers and Instructors, All Other; Tutors; others.

Skills: Writing; Reading Comprehension; Active Listening; Speaking; Social Perceptiveness; Service Orientation; Learning Strategies; Monitoring.

Work Environment: Indoors; sitting; repetitive motions.

Interviewers, Except Eligibility and Loan

- ✳ Annual Earnings: H $29,557, * $28,820
- ✳ Earnings Growth Potential: Low (33.6%)
- ✳ Growth: H 20.3%, * 15.6%
- ✳ Annual Job Openings: H 6,940, * 9,210
- ✳ Self-Employed: 0.6%

Detailed Fields with Greatest Employment: Ambulatory Health Care Services (8.8%); Educational Services, Public and Private (8.1%); Hospitals, Public and Private (41.0%); Professional, Scientific, and Technical Services (24.8%); Insurance Carriers and Related Activities (2.4%)

Detailed Fields with Highest Growth (Projected Growth for This Job): Internet Service Providers, Web Search Portals, and Data Processing Services (48.7%); General Merchandise Stores (40.9%); Ambulatory Health Care Services (33.7%); Administrative and Support Services (21.1%); Educational Services, Public and Private (19.5%)

Other Considerations for Job Outlook: Growth in market research and health-care industries is expected to generate jobs for interviewers. Prospects should be good.

Interview persons by telephone, by mail, in person, or by other means for the purpose of completing forms, applications, or questionnaires. Ask specific questions, record answers, and assist persons with completing form. May sort, classify, and file forms. Ask questions in accordance with instructions to obtain various specified information such as person's name, address, age, religious preference, and state of residency. Identify and resolve inconsistencies in interviewees' responses by means of appropriate questioning or explanation. Compile, record, and code results and data from interview or survey, using computer or specified form. Review data obtained from interview for completeness and accuracy. Contact individuals to be interviewed at home, place of business, or field location by telephone, by mail, or in person. Assist individuals in filling out applications or questionnaires. Ensure payment for services by verifying benefits with the person's insurance provider or working out financing options. Identify and report problems in obtaining valid data. Explain survey objectives and procedures to interviewees and

*C=Computer Systems Design, E=Educational Services, G=Government, H=Health Care, R=Repair and Maintenance, U=Utilities, *=All Fields*

150 Best Jobs for a Secure Future © JIST Works

249

interpret survey questions to help interviewees' comprehension.

Education/Training Required: Short-term on-the-job training. **Education and Training Program:** Receptionist Training. **Knowledge/Courses:** Clerical Practices; Customer and Personal Service; Communications and Media; Computers and Electronics.

Personality Type: Conventional-Enterprising-Social. **Career Cluster:** 04 Business, Management, and Administration. **Career Pathway:** 4.6 Administrative and Information Support. **Other Jobs in This Pathway:** Couriers and Messengers; Court Clerks; Court, Municipal, and License Clerks; Customer Service Representatives; Data Entry Keyers; Dispatchers, Except Police, Fire, and Ambulance; Executive Secretaries and Executive Administrative Assistants; File Clerks; Human Resources Assistants, Except Payroll and Timekeeping; Information and Record Clerks, All Other; Insurance Claims Clerks; Insurance Policy Processing Clerks; License Clerks; Mail Clerks and Mail Machine Operators, Except Postal Service; Office and Administrative Support Workers, All Other; Office Clerks, General; Order Clerks; Patient Representatives; Postal Service Mail Carriers; Postal Service Mail Sorters, Processors, and Processing Machine Operators; Receptionists and Information Clerks; Secretaries and Administrative Assistants, Except Legal, Medical, and Executive; Shipping, Receiving, and Traffic Clerks; Switchboard Operators, Including Answering Service; Word Processors and Typists; others.

Skills: Active Listening; Speaking; Programming; Writing; Instructing; Persuasion; Social Perceptiveness; Reading Comprehension.

Work Environment: Indoors; sitting; using hands; repetitive motions; noise.

Kindergarten Teachers, Except Special Education

- ❋ Annual Earnings: E $49,790, * $48,800
- ❋ Earnings Growth Potential: Low (35.0%)
- ❋ Growth: E 15.4%, * 15.0%
- ❋ Annual Job Openings: E 4,240, * 6,300
- ❋ Self-Employed: 1.6%

Detailed Fields with Greatest Employment: Educational Services, Public and Private (93.0%); Social Assistance (5.0%); Religious, Grantmaking, Civic, Professional, and Similar Organizations (1.6%); State and Local Government (0.2%); Private Households; Primary and Secondary Jobs (0.1%)

Detailed Fields with Highest Growth (Projected Growth for This Job): Educational Services, Public and Private (15.4%); Religious, Grantmaking, Civic, Professional, and Similar Organizations (12.7%); Social Assistance (12.6%); State and Local Government, Excluding Education and Hospitals (6.5%); Private Households; Primary and Secondary Jobs (0.0%)

Other Considerations for Job Outlook: Enrollment from 2008–2018 is expected to grow more slowly than in recent years. Prospects are usually better in urban and rural areas, for bilingual teachers, and for math and science teachers.

Teach elemental natural and social science, personal hygiene, music, art, and literature to children from 4 to 6 years of age. Promote physical, mental, and social development. May be required to hold state certification. Teach basic skills such as color, shape, number, and letter recognition; personal hygiene; and social skills. Establish and enforce rules for behavior and policies and procedures to maintain order among students. Observe and evaluate children's performance, behavior, social development, and physical health. Instruct students individually and in groups, adapting teaching methods to meet students' varying needs and interests. Read books to entire classes or to small groups. Demonstrate activities to children. Provide a variety of materials and resources for children to explore, manipulate, and use, both in learning activities and in imaginative play. Plan and conduct activities for a balanced program of instruction, demonstration, and work time that provides students with opportunities to observe, question, and investigate. Confer with parents or guardians, other teachers, counselors, and administrators to resolve students' behavioral and academic problems.

Education/Training Required: Bachelor's degree. **Education and Training Program:** Early Childhood Education and Teaching. **Knowledge/Courses:** Philosophy and Theology; Fine Arts; Geography; Sociology and Anthropology; Psychology; Education and Training.

Personality Type: Social-Artistic. **Career Cluster:** 05 Education and Training. **Career Pathway:** 5.3 Teaching/Training. **Other Jobs in This Pathway:** Adult Basic and Secondary Education and Literacy Teachers and Instructors; Athletes and Sports Competitors; Audio-Visual and Multimedia Collections Specialists; Career/Technical Education Teachers, Middle School; Career/Technical Education Teachers, Secondary School; Chemists; Coaches and Scouts; Dietitians and Nutritionists; Elementary School Teachers, Except Special Education; Fitness Trainers and Aerobics Instructors; Historians; Instructional Coordinators; Instructional Designers and Technologists; Interpreters and Translators; Librarians; Middle School Teachers, Except Special and Career/Technical Education; Physicists; Preschool Teachers, Except Special Education; Recreation Workers; Secondary School Teachers, Except Special and Career/Technical

Education; Self-Enrichment Education Teachers; Teacher Assistants; Teachers and Instructors, All Other; Tutors.

Skills: Learning Strategies; Negotiation; Social Perceptiveness; Technology Design; Service Orientation; Active Listening; Management of Personnel Resources; Active Learning.

Work Environment: Indoors; standing.

Licensed Practical and Licensed Vocational Nurses

- ❋ Annual Earnings: H $40,037, * $40,380
- ❋ Earnings Growth Potential: Low (26.5%)
- ❋ Growth: H 22.0%, * 20.6%
- ❋ Annual Job Openings: H 47,420, * 39,130
- ❋ Self-Employed: 1.2%

Detailed Fields with Greatest Employment: Administrative and Support Services (5.7%); State and Local Government (4.6%); Nursing and Residential Care Facilities (34.5%); Hospitals, Public and Private (24.9%); Ambulatory Health Care Services (23.8%)

Detailed Fields with Highest Growth (Projected Growth for This Job): Professional, Scientific, and Technical Services (62.5%); Ambulatory Health Care Services (34.8%); Social Assistance (29.8%); Administrative and Support Services (23.9%); Nursing and Residential Care Facilities (23.1%)

Other Considerations for Job Outlook: An aging population is expected to boost demand for nursing services. Job prospects are expected to be very good, especially in employment settings that serve older populations.

Care for ill, injured, convalescent, or disabled persons in hospitals, nursing homes, clinics,

*C=Computer Systems Design, E=Educational Services, G=Government, H=Health Care, R=Repair and Maintenance, U=Utilities, *=All Fields*

private homes, group homes, and similar institutions. May work under the supervision of a registered nurse. Licensing required. Administer prescribed medications or start intravenous fluids, recording times and amounts on patients' charts. Observe patients, charting and reporting changes in patients' conditions, such as adverse reactions to medication or treatment, and taking any necessary actions. Provide basic patient care and treatments such as taking temperatures or blood pressures, dressing wounds, treating bedsores, giving enemas or douches, rubbing with alcohol, massaging, or performing catheterizations. Sterilize equipment and supplies, using germicides, sterilizer, or autoclave. Answer patients' calls and determine how to assist them. Work as part of a health-care team to assess patient needs, plan and modify care, and implement interventions. Measure and record patients' vital signs, such as height, weight, temperature, blood pressure, pulse, and respiration. Collect samples such as blood, urine, and sputum from patients and perform routine laboratory tests on samples.

Education/Training Required: Postsecondary vocational training. **Education and Training Program:** Licensed Practical/Vocational Nurse Training. **Knowledge/Courses:** Psychology; Medicine and Dentistry; Therapy and Counseling; Biology; Philosophy and Theology; Customer and Personal Service.

Personality Type: Social-Realistic. **Career Cluster:** 08 Health Science. **Career Pathway:** 8.1 Therapeutic Services. **Other Jobs in This Pathway:** Clinical Psychologists; Community and Social Service Specialists, All Other; Counseling Psychologists; Dental Assistants; Dental Hygienists; Dentists, General; Health Technologists and Technicians, All Other; Healthcare Support Workers, All Other; Home Health Aides; Low Vision Therapists, Orientation and Mobility Specialists, and Vision Rehabilitation Therapists; Massage Therapists; Medical and Clinical Laboratory Technicians; Medical and Health Services Managers; Medical Scientists, Except Epidemiologists; Medical Secretaries; Occupational Therapists; Ophthalmic Medical Technologists; Pharmacists; Pharmacy Technicians; Radiologic Technologists; School Psychologists; Social and Human Service Assistants; Speech-Language Pathologists; Speech-Language Pathology Assistants; Substance Abuse and Behavioral Disorder Counselors; others.

Skills: Science; Social Perceptiveness; Service Orientation; Operation and Control; Persuasion; Negotiation; Speaking; Time Management.

Work Environment: Indoors; standing; walking and running; using hands; repetitive motions; noise; contaminants; cramped work space; exposed to disease or infections.

Logisticians

- ❋ Annual Earnings: C $73,700, U $76,950, G $77,350, * $70,800
- ❋ Earnings Growth Potential: Medium (38.5%)
- ❋ Growth: U –6.5%, G 17.8%, C 54.2%, * 19.5%
- ❋ Annual Job Openings: U 50, C 230, G 750, * 4,190
- ❋ Self-Employed: 0.0%

Detailed Fields with Greatest Employment: Transportation Equipment Manufacturing (8.9%); Management of Companies and Enterprises (7.8%); Computer and Electronic Product Manufacturing (6.3%); Warehousing and Storage (3.0%); Federal Government (25.0%)

Detailed Fields with Highest Growth (Projected Growth for This Job): Professional, Scientific, and Technical Services (63.7%); Internet Service Providers, Web Search Portals, and Data

Processing Services (63.2%); Waste Management and Remediation Services (46.2%); Other Information Services (42.9%); Wholesale Electronic Markets and Agents and Brokers (41.6%)

Other Considerations for Job Outlook: Faster than average employment growth is projected.

Job Specialization: Logistics Analysts

Analyze product delivery or supply chain processes to identify or recommend changes. May manage route activity including invoicing, electronic bills, and shipment tracing. Identify opportunities for inventory reductions. Monitor industry standards, trends, or practices to identify developments in logistics planning or execution. Enter logistics-related data into databases. Develop and maintain payment systems to ensure accuracy of vendor payments. Determine packaging requirements. Develop and maintain freight rate databases for use by supply chain departments to determine the most economical modes of transportation. Contact potential vendors to determine material availability. Contact carriers for rates or schedules. Communicate with and monitor service providers, such as ocean carriers, air freight forwarders, global consolidators, customs brokers, and trucking companies. Track product flow from origin to final delivery. Write or revise standard operating procedures for logistics processes. Review procedures such as distribution and inventory management to ensure maximum efficiency and minimum cost.

Education/Training Required: Bachelor's degree. **Education and Training Programs:** Logistics, Materials, and Supply Chain Management; Operations Management and Supervision; Transportation/Mobility Management. **Knowledge/ Courses:** No data available.

Personality Type: Conventional-Enterprising-Investigative. **Career Clusters:** 04 Business, Management, and Administration; 16 Transportation, Distribution, and Logistics. **Career Pathways:** 4.1 Management; 16.3 Warehousing and Distribution Center Operations. **Other Jobs in These Pathways:** Brownfield Redevelopment Specialists and Site Managers; Business Continuity Planners; Business Operations Specialists, All Other; Chief Executives; Chief Sustainability Officers; Compliance Managers; Computer and Information Systems Managers; Construction Managers; Customs Brokers; Energy Auditors; First-Line Supervisors of Office and Administrative Support Workers; General and Operations Managers; Investment Fund Managers; Loss Prevention Managers; Management Analysts; Managers, All Other; Regulatory Affairs Managers; Sales Managers; Security Management Specialists; Security Managers; Shipping, Receiving, and Traffic Clerks; Supply Chain Managers; Sustainability Specialists; Wind Energy Operations Managers; Wind Energy Project Managers; others.

Skills: No data available.

Work Environment: No data available.

Job Specialization: Logistics Engineers

Design and analyze operational solutions for projects such as transportation optimization, network modeling, process and methods analysis, cost containment, capacity enhancement, routing and shipment optimization, and information management. Propose logistics solutions for customers. Prepare production strategies and conceptual designs for production facilities. Interview key staff or tour facilities to identify efficiency-improvement, cost-reduction, or service-delivery opportunities. Direct the work of logistics analysts. Design plant distribution centers. Develop specifications for equipment, tools, facility layouts, or material-handling systems. Review contractual commitments, customer specifications, or related information to determine logistics and

*C=Computer Systems Design, E=Educational Services, G=Government, H=Health Care, R=Repair and Maintenance, U=Utilities, *=All Fields*

support requirements. Prepare or validate documentation on automated logistics or maintenance-data reporting and management information systems. Identify cost-reduction and process-improvement opportunities. Identify or develop business rules and standard operating procedures to streamline operating processes. Develop metrics, internal analysis tools, or key performance indicators for business units within logistics.

Education/Training Required: Bachelor's degree. **Education and Training Programs:** Logistics, Materials, and Supply Chain Management; Operations Management and Supervision; Transportation/Mobility Management. **Knowledge/Courses:** No data available.

Personality Type: Investigative-Conventional-Realistic. **Career Clusters:** 04 Business, Management, and Administration; 16 Transportation, Distribution, and Logistics. **Career Pathways:** 4.1 Management; 16.2 Logistics, Planning, and Management Services. **Other Jobs in These Pathways:** Brownfield Redevelopment Specialists and Site Managers; Business Continuity Planners; Business Operations Specialists, All Other; Chief Executives; Chief Sustainability Officers; Compliance Managers; Computer and Information Systems Managers; Construction Managers; Customs Brokers; Energy Auditors; First-Line Supervisors of Office and Administrative Support Workers; General and Operations Managers; Investment Fund Managers; Loss Prevention Managers; Management Analysts; Managers, All Other; Public Relations Specialists; Regulatory Affairs Managers; Sales Managers; Security Management Specialists; Security Managers; Supply Chain Managers; Sustainability Specialists; Wind Energy Operations Managers; Wind Energy Project Managers; others.

Skills: No data available.

Work Environment: No data available.

Machinists

- ❋ Annual Earnings: R $38,160, * $38,520
- ❋ Earnings Growth Potential: Medium (37.4%)
- ❋ Growth: R 3.2%, * –4.6%
- ❋ Annual Job Openings: R 120, * 5,560
- ❋ Self-Employed: 2.0%

Detailed Fields with Greatest Employment: Administrative and Support Services (7.6%); Merchant Wholesalers, Durable Goods (4.4%); Fabricated Metal Product Manufacturing (31.2%); Computer and Electronic Product Manufacturing (3.3%); Miscellaneous Manufacturing (2.8%)

Detailed Fields with Highest Growth (Projected Growth for This Job): Wholesale Electronic Markets and Agents and Brokers (27.5%); Administrative and Support Services (23.5%); Professional, Scientific, and Technical Services (23.2%); Building Material and Garden Equipment and Supplies Dealers (20.0%); Support Activities for Transportation (20.0%)

Other Considerations for Job Outlook: Employment growth should be affected by increased productivity requiring fewer machinists. But technology is not expected to affect their employment as significantly as that of other production workers. Opportunities should be good because of the many openings expected to arise from the need to replace workers who leave the occupation permanently.

Set up and operate a variety of machine tools to produce precision parts and instruments. Includes precision instrument makers who fabricate, modify, or repair mechanical instruments. May also fabricate and modify parts to make or repair machine tools or maintain industrial machines, applying knowledge of mechanics, shop mathematics, metal properties, layout, and

machining procedures. Calculate dimensions and tolerances, using knowledge of mathematics and instruments such as micrometers and vernier calipers. Align and secure holding fixtures, cutting tools, attachments, accessories, and materials onto machines. Select the appropriate tools, machines, and materials to be used in preparation of machinery work. Monitor the feed and speed of machines during the machining process. Machine parts to specifications, using machine tools such as lathes, milling machines, shapers, or grinders. Set up, adjust, and operate all of the basic machine tools and many specialized or advanced variation tools to perform precision machining operations. Measure, examine, and test completed units to detect defects and ensure conformance to specifications, using precision instruments such as micrometers. Set controls to regulate machining or enter commands to retrieve, input, or edit computerized machine control media. Position and fasten work pieces.

Education/Training Required: Long-term on-the-job training. **Education and Training Programs:** Machine Shop Technology/Assistant; Machine Tool Technology/Machinist. **Knowledge/Courses:** Mechanical Devices; Design; Engineering and Technology; Production and Processing; Mathematics.

Personality Type: Realistic-Conventional-Investigative. **Career Cluster:** 13 Manufacturing. **Career Pathway:** 13.1 Production. **Other Jobs in This Pathway:** Assemblers and Fabricators, All Other; Cabinetmakers and Bench Carpenters; Coating, Painting, and Spraying Machine Setters, Operators, and Tenders; Computer-Controlled Machine Tool Operators, Metal and Plastic; Cost Estimators; Cutting, Punching, and Press Machine Setters, Operators, and Tenders, Metal and Plastic; First-Line Supervisors of Mechanics, Installers, and Repairers; First-Line Supervisors of Production and Operating Workers; Geothermal Technicians; Grinding, Lapping, Polishing, and Buffing Machine Tool Setters,

Operators, and Tenders, Metal and Plastic; Helpers—Production Workers; Machine Feeders and Offbearers; Mixing and Blending Machine Setters, Operators, and Tenders; Molding, Coremaking, and Casting Machine Setters, Operators, and Tenders, Metal and Plastic; Packaging and Filling Machine Operators and Tenders; Packers and Packagers, Hand; Paper Goods Machine Setters, Operators, and Tenders; Production Workers, All Other; Recycling and Reclamation Workers; Recycling Coordinators; Sheet Metal Workers; Solderers and Brazers; Structural Metal Fabricators and Fitters; Team Assemblers; Welders, Cutters, and Welder Fitters; others.

Skills: Equipment Maintenance; Installation; Repairing; Equipment Selection; Quality Control Analysis; Technology Design; Troubleshooting; Operation and Control.

Work Environment: Standing; walking and running; using hands; repetitive motions; noise; contaminants; hazardous equipment; minor burns, cuts, bites, or stings.

Maintenance and Repair Workers, General

- ✴ Annual Earnings: R $33,480, U $49,030, * $34,730
- ✴ Earnings Growth Potential: Medium (40.1%)
- ✴ Growth: U –8.8%, R 5.6%, * 10.9%
- ✴ Annual Job Openings: U 220, R 350, * 35,750
- ✴ Self-Employed: 1.1%

Detailed Fields with Greatest Employment: State and Local Government (9.6%); Educational Services, Public and Private (7.8%); Accommodation, Including Hotels and Motels (5.4%); Administrative and Support Services (4.4%); Religious,

*C=Computer Systems Design, E=Educational Services, G=Government, H=Health Care, R=Repair and Maintenance, U=Utilities, *=All Fields*

Grantmaking, Civic, Professional, and Similar Organizations (4.1%)

Detailed Fields with Highest Growth (Projected Growth for This Job): Internet Service Providers, Web Search Portals, and Data Processing Services (54.4%); Professional, Scientific, and Technical Services (51.0%); Lessors of Nonfinancial Intangible Assets (Except Copyrighted Works) (40.7%); Other Information Services (35.3%); Waste Management and Remediation Services (34.5%)

Other Considerations for Job Outlook: Employment is related to the extent of building stock and the amount of equipment needing maintenance and repair. Opportunities should be excellent, especially for job seekers with experience or certification.

Perform work involving the skills of two or more maintenance or craft occupations to keep machines, mechanical equipment, or the structure of an establishment in repair. Duties may involve pipe fitting; boiler making; insulating; welding; machining; carpentry; repairing electrical or mechanical equipment; installing, aligning, and balancing new equipment; and repairing buildings, floors, or stairs. Repair or replace defective equipment parts, using hand tools and power tools, and reassemble equipment. Perform routine preventive maintenance to ensure that machines continue to run smoothly, building systems operate efficiently, or the physical condition of buildings does not deteriorate. Inspect drives, motors, and belts; check fluid levels; replace filters; or perform other maintenance actions, following checklists. Use tools ranging from common hand and power tools, such as hammers, hoists, saws, drills, and wrenches, to precision measuring instruments and electrical and electronic testing devices. Assemble, install, or repair wiring, electrical and electronic components, pipe systems and plumbing, machinery, and equipment. Diagnose mechanical problems and determine how to correct them, checking blueprints, repair manuals, and parts catalogs as necessary. Inspect, operate, and test machinery and equipment to diagnose machine malfunctions.

Education/Training Required: Moderate-term on-the-job training. **Education and Training Program:** Industrial Mechanics and Maintenance Technology. **Knowledge/Courses:** Building and Construction; Mechanical Devices; Design; Physics; Engineering and Technology; Public Safety and Security.

Personality Type: Realistic-Conventional-Investigative. **Career Cluster:** 13 Manufacturing. **Career Pathway:** 2.2 Construction. **Other Jobs in This Pathway:** Brickmasons and Blockmasons; Cement Masons and Concrete Finishers; Construction and Building Inspectors; Construction Carpenters; Construction Laborers; Construction Managers; Cost Estimators; Drywall and Ceiling Tile Installers; Electrical Power-Line Installers and Repairers; Electricians; Engineering Technicians, Except Drafters, All Other; First-Line Supervisors of Construction Trades and Extraction Workers; Heating and Air Conditioning Mechanics and Installers; Helpers—Carpenters; Helpers—Electricians; Helpers—Pipelayers, Plumbers, Pipefitters, and Steamfitters; Highway Maintenance Workers; Operating Engineers and Other Construction Equipment Operators; Painters, Construction and Maintenance; Pipe Fitters and Steamfitters; Plumbers; Refrigeration Mechanics and Installers; Roofers; Rough Carpenters; Solar Energy Installation Managers; others.

Skills: Repairing; Equipment Maintenance; Installation; Equipment Selection; Troubleshooting; Quality Control Analysis; Operation and Control; Technology Design.

Work Environment: More often indoors than outdoors; standing; walking and running; using hands; noise; very hot or cold; bright or inadequate lighting; contaminants; cramped work space; hazardous conditions; hazardous equipment; minor burns, cuts, bites, or stings.

Management Analysts

- ❋ Annual Earnings: E $66,100, G $74,880, U $76,000, C $87,950, * $78,160
- ❋ Earnings Growth Potential: High (43.8%)
- ❋ Growth: U –15.4%, G 8.4%, E 17.8%, C 40.2%, * 23.9%
- ❋ Annual Job Openings: U 190, E 410, C 1,930, G 2,990, * 30,650
- ❋ Self-Employed: 25.8%

Detailed Fields with Greatest Employment: Federal Government (9.1%); Insurance Carriers and Related Activities (6.2%); Management of Companies and Enterprises (5.4%); Administrative and Support Services (4.8%); Professional, Scientific, and Technical Services (38.6%)

Detailed Fields with Highest Growth (Projected Growth for This Job): Professional, Scientific, and Technical Services (68.0%); Internet Service Providers, Web Search Portals, and Data Processing Services (48.6%); Lessors of Nonfinancial Intangible Assets (Except Copyrighted Works) (36.7%); Specialty Trade Contractors (32.3%); Other Information Services (30.7%)

Other Considerations for Job Outlook: Organizations are expected to rely increasingly on outside expertise in an effort to maintain competitiveness and improve performance. Keen competition is expected. Opportunities are expected to be best for those who have a graduate degree, specialized expertise, and ability in salesmanship and public relations.

Conduct organizational studies and evaluations, design systems and procedures, conduct work simplifications and measurement studies, and prepare operations and procedures manuals to assist management in operating more efficiently and effectively. Includes program analysts and management consultants. Gather and organize information on problems or procedures. Analyze data gathered and develop solutions or alternative methods of proceeding. Confer with personnel concerned to ensure successful functioning of newly implemented systems or procedures. Develop and implement records management program for filing, protection, and retrieval of records and assure compliance with program. Review forms and reports and confer with management and users about format, distribution, and purpose and to identify problems and improvements. Document findings of study and prepare recommendations for implementation of new systems, procedures, or organizational changes. Interview personnel and conduct on-site observation to ascertain unit functions; work performed; and methods, equipment, and personnel used. Prepare manuals and train workers in use of new forms, reports, procedures, or equipment according to organizational policy. Design, evaluate, recommend, and approve changes of forms and reports.

Education/Training Required: Work experience plus degree. **Education and Training Programs:** Business Administration and Management, General; Business/Commerce, General. **Knowledge/Courses:** Personnel and Human Resources; Clerical Practices; Sales and Marketing; Economics and Accounting; Customer and Personal Service; Administration and Management.

Personality Type: Investigative-Enterprising-Conventional. **Career Cluster:** 04 Business, Management, and Administration. **Career Pathway:** 4.1 Management. **Other Jobs in This Pathway:** Administrative Services Managers; Brownfield

*C=Computer Systems Design, E=Educational Services, G=Government, H=Health Care, R=Repair and Maintenance, U=Utilities, *=All Fields*

Redevelopment Specialists and Site Managers; Business Continuity Planners; Business Operations Specialists, All Other; Chief Executives; Chief Sustainability Officers; Compliance Managers; Computer and Information Systems Managers; Construction Managers; Customs Brokers; Energy Auditors; First-Line Supervisors of Office and Administrative Support Workers; General and Operations Managers; Investment Fund Managers; Loss Prevention Managers; Managers, All Other; Public Relations Specialists; Regulatory Affairs Managers; Sales Managers; Security Management Specialists; Security Managers; Supply Chain Managers; Sustainability Specialists; Wind Energy Operations Managers; Wind Energy Project Managers; others.

Skills: Operations Analysis; Systems Evaluation; Systems Analysis; Science; Judgment and Decision Making; Management of Material Resources; Writing; Management of Personnel Resources.

Work Environment: Indoors; sitting.

Massage Therapists

- ✳ Annual Earnings: H $38,240, * $34,900
- ✳ Earnings Growth Potential: High (48.5%)
- ✳ Growth: H 44.8%, * 18.9%
- ✳ Annual Job Openings: H 710, * 3,950
- ✳ Self-Employed: 57.2%

Detailed Fields with Greatest Employment: Amusement, Gambling, and Recreation Industries (9.9%); Personal and Laundry Services (42.4%); Ambulatory Health Care Services (27.1%); Accommodation, Including Hotels and Motels (12.9%); Educational Services, Public and Private (1.8%).

Detailed Fields with Highest Growth (Projected Growth for This Job): Ambulatory Health Care Services (47.0%); Personal and Laundry Services (44.8%); Educational Services, Public and

Private (41.3%); Nursing and Residential Care Facilities (25.0%); Administrative and Support Services (22.2%)

Other Considerations for Job Outlook: Growing demand for massage services to help improve health and wellness is expected to create jobs for massage therapists. Opportunities for entry-level workers should be good. Job seekers with experience and licensure or certification should have the best prospects.

Massage customers for hygienic or remedial purposes. Confer with clients about their medical histories and any problems with stress or pain to determine whether massage would be helpful. Apply finger and hand pressure to specific points of the body. Massage and knead the muscles and soft tissues of the human body to provide courses of treatment for medical conditions and injuries or wellness maintenance. Maintain treatment records. Provide clients with guidance and information about techniques for postural improvement and stretching, strengthening, relaxation, and rehabilitative exercises. Assess clients' soft tissue condition, joint quality and function, muscle strength, and range of motion. Develop and propose client treatment plans that specify which types of massage are to be used. Refer clients to other types of therapists when necessary. Use complementary aids, such as infrared lamps, wet compresses, ice, and whirlpool baths, to promote clients' recovery, relaxation, and well-being.

Education/Training Required: Postsecondary vocational training. **Education and Training Programs:** Asian Bodywork Therapy; Massage Therapy/Therapeutic Massage; Somatic Bodywork; Somatic Bodywork and Related Therapeutic Services, Other. **Knowledge/Courses:** Therapy and Counseling; Psychology; Sales and Marketing; Medicine and Dentistry; Chemistry; English Language.

Personality Type: Social-Realistic. **Career Cluster:** 08 Health Science. **Career Pathway:** 8.1 Therapeutic Services. **Other Jobs in This Pathway:** Clinical Psychologists; Community and Social Service Specialists, All Other; Counseling Psychologists; Dental Assistants; Dental Hygienists; Dentists, General; Health Technologists and Technicians, All Other; Healthcare Support Workers, All Other; Home Health Aides; Licensed Practical and Licensed Vocational Nurses; Low Vision Therapists, Orientation and Mobility Specialists, and Vision Rehabilitation Therapists; Medical and Clinical Laboratory Technicians; Medical and Health Services Managers; Medical Scientists, Except Epidemiologists; Medical Secretaries; Occupational Therapists; Ophthalmic Medical Technologists; Pharmacists; Pharmacy Technicians; Radiologic Technologists; School Psychologists; Social and Human Service Assistants; Speech-Language Pathologists; Speech-Language Pathology Assistants; Substance Abuse and Behavioral Disorder Counselors; others.

Skills: Operations Analysis; Science; Persuasion; Service Orientation; Critical Thinking; Active Listening; Speaking; Social Perceptiveness.

Work Environment: Indoors; standing; using hands; repetitive motions.

Mechanical Engineers

- ❋ Annual Earnings: C $79,000, G $89,440, * $78,160
- ❋ Earnings Growth Potential: Low (35.3%)
- ❋ Growth: G 9.2%, C 50.2%, * 6.0%
- ❋ Annual Job Openings: C 90, G 270, * 7,570
- ❋ Self-Employed: 2.3%

Detailed Fields with Greatest Employment: Computer and Electronic Product Manufacturing (9.5%); Fabricated Metal Product Manufacturing (6.1%); Federal Government (4.5%); Professional, Scientific, and Technical Services (29.9%); Management of Companies and Enterprises (2.7%)

Detailed Fields with Highest Growth (Projected Growth for This Job): Waste Management and Remediation Services (41.7%); Specialty Trade Contractors (33.5%); Publishing Industries (Except Internet) (33.3%); Ambulatory Health Care Services (33.3%); Wholesale Electronic Markets and Agents and Brokers (32.9%)

Other Considerations for Job Outlook: Materials engineers are expected to have employment growth of 9 percent from 2008–2018, about as fast as the average for all occupations. Growth should result from increased use of composite and other nontraditional materials developed through biotechnology and nanotechnology research. As manufacturing firms contract for their materials engineering needs, most employment growth is expected in professional, scientific, and technical services industries.

Perform engineering duties in planning and designing tools, engines, machines, and other mechanically functioning equipment. Oversee installation, operation, maintenance, and repair of such equipment as centralized heat, gas, water, and steam systems. Read and interpret blueprints, technical drawings, schematics, and computer-generated reports. Confer with engineers and other personnel to implement operating procedures, resolve system malfunctions, and provide technical information. Research and analyze customer design proposals, specifications, manuals, and other data to evaluate the feasibility, cost, and maintenance requirements of designs or applications. Specify system components or direct modification of products to ensure conformance with engineering design and performance specifications. Research, design, evaluate, install, operate, and maintain mechanical products,

C=Computer Systems Design, E=Educational Services, G=Government, H=Health Care, R=Repair and Maintenance, U=Utilities, *=All Fields

150 Best Jobs for a Secure Future © JIST Works

259

equipment, systems, and processes to meet requirements, applying knowledge of engineering principles. Investigate equipment failures and difficulties to diagnose faulty operation and to make recommendations to maintenance crew.

Education/Training Required: Bachelor's degree. **Education and Training Program:** Mechanical Engineering. **Knowledge/Courses:** Design; Engineering and Technology; Physics; Mechanical Devices; Production and Processing; Mathematics.

Personality Type: Investigative-Realistic-Conventional. **Career Cluster:** 15 Science, Technology, Engineering, and Mathematics. **Career Pathway:** 15.1 Engineering and Technology. **Other Jobs in This Pathway:** Architectural and Engineering Managers; Automotive Engineers; Biochemical Engineers; Biofuels/Biodiesel Technology and Product Development Managers; Civil Engineers; Cost Estimators; Education, Training, and Library Workers, All Other; Electrical Engineers; Electronics Engineers, Except Computer; Energy Engineers; Engineers, All Other; Fuel Cell Engineers; Human Factors Engineers and Ergonomists; Industrial Engineers; Manufacturing Engineers; Mechatronics Engineers; Microsystems Engineers; Nanosystems Engineers; Photonics Engineers; Radio Frequency Identification Device Specialists; Robotics Engineers; Solar Energy Systems Engineers; Transportation Engineers; Validation Engineers; Wind Energy Engineers; others.

Skills: Technology Design; Science; Mathematics; Installation; Operations Analysis; Programming; Quality Control Analysis; Troubleshooting.

Work Environment: Indoors; sitting; noise.

Job Specialization: Automotive Engineers

Develop new or improved designs for vehicle structural members, engines, transmissions and other vehicle systems, using computer-assisted design technology. Direct building, modification, and testing of vehicle and components. Read current literature, attend meetings or conferences, and talk with colleagues to stay abreast of new technology and competitive products. Establish production or quality control standards. Prepare and present technical or project status reports. Develop or implement operating methods and procedures. Write, review, or maintain engineering documentation. Conduct research studies to develop new concepts in the field of automotive engineering. Coordinate production activities with other functional units such as procurement, maintenance, and quality control. Provide technical direction to other engineers or engineering support personnel. Perform failure, variation, or root cause analyses. Develop or integrate control feature requirements. Develop engineering specifications and cost estimates for automotive design concepts. Develop calibration methodologies, test methodologies, or tools. Conduct automotive design reviews.

Education/Training Required: Bachelor's degree. **Education and Training Program:** Mechanical Engineering. **Knowledge/Courses:** No data available.

Personality Type: No data available. **Career Cluster:** 15 Science, Technology, Engineering, and Mathematics. **Career Pathway:** 15.1 Engineering and Technology. **Other Jobs in This Pathway:** Architectural and Engineering Managers; Biochemical Engineers; Biofuels/Biodiesel Technology and Product Development Managers; Civil Engineers; Cost Estimators; Education, Training, and Library Workers, All Other; Electrical Engineers; Electronics Engineers, Except Computer; Energy Engineers; Engineers, All Other; Fuel Cell Engineers; Human Factors Engineers and Ergonomists; Industrial Engineers; Manufacturing Engineers; Mechatronics Engineers; Microsystems Engineers; Nanosystems Engineers; Photonics Engineers; Radio Frequency

Identification Device Specialists; Robotics Engineers; Solar Energy Systems Engineers; Transportation Engineers; Validation Engineers; Wind Energy Engineers; others.

Skills: No data available.

Work Environment: No data available.

Job Specialization: Fuel Cell Engineers

Design, evaluate, modify, and construct fuel cell components and systems for transportation, stationary, or portable applications. Write technical reports or proposals related to engineering projects. Read current literature, attend meetings or conferences, and talk with colleagues to stay abreast of new technology and competitive products. Prepare test stations, instrumentation, or data acquisition systems for use in specific tests. Plan or implement cost reduction or product improvement projects in collaboration with other engineers, suppliers, support personnel, or customers. Coordinate engineering or test schedules with departments outside engineering, such as manufacturing. Validate design of fuel cells, fuel cell components, or fuel cell systems. Authorize the release of parts or subsystems for production. Simulate or model fuel cell, motor, or other system information using simulation software programs. Recommend or implement changes to fuel cell system design. Provide technical consultation or direction related to the development or production of fuel cell systems.

Education/Training Required: Bachelor's degree. **Education and Training Program:** Mechanical Engineering. **Knowledge/Courses:** No data available.

Personality Type: No data available. **Career Cluster:** 15 Science, Technology, Engineering, and Mathematics. **Career Pathway:** 15.1 Engineering and Technology. **Other Jobs in This Pathway:** Architectural and Engineering Managers;

Automotive Engineers; Biochemical Engineers; Biofuels/Biodiesel Technology and Product Development Managers; Civil Engineers; Cost Estimators; Education, Training, and Library Workers, All Other; Electrical Engineers; Electronics Engineers, Except Computer; Energy Engineers; Engineers, All Other; Human Factors Engineers and Ergonomists; Industrial Engineers; Manufacturing Engineers; Mechanical Engineers; Mechatronics Engineers; Microsystems Engineers; Nanosystems Engineers; Photonics Engineers; Radio Frequency Identification Device Specialists; Robotics Engineers; Solar Energy Systems Engineers; Transportation Engineers; Validation Engineers; Wind Energy Engineers; others.

Skills: No data available.

Work Environment: No data available.

Medical and Clinical Laboratory Technicians

- ❋ Annual Earnings: H $36,057, * $36,280
- ❋ Earnings Growth Potential: Low (33.3%)
- ❋ Growth: H 16.5%, * 16.1%
- ❋ Annual Job Openings: H 6,620, * 5,460
- ❋ Self-Employed: 0.2%

Detailed Fields with Greatest Employment: Educational Services, Public and Private (8.5%); Hospitals, Public and Private (45.3%); Ambulatory Health Care Services (37.6%); Professional, Scientific, and Technical Services (2.3%); Federal Government (1.9%)

Detailed Fields with Highest Growth (Projected Growth for This Job): Ambulatory Health Care Services (39.8%); Professional, Scientific, and Technical Services (28.0%); Merchant Wholesalers, Nondurable Goods (25.0%); Administrative

*C=Computer Systems Design, E=Educational Services, G=Government, H=Health Care, R=Repair and Maintenance, U=Utilities, *=All Fields*

and Support Services (23.4%); Nursing and Residential Care Facilities (19.0%)

Other Considerations for Job Outlook: Employment of these workers is expected to rise as the volume of laboratory tests continues to increase with population growth and the development of new tests. Excellent opportunities are expected.

Perform routine medical laboratory tests for the diagnosis, treatment, and prevention of disease. May work under the supervision of a medical technologist. Conduct chemical analyses of bodily fluids, such as blood and urine, using microscope or automatic analyzer to detect abnormalities or diseases, and enter findings into computer. Set up, adjust, maintain, and clean medical laboratory equipment. Analyze the results of tests and experiments to ensure conformity to specifications, using special mechanical and electrical devices. Analyze and record test data to issue reports that use charts, graphs, and narratives. Conduct blood tests for transfusion purposes and perform blood counts. Perform medical research to further control and cure disease. Obtain specimens, cultivating, isolating, and identifying microorganisms for analysis. Examine cells stained with dye to locate abnormalities. Collect blood or tissue samples from patients, observing principles of asepsis to obtain blood sample. Consult with a pathologist to determine a final diagnosis when abnormal cells are found.

Education/Training Required: Associate degree. **Education and Training Programs:** Blood Bank Technology Specialist Training; Clinical/Medical Laboratory Assistant Training; Clinical/Medical Laboratory Technician; Hematology Technology/Technician; Histologic Technician Training. **Knowledge/Courses:** Chemistry; Medicine and Dentistry; Biology; Mechanical Devices; Computers and Electronics; Production and Processing.

Personality Type: Realistic-Investigative-Conventional. **Career Cluster:** 08 Health Science. **Career Pathways:** 8.1 Therapeutic Services; 8.2 Diagnostics Services. **Other Jobs in These Pathways:** Clinical Psychologists; Counseling Psychologists; Cytogenetic Technologists; Cytotechnologists; Dental Assistants; Dental Hygienists; Dentists, General; Emergency Medical Technicians and Paramedics; Endoscopy Technicians; Healthcare Support Workers, All Other; Histotechnologists and Histologic Technicians; Home Health Aides; Licensed Practical and Licensed Vocational Nurses; Massage Therapists; Medical and Clinical Laboratory Technologists; Medical and Health Services Managers; Medical Assistants; Medical Secretaries; Pharmacists; Pharmacy Technicians; Radiologic Technologists; School Psychologists; Social and Human Service Assistants; Speech-Language Pathologists; Speech-Language Pathology Assistants; others.

Skills: Science; Equipment Maintenance; Equipment Selection; Troubleshooting; Repairing; Operation and Control; Quality Control Analysis; Operation Monitoring.

Work Environment: Indoors; standing; walking and running; using hands; repetitive motions; noise; contaminants; exposed to disease or infections; hazardous conditions.

Medical and Clinical Laboratory Technologists

* Annual Earnings: H $55,821, * $56,130
* Earnings Growth Potential: Low (30.9%)
* Growth: H 11.7%, * 11.9%
* Annual Job Openings: H 6,740, * 5,330
* Self-Employed: 0.2%

Detailed Fields with Greatest Employment: Hospitals, Public and Private (60.8%); Educational Services, Public and Private (5.2%); Federal Government (3.3%); Ambulatory Health Care Services (26.0%); Professional, Scientific, and Technical Services (1.7%)

Detailed Fields with Highest Growth (Projected Growth for This Job): Ambulatory Health Care Services (45.9%); Professional, Scientific, and Technical Services (34.9%); Religious, Grantmaking, Civic, Professional, and Similar Organizations (25.0%); Administrative and Support Services (23.1%); Social Assistance (16.7%)

Other Considerations for Job Outlook: Employment of these workers is expected to rise as the volume of laboratory tests continues to increase with population growth and the development of new tests. Excellent opportunities are expected.

Perform complex medical laboratory tests for diagnosis, treatment, and prevention of disease. May train or supervise staff. Conduct chemical analysis of bodily fluids, including blood, urine, and spinal fluid, to determine presence of normal and abnormal components. Analyze laboratory findings to check the accuracy of the results. Enter data from analysis of medical tests and clinical results into computer for storage. Operate, calibrate, and maintain equipment used in quantitative and qualitative analysis, such as spectrophotometers, calorimeters, flame photometers, and computer-controlled analyzers. Establish and monitor quality assurance programs and activities to ensure the accuracy of laboratory results. Set up, clean, and maintain laboratory equipment. Provide technical information about test results to physicians, family members, and researchers. Supervise, train, and direct lab assistants, medical and clinical laboratory technicians and technologists, and other medical laboratory workers engaged in laboratory testing.

Education/Training Required: Bachelor's degree. **Education and Training Programs:** Clinical Laboratory Science/Medical Technology/Technologist; Clinical/Medical Laboratory Science and Allied Professions, Other; Cytogenetics/Genetics/Clinical Genetics Technology/Technologist; Cytotechnology/Cytotechnologist; Histologic Technology/Histotechnologist; Renal/Dialysis Technologist/Technician. **Knowledge/Courses:** Biology; Chemistry; Medicine and Dentistry; Mechanical Devices; Clerical Practices; Mathematics.

Personality Type: Investigative-Realistic-Conventional. **Career Cluster:** 08 Health Science. **Career Pathway:** 8.2 Diagnostics Services. **Other Jobs in This Pathway:** Ambulance Drivers and Attendants, Except Emergency Medical Technicians; Anesthesiologist Assistants; Cardiovascular Technologists and Technicians; Cytogenetic Technologists; Cytotechnologists; Diagnostic Medical Sonographers; Emergency Medical Technicians and Paramedics; Endoscopy Technicians; Health Diagnosing and Treating Practitioners, All Other; Health Technologists and Technicians, All Other; Healthcare Practitioners and Technical Workers, All Other; Histotechnologists and Histologic Technicians; Medical and Clinical Laboratory Technicians; Medical and Health Services Managers; Medical Assistants; Medical Equipment Preparers; Neurodiagnostic Technologists; Nuclear Medicine Technologists; Ophthalmic Laboratory Technicians; Physical Scientists, All Other; Physician Assistants; Radiologic Technicians; Radiologic Technologists; Surgical Technologists; Veterinary Assistants and Laboratory Animal Caretakers; others.

Skills: Science; Equipment Selection; Equipment Maintenance; Quality Control Analysis; Programming; Operation Monitoring; Troubleshooting; Operation and Control.

---

*C=Computer Systems Design, E=Educational Services, G=Government, H=Health Care, R=Repair and Maintenance, U=Utilities, *=All Fields*

Work Environment: Indoors; standing; using hands; repetitive motions; noise; contaminants; exposed to disease or infections; hazardous conditions.

Job Specialization: Cytogenetic Technologists

Analyze chromosomes found in biological specimens such as amniotic fluids, bone marrow, and blood to aid in the study, diagnosis, or treatment of genetic diseases. Develop and implement training programs for trainees, medical students, resident physicians, or postdoctoral fellows. Stain slides to make chromosomes visible for microscopy. Summarize test results and report to appropriate authorities. Select or prepare specimens and media for cell cultures using aseptic techniques, knowledge of medium components, or cell nutritional requirements. Select banding methods to permit identification of chromosome pairs Identify appropriate methods of specimen collection, preservation, or transport. Prepare slides of cell cultures following standard procedures. Select appropriate methods of preparation and storage of media to maintain potential of hydrogen (pH), sterility, or ability to support growth. Harvest cell cultures using substances such as mitotic arrestants, cell releasing agents, and cell fixatives. Create chromosome images using computer imaging systems. Determine optimal time sequences and methods for manual or robotic cell harvests.

Education/Training Required: Bachelor's degree. **Education and Training Programs:** Clinical Laboratory Science/Medical Technology/Technologist; Cytogenetics/Genetics/Clinical Genetics Technology/Technologist. **Knowledge/Courses:** Biology; Chemistry; Medicine and Dentistry; Education and Training.

Personality Type: Investigative-Realistic-Conventional. **Career Cluster:** 08 Health Science.

Career Pathway: 8.2 Diagnostics Services. **Other Jobs in This Pathway:** Ambulance Drivers and Attendants, Except Emergency Medical Technicians; Anesthesiologist Assistants; Cardiovascular Technologists and Technicians; Cytotechnologists; Diagnostic Medical Sonographers; Emergency Medical Technicians and Paramedics; Endoscopy Technicians; Health Diagnosing and Treating Practitioners, All Other; Health Technologists and Technicians, All Other; Healthcare Practitioners and Technical Workers, All Other; Histotechnologists and Histologic Technicians; Medical and Clinical Laboratory Technicians; Medical and Clinical Laboratory Technologists; Medical and Health Services Managers; Medical Assistants; Medical Equipment Preparers; Neurodiagnostic Technologists; Nuclear Medicine Technologists; Ophthalmic Laboratory Technicians; Physical Scientists, All Other; Physician Assistants; Radiologic Technicians; Radiologic Technologists; Surgical Technologists; Veterinary Assistants and Laboratory Animal Caretakers; others.

Skills: Science; Reading Comprehension; Writing; Active Learning; Speaking; Mathematics; Instructing; Active Listening.

Work Environment: Indoors; sitting; using hands; repetitive motions; contaminants; exposed to disease or infections; hazardous conditions.

Job Specialization: Cytotechnologists

Stain, mount, and study cells to detect evidence of cancer, hormonal abnormalities, and other pathological conditions following established standards and practices. Examine cell samples to detect abnormalities in the color, shape, or size of cellular components and patterns. Examine specimens using microscopes to evaluate specimen quality. Prepare and analyze samples, such as Papanicolaou (PAP) smear body fluids and fine needle aspirations (FNAs), to detect abnormal conditions. Provide patient clinical data or microscopic findings to assist pathologists in the preparation of pathology reports. Assist pathologists or other physicians to collect cell samples such as by fine needle aspiration (FNA) biopsies. Examine specimens to detect abnormal hormone conditions. Document specimens by verifying patients' and specimens' information. Maintain effective laboratory operations by adhering to standards of specimen collection, preparation, or laboratory safety. Perform karyotyping or organizing of chromosomes according to standardized ideograms.

Education/Training Required: Bachelor's degree. **Education and Training Programs:** Clinical Laboratory Science/Medical Technology/Technologist; Cytotechnology/Cytotechnologist. **Knowledge/Courses:** Biology; Medicine and Dentistry; Chemistry; Clerical Practices; Law and Government.

Personality Type: Investigative-Realistic. **Career Cluster:** 08 Health Science. **Career Pathway:** 8.2 Diagnostics Services. **Other Jobs in This Pathway:** Ambulance Drivers and Attendants, Except Emergency Medical Technicians; Anesthesiologist Assistants; Cardiovascular Technologists and Technicians; Cytogenetic Technologists; Diagnostic Medical Sonographers; Emergency Medical Technicians and Paramedics; Endoscopy Technicians; Health Diagnosing and Treating Practitioners, All Other; Health Technologists and Technicians, All Other; Healthcare Practitioners and Technical Workers, All Other; Histotechnologists and Histologic Technicians; Medical and Clinical Laboratory Technicians; Medical and Clinical Laboratory Technologists; Medical and Health Services Managers; Medical Assistants; Medical Equipment Preparers; Neurodiagnostic Technologists; Nuclear Medicine Technologists; Ophthalmic Laboratory Technicians; Physical Scientists, All Other; Physician Assistants; Radiologic Technicians; Radiologic Technologists; Surgical Technologists; Veterinary Assistants and Laboratory Animal Caretakers; others.

Skills: Science; Mathematics; Reading Comprehension; Writing; Operation Monitoring; Judgment and Decision Making; Learning Strategies; Instructing.

Work Environment: Indoors; sitting; using hands; repetitive motions; contaminants; exposed to disease or infections; hazardous conditions.

Job Specialization: Histotechnologists and Histologic Technicians

Prepare histologic slides from tissue sections for microscopic examination and diagnosis by pathologists. May assist in research studies. Cut sections of body tissues for microscopic examination using microtomes. Embed tissue specimens into paraffin wax blocks or infiltrate tissue specimens with wax. Freeze tissue specimens. Mount tissue specimens on glass slides. Stain tissue specimens with dyes or other chemicals to make cell details visible under microscopes. Examine slides under microscopes to ensure tissue preparation meets laboratory requirements. Identify tissue structures or cell components to be used in the diagnosis, prevention, or treatment of diseases. Operate computerized laboratory equipment to dehydrate, decalcify, or microincinerate tissue samples. Perform electron microscopy or mass spectrometry to analyze specimens. Perform procedures associated with histochemistry to prepare specimens for immunofluorescence or microscopy. Maintain laboratory equipment such as microscopes, mass spectrometers, microtomes, immunostainers, tissue processors, embedding centers, and water baths.

Education/Training Required: Associate degree. **Education and Training Programs:** Clinical Laboratory Science/Medical Technology/Technologist; Clinical/Medical Laboratory Science and Allied Professions, Other; Cytogenetics/Genetics/Clinical Genetics Technology/Technologist; Cytotechnology/Cytotechnologist; Histologic Technology/Histotechnologist; Renal/Dialysis Technologist/Technician.

*C=Computer Systems Design, E=Educational Services, G=Government, H=Health Care, R=Repair and Maintenance, U=Utilities, *=All Fields*

Knowledge/Courses: Biology; Chemistry; Medicine and Dentistry; Production and Processing; Mechanical Devices; Education and Training.

Personality Type: Realistic-Investigative-Conventional. **Career Cluster:** 08 Health Science. **Career Pathway:** 8.2 Diagnostics Services. **Other Jobs in This Pathway:** Ambulance Drivers and Attendants, Except Emergency Medical Technicians; Anesthesiologist Assistants; Cardiovascular Technologists and Technicians; Cytogenetic Technologists; Cytotechnologists; Diagnostic Medical Sonographers; Emergency Medical Technicians and Paramedics; Endoscopy Technicians; Health Diagnosing and Treating Practitioners, All Other; Health Technologists and Technicians, All Other; Healthcare Practitioners and Technical Workers, All Other; Medical and Clinical Laboratory Technicians; Medical and Clinical Laboratory Technologists; Medical and Health Services Managers; Medical Assistants; Medical Equipment Preparers; Neurodiagnostic Technologists; Nuclear Medicine Technologists; Ophthalmic Laboratory Technicians; Physical Scientists, All Other; Physician Assistants; Radiologic Technicians; Radiologic Technologists; Surgical Technologists; Veterinary Assistants and Laboratory Animal Caretakers; others.

Skills: Science; Equipment Maintenance; Equipment Selection; Repairing; Operation and Control; Troubleshooting; Mathematics; Operation Monitoring.

Work Environment: Indoors; sitting; using hands; repetitive motions; contaminants; exposed to disease or infections; hazardous conditions.

Medical and Health Services Managers

- ❋ Annual Earnings: H $83,271, G $89,870, E $90,440, * $84,270
- ❋ Earnings Growth Potential: Medium (39.1%)
- ❋ Growth: G 8.1%, E 12.4%, H 18.0%, * 16.0%
- ❋ Annual Job Openings: E 140, G 530, H 7,700, * 9,940
- ❋ Self-Employed: 6.0%

Detailed Fields with Greatest Employment: State and Local Government (6.6%); Hospitals, Public and Private (40.8%); Ambulatory Health Care Services (24.8%); Educational Services, Public and Private (2.8%); Federal Government (2.8%)

Detailed Fields with Highest Growth (Projected Growth for This Job): Professional, Scientific, and Technical Services (52.2%); Ambulatory Health Care Services (32.7%); Social Assistance (25.6%); Administrative and Support Services (23.9%); Merchant Wholesalers, Nondurable Goods (23.7%)

Other Considerations for Job Outlook: The health-care industry is expected to continue growing and diversifying, requiring managers increasingly to run business operations. Opportunities should be good, especially for job seekers who have work experience in health care and strong business management skills.

Plan, direct, or coordinate medicine and health services in hospitals, clinics, managed care organizations, public health agencies, or similar organizations. Conduct and administer fiscal operations, including accounting, planning budgets, authorizing expenditures, establishing rates for services, and coordinating financial reporting.

Direct, supervise, and evaluate work activities of medical, nursing, technical, clerical, service, maintenance, and other personnel. Maintain communication between governing boards, medical staff, and department heads by attending board meetings and coordinating interdepartmental functioning. Review and analyze facility activities and data to aid planning and cash and risk management and to improve service utilization. Plan, implement, and administer programs and services in a health-care or medical facility, including personnel administration, training, and coordination of medical, nursing, and physical plant staff. Direct or conduct recruitment, hiring, and training of personnel. Establish work schedules and assignments for staff, according to workload, space, and equipment availability.

Education/Training Required: Work experience plus degree. **Education and Training Programs:** Community Health and Preventive Medicine; Health and Medical Administrative Services, Other; Health Information/Medical Records Administration/Administrator; Health Services Administration; Health Unit Manager/Ward Supervisor Training; Health/Health Care Administration/Management; Hospital and Health Care Facilities Administration/Management; Public Health, General. **Knowledge/Courses:** Economics and Accounting; Personnel and Human Resources; Administration and Management; Sales and Marketing; Medicine and Dentistry; Law and Government.

Personality Type: Enterprising-Conventional-Social. **Career Cluster:** 08 Health Science. **Career Pathways:** 8.1 Therapeutic Services; 8.2 Diagnostics Services; 8.3 Health Informatics. **Other Jobs in These Pathways:** Cytogenetic Technologists; Cytotechnologists; Dental Assistants; Dental Hygienists; Emergency Medical Technicians and Paramedics; Endoscopy Technicians; Engineers, All Other; Executive Secretaries and Executive Administrative Assistants; First-Line Supervisors of Office and Administrative Support Workers; Healthcare Support Workers, All Other; Histotechnologists and Histologic Technicians; Home Health Aides; Licensed Practical and Licensed Vocational Nurses; Medical and Clinical Laboratory Technologists; Medical Assistants; Medical Records and Health Information Technicians; Medical Secretaries; Pharmacists; Pharmacy Technicians; Physical Therapists; Public Relations Specialists; Radiologic Technologists; Receptionists and Information Clerks; Social and Human Service Assistants; Speech-Language Pathology Assistants; others.

Skills: Management of Financial Resources; Operations Analysis; Management of Material Resources; Science; Management of Personnel Resources; Systems Evaluation; Coordination; Time Management.

Work Environment: Indoors; sitting; exposed to disease or infections.

Medical Equipment Repairers

- ❋ Annual Earnings: R $43,630, H $46,974, * $44,490
- ❋ Earnings Growth Potential: High (41.5%)
- ❋ Growth: R 28.0%, H 39.3%, * 27.2%
- ❋ Annual Job Openings: R 360, H 820, * 2,320
- ❋ Self-Employed: 16.4%

Detailed Fields with Greatest Employment: Ambulatory Health Care Services (8.2%); Rental and Leasing Services (7.6%); Health and Personal Care Stores (6.6%); Merchant Wholesalers, Durable Goods (27.1%); Hospitals, Public and Private (20.5%)

Detailed Fields with Highest Growth (Projected Growth for This Job): Ambulatory Health Care Services (63.0%); Wholesale Electronic Markets and Agents and Brokers (53.1%); Administrative

*C=Computer Systems Design, E=Educational Services, G=Government, H=Health Care, R=Repair and Maintenance, U=Utilities, *=All Fields*

and Support Services (47.6%); Professional, Scientific, and Technical Services (47.4%); Food Services and Drinking Places (40.0%)

Other Considerations for Job Outlook: An increased demand for health-care services and the growing complexity of medical equipment are projected to result in greater need for these repairers. Excellent job prospects are expected. Job seekers who have an associate degree should have the best prospects.

Test, adjust, or repair biomedical or electromedical equipment. Inspect and test malfunctioning medical and related equipment following manufacturers' specifications, using test and analysis instruments. Examine medical equipment and facility's structural environment and check for proper use of equipment to protect patients and staff from electrical or mechanical hazards and to ensure compliance with safety regulations. Disassemble malfunctioning equipment and remove, repair, and replace defective parts such as motors, clutches, or transformers. Keep records of maintenance, repair, and required updates of equipment. Perform preventive maintenance or service such as cleaning, lubricating, and adjusting equipment. Test and calibrate components and equipment, following manufacturers' manuals and troubleshooting techniques and using hand tools, power tools, and measuring devices. Explain and demonstrate correct operation and preventive maintenance of medical equipment to personnel.

Education/Training Required: Associate degree. **Education and Training Program:** Biomedical Technology/Technician. **Knowledge/Courses:** Mechanical Devices; Engineering and Technology; Physics; Telecommunications; Computers and Electronics; Chemistry.

Personality Type: Realistic-Investigative-Conventional. **Career Cluster:** 13 Manufacturing. **Career Pathway:** 13.3 Maintenance, Installation, and Repair. **Other Jobs in This Pathway:** Aircraft Mechanics and Service Technicians; Automotive Specialty Technicians; Biological Technicians; Civil Engineering Technicians; Computer, Automated Teller, and Office Machine Repairers; Electrical and Electronic Equipment Assemblers; Electrical and Electronics Repairers, Commercial and Industrial Equipment; Electrical Engineering Technicians; Electrical Engineering Technologists; Electromechanical Engineering Technologists; Electronics Engineering Technicians; Electronics Engineering Technologists; Engineering Technicians, Except Drafters, All Other; Fuel Cell Technicians; Helpers—Installation, Maintenance, and Repair Workers; Industrial Engineering Technologists; Industrial Machinery Mechanics; Installation, Maintenance, and Repair Workers, All Other; Manufacturing Engineering Technologists; Manufacturing Production Technicians; Mapping Technicians; Mechanical Engineering Technologists; Mobile Heavy Equipment Mechanics, Except Engines; Telecommunications Line Installers and Repairers; Tire Repairers and Changers; others.

Skills: Equipment Maintenance; Repairing; Troubleshooting; Equipment Selection; Quality Control Analysis; Operation and Control; Installation; Operation Monitoring.

Work Environment: Indoors; standing; using hands; noise; bright or inadequate lighting; contaminants; cramped work space; exposed to disease or infections; hazardous conditions; hazardous equipment; minor burns, cuts, bites, or stings.

Medical Records and Health Information Technicians

- ❈ Annual Earnings: H $31,644, * $32,350
- ❈ Earnings Growth Potential: Low (34.3%)
- ❈ Growth: H 20.7%, * 20.3%
- ❈ Annual Job Openings: H 8,570, * 7,030
- ❈ Self-Employed: 0.0%

Detailed Fields with Greatest Employment: Nursing and Residential Care Facilities (9.6%); Hospitals, Public and Private (38.8%); Ambulatory Health Care Services (34.9%); Professional, Scientific, and Technical Services (3.4%); Federal Government (3.1%)

Detailed Fields with Highest Growth (Projected Growth for This Job): Internet Service Providers, Web Search Portals, and Data Processing Services (58.3%); Professional, Scientific, and Technical Services (41.6%); Ambulatory Health Care Services (34.2%); Administrative and Support Services (25.7%); Social Assistance (25.5%)

Other Considerations for Job Outlook: Employment of these workers is expected to grow as the number of elderly—a demographic group with a higher incidence of injury and illness—increases. Job prospects should be best for technicians who have strong skills in technology and computer software.

Compile, process, and maintain medical records of hospital and clinic patients in a manner consistent with medical, administrative, ethical, legal, and regulatory requirements of the heath-care system. Protect the security of medical records to ensure that confidentiality is maintained. Review records for completeness, accuracy, and compliance with regulations. Retrieve patient medical records for physicians, technicians, or other medical personnel. Release information to persons and agencies according to regulations. Plan, develop, maintain, and operate a variety of health record indexes and storage and retrieval systems to collect, classify, store, and analyze information. Enter data such as demographic characteristics, history and extent of disease, diagnostic procedures, and treatment into computer. Process and prepare business and government forms. Compile and maintain patients' medical records to document condition and treatment and to provide data for research or cost control and care improvement efforts. Process patient admission and discharge documents. Assign the patient to diagnosis-related groups (DRGs), using appropriate computer software. Transcribe medical reports.

Education/Training Required: Associate degree. **Education and Training Programs:** Health Information/Medical Records Technology/Technician; Medical Insurance Coding Specialist/Coder Training. **Knowledge/Courses:** Clerical Practices; Law and Government; Customer and Personal Service.

Personality Type: Conventional-Enterprising. **Career Cluster:** 08 Health Science. **Career Pathway:** 8.3 Health Informatics. **Other Jobs in This Pathway:** Clinical Psychologists; Dental Laboratory Technicians; Editors; Engineers, All Other; Executive Secretaries and Executive Administrative Assistants; Fine Artists, Including Painters, Sculptors, and Illustrators; First-Line Supervisors of Office and Administrative Support Workers; Health Educators; Medical and Health Services Managers; Medical Appliance Technicians; Medical Assistants; Medical Secretaries; Medical Transcriptionists; Mental Health Counselors; Occupational Health and Safety Specialists; Occupational Health and Safety Technicians; Physical Therapists; Psychiatric Aides; Psychiatric Technicians; Public Relations Specialists; Receptionists and Information Clerks; Recreational Therapists; Rehabilitation Counselors; Substance

*C=Computer Systems Design, E=Educational Services, G=Government, H=Health Care, R=Repair and Maintenance, U=Utilities, *=All Fields*

Abuse and Behavioral Disorder Counselors; Therapists, All Other; others.

Skills: None met the criteria.

Work Environment: Indoors; sitting; using hands; repetitive motions; exposed to disease or infections.

Medical Scientists, Except Epidemiologists

❋ Annual Earnings: E $53,470, H $72,858, G $95,000, * $76,700

❋ Earnings Growth Potential: High (45.8%)

❋ Growth: G 29.8%, E 34.6%, H 42.0%, * 40.4%

❋ Annual Job Openings: G 80, E 1,320, H 1,400, * 6,620

❋ Self-Employed: 2.5%

Detailed Fields with Greatest Employment: Ambulatory Health Care Services (4.9%); Professional, Scientific, and Technical Services (35.5%); Educational Services, Public and Private (27.7%); Merchant Wholesalers, Nondurable Goods (2.3%); Chemical Manufacturing (13.2%)

Detailed Fields with Highest Growth (Projected Growth for This Job): Ambulatory Health Care Services (58.1%); Wholesale Electronic Markets and Agents and Brokers (57.9%); Professional, Scientific, and Technical Services (52.8%); Administrative and Support Services (45.9%); Merchant Wholesalers, Nondurable Goods (44.4%)

Other Considerations for Job Outlook: New discoveries in biological and medical science are expected to create strong employment growth for these workers. Medical scientists with both doctoral and medical degrees should have the best opportunities.

Conduct research dealing with the understanding of human diseases and the improvement of human health. Engage in clinical investigation or other research, production, technical writing, or related activities. Conduct research to develop methodologies, instrumentation, and procedures for medical application, analyzing data and presenting findings. Plan and direct studies to investigate human or animal disease, preventive methods, and treatments for disease. Follow strict safety procedures when handling toxic materials to avoid contamination. Evaluate effects of drugs, gases, pesticides, parasites, and microorganisms at various levels. Teach principles of medicine and medical and laboratory procedures to physicians, residents, students, and technicians. Prepare and analyze organ, tissue, and cell samples to identify toxicity, bacteria, or microorganisms or to study cell structure. Standardize drug dosages, methods of immunization, and procedures for manufacture of drugs and medicinal compounds. Investigate cause, progress, life cycle, or mode of transmission of diseases or parasites.

Education/Training Required: Doctoral degree. **Education and Training Programs:** Anatomy; Biochemistry; Biomedical Sciences, General; Biophysics; Biostatistics; Cardiovascular Science; Cell Physiology; Cell/Cellular Biology and Histology; Endocrinology; Environmental Toxicology; Epidemiology; Exercise Physiology; Human/Medical Genetics; Immunology; Medical Microbiology and Bacteriology; Medical Science; Molecular Biology; Molecular Pharmacology; Molecular Physiology; Molecular Toxicology; Neuropharmacology; Oncology and Cancer Biology; Pathology/Experimental Pathology; Pharmacology; Pharmacology and Toxicology; Pharmacology and Toxicology, Other; Physiology, General; Physiology, Pathology, and Related Sciences, Other; Reproductive Biology; Toxicology; Vision Science/Physiological Optics. **Knowledge/Courses:** Biology; Medicine and Dentistry; Chemistry; Communications and Media; Personnel and Human Resources; Mathematics.

Personality Type: Investigative-Realistic-Artistic. **Career Clusters:** 08 Health Science; 15 Science, Technology, Engineering, and Mathematics. **Career Pathways:** 8.1 Therapeutic Services; 15.2 Science and Mathematics. **Other Jobs in These Pathways:** Architectural and Engineering Managers; Biofuels/Biodiesel Technology and Product Development Managers; Clinical Psychologists; Community and Social Service Specialists, All Other; Counseling Psychologists; Dental Assistants; Dental Hygienists; Dentists, General; Education, Training, and Library Workers, All Other; Healthcare Support Workers, All Other; Home Health Aides; Licensed Practical and Licensed Vocational Nurses; Low Vision Therapists, Orientation and Mobility Specialists, and Vision Rehabilitation Therapists; Massage Therapists; Medical and Clinical Laboratory Technicians; Medical and Health Services Managers; Medical Secretaries; Occupational Therapists; Pharmacists; Pharmacy Technicians; Radiologic Technologists; School Psychologists; Social and Human Service Assistants; Speech-Language Pathologists; Speech-Language Pathology Assistants; others.

Skills: Science; Operations Analysis; Reading Comprehension; Mathematics; Systems Evaluation; Instructing; Complex Problem Solving; Systems Analysis.

Work Environment: Indoors; sitting; using hands.

Medical Secretaries

- ✳ Annual Earnings: H $30,512, * $30,530
- ✳ Earnings Growth Potential: Low (30.5%)
- ✳ Growth: H 27.4%, * 26.6%
- ✳ Annual Job Openings: H 25,630, * 18,900
- ✳ Self-Employed: 1.4%

Detailed Fields with Greatest Employment:

Ambulatory Health Care Services (67.6%); Hospitals, Public and Private (25.2%); Educational Services, Public and Private (1.5%); Nursing and Residential Care Facilities (1.5%); Professional, Scientific, and Technical Services (1.5%)

Detailed Fields with Highest Growth (Projected Growth for This Job): Professional, Scientific, and Technical Services (38.5%); Ambulatory Health Care Services (34.0%); Social Assistance (33.0%); Nursing and Residential Care Facilities (22.7%); Administrative and Support Services (20.8%)

Other Considerations for Job Outlook: Projected employment growth varies by occupational specialty. Faster than average growth is expected for medical secretaries and legal secretaries; average growth for executive secretaries and administrative assistants; and slower than average growth for secretaries other than legal, medical, or executive, who account for most of the workers in these specialties. Many opportunities are expected.

Perform secretarial duties, using specific knowledge of medical terminology and hospital, clinical, or laboratory procedures. Answer telephones and direct calls to appropriate staff. Schedule and confirm patient diagnostic appointments, surgeries, and medical consultations. Greet visitors, ascertain purpose of visit, and direct them to appropriate staff. Operate office equipment, such as voice mail messaging systems, and use word processing, spreadsheet, and other software applications to prepare reports, invoices, financial statements, letters, case histories, and medical records. Complete insurance and other claim forms. Interview patients to complete documents, case histories, and forms such as intake and insurance forms. Receive and route messages and documents such as laboratory results to appropriate staff. Compile and record medical charts, reports,

*C=Computer Systems Design, E=Educational Services, G=Government, H=Health Care, R=Repair and Maintenance, U=Utilities, *=All Fields*

and correspondence, using typewriter or personal computer. Transmit correspondence and medical records by mail, e-mail, or fax. Maintain medical records, technical library documents, and correspondence files.

Education/Training Required: Moderate-term on-the-job training. **Education and Training Programs:** Medical Administrative/Executive Assistant and Medical Secretary Training; Medical Insurance Specialist/Medical Biller Training; Medical Office Assistant/Specialist Training. **Knowledge/Courses:** Clerical Practices; Medicine and Dentistry; Customer and Personal Service; Computers and Electronics; Economics and Accounting.

Personality Type: Conventional-Social. **Career Cluster:** 08 Health Science. **Career Pathways:** 8.1 Therapeutic Services; 8.3 Health Informatics. **Other Jobs in These Pathways:** Clinical Psychologists; Counseling Psychologists; Dental Assistants; Dental Hygienists; Editors; Engineers, All Other; Executive Secretaries and Executive Administrative Assistants; First-Line Supervisors of Office and Administrative Support Workers; Healthcare Support Workers, All Other; Home Health Aides; Licensed Practical and Licensed Vocational Nurses; Medical and Clinical Laboratory Technicians; Medical and Health Services Managers; Medical Assistants; Medical Records and Health Information Technicians; Pharmacists; Pharmacy Technicians; Physical Therapists; Public Relations Specialists; Radiologic Technologists; Clerks; Receptionists and Information Rehabilitation Counselors; School Psychologists; Social and Human Service Assistants; Speech-Language Pathology Assistants; others.

Skills: Service Orientation; Active Listening; Speaking.

Work Environment: Indoors; sitting; repetitive motions; exposed to disease or infections.

Mental Health and Substance Abuse Social Workers

- ❋ Annual Earnings: H $39,270, * $38,600
- ❋ Earnings Growth Potential: Low (34.7%)
- ❋ Growth: H 23.0%, * 19.5%
- ❋ Annual Job Openings: H 6,660, * 6,130
- ❋ Self-Employed: 2.2%

Detailed Fields with Greatest Employment: Religious, Grantmaking, Civic, Professional, and Similar Organizations (3.0%); Ambulatory Health Care Services (24.9%); Social Assistance (20.4%); State and Local Government (18.0%); Nursing and Residential Care Facilities (16.5%)

Detailed Fields with Highest Growth (Projected Growth for This Job): Ambulatory Health Care Services (33.1%); Professional, Scientific, and Technical Services (32.0%); Administrative and Support Services (28.5%); Social Assistance (24.7%); Nursing and Residential Care Facilities (23.4%)

Other Considerations for Job Outlook: The rapidly increasing elderly population is expected to spur demand for social services. Job prospects should be favorable because of the need to replace the many workers who are leaving the occupation permanently.

Assess and treat individuals with mental, emotional, or substance abuse problems, including abuse of alcohol, tobacco, and/or other drugs. Activities may include individual and group therapy, crisis intervention, case management, client advocacy, prevention, and education. Counsel clients in individual and group sessions to assist them in dealing with substance abuse, mental and physical illness, poverty, unemployment, or physical abuse. Interview clients, review records, and confer with other professionals to evaluate mental or physical condition of client or patient. Collaborate with counselors, physicians, and nurses to plan and coordinate treatment, drawing on social work experience and patient needs. Monitor, evaluate, and record client progress with respect to treatment goals. Refer patient, client, or family to community resources for housing or treatment to assist in recovery from mental or physical illness, following through to ensure service efficacy. Counsel and aid family members to assist them in understanding, dealing with, and supporting the client or patient. Modify treatment plans according to changes in client status.

Education/Training Required: Master's degree. **Education and Training Program:** Clinical/Medical Social Work. **Knowledge/Courses:** Therapy and Counseling; Psychology; Sociology and Anthropology; Philosophy and Theology; Customer and Personal Service; Education and Training.

Personality Type: Social-Investigative-Artistic. **Career Cluster:** 10 Human Services. **Career Pathway:** 10.2 Counseling and Mental Health Services. **Other Jobs in This Pathway:** Clergy; Clinical Psychologists; Counseling Psychologists; Counselors, All Other; Directors, Religious Activities and Education; Epidemiologists; Health Educators; Healthcare Social Workers; Marriage and Family Therapists; Mental Health Counselors; Music Directors; Psychologists, All Other; Recreation Workers; Religious Workers, All Other; School Psychologists; Substance Abuse and Behavioral Disorder Counselors.

Skills: Social Perceptiveness; Science; Operations Analysis; Service Orientation; Learning Strategies; Active Learning; Persuasion; Negotiation.

Work Environment: Indoors; sitting; repetitive motions; noise; exposed to disease or infections.

Mental Health Counselors

* Annual Earnings: H $37,457, * $38,150
* Earnings Growth Potential: Medium (36.6%)
* Growth: H 27.6%, * 24.0%
* Annual Job Openings: H 5,720, * 5,010
* Self-Employed: 6.1%

Detailed Fields with Greatest Employment: Ambulatory Health Care Services (30.3%); Nursing and Residential Care Facilities (20.4%); Social Assistance (20.2%); Hospitals, Public and Private (12.6%); Educational Services, Public and Private (1.4%)

Detailed Fields with Highest Growth (Projected Growth for This Job): Ambulatory Health Care Services (33.9%); Nursing and Residential Care Facilities (33.7%); Administrative and Support Services (26.1%); Social Assistance (24.8%); Educational Services, Public and Private (13.9%)

Other Considerations for Job Outlook: Increasing demand for services provided by counselors is expected to result in employment growth. But growth will vary by specialty and will be faster for mental health, substance abuse and behavioral disorder, and rehabilitation counselors than for counselors of other specialties. Opportunities should be favorable, particularly in rural areas.

Counsel with emphasis on prevention. Work with individuals and groups to promote optimum mental health. May help individuals deal with addictions and substance abuse; family, parenting, and marital problems; suicide; stress management; problems with self-esteem; and issues associated with aging and mental and emotional health. Maintain confidentiality of records relating to clients' treatment. Guide clients in the development of skills and strategies for dealing

*C=Computer Systems Design, E=Educational Services, G=Government, H=Health Care, R=Repair and Maintenance, U=Utilities, *=All Fields*

with their problems. Encourage clients to express their feelings and discuss what is happening in their lives and help them to develop insight into themselves and their relationships. Prepare and maintain all required treatment records and reports. Counsel clients and patients, individually and in group sessions, to assist in overcoming dependencies, adjusting to life, and making changes. Collect information about clients through interviews, observation, and tests. Act as client advocates to coordinate required services or to resolve emergency problems in crisis situations. Develop and implement treatment plans based on clinical experience and knowledge. Collaborate with other staff members to perform clinical assessments and develop treatment plans. Evaluate clients' physical or mental condition based on review of client information.

Education/Training Required: Master's degree. **Education and Training Programs:** Clinical/Medical Social Work; Mental and Social Health Services and Allied Professions, Other; Mental Health Counseling/Counselor; Substance Abuse/Addiction Counseling. **Knowledge/Courses:** Therapy and Counseling; Psychology; Sociology and Anthropology; Philosophy and Theology; Customer and Personal Service; Medicine and Dentistry.

Personality Type: Social-Investigative-Artistic. **Career Clusters:** 08 Health Science; 10 Human Services. **Career Pathways:** 8.3 Health Informatics; 10.2 Counseling and Mental Health Services. **Other Jobs in These Pathways:** Clergy; Clinical Psychologists; Counseling Psychologists; Directors, Religious Activities and Education; Editors; Engineers, All Other; Executive Secretaries and Executive Administrative Assistants; First-Line Supervisors of Office and Administrative Support Workers; Health Educators; Healthcare Social Workers; Medical and Health Services Managers; Medical Assistants; Medical Records and Health Information Technicians; Medical Secretaries; Medical Transcriptionists; Mental Health and Substance Abuse Social Workers; Physical Therapists; Psychiatric Aides; Psychiatric Technicians; Public Relations Specialists; Receptionists and Information Clerks; Recreation Workers; Rehabilitation Counselors; School Psychologists; Substance Abuse and Behavioral Disorder Counselors; others.

Skills: Science; Social Perceptiveness; Active Listening; Operations Analysis; Service Orientation; Systems Evaluation; Persuasion; Systems Analysis.

Work Environment: Indoors; sitting.

Middle School Teachers, Except Special and Career/Technical Education

- ❋ Annual Earnings: E $51,980, * $51,960
- ❋ Earnings Growth Potential: Low (32.7%)
- ❋ Growth: E 15.4%, * 15.3%
- ❋ Annual Job Openings: E 18,290, * 25,110
- ❋ Self-Employed: 0.0%

Detailed Fields with Greatest Employment: Educational Services, Public and Private (98.9%); Administrative and Support Services (0.5%); Religious, Grantmaking, Civic, Professional, and Similar Organizations (0.3%); Hospitals, Public and Private (0.0%); Nursing and Residential Care Facilities (0.0%)

Detailed Fields with Highest Growth (Projected Growth for This Job): Administrative and Support Services (17.9%); Educational Services, Public and Private (15.4%); Religious, Grantmaking, Civic, Professional, and Similar Organizations (7.5%); Social Assistance (7.4%); Hospitals, Public and Private (0.0%)

Other Considerations for Job Outlook: Enrollment from 2008–2018 is expected to grow more slowly than in recent years. Prospects are usually better in urban and rural areas, for bilingual teachers, and for math and science teachers.

Teach students in public or private schools in one or more subjects at the middle, intermediate, or junior high level, which falls between elementary and senior high school as defined by applicable state laws and regulations. Establish and enforce rules for behavior and procedures for maintaining order among the students for whom they are responsible. Adapt teaching methods and instructional materials to meet students' varying needs and interests. Instruct through lectures, discussions, and demonstrations in one or more subjects such as English, mathematics, or social studies. Prepare, administer, and grade tests and assignments to evaluate students' progress. Establish clear objectives for all lessons, units, and projects and communicate these objectives to students. Plan and conduct activities for a balanced program of instruction, demonstration, and work time that provides students with opportunities to observe, question, and investigate. Maintain accurate, complete, and correct student records as required by laws, district policies, and administrative regulations. Observe and evaluate students' performance, behavior, social development, and physical health. Assign lessons and correct homework.

Education/Training Required: Bachelor's degree. **Education and Training Programs:** Art Teacher Education; Computer Teacher Education; English/Language Arts Teacher Education; Family and Consumer Sciences/Home Economics Teacher Education; Foreign Language Teacher Education; Health Occupations Teacher Education; Health Teacher Education; History Teacher Education; Junior High/Intermediate/Middle School Education and Teaching; Mathematics Teacher Education; Music Teacher Education; Physical Education Teaching and Coaching; Reading Teacher Education; Science Teacher Education/General Science Teacher Education; Social Science Teacher Education; Social Studies Teacher Education; Teacher Education and Professional Development, Specific Subject Areas, Other; Technology Teacher Education/Industrial Arts Teacher Education. **Knowledge/Courses:** History and Archeology; Education and Training; Sociology and Anthropology; Fine Arts; Philosophy and Theology; English Language.

Personality Type: Social-Artistic. **Career Cluster:** 05 Education and Training. **Career Pathway:** 5.3 Teaching/Training. **Other Jobs in This Pathway:** Adult Basic and Secondary Education and Literacy Teachers and Instructors; Athletes and Sports Competitors; Audio-Visual and Multimedia Collections Specialists; Career/Technical Education Teachers, Middle School; Career/Technical Education Teachers, Secondary School; Chemists; Coaches and Scouts; Dietitians and Nutritionists; Elementary School Teachers, Except Special Education; Fitness Trainers and Aerobics Instructors; Historians; Instructional Coordinators; Instructional Designers and Technologists; Interpreters and Translators; Kindergarten Teachers, Except Special Education; Librarians; Physicists; Preschool Teachers, Except Special Education; Recreation Workers; Secondary School Teachers, Except Special and Career/Technical Education; Self-Enrichment Education Teachers; Teacher Assistants; Teachers and Instructors, All Other; Tutors.

Skills: Learning Strategies; Instructing; Negotiation; Writing; Social Perceptiveness; Reading Comprehension; Active Listening; Systems Evaluation.

Work Environment: Indoors; standing; noise.

C=Computer Systems Design, E=Educational Services, G=Government, H=Health Care, R=Repair and Maintenance, U=Utilities, *=All Fields

Motorboat Mechanics and Service Technicians

❋ Annual Earnings: R $35,420, * $35,600

❋ Earnings Growth Potential: Medium (36.5%)

❋ Growth: R −11.4%, * 5.6%

❋ Annual Job Openings: R 100, * 580

❋ Self-Employed: 12.8%

Detailed Fields with Greatest Employment: Motor Vehicle and Parts Dealers (51.0%); Transportation Equipment Manufacturing (3.2%); Amusement, Gambling, and Recreation Industries (20.3%); Repair and Maintenance (18.2%); Merchant Wholesalers, Durable Goods (1.7%)

Detailed Fields with Highest Growth (Projected Growth for This Job): Scenic and Sightseeing Transportation (18.2%); Motor Vehicle and Parts Dealers (10.3%); Amusement, Gambling, and Recreation Industries (9.9%); Support Activities for Transportation (3.3%); Merchant Wholesalers, Durable Goods (3.0%)

Other Considerations for Job Outlook: Employment growth is projected to be greatest for workers who repair motorcycles as the number of registered motorcycles continues to increase. Excellent job prospects are expected for job seekers with formal training.

Repair and adjust electrical and mechanical equipment of gasoline or diesel-powered inboard or inboard-outboard boat engines. Disassemble and inspect motors to locate defective parts, using mechanic's hand tools and gauges. Adjust generators and replace faulty wiring, using hand tools and soldering irons. Start motors and monitor performance for signs of malfunctioning such as smoke, excessive vibration, and misfiring. Adjust carburetor mixtures, electrical point settings, and timing while motors are running in water-filled test tanks. Idle motors and observe thermometers to determine the effectiveness of cooling systems. Inspect and repair or adjust propellers and propeller shafts. Mount motors to boats and operate boats at various speeds on waterways to conduct operational tests. Replace parts such as gears, magneto points, piston rings, and spark plugs, then reassemble engines. Repair or rework parts, using machine tools such as lathes, mills, drills, and grinders. Repair engine mechanical equipment such as power-tilts, bilge pumps, or power take-offs.

Education/Training Required: Long-term on-the-job training. **Education and Training Programs:** Marine Maintenance/Fitter and Ship Repair Technology/Technician; Small Engine Mechanics and Repair Technology/Technician. **Knowledge/Courses:** Mechanical Devices; Engineering and Technology; Design; Physics; Chemistry; Transportation.

Personality Type: Realistic-Conventional-Investigative. **Career Cluster:** 16 Transportation, Distribution, and Logistics. **Career Pathway:** 16.4 Facility and Mobile Equipment Maintenance. **Other Jobs in This Pathway:** Aircraft Mechanics and Service Technicians; Aircraft Structure, Surfaces, Rigging, and Systems Assemblers; Automotive Body and Related Repairers; Automotive Glass Installers and Repairers; Automotive Master Mechanics; Automotive Specialty Technicians; Bicycle Repairers; Bus and Truck Mechanics and Diesel Engine Specialists; Cleaners of Vehicles and Equipment; Electrical and Electronics Installers and Repairers, Transportation Equipment; Electronic Equipment Installers and Repairers, Motor Vehicles; Engine and Other Machine Assemblers; Gem and Diamond Workers; Installation, Maintenance, and Repair Workers, All Other; Motorcycle Mechanics; Outdoor Power Equipment and Other Small Engine Mechanics; Painters, Transportation Equipment.

Skills: Equipment Maintenance; Repairing; Troubleshooting; Operation and Control; Equipment Selection; Operation Monitoring; Quality Control Analysis; Installation.

Work Environment: Outdoors; standing; walking and running; using hands; bending or twisting the body; repetitive motions; noise; very hot or cold; bright or inadequate lighting; contaminants; cramped work space; hazardous conditions; hazardous equipment; minor burns, cuts, bites, or stings.

Network and Computer Systems Administrators

- ❋ Annual Earnings: E $59,230, H $65,616, G $67,070, U $74,180, C $74,230, * $69,160
- ❋ Earnings Growth Potential: Medium (38.7%)
- ❋ Growth: U −15.0%, G 8.3%, E 11.5%, H 46.3%, C 71.7%, * 23.2%
- ❋ Annual Job Openings: G 522, H 1,050, E 1,212, C 2,793, U 2,793, * 13,550
- ❋ Self-Employed: 0.8%

Detailed Fields with Greatest Employment: Management of Companies and Enterprises (6.5%); Telecommunications (6.2%); State and Local Government (4.9%); Credit Intermediation and Related Activities (3.7%); Insurance Carriers and Related Activities (3.7%)

Detailed Fields with Highest Growth (Projected Growth for This Job): Internet Service Providers, Web Search Portals, and Data Processing Services (81.3%); Hospitals, Public and Private (57.4%); Professional, Scientific, and Technical Services (56.1%); Publishing Industries (Except Internet) (35.4%); Lessors of Nonfinancial Intangible Assets (Except Copyrighted Works) (33.3%)

Other Considerations for Job Outlook: Employment of these workers should grow as organizations increasingly use network technologies. Job prospects are expected to be excellent.

Install, configure, and support organizations' local area networks (LANs), wide area networks (WANs), and Internet systems or segments of network systems. Maintain network hardware and software. Monitor networks to ensure network availability to all system users and perform necessary maintenance to support network availability. May supervise other network support and client server specialists and plan, coordinate, and implement network security measures. Perform data backups and disaster recovery operations. Maintain and administer computer networks and related computing environments including computer hardware, systems software, applications software, and all configurations. Plan, coordinate, and implement network security measures to protect data, software, and hardware. Operate master consoles to monitor the performance of computer systems and networks, and to coordinate computer network access and use. Perform routine network startup and shutdown procedures, and maintain control records. Design, configure, and test computer hardware, networking software, and operating system software. Recommend changes to improve systems and network configurations, and determine hardware or software requirements related to such changes. Confer with network users about how to solve existing system problems. Monitor network performance to determine whether adjustments need to be made, and to determine where changes will need to be made in the future.

Education/Training Required: Bachelor's degree. **Education and Training Programs:** Network and System Administration/Administrator; System, Networking, and LAN/WAN Management/Manager. **Knowledge/Courses:** Telecommunications;

*C=Computer Systems Design, E=Educational Services, G=Government, H=Health Care, R=Repair and Maintenance, U=Utilities, *=All Fields*

Computers and Electronics; Clerical Practices; Administration and Management; Engineering and Technology.

Personality Type: Investigative-Realistic-Conventional. **Career Cluster:** 11 Information Technology. **Career Pathways:** 11.1 Network Systems; 11.2 Information Support Services; 11.4 Programming and Software Development. **Other Jobs in These Pathways:** Architectural and Engineering Managers; Bioinformatics Scientists; Computer and Information Systems Managers; Computer Hardware Engineers; Computer Numerically Controlled Machine Tool Programmers, Metal and Plastic; Computer Operators; Graphic Designers; Multimedia Artists and Animators; Remote Sensing Scientists and Technologists; Remote Sensing Technicians.

Skills: Programming; Equipment Maintenance; Troubleshooting; Equipment Selection; Technology Design; Repairing; Installation; Quality Control Analysis.

Work Environment: Indoors; sitting; using hands; repetitive motions; noise.

Nuclear Medicine Technologists

- ❋ Annual Earnings: H $68,713, * $68,560
- ❋ Earnings Growth Potential: Low (28.3%)
- ❋ Growth: H 16.3%, * 16.3%
- ❋ Annual Job Openings: H 940, * 670
- ❋ Self-Employed: 0.8%

Detailed Fields with Greatest Employment: Hospitals, Public and Private (66.2%); Ambulatory Health Care Services (31.2%); Educational Services, Public and Private (0.8%); Administrative and Support Services (0.5%); Federal Government (0.5%)

Detailed Fields with Highest Growth (Projected Growth for This Job): Professional, Scientific, and Technical Services (80.0%); Ambulatory Health Care Services (35.3%); Administrative and Support Services (30.0%); Educational Services, Public and Private (17.6%); Federal Government (10.0%)

Other Considerations for Job Outlook: Job growth is expected to result from advancements in nuclear medicine and an increase in the number of older people requiring diagnostic procedures. Competition is expected to be keen.

Prepare, administer, and measure radioactive isotopes in therapeutic, diagnostic, and tracer studies, using a variety of radioisotope equipment. Prepare stock solutions of radioactive materials and calculate doses to be administered by radiologists. Subject patients to radiation. Execute blood volume, red cell survival, and fat absorption studies, following standard laboratory techniques. Detect and map radiopharmaceuticals in patients' bodies, using a camera to produce photographic or computer images. Administer radiopharmaceuticals or radiation intravenously to detect or treat diseases, using radioisotope equipment, under direction of a physician. Produce computer-generated or film images for interpretation by physicians. Calculate, measure, and record radiation dosages or radiopharmaceuticals received, used, and disposed, using computers and following physicians' prescriptions. Perform quality control checks on laboratory equipment and cameras. Maintain and calibrate radioisotope and laboratory equipment. Dispose of radioactive materials and store radiopharmaceuticals, following radiation safety procedures. Process cardiac function studies, using computers. Prepare stock radiopharmaceuticals, adhering to safety standards that minimize radiation exposure to workers and patients. Record and process results of procedures.

Education/Training Required: Associate degree. **Education and Training Programs:** Nuclear

Medical Technology/Technologist; Radiation Protection/Health Physics Technician Training. **Knowledge/Courses:** Medicine and Dentistry; Biology; Chemistry; Physics; Customer and Personal Service; Therapy and Counseling.

Personality Type: Investigative-Realistic-Social. **Career Cluster:** 08 Health Science. **Career Pathways:** 8.1 Therapeutic Services; 8.2 Diagnostics Services. **Other Jobs in These Pathways:** Clinical Psychologists; Counseling Psychologists; Cytogenetic Technologists; Cytotechnologists; Dental Assistants; Dental Hygienists; Dentists, General; Emergency Medical Technicians and Paramedics; Endoscopy Technicians; Healthcare Support Workers, All Other; Histotechnologists and Histologic Technicians; Home Health Aides; Licensed Practical and Licensed Vocational Nurses; Massage Therapists; Medical and Clinical Laboratory Technicians; Medical and Clinical Laboratory Technologists; Medical and Health Services Managers; Medical Assistants; Medical Secretaries; Pharmacists; Pharmacy Technicians; Radiologic Technologists; School Psychologists; Social and Human Service Assistants; Speech-Language Pathology Assistants; others.

Skills: Science; Equipment Maintenance; Quality Control Analysis; Operation Monitoring; Repairing; Troubleshooting; Operation and Control; Service Orientation.

Work Environment: Indoors; standing; walking and running; using hands; contaminants; exposed to radiation; exposed to disease or infections; hazardous conditions.

Occupational Therapists

- ❋ Annual Earnings: H $74,360, * $72,320
- ❋ Earnings Growth Potential: Low (32.4%)
- ❋ Growth: H 31.6%, * 25.6%
- ❋ Annual Job Openings: H 4,910, * 4,580
- ❋ Self-Employed: 7.0%

Detailed Fields with Greatest Employment: Social Assistance (6.4%); Ambulatory Health Care Services (31.2%); Hospitals, Public and Private (30.4%); Educational Services, Public and Private (13.5%); Nursing and Residential Care Facilities (11.0%)

Detailed Fields with Highest Growth (Projected Growth for This Job): Professional, Scientific, and Technical Services (72.7%); Ambulatory Health Care Services (50.9%); Social Assistance (41.8%); Nursing and Residential Care Facilities (23.4%); Administrative and Support Services (20.4%)

Other Considerations for Job Outlook: Employment growth for occupational therapists should continue as the population ages and better medical technology increases the survival rates of people who become injured or ill. Job opportunities are expected be good.

Assess, plan, organize, and participate in rehabilitative programs that help restore vocational, homemaking, and daily living skills, as well as general independence, to disabled persons. Plan, organize, and conduct occupational therapy programs in hospital, institutional, or community settings to help rehabilitate those impaired because of illness, injury, or psychological or developmental problems. Test and evaluate patients' physical and mental abilities and analyze medical data to determine realistic rehabilitation goals for patients. Select activities that will help individuals

*C=Computer Systems Design, E=Educational Services, G=Government, H=Health Care, R=Repair and Maintenance, U=Utilities, *=All Fields*

learn work and life-management skills within limits of their mental and physical capabilities. Evaluate patients' progress and prepare reports that detail progress. Complete and maintain necessary records. Train caregivers to provide for the needs of patients during and after therapies. Recommend changes in patients' work or living environments, consistent with their needs and capabilities. Develop and participate in health promotion programs, group activities, or discussions to promote client health, facilitate social adjustment, alleviate stress, and prevent physical or mental disability.

Education/Training Required: Master's degree. **Education and Training Program:** Occupational Therapy/Therapist. **Knowledge/Courses:** Therapy and Counseling; Psychology; Sociology and Anthropology; Medicine and Dentistry; Biology; Philosophy and Theology.

Personality Type: Social-Investigative. **Career Cluster:** 08 Health Science. **Career Pathway:** 8.1 Therapeutic Services. **Other Jobs in This Pathway:** Clinical Psychologists; Community and Social Service Specialists, All Other; Counseling Psychologists; Dental Assistants; Dental Hygienists; Dentists, General; Health Technologists and Technicians, All Other; Healthcare Support Workers, All Other; Home Health Aides; Licensed Practical and Licensed Vocational Nurses; Low Vision Therapists, Orientation and Mobility Specialists, and Vision Rehabilitation Therapists; Massage Therapists; Medical and Clinical Laboratory Technicians; Medical and Health Services Managers; Medical Scientists, Except Epidemiologists; Medical Secretaries; Ophthalmic Medical Technologists; Pharmacists; Pharmacy Technicians; Radiologic Technologists; School Psychologists; Social and Human Service Assistants; Speech-Language Pathologists; Speech-Language Pathology Assistants; Substance Abuse and Behavioral Disorder Counselors; others.

Skills: Operations Analysis; Science; Service Orientation; Social Perceptiveness; Active Listening; Writing; Learning Strategies; Instructing.

Work Environment: Indoors; standing; using hands; bending or twisting the body; exposed to disease or infections.

Job Specialization: Low Vision Therapists, Orientation and Mobility Specialists, and Vision Rehabilitation Therapists

Provide therapy to patients with visual impairments to improve their functioning in daily life activities. May train patients in activities such as computer use, communication skills, or home management skills. Teach cane skills including cane use with a guide, diagonal techniques, and two-point touches. Refer clients to services, such as eye care, health care, rehabilitation, and counseling, to enhance visual and life functioning or when condition exceeds scope of practice. Provide consultation, support, or education to groups such as parents and teachers. Participate in professional development activities such as reading literature, continuing education, attending conferences, and collaborating with colleagues. Obtain, distribute, or maintain low vision devices. Design instructional programs to improve communication using devices such as slates and styluses, braillers, keyboards, adaptive handwriting devices, talking book machines, digital books, and optical character readers (OCRs). Collaborate with specialists, such as rehabilitation counselors, speech pathologists, and occupational therapists, to provide client solutions.

Education/Training Required: Master's degree. **Education and Training Program:** Occupational Therapy/Therapist. **Knowledge/Courses:** Therapy and Counseling; Psychology; Sociology and Anthropology; Education and Training; Transportation; Medicine and Dentistry.

Personality Type: Social-Investigative-Realistic. **Career Cluster:** 08 Health Science. **Career Pathway:** 8.1 Therapeutic Services. **Other Jobs in This Pathway:** Clinical Psychologists; Community and Social Service Specialists, All Other; Counseling Psychologists; Dental Assistants; Dental Hygienists; Dentists, General; Health Technologists and Technicians, All Other; Healthcare Support Workers, All Other; Home Health Aides; Licensed Practical and Licensed Vocational Nurses; Massage Therapists; Medical and Clinical Laboratory Technicians; Medical and Health Services Managers; Medical Scientists, Except Epidemiologists; Medical Secretaries; Occupational Therapists; Ophthalmic Medical Technologists; Pharmacists; Pharmacy Technicians; Radiologic Technologists; School Psychologists; Social and Human Service Assistants; Speech-Language Pathologists; Speech-Language Pathology Assistants; Substance Abuse and Behavioral Disorder Counselors; others.

Skills: Technology Design; Learning Strategies; Writing; Social Perceptiveness; Reading Comprehension; Service Orientation; Negotiation; Systems Evaluation.

Work Environment: More often outdoors than indoors; standing.

Occupational Therapy Assistants

- ❋ Annual Earnings: H $52,213, * $51,010
- ❋ Earnings Growth Potential: Low (35.1%)
- ❋ Growth: H 33.0%, * 29.8%
- ❋ Annual Job Openings: H 1,470, * 1,180
- ❋ Self-Employed: 2.1%

Detailed Fields with Greatest Employment: Educational Services, Public and Private (7.3%); Ambulatory Health Care Services (37.1%); Social Assistance (3.1%); Hospitals, Public and Private (26.4%); Nursing and Residential Care Facilities (20.6%)

Detailed Fields with Highest Growth (Projected Growth for This Job): Ambulatory Health Care Services (52.3%); Social Assistance (38.3%); Nursing and Residential Care Facilities (24.0%); Administrative and Support Services (20.0%); Hospitals, Public and Private (12.2%)

Other Considerations for Job Outlook: Employment growth for occupational therapist assistants should continue as the population ages and better medical technology increases the survival rates of people who become injured or ill. Job prospects should be very good for assistants who have credentials.

Assist occupational therapists in providing occupational therapy treatments and procedures. May, in accordance with state laws, assist in development of treatment plans, carry out routine functions, direct activity programs, and document the progress of treatments. Generally requires formal training. Observe and record patients' progress, attitudes, and behavior and maintain this information in client records. Maintain and promote a positive attitude toward clients and their treatment programs. Monitor patients' performance in therapy activities, providing encouragement. Select therapy activities to fit patients' needs and capabilities. Instruct, or assist in instructing, patients and families in home programs, basic living skills, and the care and use of adaptive equipment. Evaluate the daily living skills and capacities of physically, developmentally, or emotionally disabled clients. Aid patients in dressing and grooming themselves. Implement, or assist occupational therapists with implementing, treatment plans designed to help clients function independently. Report to supervisors, verbally or in writing, on patients' progress, attitudes, and

*C=Computer Systems Design, E=Educational Services, G=Government, H=Health Care, R=Repair and Maintenance, U=Utilities, *=All Fields*

behavior. Alter treatment programs to obtain better results if treatment is not having the intended effect.

Education/Training Required: Associate degree. **Education and Training Program:** Occupational Therapist Assistant Training. **Knowledge/Courses:** Psychology; Therapy and Counseling; Philosophy and Theology; Medicine and Dentistry; Sociology and Anthropology; Education and Training.

Personality Type: Social-Realistic. **Career Cluster:** 08 Health Science. **Career Pathway:** 8.1 Therapeutic Services. **Other Jobs in This Pathway:** Clinical Psychologists; Community and Social Service Specialists, All Other; Counseling Psychologists; Dental Assistants; Dental Hygienists; Dentists, General; Health Technologists and Technicians, All Other; Healthcare Support Workers, All Other; Home Health Aides; Licensed Practical and Licensed Vocational Nurses; Low Vision Therapists, Orientation and Mobility Specialists, and Vision Rehabilitation Therapists; Massage Therapists; Medical and Clinical Laboratory Technicians; Medical and Health Services Managers; Medical Scientists, Except Epidemiologists; Medical Secretaries; Occupational Therapists; Pharmacists; Pharmacy Technicians; Radiologic Technologists; School Psychologists; Social and Human Service Assistants; Speech-Language Pathologists; Speech-Language Pathology Assistants; Substance Abuse and Behavioral Disorder Counselors; others.

Skills: Learning Strategies; Social Perceptiveness; Service Orientation; Negotiation; Instructing; Persuasion; Operation Monitoring; Writing.

Work Environment: Indoors; standing; using hands; noise; exposed to disease or infections.

Operations Research Analysts

- ✽ Annual Earnings: E $53,220, H $59,671, G $71,110, C $78,620, * $70,960
- ✽ Earnings Growth Potential: High (43.7%)
- ✽ Growth: G 17.5%, E 24.4%, H 25.1%, C 30.4%, * 22.0%
- ✽ Annual Job Openings: E 120, H 150, G 340, C 350, * 3,220
- ✽ Self-Employed: 0.2%

Detailed Fields with Greatest Employment: Insurance Carriers and Related Activities (8.6%); Credit Intermediation and Related Activities (8.3%); Federal Government (6.9%); Management of Companies and Enterprises (6.5%); Educational Services, Public and Private (5.1%)

Detailed Fields with Highest Growth (Projected Growth for This Job): Internet Service Providers, Web Search Portals, and Data Processing Services (63.4%); Wholesale Electronic Markets and Agents and Brokers (46.2%); Other Information Services (45.5%); Professional, Scientific, and Technical Services (45.4%); Ambulatory Health Care Services (45.0%)

Other Considerations for Job Outlook: As technology advances and companies further emphasize efficiency, demand for operations research analysis should continue to grow. Excellent opportunities are expected, especially for those who have an advanced degree.

Formulate and apply mathematical modeling and other optimizing methods, using a computer to develop and interpret information that assists management with decision making, policy formulation, or other managerial functions. May develop related software, service, or products. Frequently concentrates on collecting and

analyzing data and developing decision support software. **May develop and supply optimal time, cost, or logistics networks for program evaluation, review, or implementation.** Formulate mathematical or simulation models of problems, relating constants and variables, restrictions, alternatives, and conflicting objectives and their numerical parameters. Collaborate with others in the organization to ensure successful implementation of chosen problem solutions. Analyze information obtained from management in order to conceptualize and define operational problems. Perform validation and testing of models to ensure adequacy; reformulate models as necessary. Collaborate with senior managers and decision makers to identify and solve a variety of problems and to clarify management objectives. Define data requirements; then gather and validate information, applying judgment and statistical tests. Study and analyze information about alternative courses of action in order to determine which plan will offer the best outcomes. Prepare management reports defining and evaluating problems and recommending solutions.

Education/Training Required: Master's degree. **Education and Training Programs:** Management Science; Management Sciences and Quantitative Methods, Other; Operations Research. **Knowledge/Courses:** Mathematics; Engineering and Technology; Computers and Electronics; Production and Processing; Economics and Accounting; Administration and Management.

Personality Type: Investigative-Conventional-Enterprising. **Career Clusters:** 04 Business, Management, and Administration; 15 Science, Technology, Engineering, and Mathematics. **Career Pathways:** 4.1 Management; 4.4 Business Analysis; 15.2 Science and Mathematics. **Other Jobs in These Pathways:** Brownfield Redevelopment Specialists and Site Managers; Business Continuity Planners; Business Operations Specialists, All Other; Chief Executives; Chief Sustainability Officers; Compliance Managers; Computer and Information Systems Managers; Construction Managers; Customs Brokers; Energy Auditors; First-Line Supervisors of Office and Administrative Support Workers; General and Operations Managers; Investment Fund Managers; Loss Prevention Managers; Management Analysts; Managers, All Other; Public Relations Specialists; Regulatory Affairs Managers; Sales Managers; Security Management Specialists; Security Managers; Supply Chain Managers; Sustainability Specialists; Wind Energy Operations Managers; Wind Energy Project Managers; others.

Skills: Operations Analysis; Science; Mathematics; Systems Evaluation; Systems Analysis; Programming; Complex Problem Solving; Active Learning.

Work Environment: Indoors; sitting.

Optometrists

- ❋ Annual Earnings: H $95,066, * $94,990
- ❋ Earnings Growth Potential: High (47.8%)
- ❋ Growth: H 35.0%, * 24.4%
- ❋ Annual Job Openings: H 1,900, * 2,010
- ❋ Self-Employed: 24.6%

Detailed Fields with Greatest Employment: Health and Personal Care Stores (9.5%); Ambulatory Health Care Services (84.0%); Hospitals, Public and Private (2.0%); Educational Services, Public and Private (1.3%); Federal Government (1.3%)

Detailed Fields with Highest Growth (Projected Growth for This Job): Ambulatory Health Care Services (35.6%); Educational Services, Public and Private (14.3%); Religious, Grantmaking, Civic, Professional, and Similar Organizations (12.5%); Hospitals, Public and Private (9.4%); Federal Government (9.1%)

---

*C=Computer Systems Design, E=Educational Services, G=Government, H=Health Care, R=Repair and Maintenance, U=Utilities, *=All Fields*

Other Considerations for Job Outlook: An aging population and increasing insurance coverage for vision care are expected to lead to employment growth for optometrists. Excellent opportunities are expected.

Diagnose, manage, and treat conditions and diseases of the human eye and visual system. Examine eyes and visual systems, diagnose problems or impairments, prescribe corrective lenses, and provide treatment. May prescribe therapeutic drugs to treat specific eye conditions. Examine eyes, using observation, instruments, and pharmaceutical agents, to determine visual acuity and perception, focus, and coordination and to diagnose diseases and other abnormalities such as glaucoma or color blindness. Prescribe medications to treat eye diseases if state laws permit. Analyze test results and develop treatment plans. Prescribe, supply, fit, and adjust eyeglasses, contact lenses, and other vision aids. Educate and counsel patients on contact lens care, visual hygiene, lighting arrangements, and safety factors. Remove foreign bodies from eyes. Consult with and refer patients to ophthalmologist or other health care practitioners if additional medical treatment is determined necessary. Provide patients undergoing eye surgeries such as cataract and laser vision correction, with pre- and post-operative care. Prescribe therapeutic procedures to correct or conserve vision. Provide vision therapy and low vision rehabilitation.

Education/Training Required: First professional degree. **Education and Training Program:** Optometry (OD). **Knowledge/Courses:** Medicine and Dentistry; Biology; Therapy and Counseling; Physics; Sales and Marketing; Economics and Accounting.

Personality Type: Investigative-Social-Realistic. **Career Cluster:** 08 Health Science. **Career Pathway:** 8.1 Therapeutic Services. **Other Jobs in This Pathway:** Clinical Psychologists; Community and Social Service Specialists, All Other; Counseling Psychologists; Dental Assistants; Dental Hygienists; Dentists, General; Health Technologists and Technicians, All Other; Healthcare Support Workers, All Other; Home Health Aides; Licensed Practical and Licensed Vocational Nurses; Low Vision Therapists, Orientation and Mobility Specialists, and Vision Rehabilitation Therapists; Massage Therapists; Medical and Clinical Laboratory Technicians; Medical and Health Services Managers; Medical Scientists, Except Epidemiologists; Medical Secretaries; Occupational Therapists; Pharmacists; Pharmacy Technicians; Radiologic Technologists; School Psychologists; Social and Human Service Assistants; Speech-Language Pathologists; Speech-Language Pathology Assistants; Substance Abuse and Behavioral Disorder Counselors; others.

Skills: Science; Reading Comprehension; Management of Financial Resources; Operations Analysis; Quality Control Analysis; Management of Material Resources; Operation and Control; Service Orientation.

Work Environment: Indoors; sitting; using hands; exposed to disease or infections.

Orthotists and Prosthetists

- Annual Earnings: H $53,331, * $65,060
- Earnings Growth Potential: High (48.2%)
- Growth: H 30.1%, * 15.4%
- Annual Job Openings: H 80, * 210
- Self-Employed: 5.8%

Detailed Fields with Greatest Employment: Federal Government (8.8%); Miscellaneous Manufacturing (37.7%); Health and Personal Care Stores (20.0%); Ambulatory Health Care Services (16.0%); Hospitals, Public and Private (11.0%)

Detailed Fields with Highest Growth (Projected Growth for This Job): Ambulatory Health Care Services (40.4%); Miscellaneous Manufacturing (14.8%); Hospitals, Public and Private (14.8%); Federal Government (10.2%); Health and Personal Care Stores (2.7%)

Other Considerations for Job Outlook: Faster than average employment growth is projected.

Assist patients with disabling conditions of limbs and spine or with partial or total absence of limb by fitting and preparing orthopedic braces or prostheses. Examine, interview, and measure patients in order to determine their appliance needs and to identify factors that could affect appliance fit. Fit, test, and evaluate devices on patients and make adjustments for proper fit, function, and comfort. Instruct patients in the use and care of orthoses and prostheses. Design orthopedic and prosthetic devices based on physicians' prescriptions and examination and measurement of patients. Maintain patients' records. Make and modify plaster casts of areas that will be fitted with prostheses or orthoses for use in the device construction process. Select materials and components to be used, based on device design. Confer with physicians to formulate specifications and prescriptions for orthopedic or prosthetic devices. Repair, rebuild, and modify prosthetic and orthopedic appliances. Construct and fabricate appliances or supervise others who are constructing the appliances.

Education/Training Required: Bachelor's degree. **Education and Training Programs:** Assistive/Augmentative Technology and Rehabilitation Engineering; Orthotist/Prosthetist. **Knowledge/Courses:** Engineering and Technology; Medicine and Dentistry; Design; Therapy and Counseling; Production and Processing; Psychology.

Personality Type: Social-Realistic-Investigative. **Career Cluster:** 08 Health Science. **Career**

Pathway: 8.3 Health Informatics. **Other Jobs in This Pathway:** Clinical Psychologists; Dental Laboratory Technicians; Editors; Engineers, All Other; Executive Secretaries and Executive Administrative Assistants; Fine Artists, Including Painters, Sculptors, and Illustrators; First-Line Supervisors of Office and Administrative Support Workers; Health Educators; Medical and Health Services Managers; Medical Appliance Technicians; Medical Assistants; Medical Records and Health Information Technicians; Medical Secretaries; Medical Transcriptionists; Mental Health Counselors; Occupational Health and Safety Specialists; Physical Therapists; Psychiatric Aides; Psychiatric Technicians; Public Relations Specialists; Receptionists and Information Clerks; Recreational Therapists; Rehabilitation Counselors; Substance Abuse and Behavioral Disorder Counselors; Therapists, All Other; others.

Skills: Operations Analysis; Technology Design; Science; Instructing; Service Orientation; Writing; Troubleshooting; Active Listening.

Work Environment: Indoors; standing; using hands; noise; contaminants; exposed to disease or infections; hazardous equipment; minor burns, cuts, bites, or stings.

Painters, Transportation Equipment

- ✸ Annual Earnings: R $39,170, * $39,040
- ✸ Earnings Growth Potential: Medium (36.7%)
- ✸ Growth: R 12.8%, * 0.8%
- ✸ Annual Job Openings: R 730, * 1,410
- ✸ Self-Employed: 5.8%

Detailed Fields with Greatest Employment: Repair and Maintenance (50.3%); Support Activities

*C=Computer Systems Design, E=Educational Services, G=Government, H=Health Care, R=Repair and Maintenance, U=Utilities, *=All Fields*

150 Best Jobs for a Secure Future © JIST Works — **285**

for Transportation (3.9%); Transportation Equipment Manufacturing (28.8%); Motor Vehicle and Parts Dealers (10.5%); Merchant Wholesalers, Durable Goods (1.6%)

Detailed Fields with Highest Growth (Projected Growth for This Job): Professional, Scientific, and Technical Services (17.6%); Support Activities for Transportation (14.3%); Repair and Maintenance (12.8%); Administrative and Support Services (11.8%); Waste Management and Remediation Services (11.1%)

Other Considerations for Job Outlook: Projected employment growth will be driven by the increased number of goods that need painting and coating. Good job prospects are expected, due to the need to replace workers who leave the occupation.

Operate or tend painting machines to paint surfaces of transportation equipment, such as automobiles, buses, trucks, trains, boats, and airplanes. Dispose of hazardous waste in an appropriate manner. Select paint according to company requirements and match colors of paint following specified color charts. Mix paints to match color specifications or vehicles' original colors; then stir and thin the paints, using spatulas or power mixing equipment. Remove grease, dirt, paint, and rust from vehicle surfaces in preparation for paint application, using abrasives, solvents, brushes, blowtorches, washing tanks, or sandblasters. Pour paint into spray guns and adjust nozzles and paint mixes to get the proper paint flow and coating thickness. Monitor painting operations to identify flaws such as blisters and streaks so that their causes can be corrected. Sand vehicle surfaces between coats of paint or primer to remove flaws and enhance adhesion for subsequent coats. Disassemble, clean, and reassemble sprayers and power equipment, using solvents, wire brushes, and cloths for cleaning duties.

Education/Training Required: Moderate-term on-the-job training. **Education and Training Program:** Autobody/Collision and Repair Technology/Technician. **Knowledge/Courses:** Chemistry; Mechanical Devices; Production and Processing.

Personality Type: Realistic-Conventional. **Career Cluster:** 16 Transportation, Distribution, and Logistics. **Career Pathway:** 16.4 Facility and Mobile Equipment Maintenance. **Other Jobs in This Pathway:** Aircraft Mechanics and Service Technicians; Aircraft Structure, Surfaces, Rigging, and Systems Assemblers; Automotive Body and Related Repairers; Automotive Glass Installers and Repairers; Automotive Master Mechanics; Automotive Specialty Technicians; Bicycle Repairers; Bus and Truck Mechanics and Diesel Engine Specialists; Cleaners of Vehicles and Equipment; Electrical and Electronics Installers and Repairers, Transportation Equipment; Electronic Equipment Installers and Repairers, Motor Vehicles; Engine and Other Machine Assemblers; Gem and Diamond Workers; Installation, Maintenance, and Repair Workers, All Other; Motorboat Mechanics and Service Technicians; Motorcycle Mechanics; Outdoor Power Equipment and Other Small Engine Mechanics.

Skills: Equipment Selection; Equipment Maintenance; Operation and Control; Quality Control Analysis; Repairing; Troubleshooting; Operation Monitoring.

Work Environment: Indoors; standing; kneeling, crouching, stooping, or crawling; using hands; bending or twisting the body; repetitive motions; noise; very hot or cold; contaminants; cramped work space; high places; hazardous conditions; hazardous equipment; minor burns, cuts, bites, or stings.

Paralegals and Legal Assistants

❋ Annual Earnings: G $51,630, * $46,680

❋ Earnings Growth Potential: Medium (36.9%)

❋ Growth: G 18.7%, * 28.1%

❋ Annual Job Openings: G 980, * 10,400

❋ Self-Employed: 3.2%

Detailed Fields with Greatest Employment: Professional, Scientific, and Technical Services (74.1%); Federal Government (5.7%); Management of Companies and Enterprises (2.3%); Administrative and Support Services (2.0%); Insurance Carriers and Related Activities (2.0%)

Detailed Fields with Highest Growth (Projected Growth for This Job): Internet Service Providers, Web Search Portals, and Data Processing Services (68.8%); Wholesale Electronic Markets and Agents and Brokers (50.0%); Lessors of Nonfinancial Intangible Assets (Except Copyrighted Works) (47.1%); Other Information Services (46.2%); Ambulatory Health Care Services (46.2%)

Other Considerations for Job Outlook: Increased demand for accessible, cost-efficient legal services is expected to increase employment for paralegals, who may perform more tasks previously done by lawyers. Keen competition is expected. Experienced, formally trained paralegals should have the best job prospects.

Assist lawyers by researching legal precedent, investigating facts, or preparing legal documents. Conduct research to support a legal proceeding, to formulate a defense, or to initiate legal action. Prepare legal documents, including briefs, pleadings, appeals, wills, contracts, and real estate closing statements. Prepare affidavits or other documents, maintain document file, and file pleadings with court clerk. Gather and analyze research data, such as statutes; decisions; and legal articles, codes, and documents. Investigate facts and law of cases to determine causes of action and to prepare cases. Call upon witnesses to testify at hearing. Direct and coordinate law office activity, including delivery of subpoenas. Arbitrate disputes between parties and assist in real estate closing process. Keep and monitor legal volumes to ensure that law library is up to date. Appraise and inventory real and personal property for estate planning.

Education/Training Required: Associate degree. **Education and Training Program:** Legal Assistant/Paralegal Training. **Knowledge/Courses:** Clerical Practices; Law and Government; English Language; Computers and Electronics; Communications and Media.

Personality Type: Conventional-Investigative-Enterprising. **Career Cluster:** 12 Law, Public Safety, Corrections, and Security. **Career Pathway:** 12.5 Legal Services. **Other Jobs in This Pathway:** Administrative Law Judges, Adjudicators, and Hearing Officers; Arbitrators, Mediators, and Conciliators; Court Reporters; Farm and Home Management Advisors; Judges, Magistrate Judges, and Magistrates; Lawyers; Legal Secretaries; Legal Support Workers, All Other; Title Examiners, Abstractors, and Searchers.

Skills: Writing; Active Listening; Speaking; Service Orientation.

Work Environment: Indoors; sitting; repetitive motions.

P

*C=Computer Systems Design, E=Educational Services, G=Government, H=Health Care, R=Repair and Maintenance, U=Utilities, *=All Fields*

Pharmacists

- ❋ Annual Earnings: G $107,500, H $110,597, * $111,570
- ❋ Earnings Growth Potential: Low (26.4%)
- ❋ Growth: G 8.5%, H 14.0%, * 17.0%
- ❋ Annual Job Openings: G 240, H 3,860, * 10,580
- ❋ Self-Employed: 0.6%

Detailed Fields with Greatest Employment: Food and Beverage Stores (8.1%); Hospitals, Public and Private (22.4%); Ambulatory Health Care Services (2.5%); Federal Government (2.5%); General Merchandise Stores (10.7%)

Detailed Fields with Highest Growth (Projected Growth for This Job): Internet Service Providers, Web Search Portals, and Data Processing Services (66.7%); Ambulatory Health Care Services (64.0%); Professional, Scientific, and Technical Services (58.3%); Nonstore Retailers (47.5%); Wholesale Electronic Markets and Agents and Brokers (32.4%)

Other Considerations for Job Outlook: The increasing numbers of middle-aged and elderly people—who use more prescription drugs than younger people—should continue to spur employment growth for pharmacists. Job prospects are expected to be excellent.

Compound and dispense medications, following prescriptions issued by physicians, dentists, or other authorized medical practitioners. Review prescriptions to assure accuracy, to ascertain the needed ingredients, and to evaluate their suitability. Provide information and advice regarding drug interactions, side effects, dosage, and proper medication storage. Analyze prescribing trends to monitor patient compliance and to prevent excessive usage or harmful interactions. Order and purchase pharmaceutical supplies, medical supplies, and drugs, maintaining stock and storing and handling it properly. Maintain records such as pharmacy files; patient profiles; charge system files; inventories; control records for radioactive nuclei; and registries of poisons, narcotics, and controlled drugs. Provide specialized services to help patients manage conditions such as diabetes, asthma, smoking cessation, or high blood pressure. Advise customers on the selection of medication brands, medical equipment, and health-care supplies.

Education/Training Required: First professional degree. **Education and Training Programs:** Clinical, Hospital, and Managed Care Pharmacy (MS, PhD); Industrial and Physical Pharmacy and Cosmetic Sciences (MS, PhD); Medicinal and Pharmaceutical Chemistry (MS, PhD); Natural Products Chemistry and Pharmacognosy (MS, PhD); Pharmaceutics and Drug Design (MS, PhD); Pharmacoeconomics/Pharmaceutical Economics (MS, PhD); Pharmacy (PharmD [USA], PharmD or BS/BPharm [Canada]); Pharmacy Administration and Pharmacy Policy and Regulatory Affairs (MS, PhD); Pharmacy, Pharmaceutical Sciences, and Administration, Other. **Knowledge/Courses:** Biology; Medicine and Dentistry; Chemistry; Therapy and Counseling; Psychology; Clerical.

Personality Type: Investigative-Conventional-Social. **Career Cluster:** 08 Health Science. **Career Pathways:** 8.1 Therapeutic Services; 8.5 Biotechnology Research and Development. **Other Jobs in These Pathways:** Clinical Psychologists; Community and Social Service Specialists, All Other; Counseling Psychologists; Dental Assistants; Dental Hygienists; Dentists, General; Health Technologists and Technicians, All Other; Healthcare Support Workers, All Other; Home Health Aides; Licensed Practical and Licensed Vocational Nurses; Low Vision Therapists, Orientation and Mobility Specialists, and Vision Rehabilitation Therapists; Massage Therapists; Medical and Clinical

Laboratory Technicians; Medical and Health Services Managers; Medical Scientists, Except Epidemiologists; Medical Secretaries; Occupational Therapists; Ophthalmic Medical Technologists; Pharmacy Technicians; Radiologic Technologists; School Psychologists; Social and Human Service Assistants; Speech-Language Pathologists; Speech-Language Pathology Assistants; Substance Abuse and Behavioral Disorder Counselors; others.

Skills: Science; Operations Analysis; Reading Comprehension; Management of Material Resources; Active Listening; Writing; Instructing; Management of Financial Resources.

Work Environment: Indoors; standing; using hands; repetitive motions; exposed to disease or infections.

Pharmacy Technicians

* ❈ Annual Earnings: H $32,518, * $28,400
* ❈ Earnings Growth Potential: Low (30.1%)
* ❈ Growth: H 25.3%, * 30.6%
* ❈ Annual Job Openings: H 5,360, * 18,200
* ❈ Self-Employed: 0.2%

Detailed Fields with Greatest Employment: Food and Beverage Stores (6.2%); Ambulatory Health Care Services (2.3%); Hospitals, Public and Private (17.7%); General Merchandise Stores (10.7%); Federal Government (1.7%)

Detailed Fields with Highest Growth (Projected Growth for This Job): Ambulatory Health Care Services (76.7%); Nonstore Retailers (63.7%); Professional, Scientific, and Technical Services (50.0%); Wholesale Electronic Markets and Agents and Brokers (41.5%); Administrative and Support Services (34.5%)

Other Considerations for Job Outlook: Growth in the population of middle-aged and elderly people —who use more prescription drugs than younger people—should spur employment increases for these workers. Job prospects are expected to be good.

Prepare medications under the direction of a pharmacist. May measure, mix, count out, label, and record amounts and dosages of medications. Receive written prescription or refill requests and verify that information is complete and accurate. Maintain proper storage and security conditions for drugs. Answer telephones, responding to questions or requests. Fill bottles with prescribed medications and type and affix labels. Assist customers by answering simple questions, locating items, or referring them to the pharmacist for medication information. Price and file prescriptions that have been filled. Clean and help maintain equipment and work areas and sterilize glassware according to prescribed methods. Establish and maintain patient profiles, including lists of medications taken by individual patients. Order, label, and count stock of medications, chemicals, and supplies and enter inventory data into computer. Receive and store incoming supplies, verify quantities against invoices, and inform supervisors of stock needs and shortages.

Education/Training Required: Moderate-term on-the-job training. **Education and Training Program:** Pharmacy Technician/Assistant Training. **Knowledge/Courses:** Medicine and Dentistry; Clerical Practices; Computers and Electronics; Customer and Personal Service; Chemistry; Mathematics.

Personality Type: Conventional-Realistic. **Career Cluster:** 08 Health Science. **Career Pathway:** 8.1 Therapeutic Services. **Other Jobs in This Pathway:** Clinical Psychologists; Community and Social Service Specialists, All Other; Counseling Psychologists; Dental Assistants; Dental Hygienists; Dentists, General; Health Technologists and Technicians, All Other; Healthcare Support Workers, All Other; Home Health Aides; Licensed Practical and Licensed Vocational Nurses; Low

*C=Computer Systems Design, E=Educational Services, G=Government, H=Health Care, R=Repair and Maintenance, U=Utilities, *=All Fields*

150 Best Jobs for a Secure Future © JIST Works

289

Vision Therapists, Orientation and Mobility Specialists, and Vision Rehabilitation Therapists; Massage Therapists; Medical and Clinical Laboratory Technicians; Medical and Health Services Managers; Medical Scientists, Except Epidemiologists; Medical Secretaries; Occupational Therapists; Ophthalmic Medical Technologists; Pharmacists; Radiologic Technologists; School Psychologists; Social and Human Service Assistants; Speech-Language Pathologists; Speech-Language Pathology Assistants; Substance Abuse and Behavioral Disorder Counselors; others.

Skills: Management of Financial Resources; Service Orientation; Mathematics; Programming; Science; Active Listening.

Work Environment: Indoors; standing; walking and running; using hands; repetitive motions; exposed to disease or infections.

Physical Therapist Assistants

- ❋ Annual Earnings: H $49,717, * $49,690
- ❋ Earnings Growth Potential: Medium (37.5%)
- ❋ Growth: H 34.7%, * 33.3%
- ❋ Annual Job Openings: H 4,170, * 3,050
- ❋ Self-Employed: 1.3%

Detailed Fields with Greatest Employment: Ambulatory Health Care Services (52.2%); Hospitals, Public and Private (31.1%); Nursing and Residential Care Facilities (11.0%); Administrative and Support Services (1.7%); State and Local Government (1.2%).

Detailed Fields with Highest Growth (Projected Growth for This Job): Ambulatory Health Care Services (50.8%); Social Assistance (39.5%); Nursing and Residential Care Facilities (23.8%); Administrative and Support Services (20.8%); Amusement, Gambling, and Recreation Industries (20.0%).

Other Considerations for Job Outlook: Projected growth stems from an expected increase in the elderly population and better medical technology that increases the survival rates of people who become injured or ill. Job opportunities should be good in settings that treat the elderly.

Assist physical therapists in providing physical therapy treatments and procedures. May, in accordance with state laws, assist in the development of treatment plans, carry out routine functions, document the progress of treatment, and modify specific treatments in accordance with patient status and within the scope of treatment plans established by physical therapists. Generally requires formal training. Instruct, motivate, safeguard, and assist patients as they practice exercises and functional activities. Observe patients during treatments to compile and evaluate data on their responses and progress; provide results to physical therapists in person or through progress notes. Confer with physical therapy staffs or others to discuss and evaluate patient information for planning, modifying, and coordinating treatment. Transport patients to and from treatment areas, lifting and transferring them according to positioning requirements. Secure patients into or onto therapy equipment. Administer active and passive manual therapeutic exercises; therapeutic massages; aquatic physical therapy; and heat, light, sound, and electrical modality treatments such as ultrasound. Communicate with or instruct caregivers and family members on patient therapeutic activities and treatment plans.

Education/Training Required: Associate degree. **Education and Training Program:** Physical Therapy Technician/Assistant Training. **Knowledge/Courses:** Therapy and Counseling; Medicine and Dentistry; Psychology; Biology; Customer and Personal Service; Education and Training.

Personality Type: Social-Realistic-Investigative. **Career Cluster:** 08 Health Science. **Career Pathway:** 8.1 Therapeutic Services. **Other Jobs in This Pathway:** Clinical Psychologists; Community and Social Service Specialists, All Other; Counseling Psychologists; Dental Assistants; Dental Hygienists; Dentists, General; Health Technologists and Technicians, All Other; Healthcare Support Workers, All Other; Home Health Aides; Licensed Practical and Licensed Vocational Nurses; Low Vision Therapists, Orientation and Mobility Specialists, and Vision Rehabilitation Therapists; Massage Therapists; Medical and Clinical Laboratory Technicians; Medical and Health Services Managers; Medical Scientists, Except Epidemiologists; Medical Secretaries; Occupational Therapists; Pharmacists; Pharmacy Technicians; Radiologic Technologists; School Psychologists; Social and Human Service Assistants; Speech-Language Pathologists; Speech-Language Pathology Assistants; Substance Abuse and Behavioral Disorder Counselors; others.

Skills: Service Orientation; Quality Control Analysis; Social Perceptiveness; Science; Learning Strategies; Speaking; Reading Comprehension; Systems Evaluation.

Work Environment: Indoors; standing; walking and running; exposed to disease or infections.

Physical Therapists

- ❈ Annual Earnings: H $76,653, * $76,310
- ❈ Earnings Growth Potential: Low (29.7%)
- ❈ Growth: H 34.3%, * 30.3%
- ❈ Annual Job Openings: H 9,640, * 7,860
- ❈ Self-Employed: 8.0%

Detailed Fields with Greatest Employment: Nursing and Residential Care Facilities (7.2%); Ambulatory Health Care Services (50.7%); Educational Services, Public and Private (4.0%); Hospitals, Public and Private (32.3%); Administrative and Support Services (1.5%)

Detailed Fields with Highest Growth (Projected Growth for This Job): Professional, Scientific, and Technical Services (59.1%); Ambulatory Health Care Services (50.0%); Social Assistance (38.7%); Amusement, Gambling, and Recreation Industries (28.6%); Nursing and Residential Care Facilities (23.7%)

Other Considerations for Job Outlook: Employment of physical therapists is expected to increase as the population ages and as better medical technology increases survival rates of people who become injured or ill. Job opportunities should be good in settings that treat primarily the elderly.

Assess, plan, organize, and participate in rehabilitative programs that improve mobility, relieve pain, increase strength, and decrease or prevent deformity of patients suffering from disease or injury. Perform and document initial exams, evaluating data to identify problems and determine diagnoses prior to interventions. Plan, prepare, and carry out individually designed programs of physical treatment to maintain, improve, or restore physical functioning; alleviate pain; and prevent physical dysfunction in patients. Record prognoses, treatments, responses, and progresses in patients' charts or enter information into computers. Identify and document goals, anticipated prog- resses, and plans for reevaluation. Evaluate effects of treatments at various stages and adjust treatments to achieve maximum benefits. Administer manual exercises, massages, or traction to help relieve pain, increase patient strength, or decrease or prevent deformity or crippling. Test and measure patients' strength, motor development and function, sensory perception, functional capacity, and respiratory and circulatory efficiency and record data.

---

*C=Computer Systems Design, E=Educational Services, G=Government, H=Health Care, R=Repair and Maintenance, U=Utilities, *=All Fields*

Education/Training Required: Master's degree. **Education and Training Programs:** Kinesiotherapy/Kinesiotherapist; Physical Therapy/Therapist. **Knowledge/Courses:** Therapy and Counseling; Medicine and Dentistry; Psychology; Education and Training; Biology; Customer and Personal Service.

Personality Type: Social-Investigative-Realistic. **Career Cluster:** 08 Health Science. **Career Pathway:** 8.3 Health Informatics. **Other Jobs in This Pathway:** Clinical Psychologists; Dental Laboratory Technicians; Editors; Engineers, All Other; Executive Secretaries and Executive Administrative Assistants; Fine Artists, Including Painters, Sculptors, and Illustrators; First-Line Supervisors of Office and Administrative Support Workers; Health Educators; Medical and Health Services Managers; Medical Appliance Technicians; Medical Assistants; Medical Records and Health Information Technicians; Medical Secretaries; Medical Transcriptionists; Mental Health Counselors; Occupational Health and Safety Specialists; Occupational Health and Safety Technicians; Psychiatric Aides; Psychiatric Technicians; Public Relations Specialists; Receptionists and Information Clerks; Recreational Therapists; Rehabilitation Counselors; Substance Abuse and Behavioral Disorder Counselors; Therapists, All Other; others.

Skills: Science; Operations Analysis; Service Orientation; Instructing; Persuasion; Time Management; Social Perceptiveness; Reading Comprehension.

Work Environment: Indoors; standing; exposed to disease or infections.

Physician Assistants

- ❋ Annual Earnings: E $80,890, G $85,170, H $86,462, * $86,410
- ❋ Earnings Growth Potential: Low (33.5%)
- ❋ Growth: G 18.8%, E 23.1%, H 41.3%, * 39.0%
- ❋ Annual Job Openings: E 110, G 130, H 5,530, * 4,280
- ❋ Self-Employed: 1.4%

Detailed Fields with Greatest Employment: Ambulatory Health Care Services (65.2%); Educational Services, Public and Private (3.5%); Federal Government (3.1%); Hospitals, Public and Private (24.5%); State and Local Government (1.4%)

Detailed Fields with Highest Growth (Projected Growth for This Job): Ambulatory Health Care Services (49.7%); Professional, Scientific, and Technical Services (44.1%); Administrative and Support Services (35.3%); Social Assistance (33.3%); Nursing and Residential Care Facilities (27.3%)

Other Considerations for Job Outlook: Employment growth for these workers should be driven by an aging population and by health-care providers' increasing use of physician assistants to contain costs. Opportunities should be good, particularly in underserved areas.

Under the supervision of physicians, provide health-care services typically performed by a physician. Conduct complete physicals, provide treatment, and counsel patients. May, in some cases, prescribe medication. Must graduate from an accredited educational program for physician assistants. Examine patients to obtain information about their physical conditions. Obtain, compile, and record patient medical data, including health history, progress notes, and results of physical examinations. Interpret diagnostic test results for deviations from normal. Make tentative diagnoses and decisions about management and treatment of patients. Prescribe therapy or medication with physician approval. Administer or order diagnostic tests, such as X-ray, electrocardiogram, and laboratory tests. Instruct and counsel patients about prescribed therapeutic regimens, normal growth and development, family planning, emotional problems of daily living, and health maintenance. Perform therapeutic procedures such as injections, immunizations, suturing and wound care, and infection management. Provide physicians with assistance during surgery or complicated medical procedures.

Education/Training Required: Master's degree. **Education and Training Program:** Physician Assistant Training. **Knowledge/Courses:** Medicine and Dentistry; Biology; Therapy and Counseling; Psychology; Chemistry; Sociology and Anthropology.

Personality Type: Social-Investigative-Realistic. **Career Cluster:** 08 Health Science. **Career Pathway:** 8.2 Diagnostics Services. **Other Jobs in This Pathway:** Ambulance Drivers and Attendants, Except Emergency Medical Technicians; Anesthesiologist Assistants; Cardiovascular Technologists and Technicians; Cytogenetic Technologists; Cytotechnologists; Diagnostic Medical Sonographers; Emergency Medical Technicians and Paramedics; Endoscopy Technicians; Health Diagnosing and Treating Practitioners, All Other; Health Technologists and Technicians, All Other; Healthcare Practitioners and Technical Workers, All Other; Histotechnologists and Histologic Technicians; Medical and Clinical Laboratory Technicians; Medical and Clinical Laboratory Technologists; Medical and Health Services Managers; Medical Assistants; Medical Equipment Preparers; Neurodiagnostic Technologists; Nuclear Medicine Technologists; Ophthalmic Laboratory Technicians; Physical

Scientists, All Other; Radiologic Technicians; Radiologic Technologists; Surgical Technologists; Veterinary Assistants and Laboratory Animal Caretakers; others.

Skills: Science; Instructing; Service Orientation; Judgment and Decision Making; Social Perceptiveness; Reading Comprehension; Operations Analysis; Systems Evaluation.

Work Environment: Indoors; standing; using hands; exposed to disease or infections.

Job Specialization: Anesthesiologist Assistants

Assist anesthesiologists in the administration of anesthesia for surgical and nonsurgical procedures. Monitor patient status and provide patient care during surgical treatment. Verify availability of operating room supplies, medications, and gases. Provide clinical instruction, supervision, or training to staff in areas such as anesthesia practices. Collect samples or specimens for diagnostic testing. Participate in seminars, workshops, or other professional activities to keep abreast of developments in anesthesiology. Collect and document patients' pre-anesthetic health histories. Provide airway management interventions including tracheal intubation, fiber optics, or ventilary support. Respond to emergency situations by providing cardiopulmonary resuscitation (CPR), basic cardiac life support (BLS), advanced cardiac life support (ACLS), or pediatric advanced life support (PALS). Monitor and document patients' progress during postanesthesia period. Pretest and calibrate anesthesia delivery systems and monitors.

Education/Training Required: Master's degree. **Education and Training Program:** Physician Assistant Training. **Knowledge/Courses:** No data available.

Personality Type: Realistic-Social-Investigative. **Career Cluster:** 08 Health Science. **Career**

---

*C=Computer Systems Design, E=Educational Services, G=Government, H=Health Care, R=Repair and Maintenance, U=Utilities, *=All Fields*

Pathway: 8.2 Diagnostics Services. **Other Jobs in This Pathway:** Ambulance Drivers and Attendants, Except Emergency Medical Technicians; Cardiovascular Technologists and Technicians; Cytogenetic Technologists; Cytotechnologists; Diagnostic Medical Sonographers; Emergency Medical Technicians and Paramedics; Endoscopy Technicians; Health Diagnosing and Treating Practitioners, All Other; Health Technologists and Technicians, All Other; Healthcare Practitioners and Technical Workers, All Other; Histotechnologists and Histologic Technicians; Medical and Clinical Laboratory Technicians; Medical and Clinical Laboratory Technologists; Medical and Health Services Managers; Medical Assistants; Medical Equipment Preparers; Neurodiagnostic Technologists; Nuclear Medicine Technologists; Ophthalmic Laboratory Technicians; Physical Scientists, All Other; Physician Assistants; Radiologic Technicians; Radiologic Technologists; Surgical Technologists; Veterinary Assistants and Laboratory Animal Caretakers; others.

Skills: No data available.

Work Environment: No data available.

Physicians and Surgeons

- ❋ Annual Earnings: E $74,135, H $153,970, * $165,279
- ❋ Earnings Growth Potential: Very High (55.2%)
- ❋ Growth: E 12.4%, H 26.0%, * 21.8%
- ❋ Annual Job Openings: E 700, H 29,480, * 26,050
- ❋ Self-Employed: 11.7%

Detailed Fields with Greatest Employment: Ambulatory Health Care Services (65.8%); Federal Government (4.7%); Educational Services, Public and Private (4.2%); Hospitals, Public and Private (21.7%); State and Local Government (2.3%)

Detailed Fields with Highest Growth (Projected Growth for This Job): Professional, Scientific, and Technical Services (37.1%); Ambulatory Health Care Services (32.1%); Personal and Laundry Services (27.3%); Administrative and Support Services (24.8%); Social Assistance (22.1%)

Other Considerations for Job Outlook: Employment growth is expected to be tied to increases in the aging population and in new medical technologies that allow more maladies to be diagnosed and treated. Job prospects should be very good, particularly in underserved areas.

Job Specialization: Anesthesiologists

Administer anesthetics during surgery or other medical procedures. Administer anesthetic or sedation during medical procedures, using local, intravenous, spinal, or caudal methods. Monitor patient before, during, and after anesthesia and counteract adverse reactions or complications. Provide and maintain life support and airway management and help prepare patients for emergency surgery. Record type and amount of anesthesia and patient condition throughout procedure. Examine patient; obtain medical history; and use diagnostic tests to determine risk during surgical, obstetrical, and other medical procedures. Position patient on operating table to maximize patient comfort and surgical accessibility. Decide when patients have recovered or stabilized enough to be sent to another room or ward or to be sent home following outpatient surgery. Coordinate administration of anesthetics with surgeons during operation. Confer with other medical professionals to determine type and method of anesthetic or sedation to render patient insensible to pain.

Education/Training Required: First professional degree. **Education and Training Program:** Medicine (MD). **Knowledge/Courses:** Medicine and Dentistry; Biology; Chemistry; Psychology; Physics; Therapy and Counseling.

Personality Type: Investigative-Realistic-Social. **Career Cluster:** 08 Health Science. **Career Pathway:** 8.1 Therapeutic Services. **Other Jobs in This Pathway:** Clinical Psychologists; Community and Social Service Specialists, All Other; Counseling Psychologists; Dental Assistants; Dental Hygienists; Dentists, General; Health Technologists and Technicians, All Other; Healthcare Support Workers, All Other; Home Health Aides; Licensed Practical and Licensed Vocational Nurses; Low Vision Therapists, Orientation and Mobility Specialists, and Vision Rehabilitation Therapists; Massage Therapists; Medical and Clinical Laboratory Technicians; Medical and Health Services Managers; Medical Scientists, Except Epidemiologists; Medical Secretaries; Occupational Therapists; Pharmacists; Pharmacy Technicians; Radiologic Technologists; School Psychologists; Social and Human Service Assistants; Speech-Language Pathologists; Speech-Language Pathology Assistants; Substance Abuse and Behavioral Disorder Counselors; 19 other physician occupations; others.

Skills: Science; Operation Monitoring; Reading Comprehension; Operations Analysis; Operation and Control; Judgment and Decision Making; Time Management; Management of Personnel Resources.

Work Environment: Indoors; more often sitting than standing; using hands; noise; contaminants; exposed to radiation; exposed to disease or infections; hazardous conditions.

Job Specialization: Family and General Practitioners

Diagnose, treat, and help prevent diseases and injuries that commonly occur in the general population. Prescribe or administer treatment, therapy, medication, vaccination, and other specialized medical care to treat or prevent illness, disease, or injury. Order, perform, and interpret tests and analyze records, reports, and examination information to diagnose patients' condition. Monitor the patients' conditions and progress and re-evaluate treatments as necessary. Explain procedures and discuss test results or prescribed treatments with patients. Collect, record, and maintain patient information, such as medical history, reports, and examination results. Advise patients and community members concerning diet, activity, hygiene, and disease prevention. Refer patients to medical specialists or other practitioners when necessary. Direct and coordinate activities of nurses, students, assistants, specialists, therapists, and other medical staff. Coordinate work with nurses, social workers, rehabilitation therapists, pharmacists, psychologists, and other health-care providers. Deliver babies.

Education/Training Required: First professional degree. **Education and Training Programs:** Medicine (MD); Osteopathic Medicine/Osteopathy (DO). **Knowledge/Courses:** Medicine and Dentistry; Therapy and Counseling; Biology; Psychology; Sociology and Anthropology; Chemistry.

Personality Type: Investigative-Social. **Career Clusters:** 08 Health Science; 15 Science, Technology, Engineering, and Mathematics. **Career Pathways:** 8.1 Therapeutic Services; 15.2 Science and Mathematics. **Other Jobs in These Pathways:** Architectural and Engineering Managers; Biofuels/Biodiesel Technology and Product Development Managers; Clinical Psychologists; Community and Social Service Specialists, All Other; Counseling Psychologists; Dental Assistants; Dental Hygienists; Dentists, General; Education, Training, and Library Workers, All Other; Healthcare Support Workers, All Other; Home Health Aides; Licensed Practical and Licensed Vocational Nurses; Low Vision Therapists, Orientation and Mobility Specialists, and Vision Rehabilitation Therapists; Massage Therapists; Medical and Clinical Laboratory Technicians; Medical and Health

C=Computer Systems Design, E=Educational Services, G=Government, H=Health Care, R=Repair and Maintenance, U=Utilities, *=All Fields

Services Managers; Medical Scientists, Except Epidemiologists; Medical Secretaries; Pharmacists; Pharmacy Technicians; Radiologic Technologists; School Psychologists; Social and Human Service Assistants; Speech-Language Pathologists; Speech-Language Pathology Assistants; 19 other physician occupations; others.

Skills: Science; Operations Analysis; Judgment and Decision Making; Social Perceptiveness; Reading Comprehension; Service Orientation; Active Listening; Persuasion.

Work Environment: Indoors; standing; using hands; exposed to disease or infections.

Job Specialization: Internists, General

Diagnose and provide nonsurgical treatment of diseases and injuries of internal organ systems. Provide care mainly for adults who have a wide range of problems associated with the internal organs. Treat internal disorders, such as hypertension; heart disease; diabetes; and problems of the lung, brain, kidney, and gastrointestinal tract. Analyze records, reports, test results, or examination information to diagnose medical condition of patient. Prescribe or administer medication, therapy, and other specialized medical care to treat or prevent illness, disease, or injury. Provide and manage long-term, comprehensive medical care, including diagnosis and nonsurgical treatment of diseases, for adult patients in an office or hospital. Manage and treat common health problems, such as infections, influenza and pneumonia, as well as serious, chronic, and complex illnesses, in adolescents, adults, and the elderly. Monitor patients' conditions and progress and re-evaluate treatments as necessary. Collect, record, and maintain patient information, such as medical history, reports, and examination results.

Education/Training Required: First professional degree. **Education and Training Program:** Medicine (MD). **Knowledge/Courses:** Medicine and

Dentistry; Biology; Therapy and Counseling; Psychology; Chemistry; Education and Training.

Personality Type: Investigative-Social-Realistic. **Career Cluster:** 08 Health Science. **Career Pathway:** 8.1 Therapeutic Services. **Other Jobs in This Pathway:** Clinical Psychologists; Community and Social Service Specialists, All Other; Counseling Psychologists; Dental Assistants; Dental Hygienists; Dentists, General; Health Technologists and Technicians, All Other; Healthcare Support Workers, All Other; Home Health Aides; Licensed Practical and Licensed Vocational Nurses; Low Vision Therapists, Orientation and Mobility Specialists, and Vision Rehabilitation Therapists; Massage Therapists; Medical and Clinical Laboratory Technicians; Medical and Health Services Managers; Medical Scientists, Except Epidemiologists; Medical Secretaries; Occupational Therapists; Pharmacists; Pharmacy Technicians; Radiologic Technologists; School Psychologists; Social and Human Service Assistants; Speech-Language Pathologists; Speech-Language Pathology Assistants; Substance Abuse and Behavioral Disorder Counselors; 19 other physician occupations; others.

Skills: Science; Operations Analysis; Reading Comprehension; Active Learning; Service Orientation; Complex Problem Solving; Systems Evaluation; Writing.

Work Environment: Indoors; standing; exposed to disease or infections.

Job Specialization: Obstetricians and Gynecologists

Diagnose, treat, and help prevent diseases of women, especially those affecting the reproductive system and the process of childbirth. Care for and treat women during prenatal, natal, and postnatal periods. Explain procedures and discuss test results or prescribed treatments with patients. Treat diseases of female organs. Monitor patients' condition and progress and re-evaluate treatments as necessary. Perform cesarean sections or other surgical procedures as needed to preserve patients' health and deliver babies safely. Prescribe or administer therapy, medication, and other specialized medical care to treat or prevent illness, disease, or injury. Analyze records, reports, test results, or examination information to diagnose medical condition of patient. Collect, record, and maintain patient information, such as medical histories, reports, and examination results. Advise patients and community members concerning diet, activity, hygiene, and disease prevention. Refer patient to medical specialist or other practitioner when necessary. Consult with, or provide consulting services to, other physicians.

Education/Training Required: First professional degree. **Education and Training Program:** Medicine (MD). **Knowledge/Courses:** Medicine and Dentistry; Therapy and Counseling; Biology; Psychology; Sociology and Anthropology; Chemistry.

Personality Type: Investigative-Social-Realistic. **Career Cluster:** 08 Health Science. **Career Pathway:** 8.1 Therapeutic Services. **Other Jobs in This Pathway:** Clinical Psychologists; Community and Social Service Specialists, All Other; Counseling Psychologists; Dental Assistants; Dental Hygienists; Dentists, General; Health Technologists and Technicians, All Other; Healthcare Support Workers, All Other; Home Health Aides; Licensed Practical and Licensed Vocational Nurses; Low Vision Therapists, Orientation and Mobility Specialists, and Vision Rehabilitation Therapists; Massage Therapists; Medical and Clinical Laboratory Technicians; Medical and Health Services Managers; Medical Scientists, Except Epidemiologists; Medical Secretaries; Occupational Therapists; Pharmacists; Pharmacy Technicians; Radiologic Technologists; School Psychologists; Social and Human Service Assistants; Speech-Language Pathologists; Speech-Language Pathology Assistants; Substance Abuse and Behavioral Disorder Counselors; 19 other physician occupations; others.

Skills: Science; Operations Analysis; Reading Comprehension; Social Perceptiveness; Active Listening; Active Learning; Critical Thinking; Monitoring.

Work Environment: Indoors; standing; using hands; exposed to disease or infections.

Job Specialization: Pediatricians, General

Diagnose, treat, and help prevent children's diseases and injuries. Examine patients or order, perform, and interpret diagnostic tests to obtain information on medical condition and determine diagnosis. Examine children regularly to assess their growth and development. Prescribe or administer treatment, therapy, medication, vaccination, and other specialized medical care to treat or prevent illness, disease, or injury in infants and children. Collect, record, and maintain patient information, such as medical history, reports, and examination results. Advise patients, parents or guardians, and community members concerning diet, activity, hygiene, and disease prevention. Treat children who have minor illnesses, acute and chronic health problems, and growth and development concerns. Explain procedures and discuss test results or prescribed treatments with patients and parents or guardians. Monitor patients' condition and progress and re-evaluate treatments as necessary.

Education/Training Required: First professional degree. **Education and Training Program:** Medicine (MD). **Knowledge/Courses:** Medicine and Dentistry; Therapy and Counseling; Biology; Psychology; Chemistry; Sociology and Anthropology.

Personality Type: Investigative-Social. **Career Cluster:** 08 Health Science. **Career Pathway:** 8.1 Therapeutic Services. **Other Jobs in This Pathway:** Clinical Psychologists; Community and Social Service Specialists, All Other; Counseling Psychologists; Dental Assistants; Dental

C=Computer Systems Design, E=Educational Services, G=Government, H=Health Care, R=Repair and Maintenance, U=Utilities, *=All Fields

150 Best Jobs for a Secure Future © JIST Works — 297

Hygienists; Dentists, General; Health Technologists and Technicians, All Other; Healthcare Support Workers, All Other; Home Health Aides; Licensed Practical and Licensed Vocational Nurses; Low Vision Therapists, Orientation and Mobility Specialists, and Vision Rehabilitation Therapists; Massage Therapists; Medical and Clinical Laboratory Technicians; Medical and Health Services Managers; Medical Scientists, Except Epidemiologists; Medical Secretaries; Occupational Therapists; Pharmacists; Pharmacy Technicians; Radiologic Technologists; School Psychologists; Social and Human Service Assistants; Speech-Language Pathologists; Speech-Language Pathology Assistants; Substance Abuse and Behavioral Disorder Counselors; 19 other physician occupations; others.

Skills: Science; Operations Analysis; Reading Comprehension; Systems Evaluation; Active Learning; Judgment and Decision Making; Service Orientation; Speaking.

Work Environment: Indoors; standing; using hands; exposed to disease or infections.

Job Specialization: Physicians and Surgeons, All Other

This occupation includes all physicians and surgeons not listed separately. No task data available.

Education/Training Required: First professional degree. **Education and Training Program:** Medicine (MD). **Knowledge/Courses:** No data available.

Personality Type: No data available. **Career Clusters:** 08 Health Science; 10 Human Services. **Career Pathways:** 8.1 Therapeutic Services; 10.2 Counseling and Mental Health Services. **Other Jobs in These Pathways:** Clergy; Clinical Psychologists; Community and Social Service Specialists, All Other; Counseling Psychologists; Dental Assistants; Dental Hygienists; Dentists, General;

Healthcare Social Workers; Healthcare Support Workers, All Other; Home Health Aides; Licensed Practical and Licensed Vocational Nurses; Massage Therapists; Medical and Clinical Laboratory Technicians; Medical and Health Services Managers; Medical Secretaries; Mental Health and Substance Abuse Social Workers; Mental Health Counselors; Pharmacists; Pharmacy Technicians; Radiologic Technologists; Recreation Workers; School Psychologists; Social and Human Service Assistants; Speech-Language Pathologists; Speech-Language Pathology Assistants; 19 other physician occupations; others.

Skills: No data available.

Work Environment: No data available.

Job Specialization: Psychiatrists

Diagnose, treat, and help prevent disorders of the mind. Prescribe, direct, and administer psychotherapeutic treatments or medications to treat mental, emotional, or behavioral disorders. Analyze and evaluate patient data and test findings to diagnose nature and extent of mental disorders. Collaborate with physicians, psychologists, social workers, psychiatric nurses, or other professionals to discuss treatment plans and progress. Gather and maintain patient information and records, including social and medical histories obtained from patients, relatives, and other professionals. Design individualized care plans, using a variety of treatments. Counsel outpatients and other patients during office visits. Examine or conduct laboratory or diagnostic tests on patients to provide information on general physical conditions and mental disorders. Advise and inform guardians, relatives, and significant others of patients' conditions and treatments.

Education/Training Required: First professional degree. **Education and Training Program:** Medicine (MD). **Knowledge/Courses:** Therapy and Counseling; Medicine and Dentistry; Psychology;

Biology; Sociology and Anthropology; Philosophy and Theology.

Personality Type: Investigative-Social-Artistic. **Career Cluster:** 08 Health Science. **Career Pathway:** 8.1 Therapeutic Services. **Other Jobs in This Pathway:** Clinical Psychologists; Community and Social Service Specialists, All Other; Counseling Psychologists; Dental Assistants; Dental Hygienists; Dentists, General; Health Technologists and Technicians, All Other; Healthcare Support Workers, All Other; Home Health Aides; Licensed Practical and Licensed Vocational Nurses; Low Vision Therapists, Orientation and Mobility Specialists, and Vision Rehabilitation Therapists; Massage Therapists; Medical and Clinical Laboratory Technicians; Medical and Health Services Managers; Medical Scientists, Except Epidemiologists; Medical Secretaries; Occupational Therapists; Pharmacists; Pharmacy Technicians; Radiologic Technologists; School Psychologists; Social and Human Service Assistants; Speech-Language Pathologists; Speech-Language Pathology Assistants; Substance Abuse and Behavioral Disorder Counselors; 19 other physician occupations; others.

Skills: Science; Social Perceptiveness; Operations Analysis; Persuasion; Negotiation; Service Orientation; Instructing; Judgment and Decision Making.

Work Environment: Indoors; sitting; exposed to disease or infections.

Job Specialization: Surgeons

Treat diseases, injuries, and deformities by invasive methods, such as manual manipulation, or by using instruments and appliances. Analyze patient's medical history, medication allergies, physical condition, and examination results to verify operation's necessity and to determine best procedure. Operate on patients to correct deformities, repair injuries, prevent and treat diseases, or improve or restore patients' functions. Follow established surgical techniques during the operation. Prescribe preoperative and postoperative treatments and procedures, such as sedatives, diets, antibiotics, and preparation and treatment of the patient's operative area. Examine patient to provide information on medical condition and surgical risk. Diagnose bodily disorders and orthopedic conditions and provide treatments, such as medicines and surgeries, in clinics, hospital wards, and operating rooms. Direct and coordinate activities of nurses, assistants, specialists, residents, and other medical staff. Provide consultation and surgical assistance to other physicians and surgeons.

Education/Training Required: First professional degree. **Education and Training Program:** Medicine (MD). **Knowledge/Courses:** Medicine and Dentistry; Biology; Therapy and Counseling; Psychology; Chemistry; Customer and Personal Service.

Personality Type: Investigative-Realistic-Social. **Career Cluster:** 08 Health Science. **Career Pathway:** 8.1 Therapeutic Services. **Other Jobs in This Pathway:** Clinical Psychologists; Community and Social Service Specialists, All Other; Counseling Psychologists; Dental Assistants; Dental Hygienists; Dentists, General; Health Technologists and Technicians, All Other; Healthcare Support Workers, All Other; Home Health Aides; Licensed Practical and Licensed Vocational Nurses; Low Vision Therapists, Orientation and Mobility Specialists, and Vision Rehabilitation Therapists; Massage Therapists; Medical and Clinical Laboratory Technicians; Medical and Health Services Managers; Medical Scientists, Except Epidemiologists; Medical Secretaries; Occupational Therapists; Pharmacists; Pharmacy Technicians; Radiologic Technologists; School Psychologists; Social and Human Service Assistants; Speech-Language Pathologists; Speech-Language Pathology Assistants; Substance Abuse and Behavioral Disorder Counselors; 19 other physician occupations; others.

C=Computer Systems Design, E=Educational Services, G=Government, H=Health Care, R=Repair and Maintenance, U=Utilities, *=All Fields

Skills: Science; Reading Comprehension; Active Learning; Instructing; Operations Analysis; Judgment and Decision Making; Learning Strategies; Social Perceptiveness.

Work Environment: Indoors; standing; using hands; contaminants; exposed to radiation; exposed to disease or infections.

Physicists

* ❋ Annual Earnings: H $152,545, * $106,370
* ❋ Earnings Growth Potential: High (44.7%)
* ❋ Growth: H 16.7%, * 15.9%
* ❋ Annual Job Openings: H 70, * 690
* ❋ Self-Employed: 0.0%

Detailed Fields with Greatest Employment: Hospitals, Public and Private (5.6%); Professional, Scientific, and Technical Services (48.8%); Federal Government (21.3%); Computer and Electronic Product Manufacturing (2.4%); Utilities (2.4%)

Detailed Fields with Highest Growth (Projected Growth for This Job): Ambulatory Health Care Services (38.5%); Waste Management and Remediation Services (28.6%); Professional, Scientific, and Technical Services (24.4%); Educational Services, Public and Private (11.9%); Hospitals, Public and Private (10.2%)

Other Considerations for Job Outlook: An increased focus on basic research, particularly that related to energy, is expected to drive employment growth for these workers. Prospects should be favorable for physicists in applied research, development, and related technical fields.

Conduct research into phases of physical phenomena, develop theories and laws on basis of observation and experiments, and devise methods to apply laws and theories to industry and other fields. Perform complex calculations as part of the analysis and evaluation of data, using computers. Describe and express observations and conclusions in mathematical terms. Analyze data from research conducted to detect and measure physical phenomena. Report experimental results by writing papers for scientific journals or by presenting information at scientific conferences. Design computer simulations to model physical data so that it can be better understood. Collaborate with other scientists in the design, development, and testing of experimental, industrial, or medical equipment, instrumentation, and procedures. Direct testing and monitoring of contamination of radioactive equipment and recording of personnel and plant area radiation exposure data. Observe the structure and properties of matter and the transformation and propagation of energy, using equipment such as masers, lasers, and telescopes, in order to explore and identify the basic principles governing these phenomena.

Education/Training Required: Doctoral degree. **Education and Training Programs:** Acoustics; Astrophysics; Atomic/Molecular Physics; Condensed Matter and Materials Physics; Elementary Particle Physics; Health/Medical Physics; Nuclear Physics; Optics/Optical Sciences; Physics, General; Physics, Other; Plasma and High-Temperature Physics; Theoretical and Mathematical Physics. **Knowledge/Courses:** Physics; Mathematics; Engineering and Technology; Computers and Electronics; English Language; Telecommunications.

Personality Type: Investigative-Realistic. **Career Clusters:** 05 Education and Training; 15 Science, Technology, Engineering, and Mathematics. **Career Pathways:** 5.3 Teaching/Training; 15.2 Science and Mathematics. **Other Jobs in These Pathways:** Adult Basic and Secondary Education and Literacy Teachers and Instructors; Architectural and Engineering Managers; Biofuels/Biodiesel Technology and Product Development Managers; Biologists; Career/Technical Education Teachers,

Secondary School; Chemists; Coaches and Scouts; Community and Social Service Specialists, All Other; Education, Training, and Library Workers, All Other; Elementary School Teachers, Except Special Education; Fitness Trainers and Aerobics Instructors; Instructional Coordinators; Instructional Designers and Technologists; Kindergarten Teachers, Except Special Education; Librarians; Medical Scientists, Except Epidemiologists; Middle School Teachers, Except Special and Career/Technical Education; Operations Research Analysts; Preschool Teachers, Except Special Education; Recreation Workers; Secondary School Teachers, Except Special and Career/Technical Education; Self-Enrichment Education Teachers; Teacher Assistants; Teachers and Instructors, All Other; Tutors; others.

Skills: Science; Programming; Mathematics; Technology Design; Active Learning; Reading Comprehension; Learning Strategies; Writing.

Work Environment: Indoors; sitting.

Police and Sheriff's Patrol Officers

- ❋ Annual Earnings: E $44,410, G $53,800, * $53,540
- ❋ Earnings Growth Potential: Medium (40.8%)
- ❋ Growth: G 8.1%, E 30.3%, * 8.7%
- ❋ Annual Job Openings: E 430, G 14,660, * 22,790
- ❋ Self-Employed: 0.0%

Detailed Fields with Greatest Employment: State and Local Government (95.4%); Educational Services, Public and Private (2.6%); Hospitals, Public and Private (0.1%)

Detailed Fields with Highest Growth (Projected Growth for This Job): Educational Services,

Public and Private (30.3%); Hospitals, Public and Private (12.4%); State and Local Government, Excluding Education and Hospitals (8.1%)

Other Considerations for Job Outlook: Population growth is the main source of demand for police services. Overall, opportunities in local police departments should be favorable for qualified applicants.

Job Specialization: Police Patrol Officers

Patrol assigned areas to enforce laws and ordinances, regulate traffic, control crowds, prevent crime, and arrest violators. Provide for public safety by maintaining order, responding to emergencies, protecting people and property, enforcing motor vehicle and criminal laws, and promoting good community relations. Monitor, note, report, and investigate suspicious persons and situations, safety hazards, and unusual or illegal activity in patrol area. Record facts to prepare reports that document incidents and activities. Identify, pursue, and arrest suspects and perpetrators of criminal acts. Patrol specific areas on foot, horseback, or motorized conveyance, responding promptly to calls for assistance. Review facts of incidents to determine whether criminal acts or statute violations were involved. Investigate traffic accidents and other accidents to determine causes and to determine whether crimes have been committed. Render aid to accident victims and other persons requiring first aid for physical injuries. Testify in court to present evidence or act as witness in traffic and criminal cases.

Education/Training Required: Long-term on-the-job training. **Education and Training Programs:** Criminal Justice/Police Science; Criminalistics and Criminal Science. **Knowledge/Courses:** Psychology; Public Safety and Security; Law and Government; Customer and Personal Service; Therapy and Counseling; Sociology and Anthropology.

Personality Type: Realistic-Enterprising-Conventional. **Career Cluster:** 12 Law, Public Safety,

P

*C=Computer Systems Design, E=Educational Services, G=Government, H=Health Care, R=Repair and Maintenance, U=Utilities, *=All Fields*

Corrections, and Security. **Career Pathway:** 12.4 Law Enforcement Services. **Other Jobs in This Pathway:** Bailiffs; Correctional Officers and Jailers; Criminal Investigators and Special Agents; First-Line Supervisors of Police and Detectives; Forensic Science Technicians; Immigration and Customs Inspectors; Intelligence Analysts; Police Detectives; Police Identification and Records Officers; Remote Sensing Scientists and Technologists; Sheriffs and Deputy Sheriffs.

Skills: Negotiation; Persuasion; Service Orientation; Operation and Control; Social Perceptiveness; Active Listening; Critical Thinking; Coordination.

Work Environment: More often outdoors than indoors; sitting; using hands; noise; very hot or cold; bright or inadequate lighting; contaminants; exposed to disease or infections; hazardous equipment; minor burns, cuts, bites, or stings.

Job Specialization: Sheriffs and Deputy Sheriffs

Enforce law and order in rural or unincorporated districts or serve legal processes of courts. May patrol courthouse, guard court or grand jury, or escort defendants. Drive vehicles or patrol specific areas to detect law violators, issue citations, and make arrests. Investigate illegal or suspicious activities. Verify that the proper legal charges have been made against law offenders. Execute arrest warrants, locating and taking persons into custody. Record daily activities and submit logs and other related reports and paperwork to appropriate authorities. Patrol and guard courthouses, grand jury rooms, or assigned areas to provide security, enforce laws, maintain order, and arrest violators. Notify patrol units to take violators into custody or to provide needed assistance or medical aid. Place people in protective custody. Serve statements of claims, subpoenas, summonses, jury summonses, orders to pay alimony, and other court orders. Take control of accident scenes to maintain traffic flow, to assist accident victims, and to investigate causes.

Education/Training Required: Long-term on-the-job training. **Education and Training Programs:** Criminal Justice/Police Science; Criminalistics and Criminal Science. **Knowledge/Courses:** Public Safety and Security; Law and Government; Telecommunications; Psychology; Therapy and Counseling; Philosophy and Theology.

Personality Type: Enterprising-Realistic-Social. **Career Cluster:** 12 Law, Public Safety, Corrections, and Security. **Career Pathways:** 12.3 Security and Protective Services; 12.4 Law Enforcement Services. **Other Jobs in These Pathways:** Animal Control Workers; Bailiffs; Correctional Officers and Jailers; Criminal Investigators and Special Agents; Crossing Guards; First-Line Supervisors of Police and Detectives; First-Line Supervisors of Protective Service Workers, All Other; Forensic Science Technicians; Forest Firefighters; Gaming Surveillance Officers and Gaming Investigators; Immigration and Customs Inspectors; Intelligence Analysts; Lifeguards, Ski Patrol, and Other Recreational Protective Service Workers; Parking Enforcement Workers; Police Detectives; Police Identification and Records Officers; Police Patrol Officers; Police, Fire, and Ambulance Dispatchers; Private Detectives and Investigators; Remote Sensing Scientists and Technologists; Retail Loss Prevention Specialists; Security Guards; Transit and Railroad Police.

Skills: Negotiation; Social Perceptiveness; Persuasion; Service Orientation; Management of Personnel Resources; Critical Thinking; Time Management; Reading Comprehension.

Work Environment: More often outdoors than indoors; sitting; using hands; repetitive motions; noise; very hot or cold; bright or inadequate lighting; contaminants; cramped work space; exposed to disease or infections; hazardous equipment.

Police, Fire, and Ambulance Dispatchers

❀ Annual Earnings: G $35,880, * $35,370

❀ Earnings Growth Potential: Medium (36.9%)

❀ Growth: G 18.6%, * 17.8%

❀ Annual Job Openings: G 2,350, * 3,840

❀ Self-Employed: 0.0%

Detailed Fields with Greatest Employment: State and Local Government, Excluding Education and Hospitals (89.8%); Ambulatory Health Care Services (5.2%); Educational Services, Public and Private (2.0%); Hospitals, Public and Private (1.6%); Administrative and Support Services (0.7%)

Detailed Fields with Highest Growth (Projected Growth for This Job): Administrative and Support Services (21.2%); State and Local Government, Excluding Education and Hospitals (18.6%); Educational Services, Public and Private (12.2%) Ambulatory Health Care Services (9.2%); Hospitals, Public and Private (8.2%)

Other Considerations for Job Outlook: The growing and aging population will increase demand for emergency services, leading to employment increases for these dispatchers. Job opportunities should be favorable.

Receive complaints from public concerning crimes and police emergencies. Broadcast orders to police patrol units in vicinity of complaint to investigate. Operate radio, telephone, or computer equipment to receive reports of fires and medical emergencies and relay information or orders to proper officials. Question callers about their locations and the nature of their problems to determine types of response needed. Receive incoming telephone or alarm system calls regarding emergency and nonemergency police and fire service, emergency ambulance service, information, and after-hours calls for departments within a city. Determine response requirements and relative priorities of situations and dispatch units in accordance with established procedures. Record details of calls, dispatches, and messages. Enter, update, and retrieve information from teletype networks and computerized data systems regarding such things as wanted persons, stolen property, vehicle registration, and stolen vehicles. Maintain access to and security of highly sensitive materials. Relay information and messages to and from emergency sites, to law enforcement agencies, and to all other individuals or groups requiring notification.

Education/Training Required: Moderate-term on-the-job training. **Education and Training Programs:** No related CIP programs; this job is learned through moderate-term on-the-job training. **Knowledge/Courses:** Telecommunications; Customer and Personal Service; Clerical Practices; Law and Government; Public Safety and Security; Psychology.

Personality Type: Conventional-Realistic-Enterprising. **Career Cluster:** 12 Law, Public Safety, Corrections, and Security. **Career Pathway:** 12.3 Security and Protective Services. **Other Jobs in This Pathway:** Animal Control Workers; Crossing Guards; First-Line Supervisors of Protective Service Workers, All Other; Forest Firefighters; Gaming Surveillance Officers and Gaming Investigators; Lifeguards, Ski Patrol, and Other Recreational Protective Service Workers; Parking Enforcement Workers; Private Detectives and Investigators; Retail Loss Prevention Specialists; Security Guards; Sheriffs and Deputy Sheriffs; Transit and Railroad Police.

Skills: Active Listening; Critical Thinking; Persuasion; Social Perceptiveness; Service Orientation; Operation and Control; Programming; Operations Analysis.

*C=Computer Systems Design, E=Educational Services, G=Government, H=Health Care, R=Repair and Maintenance, U=Utilities, *=All Fields*

Work Environment: Indoors; sitting; using hands; repetitive motions; noise; contaminants.

Political Scientists

- ❋ Annual Earnings: G $115,730, * $107,420
- ❋ Earnings Growth Potential: Very High (54.6%)
- ❋ Growth: G 18.4%, * 19.4%
- ❋ Annual Job Openings: G 130, * 280
- ❋ Self-Employed: 1.4%

Detailed Fields with Greatest Employment: Educational Services, Public and Private (7.7%); Religious, Grantmaking, Civic, Professional, and Similar Organizations (7.7%); Federal Government (63.6%); Professional, Scientific, and Technical Services (12.7%); Private Households; Primary and Secondary Jobs (1.7%)

Detailed Fields with Highest Growth (Projected Growth for This Job): Educational Services, Public and Private (22.6%); Religious, Grantmaking, Civic, Professional, and Similar Organizations (22.6%); Professional, Scientific, and Technical Services (21.6%); Federal Government (18.4%); Private Households; Primary and Secondary Jobs (14.3%)

Other Considerations for Job Outlook: Political scientists are expected to experience employment growth especially in nonprofit, political lobbying, and civic organizations. Opportunities should be best for job seekers who have an advanced degree.

Study the origin, development, and operation of political systems. Research a wide range of subjects, such as relations between the United States and foreign countries, the beliefs and institutions of foreign nations, or the politics of small towns or a major metropolis. May study topics such as public opinion, political decision making, and ideology. May analyze the structure and operation of governments, as well as various political entities. May conduct public opinion surveys, analyze election results, or analyze public documents. Teach political science. Disseminate research results through academic publications, written reports, or public presentations. Identify issues for research and analysis. Develop and test theories, using information from interviews, newspapers, periodicals, case law, historical papers, polls, and/or statistical sources. Maintain current knowledge of government policy decisions. Collect, analyze, and interpret data such as election results and public opinion surveys; report on findings, recommendations, and conclusions. Interpret and analyze policies; public issues; legislation; and the operations of governments, businesses, and organizations. Evaluate programs and policies and make related recommendations to institutions and organizations. Write drafts of legislative proposals and prepare speeches, correspondence, and policy papers for governmental use. Forecast political, economic, and social trends.

Education/Training Required: Master's degree. **Education and Training Programs:** American Government and Politics (United States); Canadian Government and Politics; International Relations and Affairs; International/Global Studies; Political Science and Government, General; Political Science and Government, Other. **Knowledge/ Courses:** History and Archeology; Law and Government; Philosophy and Theology; Sociology and Anthropology; Foreign Language; Geography.

Personality Type: Investigative-Artistic-Social. **Career Clusters:** 07 Government and Public Administration; 15 Science, Technology, Engineering, and Mathematics. **Career Pathways:** 7.1 Governance; 15.2 Science and Mathematics. **Other Jobs in These Pathways:** Administrative Services Managers; Architectural and Engineering Managers; Biofuels/Biodiesel Technology and Product Development Managers; Biologists; Chemists;

Chief Executives; Chief Sustainability Officers; Clinical Research Coordinators; Community and Social Service Specialists, All Other; Compliance Managers; Dietitians and Nutritionists; Education, Training, and Library Workers, All Other; General and Operations Managers; Legislators; Managers, All Other; Mapping Technicians; Medical Scientists, Except Epidemiologists; Natural Sciences Managers; Operations Research Analysts; Regulatory Affairs Managers; Reporters and Correspondents; Social and Community Service Managers; Storage and Distribution Managers; Surveying Technicians; Transportation Managers; others.

Skills: Science; Speaking; Writing; Critical Thinking; Active Listening; Active Learning; Systems Analysis; Reading Comprehension.

Work Environment: Indoors; sitting.

Power Distributors and Dispatchers

- ❋ Annual Earnings: U $68,010, * $68,900
- ❋ Earnings Growth Potential: Low (30.8%)
- ❋ Growth: U –1.0%, * –2.2%
- ❋ Annual Job Openings: U 200, * 350
- ❋ Self-Employed: 0.0%

Detailed Fields with Greatest Employment: Federal Government (9.1%); Utilities (73.6%); Heavy and Civil Engineering Construction (2.2%); Management of Companies and Enterprises (1.4%);

Detailed Fields with Highest Growth (Projected Growth for This Job): Management of Companies and Enterprises (0.0%); Utilities (–1.0%); Federal Government (–3.3%); Heavy and Civil Engineering Construction (–22.7%)

Other Considerations for Job Outlook: Although annual energy use continues to grow in the United States, greater power plant efficiency is expected to temper employment gains resulting from that growth. Job opportunities should be excellent, however, because of the need to replace a large number of retiring workers.

Coordinate, regulate, or distribute electricity or steam. Respond to emergencies, such as transformer or transmission line failures, and route current around affected areas. Prepare switching orders that will isolate work areas without causing power outages, referring to drawings of power systems. Control, monitor, or operate equipment that regulates or distributes electricity or steam, using data obtained from instruments or computers. Coordinate with engineers, planners, field personnel, and other utility workers to provide information such as clearances, switching orders, and distribution process changes. Direct personnel engaged in controlling and operating distribution equipment and machinery, for example, instructing control room operators to start boilers and generators. Distribute and regulate the flow of power between entities such as generating stations, substations, distribution lines, and users, keeping track of the status of circuits and connections.

Education/Training Required: Long-term on-the-job training. **Education and Training Program:** Mechanic and Repair Technologies/Technicians, Other. **Knowledge/Courses:** Public Safety and Security; Mechanical Devices; Telecommunications; Customer and Personal Service; Physics; Engineering and Technology.

Personality Type: Realistic-Investigative-Conventional. **Career Cluster:** 13 Manufacturing. **Career Pathway:** 13.1 Production. **Other Jobs in This Pathway:** Assemblers and Fabricators, All Other; Cabinetmakers and Bench Carpenters; Coating, Painting, and Spraying Machine Setters, Operators, and Tenders; Computer-Controlled Machine Tool Operators, Metal and Plastic; Cost

P

*C=Computer Systems Design, E=Educational Services, G=Government, H=Health Care, R=Repair and Maintenance, U=Utilities, *=All Fields*

150 Best Jobs for a Secure Future © JIST Works 305

Estimators; Cutting, Punching, and Press Machine Setters, Operators, and Tenders, Metal and Plastic; First-Line Supervisors of Mechanics, Installers, and Repairers; First-Line Supervisors of Production and Operating Workers; Geothermal Technicians; Helpers—Production Workers; Machine Feeders and Offbearers; Machinists; Mixing and Blending Machine Setters, Operators, and Tenders; Molding, Coremaking, and Casting Machine Setters, Operators, and Tenders, Metal and Plastic; Packaging and Filling Machine Operators and Tenders; Packers and Packagers, Hand; Paper Goods Machine Setters, Operators, and Tenders; Production Workers, All Other; Recycling and Reclamation Workers; Recycling Coordinators; Sheet Metal Workers; Solderers and Brazers; Structural Metal Fabricators and Fitters; Team Assemblers; Welders, Cutters, and Welder Fitters; others.

Skills: Operation Monitoring; Operation and Control; Troubleshooting; Quality Control Analysis; Management of Personnel Resources; Systems Analysis; Instructing; Time Management.

Work Environment: Indoors; sitting; using hands.

Power Plant Operators

- ❀ Annual Earnings: U $64,440, * $63,080
- ❀ Earnings Growth Potential: Low (35.6%)
- ❀ Growth: U –2.7%, * –1.6%
- ❀ Annual Job Openings: U 700, * 1,220
- ❀ Self-Employed: 0.0%

Detailed Fields with Greatest Employment: Utilities (72.0%); Educational Services, Public and Private (2.9%); State and Local Government (16.5%); Hospitals, Public and Private (1.0%); Professional, Scientific, and Technical Services (0.7%)

Detailed Fields with Highest Growth (Projected Growth for This Job): Professional, Scientific, and Technical Services (17.4%); Educational Services, Public and Private (14.6%); State and Local Government, Excluding Education and Hospitals (1.2%); Utilities (–2.7%); Hospitals, Public and Private (–5.4%)

Other Considerations for Job Outlook: Although annual energy use continues to grow in the United States, greater power plant efficiency is expected to temper employment gains resulting from that growth. Job opportunities should be excellent, however, because of the need to replace a large number of retiring workers.

Control, operate, or maintain machinery to generate electric power. Includes auxiliary equipment operators. Operate or control power-generating equipment, including boilers, turbines, generators, and reactors, using control boards or semi-automatic equipment. Monitor and inspect power plant equipment and indicators to detect evidence of operating problems. Adjust controls to generate specified electrical power or to regulate the flow of power between generating stations and substations. Regulate equipment operations and conditions such as water levels based on data from recording and indicating instruments or from computers. Take readings from charts, meters, and gauges at established intervals and take corrective steps as necessary. Inspect records and logbook entries and communicate with other plant personnel to assess equipment operating status. Start or stop generators, auxiliary pumping equipment, turbines, and other power plant equipment and connect or disconnect equipment from circuits.

Education/Training Required: Long-term on-the-job training. **Education and Training Programs:** No related CIP programs; this job is learned through long-term on-the-job training. **Knowledge/Courses:** Mechanical Devices; Physics; Chemistry;

Engineering and Technology; Public Safety and Security; Computers and Electronics.

Personality Type: Realistic-Conventional. **Career Cluster:** 13 Manufacturing. **Career Pathway:** 13.1 Production. **Other Jobs in This Pathway:** Assemblers and Fabricators, All Other; Cabinetmakers and Bench Carpenters; Coating, Painting, and Spraying Machine Setters, Operators, and Tenders; Computer-Controlled Machine Tool Operators, Metal and Plastic; Cost Estimators; Cutting, Punching, and Press Machine Setters, Operators, and Tenders, Metal and Plastic; First-Line Supervisors of Mechanics, Installers, and Repairers; First-Line Supervisors of Production and Operating Workers; Geothermal Technicians; Helpers—Production Workers; Machine Feeders and Offbearers; Machinists; Mixing and Blending Machine Setters, Operators, and Tenders; Molding, Coremaking, and Casting Machine Setters, Operators, and Tenders, Metal and Plastic; Packaging and Filling Machine Operators and Tenders; Packers and Packagers, Hand; Paper Goods Machine Setters, Operators, and Tenders; Production Workers, All Other; Recycling and Reclamation Workers; Recycling Coordinators; Sheet Metal Workers; Solderers and Brazers; Structural Metal Fabricators and Fitters; Team Assemblers; Welders, Cutters, and Welder Fitters; others.

Skills: Equipment Maintenance; Repairing; Troubleshooting; Operation and Control; Operation Monitoring; Quality Control Analysis; Equipment Selection; Installation.

Work Environment: More often indoors than outdoors; sitting; using hands; noise; very hot or cold; contaminants; high places; hazardous conditions; hazardous equipment.

Probation Officers and Correctional Treatment Specialists

- ❋ Annual Earnings: G $47,700, * $47,200
- ❋ Earnings Growth Potential: Low (34.5%)
- ❋ Growth: G 19.2%, * 19.3%
- ❋ Annual Job Openings: G 2,740, * 4,180
- ❋ Self-Employed: 0.3%

Detailed Fields with Greatest Employment: State and Local Government (96.6%); Social Assistance (1.5%); Administrative and Support Services (0.7%); Nursing and Residential Care Facilities (0.6%); Educational Services, Public and Private (0.2%)

Detailed Fields with Highest Growth (Projected Growth for This Job): Administrative and Support Services (32.4%); Social Assistance (28.1%); State and Local Government, Excluding Education and Hospitals (19.2%); Nursing and Residential Care Facilities (11.1%); Educational Services, Public and Private (5.9%)

Other Considerations for Job Outlook: Many states are expected to emphasize alternatives to incarceration, such as probation. As a result, employment growth should be strong for these workers. Opportunities should be excellent.

Provide social services to assist in rehabilitation of law offenders in custody or on probation or parole. Make recommendations for actions involving formulation of rehabilitation plan and treatment of offender, including conditional release and education and employment stipulations. Prepare and maintain case folder for each assigned inmate or offender. Write reports describing offenders' progress. Inform offenders or inmates of requirements of conditional release, such

*C=Computer Systems Design, E=Educational Services, G=Government, H=Health Care, R=Repair and Maintenance, U=Utilities, *=All Fields*

as office visits, restitution payments, or educational and employment stipulations. Discuss with offenders how such issues as drug and alcohol abuse and anger management problems might have played roles in their criminal behavior. Gather information about offenders' backgrounds by talking to offenders, their families and friends, and other people who have relevant information. Develop rehabilitation programs for assigned offenders or inmates, establishing rules of conduct, goals, and objectives. Develop liaisons and networks with other parole officers, community agencies, staff in correctional institutions, psychiatric facilities, and after-care agencies to make plans for helping offenders with life adjustments.

Education/Training Required: Bachelor's degree. **Education and Training Program:** Social Work. **Knowledge/Courses:** Therapy and Counseling; Psychology; Sociology and Anthropology; Philosophy and Theology; Law and Government; Public Safety and Security.

Personality Type: Social-Enterprising-Conventional. **Career Cluster:** 10 Human Services. **Career Pathway:** 10.3 Family and Community Services. **Other Jobs in This Pathway:** Chief Executives; Child, Family, and School Social Workers; Childcare Workers; City and Regional Planning Aides; Counselors, All Other; Eligibility Interviewers, Government Programs; Farm and Home Management Advisors; Legislators; Managers, All Other; Marriage and Family Therapists; Nannies; Personal Care Aides; Protective Service Workers, All Other; Social and Community Service Managers; Social Science Research Assistants; Social Scientists and Related Workers, All Other; Social Workers, All Other; Sociologists; Supply Chain Managers.

Skills: Social Perceptiveness; Negotiation; Service Orientation; Persuasion; Monitoring; Critical Thinking; Speaking; Judgment and Decision Making.

Work Environment: More often indoors than outdoors; sitting; very hot or cold; exposed to disease or infections.

Production, Planning, and Expediting Clerks

- ❋ Annual Earnings: U $53,380, * $42,220
- ❋ Earnings Growth Potential: Medium (39.5%)
- ❋ Growth: U –15.9%, * 1.5%
- ❋ Annual Job Openings: U 70, * 7,410
- ❋ Self-Employed: 0.5%

Detailed Fields with Greatest Employment: Professional, Scientific, and Technical Services (7.2%); Transportation Equipment Manufacturing (6.2%); Merchant Wholesalers, Durable Goods (5.3%); Computer and Electronic Product Manufacturing (4.8%); Administrative and Support Services (4.6%)

Detailed Fields with Highest Growth (Projected Growth for This Job): Internet Service Providers, Web Search Portals, and Data Processing Services (48.6%); Professional, Scientific, and Technical Services (34.6%); Waste Management and Remediation Services (28.6%); Museums, Historical Sites, and Similar Institutions (28.6%); Ambulatory Health Care Services (27.0%)

Other Considerations for Job Outlook: Job openings are expected to arise from the need to replace workers who leave the occupation. Opportunities should be limited in manufacturing but better in industries with faster growth, such as wholesale trade and warehousing.

Coordinate and expedite the flow of work and materials within or between departments of an establishment according to production schedules, inventory levels, costs, and production problems. Examine documents, materials, and products, and monitor work processes to assess completeness, accuracy, and conformance to standards and specifications. Review documents such as production schedules, work orders, and staffing tables to determine personnel and materials requirements and material priorities. Revise production schedules when required due to design changes, labor or material shortages, backlogs, or other interruptions, collaborating with management, marketing, sales, production, and engineering. Confer with department supervisors and other personnel to assess progress and discuss needed changes. Confer with establishment personnel, vendors, and customers to coordinate production and shipping activities, and to resolve complaints or eliminate delays. Record production data, including volume produced, consumption of raw materials, and quality control measures. Requisition and maintain inventories of materials and supplies necessary to meet production demands.

Education/Training Required: Moderate-term on-the-job training. **Education and Training Program:** Parts, Warehousing, and Inventory Management Operations. **Knowledge/Courses:** Production and Processing; Clerical Practices; Computers and Electronics; Administration and Management; Mathematics; Customer and Personal Service.

Personality Type: Conventional-Enterprising. **Career Cluster:** 16 Transportation, Distribution, and Logistics. **Career Pathway:** 16.3 Warehousing and Distribution Center Operations. **Other Jobs in This Pathway:** Logistics Analysts; Shipping, Receiving, and Traffic Clerks; Traffic Technicians.

Skills: Management of Material Resources; Negotiation; Management of Financial Resources; Reading Comprehension; Persuasion; Time Management; Programming; Speaking.

Work Environment: Indoors; sitting; noise; contaminants.

Psychologists, All Other

- ❋ Annual Earnings: H $83,340, * $89,900
- ❋ Earnings Growth Potential: Very High (54.2%)
- ❋ Growth: H 39.5%, * 14.4%
- ❋ Annual Job Openings: H 190, * 680
- ❋ Self-Employed: 32.8%

Detailed Fields with Greatest Employment: State and Local Government (5.6%); Federal Government (45.6%); Professional, Scientific, and Technical Services (3.2%); Ambulatory Health Care Services (16.3%); Educational Services, Public and Private (15.8%)

Detailed Fields with Highest Growth (Projected Growth for This Job): Ambulatory Health Care Services (62.9%); Professional, Scientific, and Technical Services (38.2%); Social Assistance (20.0%); Educational Services, Public and Private (13.0%); State and Local Government, Excluding Education and Hospitals (10.0%)

Other Considerations for Job Outlook: Employment growth is expected due to increased emphasis on mental health in a variety of specializations, including school counseling, depression, and substance abuse. Job seekers with a doctoral degree should have the best opportunities.

This occupation includes all psychologists not listed separately. No task data available.

Education/Training Required: Master's degree. **Education and Training Program:** Psychology, Other. **Knowledge/Courses:** No data available.

Personality Type: No data available. **Career Clusters:** 08 Health Science; 10 Human Services; 15 Science, Technology, Engineering, and Mathematics. **Career Pathways:** 8.1 Therapeutic Services; 10.2 Counseling and Mental Health Services; 15.2

*C=Computer Systems Design, E=Educational Services, G=Government, H=Health Care, R=Repair and Maintenance, U=Utilities, *=All Fields*

Science and Mathematics. **Other Jobs in These Pathways:** Architectural and Engineering Managers; Biofuels/Biodiesel Technology and Product Development Managers; Clergy; Clinical Psychologists; Counseling Psychologists; Dental Assistants; Dental Hygienists; Dentists, General; Healthcare Social Workers; Healthcare Support Workers, All Other; Home Health Aides; Licensed Practical and Licensed Vocational Nurses; Massage Therapists; Medical and Clinical Laboratory Technicians; Medical and Health Services Managers; Medical Secretaries; Mental Health and Substance Abuse Social Workers; Pharmacists; Pharmacy Technicians; Radiologic Technologists; Recreation Workers; School Psychologists; Social and Human Service Assistants; Speech-Language Pathologists; Speech-Language Pathology Assistants; others.

Skills: No data available.

Work Environment: No data available.

Job Specialization: Neuropsychologists and Clinical Neuropsychologists

Apply theories and principles of neuropsychology to diagnose and treat disorders of higher cerebral functioning. Write or prepare detailed clinical neuropsychological reports using data from psychological or neuropsychological tests, self-report measures, rating scales, direct observations, or interviews. Provide psychotherapy, behavior therapy, or other counseling interventions to patients with neurological disorders. Provide education or counseling to individuals and families. Participate in educational programs, inservice training, or workshops to remain current in methods and techniques. Read current literature, talk with colleagues, and participate in professional organizations or conferences to keep abreast of developments in neuropsychology. Interview patients to obtain comprehensive medical histories. Identify and communicate risks associated with specific neurological surgical procedures such as epilepsy surgery. Educate and supervise practicum students, psychology interns, or hospital staff.

Education/Training Required: Doctoral degree. **Education and Training Program:** Physiological Psychology/Psychobiology. **Knowledge/Courses:** Therapy and Counseling; Psychology; Biology; Medicine and Dentistry; Sociology and Anthropology; Philosophy and Theology.

Personality Type: Investigative-Social-Artistic. **Career Cluster:** 15 Science, Technology, Engineering, and Mathematics. **Career Pathway:** 15.2 Science and Mathematics. **Other Jobs in This Pathway:** Architectural and Engineering Managers; Biochemists and Biophysicists; Biofuels/Biodiesel Technology and Product Development Managers; Bioinformatics Scientists; Biological Scientists, All Other; Biologists; Biostatisticians; Chemists; Clinical Data Managers; Clinical Research Coordinators; Community and Social Service Specialists, All Other; Dietitians and Nutritionists; Education, Training, and Library Workers, All Other; Geneticists; Geoscientists, Except Hydrologists and Geographers; Medical Scientists, Except Epidemiologists; Molecular and Cellular Biologists; Natural Sciences Managers; Operations Research Analysts; Physical Scientists, All Other; Social Scientists and Related Workers, All Other; Statisticians; Survey Researchers; Transportation Planners; Water Resource Specialists; others.

Skills: Science; Social Perceptiveness; Reading Comprehension; Active Learning; Writing; Learning Strategies; Systems Evaluation; Instructing.

Work Environment: Indoors; sitting; using hands; exposed to disease or infections.

Public Relations Specialists

* Annual Earnings: E $48,700, H $48,719, G $57,690, U $63,030, C $68,760, * $52,090
* Earnings Growth Potential: High (41.3%)
* Growth: U –6.5%, G 18.8%, E 26.5%, H 29.2%, C 54.2%, * 24.0%
* Annual Job Openings: U 60, C 230, G 680, E 970, H 1,440, * 13,130
* Self-Employed: 4.5%

Detailed Fields with Greatest Employment: State and Local Government (6.1%); Management of Companies and Enterprises (3.6%); Social Assistance (3.0%); Professional, Scientific, and Technical Services (21.5%); Religious, Grantmaking, Civic, Professional, and Similar Organizations (21.3%)

Detailed Fields with Highest Growth (Projected Growth for This Job): Internet Service Providers, Web Search Portals, and Data Processing Services (65.0%); Lessors of Nonfinancial Intangible Assets (Except Copyrighted Works) (49.1%); Waste Management and Remediation Services (45.5%); Other Information Services (43.7%); Ambulatory Health Care Services (36.0%)

Other Considerations for Job Outlook: As the business environment becomes increasingly globalized, the need for good public relations and communications is growing rapidly. Opportunities should be best for workers with knowledge of more than one language.

Engage in promoting or creating goodwill for individuals, groups, or organizations by writing or selecting favorable publicity material and releasing it through various communications media. May prepare and arrange displays and make speeches. Prepare or edit organizational publications for internal and external audiences, including employee newsletters and stockholders' reports. Respond to requests for information from the media or designate another appropriate spokesperson or information source. Establish and maintain cooperative relationships with representatives of community, consumer, employee, and public interest groups. Plan and direct development and communication of informational programs to maintain favorable public and stockholder perceptions of an organization's accomplishments and agenda. Confer with production and support personnel to produce or coordinate production of advertisements and promotions. Arrange public appearances, lectures, contests, or exhibits for clients to increase product and service awareness and to promote goodwill.

Education/Training Required: Bachelor's degree. **Education and Training Programs:** Family and Consumer Sciences/Human Sciences Communication; Health Communication; Political Communication; Public Relations/Image Management; Speech Communication and Rhetoric. **Knowledge/Courses:** Communications and Media; Sales and Marketing; English Language; Geography; Computers and Electronics; Customer and Personal Service.

Personality Type: Enterprising-Artistic-Social. **Career Clusters:** 03 Arts, Audio/Video Technology, and Communications; 04 Business, Management, and Administration; 08 Health Science; 10 Human Services. **Career Pathways:** 3.5 Journalism and Broadcasting; 4.1 Management; 8.3 Health Informatics; 10.5 Consumer Services Career. **Other Jobs in These Pathways:** Brownfield Redevelopment Specialists and Site Managers; Business Continuity Planners; Business Operations Specialists, All Other; Compliance Managers; Construction Managers; Customs Brokers; Energy Auditors; Executive Secretaries and Executive Administrative Assistants; First-Line

P

*C=Computer Systems Design, E=Educational Services, G=Government, H=Health Care, R=Repair and Maintenance, U=Utilities, *=All Fields*

Supervisors of Office and Administrative Support Workers; First-Line Supervisors of Retail Sales Workers; General and Operations Managers; Investment Fund Managers; Loss Prevention Managers; Management Analysts; Managers, All Other; Medical Assistants; Medical Secretaries; Receptionists and Information Clerks; Regulatory Affairs Managers; Security Management Specialists; Security Managers; Supply Chain Managers; Sustainability Specialists; Wind Energy Operations Managers; Wind Energy Project Managers; others.

Skills: Operations Analysis; Social Perceptiveness; Negotiation; Writing; Systems Evaluation; Speaking; Persuasion; Time Management.

Work Environment: Indoors; sitting.

Radiation Therapists

- ❋ Annual Earnings: H $74,625, * $74,980
- ❋ Earnings Growth Potential: Low (32.0%)
- ❋ Growth: H 27.0%, * 27.1%
- ❋ Annual Job Openings: H 940, * 690
- ❋ Self-Employed: 0.0%

Detailed Fields with Greatest Employment: Hospitals, Public and Private (69.6%); Educational Services, Public and Private (3.5%); Ambulatory Health Care Services (23.6%); Administrative and Support Services (2.7%)

Detailed Fields with Highest Growth (Projected Growth for This Job): Ambulatory Health Care Services (49.3%); Administrative and Support Services (36.6%); Educational Services, Public and Private (22.6%); Hospitals, Public and Private (19.4%)

Other Considerations for Job Outlook: The increasing number of elderly people, who are more likely than younger people to need radiation treatment, is expected to lead to employment growth for these workers. Prospects are expected to be good; job seekers with a bachelor's degree should have the best opportunities.

Provide radiation therapy to patients as prescribed by radiologists according to established practices and standards. Duties may include reviewing prescriptions and diagnoses; acting as liaisons with physicians and supportive care personnel; preparing equipment such as immobilization, treatment, and protection devices; and maintaining records, reports, and files. May assist in dosimetry procedures and tumor localization. Position patients for treatment with accuracy according to prescription. Administer prescribed doses of radiation to specific body parts, using radiation therapy equipment according to established practices and standards. Check radiation therapy equipment to ensure proper operation. Review prescriptions, diagnoses, patient charts, and identification. Follow principles of radiation protection for patients, radiation therapists, and others. Maintain records, reports, and files as required, including such information as radiation dosages, equipment settings, and patients' reactions. Conduct most treatment sessions independently, in accordance with long-term treatment plans and under general direction of patients' physicians. Enter data into computers and set controls to operate and adjust equipment and regulate dosages. Observe and reassure patients during treatments and report unusual reactions to physicians or turn equipment off if unexpected adverse reactions occur.

Education/Training Required: Associate degree. **Education and Training Program:** Medical Radiologic Technology/Science—Radiation Therapist. **Knowledge/Courses:** Medicine and Dentistry; Biology; Physics; Psychology; Philosophy and Theology; Therapy and Counseling.

Personality Type: Social-Realistic-Conventional. **Career Cluster:** 08 Health Science. **Career**

Pathway: 8.2 Diagnostics Services. **Other Jobs in This Pathway:** Ambulance Drivers and Attendants, Except Emergency Medical Technicians; Anesthesiologist Assistants; Cardiovascular Technologists and Technicians; Cytogenetic Technologists; Cytotechnologists; Diagnostic Medical Sonographers; Emergency Medical Technicians and Paramedics; Endoscopy Technicians; Health Diagnosing and Treating Practitioners, All Other; Health Technologists and Technicians, All Other; Healthcare Practitioners and Technical Workers, All Other; Histotechnologists and Histologic Technicians; Medical and Clinical Laboratory Technicians; Medical and Clinical Laboratory Technologists; Medical and Health Services Managers; Medical Assistants; Medical Equipment Preparers; Neurodiagnostic Technologists; Ophthalmic Laboratory Technicians; Physical Scientists, All Other; Physician Assistants; Radiologic Technicians; Radiologic Technologists; Surgical Technologists; Veterinary Assistants and Laboratory Animal Caretakers; others.

Skills: Operation and Control; Equipment Selection; Equipment Maintenance; Science; Quality Control Analysis; Operation Monitoring; Troubleshooting; Repairing.

Work Environment: Indoors; standing; walking and running; using hands; bending or twisting the body; repetitive motions; contaminants; exposed to radiation; exposed to disease or infections.

Radiologic Technologists

- ❀ Annual Earnings: H $54,116, * $54,340
- ❀ Earnings Growth Potential: Low (32.8%)
- ❀ Growth: H 17.5%, * 17.2%
- ❀ Annual Job Openings: H 9,300, * 6,800
- ❀ Self-Employed: 0.8%

Detailed Fields with Greatest Employment: Hospitals, Public and Private (61.4%); Ambulatory

Health Care Services (33.1%); Federal Government (2.0%); Administrative and Support Services (1.1%); Educational Services, Public and Private (0.9%)

Detailed Fields with Highest Growth (Projected Growth for This Job): Professional, Scientific, and Technical Services (45.6%); Ambulatory Health Care Services (35.6%); Administrative and Support Services (22.2%); Nursing and Residential Care Facilities (20.0%); Educational Services, Public and Private (12.0%)

Other Considerations for Job Outlook: As the population grows and ages, demand for diagnostic imaging is expected to increase. Job seekers who have knowledge of multiple technologies should have the best prospects.

Take X-rays and CAT scans or administer nonradioactive materials into patient's bloodstream for diagnostic purposes. Includes technologists who specialize in other modalities, such as computed tomography and magnetic resonance. Includes workers whose primary duties are to demonstrate portions of the human body on X-ray film or fluoroscopic screen. Review and evaluate developed X-rays, video tape, or computer-generated information to determine if images are satisfactory for diagnostic purposes. Use radiation safety measures and protection devices to comply with government regulations and to ensure safety of patients and staff. Explain procedures and observe patients to ensure safety and comfort during scan. Operate or oversee operation of radiologic and magnetic imaging equipment to produce images of the body for diagnostic purposes. Position and immobilize patient on examining table. Position imaging equipment and adjust controls to set exposure time and distance, according to specification of examination. Key commands and data into computer to document and specify scan sequences, adjust transmitters and receivers, or photograph certain images. Monitor video display of area being

C=Computer Systems Design, E=Educational Services, G=Government, H=Health Care, R=Repair and Maintenance, U=Utilities, *=All Fields

150 Best Jobs for a Secure Future © JIST Works

313

scanned and adjust density or contrast to improve picture quality. Monitor patients' conditions and reactions, reporting abnormal signs to physician.

Education/Training Required: Associate degree. **Education and Training Programs:** Allied Health Diagnostic, Intervention, and Treatment Professions, Other; Medical Radiologic Technology/Science—Radiation Therapist; Radiologic Technology/Science—Radiographer. **Knowledge/Courses:** Medicine and Dentistry; Physics; Customer and Personal Service; Biology; Psychology; Chemistry.

Personality Type: Realistic-Social. **Career Cluster:** 08 Health Science. **Career Pathways:** 8.1 Therapeutic Services; 8.2 Diagnostics Services. **Other Jobs in These Pathways:** Clinical Psychologists; Counseling Psychologists; Cytogenetic Technologists; Cytotechnologists; Dental Assistants; Dental Hygienists; Dentists, General; Emergency Medical Technicians and Paramedics; Endoscopy Technicians; Healthcare Support Workers, All Other; Histotechnologists and Histologic Technicians; Home Health Aides; Licensed Practical and Licensed Vocational Nurses; Massage Therapists; Medical and Clinical Laboratory Technicians; Medical and Clinical Laboratory Technologists; Medical and Health Services Managers; Medical Assistants; Medical Secretaries; Pharmacists; Pharmacy Technicians; School Psychologists; Social and Human Service Assistants; Speech-Language Pathologists; Speech-Language Pathology Assistants; others.

Skills: Science; Operation and Control; Service Orientation; Operation Monitoring; Quality Control Analysis; Programming; Instructing; Social Perceptiveness.

Work Environment: Indoors; standing; walking and running; using hands; bending or twisting the body; repetitive motions; contaminants; exposed to radiation; exposed to disease or infections.

Receptionists and Information Clerks

* Annual Earnings: R $22,980, * $25,240
* Earnings Growth Potential: Low (30.4%)
* Growth: R 5.3%, * 15.2%
* Annual Job Openings: R 230, * 48,020
* Self-Employed: 0.8%

Detailed Fields with Greatest Employment: Administrative and Support Services (6.1%); Personal and Laundry Services (5.8%); Educational Services, Public and Private (4.5%); Religious, Grantmaking, Civic, Professional, and Similar Organizations (4.1%); Hospitals, Public and Private (3.9%)

Detailed Fields with Highest Growth (Projected Growth for This Job): Internet Service Providers, Web Search Portals, and Data Processing Services (50.0%); Lessors of Nonfinancial Intangible Assets (Except Copyrighted Works) (36.8%); Professional, Scientific, and Technical Services (34.4%); Other Information Services (32.1%); Wholesale Electronic Markets and Agents and Brokers (29.5%)

Other Considerations for Job Outlook: Although technology makes these workers more productive, many new jobs are expected as clerical work is consolidated and involves more tasks. Employment growth is expected in offices of physicians and other health practitioners and in the legal services, personal care services, construction, and management and technical consulting industries. Plentiful opportunities are expected.

Answer inquiries and obtain information for general public, customers, visitors, and other interested parties. Provide information regarding activities conducted at establishment

and location of departments, offices, and employees within organization. Operate telephone switchboard to answer, screen, and forward calls, providing information, taking messages, and scheduling appointments. Receive payment and record receipts for services. Perform administrative support tasks such as proofreading, transcribing handwritten information, and operating calculators or computers to work with pay records, invoices, balance sheets, and other documents. Greet persons entering establishment, determine nature and purpose of visit, and direct or escort them to specific destinations. Hear and resolve complaints from customers and public. File and maintain records. Transmit information or documents to customers, using computer, mail, or facsimile machine. Schedule appointments and maintain and update appointment calendars. Analyze data to determine answers to questions from customers or members of the public. Provide information about establishment such as location of departments or offices, employees within the organization, or services provided.

Education/Training Required: Short-term on-the-job training. **Education and Training Programs:** General Office Occupations and Clerical Services; Health Unit Coordinator/Ward Clerk Training; Medical Reception/Receptionist; Receptionist Training. **Knowledge/Courses:** Clerical Practices; Customer and Personal Service; Computers and Electronics; Communications and Media.

Personality Type: Conventional-Enterprising-Social. **Career Clusters:** 04 Business, Management, and Administration; 08 Health Science. **Career Pathways:** 4.6 Administrative and Information Support; 8.3 Health Informatics. **Other Jobs in These Pathways:** Customer Service Representatives; Data Entry Keyers; Dispatchers, Except Police, Fire, and Ambulance; Engineers, All Other; Executive Secretaries and Executive Administrative Assistants; File Clerks; First-Line Supervisors

of Office and Administrative Support Workers; Information and Record Clerks, All Other; Insurance Claims Clerks; Insurance Policy Processing Clerks; Interviewers, Except Eligibility and Loan; Medical and Health Services Managers; Medical Assistants; Medical Records and Health Information Technicians; Medical Secretaries; Office and Administrative Support Workers, All Other; Office Clerks, General; Order Clerks; Patient Representatives; Physical Therapists; Postal Service Mail Carriers; Postal Service Mail Sorters, Processors, and Processing Machine Operators; Public Relations Specialists; Secretaries and Administrative Assistants, Except Legal, Medical, and Executive; Shipping, Receiving, and Traffic Clerks; others.

Skills: Service Orientation; Speaking; Active Listening.

Work Environment: Indoors; sitting; using hands; repetitive motions.

Registered Nurses

- Annual Earnings: E $57,210, H $64,717, G $67,930, * $64,690
- Earnings Growth Potential: Low (31.7%)
- Growth: E 12.3%, G 13.9%, H 23.4%, * 22.2%
- Annual Job Openings: E 2,570, G 4,190, H 127,890, * 103,900
- Self-Employed: 0.6%

Detailed Fields with Greatest Employment: Hospitals, Public and Private (60.3%); Nursing and Residential Care Facilities (6.2%); State and Local Government (3.6%); Administrative and Support Services (3.5%); Educational Services, Public and Private (3.4%)

Detailed Fields with Highest Growth (Projected Growth for This Job): Professional, Scientific, and

R

*C=Computer Systems Design, E=Educational Services, G=Government, H=Health Care, R=Repair and Maintenance, U=Utilities, *=All Fields*

Technical Services (59.5%); Internet Service Providers, Web Search Portals, and Data Processing Services (57.1%); Ambulatory Health Care Services (44.1%); Social Assistance (30.2%); Miscellaneous Manufacturing (28.6%)

Other Considerations for Job Outlook: Employment growth for registered nurses will be driven by the medical needs of an aging population. In addition, registered nurses are expected to provide more primary care as a low-cost alternative to physician-provided care. Job opportunities should be excellent.

Assess patient health problems and needs, develop and implement nursing care plans, and maintain medical records. Administer nursing care to ill, injured, convalescent, or disabled patients. May advise patients on health maintenance and disease prevention or provide case management. Licensing or registration required. Includes advance practice nurses such as nurse practitioners, clinical nurse specialists, certified nurse midwives, and certified registered nurse anesthetists. Advanced practice nursing is practiced by RNs who have specialized formal, postbasic education and who function in highly autonomous and specialized roles. Maintain accurate, detailed reports and records. Monitor, record, and report symptoms and changes in patients' conditions. Record patients' medical information and vital signs. Modify patient treatment plans as indicated by patients' responses and conditions. Consult and coordinate with health care team members to assess, plan, implement, and evaluate patient care plans. Order, interpret, and evaluate diagnostic tests to identify and assess patient's condition. Monitor all aspects of patient care, including diet and physical activity. Direct and supervise less skilled nursing or health-care personnel or supervise a particular unit. Prepare patients for, and assist with, examinations and treatments. Observe nurses and visit patients to ensure proper nursing care. Assess the needs of individuals, families, or communities, including assessment of individuals' home or work environments to identify potential health or safety problems.

Education/Training Required: Associate degree. **Education and Training Programs:** Adult Health Nurse/Nursing; Clinical Nurse Specialist Training; Critical Care Nursing; Family Practice Nurse/Nursing; Maternal/Child Health and Neonatal Nurse/Nursing; Nurse Anesthetist Training; Nurse Midwife/Nursing Midwifery; Nursing Science; Occupational and Environmental Health Nursing; Pediatric Nurse/Nursing; Perioperative/Operating Room and Surgical Nurse/Nursing; Psychiatric/Mental Health Nurse/Nursing; Public Health/Community Nurse/Nursing; Registered Nursing/Registered Nurse Training. **Knowledge/Courses:** Medicine and Dentistry; Psychology; Therapy and Counseling; Biology; Philosophy and Theology; Sociology and Anthropology.

Personality Type: Social-Investigative-Conventional. **Career Cluster:** 08 Health Science. **Career Pathway:** 8.1 Therapeutic Services. **Other Jobs in This Pathway:** Clinical Psychologists; Community and Social Service Specialists, All Other; Counseling Psychologists; Dental Assistants; Dental Hygienists; Dentists, General; Health Technologists and Technicians, All Other; Healthcare Support Workers, All Other; Home Health Aides; Licensed Practical and Licensed Vocational Nurses; Low Vision Therapists, Orientation and Mobility Specialists, and Vision Rehabilitation Therapists; Massage Therapists; Medical and Clinical Laboratory Technicians; Medical and Health Services Managers; Medical Scientists, Except Epidemiologists; Medical Secretaries; Occupational Therapists; Pharmacists; Pharmacy Technicians; Radiologic Technologists; School Psychologists; Social and Human Service Assistants; Speech-Language Pathologists; Speech-Language Pathology Assistants; Substance Abuse and Behavioral Disorder Counselors; others.

Skills: Science; Social Perceptiveness; Quality Control Analysis; Service Orientation; Learning Strategies; Management of Material Resources; Coordination; Instructing.

Work Environment: Indoors; standing; walking and running; using hands; exposed to disease or infections.

Job Specialization: Acute Care Nurses

Provide advanced nursing care for patients with acute conditions such as heart attacks, respiratory distress syndrome, or shock. May care for pre- and postoperative patients or perform advanced, invasive diagnostic, or therapeutic procedures. Analyze the indications, contraindications, risk complications, and cost-benefit trade-offs of therapeutic interventions. Diagnose acute or chronic conditions that could result in rapid physiological deterioration or life-threatening instability. Distinguish between normal and abnormal developmental and age-related physiological and behavioral changes in acute, critical, and chronic illness. Manage patients' pain relief and sedation by providing pharmacologic and nonpharmacologic interventions, monitoring patients' responses, and changing care plans accordingly. Interpret information obtained from electrocardiograms (EKGs) or radiographs (X-rays). Perform emergency medical procedures, such as basic cardiac life support (BLS), advanced cardiac life support (ACLS), and other condition-stabilizing interventions. Assess urgent and emergent health conditions using both physiologically and technologically derived data.

Education/Training Required: Associate degree. **Education and Training Program:** Critical Care Nursing. **Knowledge/Courses:** Medicine and Dentistry; Therapy and Counseling; Psychology; Biology; Sociology and Anthropology; Philosophy and Theology.

Personality Type: Social-Investigative-Realistic. **Career Cluster:** 08 Health Science. **Career**

Pathway: 8.1 Therapeutic Services. **Other Jobs in This Pathway:** Clinical Psychologists; Community and Social Service Specialists, All Other; Counseling Psychologists; Dental Assistants; Dental Hygienists; Dentists, General; Health Technologists and Technicians, All Other; Healthcare Support Workers, All Other; Home Health Aides; Licensed Practical and Licensed Vocational Nurses; Low Vision Therapists, Orientation and Mobility Specialists, and Vision Rehabilitation Therapists; Massage Therapists; Medical and Clinical Laboratory Technicians; Medical and Health Services Managers; Medical Scientists, Except Epidemiologists; Medical Secretaries; Occupational Therapists; Pharmacists; Pharmacy Technicians; Radiologic Technologists; School Psychologists; Social and Human Service Assistants; Speech-Language Pathologists; Speech-Language Pathology Assistants; Substance Abuse and Behavioral Disorder Counselors; others.

Skills: Science; Social Perceptiveness; Reading Comprehension; Operation Monitoring; Service Orientation; Systems Evaluation; Operation and Control; Active Learning.

Work Environment: Indoors; standing; walking and running; using hands; noise; contaminants; cramped work space; exposed to radiation; exposed to disease or infections.

Job Specialization: Advanced Practice Psychiatric Nurses

Provide advanced nursing care for patients with psychiatric disorders. May provide psychotherapy under the direction of a psychiatrist. Teach classes in mental health topics such as stress reduction. Participate in activities aimed at professional growth and development including conferences or continuing education activities. Direct or provide home health services. Monitor the use and status of medical and pharmaceutical supplies. Develop practice protocols for mental health problems based on

R

*C=Computer Systems Design, E=Educational Services, G=Government, H=Health Care, R=Repair and Maintenance, U=Utilities, *=All Fields*

review and evaluation of published research. Develop, implement, or evaluate programs such as outreach activities, community mental health programs, and crisis situation response activities. Treat patients for routine physical health problems. Write prescriptions for psychotropic medications as allowed by state regulations and collaborative practice agreements. Refer patients requiring more specialized or complex treatment to psychiatrists, primary care physicians, or other medical specialists. Provide routine physical health screenings to detect or monitor problems such as heart disease and diabetes.

Education/Training Required: Master's degree. **Education and Training Program:** Psychiatric/Mental Health Nurse Training/Nursing. **Knowledge/Courses:** Therapy and Counseling; Psychology; Medicine and Dentistry; Sociology and Anthropology; Philosophy and Theology; Biology.

Personality Type: Social-Investigative. **Career Cluster:** 08 Health Science. **Career Pathway:** 8.1 Therapeutic Services. **Other Jobs in This Pathway:** Clinical Psychologists; Community and Social Service Specialists, All Other; Counseling Psychologists; Dental Assistants; Dental Hygienists; Dentists, General; Health Technologists and Technicians, All Other; Healthcare Support Workers, All Other; Home Health Aides; Licensed Practical and Licensed Vocational Nurses; Low Vision Therapists, Orientation and Mobility Specialists, and Vision Rehabilitation Therapists; Massage Therapists; Medical and Clinical Laboratory Technicians; Medical and Health Services Managers; Medical Scientists, Except Epidemiologists; Medical Secretaries; Occupational Therapists; Pharmacists; Pharmacy Technicians; Radiologic Technologists; School Psychologists; Social and Human Service Assistants; Speech-Language Pathologists; Speech-Language Pathology Assistants; Substance Abuse and Behavioral Disorder Counselors; others.

Skills: Social Perceptiveness; Science; Negotiation; Service Orientation; Systems Evaluation; Persuasion; Learning Strategies; Reading Comprehension.

Work Environment: Indoors; sitting; exposed to disease or infections.

Job Specialization: Clinical Nurse Specialists

Plan, direct, or coordinate daily patient care activities in a clinical practice. Ensure adherence to established clinical policies, protocols, regulations, and standards. Coordinate or conduct educational programs or in-service training sessions on topics such as clinical procedures. Observe, interview, and assess patients to identify care needs. Evaluate the quality and effectiveness of nursing practice or organizational systems. Provide direct care by performing comprehensive health assessments, developing differential diagnoses, conducting specialized tests, or prescribing medications or treatments. Provide specialized direct and indirect care to inpatients and outpatients within a designated specialty such as obstetrics, neurology, oncology, or neonatal care. Maintain departmental policies, procedures, objectives, or infection control standards. Collaborate with other health-care professionals and service providers to ensure optimal patient care. Develop nursing service philosophies, goals, policies, priorities, or procedures.

Education/Training Required: Master's degree. **Education and Training Program:** Clinical Nurse Specialist Training. **Knowledge/Courses:** Medicine and Dentistry; Biology; Therapy and Counseling; Psychology; Sociology and Anthropology; Philosophy and Theology.

Personality Type: Enterprising-Social-Conventional. **Career Cluster:** 08 Health Science. **Career Pathways:** 8.1 Therapeutic Services; 8.3

Health Informatics. **Other Jobs in These Pathways:** Clinical Psychologists; Counseling Psychologists; Dental Assistants; Dental Hygienists; Editors; Engineers, All Other; Executive Secretaries and Executive Administrative Assistants; First-Line Supervisors of Office and Administrative Support Workers; Healthcare Support Workers, All Other; Home Health Aides; Licensed Practical and Licensed Vocational Nurses; Medical and Clinical Laboratory Technicians; Medical and Health Services Managers; Medical Assistants; Medical Records and Health Information Technicians; Medical Secretaries; Pharmacists; Pharmacy Technicians; Physical Therapists; Public Relations Specialists; Radiologic Technologists; Receptionists and Information Clerks; School Psychologists; Social and Human Service Assistants; Speech-Language Pathology Assistants; others.

Skills: Science; Operations Analysis; Instructing; Service Orientation; Negotiation; Persuasion; Judgment and Decision Making; Systems Evaluation.

Work Environment: Indoors; standing; using hands; noise; contaminants; exposed to radiation; exposed to disease or infections.

Job Specialization: Critical Care Nurses

Provide advanced nursing care for patients in critical or coronary care units. Identify patients' age-specific needs and alter care plans as necessary to meet those needs. Provide postmortem care. Evaluate patients' vital signs and laboratory data to determine emergency intervention needs. Perform approved therapeutic or diagnostic procedures based upon patients' clinical status. Administer blood and blood products, monitoring patients for signs and symptoms related to transfusion reactions. Administer medications intravenously, by injection, orally, through gastric tubes, or by other methods. Advocate for patients' and families' needs, or provide emotional support for patients and their families. Set up and monitor medical equipment and devices such as cardiac monitors, mechanical ventilators and alarms, oxygen delivery devices, transducers, and pressure lines. Monitor patients' fluid intake and output to detect emerging problems such as fluid and electrolyte imbalances.

Education/Training Required: Associate degree. **Education and Training Program:** Critical Care Nursing. **Knowledge/Courses:** Medicine and Dentistry; Biology; Psychology; Therapy and Counseling; Sociology and Anthropology; Philosophy and Theology.

Personality Type: Social-Investigative-Realistic. **Career Cluster:** 08 Health Science. **Career Pathway:** 8.1 Therapeutic Services. **Other Jobs in This Pathway:** Clinical Psychologists; Community and Social Service Specialists, All Other; Counseling Psychologists; Dental Assistants; Dental Hygienists; Dentists, General; Health Technologists and Technicians, All Other; Healthcare Support Workers, All Other; Home Health Aides; Licensed Practical and Licensed Vocational Nurses; Low Vision Therapists, Orientation and Mobility Specialists, and Vision Rehabilitation Therapists; Massage Therapists; Medical and Clinical Laboratory Technicians; Medical and Health Services Managers; Medical Scientists, Except Epidemiologists; Medical Secretaries; Occupational Therapists; Pharmacists; Pharmacy Technicians; Radiologic Technologists; School Psychologists; Social and Human Service Assistants; Speech-Language Pathologists; Speech-Language Pathology Assistants; Substance Abuse and Behavioral Disorder Counselors; others.

Skills: Science; Social Perceptiveness; Operation and Control; Operation Monitoring; Quality Control Analysis; Service Orientation; Monitoring; Learning Strategies.

C=Computer Systems Design, E=Educational Services, G=Government, H=Health Care, R=Repair and Maintenance, U=Utilities, *=All Fields

Work Environment: Indoors; standing; walking and running; using hands; bending or twisting the body; noise; contaminants; cramped work space; exposed to radiation; exposed to disease or infections.

Rehabilitation Counselors

- ❋ Annual Earnings: H $31,182, * $32,350
- ❋ Earnings Growth Potential: Low (35.8%)
- ❋ Growth: H 23.2%, * 18.9%
- ❋ Annual Job Openings: H 5,240, * 5,070
- ❋ Self-Employed: 5.7%

Detailed Fields with Greatest Employment: Ambulatory Health Care Services (5.2%); Social Assistance (46.5%); Nursing and Residential Care Facilities (21.0%); State and Local Government (20.5%); Hospitals, Public and Private (2.5%)

Detailed Fields with Highest Growth (Projected Growth for This Job): Social Assistance (30.3%); Educational Services, Public and Private (20.4%); Ambulatory Health Care Services (18.7%); Miscellaneous Store Retailers (16.0%); Religious, Grantmaking, Civic, Professional, and Similar Organizations (12.4%)

Other Considerations for Job Outlook: Increasing demand for services provided by counselors is expected to result in employment growth. But growth will vary by specialty and will be faster for mental health, substance abuse and behavioral disorder, and rehabilitation counselors than for counselors of other specialties. Opportunities should be favorable, particularly in rural areas.

Counsel individuals to maximize the independence and employability of persons coping with personal, social, and vocational difficulties that result from birth defects, illness, disease, accidents, or the stress of daily life. Coordinate activities for residents of care and treatment facilities. Assess client needs and design and implement rehabilitation programs that may include personal and vocational counseling, training, and job placement. Monitor and record clients' progress in order to ensure that goals and objectives are met. Confer with clients to discuss their options and goals so that rehabilitation programs and plans for accessing needed services can be developed. Prepare and maintain records and case files, including documentation such as clients' personal and eligibility information, services provided, narratives of client contacts, and relevant correspondence. Arrange for physical, mental, academic, vocational, and other evaluations to obtain information for assessing clients' needs and developing rehabilitation plans. Analyze information from interviews, educational and medical records, consultation with other professionals, and diagnostic evaluations to assess clients' abilities, needs, and eligibility for services. Develop rehabilitation plans that fit clients' aptitudes, education levels, physical abilities, and career goals.

Education/Training Required: Master's degree. **Education and Training Programs:** Assistive/Augmentative Technology and Rehabilitation Engineering; Vocational Rehabilitation Counseling/Counselor. **Knowledge/Courses:** Therapy and Counseling; Psychology; Philosophy and Theology; Education and Training; Personnel and Human Resources; Sociology and Anthropology.

Personality Type: Social-Investigative. **Career Cluster:** 08 Health Science. **Career Pathway:** 8.3 Health Informatics. **Other Jobs in This Pathway:** Clinical Psychologists; Dental Laboratory Technicians; Editors; Engineers, All Other; Executive Secretaries and Executive Administrative Assistants; Fine Artists, Including Painters, Sculptors, and Illustrators; First-Line Supervisors of Office and Administrative Support Workers; Health Educators; Medical and Health Services Managers; Medical

Appliance Technicians; Medical Assistants; Medical Records and Health Information Technicians; Medical Secretaries; Medical Transcriptionists; Mental Health Counselors; Occupational Health and Safety Specialists; Occupational Health and Safety Technicians; Physical Therapists; Psychiatric Aides; Psychiatric Technicians; Public Relations Specialists; Receptionists and Information Clerks; Recreational Therapists; Substance Abuse and Behavioral Disorder Counselors; Therapists, All Other; others.

Skills: Operations Analysis; Social Perceptiveness; Systems Analysis; Service Orientation; Science; Systems Evaluation; Learning Strategies; Monitoring.

Work Environment: More often indoors than outdoors; sitting; walking and running.

Respiratory Therapists

- ❋ Annual Earnings: H $54,350, * $54,280
- ❋ Earnings Growth Potential: Low (26.3%)
- ❋ Growth: H 21.3%, * 20.9%
- ❋ Annual Job Openings: H 5,450, * 4,140
- ❋ Self-Employed: 0.0%

Detailed Fields with Greatest Employment: Hospitals, Public and Private (81.3%); Ambulatory Health Care Services (5.7%); Nursing and Residential Care Facilities (3.4%); Administrative and Support Services (3.1%); Rental and Leasing Services (2.6%)

Detailed Fields with Highest Growth (Projected Growth for This Job): Ambulatory Health Care Services (44.3%); Nursing and Residential Care Facilities (35.7%); Rental and Leasing Services (23.8%); Administrative and Support Services (23.3%); Hospitals, Public and Private (19.1%)

Other Considerations for Job Outlook: Growth of the elderly population is expected to increase employment for these workers, especially as they take on additional duties related to case management, disease prevention, and emergency care. Opportunities are expected to be very good.

Assess, treat, and care for patients with breathing disorders. Assume primary responsibility for all respiratory care modalities, including the supervision of respiratory therapy technicians. Initiate and conduct therapeutic procedures; maintain patient records; and select, assemble, check, and operate equipment. Set up and operate devices such as mechanical ventilators, therapeutic gas administration apparatus, environmental control systems, and aerosol generators, following specified parameters of treatment. Provide emergency care, including artificial respiration, external cardiac massage, and assistance with cardiopulmonary resuscitation. Determine requirements for treatment, such as type, method, and duration of therapy; precautions to be taken; and medication and dosages, compatible with physicians' orders. Monitor patient's physiological responses to therapy, such as vital signs, arterial blood gases, and blood chemistry changes, and consult with physician if adverse reactions occur. Read prescription, measure arterial blood gases, and review patient information to assess patient condition. Work as part of a team of physicians, nurses, and other health-care professionals to manage patient care. Enforce safety rules and ensure careful adherence to physicians' orders.

Education/Training Required: Associate degree. **Education and Training Program:** Respiratory Care Therapy/Therapist. **Knowledge/Courses:** Medicine and Dentistry; Biology; Customer and Personal Service; Therapy and Counseling; Psychology; Chemistry.

Personality Type: Social-Investigative-Realistic. **Career Cluster:** 08 Health Science. **Career Pathway:** 8.1 Therapeutic Services. **Other Jobs in This**

R

*C=Computer Systems Design, E=Educational Services, G=Government, H=Health Care, R=Repair and Maintenance, U=Utilities, *=All Fields*

Pathway: Clinical Psychologists; Community and Social Service Specialists, All Other; Counseling Psychologists; Dental Assistants; Dental Hygienists; Dentists, General; Health Technologists and Technicians, All Other; Healthcare Support Workers, All Other; Home Health Aides; Licensed Practical and Licensed Vocational Nurses; Low Vision Therapists, Orientation and Mobility Specialists, and Vision Rehabilitation Therapists; Massage Therapists; Medical and Clinical Laboratory Technicians; Medical and Health Services Managers; Medical Scientists, Except Epidemiologists; Medical Secretaries; Occupational Therapists; Pharmacists; Pharmacy Technicians; Radiologic Technologists; School Psychologists; Social and Human Service Assistants; Speech-Language Pathologists; Speech-Language Pathology Assistants; Substance Abuse and Behavioral Disorder Counselors; others.

Skills: Science; Repairing; Equipment Maintenance; Equipment Selection; Operation and Control; Operation Monitoring; Quality Control Analysis; Service Orientation.

Work Environment: Indoors; standing; walking and running; using hands; repetitive motions; contaminants; exposed to radiation; exposed to disease or infections.

Secretaries and Administrative Assistants, Except Legal, Medical, and Executive

- ❋ Annual Earnings: R $25,930, H $30,919, * $30,830
- ❋ Earnings Growth Potential: Medium (36.1%)
- ❋ Growth: R –4.9%, H 27.5%, * 4.6%
- ❋ Annual Job Openings: R 510, H 6,480, * 36,550
- ❋ Self-Employed: 1.3%

Detailed Fields with Greatest Employment: Professional, Scientific, and Technical Services (9.6%); State and Local Government (7.3%); Religious, Grantmaking, Civic, Professional, and Similar Organizations (6.9%); Ambulatory Health Care Services (6.4%); Administrative and Support Services (5.7%)

Detailed Fields with Highest Growth (Projected Growth for This Job): Ambulatory Health Care Services (49.1%); Internet Service Providers, Web Search Portals, and Data Processing Services (37.3%); Lessors of Nonfinancial Intangible Assets (Except Copyrighted Works) (20.2%); Professional, Scientific, and Technical Services (19.8%); Other Information Services (18.8%)

Other Considerations for Job Outlook: Projected employment growth varies by occupational specialty. Faster than average growth is expected for medical secretaries and legal secretaries; average growth for executive secretaries and administrative assistants; and slower than average growth for secretaries other than legal, medical, or executive, who account for most of the workers in these specialties. Many opportunities are expected.

Perform routine clerical and administrative functions such as drafting correspondence, scheduling appointments, organizing and maintaining paper and electronic files, or providing information to callers. Operate office equipment such as fax machines, copiers, and phone systems and use computers for spreadsheet, word-processing, database management, and other applications. Answer telephones and give information to callers, take messages, or transfer calls to appropriate individuals. Greet visitors and callers, handle their inquiries, and direct them to the appropriate persons according to their needs. Set up and maintain paper and electronic filing systems for records, correspondence, and other material. Locate and attach appropriate files to incoming correspondence requiring replies. Open, read, route, and distribute incoming mail and other material and prepare answers to routine letters. Complete forms in accordance with company procedures. Make copies of correspondence and other printed material. Review work done by others to check for correct spelling and grammar, ensure that company format policies are followed, and recommend revisions.

Education/Training Required: Moderate-term on-the-job training. **Education and Training Programs:** Administrative Assistant and Secretarial Science, General; Executive Assistant/Executive Secretary Training. **Knowledge/Courses:** Clerical Practices; Customer and Personal Service; Economics and Accounting; Computers and Electronics; English Language; Personnel and Human Resources.

Personality Type: Conventional-Enterprising. **Career Cluster:** 04 Business, Management, and Administration. **Career Pathway:** 4.6 Administrative and Information Support. **Other Jobs in This Pathway:** Couriers and Messengers; Court Clerks; Court, Municipal, and License Clerks; Customer Service Representatives; Data Entry Keyers; Dispatchers, Except Police, Fire, and Ambulance; Executive Secretaries and Executive Administrative Assistants; File Clerks; Human Resources Assistants, Except Payroll and Timekeeping; Information and Record Clerks, All Other; Insurance Claims Clerks; Insurance Policy Processing Clerks; Interviewers, Except Eligibility and Loan; License Clerks; Mail Clerks and Mail Machine Operators, Except Postal Service; Office and Administrative Support Workers, All Other; Office Clerks, General; Order Clerks; Patient Representatives; Postal Service Mail Carriers; Postal Service Mail Sorters, Processors, and Processing Machine Operators; Receptionists and Information Clerks; Shipping, Receiving, and Traffic Clerks; Switchboard Operators, Including Answering Service; Word Processors and Typists; others.

Skills: Service Orientation; Management of Financial Resources; Writing; Time Management; Management of Material Resources; Active Listening; Reading Comprehension; Speaking.

Work Environment: Indoors; sitting; repetitive motions.

Security Guards

- ❋ Annual Earnings: U $46,070, * $23,920
- ❋ Earnings Growth Potential: Low (28.4%)
- ❋ Growth: U –16.6%, * 14.2%
- ❋ Annual Job Openings: U 100, * 37,390
- ❋ Self-Employed: 1.3%

Detailed Fields with Greatest Employment: Educational Services, Public and Private (6.1%); Administrative and Support Services (58.9%); State and Local Government (4.3%); Hospitals, Public and Private (4.0%); Accommodation, Including Hotels and Motels (2.8%)

Detailed Fields with Highest Growth (Projected Growth for This Job): Internet Service Providers, Web Search Portals, and Data Processing Services (47.1%); Professional, Scientific, and Technical Services (41.4%); Ambulatory Health Care Services (31.3%); Other Information Services (30.0%); Waste Management and Remediation Services (29.8%)

Other Considerations for Job Outlook: Concern about crime, vandalism, and terrorism are expected to result in increased demand for security services. This increased demand, along with the need to replace workers leaving the occupation permanently, should result in favorable job opportunities.

Guard, patrol, or monitor premises to prevent theft, violence, or infractions of rules. Monitor and authorize entrance and departure of employees,

*C=Computer Systems Design, E=Educational Services, G=Government, H=Health Care, R=Repair and Maintenance, U=Utilities, *=All Fields*

visitors, and other persons to guard against theft and maintain security of premises. Write reports of daily activities and irregularities, such as equipment or property damage, theft, presence of unauthorized persons, or unusual occurrences. Call police or fire departments in cases of emergency, such as fire or presence of unauthorized persons. Answer alarms and investigate disturbances. Circulate among visitors, patrons, or employees to preserve order and protect property. Patrol industrial or commercial premises to prevent and detect signs of intrusion and ensure security of doors, windows, and gates. Escort or drive motor vehicle to transport individuals to specified locations or to provide personal protection. Operate detecting devices to screen individuals and prevent passage of prohibited articles into restricted areas.

Education/Training Required: Short-term on-the-job training. **Education and Training Programs:** Securities Services Administration/Management; Security and Loss Prevention Services. **Knowledge/Courses:** Public Safety and Security.

Personality Type: Realistic-Conventional-Enterprising. **Career Cluster:** 12 Law, Public Safety, Corrections, and Security. **Career Pathways:** 12.1 Correction Services; 12.3 Security and Protective Services. **Other Jobs in These Pathways:** Animal Control Workers; Child, Family, and School Social Workers; Crossing Guards; First-Line Supervisors of Correctional Officers; First-Line Supervisors of Police and Detectives; First-Line Supervisors of Protective Service Workers, All Other; Forest Firefighters; Gaming Surveillance Officers and Gaming Investigators; Lifeguards, Ski Patrol, and Other Recreational Protective Service Workers; Parking Enforcement Workers; Police, Fire, and Ambulance Dispatchers; Private Detectives and Investigators; Protective Service Workers, All Other; Retail Loss Prevention Specialists; Sheriffs and Deputy Sheriffs; Transit and Railroad Police.

Skills: Operation and Control.

Work Environment: More often indoors than outdoors; standing; walking and running; using hands; noise; contaminants.

Self-Enrichment Education Teachers

- ❈ Annual Earnings: E $37,400, * $36,340
- ❈ Earnings Growth Potential: High (48.3%)
- ❈ Growth: E 49.6%, * 32.0%
- ❈ Annual Job Openings: E 3,720, * 12,030
- ❈ Self-Employed: 17.3%

Detailed Fields with Greatest Employment: Social Assistance (7.7%); Educational Services, Public and Private (50.8%); Religious, Grantmaking, Civic, Professional, and Similar Organizations (29.4%); State and Local Government (2.0%); Amusement, Gambling, and Recreation Industries (1.9%)

Detailed Fields with Highest Growth (Projected Growth for This Job): Educational Services, Public and Private (49.6%); Air Transportation (40.0%); Ambulatory Health Care Services (40.0%); Support Activities for Transportation (38.9%); Professional, Scientific, and Technical Services (34.1%)

Other Considerations for Job Outlook: Demand for self-enrichment education will increase as more people embrace lifelong learning or seek to acquire or improve skills that make them more attractive to prospective employers. Opportunities should be favorable.

Teach or instruct courses other than those that normally lead to an occupational objective or degree. Courses may include self-improvement, nonvocational, and nonacademic subjects. Teaching may or may not take place in a traditional educational institution. Adapt teaching methods and instructional materials to meet students' varying needs and interests. Conduct classes, workshops, and demonstrations and provide individual instruction to teach topics and skills such as cooking, dancing, writing, physical fitness, photography, personal finance, and flying. Monitor students' performance to make suggestions for improvement and to ensure that they satisfy course standards, training requirements, and objectives. Observe students to determine qualifications, limitations, abilities, interests, and other individual characteristics. Instruct students individually and in groups, using various teaching methods such as lectures, discussions, and demonstrations. Establish clear objectives for all lessons, units, and projects and communicate those objectives to students. Instruct and monitor students in use and care of equipment and materials to prevent injury and damage.

Education/Training Required: Work experience in a related occupation. **Education and Training Program:** Adult and Continuing Education and Teaching. **Knowledge/Courses:** Fine Arts; Education and Training; Psychology; Customer and Personal Service; Sales and Marketing; Administration and Management.

Personality Type: Social-Artistic-Enterprising. **Career Cluster:** 05 Education and Training. **Career Pathway:** 5.3 Teaching/Training. **Other Jobs in This Pathway:** Adult Basic and Secondary Education and Literacy Teachers and Instructors; Athletes and Sports Competitors; Audio-Visual and Multimedia Collections Specialists; Career/Technical Education Teachers, Middle School; Career/Technical Education Teachers, Secondary School; Chemists; Coaches and Scouts; Dietitians and Nutritionists; Elementary School Teachers, Except Special Education; Fitness Trainers and Aerobics Instructors; Historians; Instructional Coordinators; Instructional Designers and Technologists; Interpreters and Translators; Kindergarten Teachers, Except Special Education; Librarians; Middle School Teachers,

Except Special and Career/Technical Education; Physicists; Preschool Teachers, Except Special Education; Recreation Workers; Secondary School Teachers, Except Special and Career/Technical Education; Teacher Assistants; Teachers and Instructors, All Other; Tutors.

Skills: Operations Analysis; Learning Strategies; Instructing; Persuasion; Active Learning; Speaking; Technology Design; Social Perceptiveness.

Work Environment: Indoors; standing.

Social and Community Service Managers

- ❋ Annual Earnings: E $62,690, * $57,950
- ❋ Earnings Growth Potential: Medium (40.8%)
- ❋ Growth: E 18.2%, * 13.8%
- ❋ Annual Job Openings: E 120, * 4,820
- ❋ Self-Employed: 3.1%

Detailed Fields with Greatest Employment: Social Assistance (33.6%); Educational Services, Public and Private (3.5%); Ambulatory Health Care Services (3.3%); Hospitals, Public and Private (3.2%); State and Local Government (23.2%)

Detailed Fields with Highest Growth (Projected Growth for This Job): Professional, Scientific, and Technical Services (42.9%); Administrative and Support Services (24.4%); Museums, Historical Sites, and Similar Institutions (22.7%); Social Assistance (20.9%); Educational Services, Public and Private (18.3%)

Other Considerations for Job Outlook: Faster than average employment growth is projected.

Plan, organize, or coordinate the activities of a social service program or community outreach organization. Oversee the program or

*C=Computer Systems Design, E=Educational Services, G=Government, H=Health Care, R=Repair and Maintenance, U=Utilities, *=All Fields*

organization's budget and policies regarding participant involvement, program requirements, and benefits. Work may involve directing social workers, counselors, or probation officers. Establish and maintain relationships with other agencies and organizations in community to meet community needs and to ensure that services are not duplicated. Prepare and maintain records and reports, such as budgets, personnel records, or training manuals. Direct activities of professional and technical staff members and volunteers. Evaluate the work of staff and volunteers to ensure that programs are of appropriate quality and that resources are used effectively. Establish and oversee administrative procedures to meet objectives set by boards of directors or senior management. Participate in the determination of organizational policies regarding such issues as participant eligibility, program requirements, and program benefits. Research and analyze member or community needs to determine program directions and goals. Speak to community groups to explain and interpret agency purposes, programs, and policies. Recruit, interview, and hire or sign up volunteers and staff.

Education/Training Required: Bachelor's degree. **Education and Training Programs:** Business Administration and Management, General; Business, Management, Marketing, and Related Support Services, Other; Business/Commerce, General; Community Organization and Advocacy; Entrepreneurship/Entrepreneurial Studies; Human Services, General; Non-Profit/Public/Organizational Management; Public Administration. **Knowledge/Courses:** Therapy and Counseling; Psychology; Sociology and Anthropology; Philosophy and Theology; Personnel and Human Resources; Customer and Personal Service.

Personality Type: Enterprising-Social. **Career Clusters:** 04 Business, Management, and Administration; 07 Government and Public Administration; 10 Human Services. **Career Pathways:** 4.1

Management; 7.1 Governance; 7.7 Public Management and Administration; 10.3 Family and Community Services. **Other Jobs in These Pathways:** Brownfield Redevelopment Specialists and Site Managers; Business Continuity Planners; Business Operations Specialists, All Other; Chief Executives; Chief Sustainability Officers; Childcare Workers; Compliance Managers; Construction Managers; Customs Brokers; Energy Auditors; First-Line Supervisors of Office and Administrative Support Workers; General and Operations Managers; Investment Fund Managers; Loss Prevention Managers; Management Analysts; Managers, All Other; Nannies; Personal Care Aides; Regulatory Affairs Managers; Security Management Specialists; Security Managers; Supply Chain Managers; Sustainability Specialists; Wind Energy Operations Managers; Wind Energy Project Managers; others.

Skills: Management of Financial Resources; Management of Personnel Resources; Management of Material Resources; Systems Evaluation; Operations Analysis; Social Perceptiveness; Systems Analysis; Learning Strategies.

Work Environment: Indoors; sitting.

Social Scientists and Related Workers, All Other

- ❋ Annual Earnings: E $59,280, G $76,120, * $74,620
- ❋ Earnings Growth Potential: High (41.8%)
- ❋ Growth: G 19.3%, E 24.1%, * 22.5%
- ❋ Annual Job Openings: E 270, G 860, * 2,380
- ❋ Self-Employed: 1.5%

Detailed Fields with Greatest Employment: Federal Government (43.8%); Merchant Wholesalers,

Durable Goods (2.1%); Professional, Scientific, and Technical Services (18.9%); Educational Services, Public and Private (15.4%); Private Households; Primary and Secondary Jobs (1.6%)

Detailed Fields with Highest Growth (Projected Growth for This Job): Ambulatory Health Care Services (48.6%); Social Assistance (41.7%); Professional, Scientific, and Technical Services (31.2%); Miscellaneous Manufacturing (27.3%); Nursing and Residential Care Facilities (25.0%)

Other Considerations for Job Outlook: Much faster than average employment growth is projected.

This occupation includes all social scientists and related workers not listed separately. No task data available.

Education/Training Required: Master's degree. **Education and Training Program:** Social Sciences, Other. **Knowledge/Courses:** No data available.

Personality Type: No data available. **Career Clusters:** 02 Architecture and Construction; 10 Human Services; 15 Science, Technology, Engineering, and Mathematics. **Career Pathways:** 2.2 Construction; 10.3 Family and Community Services; 15.2 Science and Mathematics. **Other Jobs in These Pathways:** Architectural and Engineering Managers; Biofuels/Biodiesel Technology and Product Development Managers; Cement Masons and Concrete Finishers; Chief Executives; Child, Family, and School Social Workers; Childcare Workers; Construction Carpenters; Construction Laborers; Construction Managers; Cost Estimators; Drywall and Ceiling Tile Installers; Electricians; First-Line Supervisors of Construction Trades and Extraction Workers; Heating and Air Conditioning Mechanics and Installers; Managers, All Other; Nannies; Operating Engineers and Other Construction Equipment Operators; Painters, Construction and Maintenance; Personal Care Aides; Pipe Fitters and Steamfitters; Plumbers; Refrigeration Mechanics and Installers; Rough Carpenters; Solar Energy Installation Managers; Supply Chain Managers; others.

Skills: No data available.

Work Environment: No data available.

Job Specialization: Transportation Planners

Prepare studies for proposed transportation projects. Gather, compile, and analyze data. Study the use and operation of transportation systems. Develop transportation models or simulations. Prepare or review engineering studies or specifications. Represent jurisdictions in the legislative and administrative approval of land development projects. Prepare necessary documents to obtain project approvals or permits. Direct urban traffic counting programs. Develop or test new methods and models of transportation analysis. Define or update information such as urban boundaries and classification of roadways. Analyze transportation-related consequences of federal and state legislative proposals. Analyze information from traffic counting programs. Review development plans for transportation system effects, infrastructure requirements, or compliance with applicable transportation regulations. Prepare reports and recommendations on transportation planning. Produce environmental documents, such as environmental assessments and environmental impact statements.

Education/Training Required: Master's degree. **Education and Training Program:** City/Urban, Community and Regional Planning. **Knowledge/Courses:** No data available.

Personality Type: Investigative-Conventional-Realistic. **Career Cluster:** 15 Science, Technology, Engineering, and Mathematics. **Career Pathway:** 15.2 Science and Mathematics. **Other Jobs in This**

---

*C=Computer Systems Design, E=Educational Services, G=Government, H=Health Care, R=Repair and Maintenance, U=Utilities, *=All Fields*

Pathway: Architectural and Engineering Managers; Biochemists and Biophysicists; Biofuels/Biodiesel Technology and Product Development Managers; Bioinformatics Scientists; Biological Scientists, All Other; Biologists; Biostatisticians; Chemists; Clinical Data Managers; Clinical Research Coordinators; Community and Social Service Specialists, All Other; Dietitians and Nutritionists; Education, Training, and Library Workers, All Other; Geneticists; Geoscientists, Except Hydrologists and Geographers; Medical Scientists, Except Epidemiologists; Molecular and Cellular Biologists; Natural Sciences Managers; Operations Research Analysts; Physical Scientists, All Other; Social Scientists and Related Workers, All Other; Statisticians; Survey Researchers; Water Resource Specialists; Zoologists and Wildlife Biologists; others.

Skills: No data available.

Work Environment: No data available.

Sociologists

- ❋ Annual Earnings: E $68,860, * $72,360
- ❋ Earnings Growth Potential: Medium (39.2%)
- ❋ Growth: E 23.1%, * 22.0%
- ❋ Annual Job Openings: E 50, * 200
- ❋ Self-Employed: 0.0%

Detailed Fields with Greatest Employment: Religious, Grantmaking, Civic, Professional, and Similar Organizations (8.7%); State and Local Government, Excluding Education and Hospitals (7.9%); Professional, Scientific, and Technical Services (45.1%): Educational Services, Public and Private (37.0%)

Detailed Fields with Highest Growth (Projected Growth for This Job): Educational Services, Public and Private (23.3%); Religious, Grantmaking, Civic, Professional, and Similar

Organizations (21.3%); Professional, Scientific, and Technical Services (21.2%); State and Local Government (19.1%)

Other Considerations for Job Outlook: Employment growth of sociologists in a variety of fields is tied to expected demand for their research and analytical skills. Opportunities should be best for job seekers who have an advanced degree.

Study human society and social behavior by examining the groups and social institutions that people form, as well as various social, religious, political, and business organizations. May study the behavior and interaction of groups, trace their origin and growth, and analyze the influence of group activities on individual members. Analyze and interpret data in order to increase the understanding of human social behavior. Prepare publications and reports containing research findings. Plan and conduct research to develop and test theories about societal issues such as crime, group relations, poverty, and aging. Collect data about the attitudes, values, and behaviors of people in groups, using observation, interviews, and review of documents. Develop, implement, and evaluate methods of data collection, such as questionnaires or interviews. Teach sociology. Direct work of statistical clerks, statisticians, and others who compile and evaluate research data. Consult with and advise individuals such as administrators, social workers, and legislators regarding social issues and policies, as well as the implications of research findings. Collaborate with research workers in other disciplines. Develop approaches to the solution of groups' problems based on research findings in sociology and related disciplines.

Education/Training Required: Master's degree. **Education and Training Programs:** Criminology; Demography and Population Studies; Sociology; Urban Studies/Affairs. **Knowledge/Courses:**

Sociology and Anthropology; Philosophy and Theology; History and Archeology; Psychology; English Language; Mathematics.

Personality Type: Investigative-Artistic-Social. **Career Clusters:** 10 Human Services; 15 Science, Technology, Engineering, and Mathematics. **Career Pathways:** 10.3 Family and Community Services; 15.2 Science and Mathematics. **Other Jobs in These Pathways:** Architectural and Engineering Managers; Biofuels/Biodiesel Technology and Product Development Managers; Biologists; Chemists; Chief Executives; Child, Family, and School Social Workers; Childcare Workers; Clinical Research Coordinators; Community and Social Service Specialists, All Other; Dietitians and Nutritionists; Education, Training, and Library Workers, All Other; Eligibility Interviewers, Government Programs; Legislators; Managers, All Other; Medical Scientists, Except Epidemiologists; Nannies; Natural Sciences Managers; Operations Research Analysts; Personal Care Aides; Probation Officers and Correctional Treatment Specialists; Protective Service Workers, All Other; Social and Community Service Managers; Social Workers, All Other; Supply Chain Managers; Water Resource Specialists; others.

Skills: Science; Reading Comprehension; Writing; Speaking; Mathematics; Active Listening; Learning Strategies; Active Learning.

Work Environment: Indoors; sitting.

Software Developers, Applications

- ❈ Annual Earnings: E $71,990, G $73,640, H $78,233, U $85,170, C $87,220, * $87,790
- ❈ Earnings Growth Potential: Medium (38.1%)
- ❈ Growth: U –5.7%, G 19.3%, E 25.5%, H 28.4%, C 57.3%, * 34.0%
- ❈ Annual Job Openings: U 70, E 370, G 400, H 420, C 10,300, * 21,840
- ❈ Self-Employed: 2.7%

Detailed Fields with Greatest Employment: Publishing Industries (Except Internet) (8.5%); Computer and Electronic Product Manufacturing (6.3%); Management of Companies and Enterprises (5.4%); Professional, Scientific, and Technical Services (43.6%); Insurance Carriers and Related Activities (4.8%)

Detailed Fields with Highest Growth (Projected Growth for This Job): Internet Service Providers, Web Search Portals, and Data Processing Services (66.2%); Professional, Scientific, and Technical Services (56.7%); Ambulatory Health Care Services (46.2%); Lessors of Nonfinancial Intangible Assets (Except Copyrighted Works) (46.2%); Museums, Historical Sites, and Similar Institutions (42.9%)

Other Considerations for Job Outlook: Employment is expected to increase as businesses and other organizations continue to demand newer, more sophisticated software products. As a result of rapid growth, job prospects for software engineers should be excellent. The need to replace workers who leave the occupation is expected to generate numerous openings for programmers.

*C=Computer Systems Design, E=Educational Services, G=Government, H=Health Care, R=Repair and Maintenance, U=Utilities, *=All Fields*

Develop, create, and modify general computer applications software or specialized utility programs. Analyze user needs and develop software solutions. Design software or customize software for client use with the aim of optimizing operational efficiency. May analyze and design databases within an application area, working individually or coordinating database development as part of a team. Confer with systems analysts, engineers, programmers and others to design system and to obtain information on project limitations and capabilities, performance requirements and interfaces. Modify existing software to correct errors, allow it to adapt to new hardware, or to improve its performance. Analyze user needs and software requirements to determine feasibility of design within time and cost constraints. Consult with customers about software system design and maintenance. Coordinate software system installation and monitor equipment functioning to ensure specifications are met. Design, develop and modify software systems, using scientific analysis and mathematical models to predict and measure outcome and consequences of design. Develop and direct software system testing and validation procedures, programming, and documentation. Analyze information to determine, recommend, and plan computer specifications and layouts, and peripheral equipment modifications.

Education/Training Required: Bachelor's degree. **Education and Training Programs:** Computer Graphics; Computer Science; Computer Software and Media Applications, Other; Data Modeling/Warehousing and Database Administration; Modeling, Virtual Environments and Simulation; Web Page, Digital/Multimedia, and Information Resources Design. **Knowledge/Courses:** Computers and Electronics; Mathematics; Engineering and Technology; Design; English Language.

Personality Type: Investigative-Realistic-Conventional. **Career Cluster:** 11 Information Technology. **Career Pathways:** 8.3 Health Informatics;

11.1 Network Systems; 11.2 Information Support Services; 11.3 Interactive Media; 11.4 Programming and Software Development; 13.3 Maintenance, Installation, and Repair; 15.2 Science and Mathematics. **Other Jobs in These Pathways:** Architectural and Engineering Managers; Automotive Specialty Technicians; Biofuels/Biodiesel Technology and Product Development Managers; Clinical Psychologists; Computer and Information Systems Managers; Computer, Automated Teller, and Office Machine Repairers; Electrical and Electronic Equipment Assemblers; Electrical Engineering Technicians; Electronics Engineering Technicians; Engineers, All Other; Executive Secretaries and Executive Administrative Assistants; First-Line Supervisors of Office and Administrative Support Workers; Graphic Designers; Helpers—Installation, Maintenance, and Repair Workers; Industrial Machinery Mechanics; Installation, Maintenance, and Repair Workers, All Other; Medical and Health Services Managers; Medical Assistants; Medical Records and Health Information Technicians; Medical Secretaries; Mobile Heavy Equipment Mechanics, Except Engines; Physical Therapists; Public Relations Specialists; Receptionists and Information Clerks; Telecommunications Line Installers and Repairers; others.

Skills: Programming; Troubleshooting; Technology Design; Systems Evaluation; Operations Analysis; Mathematics; Systems Analysis; Quality Control Analysis.

Work Environment: Indoors; sitting; repetitive motions.

Software Developers, Systems Software

❀ Annual Earnings: E $75,000, H $82,895, C $92,130, * $94,180

❀ Earnings Growth Potential: Low (35.2%)

❀ Growth: E 24.1%, H 26.0%, C 57.4%, * 30.4%

❀ Annual Job Openings: H 100, E 110, C 6,120, * 15,340

❀ Self-Employed: 2.7%

Detailed Fields with Greatest Employment: Publishing Industries (Except Internet) (7.0%); Professional, Scientific, and Technical Services (42.6%); Telecommunications (4.8%); Merchant Wholesalers, Durable Goods (4.7%); Internet Service Providers, Web Search Portals, and Data Processing Services (3.8%)

Detailed Fields with Highest Growth (Projected Growth for This Job): Internet Service Providers, Web Search Portals, and Data Processing Services (66.1%); Professional, Scientific, and Technical Services (55.7%); Waste Management and Remediation Services (45.5%); Specialty Trade Contractors (44.4%); Ambulatory Health Care Services (44.0%)

Other Considerations for Job Outlook: Employment is expected to increase as businesses and other organizations continue to demand newer, more sophisticated software products. As a result of rapid growth, job prospects for software engineers should be excellent. The need to replace workers who leave the occupation is expected to generate numerous openings for programmers.

Research, design, develop, and test operating systems–level software, compilers, and network distribution software for medical, industrial, military, communications, aerospace, business, scientific, and general computing applications. **Set operational specifications and formulate and analyze software requirements. Apply principles and techniques of computer science, engineering, and mathematical analysis.** Modify existing software to correct errors, to adapt it to new hardware or to upgrade interfaces and improve performance. Design and develop software systems, using scientific analysis and mathematical models to predict and measure outcome and consequences of design. Consult with engineering staff to evaluate interface between hardware and software, develop specifications and performance requirements and resolve customer problems. Analyze information to determine, recommend, and plan installation of a new system or modification of an existing system. Develop and direct software system testing and validation procedures. Direct software programming and development of documentation. Consult with customers or other departments on project status, proposals, and technical issues such as software system design and maintenance. Advise customer about, or perform, maintenance of software system. Coordinate installation of software system.

Education/Training Required: Bachelor's degree. **Education and Training Programs:** Computer Graphics; Computer Science; Computer Software and Media Applications, Other; Data Modeling/Warehousing and Database Administration; Modeling, Virtual Environments and Simulation; Web Page, Digital/Multimedia, and Information Resources Design. **Knowledge/Courses:** Computers and Electronics; Engineering and Technology; Design; Telecommunications; Mathematics; Communications and Media.

Personality Type: Investigative-Conventional-Realistic. **Career Cluster:** 11 Information Technology. **Career Pathways:** 11.1 Network Systems; 11.2 Information Support Services; 11.3 Interactive Media; 11.4 Programming and Software Development. **Other Jobs in These Pathways:** Architectural

*C=Computer Systems Design, E=Educational Services, G=Government, H=Health Care, R=Repair and Maintenance, U=Utilities, *=All Fields*

and Engineering Managers; Bioinformatics Scientists; Computer and Information Systems Managers; Computer Hardware Engineers; Computer Numerically Controlled Machine Tool Programmers, Metal and Plastic; Computer Operators; Graphic Designers; Multimedia Artists and Animators; Remote Sensing Scientists and Technologists; Remote Sensing Technicians.

Skills: Programming; Technology Design; Operations Analysis; Science; Equipment Selection; Quality Control Analysis; Systems Evaluation; Mathematics.

Work Environment: Indoors; sitting; repetitive motions.

Special Education Teachers, Preschool, Kindergarten, and Elementary School

❋ Annual Earnings: H $50,027, E $52,650, * $52,250

❋ Earnings Growth Potential: Very High (66.4%)

❋ Growth: E 18.5%, H 37.9%, * 19.6%

❋ Annual Job Openings: H 850, E 7,060, * 10,290

❋ Self-Employed: 0.2%

Detailed Fields with Greatest Employment: Educational Services, Public and Private (93.3%); Social Assistance (4.4%); Ambulatory Health Care Services (0.7%); Nursing and Residential Care Facilities (0.5%); Hospitals, Public and Private (0.1%)

Detailed Fields with Highest Growth (Projected Growth for This Job): Ambulatory Health Care Services (66.0%); Social Assistance (35.3%); Nursing and Residential Care Facilities (25.0%);

Religious, Grantmaking, Civic, Professional, and Similar Organizations (25.0%); Hospitals, Public and Private (22.6%)

Other Considerations for Job Outlook: Employment of these teachers is expected to rise as more students qualify for special education services. Excellent job prospects are expected.

Job Specialization: Special Education Teachers, Kindergarten and Elementary School

Teach elementary school subjects to educationally and physically handicapped students. Includes teachers who specialize and work with audibly and visually handicapped students and those who teach basic academic and life processes skills to the mentally impaired. Administer standardized ability and achievement tests to kindergarten or elementary students with special needs. Collaborate with other teachers or administrators to develop, evaluate, or revise kindergarten or elementary school programs. Confer with other staff members to plan or schedule lessons promoting learning, following approved curricula. Confer with parents, administrators, testing specialists, social workers, or other professionals to develop individual education plans (IEPs). Confer with parents, guardians, teachers, counselors, or administrators to resolve students' behavioral or academic problems. Coordinate placement of students with special needs into mainstream classes. Develop individual educational plans (IEPs) designed to promote students' educational, physical, or social development. Develop or implement strategies to meet the needs of students with a variety of disabilities.

Education/Training Required: Bachelor's degree. **Education and Training Programs:** Education/ Teaching of Individuals in Early Childhood Special Education Programs; Education/Teaching of

Individuals in Elementary Special Education Programs. **Knowledge/Courses:** No data available.

Personality Type: No data available. **Career Cluster:** 05 Education and Training. **Career Pathway:** 5.3 Teaching/Training. **Other Jobs in This Pathway:** Adult Basic and Secondary Education and Literacy Teachers and Instructors; Athletes and Sports Competitors; Audio-Visual and Multimedia Collections Specialists; Career/Technical Education Teachers, Middle School; Career/Technical Education Teachers, Secondary School; Chemists; Coaches and Scouts; Dietitians and Nutritionists; Elementary School Teachers, Except Special Education; Fitness Trainers and Aerobics Instructors; Historians; Instructional Coordinators; Instructional Designers and Technologists; Interpreters and Translators; Kindergarten Teachers, Except Special Education; Librarians; Middle School Teachers, Except Special and Career/Technical Education; Physicists; Preschool Teachers, Except Special Education; Recreation Workers; Secondary School Teachers, Except Special and Career/Technical Education; Self-Enrichment Education Teachers; Teacher Assistants; Teachers and Instructors, All Other; Tutors.

Skills: No data available.

Work Environment: No data available.

Job Specialization: Special Education Teachers, Preschool

Teach elementary and preschool school subjects to educationally and physically handicapped students. Includes teachers who specialize and work with audibly and visually handicapped students and those who teach basic academic and life processes skills to the mentally impaired. Arrange indoor or outdoor space to facilitate creative play, motor-skill activities, or safety. Attend to children's basic needs by feeding them, dressing them, or changing their diapers. Communicate nonverbally with children to provide them with comfort, encouragement, or positive reinforcement. Confer with parents, guardians, teachers, counselors, or administrators to resolve students' behavioral or academic problems. Develop individual educational plans (IEPs) designed to promote students' educational, physical, or social development. Develop or implement strategies to meet the needs of students with a variety of disabilities. Employ special educational strategies or techniques during instruction to improve the development of sensory- and perceptual-motor skills, language, cognition, or memory. Encourage students to explore learning opportunities or persevere with challenging tasks to prepare them for later grades.

Education/Training Required: Bachelor's degree. **Education and Training Program:** Education/Teaching of Individuals in Early Childhood Special Education Programs. **Knowledge/Courses:** No data available.

Personality Type: No data available. **Career Cluster:** 05 Education and Training. **Career Pathway:** 5.3 Teaching/Training. **Other Jobs in This Pathway:** Adult Basic and Secondary Education and Literacy Teachers and Instructors; Athletes and Sports Competitors; Audio-Visual and Multimedia Collections Specialists; Career/Technical Education Teachers, Middle School; Career/Technical Education Teachers, Secondary School; Chemists; Coaches and Scouts; Dietitians and Nutritionists; Elementary School Teachers, Except Special Education; Fitness Trainers and Aerobics Instructors; Historians; Instructional Coordinators; Instructional Designers and Technologists; Interpreters and Translators; Kindergarten Teachers, Except Special Education; Librarians; Middle School Teachers, Except Special and Career/Technical Education; Physicists; Preschool Teachers, Except Special Education; Recreation Workers; Secondary School Teachers, Except Special and Career/Technical Education; Self-Enrichment Education Teachers; Teacher Assistants; Teachers and Instructors, All Other; Tutors.

C=Computer Systems Design, E=Educational Services, G=Government, H=Health Care, R=Repair and Maintenance, U=Utilities, *=All Fields

150 Best Jobs for a Secure Future © JIST Works

333

Skills: No data available.

Work Environment: No data available.

Special Education Teachers, Secondary School

- ❋ Annual Earnings: E $54,900, * $54,810
- ❋ Earnings Growth Potential: Low (33.2%)
- ❋ Growth: E 13.3%, * 13.3%
- ❋ Annual Job Openings: E 4,100, * 5,750
- ❋ Self-Employed: 0.2%

Detailed Fields with Greatest Employment: Educational Services, Public and Private (97.0%); Nursing and Residential Care Facilities (0.6%); Social Assistance (0.3%); Ambulatory Health Care Services (0.1%); Hospitals, Public and Private (0.1%)

Detailed Fields with Highest Growth (Projected Growth for This Job): Ambulatory Health Care Services (36.4%); Social Assistance (22.4%); Educational Services, Public and Private (13.3%); Nursing and Residential Care Facilities (4.2%); Hospitals, Public and Private (0.0%)

Other Considerations for Job Outlook: Employment of these teachers is expected to rise as more students qualify for special education services. Excellent job prospects are expected.

Teach secondary school subjects to educationally and physically handicapped students. Includes teachers who specialize and work with audibly and visually handicapped students and those who teach basic academic and life processes skills to the mentally impaired. Maintain accurate and complete student records, and prepare reports on children and activities, as required by laws, district policies, and administrative regulations. Teach socially acceptable behavior, employing techniques such as behavior modification and positive reinforcement. Prepare materials and classrooms for class activities. Establish and enforce rules for behavior and policies and procedures to maintain order among students. Confer with parents, administrators, testing specialists, social workers, and professionals to develop individual educational plans designed to promote students' educational, physical, and social development. Instruct through lectures, discussions, and demonstrations in one or more subjects, such as English, mathematics, or social studies. Employ special educational strategies and techniques during instruction to improve the development of sensory- and perceptual-motor skills, language, cognition, and memory.

Education/Training Required: Bachelor's degree. **Education and Training Program:** Education/Teaching of Individuals in Secondary Special Education Programs. **Knowledge/Courses:** Therapy and Counseling; History and Archeology; Psychology; Geography; Philosophy and Theology; Sociology and Anthropology.

Personality Type: Social-Investigative. **Career Cluster:** 05 Education and Training. **Career Pathway:** 5.3 Teaching/Training. **Other Jobs in This Pathway:** Adult Basic and Secondary Education and Literacy Teachers and Instructors; Athletes and Sports Competitors; Audio-Visual and Multimedia Collections Specialists; Career/Technical Education Teachers, Middle School; Career/Technical Education Teachers, Secondary School; Chemists; Coaches and Scouts; Dietitians and Nutritionists; Elementary School Teachers, Except Special Education; Fitness Trainers and Aerobics Instructors; Historians; Instructional Coordinators; Instructional Designers and Technologists; Interpreters and Translators; Kindergarten Teachers, Except Special Education;

Librarians; Middle School Teachers, Except Special and Career/Technical Education; Physicists; Preschool Teachers, Except Special Education; Recreation Workers; Secondary School Teachers, Except Special and Career/Technical Education; Self-Enrichment Education Teachers; Teacher Assistants; Teachers and Instructors, All Other; Tutors.

Skills: Learning Strategies; Social Perceptiveness; Service Orientation; Instructing; Monitoring; Active Learning; Operations Analysis; Reading Comprehension.

Work Environment: Indoors; standing; noise.

Speech-Language Pathologists

- ❋ Annual Earnings: H $74,247, * $66,920
- ❋ Earnings Growth Potential: Low (35.8%)
- ❋ Growth: H 34.0%, * 18.5%
- ❋ Annual Job Openings: H 2,470, * 4,380
- ❋ Self-Employed: 9.0%

Detailed Fields with Greatest Employment: Educational Services, Public and Private (52.5%); Nursing and Residential Care Facilities (4.8%); Social Assistance (3.1%); Ambulatory Health Care Services (20.3%); State and Local Government (2.4%)

Detailed Fields with Highest Growth (Projected Growth for This Job): Ambulatory Health Care Services (52.6%); Social Assistance (34.0%); Professional, Scientific, and Technical Services (27.3%); Administrative and Support Services (26.1%); Nursing and Residential Care Facilities (21.8%)

Other Considerations for Job Outlook: The aging population, better medical technology that increases the survival rates of people who become injured or ill, and growing enrollments in elementary and secondary schools are expected to increase employment of these workers. Job prospects are expected to be favorable.

Assess and treat persons with speech, language, voice, and fluency disorders. May select alternative communication systems and teach their use. May perform research related to speech and language problems. Monitor patients' progress and adjust treatments accordingly. Evaluate hearing and speech/language test results and medical or background information to diagnose and plan treatment for speech, language, fluency, voice, and swallowing disorders. Administer hearing or speech and language evaluations, tests, or examinations to patients to collect information on type and degree of impairments, using written and oral tests and special instruments. Record information on the initial evaluation, treatment, progress, and discharge of clients. Develop and implement treatment plans for problems such as stuttering, delayed language, swallowing disorders, and inappropriate pitch or harsh voice problems based on own assessments and recommendations of physicians, psychologists, or social workers. Develop individual or group programs in schools to deal with speech or language problems.

Education/Training Required: Master's degree. **Education and Training Programs:** Audiology/Audiologist and Speech-Language Pathology/Pathologist; Communication Disorders Sciences and Services, Other; Communication Disorders, General; Communication Sciences and Disorders, General; Speech-Language Pathology/Pathologist. **Knowledge/Courses:** Therapy and Counseling; English Language; Psychology; Sociology and Anthropology; Education and Training; Medicine and Dentistry.

Personality Type: Social-Investigative-Artistic. **Career Cluster:** 08 Health Science. **Career Pathway:** 8.1 Therapeutic Services. **Other Jobs in This Pathway:** Clinical Psychologists; Community and

---

*C=Computer Systems Design, E=Educational Services, G=Government, H=Health Care, R=Repair and Maintenance, U=Utilities, *=All Fields*

Social Service Specialists, All Other; Counseling Psychologists; Dental Assistants; Dental Hygienists; Dentists, General; Health Technologists and Technicians, All Other; Healthcare Support Workers, All Other; Home Health Aides; Licensed Practical and Licensed Vocational Nurses; Low Vision Therapists, Orientation and Mobility Specialists, and Vision Rehabilitation Therapists; Massage Therapists; Medical and Clinical Laboratory Technicians; Medical and Health Services Managers; Medical Scientists, Except Epidemiologists; Medical Secretaries; Occupational Therapists; Ophthalmic Medical Technologists; Pharmacists; Pharmacy Technicians; Radiologic Technologists; School Psychologists; Social and Human Service Assistants; Speech-Language Pathology Assistants; Substance Abuse and Behavioral Disorder Counselors; others.

Skills: Science; Learning Strategies; Social Perceptiveness; Writing; Monitoring; Systems Evaluation; Active Learning; Technology Design.

Work Environment: Indoors; sitting; noise; exposed to disease or infections.

Stationary Engineers and Boiler Operators

- Annual Earnings: U $58,050, * $52,140
- Earnings Growth Potential: Medium (37.4%)
- Growth: U –14.8%, * 5.2%
- Annual Job Openings: U 50, * 920
- Self-Employed: 2.0%

Detailed Fields with Greatest Employment: Utilities (7.6%); Paper Manufacturing (6.9%); Real Estate (4.8%); Wood Product Manufacturing (3.8%); Administrative and Support Services (2.1%)

Detailed Fields with Highest Growth (Projected Growth for This Job): Ambulatory Health Care Services (35.0%); Waste Management and Remediation Services (33.9%); Professional, Scientific, and Technical Services (29.6%); Educational Services, Public and Private (26.2%); Administrative and Support Services (23.0%)

Other Considerations for Job Outlook: Commercial and industrial development is expected to increase the amount of equipment to be operated and maintained. Job seekers face competition; those who have completed an apprenticeship or other formal training should have the best prospects.

Operate or maintain stationary engines, boilers, or other mechanical equipment to provide utilities for buildings or industrial processes. Operate equipment such as steam engines, generators, motors, turbines, and steam boilers. Operate or tend stationary engines; boilers; and auxiliary equipment such as pumps, compressors, and air-conditioning equipment to supply and maintain steam or heat for buildings, marine vessels, or pneumatic tools. Observe and interpret readings on gauges, meters, and charts registering various aspects of boiler operation to ensure that boilers are operating properly. Test boiler water quality or arrange for testing and take any necessary corrective action, such as adding chemicals to prevent corrosion and harmful deposits. Activate valves to maintain required amounts of water in boilers, to adjust supplies of combustion air, and to control the flow of fuel into burners. Monitor boiler water, chemical, and fuel levels and make adjustments to maintain required levels. Fire coal furnaces by hand or with stokers and gas- or oil-fed boilers, using automatic gas feeds or oil pumps.

Education/Training Required: Long-term on-the-job training. **Education and Training Program:** Building/Property Maintenance. **Knowledge/Courses:** Mechanical Devices; Building and Construction; Chemistry; Physics; Engineering and Technology; Design.

Personality Type: Realistic-Investigative-Conventional. **Career Cluster:** 13 Manufacturing. **Career Pathway:** 13.3 Maintenance, Installation, and Repair. **Other Jobs in This Pathway:** Aircraft Mechanics and Service Technicians; Automotive Specialty Technicians; Biological Technicians; Civil Engineering Technicians; Computer, Automated Teller, and Office Machine Repairers; Electrical and Electronic Equipment Assemblers; Electrical and Electronics Repairers, Commercial and Industrial Equipment; Electrical Engineering Technicians; Electrical Engineering Technologists; Electromechanical Engineering Technologists; Electronics Engineering Technicians; Electronics Engineering Technologists; Engineering Technicians, Except Drafters, All Other; Fuel Cell Technicians; Helpers—Installation, Maintenance, and Repair Workers; Industrial Engineering Technologists; Industrial Machinery Mechanics; Installation, Maintenance, and Repair Workers, All Other; Manufacturing Engineering Technologists; Manufacturing Production Technicians; Mapping Technicians; Mechanical Engineering Technologists; Mobile Heavy Equipment Mechanics, Except Engines; Telecommunications Line Installers and Repairers; Tire Repairers and Changers; others.

Skills: Repairing; Equipment Maintenance; Troubleshooting; Operation and Control; Equipment Selection; Operation Monitoring; Science; Installation.

Work Environment: More often indoors than outdoors; standing; using hands; noise; very hot or cold; bright or inadequate lighting; contaminants; cramped work space; high places; hazardous conditions; hazardous equipment; minor burns, cuts, bites, or stings.

Stock Clerks and Order Fillers

- ❋ Annual Earnings: R $27,330, * $21,290
- ❋ Earnings Growth Potential: Very Low (23.3%)
- ❋ Growth: R 4.1%, * 7.2%
- ❋ Annual Job Openings: R 140, * 56,260
- ❋ Self-Employed: 0.3%

Detailed Fields with Greatest Employment: Merchant Wholesalers, Nondurable Goods (5.3%); Merchant Wholesalers, Durable Goods (4.6%); Clothing and Clothing Accessories Stores (3.8%); Administrative and Support Services (3.7%); Warehousing and Storage (3.1%)

Detailed Fields with Highest Growth (Projected Growth for This Job): Internet Service Providers, Web Search Portals, and Data Processing Services (46.8%); Wholesale Electronic Markets and Agents and Brokers (39.5%); Lessors of Nonfinancial Intangible Assets (Except Copyrighted Works) (36.4%); Professional, Scientific, and Technical Services (34.6%); Waste Management and Remediation Services (28.6%)

Other Considerations for Job Outlook: Steady growth is expected, especially in retail trade where workers handling individual items and small quantities make job tasks difficult to automate. Job prospects should be good because of the need to replace workers who leave the occupation.

Job Specialization: Marking Clerks

Print and attach price tickets to articles of merchandise using one or several methods, such as marking price on tickets by hand or using ticket-printing machine. Put price information on tickets, marking by hand or using ticket-printing machine. Compare printed price tickets with entries on purchase orders to verify accuracy and notify supervisor of discrepancies. Pin, paste, sew, tie, or

C=Computer Systems Design, E=Educational Services, G=Government, H=Health Care, R=Repair and Maintenance, U=Utilities, *=All Fields

staple tickets, tags, or labels to article. Record number and types of articles marked and pack articles in boxes. Mark selling price by hand on boxes containing merchandise. Record price, buyer, and grade of product on tickets attached to products auctioned. Keep records of production, returned goods, and related transactions. Indicate item size, style, color, and inspection results on tags, tickets, and labels, using rubber stamp or writing instrument. Change the price of books in a warehouse.

Education/Training Required: Short-term on-the-job training. **Education and Training Program:** Retailing and Retail Operations. **Knowledge/Courses:** Production and Processing; Sales and Marketing; Mathematics.

Personality Type: Conventional-Realistic-Enterprising. **Career Cluster:** 14 Marketing, Sales, and Service. **Career Pathway:** 14.2 Professional Sales and Marketing. **Other Jobs in This Pathway:** Cashiers; Counter and Rental Clerks; Door-To-Door Sales Workers, News and Street Vendors, and Related Workers; Driver/Sales Workers; Energy Brokers; First-Line Supervisors of Non-Retail Sales Workers; First-Line Supervisors of Retail Sales Workers; Hotel, Motel, and Resort Desk Clerks; Marketing Managers; Online Merchants; Order Fillers, Wholesale and Retail Sales; Parts Salespersons; Property, Real Estate, and Community Association Managers; Real Estate Sales Agents; Reservation and Transportation Ticket Agents and Travel Clerks; Retail Salespersons; Sales and Related Workers, All Other; Sales Representatives, Services, All Other; Sales Representatives, Wholesale and Manufacturing, Except Technical and Scientific Products; Sales Representatives, Wholesale and Manufacturing, Technical and Scientific Products; Solar Sales Representatives and Assessors; Stock Clerks—Stockroom, Warehouse, or Storage Yard; Stock Clerks, Sales Floor; Telemarketers; Wholesale and Retail Buyers, Except Farm Products; others.

Skills: None met the criteria.

Work Environment: Indoors; standing; walking and running; using hands; bending or twisting the body; repetitive motions.

Job Specialization: Order Fillers, Wholesale and Retail Sales

Fill customers' mail and telephone orders from stored merchandise in accordance with specifications on sales slips or order forms. Read orders to ascertain catalog numbers, sizes, colors, and quantities of merchandise. Obtain merchandise from bins or shelves. Compute prices of items or groups of items. Complete order receipts. Keep records of outgoing orders. Place merchandise on conveyors leading to wrapping areas. Requisition additional materials, supplies, and equipment.

Education/Training Required: Short-term on-the-job training. **Education and Training Program:** Retailing and Retail Operations. **Knowledge/Courses:** Sales and Marketing.

Personality Type: Conventional-Realistic. **Career Cluster:** 14 Marketing, Sales, and Service. **Career Pathway:** 14.2 Professional Sales and Marketing. **Other Jobs in This Pathway:** Cashiers; Counter and Rental Clerks; Door-To-Door Sales Workers, News and Street Vendors, and Related Workers; Driver/Sales Workers; Energy Brokers; First-Line Supervisors of Non-Retail Sales Workers; First-Line Supervisors of Retail Sales Workers; Hotel, Motel, and Resort Desk Clerks; Marketing Managers; Marking Clerks; Online Merchants; Parts Salespersons; Property, Real Estate, and Community Association Managers; Real Estate Sales Agents; Reservation and Transportation Ticket Agents and Travel Clerks; Retail Salespersons; Sales and Related Workers, All Other; Sales Representatives, Services, All Other; Sales Representatives, Wholesale and Manufacturing, Except Technical and Scientific Products; Sales Representatives, Wholesale and Manufacturing, Technical and Scientific Products; Solar Sales Representatives and Assessors; Stock Clerks—Stockroom,

Warehouse, or Storage Yard; Stock Clerks, Sales Floor; Telemarketers; Wholesale and Retail Buyers, Except Farm Products; others.

Skills: None met the criteria.

Work Environment: Indoors; standing; using hands; repetitive motions; noise; contaminants.

Job Specialization: Stock Clerks, Sales Floor

Receive, store, and issue sales floor merchandise. Stock shelves, racks, cases, bins, and tables with merchandise and arrange merchandise displays to attract customers. May periodically take physical count of stock or check and mark merchandise. Answer customers' questions about merchandise and advise customers on merchandise selection. Itemize and total customer merchandise selection at checkout counter, using cash register, and accept cash or charge card for purchases. Take inventory or examine merchandise to identify items to be reordered or replenished. Pack customer purchases in bags or cartons. Stock shelves, racks, cases, bins, and tables with new or transferred merchandise. Receive, open, unpack, and issue sales floor merchandise. Clean display cases, shelves, and aisles. Compare merchandise invoices to items actually received to ensure that shipments are correct. Requisition merchandise from supplier based on available space, merchandise on hand, customer demand, or advertised specials. Transport packages to customers' vehicles. Stamp, attach, or change price tags on merchandise, referring to price list.

Education/Training Required: Short-term on-the-job training. **Education and Training Program:** Retailing and Retail Operations. **Knowledge/Courses:** No data available.

Personality Type: Conventional-Realistic-Enterprising. **Career Cluster:** 14 Marketing, Sales, and Service. **Career Pathway:** 14.2 Professional Sales and Marketing. **Other Jobs in This Pathway:**

Cashiers; Counter and Rental Clerks; Door-To-Door Sales Workers, News and Street Vendors, and Related Workers; Driver/Sales Workers; Energy Brokers; First-Line Supervisors of Non-Retail Sales Workers; First-Line Supervisors of Retail Sales Workers; Hotel, Motel, and Resort Desk Clerks; Marketing Managers; Marking Clerks; Online Merchants; Order Fillers, Wholesale and Retail Sales; Parts Salespersons; Property, Real Estate, and Community Association Managers; Real Estate Sales Agents; Reservation and Transportation Ticket Agents and Travel Clerks; Retail Salespersons; Sales and Related Workers, All Other; Sales Representatives, Services, All Other; Sales Representatives, Wholesale and Manufacturing, Except Technical and Scientific Products; Sales Representatives, Wholesale and Manufacturing, Technical and Scientific Products; Solar Sales Representatives and Assessors; Stock Clerks—Stockroom, Warehouse, or Storage Yard; Telemarketers; Wholesale and Retail Buyers, Except Farm Products; others.

Skills: None met the criteria.

Work Environment: Indoors; standing; walking and running; kneeling, crouching, stooping, or crawling; using hands; bending or twisting the body; repetitive motions.

Job Specialization: Stock Clerks— Stockroom, Warehouse, or Storage Yard

Receive, store, and issue materials, equipment, and other items from stockroom, warehouse, or storage yard. Keep records and compile stock reports. Receive and count stock items and record data manually or by using computer. Pack and unpack items to be stocked on shelves in stockrooms, warehouses, or storage yards. Verify inventory computations by comparing them to physical counts of stock and investigate discrepancies or adjust errors. Store items in an orderly and accessible manner in warehouses, tool rooms, supply rooms, or

*C=Computer Systems Design, E=Educational Services, G=Government, H=Health Care, R=Repair and Maintenance, U=Utilities, *=All Fields*

150 Best Jobs for a Secure Future © JIST Works

339

other areas. Mark stock items, using identification tags, stamps, electric marking tools, or other labeling equipment. Clean and maintain supplies, tools, equipment, and storage areas to ensure compliance with safety regulations. Determine proper storage methods, identification, and stock location based on turnover, environmental factors, and physical capabilities of facilities. Keep records on the use and damage of stock or stock handling equipment. Examine and inspect stock items for wear or defects, reporting any damage to supervisors.

Education/Training Required: Short-term on-the-job training. **Education and Training Program:** Retailing and Retail Operations. **Knowledge/Courses:** No data available.

Personality Type: Realistic-Conventional. **Career Cluster:** 14 Marketing, Sales, and Service. **Career Pathway:** 14.2 Professional Sales and Marketing. **Other Jobs in This Pathway:** Cashiers; Counter and Rental Clerks; Door-To-Door Sales Workers, News and Street Vendors, and Related Workers; Driver/Sales Workers; Energy Brokers; First-Line Supervisors of Non-Retail Sales Workers; First-Line Supervisors of Retail Sales Workers; Hotel, Motel, and Resort Desk Clerks; Marketing Managers; Marking Clerks; Online Merchants; Order Fillers, Wholesale and Retail Sales; Parts Salespersons; Property, Real Estate, and Community Association Managers; Real Estate Sales Agents; Reservation and Transportation Ticket Agents and Travel Clerks; Retail Salespersons; Sales and Related Workers, All Other; Sales Representatives, Services, All Other; Sales Representatives, Wholesale and Manufacturing, Except Technical and Scientific Products; Sales Representatives, Wholesale and Manufacturing, Technical and Scientific Products; Solar Sales Representatives and Assessors; Stock Clerks, Sales Floor; Telemarketers; Wholesale and Retail Buyers, Except Farm Products; others.

Skills: Management of Material Resources; Persuasion; Negotiation; Service Orientation.

Work Environment: Indoors; standing; walking and running; using hands; bending or twisting the body; repetitive motions; contaminants.

Substance Abuse and Behavioral Disorder Counselors

- ❀ Annual Earnings: H $36,902, * $38,120
- ❀ Earnings Growth Potential: Low (35.2%)
- ❀ Growth: H 25.1%, * 21.0%
- ❀ Annual Job Openings: H 3,780, * 3,550
- ❀ Self-Employed: 6.0%

Detailed Fields with Greatest Employment: Educational Services, Public and Private (5.8%); Ambulatory Health Care Services (24.7%); Nursing and Residential Care Facilities (22.0%); Religious, Grantmaking, Civic, Professional, and Similar Organizations (2.1%); Social Assistance (17.8%)

Detailed Fields with Highest Growth (Projected Growth for This Job): Professional, Scientific, and Technical Services (36.8%); Administrative and Support Services (33.9%); Nursing and Residential Care Facilities (30.9%); Ambulatory Health Care Services (24.9%); Social Assistance (22.0%)

Other Considerations for Job Outlook: Increasing demand for services provided by counselors is expected to result in employment growth. But growth will vary by specialty and will be faster for mental health, substance abuse and behavioral disorder, and rehabilitation counselors than for counselors of other specialties. Opportunities should be favorable, particularly in rural areas.

Counsel and advise individuals with alcohol; tobacco; drug; or other problems, such as gambling and eating disorders. May counsel individuals, families, or groups or engage in prevention programs. Counsel clients and patients individually and in group sessions to assist in overcoming dependencies, adjusting to life, and making changes. Complete and maintain accurate records and reports regarding the patients' histories and progress, services provided, and other required information. Develop client treatment plans based on research, clinical experience, and client histories. Review and evaluate clients' progress in relation to measurable goals described in treatment and care plans. Interview clients, review records, and confer with other professionals to evaluate individuals' mental and physical condition and to determine their suitability for participation in a specific program. Intervene as advocate for clients or patients to resolve emergency problems in crisis situations. Provide clients or family members with information about addiction issues and about available services and programs, making appropriate referrals when necessary.

Education/Training Required: Bachelor's degree. **Education and Training Programs:** Clinical/ Medical Social Work; Mental and Social Health Services and Allied Professions, Other; Substance Abuse/Addiction Counseling. **Knowledge/ Courses:** Therapy and Counseling; Psychology; Sociology and Anthropology; Philosophy and Theology; Education and Training; Clerical Practices.

Personality Type: Social-Artistic-Investigative. **Career Clusters:** 08 Health Science; 10 Human Services. **Career Pathways:** 8.1 Therapeutic Services; 8.3 Health Informatics; 10.2 Counseling and Mental Health Services. **Other Jobs in These Pathways:** Clergy; Clinical Psychologists; Counseling Psychologists; Dental Assistants; Dental Hygienists; Engineers, All Other; Executive Secretaries and Executive Administrative Assistants; First-Line Supervisors of Office and Administrative Support Workers; Healthcare Support Workers, All Other; Home Health Aides; Licensed Practical and Licensed Vocational Nurses; Medical and Clinical Laboratory Technicians; Medical and Health Services Managers; Medical Assistants; Medical Records and Health Information Technicians; Medical Secretaries; Pharmacists; Pharmacy Technicians; Physical Therapists; Public Relations Specialists; Radiologic Technologists; Receptionists and Information Clerks; Recreation Workers; Social and Human Service Assistants; Speech-Language Pathology Assistants; others.

Skills: Social Perceptiveness; Service Orientation; Persuasion; Learning Strategies; Active Listening; Negotiation; Monitoring; Systems Analysis.

Work Environment: Indoors; sitting.

Surgical Technologists

- ❀ Annual Earnings: H $39,876, * $39,920
- ❀ Earnings Growth Potential: Low (29.6%)
- ❀ Growth: H 25.5%, * 25.3%
- ❀ Annual Job Openings: H 6,460, * 4,630
- ❀ Self-Employed: 0.2%

Detailed Fields with Greatest Employment: Hospitals, Public and Private (71.6%); Ambulatory Health Care Services (24.3%); Administrative and Support Services (2.0%); Educational Services, Public and Private (1.0%); Professional, Scientific, and Technical Services (0.2%)

Detailed Fields with Highest Growth (Projected Growth for This Job): Professional, Scientific, and Technical Services (70.6%); Ambulatory Health Care Services (48.3%); Administrative and Support Services (25.1%); Hospitals, Public and Private

*C=Computer Systems Design, E=Educational Services, G=Government, H=Health Care, R=Repair and Maintenance, U=Utilities, *=All Fields*

(17.8%); Educational Services, Public and Private (16.1%)

Other Considerations for Job Outlook: Employment growth for these workers is expected as a growing and aging population has more surgeries and as advances allow technologists to assist surgeons more often. Job opportunities should be best for technologists who are certified.

Assist in operations under the supervision of surgeons, registered nurses, or other surgical personnel. May help set up operating rooms; prepare and transport patients for surgery; adjust lights and equipment; pass instruments and other supplies to surgeons and surgeons' assistants; hold retractors; cut sutures; and help count sponges, needles, supplies, and instruments. Count sponges, needles, and instruments before and after operations. Maintain a proper sterile field during surgical procedures. Hand instruments and supplies to surgeons and surgeons' assistants, hold retractors and cut sutures, and perform other tasks as directed by surgeons during operations. Prepare patients for surgery, including positioning patients on operating tables and covering them with sterile surgical drapes to prevent exposure. Scrub arms and hands and assist surgical teams to scrub and put on gloves, masks, and surgical clothing. Wash and sterilize equipment, using germicides and sterilizers. Monitor and continually assess operating room conditions, including needs of the patient and surgical team. Prepare dressings or bandages and apply or assist with their application following surgeries. Clean and restock operating rooms, gathering and placing equipment and supplies and arranging instruments according to instructions such as those found on a preference card.

Education/Training Required: Postsecondary vocational training. **Education and Training Programs:** Pathology/Pathologist Assistant Training; Surgical Technology/Technologist. **Knowledge/Courses:** Medicine and Dentistry; Biology;

Psychology; Chemistry; Therapy and Counseling; Customer and Personal Service.

Personality Type: Realistic-Social-Conventional. **Career Cluster:** 08 Health Science. **Career Pathway:** 8.2 Diagnostics Services. **Other Jobs in This Pathway:** Ambulance Drivers and Attendants, Except Emergency Medical Technicians; Anesthesiologist Assistants; Cardiovascular Technologists and Technicians; Cytogenetic Technologists; Cytotechnologists; Diagnostic Medical Sonographers; Emergency Medical Technicians and Paramedics; Endoscopy Technicians; Health Diagnosing and Treating Practitioners, All Other; Health Technologists and Technicians, All Other; Healthcare Practitioners and Technical Workers, All Other; Histotechnologists and Histologic Technicians; Medical and Clinical Laboratory Technicians; Medical and Clinical Laboratory Technologists; Medical and Health Services Managers; Medical Assistants; Medical Equipment Preparers; Neurodiagnostic Technologists; Nuclear Medicine Technologists; Ophthalmic Laboratory Technicians; Physical Scientists, All Other; Physician Assistants; Radiologic Technicians; Radiologic Technologists; Veterinary Assistants and Laboratory Animal Caretakers; others.

Skills: Equipment Maintenance; Equipment Selection; Operation Monitoring; Repairing; Quality Control Analysis; Operation and Control; Management of Material Resources; Coordination.

Work Environment: Indoors; standing; using hands; bending or twisting the body; repetitive motions; contaminants; exposed to radiation; exposed to disease or infections; hazardous conditions; hazardous equipment; minor burns, cuts, bites, or stings.

Tax Examiners and Collectors, and Revenue Agents

- ❋ Annual Earnings: G $49,360, * $49,360
- ❋ Earnings Growth Potential: Medium (40.2%)
- ❋ Growth: G 13.2%, * 13.0%
- ❋ Annual Job Openings: G 2,340, * 3,520
- ❋ Self-Employed: 2.3%

Detailed Fields with Greatest Employment: Federal Government (44.2%); Federal, State, and Local Government (100.0%);

Detailed Fields with Highest Growth (Projected Growth for This Job): Federal Government (19.5%); Federal, State, and Local Government (13.2%)

Other Considerations for Job Outlook: Employment growth of revenue agents and tax collectors should remain strong. The Federal Government is expected to increase its tax enforcement efforts, but demand for these workers' services is expected to be adversely affected by the automation of examiners' tasks and outsourcing of collection duties to private agencies.

Determine tax liability or collect taxes from individuals or business firms according to prescribed laws and regulations. Collect taxes from individuals or businesses according to prescribed laws and regulations. Maintain knowledge of tax code changes and of accounting procedures and theory to properly evaluate financial information. Maintain records for each case, including contacts, telephone numbers, and actions taken. Confer with taxpayers or their representatives to discuss the issues, laws, and regulations involved in returns and to resolve problems with returns. Contact taxpayers by mail or telephone to address discrepancies and to request supporting documentation. Send notices to taxpayers when accounts are delinquent. Notify taxpayers of any overpayment or underpayment and either issue a refund or request further payment. Conduct independent field audits and investigations of income tax returns to verify information or to amend tax liabilities. Review filed tax returns to determine whether claimed tax credits and deductions are allowed by law.

Education/Training Required: Bachelor's degree. **Education and Training Programs:** Accounting; Taxation. **Knowledge/Courses:** Law and Government; Customer and Personal Service; Economics and Accounting; Computers and Electronics; Clerical Practices; Mathematics.

Personality Type: Conventional-Enterprising. **Career Cluster:** 07 Government and Public Administration. **Career Pathway:** 7.5 Revenue and Taxation. **Other Jobs in This Pathway:** Financial Examiners; Tax Preparers.

Skills: Programming; Reading Comprehension; Mathematics; Active Learning; Operations Analysis; Judgment and Decision Making; Negotiation; Active Listening.

Work Environment: Indoors; sitting; repetitive motions.

Teachers and Instructors, All Other

- ❋ Annual Earnings: E $29,070, * $29,820
- ❋ Earnings Growth Potential: Medium (40.5%)
- ❋ Growth: E 18.0%, * 14.7%
- ❋ Annual Job Openings: E 11,300, * 22,570
- ❋ Self-Employed: 20.6%

Detailed Fields with Greatest Employment: Educational Services, Public and Private (85.6%);

*C=Computer Systems Design, E=Educational Services, G=Government, H=Health Care, R=Repair and Maintenance, U=Utilities, *=All Fields*

State and Local Government, Excluding Education and Hospitals (3.0%); Federal Government (2.8%); Social Assistance (2.4%); Religious, Grantmaking, Civic, Professional, and Similar Organizations (2.0%)

Detailed Fields with Highest Growth (Projected Growth for This Job): Management, Scientific, and Technical Consulting Services (86.2%); Offices of Physical, Occupational and Speech Therapists, and Audiologists (58.7%); Offices of Other Health Practitioners (52.6%); Computer Systems Design and Related Services (40.8%); Offices of Mental Health Practitioners (Except Physicians) (34.4%)

Other Considerations for Job Outlook: Faster than average employment growth is projected.

This occupation includes all teachers and instructors not listed separately. No task data available.

Education/Training Required: Bachelor's degree. **Education and Training Program:** Education, Other. **Knowledge/Courses:** No data available.

Personality Type: No data available. **Career Cluster:** 05 Education and Training. **Career Pathway:** 5.3 Teaching/Training. **Other Jobs in This Pathway:** Adult Basic and Secondary Education and Literacy Teachers and Instructors; Athletes and Sports Competitors; Audio-Visual and Multimedia Collections Specialists; Career/Technical Education Teachers, Middle School; Career/Technical Education Teachers, Secondary School; Chemists; Coaches and Scouts; Dietitians and Nutritionists; Elementary School Teachers, Except Special Education; Fitness Trainers and Aerobics Instructors; Historians; Instructional Coordinators; Instructional Designers and Technologists; Interpreters and Translators; Kindergarten Teachers, Except Special Education; Librarians; Middle School Teachers, Except Special and Career/Technical Education;

Physicists; Preschool Teachers, Except Special Education; Recreation Workers; Secondary School Teachers, Except Special and Career/Technical Education; Self-Enrichment Education Teachers; Teacher Assistants; Tutors.

Skills: No data available.

Work Environment: No data available.

Job Specialization: Tutors

Provide nonclassroom, academic instruction to students on an individual or small-group basis for proactive or remedial purposes. Travel to students' homes, libraries, or schools to conduct tutoring sessions. Schedule tutoring appointments with students or their parents. Research or recommend textbooks, software, equipment, or other learning materials to complement tutoring. Prepare and facilitate tutoring workshops, collaborative projects, or academic support sessions for small groups of students. Participate in training and development sessions to improve tutoring practices or learn new tutoring techniques. Organize tutoring environment to promote productivity and learning. Monitor student performance or assist students in academic environments, such as classrooms, laboratories, or computing centers. Review class material with students by discussing text, working solutions to problems, or reviewing worksheets or other assignments. Provide feedback to students using positive reinforcement techniques to encourage, motivate, or build confidence in students.

Education/Training Required: Short-term on-the-job training. **Education and Training Programs:** Adult Literacy Tutor/Instructor Training; Teaching Assistants/Aides, Other, Training. **Knowledge/Courses:** No data available.

Personality Type: No data available. **Career Cluster:** 05 Education and Training. **Career Pathway:** 5.3 Teaching/Training. **Other Jobs in This Pathway:** Adult Basic and Secondary Education and

Literacy Teachers and Instructors; Athletes and Sports Competitors; Audio-Visual and Multimedia Collections Specialists; Career/Technical Education Teachers, Middle School; Career/Technical Education Teachers, Secondary School; Chemists; Coaches and Scouts; Dietitians and Nutritionists; Elementary School Teachers, Except Special Education; Fitness Trainers and Aerobics Instructors; Historians; Instructional Coordinators; Instructional Designers and Technologists; Interpreters and Translators; Kindergarten Teachers, Except Special Education; Librarians; Middle School Teachers, Except Special and Career/Technical Education; Physicists; Preschool Teachers, Except Special Education; Recreation Workers; Secondary School Teachers, Except Special and Career/Technical Education; Self-Enrichment Education Teachers; Teacher Assistants; Teachers and Instructors, All Other.

Skills: No data available.

Work Environment: No data available.

Teachers, Postsecondary

- ❋ Annual Earnings: E $64,086, * $64,109
- ❋ Earnings Growth Potential: Very High (52.4%)
- ❋ Growth: E 15.2%, * 15.1%
- ❋ Annual Job Openings: E 39,780, * 55,290
- ❋ Self-Employed: 0.2%

Detailed Fields with Greatest Employment: Educational Services, Public and Private (97.9%); Hospitals, Public and Private (0.7%); Professional, Scientific, and Technical Services (0.3%); Religious, Grantmaking, Civic, Professional, and Similar Organizations (0.3%); Administrative and Support Services (0.2%)

Detailed Fields with Highest Growth (Projected Growth for This Job): Support Activities for Transportation (33.3%); Professional, Scientific, and Technical Services (26.8%); Social Assistance (24.4%); Administrative and Support Services (20.7%); Educational Services, Public and Private (15.2%).

Other Considerations for Job Outlook: Enrollments in postsecondary institutions are expected to continue rising as more people attend college and as workers return to school to update their skills. Opportunities for part-time or temporary positions should be favorable, but significant competition exists for tenure-track positions.

Job Specialization: Agricultural Sciences Teachers, Postsecondary

Teach courses in the agricultural sciences, including agronomy, dairy sciences, fisheries management, horticultural sciences, poultry sciences, range management, and agricultural soil conservation. Prepare course materials such as syllabi, homework assignments, and handouts. Evaluate and grade students' classwork, laboratory work, assignments, and papers. Keep abreast of developments in agriculture by reading current literature, talking with colleagues, and participating in professional conferences. Prepare and deliver lectures to undergraduate and/or graduate students on topics such as crop production, plant genetics, and soil chemistry. Initiate, facilitate, and moderate classroom discussions. Conduct research in a particular field of knowledge and publish findings in professional journals, books, and/or electronic media. Supervise laboratory sessions and fieldwork and coordinate laboratory operations. Supervise undergraduate and/or graduate teaching, internship, and research work. Compile, administer, and grade examinations or assign this work to others. Advise students on academic and vocational curricula and on career issues.

Education/Training Required: Doctoral degree. **Education and Training Programs:** Agribusiness/Agricultural Business Operations; Agricultural

*C=Computer Systems Design, E=Educational Services, G=Government, H=Health Care, R=Repair and Maintenance, U=Utilities, *=All Fields*

150 Best Jobs for a Secure Future © *JIST Works*

345

and Food Products Processing; Agricultural and Horticultural Plant Breeding; Agricultural Animal Breeding; Agricultural Business and Management, General; Agricultural Economics; Agricultural Mechanization, General; Agricultural Power Machinery Operation; Agricultural Production Operations, General; Agricultural Teacher Education; Agricultural/Farm Supplies Retailing and Wholesaling; Agriculture, General; Animal Health; Animal Nutrition; Animal Training; Animal/Livestock Husbandry and Production; Applied Horticulture/Horticulture Operations, General; Aquaculture; Crop Production; Dairy Science; Equestrian/Equine Studies; Farm/Farm and Ranch Management; Food Science; Greenhouse Operations and Management; Horticultural Science; International Agriculture; Landscaping and Groundskeeping; Livestock Management; Ornamental Horticulture; Plant Nursery Operations and Management; Plant Protection and Integrated Pest Management; Plant Sciences, General; Poultry Science; Range Science and Management; Soil Science and Agronomy, General; Turf and Turfgrass Management; others. **Knowledge/Courses:** Biology; Food Production; Education and Training; Geography; Chemistry; Communications and Media.

Personality Type: Social-Investigative-Realistic. **Career Clusters:** 01 Agriculture, Food, and Natural Resources; 05 Education and Training. **Career Pathways:** 1.1 Food Products and Processing Systems; 1.2 Plant Systems; 1.3 Animal Systems; 1.4 Power Structure and Technical Systems; 1.7 Agribusiness Systems; 5.3 Teaching/Training. **Other Jobs in These Pathways:** Career/Technical Education Teachers, Secondary School; Coaches and Scouts; Elementary School Teachers, Except Special Education; First-Line Supervisors of Landscaping, Lawn Service, and Groundskeeping Workers; First-Line Supervisors of Office and Administrative Support Workers; First-Line Supervisors of Retail Sales Workers; Fitness Trainers and Aerobics Instructors; Food Batchmakers; Graphic Designers;

Instructional Coordinators; Instructional Designers and Technologists; Kindergarten Teachers, Except Special Education; Landscaping and Groundskeeping Workers; Librarians; Middle School Teachers, Except Special and Career/Technical Education; Mobile Heavy Equipment Mechanics, Except Engines; Nonfarm Animal Caretakers; Preschool Teachers, Except Special Education; Recreation Workers; Retail Salespersons; Secondary School Teachers, Except Special and Career/Technical Education; Self-Enrichment Education Teachers; Teacher Assistants; Tutors; 37 other postsecondary teaching occupations; others.

Skills: Instructing; Science; Writing; Speaking; Reading Comprehension; Active Learning; Learning Strategies; Operations Analysis.

Work Environment: Indoors; sitting.

Job Specialization: Anthropology and Archeology Teachers, Postsecondary

Teach courses in anthropology or archeology. Conduct research in a particular field of knowledge and publish findings in professional journals, books, and electronic media. Keep abreast of developments in their field by reading current literature, talking with colleagues, and participating in professional conferences. Prepare and deliver lectures to undergraduate and graduate students on topics such as research methods, urban anthropology, and language and culture. Evaluate and grade students' classwork, assignments, and papers. Initiate, facilitate, and moderate classroom discussions. Write grant proposals to procure external research funding. Supervise undergraduate and/or graduate teaching, internship, and research work. Prepare course materials such as syllabi, homework assignments, and handouts. Compile, administer, and grade examinations or assign this work to others. Supervise students' laboratory work or fieldwork. Plan, evaluate, and revise curricula, course content, and course materials and methods of instruction.

Education/Training Required: Doctoral degree. **Education and Training Programs:** Anthropology; Archeology; Humanities/Humanistic Studies; Physical and Biological Anthropology; Social Science Teacher Education. **Knowledge/Courses:** Sociology and Anthropology; History and Archeology; Geography; Foreign Language; Philosophy and Theology; English Language.

Personality Type: Social-Investigative. **Career Clusters:** 05 Education and Training; 12 Law, Public Safety, Corrections, and Security; 15 Science, Technology, Engineering, and Mathematics. **Career Pathways:** 5.3 Teaching/Training; 12.4 Law Enforcement Services; 15.2 Science and Mathematics. **Other Jobs in These Pathways:** Architectural and Engineering Managers; Biofuels/Biodiesel Technology and Product Development Managers; Coaches and Scouts; Community and Social Service Specialists, All Other; Correctional Officers and Jailers; Criminal Investigators and Special Agents; Education, Training, and Library Workers, All Other; Elementary School Teachers, Except Special Education; Fitness Trainers and Aerobics Instructors; Immigration and Customs Inspectors; Instructional Coordinators; Instructional Designers and Technologists; Intelligence Analysts; Kindergarten Teachers, Except Special Education; Librarians; Middle School Teachers, Except Special and Career/Technical Education; Police Patrol Officers; Preschool Teachers, Except Special Education; Recreation Workers; Secondary School Teachers, Except Special and Career/Technical Education; Self-Enrichment Education Teachers; Sheriffs and Deputy Sheriffs; Teacher Assistants; Tutors; 37 other postsecondary teaching occupations; others.

Skills: Science; Writing; Speaking; Judgment and Decision Making; Operations Analysis; Reading Comprehension; Active Listening; Systems Evaluation.

Work Environment: Indoors; sitting.

Job Specialization: Architecture Teachers, Postsecondary

Teach courses in architecture and architectural design, such as architectural environmental design, interior architecture/design, and landscape architecture. Evaluate and grade students' work, including work performed in design studios. Prepare and deliver lectures to undergraduate and/or graduate students on topics such as architectural design methods, aesthetics and design, and structures and materials. Prepare course materials such as syllabi, homework assignments, and handouts. Initiate, facilitate, and moderate classroom discussions. Plan, evaluate, and revise curricula, course content, and course materials and methods of instruction. Keep abreast of developments in their field by reading current literature, talking with colleagues, and participating in professional conferences. Maintain student attendance records, grades, and other required records. Maintain regularly scheduled office hours to advise and assist students. Compile, administer, and grade examinations or assign this work to others. Conduct research in a particular field of knowledge and publish findings in professional journals, books, and/or electronic media.

Education/Training Required: Doctoral degree. **Education and Training Programs:** Architectural Engineering; Architecture (BArch, BA/BS, MArch, MA/MS, PhD); City/Urban, Community and Regional Planning; Environmental Design/Architecture; Interior Architecture; Landscape Architecture (BS, BSLA, BLA, MSLA, MLA, PhD); Teacher Education and Professional Development, Specific Subject Areas, Other. **Knowledge/Courses:** Fine Arts; Building and Construction; Design; History and Archeology; Philosophy and Theology; Geography.

Personality Type: Social-Artistic. **Career Clusters:** 02 Architecture and Construction; 05 Education and Training; 15 Science, Technology, Engineering, and Mathematics. **Career Pathways:** 2.1

*C=Computer Systems Design, E=Educational Services, G=Government, H=Health Care, R=Repair and Maintenance, U=Utilities, *=All Fields*

Design/Pre-Construction; 5.3 Teaching/Training; 15.1 Engineering and Technology. **Other Jobs in These Pathways:** Architectural and Engineering Managers; Automotive Engineers; Biochemical Engineers; Biofuels/Biodiesel Technology and Product Development Managers; Civil Engineers; Coaches and Scouts; Cost Estimators; Elementary School Teachers, Except Special Education; Energy Engineers; Engineers, All Other; Fitness Trainers and Aerobics Instructors; Fuel Cell Engineers; Human Factors Engineers and Ergonomists; Industrial Engineers; Manufacturing Engineers; Mechanical Engineers; Middle School Teachers, Except Special and Career/Technical Education; Preschool Teachers, Except Special Education; Recreation Workers; Secondary School Teachers, Except Special and Career/Technical Education; Self-Enrichment Education Teachers; Teacher Assistants; Transportation Engineers; Tutors; 37 other postsecondary teaching occupations; others.

Skills: Writing; Reading Comprehension; Speaking; Instructing; Operations Analysis; Learning Strategies; Active Learning; Critical Thinking.

Work Environment: Indoors; sitting.

Job Specialization: Area, Ethnic, and Cultural Studies Teachers, Postsecondary

Teach courses pertaining to the culture and development of an area (e.g., Latin America), an ethnic group, or any other group (e.g., women's studies, urban affairs). Keep abreast of developments in their field by reading current literature, talking with colleagues, and participating in professional conferences. Conduct research in a particular field of knowledge and publish findings in professional journals, books, and/or electronic media. Evaluate and grade students' classwork, assignments, and papers. Prepare course materials such as syllabi, homework assignments, and handouts. Prepare and deliver lectures to undergraduate and/or graduate students on topics such as race and ethnic relations, gender studies, and cross-cultural perspectives. Initiate, facilitate, and moderate classroom discussions. Compile, administer, and grade examinations or assign this work to others. Maintain regularly scheduled office hours in order to advise and assist students. Plan, evaluate, and revise curricula, course content, and course materials and methods of instruction. Maintain student attendance records, grades, and other required records.

Education/Training Required: Doctoral degree. **Education and Training Programs:** African Studies; African-American/Black Studies; American Indian/Native American Studies; American Studies; Asian Studies/Civilization; Asian-American Studies; Balkans Studies; Baltic Studies; Canadian Studies; Caribbean Studies; Chinese Studies; Commonwealth Studies; East Asian Studies; European Studies; French Studies; Gay/Lesbian Studies; German Studies; Hispanic-American, Puerto Rican, and Mexican-American/Chicano Studies; Humanities; Intercultural/Multicultural and Diversity Studies; Islamic Studies; Italian Studies; Japanese Studies; Jewish Studies; Korean Studies; Latin American Studies; Near and Middle Eastern Studies; Pacific Area/Pacific Rim Studies; Polish Studies; Regional Studies; Russian Studies; Russian, Central European, East European and Eurasian Studies; Scandinavian Studies; Slavic Studies; Social Studies Teacher Education; South Asian Studies; Southeast Asian Studies; Spanish and Iberian Studies; Tibetan Studies; Ukraine Studies; Ural-Altaic and Central Asian Studies; Western European Studies; Women's Studies; others. **Knowledge/Courses:** History and Archeology; Sociology and Anthropology; Foreign Language; Philosophy and Theology; Geography; Education and Training.

Personality Type: Social-Investigative-Artistic. **Career Clusters:** 05 Education and Training; 10 Human Services. **Career Pathways:** 5.3 Teaching/

Training; 10.2 Counseling and Mental Health Services. **Other Jobs in These Pathways:** Adult Basic and Secondary Education and Literacy Teachers and Instructors; Career/Technical Education Teachers, Secondary School; Clergy; Clinical Psychologists; Coaches and Scouts; Counseling Psychologists; Elementary School Teachers, Except Special Education; Fitness Trainers and Aerobics Instructors; Healthcare Social Workers; Instructional Coordinators; Instructional Designers and Technologists; Kindergarten Teachers, Except Special Education; Librarians; Mental Health and Substance Abuse Social Workers; Mental Health Counselors; Middle School Teachers, Except Special and Career/Technical Education; Preschool Teachers, Except Special Education; Recreation Workers; School Psychologists; Secondary School Teachers, Except Special and Career/Technical Education; Self-Enrichment Education Teachers; Substance Abuse and Behavioral Disorder Counselors; Teacher Assistants; Tutors; 37 other postsecondary teaching occupations; others.

Skills: Science; Writing; Operations Analysis; Learning Strategies; Speaking; Reading Comprehension; Active Learning; Active Listening.

Work Environment: Indoors; sitting.

Job Specialization: Art, Drama, and Music Teachers, Postsecondary

Teach courses in drama; music; and the arts, including fine and applied art, such as painting and sculpture, or design and crafts. Evaluate and grade students' classwork, performances, projects, assignments, and papers. Explain and demonstrate artistic techniques. Prepare students for performances, exams, or assessments. Prepare and deliver lectures to undergraduate or graduate students on topics such as acting techniques, fundamentals of music, and art history. Organize performance groups and direct their rehearsals. Prepare course materials such as syllabi, homework assignments, and handouts. Initiate, facilitate, and moderate classroom discussions. Keep abreast of developments in their field by reading current literature, talking with colleagues, and participating in professional conferences. Advise students on academic and vocational curricula and on career issues. Maintain student attendance records, grades, and other required records. Conduct research in a particular field of knowledge and publish findings in professional journals, books, or electronic media.

Education/Training Required: Doctoral degree. **Education and Training Programs:** Art History, Criticism and Conservation; Art, General; Ceramic Arts and Ceramics; Cinematography and Film/Video Production; Commercial Photography; Conducting; Crafts/Craft Design, Folk Art and Artisanry; Dance, General; Design and Visual Communications, General; Directing and Theatrical Production; Drama and Dramatics/Theatre Arts, General; Fashion/Apparel Design; Fiber, Textile and Weaving Arts; Film/Cinema/Video Studies; Fine/Studio Arts, General; Graphic Design; Humanities/Humanistic Studies; Industrial and Product Design; Interior Design; Intermedia/Multimedia; Jazz/Jazz Studies; Keyboard Instruments; Metal and Jewelry Arts; Music History, Literature, and Theory; Music Pedagogy; Music Performance, General; Music Theory and Composition; Musicology and Ethnomusicology; Painting; Photography; Playwriting and Screenwriting; Printmaking; Sculpture; Stringed Instruments; Technical Theatre/Theatre Design and Technology; Theatre Literature, History and Criticism; Visual and Performing Arts, General; Voice and Opera; others. **Knowledge/Courses:** Fine Arts; History and Archeology; Philosophy and Theology; Education and Training; Communications and Media; Sociology and Anthropology.

Personality Type: Social-Artistic. **Career Clusters:** 03 Arts, Audio/Video Technology, and Communications; 05 Education and Training. **Career**

---

*C=Computer Systems Design, E=Educational Services, G=Government, H=Health Care, R=Repair and Maintenance, U=Utilities, *=All Fields*

Pathways: 3.1 Audio and Video Technology and Film; 3.2 Printing Technology; 3.3 Visual Arts; 3.4 Performing Arts; 5.3 Teaching/Training. **Other Jobs in These Pathways:** Career/Technical Education Teachers, Secondary School; Coaches and Scouts; Data Entry Keyers; Directors—Stage, Motion Pictures, Television, and Radio; Elementary School Teachers, Except Special Education; Fitness Trainers and Aerobics Instructors; Graphic Designers; Instructional Coordinators; Instructional Designers and Technologists; Kindergarten Teachers, Except Special Education; Librarians; Managers, All Other; Middle School Teachers, Except Special and Career/Technical Education; Musicians, Instrumental; Photographers; Poets, Lyricists and Creative Writers; Preschool Teachers, Except Special Education; Producers; Recreation Workers; Secondary School Teachers, Except Special and Career/Technical Education; Self-Enrichment Education Teachers; Singers; Teacher Assistants; Tutors; 37 other postsecondary teaching occupations; others.

Skills: Instructing; Learning Strategies; Speaking; Reading Comprehension; Monitoring; Writing; Management of Material Resources; Active Learning.

Work Environment: Indoors; sitting; noise.

Job Specialization: Atmospheric, Earth, Marine, and Space Sciences Teachers, Postsecondary

Teach courses in the physical sciences, except chemistry and physics. Conduct research in a particular field of knowledge and publish findings in professional journals, books, and/or electronic media. Write grant proposals to procure external research funding. Keep abreast of developments in their field by reading current literature, talking with colleagues, and participating in professional conferences. Supervise undergraduate and/or graduate teaching, internships, and research work. Prepare and deliver lectures to undergraduate and/or graduate students on topics such as structural geology, micrometeorology, and atmospheric thermodynamics. Supervise laboratory work and fieldwork. Evaluate and grade students' classwork, assignments, and papers. Prepare course materials such as syllabi, homework assignments, and handouts. Collaborate with colleagues to address teaching and research issues. Compile, administer, and grade examinations or assign this work to others.

Education/Training Required: Doctoral degree. **Education and Training Programs:** Acoustics; Astronomy; Astrophysics; Atmospheric Chemistry and Climatology; Atmospheric Physics and Dynamics; Atmospheric Sciences and Meteorology, General; Atmospheric Sciences and Meteorology, Other; Atomic/Molecular Physics; Condensed Matter and Materials Physics; Elementary Particle Physics; Geochemistry; Geochemistry and Petrology; Geological and Earth Sciences/Geosciences, Other; Geology/Earth Science, General; Geophysics and Seismology; Hydrology and Water Resources Science; Meteorology; Nuclear Physics; Oceanography, Chemical and Physical; Optics/Optical Sciences; Paleontology; Physics Teacher Education; Physics, Other; Planetary Astronomy and Science; Plasma and High-Temperature Physics; Science Teacher Education/General Science Teacher Education; Theoretical and Mathematical Physics. **Knowledge/Courses:** Physics; Geography; Chemistry; Biology; Mathematics; Education and Training.

Personality Type: Social-Investigative. **Career Clusters:** 05 Education and Training; 15 Science, Technology, Engineering, and Mathematics. **Career Pathways:** 5.3 Teaching/Training; 15.2 Science and Mathematics. **Other Jobs in These Pathways:** Adult Basic and Secondary Education and Literacy Teachers and Instructors; Architectural and Engineering Managers; Biofuels/Biodiesel Technology and Product Development

Managers; Biologists; Career/Technical Education Teachers, Secondary School; Chemists; Coaches and Scouts; Community and Social Service Specialists, All Other; Education, Training, and Library Workers, All Other; Elementary School Teachers, Except Special Education; Fitness Trainers and Aerobics Instructors; Instructional Coordinators; Instructional Designers and Technologists; Kindergarten Teachers, Except Special Education; Librarians; Medical Scientists, Except Epidemiologists; Middle School Teachers, Except Special and Career/Technical Education; Operations Research Analysts; Preschool Teachers, Except Special Education; Recreation Workers; Secondary School Teachers, Except Special and Career/Technical Education; Self-Enrichment Education Teachers; Teacher Assistants; Tutors; 37 other postsecondary teaching occupations; others.

Skills: Science; Learning Strategies; Writing; Instructing; Reading Comprehension; Speaking; Mathematics; Active Listening.

Work Environment: Indoors; sitting.

Job Specialization: Biological Science Teachers, Postsecondary

Teach courses in biological sciences. Prepare and deliver lectures to undergraduate and/or graduate students on topics such as molecular biology, marine biology, and botany. Evaluate and grade students' classwork, laboratory work, assignments, and papers. Prepare course materials such as syllabi, homework assignments, and handouts. Compile, administer, and grade examinations or assign this work to others. Supervise students' laboratory work. Keep abreast of developments in their field by reading current literature, talking with colleagues, and participating in professional conferences. Maintain student attendance records, grades, and other required records. Initiate, facilitate, and moderate classroom discussions. Plan, evaluate, and revise curricula, course content,

course materials, and methods of instruction. Advise students on academic and vocational curricula and on career issues. Maintain regularly scheduled office hours to advise and assist students.

Education/Training Required: Doctoral degree. **Education and Training Programs:** Anatomy; Animal Physiology; Biochemistry; Biological and Biomedical Sciences, Other; Biology/Biological Sciences, General; Biometry/Biometrics; Biophysics; Biotechnology; Botany/Plant Biology; Cell/Cellular Biology and Histology; Ecology; Ecology, Evolution, Systematics and Population Biology, Other; Entomology; Evolutionary Biology; Immunology; Marine Biology and Biological Oceanography; Microbiology, General; Molecular Biology; Nutrition Sciences; Parasitology; Pathology/Experimental Pathology; Pharmacology; Plant Genetics; Plant Pathology/Phytopathology; Plant Physiology; Radiation Biology/Radiobiology; Toxicology; Virology; Zoology/Animal Biology. **Knowledge/Courses:** Biology; Chemistry; Education and Training; Medicine and Dentistry; Physics; Geography.

Personality Type: Social-Investigative. **Career Clusters:** 01 Agriculture, Food, and Natural Resources; 05 Education and Training; 15 Science, Technology, Engineering, and Mathematics. **Career Pathways:** 1.5 Natural Resources Systems; 5.3 Teaching/Training; 15.2 Science and Mathematics. **Other Jobs in These Pathways:** Adult Basic and Secondary Education and Literacy Teachers and Instructors; Architectural and Engineering Managers; Biofuels/Biodiesel Technology and Product Development Managers; Biologists; Career/Technical Education Teachers, Secondary School; Coaches and Scouts; Community and Social Service Specialists, All Other; Education, Training, and Library Workers, All Other; Elementary School Teachers, Except Special Education; Fitness Trainers and Aerobics Instructors; Industrial Truck and Tractor Operators; Instructional Coordinators; Instructional Design-

C=Computer Systems Design, E=Educational Services, G=Government, H=Health Care, R=Repair and Maintenance, U=Utilities, *=All Fields

150 Best Jobs for a Secure Future © JIST Works 351

ers and Technologists; Kindergarten Teachers, Except Special Education; Librarians; Medical Scientists, Except Epidemiologists; Middle School Teachers, Except Special and Career/Technical Education; Preschool Teachers, Except Special Education; Recreation Workers; Refuse and Recyclable Material Collectors; Secondary School Teachers, Except Special and Career/Technical Education; Self-Enrichment Education Teachers; Teacher Assistants; Tutors; 37 other postsecondary teaching occupations; others.

Skills: Science; Instructing; Writing; Learning Strategies; Speaking; Reading Comprehension; Active Learning; Operations Analysis.

Work Environment: Indoors; sitting; standing.

Job Specialization: Business Teachers, Postsecondary

Teach courses in business administration and management, such as accounting, finance, human resources, labor relations, marketing, and operations research. Prepare and deliver lectures to undergraduate and/or graduate students on topics such as financial accounting, principles of marketing, and operations management. Evaluate and grade students' classwork, assignments, and papers. Compile, administer, and grade examinations or assign this work to others. Prepare course materials such as syllabi, homework assignments, and handouts. Maintain student attendance records, grades, and other required records. Initiate, facilitate, and moderate classroom discussions. Plan, evaluate, and revise curricula, course content, and course materials and methods of instruction. Keep abreast of developments in their field by reading current literature, talking with colleagues, and participating in professional organizations and conferences. Maintain regularly scheduled office hours to advise and assist students. Advise students on academic and vocational curricula and on career issues.

Select and obtain materials and supplies such as textbooks.

Education/Training Required: Doctoral degree. **Education and Training Programs:** Accounting; Actuarial Science; Business Administration and Management, General; Business Statistics; Business Teacher Education; Business/Commerce, General; Business/Corporate Communications; Entrepreneurship/Entrepreneurial Studies; Finance, General; Financial Planning and Services; Franchising and Franchise Operations; Human Resources Management/Personnel Administration, General; Insurance; International Business/Trade/Commerce; International Finance; International Marketing; Investments and Securities; Labor and Industrial Relations; Logistics, Materials, and Supply Chain Management; Management Science; Marketing Research; Marketing/Marketing Management, General; Operations Management and Supervision; Organizational Behavior Studies; Public Finance; Purchasing, Procurement/Acquisitions and Contracts Management. **Knowledge/Courses:** Economics and Accounting; Education and Training; Sociology and Anthropology; Sales and Marketing; Philosophy and Theology; English Language.

Personality Type: Social-Enterprising-Investigative. **Career Clusters:** 04 Business, Management, and Administration; 05 Education and Training; 06 Finance; 14 Marketing, Sales, and Service. **Career Pathways:** 4.1 Management; 4.2 Business, Financial Management, and Accounting; 4.3 Human Resources; 4.5 Marketing; 5.3 Teaching/Training; 6.1 Financial and Investment Planning; 6.4 Insurance Services; 14.1 Management and Entrepreneurship; 14.5 Marketing Information Management and Research. **Other Jobs in These Pathways:** Accountants; Auditors; Bookkeeping, Accounting, and Auditing Clerks; Brownfield Redevelopment Specialists and Site Managers; Business Continuity Planners; Business Operations

Specialists, All Other; Compliance Managers; Customs Brokers; Elementary School Teachers, Except Special Education; Energy Auditors; First-Line Supervisors of Office and Administrative Support Workers; First-Line Supervisors of Retail Sales Workers; General and Operations Managers; Investment Fund Managers; Loss Prevention Managers; Managers, All Other; Regulatory Affairs Managers; Secondary School Teachers, Except Special and Career/Technical Education; Security Management Specialists; Security Managers; Supply Chain Managers; Sustainability Specialists; Teacher Assistants; Wind Energy Operations Managers; Wind Energy Project Managers; 37 other postsecondary teaching occupations; others.

Skills: Learning Strategies; Instructing; Reading Comprehension; Writing; Active Learning; Speaking; Judgment and Decision Making; Systems Analysis.

Work Environment: Indoors; sitting.

Job Specialization: Chemistry Teachers, Postsecondary

Teach courses pertaining to the chemical and physical properties and compositional changes of substances. Work may include instruction in the methods of qualitative and quantitative chemical analysis. Includes both teachers primarily engaged in teaching and those who do a combination of both teaching and research. Prepare and deliver lectures to undergraduate and/or graduate students on topics such as organic chemistry, analytical chemistry, and chemical separation. Supervise students' laboratory work. Evaluate and grade students' classwork, laboratory performance, assignments, and papers. Compile, administer, and grade examinations or assign this work to others. Maintain student attendance records, grades, and other required records. Prepare course materials such as syllabi, homework assignments, and handouts. Maintain regularly scheduled office hours to advise and assist students. Plan, evaluate, and revise curricula, course content, course materials, and methods of instruction. Supervise undergraduate and/or graduate teaching, internships, and research work. Keep abreast of developments in the field by reading current literature, talking with colleagues, and participating in professional conferences. Initiate, facilitate, and moderate classroom discussions.

Education/Training Required: Doctoral degree. **Education and Training Programs:** Analytical Chemistry; Chemical Physics; Chemistry, General; Chemistry, Other; Geochemistry; Inorganic Chemistry; Organic Chemistry; Physical Chemistry; Polymer Chemistry. **Knowledge/Courses:** Chemistry; Biology; Physics; Education and Training; Mathematics; English Language.

Personality Type: Social-Investigative-Realistic. **Career Cluster:** 15 Science, Technology, Engineering, and Mathematics. **Career Pathway:** 15.2 Science and Mathematics. **Other Jobs in This Pathway:** Architectural and Engineering Managers; Biochemists and Biophysicists; Biofuels/Biodiesel Technology and Product Development Managers; Bioinformatics Scientists; Biological Scientists, All Other; Biologists; Biostatisticians; Chemists; Clinical Data Managers; Clinical Research Coordinators; Community and Social Service Specialists, All Other; Dietitians and Nutritionists; Education, Training, and Library Workers, All Other; Geneticists; Geoscientists, Except Hydrologists and Geographers; Medical Scientists, Except Epidemiologists; Molecular and Cellular Biologists; Natural Sciences Managers; Operations Research Analysts; Physical Scientists, All Other; Social Scientists and Related Workers, All Other; Statisticians; Survey Researchers; Transportation Planners; Water Resource Specialists; 37 other postsecondary teaching occupations; others.

C=Computer Systems Design, E=Educational Services, G=Government, H=Health Care, R=Repair and Maintenance, U=Utilities, *=All Fields

Skills: Science; Reading Comprehension; Speaking; Writing; Learning Strategies; Instructing; Operations Analysis; Active Learning.

Work Environment: Indoors; sitting; contaminants; hazardous conditions.

Job Specialization: Communications Teachers, Postsecondary

Teach courses in communications, such as organizational communications, public relations, radio/television broadcasting, and journalism. Evaluate and grade students' classwork, assignments, and papers. Prepare course materials such as syllabi, homework assignments, and handouts. Initiate, facilitate, and moderate classroom discussions. Prepare and deliver lectures to undergraduate or graduate students on topics such as public speaking, media criticism, and oral traditions. Compile, administer, and grade examinations or assign this work to others. Maintain student attendance records, grades, and other required records. Plan, evaluate, and revise curricula, course content, and course materials and methods of instruction. Maintain regularly scheduled office hours to advise and assist students. Keep abreast of developments in their field by reading current literature, talking with colleagues, and participating in professional conferences. Advise students on academic and vocational curricula and on career issues. Supervise undergraduate or graduate teaching, internship, and research work.

Education/Training Required: Doctoral degree. **Education and Training Programs:** Advertising; Broadcast Journalism; Communication, Journalism, and Related Programs, Other; Digital Communication and Media/Multimedia; Health Communication; Humanities/Humanistic Studies; Journalism; Journalism, Other; Mass Communication/Media Studies; Political Communication; Public Relations/Image Management; Radio and Television; Speech Communication and Rhetoric. **Knowledge/**

Courses: Communications and Media; Education and Training; Philosophy and Theology; Sociology and Anthropology; English Language; History and Archeology.

Personality Type: Social-Artistic. **Career Clusters:** 03 Arts, Audio/Video Technology, and Communications; 04 Business, Management, and Administration; 05 Education and Training; 08 Health Science. **Career Pathways:** 3.5 Journalism and Broadcasting; 4.1 Management; 4.5 Marketing; 5.3 Teaching/Training; 8.3 Health Informatics. **Other Jobs in These Pathways:** Brownfield Redevelopment Specialists and Site Managers; Business Continuity Planners; Business Operations Specialists, All Other; Compliance Managers; Customs Brokers; Elementary School Teachers, Except Special Education; Energy Auditors; Executive Secretaries and Executive Administrative Assistants; First-Line Supervisors of Office and Administrative Support Workers; General and Operations Managers; Investment Fund Managers; Loss Prevention Managers; Managers, All Other; Receptionists and Information Clerks; Regulatory Affairs Managers; Secondary School Teachers, Except Special and Career/Technical Education; Security Management Specialists; Security Managers; Supply Chain Managers; Sustainability Specialists; Teacher Assistants; Tutors; Wind Energy Operations Managers; Wind Energy Project Managers; 37 other postsecondary teaching occupations; others.

Skills: Learning Strategies; Instructing; Speaking; Active Learning; Reading Comprehension; Writing; Active Listening; Monitoring.

Work Environment: Indoors; sitting.

Job Specialization: Computer Science Teachers, Postsecondary

Teach courses in computer science. May specialize in a field of computer science, such as the design and function of computers or operations

and research analysis. Evaluate and grade students' classwork, laboratory work, assignments, and papers. Maintain student attendance records, grades, and other required records. Prepare and deliver lectures to undergraduate and/or graduate students on topics such as programming, data structures, and software design. Prepare course materials such as syllabi, homework assignments, and handouts. Compile, administer, and grade examinations or assign this work to others. Keep abreast of developments in their field by reading current literature, talking with colleagues, and participating in professional conferences. Initiate, facilitate, and moderate classroom discussions. Plan, evaluate, and revise curricula, course content, and course materials and methods of instruction. Supervise students' laboratory work. Maintain regularly scheduled office hours to advise and assist students. Select and obtain materials and supplies such as textbooks and laboratory equipment.

Education/Training Required: Doctoral degree. **Education and Training Programs:** Computer and Information Sciences, General; Computer Programming/Programmer, General; Computer Science; Computer Systems Analysis/Analyst; Information Science/Studies. **Knowledge/Courses:** Computers and Electronics; Education and Training; Telecommunications; Mathematics; Engineering and Technology; English Language.

Personality Type: Social-Investigative-Conventional. **Career Clusters:** 05 Education and Training; 11 Information Technology. **Career Pathways:** 5.3 Teaching/Training; 11.1 Network Systems; 11.2 Information Support Services; 11.4 Programming and Software Development. **Other Jobs in These Pathways:** Adult Basic and Secondary Education and Literacy Teachers and Instructors; Architectural and Engineering Managers; Career/Technical Education Teachers, Secondary School; Chemists; Coaches and Scouts; Computer and Information Systems Managers; Computer Hardware

Engineers; Computer Operators; Elementary School Teachers, Except Special Education; Fitness Trainers and Aerobics Instructors; Graphic Designers; Instructional Coordinators; Instructional Designers and Technologists; Kindergarten Teachers, Except Special Education; Librarians; Middle School Teachers, Except Special and Career/Technical Education; Multimedia Artists and Animators; Preschool Teachers, Except Special Education; Recreation Workers; Remote Sensing Technicians; Secondary School Teachers, Except Special and Career/Technical Education; Self-Enrichment Education Teachers; Teacher Assistants; Tutors; 37 other postsecondary teaching occupations; others.

Skills: Programming; Writing; Learning Strategies; Instructing; Reading Comprehension; Active Learning; Speaking; Systems Analysis.

Work Environment: Indoors; sitting.

Job Specialization: Criminal Justice and Law Enforcement Teachers, Postsecondary

Teach courses in criminal justice, corrections, and law enforcement administration. Initiate, facilitate, and moderate classroom discussions. Keep abreast of developments in their field by reading current literature, talking with colleagues, and participating in professional conferences. Evaluate and grade students' classwork, assignments, and papers. Compile, administer, and grade examinations or assign this work to others. Prepare and deliver lectures to undergraduate or graduate students on topics such as criminal law, defensive policing, and investigation techniques. Prepare course materials such as syllabi, homework assignments, and handouts. Conduct research in a particular field of knowledge and publish findings in professional journals, books, and/or electronic media. Plan, evaluate, and revise curricula, course content, and course materials and methods of instruction. Supervise undergraduate and/or

C=Computer Systems Design, E=Educational Services, G=Government, H=Health Care, R=Repair and Maintenance, U=Utilities, *=All Fields

graduate teaching, internship, and research work. Maintain student attendance records, grades, and other required records.

Education/Training Required: Doctoral degree. **Education and Training Programs:** Corrections; Corrections Administration; Corrections and Criminal Justice, Other; Criminal Justice/Law Enforcement Administration; Criminal Justice/Police Science; Criminal Justice/Safety Studies; Criminalistics and Criminal Science; Forensic Science and Technology; Juvenile Corrections; Security and Loss Prevention Services; Teacher Education and Professional Development, Specific Subject Areas, Other. **Knowledge/Courses:** Sociology and Anthropology; Philosophy and Theology; History and Archeology; Law and Government; English Language; Education and Training.

Personality Type: Social-Investigative. **Career Clusters:** 05 Education and Training; 12 Law, Public Safety, Corrections, and Security. **Career Pathways:** 5.3 Teaching/Training; 12.1 Correction Services; 12.3 Security and Protective Services; 12.4 Law Enforcement Services. **Other Jobs in These Pathways:** Child, Family, and School Social Workers; Coaches and Scouts; Correctional Officers and Jailers; Criminal Investigators and Special Agents; Elementary School Teachers, Except Special Education; Fitness Trainers and Aerobics Instructors; Forest Firefighters; Immigration and Customs Inspectors; Instructional Coordinators; Instructional Designers and Technologists; Intelligence Analysts; Kindergarten Teachers, Except Special Education; Librarians; Lifeguards, Ski Patrol, and Other Recreational Protective Service Workers; Middle School Teachers, Except Special and Career/Technical Education; Police Patrol Officers; Preschool Teachers, Except Special Education; Recreation Workers; Secondary School Teachers, Except Special and Career/Technical Education; Security Guards; Self-Enrichment Education Teachers; Sheriffs and Deputy Sheriffs; Teacher Assistants; Tutors; 37 other postsecondary teaching occupations; others.

Skills: Writing; Learning Strategies; Speaking; Reading Comprehension; Instructing; Active Listening; Active Learning; Systems Analysis.

Work Environment: Indoors; sitting.

Job Specialization: Economics Teachers, Postsecondary

Teach courses in economics. Prepare and deliver lectures to undergraduate and/or graduate students on topics such as econometrics, price theory, and macroeconomics. Prepare course materials such as syllabi, homework assignments, and handouts. Evaluate and grade students' classwork, assignments, and papers. Compile, administer, and grade examinations or assign this work to others. Keep abreast of developments in their field by reading current literature, talking with colleagues, and participating in professional conferences. Maintain student attendance records, grades, and other required records. Initiate, facilitate, and moderate classroom discussions. Maintain regularly scheduled office hours in order to advise and assist students. Select and obtain materials and supplies such as textbooks. Plan, evaluate, and revise curricula, course content, and course materials and methods of instruction.

Education/Training Required: Doctoral degree. **Education and Training Programs:** Applied Economics; Business/Managerial Economics; Development Economics and International Development; Econometrics and Quantitative Economics; Economics, General; Economics, Other; Humanities/Humanistic Studies; International Economics; Social Science Teacher Education. **Knowledge/Courses:** Economics and Accounting; History and Archeology; Mathematics; Philosophy and Theology; Education and Training; English Language.

Personality Type: Social-Investigative. **Career Clusters:** 04 Business, Management, and Administration; 15 Science, Technology, Engineering, and Mathematics. **Career Pathways:** 4.1 Management; 15.2 Science and Mathematics. **Other Jobs in These Pathways:** Brownfield Redevelopment Specialists and Site Managers; Business Continuity Planners; Business Operations Specialists, All Other; Chief Executives; Chief Sustainability Officers; Compliance Managers; Computer and Information Systems Managers; Construction Managers; Customs Brokers; Energy Auditors; First-Line Supervisors of Office and Administrative Support Workers; General and Operations Managers; Investment Fund Managers; Loss Prevention Managers; Management Analysts; Managers, All Other; Public Relations Specialists; Regulatory Affairs Managers; Sales Managers; Security Management Specialists; Security Managers; Supply Chain Managers; Sustainability Specialists; Wind Energy Operations Managers; Wind Energy Project Managers; 37 other postsecondary teaching occupations; others.

Skills: Science; Operations Analysis; Learning Strategies; Instructing; Writing; Speaking; Programming; Mathematics.

Work Environment: Indoors; sitting.

Job Specialization: Education Teachers, Postsecondary

Teach courses pertaining to education, such as counseling, curriculum, guidance, instruction, teacher education, and teaching English as a second language. Prepare course materials such as syllabi, homework assignments, and handouts. Prepare and deliver lectures to undergraduate and/or graduate students on topics such as children's literature, learning and development, and reading instruction. Initiate, facilitate, and moderate classroom discussions. Evaluate and grade students' classwork, assignments, and papers. Plan, evaluate, and revise curricula, course content, and course materials and methods of instruction. Supervise students' fieldwork, internship, and research work. Keep abreast of developments in their field by reading current literature, talking with colleagues, and participating in professional conferences. Advise students on academic and vocational curricula and on career issues. Maintain regularly scheduled office hours to advise and assist students. Maintain student attendance records, grades, and other required records. Collaborate with colleagues to address teaching and research issues.

Education/Training Required: Doctoral degree. **Education and Training Programs:** Agricultural Teacher Education; Art Teacher Education; Biology Teacher Education; Business Teacher Education; Chemistry Teacher Education; Computer Teacher Education; Drama and Dance Teacher Education; Driver and Safety Teacher Education; Education, General; English/Language Arts Teacher Education; Family and Consumer Sciences/Home Economics Teacher Education; Foreign Language Teacher Education; French Language Teacher Education; Geography Teacher Education; German Language Teacher Education; Health Occupations Teacher Education; Health Teacher Education; History Teacher Education; Humanities; Mathematics Teacher Education; Music Teacher Education; Physical Education Teaching and Coaching; Physics Teacher Education; Reading Teacher Education; Marketing and Distribution Teacher Education; Science Teacher Education; Social Science Teacher Education; Social Studies Teacher Education; Spanish Language Teacher Education; Speech Teacher Education; Technical Teacher Education; Technology Teacher Education/Industrial Arts Teacher Education; Trade and Industrial Teacher Education; others. **Knowledge/Courses:** Therapy and Counseling; Education and Training; Sociology and Anthropology; Philosophy and Theology; Psychology; English Language.

---

*C=Computer Systems Design, E=Educational Services, G=Government, H=Health Care, R=Repair and Maintenance, U=Utilities, *=All Fields*

Personality Type: Social-Artistic-Investigative. **Career Cluster:** 05 Education and Training. **Career Pathway:** 5.3 Teaching/Training. **Other Jobs in This Pathway:** Adult Basic and Secondary Education and Literacy Teachers and Instructors; Athletes and Sports Competitors; Audio-Visual and Multimedia Collections Specialists; Career/Technical Education Teachers, Middle School; Career/Technical Education Teachers, Secondary School; Chemists; Coaches and Scouts; Dietitians and Nutritionists; Elementary School Teachers, Except Special Education; Fitness Trainers and Aerobics Instructors; Historians; Instructional Coordinators; Instructional Designers and Technologists; Interpreters and Translators; Kindergarten Teachers, Except Special Education; Librarians; Middle School Teachers, Except Special and Career/Technical Education; Physicists; Preschool Teachers, Except Special Education; Recreation Workers; Secondary School Teachers, Except Special and Career/Technical Education; Self-Enrichment Education Teachers; Teacher Assistants; Tutors; 37 other postsecondary teaching occupations.

Skills: Learning Strategies; Writing; Speaking; Active Learning; Instructing; Reading Comprehension; Science; Active Listening.

Work Environment: Indoors; sitting.

Job Specialization: Engineering Teachers, Postsecondary

Teach courses pertaining to the application of physical laws and principles of engineering for the development of machines, materials, instruments, processes, and services. Includes teachers of subjects such as chemical, civil, electrical, industrial, mechanical, mineral, and petroleum engineering. Includes both teachers primarily engaged in teaching and those who do a combination of both teaching and research. Prepare and deliver lectures to undergraduate and/or graduate students on topics such as mechanics, hydraulics, and robotics. Keep abreast of developments in their field by reading current literature, talking with colleagues, and participating in professional conferences. Supervise undergraduate and/or graduate teaching, internship, and research work. Evaluate and grade students' classwork, laboratory work, assignments, and papers. Conduct research in a particular field of knowledge and publish findings in professional journals, books, and/or electronic media. Prepare course materials such as syllabi, homework assignments, and handouts. Compile, administer, and grade examinations or assign this work to others. Write grant proposals to procure external research funding. Supervise students' laboratory work. Initiate, facilitate, and moderate class discussions. Maintain regularly scheduled office hours to advise and assist students.

Education/Training Required: Doctoral degree. **Education and Training Programs:** Aerospace, Aeronautical, and Astronautical/Space Engineering; Agricultural Engineering; Architectural Engineering; Bioengineering and Biomedical Engineering; Ceramic Sciences and Engineering; Chemical Engineering; Civil Engineering, General; Computer Engineering, General; Computer Hardware Engineering; Computer Software Engineering; Construction Engineering; Electrical and Electronics Engineering; Engineering Mechanics; Engineering Physics/Applied Physics; Engineering Science; Engineering, General; Environmental/Environmental Health Engineering; Forest Engineering; Geological/Geophysical Engineering; Geotechnical and Geoenvironmental Engineering; Industrial Engineering; Manufacturing Engineering; Materials Engineering; Mechanical Engineering; Metallurgical Engineering; Mining and Mineral Engineering; Naval Architecture and Marine Engineering; Nuclear Engineering; Ocean Engineering; Petroleum Engineering; Polymer/Plastics Engineering; Structural Engineering; Surveying Engineering; Systems Engineering; Textile Sciences and Engineering; Transportation and

Highway Engineering; Water Resources Engineering; others. **Knowledge/Courses:** Engineering and Technology; Physics; Design; Mathematics; Education and Training; Telecommunications.

Personality Type: Investigative-Realistic-Social. **Career Clusters:** 02 Architecture and Construction; 05 Education and Training; 11 Information Technology; 15 Science, Technology, Engineering, and Mathematics. **Career Pathways:** 2.1 Design/Pre-Construction; 5.3 Teaching/Training; 11.4 Programming and Software Development; 15.1 Engineering and Technology; 15.2 Science and Mathematics. **Other Jobs in These Pathways:** Architectural and Engineering Managers; Automotive Engineers; Biochemical Engineers; Biofuels/Biodiesel Technology and Product Development Managers; Civil Engineers; Coaches and Scouts; Cost Estimators; Elementary School Teachers, Except Special Education; Energy Engineers; Engineers, All Other; Fitness Trainers and Aerobics Instructors; Fuel Cell Engineers; Human Factors Engineers and Ergonomists; Industrial Engineers; Manufacturing Engineers; Mechanical Engineers; Middle School Teachers, Except Special and Career/Technical Education; Preschool Teachers, Except Special Education; Recreation Workers; Secondary School Teachers, Except Special and Career/Technical Education; Self-Enrichment Education Teachers; Teacher Assistants; Transportation Engineers; Tutors; 37 other postsecondary teaching occupations; others.

Skills: Instructing; Mathematics; Operations Analysis; Science; Programming; Writing; Speaking; Reading Comprehension.

Work Environment: Indoors; sitting.

Job Specialization: English Language and Literature Teachers, Postsecondary

Teach courses in English language and literature, including linguistics and comparative literature. Initiate, facilitate, and moderate classroom discussions. Evaluate and grade students' classwork, assignments, and papers. Prepare course materials such as syllabi, homework assignments, and handouts. Prepare and deliver lectures to undergraduate and graduate students on topics such as poetry, novel structure, and translation and adaptation. Maintain student attendance records, grades, and other required records. Plan, evaluate, and revise curricula, course content, and course materials and methods of instruction. Compile, administer, and grade examinations or assign this work to others. Maintain regularly scheduled office hours in order to advise and assist students. Keep abreast of developments in their field by reading current literature, talking with colleagues, and participating in professional conferences. Select and obtain materials and supplies such as textbooks. Advise students on academic and vocational curricula and on career issues.

Education/Training Required: Doctoral degree. **Education and Training Programs:** Comparative Literature; English Language and Literature, General; English Language and Literature/Letters, Other; Humanities/Humanistic Studies. **Knowledge/Courses:** Philosophy and Theology; History and Archeology; English Language; Education and Training; Fine Arts; Sociology and Anthropology.

Personality Type: Social-Artistic-Investigative. **Career Clusters:** 03 Arts, Audio/Video Technology, and Communications; 05 Education and Training. **Career Pathways:** 3.5 Journalism and Broadcasting; 5.3 Teaching/Training. **Other Jobs in These Pathways:** Career/Technical Education Teachers, Secondary School; Coaches and Scouts; Copy Writers; Directors—Stage, Motion Pictures, Television, and Radio; Editors; Elementary School Teachers, Except Special Education; Fitness Trainers and Aerobics Instructors; Instructional Coordinators; Instructional Designers and Technologists; Kindergarten Teachers, Except Special Education;

*C=Computer Systems Design, E=Educational Services, G=Government, H=Health Care, R=Repair and Maintenance, U=Utilities, *=All Fields*

150 Best Jobs for a Secure Future © JIST Works — 359

Librarians; Middle School Teachers, Except Special and Career/Technical Education; Photographers; Preschool Teachers, Except Special Education; Producers; Program Directors; Public Relations Specialists; Recreation Workers; Secondary School Teachers, Except Special and Career/Technical Education; Self-Enrichment Education Teachers; Talent Directors; Teacher Assistants; Technical Directors/Managers; Tutors; 37 other postsecondary teaching occupations; others.

Skills: Learning Strategies; Writing; Instructing; Reading Comprehension; Speaking; Active Listening; Monitoring; Active Learning.

Work Environment: Indoors; sitting.

Job Specialization: Environmental Science Teachers, Postsecondary

Teach courses in environmental science. Supervise undergraduate and/or graduate teaching, internship, and research work. Conduct research in a particular field of knowledge and publish findings in professional journals, books, and/or electronic media. Keep abreast of developments in their field by reading current literature, talking with colleagues, and participating in professional conferences. Evaluate and grade students' classwork, laboratory work, assignments, and papers. Write grant proposals to procure external research funding. Supervise students' laboratory work and fieldwork. Prepare course materials such as syllabi, homework assignments, and handouts. Plan, evaluate, and revise curricula, course content, and course materials and methods of instruction. Compile, administer, and grade examinations or assign this work to others. Initiate, facilitate, and moderate classroom discussions. Advise students on academic and vocational curricula and on career issues.

Education/Training Required: Doctoral degree. **Education and Training Programs:** Environmental Science; Environmental Studies; Science

Teacher Education/General Science Teacher Education. **Knowledge/Courses:** Biology; Geography; Chemistry; Education and Training; History and Archeology; Physics.

Personality Type: Social-Investigative-Artistic. **Career Clusters:** 01 Agriculture, Food, and Natural Resources; 05 Education and Training. **Career Pathways:** 1.5 Natural Resources Systems; 5.3 Teaching/Training. **Other Jobs in These Pathways:** Adult Basic and Secondary Education and Literacy Teachers and Instructors; Career/Technical Education Teachers, Secondary School; Chemists; Climate Change Analysts; Coaches and Scouts; Elementary School Teachers, Except Special Education; Engineering Technicians, Except Drafters, All Other; Environmental Restoration Planners; Environmental Scientists and Specialists, Including Health; Fitness Trainers and Aerobics Instructors; Industrial Ecologists; Industrial Truck and Tractor Operators; Instructional Coordinators; Instructional Designers and Technologists; Kindergarten Teachers, Except Special Education; Librarians; Middle School Teachers, Except Special and Career/Technical Education; Preschool Teachers, Except Special Education; Recreation Workers; Refuse and Recyclable Material Collectors; Secondary School Teachers, Except Special and Career/Technical Education; Self-Enrichment Education Teachers; Teacher Assistants; Tutors; 37 other postsecondary teaching occupations; others.

Skills: Science; Writing; Reading Comprehension; Operations Analysis; Learning Strategies; Active Learning; Instructing; Systems Evaluation.

Work Environment: Indoors; sitting.

Job Specialization: Foreign Language and Literature Teachers, Postsecondary

Teach courses in foreign (i.e., other than English) languages and literature. Evaluate and grade students' classwork, assignments, and papers.

Prepare course materials such as syllabi, homework assignments, and handouts. Initiate, facilitate, and moderate classroom discussions. Maintain student attendance records, grades, and other required records. Compile, administer, and grade examinations or assign this work to others. Plan, evaluate, and revise curricula, course content, and course materials and methods of instruction. Prepare and deliver lectures to undergraduate and graduate students on topics such as how to speak and write a foreign language and the cultural aspects of areas where a particular language is used. Maintain regularly scheduled office hours to advise and assist students. Select and obtain materials and supplies such as textbooks. Keep abreast of developments in their field by reading current literature, talking with colleagues, and participating in professional organizations and activities.

Education/Training Required: Doctoral degree. **Education and Training Programs:** Ancient Near Eastern and Biblical Languages, Literatures, and Linguistics; Ancient/Classical Greek Language and Literature; Arabic Language and Literature; Celtic Languages, Literatures, and Linguistics; Chinese Language and Literature; Classics and Classical Languages, Literatures, and Linguistics, General; East Asian Languages, Literatures, and Linguistics, Other; Filipino/Tagalog Language and Literature; Foreign Languages and Literatures, General; Foreign Languages, Literatures, and Linguistics, Other; French Language and Literature; German Language and Literature; Germanic Languages, Literatures, and Linguistics, Other; Hebrew Language and Literature; Hindi Language and Literature; Italian Language and Literature; Japanese Language and Literature; Language Interpretation and Translation; Latin Language and Literature; Linguistics; Middle/Near Eastern and Semitic Languages, Literatures, and Linguistics, Other; others. **Knowledge/Courses:** Foreign Language; Philosophy and Theology; History and Archeology;

Sociology and Anthropology; Geography; English Language.

Personality Type: Social-Artistic-Investigative. **Career Cluster:** 05 Education and Training. **Career Pathway:** 5.3 Teaching/Training. **Other Jobs in This Pathway:** Adult Basic and Secondary Education and Literacy Teachers and Instructors; Athletes and Sports Competitors; Audio-Visual and Multimedia Collections Specialists; Career/Technical Education Teachers, Middle School; Career/Technical Education Teachers, Secondary School; Chemists; Coaches and Scouts; Dietitians and Nutritionists; Elementary School Teachers, Except Special Education; Fitness Trainers and Aerobics Instructors; Historians; Instructional Coordinators; Instructional Designers and Technologists; Interpreters and Translators; Kindergarten Teachers, Except Special Education; Librarians; Middle School Teachers, Except Special and Career/Technical Education; Physicists; Preschool Teachers, Except Special Education; Recreation Workers; Secondary School Teachers, Except Special and Career/Technical Education; Self-Enrichment Education Teachers; Teacher Assistants; Tutors; 37 other postsecondary teaching occupations.

Skills: Writing; Learning Strategies; Instructing; Speaking; Reading Comprehension; Operations Analysis; Active Listening; Active Learning.

Work Environment: Indoors; sitting.

Job Specialization: Forestry and Conservation Science Teachers, Postsecondary

Teach courses in environmental and conservation science. Conduct research in a particular field of knowledge and publish findings in books, professional journals, and/or electronic media. Keep abreast of developments in their field by reading current literature, talking with colleagues, and

---

*C=Computer Systems Design, E=Educational Services, G=Government, H=Health Care, R=Repair and Maintenance, U=Utilities, *=All Fields*

participating in professional conferences. Prepare and deliver lectures to undergraduate and/or graduate students on topics such as forest resource policy, forest pathology, and mapping. Evaluate and grade students' classwork, assignments, and papers. Write grant proposals to procure external research funding. Supervise undergraduate and/or graduate teaching, internship, and research work. Plan, evaluate, and revise curricula, course content, and course materials and methods of instruction. Prepare course materials such as syllabi, homework assignments, and handouts. Compile, administer, and grade examinations or assign this work to others. Advise students on academic and vocational curricula and on career issues.

Education/Training Required: Doctoral degree. **Education and Training Program:** Science Teacher Education/General Science Teacher Education. **Knowledge/Courses:** Biology; Geography; Education and Training; Mathematics; History and Archeology; Chemistry.

Personality Type: Social-Investigative-Realistic. **Career Clusters:** 01 Agriculture, Food, and Natural Resources; 05 Education and Training. **Career Pathways:** 1.5 Natural Resources Systems; 5.3 Teaching/Training. **Other Jobs in These Pathways:** Adult Basic and Secondary Education and Literacy Teachers and Instructors; Career/Technical Education Teachers, Secondary School; Chemists; Climate Change Analysts; Coaches and Scouts; Elementary School Teachers, Except Special Education; Engineering Technicians, Except Drafters, All Other; Environmental Restoration Planners; Environmental Scientists and Specialists, Including Health; Fitness Trainers and Aerobics Instructors; Industrial Ecologists; Industrial Truck and Tractor Operators; Instructional Coordinators; Instructional Designers and Technologists; Kindergarten Teachers, Except Special Education; Librarians; Middle School Teachers, Except Special and Career/Technical Education;

Preschool Teachers, Except Special Education; Recreation Workers; Refuse and Recyclable Material Collectors; Secondary School Teachers, Except Special and Career/Technical Education; Self-Enrichment Education Teachers; Teacher Assistants; Tutors; 37 other postsecondary teaching occupations; others.

Skills: Writing; Science; Learning Strategies; Instructing; Reading Comprehension; Active Learning; Speaking; Operations Analysis.

Work Environment: Indoors; sitting.

Job Specialization: Geography Teachers, Postsecondary

Teach courses in geography. Prepare and deliver lectures to undergraduate and/or graduate students on topics such as urbanization, environmental systems, and cultural geography. Evaluate and grade students' classwork, assignments, and papers. Compile, administer, and grade examinations or assign this work to others. Initiate, facilitate, and moderate classroom discussions. Maintain student attendance records, grades, and other required records. Prepare course materials such as syllabi, homework assignments, and handouts. Keep abreast of developments in their field by reading current literature, talking with colleagues, and participating in professional conferences. Supervise undergraduate and/or graduate teaching, internship, and research work. Plan, evaluate, and revise curricula, course content, and course materials and methods of instruction. Maintain regularly scheduled office hours to advise and assist students. Supervise students' laboratory work and fieldwork.

Education/Training Required: Doctoral degree. **Education and Training Programs:** Geography; Geography Teacher Education; Humanities/Humanistic Studies. **Knowledge/Courses:** Geography; Sociology and Anthropology; History and Archeology; Philosophy and Theology; Education and Training; Communications and Media.

Personality Type: Social-Investigative. **Career Clusters:** 05 Education and Training; 15 Science, Technology, Engineering, and Mathematics. **Career Pathways:** 5.3 Teaching/Training; 15.2 Science and Mathematics. **Other Jobs in These Pathways:** Adult Basic and Secondary Education and Literacy Teachers and Instructors; Architectural and Engineering Managers; Biofuels/Biodiesel Technology and Product Development Managers; Biologists; Career/Technical Education Teachers, Secondary School; Chemists; Coaches and Scouts; Community and Social Service Specialists, All Other; Education, Training, and Library Workers, All Other; Elementary School Teachers, Except Special Education; Fitness Trainers and Aerobics Instructors; Instructional Coordinators; Instructional Designers and Technologists; Kindergarten Teachers, Except Special Education; Librarians; Medical Scientists, Except Epidemiologists; Middle School Teachers, Except Special and Career/Technical Education; Operations Research Analysts; Preschool Teachers, Except Special Education; Recreation Workers; Secondary School Teachers, Except Special and Career/Technical Education; Self-Enrichment Education Teachers; Teacher Assistants; Tutors; 37 other postsecondary teaching occupations; others.

Skills: Science; Instructing; Writing; Learning Strategies; Active Learning; Operations Analysis; Speaking; Reading Comprehension.

Work Environment: Indoors; sitting.

Job Specialization: Graduate Teaching Assistants

Assist department chairperson, faculty members, or other professional staff members in colleges or universities by performing teaching or teaching-related duties such as teaching lower-level courses, developing teaching materials, preparing and giving examinations, and grading examinations or papers. Graduate assistants must be enrolled in graduate school programs. Graduate assistants who primarily perform nonteaching duties such as laboratory research should be reported in the occupational category related to the work performed. Lead discussion sections, tutorials, and laboratory sections. Evaluate and grade examinations, assignments, and papers, and record grades. Return assignments to students in accordance with established deadlines. Schedule and maintain regular office hours to meet with students. Inform students of the procedures for completing and submitting class work such as lab reports. Prepare and proctor examinations. Notify instructors of errors or problems with assignments. Meet with supervisors to discuss students' grades, and to complete required grade-related paperwork. Copy and distribute classroom materials. Demonstrate use of laboratory equipment and enforce laboratory rules. Teach undergraduate-level courses. Complete laboratory projects prior to assigning them to students so that any needed modifications can be made. Develop teaching materials such as syllabi, visual aids, answer keys, supplementary notes, and course websites.

Education/Training Required: Bachelor's degree. **Education and Training Program:** Humanities/Humanistic Studies. **Knowledge/Courses:** Sociology and Anthropology; Education and Training; Philosophy and Theology; English Language; Communications and Media; Psychology.

Personality Type: Social-Conventional. **Career Cluster:** 05 Education and Training. **Career Pathway:** 5.3 Teaching/Training. **Other Jobs in This Pathway:** Adult Basic and Secondary Education and Literacy Teachers and Instructors; Athletes and Sports Competitors; Audio-Visual and Multimedia Collections Specialists; Career/Technical Education Teachers, Middle School; Career/Technical

---

*C=Computer Systems Design, E=Educational Services, G=Government, H=Health Care, R=Repair and Maintenance, U=Utilities, *=All Fields*

150 Best Jobs for a Secure Future © JIST Works

363

Education Teachers, Secondary School; Chemists; Coaches and Scouts; Dietitians and Nutritionists; Elementary School Teachers, Except Special Education; Fitness Trainers and Aerobics Instructors; Historians; Instructional Coordinators; Instructional Designers and Technologists; Interpreters and Translators; Kindergarten Teachers, Except Special Education; Librarians; Middle School Teachers, Except Special and Career/Technical Education; Physicists; Preschool Teachers, Except Special Education; Recreation Workers; Secondary School Teachers, Except Special and Career/Technical Education; Self-Enrichment Education Teachers; Teacher Assistants; Tutors; 37 other postsecondary teaching occupations.

Skills: Instructing; Reading Comprehension; Service Orientation; Active Listening; Writing; Learning Strategies; Speaking; Operations Analysis.

Work Environment: Indoors; sitting.

Job Specialization: Health Specialties Teachers, Postsecondary

Teach courses in health specialties, such as veterinary medicine, dentistry, pharmacy, therapy, laboratory technology, and public health. Initiate, facilitate, and moderate classroom discussions. Keep abreast of developments in their field by reading current literature, talking with colleagues, and participating in professional conferences. Compile, administer, and grade examinations or assign this work to others. Evaluate and grade students' classwork, assignments, and papers. Prepare course materials such as syllabi, homework assignments, and handouts. Prepare and deliver lectures to undergraduate or graduate students on topics such as public health, stress management, and worksite health promotion. Plan, evaluate, and revise curricula, course content, and course materials and methods of instruction. Supervise undergraduate or graduate teaching, internship, and research work. Conduct research in a particular field of knowledge and publish findings in professional journals, books, or electronic media. Collaborate with colleagues to address teaching and research issues. Supervise laboratory sessions.

Education/Training Required: Doctoral degree. **Education and Training Programs:** Art Therapy; Asian Bodywork Therapy; Audiology and Speech-Language Pathology; Biostatistics; Blood Bank Technology Specialist Training; Cardiovascular Technology; Chiropractic; Clinical Laboratory Science/Medical Technology; Clinical Laboratory Assistant Training; Clinical Laboratory Technician; Cytotechnology; Dance Therapy; Dental Assisting; Dental Hygiene; Dental Laboratory Technology; Dentistry; Diagnostic Medical Sonography and Ultrasound Technician Training; Electrocardiograph Technology; Emergency Medical Technology; Environmental Health; Medical Radiologic Technology; Music Therapy; Nuclear Medical Technology; Occupational Health and Industrial Hygiene; Occupational Therapist Assistant Training; Occupational Therapy; Orthotist/Prosthetist; Pharmacy; Pharmacy Technician Training; Physical Therapy Assistant Training; Physical Therapy; Physician Assistant Training; Respiratory Care Therapy; Speech-Language Pathology; Surgical Technology; Therapeutic Recreation/Recreational Therapy; Veterinary Medicine; Veterinary Clinical Sciences, General; Veterinary Technology; Vocational Rehabilitation Counseling; others. **Knowledge/Courses:** Biology; Medicine and Dentistry; Education and Training; Therapy and Counseling; Sociology and Anthropology; Psychology.

Personality Type: Social-Investigative. **Career Clusters:** 05 Education and Training; 08 Health Science; 15 Science, Technology, Engineering, and Mathematics. **Career Pathways:** 5.3 Teaching/Training; 8.1 Therapeutic Services; 8.2 Diagnostics Services; 8.3 Health Informatics; 8.5 Biotechnology Research and Development; 15.2 Science and Mathematics. **Other Jobs in These Pathways:**

Coaches and Scouts; Dental Assistants; Elementary School Teachers, Except Special Education; Executive Secretaries and Executive Administrative Assistants; First-Line Supervisors of Office and Administrative Support Workers; Fitness Trainers and Aerobics Instructors; Home Health Aides; Licensed Practical and Licensed Vocational Nurses; Medical and Health Services Managers; Medical Assistants; Medical Secretaries; Middle School Teachers, Except Special and Career/Technical Education; Pharmacists; Pharmacy Technicians; Preschool Teachers, Except Special Education; Public Relations Specialists; Radiologic Technologists; Receptionists and Information Clerks; Recreation Workers; Secondary School Teachers, Except Special and Career/Technical Education; Self-Enrichment Education Teachers; Social and Human Service Assistants; Teacher Assistants; Tutors; 37 other postsecondary teaching occupations; others.

Skills: Instructing; Learning Strategies; Reading Comprehension; Writing; Science; Active Learning; Speaking; Active Listening.

Work Environment: Indoors; sitting.

Job Specialization: History Teachers, Postsecondary

Teach courses in human history and historiography. Prepare and deliver lectures to undergraduate and/or graduate students on topics such as ancient history, postwar civilizations, and the history of third-world countries. Evaluate and grade students' classwork, assignments, and papers. Prepare course materials such as syllabi, homework assignments, and handouts. Compile, administer, and grade examinations or assign this work to others. Initiate, facilitate, and moderate classroom discussions. Keep abreast of developments in their field by reading current literature, talking with colleagues, and participating in professional conferences. Plan, evaluate, and revise curricula,

course content, and course materials and methods of instruction. Maintain student attendance records, grades, and other required records. Maintain regularly scheduled office hours to advise and assist students. Conduct research in a particular field of knowledge and publish findings in professional journals, books, or electronic media.

Education/Training Required: Doctoral degree. **Education and Training Programs:** American History (United States); Asian History; Canadian History; European History; History and Philosophy of Science and Technology; History, General; History, Other; Humanities/Humanistic Studies; Public/Applied History. **Knowledge/Courses:** History and Archeology; Philosophy and Theology; Geography; Sociology and Anthropology; Education and Training; English Language.

Personality Type: Social-Investigative-Artistic. **Career Clusters:** 05 Education and Training; 15 Science, Technology, Engineering, and Mathematics. **Career Pathways:** 5.3 Teaching/Training; 15.2 Science and Mathematics. **Other Jobs in These Pathways:** Adult Basic and Secondary Education and Literacy Teachers and Instructors; Architectural and Engineering Managers; Biofuels/Biodiesel Technology and Product Development Managers; Biologists; Career/Technical Education Teachers, Secondary School; Chemists; Coaches and Scouts; Community and Social Service Specialists, All Other; Education, Training, and Library Workers, All Other; Elementary School Teachers, Except Special Education; Fitness Trainers and Aerobics Instructors; Instructional Coordinators; Instructional Designers and Technologists; Kindergarten Teachers, Except Special Education; Librarians; Medical Scientists, Except Epidemiologists; Middle School Teachers, Except Special and Career/Technical Education; Operations Research Analysts; Preschool Teachers, Except Special Education; Recreation Workers; Secondary School Teachers, Except Special and Career/Technical Education;

*C=Computer Systems Design, E=Educational Services, G=Government, H=Health Care, R=Repair and Maintenance, U=Utilities, *=All Fields*

150 Best Jobs for a Secure Future © JIST Works

365

Self-Enrichment Education Teachers; Teacher Assistants; Tutors; 37 other postsecondary teaching occupations; others.

Skills: Learning Strategies; Writing; Speaking; Operations Analysis; Reading Comprehension; Active Learning; Instructing; Science.

Work Environment: Indoors; sitting.

Job Specialization: Home Economics Teachers, Postsecondary

Teach courses in child care, family relations, finance, nutrition, and related subjects as pertaining to home management. Evaluate and grade students' classwork, laboratory work, projects, assignments, and papers. Initiate, facilitate, and moderate classroom discussions. Prepare and deliver lectures to undergraduate or graduate students on topics such as food science, nutrition, and child care. Prepare course materials such as syllabi, homework assignments, and handouts. Keep abreast of developments in their field by reading current literature, talking with colleagues, and participating in professional conferences. Maintain student attendance records, grades, and other required records. Plan, evaluate, and revise curricula, course content, and course materials and methods of instruction. Compile, administer, and grade examinations or assign this work to others. Advise students on academic and vocational curricula and on career issues. Maintain regularly scheduled office hours to advise and assist students. Supervise undergraduate or graduate teaching, internship, and research work.

Education/Training Required: Doctoral degree. **Education and Training Programs:** Business Family and Consumer Sciences/Human Sciences; Child Care and Support Services Management; Family and Consumer Sciences/Human Sciences, General; Foodservice Systems Administration/ Management; Human Development and Family Studies, General. **Knowledge/Courses:** Sociology and Anthropology; Philosophy and Theology; Education and Training; Therapy and Counseling; Psychology; English Language.

Personality Type: Social-Investigative-Artistic. **Career Clusters:** 05 Education and Training; 08 Health Science; 10 Human Services. **Career Pathways:** 5.3 Teaching/Training; 8.4 Support Services; 10.1 Early Childhood Development and Services; 10.3 Family and Community Services; 10.5 Consumer Services Career. **Other Jobs in These Pathways:** Chief Executives; Child, Family, and School Social Workers; Childcare Workers; Coaches and Scouts; Cooks, Institution and Cafeteria; Elementary School Teachers, Except Special Education; First-Line Supervisors of Food Preparation and Serving Workers; First-Line Supervisors of Retail Sales Workers; Fitness Trainers and Aerobics Instructors; Kindergarten Teachers, Except Special Education; Librarians; Managers, All Other; Middle School Teachers, Except Special and Career/Technical Education; Nannies; Personal Care Aides; Preschool Teachers, Except Special Education; Public Relations Specialists; Recreation Workers; Sales Managers; Secondary School Teachers, Except Special and Career/ Technical Education; Self-Enrichment Education Teachers; Supply Chain Managers; Teacher Assistants; Tutors; 37 other postsecondary teaching occupations; others.

Skills: Learning Strategies; Instructing; Writing; Active Learning; Speaking; Reading Comprehension; Active Listening; Systems Evaluation.

Work Environment: Indoors; sitting.

Job Specialization: Law Teachers, Postsecondary

Teach courses in law. Evaluate and grade students' classwork, assignments, papers, and oral presentations. Compile, administer, and grade examinations or assign this work to others. Prepare and deliver lectures to undergraduate or graduate students on topics such as civil procedure, contracts, and torts. Initiate, facilitate, and moderate classroom discussions. Prepare course materials such as syllabi, homework assignments, and handouts. Keep abreast of developments in their field by reading current literature, talking with colleagues, and participating in professional conferences. Plan, evaluate, and revise curricula, course content, and course materials and methods of instruction. Maintain regularly scheduled office hours to advise and assist students. Conduct research in a particular field of knowledge and publish findings in professional journals, books, or electronic media. Advise students on academic and vocational curricula and on career issues.

Education/Training Required: First professional degree. **Education and Training Program:** Law (LL.B., J.D.). **Knowledge/Courses:** Law and Government; English Language; History and Archeology; Philosophy and Theology; Education and Training; Communications and Media.

Personality Type: Social-Investigative-Enterprising. **Career Clusters:** 05 Education and Training; 12 Law, Public Safety, Corrections, and Security. **Career Pathways:** 5.3 Teaching/Training; 12.5 Legal Services. **Other Jobs in These Pathways:** Adult Basic and Secondary Education and Literacy Teachers and Instructors; Career/Technical Education Teachers, Secondary School; Chemists; Coaches and Scouts; Dietitians and Nutritionists; Elementary School Teachers, Except Special Education; Fitness Trainers and Aerobics Instructors; Instructional Coordinators; Instructional Designers and Technologists; Interpreters and Translators; Kindergarten Teachers, Except Special Education; Lawyers; Legal Secretaries; Legal Support Workers, All Other; Librarians; Middle School Teachers, Except Special and Career/Technical Education; Paralegals and Legal Assistants; Preschool Teachers, Except Special Education; Recreation Workers; Secondary School

Teachers, Except Special and Career/Technical Education; Self-Enrichment Education Teachers; Teacher Assistants; Title Examiners, Abstractors, and Searchers; Tutors; 37 other postsecondary teaching occupations; others.

Skills: Reading Comprehension; Speaking; Writing; Active Learning; Instructing; Learning Strategies; Critical Thinking; Active Listening.

Work Environment: Indoors; sitting.

Job Specialization: Library Science Teachers, Postsecondary

Teach courses in library science. Prepare course materials such as syllabi, homework assignments, and handouts. Prepare and deliver lectures to undergraduate or graduate students on topics such as collection development, archival methods, and indexing and abstracting. Evaluate and grade students' classwork, assignments, and papers. Keep abreast of developments in their field by reading current literature, talking with colleagues, and participating in professional conferences. Initiate, facilitate, and moderate classroom discussions. Plan, evaluate, and revise curricula, course content, and course materials and methods of instruction. Conduct research in a particular field of knowledge and publish findings in professional journals, books, and/or electronic media. Maintain student attendance records, grades, and other required records. Collaborate with colleagues to address teaching and research issues. Advise students on academic and vocational curricula and on career issues.

Education/Training Required: Doctoral degree. **Education and Training Programs:** Humanities/Humanistic Studies; Library and Information Science; Teacher Education and Professional Development, Specific Subject Areas, Other. **Knowledge/Courses:** Education and Training; Sociology and Anthropology; Communications and Media;

C=Computer Systems Design, E=Educational Services, G=Government, H=Health Care, R=Repair and Maintenance, U=Utilities, *=All Fields

150 Best Jobs for a Secure Future © JIST Works   367

English Language; History and Archeology; Philosophy and Theology.

Personality Type: Social-Investigative-Conventional. **Career Cluster:** 05 Education and Training. **Career Pathways:** 5.2 Professional Support Services; 5.3 Teaching/Training. **Other Jobs in These Pathways:** Adult Basic and Secondary Education and Literacy Teachers and Instructors; Athletes and Sports Competitors; Career/Technical Education Teachers, Middle School; Career/Technical Education Teachers, Secondary School; Chemists; Coaches and Scouts; Dietitians and Nutritionists; Educational, Guidance, School, and Vocational Counselors; Elementary School Teachers, Except Special Education; Fitness Trainers and Aerobics Instructors; Instructional Coordinators; Instructional Designers and Technologists; Interpreters and Translators; Kindergarten Teachers, Except Special Education; Librarians; Library Assistants, Clerical; Library Technicians; Middle School Teachers, Except Special and Career/Technical Education; Preschool Teachers, Except Special Education; Recreation Workers; Secondary School Teachers, Except Special and Career/Technical Education; Self-Enrichment Education Teachers; Teacher Assistants; Tutors; 37 other postsecondary teaching occupations; others.

Skills: Writing; Instructing; Learning Strategies; Systems Analysis; Speaking; Reading Comprehension; Active Listening; Active Learning.

Work Environment: Indoors; sitting.

Job Specialization: Mathematical Science Teachers, Postsecondary

Teach courses pertaining to mathematical concepts, statistics, and actuarial science and to the application of original and standardized mathematical techniques in solving specific problems and situations. Evaluate and grade students' classwork, assignments, and papers. Compile, administer, and grade examinations or assign this work to others. Prepare and deliver lectures to undergraduate and/or graduate students on topics such as linear algebra, differential equations, and discrete mathematics. Prepare course materials such as syllabi, homework assignments, and handouts. Maintain student attendance records, grades, and other required records. Maintain regularly scheduled office hours to advise and assist students. Plan, evaluate, and revise curricula, course content, and course materials and methods of instruction. Initiate, facilitate, and moderate classroom discussions. Select and obtain materials and supplies such as textbooks. Keep abreast of developments in their field by reading current literature, talking with colleagues, and participating in professional conferences. Advise students on academic and vocational curricula and on career issues.

Education/Training Required: Doctoral degree. **Education and Training Programs:** Algebra and Number Theory; Analysis and Functional Analysis; Applied Mathematics, General; Business Statistics; Geometry/Geometric Analysis; Logic; Mathematical Statistics and Probability; Mathematics and Statistics, Other; Mathematics, General; Mathematics, Other; Statistics, General; Topology and Foundations. **Knowledge/Courses:** Mathematics; Education and Training; Physics; Computers and Electronics; English Language; Communications and Media.

Personality Type: Social-Investigative-Artistic. **Career Cluster:** 15 Science, Technology, Engineering, and Mathematics. **Career Pathway:** 15.2 Science and Mathematics. **Other Jobs in This Pathway:** Architectural and Engineering Managers; Biochemists and Biophysicists; Biofuels/Biodiesel Technology and Product Development Managers; Bioinformatics Scientists; Biological Scientists, All Other; Biologists; Biostatisticians; Chemists; Clinical Data Managers; Clinical Research

Coordinators; Community and Social Service Specialists, All Other; Dietitians and Nutritionists; Education, Training, and Library Workers, All Other; Geneticists; Geoscientists, Except Hydrologists and Geographers; Medical Scientists, Except Epidemiologists; Molecular and Cellular Biologists; Natural Sciences Managers; Operations Research Analysts; Physical Scientists, All Other; Social Scientists and Related Workers, All Other; Statisticians; Survey Researchers; Transportation Planners; Water Resource Specialists; 37 other postsecondary teaching occupations; others.

Skills: Mathematics; Writing; Learning Strategies; Instructing; Reading Comprehension; Systems Evaluation; Active Learning; Speaking.

Work Environment: Indoors; sitting; standing.

Job Specialization: Nursing Instructors and Teachers, Postsecondary

Demonstrate and teach patient care in classroom and clinical units to nursing students. Includes both teachers primarily engaged in teaching and those who do a combination of both teaching and research. Initiate, facilitate, and moderate classroom discussions. Prepare and deliver lectures to undergraduate or graduate students on topics such as pharmacology, mental health nursing, and community health-care practices. Keep abreast of developments in their field by reading current literature, talking with colleagues, and participating in professional conferences. Prepare course materials such as syllabi, homework assignments, and handouts. Supervise students' laboratory and clinical work. Evaluate and grade students' classwork, laboratory and clinic work, assignments, and papers. Collaborate with colleagues to address teaching and research issues. Plan, evaluate, and revise curricula, course content, and course materials and methods of instruction. Assess clinical education needs and patient and client teaching needs, utilizing a variety of methods. Compile, administer, and grade examinations or assign this work to others.

Education/Training Required: Doctoral degree. **Education and Training Program:** Pre-Nursing Studies. **Knowledge/Courses:** Therapy and Counseling; Sociology and Anthropology; Biology; Medicine and Dentistry; Philosophy and Theology; Psychology.

Personality Type: Social-Investigative. **Career Clusters:** 05 Education and Training; 08 Health Science. **Career Pathways:** 5.3 Teaching/Training; 8.1 Therapeutic Services. **Other Jobs in These Pathways:** Coaches and Scouts; Dental Assistants; Dental Hygienists; Elementary School Teachers, Except Special Education; Fitness Trainers and Aerobics Instructors; Healthcare Support Workers, All Other; Home Health Aides; Kindergarten Teachers, Except Special Education; Librarians; Licensed Practical and Licensed Vocational Nurses; Medical and Health Services Managers; Medical Secretaries; Middle School Teachers, Except Special and Career/Technical Education; Pharmacists; Pharmacy Technicians; Preschool Teachers, Except Special Education; Radiologic Technologists; Recreation Workers; Secondary School Teachers, Except Special and Career/Technical Education; Self-Enrichment Education Teachers; Social and Human Service Assistants; Speech-Language Pathology Assistants; Teacher Assistants; Tutors; 37 other postsecondary teaching occupations; others.

Skills: Instructing; Science; Writing; Learning Strategies; Speaking; Reading Comprehension; Active Learning; Active Listening.

Work Environment: Indoors; sitting; exposed to disease or infections.

Job Specialization: Philosophy and Religion Teachers, Postsecondary

Teach courses in philosophy, religion, and theology. Evaluate and grade students' classwork,

*C=Computer Systems Design, E=Educational Services, G=Government, H=Health Care, R=Repair and Maintenance, U=Utilities, *=All Fields*

150 Best Jobs for a Secure Future © JIST Works

369

assignments, and papers. Initiate, facilitate, and moderate classroom discussions. Prepare and deliver lectures to undergraduate and graduate students on topics such as ethics, logic, and contemporary religious thought. Prepare course materials such as syllabi, homework assignments, and handouts. Compile, administer, and grade examinations or assign this work to others. Keep abreast of developments in their field by reading current literature, talking with colleagues, and participating in professional conferences. Maintain student attendance records, grades, and other required records. Plan, evaluate, and revise curricula, course content, and course materials and methods of instruction. Maintain regularly scheduled office hours to advise and assist students. Select and obtain materials and supplies such as textbooks. Advise students on academic and vocational curricula and on career issues.

Education/Training Required: Doctoral degree. **Education and Training Programs:** Bible/Biblical Studies; Buddhist Studies; Christian Studies; Divinity/Ministry (BD, MDiv.); Ethics; Hindu Studies; Humanities/Humanistic Studies; Missions/Missionary Studies and Missiology; Pastoral Counseling and Specialized Ministries, Other; Pastoral Studies/Counseling; Philosophy; Philosophy and Religious Studies, Other; Philosophy, Other; Pre-Theology/Pre-Ministerial Studies; Rabbinical Studies (M.H.L./Rav); Religion/Religious Studies; Religious Education; Religious/Sacred Music; Talmudic Studies; Theological and Ministerial Studies, Other; Theology and Religious Vocations, Other; Theology/Theological Studies. **Knowledge/Courses:** Philosophy and Theology; History and Archeology; Sociology and Anthropology; Foreign Language; English Language; Education and Training.

Personality Type: Social-Artistic-Investigative. **Career Clusters:** 05 Education and Training; 10 Human Services. **Career Pathways:** 5.3 Teaching/Training; 10.2 Counseling and Mental Health Services. **Other Jobs in These Pathways:** Adult Basic and Secondary Education and Literacy Teachers and Instructors; Career/Technical Education Teachers, Secondary School; Clergy; Clinical Psychologists; Coaches and Scouts; Counseling Psychologists; Elementary School Teachers, Except Special Education; Fitness Trainers and Aerobics Instructors; Healthcare Social Workers; Instructional Coordinators; Instructional Designers and Technologists; Kindergarten Teachers, Except Special Education; Librarians; Mental Health and Substance Abuse Social Workers; Mental Health Counselors; Middle School Teachers, Except Special and Career/Technical Education; Preschool Teachers, Except Special Education; Recreation Workers; School Psychologists; Secondary School Teachers, Except Special and Career/Technical Education; Self-Enrichment Education Teachers; Substance Abuse and Behavioral Disorder Counselors; Teacher Assistants; Tutors; 37 other postsecondary teaching occupations; others.

Skills: Writing; Operations Analysis; Reading Comprehension; Learning Strategies; Speaking; Science; Critical Thinking; Active Listening.

Work Environment: Indoors; sitting.

Job Specialization: Physics Teachers, Postsecondary

Teach courses pertaining to the laws of matter and energy. Includes both teachers primarily engaged in teaching and those who do a combination of both teaching and research. Evaluate and grade students' classwork, laboratory work, assignments, and papers. Prepare and deliver lectures to undergraduate and/or graduate students on topics such as quantum mechanics, particle physics, and optics. Compile, administer, and grade examinations or assign this work to others. Maintain student attendance records, grades, and other required records. Supervise students' laboratory work. Prepare course materials such as syllabi, homework assignments, and handouts. Maintain regularly scheduled office hours to advise and assist students. Supervise undergraduate and/or graduate teaching, internship, and research work. Keep abreast of developments in their field by reading current literature, talking with colleagues, and participating in professional conferences. Plan, evaluate, and revise curricula, course content, and course materials and methods of instruction. Initiate, facilitate, and moderate classroom discussions.

Education/Training Required: Doctoral degree. **Education and Training Programs:** Acoustics; Atomic/Molecular Physics; Condensed Matter and Materials Physics; Elementary Particle Physics; Nuclear Physics; Optics/Optical Sciences; Physics, General; Physics, Other; Plasma and High-Temperature Physics; Theoretical and Mathematical Physics. **Knowledge/Courses:** Physics; Mathematics; Chemistry; Engineering and Technology; Education and Training; Computers and Electronics.

Personality Type: Social-Investigative. **Career Cluster:** 15 Science, Technology, Engineering, and Mathematics. **Career Pathway:** 15.2 Science and Mathematics. **Other Jobs in This Pathway:** Architectural and Engineering Managers; Biochemists and Biophysicists; Biofuels/Biodiesel Technology and Product Development Managers; Bioinformatics Scientists; Biological Scientists, All Other; Biologists; Biostatisticians; Chemists; Clinical Data Managers; Clinical Research Coordinators; Community and Social Service Specialists, All Other; Dietitians and Nutritionists; Education, Training, and Library Workers, All Other; Geneticists; Geoscientists, Except Hydrologists and Geographers; Medical Scientists, Except Epidemiologists; Molecular and Cellular Biologists; Natural Sciences Managers; Operations Research Analysts; Physical Scientists, All Other; Social Scientists and Related Workers, All Other; Statisticians; Survey Researchers; Transportation Planners; Water Resource Specialists; 37 other postsecondary teaching occupations; others.

Skills: Science; Writing; Reading Comprehension; Speaking; Operations Analysis; Learning Strategies; Instructing; Active Listening.

Work Environment: Indoors; sitting.

Job Specialization: Political Science Teachers, Postsecondary

Teach courses in political science, international affairs, and international relations. Initiate, facilitate, and moderate classroom discussions. Prepare and deliver lectures to undergraduate or graduate students on topics such as classical political thought, international relations, and democracy and citizenship. Evaluate and grade students' classwork, assignments, and papers. Compile, administer, and grade examinations or assign this work to others. Prepare course materials such as syllabi, homework assignments, and handouts. Keep abreast of developments in their field by reading current literature, talking with colleagues, and participating in professional conferences. Plan, evaluate, and revise curricula, course content, and course materials and methods of instruction. Maintain student attendance records, grades, and other required records. Maintain regularly scheduled office hours in order to advise and assist students. Advise students on academic and vocational curricula and on career issues. Select and obtain materials and supplies such as textbooks.

Education/Training Required: Doctoral degree. **Education and Training Programs:** American Government and Politics (United States); Humanities/Humanistic Studies; International Relations and Affairs; Political Science and Government, General; Political Science and Government, Other; Social Science Teacher Education. **Knowledge/Courses:** History and Archeology; Philosophy and Theology; Sociology

C=Computer Systems Design, E=Educational Services, G=Government, H=Health Care, R=Repair and Maintenance, U=Utilities, *=All Fields

150 Best Jobs for a Secure Future © *JIST Works* — 371

and Anthropology; Geography; Law and Government; English Language.

Personality Type: Social-Enterprising-Artistic. **Career Clusters:** 05 Education and Training; 07 Government and Public Administration; 15 Science, Technology, Engineering, and Mathematics. **Career Pathways:** 5.3 Teaching/Training; 7.1 Governance; 7.4 Planning; 15.2 Science and Mathematics. **Other Jobs in These Pathways:** Administrative Services Managers; Architectural and Engineering Managers; Biofuels/Biodiesel Technology and Product Development Managers; Chief Executives; Chief Sustainability Officers; Coaches and Scouts; Compliance Managers; Elementary School Teachers, Except Special Education; Fitness Trainers and Aerobics Instructors; General and Operations Managers; Instructional Coordinators; Instructional Designers and Technologists; Kindergarten Teachers, Except Special Education; Librarians; Managers, All Other; Middle School Teachers, Except Special and Career/Technical Education; Preschool Teachers, Except Special Education; Recreation Workers; Regulatory Affairs Managers; Secondary School Teachers, Except Special and Career/Technical Education; Self-Enrichment Education Teachers; Social and Community Service Managers; Teacher Assistants; Tutors; 37 other postsecondary teaching occupations; others.

Skills: Science; Instructing; Writing; Speaking; Operations Analysis; Active Learning; Reading Comprehension; Learning Strategies.

Work Environment: Indoors; sitting.

Job Specialization: Postsecondary Teachers, All Other

This occupation includes all postsecondary teachers not listed separately. No task data available.

Education/Training Required: Doctoral degree.

Education and Training Program: Education, Other. **Knowledge/Courses:** No data available.

Personality Type: No data available. **Career Clusters:** 03 Arts, Audio/Video Technology, and Communications; 05 Education and Training. **Career Pathways:** 3.5 Journalism and Broadcasting; 5.2 Professional Support Services; 5.3 Teaching/Training. **Other Jobs in These Pathways:** Career/Technical Education Teachers, Secondary School; Coaches and Scouts; Copy Writers; Directors—Stage, Motion Pictures, Television, and Radio; Editors; Educational, Guidance, School, and Vocational Counselors; Elementary School Teachers, Except Special Education; Fitness Trainers and Aerobics Instructors; Instructional Coordinators; Instructional Designers and Technologists; Kindergarten Teachers, Except Special Education; Librarians; Library Assistants, Clerical; Library Technicians; Middle School Teachers, Except Special and Career/Technical Education; Photographers; Preschool Teachers, Except Special Education; Producers; Public Relations Specialists; Recreation Workers; Secondary School Teachers, Except Special and Career/Technical Education; Self-Enrichment Education Teachers; Teacher Assistants; Tutors; 37 other postsecondary teaching occupations; others.

Skills: No data available.

Work Environment: No data available.

Job Specialization: Psychology Teachers, Postsecondary

Teach courses in psychology, such as child, clinical, and developmental psychology and psychological counseling. Prepare and deliver lectures to undergraduate and/or graduate students on topics such as abnormal psychology, cognitive processes, and work motivation. Evaluate and grade students' classwork, laboratory work, assignments, and papers. Initiate, facilitate, and moderate classroom discussions. Compile, administer, and grade examinations or assign this work to others. Keep abreast of developments in their field by reading current literature, talking with colleagues, and participating in professional conferences. Prepare course materials such as syllabi, homework assignments, and handouts. Plan, evaluate, and revise curricula, course content, and course materials and methods of instruction. Maintain student attendance records, grades, and other required records. Supervise undergraduate and/or graduate teaching, internship, and research work. Maintain regularly scheduled office hours to advise and assist students.

Education/Training Required: Doctoral degree. **Education and Training Programs:** Humanities/Humanistic Studies; Marriage and Family Therapy/Counseling; Psychology Teacher Education; Psychology, General; Psychology, Other; Social Science Teacher Education. **Knowledge/Courses:** Therapy and Counseling; Psychology; Sociology and Anthropology; Philosophy and Theology; Education and Training; English Language.

Personality Type: Social-Investigative-Artistic. **Career Clusters:** 05 Education and Training; 08 Health Science; 10 Human Services; 12 Law, Public Safety, Corrections, and Security. **Career Pathways:** 5.3 Teaching/Training; 8.1 Therapeutic Services; 10.2 Counseling and Mental Health Services; 12.1 Correction Services. **Other Jobs in These Pathways:** Child, Family, and School Social Workers; Clergy; Coaches and Scouts; Dental Assistants; Elementary School Teachers, Except Special Education; Fitness Trainers and Aerobics Instructors; Healthcare Support Workers, All Other; Home Health Aides; Licensed Practical and Licensed Vocational Nurses; Medical and Health Services Managers; Medical Secretaries; Middle School Teachers, Except Special and Career/Technical Education; Pharmacists; Pharmacy Technicians; Preschool Teachers, Except Special

Education; Radiologic Technologists; Recreation Workers; Secondary School Teachers, Except Special and Career/Technical Education; Security Guards; Self-Enrichment Education Teachers; Social and Human Service Assistants; Speech-Language Pathology Assistants; Teacher Assistants; Tutors; 37 other postsecondary teaching occupations; others.

Skills: Science; Learning Strategies; Instructing; Writing; Operations Analysis; Reading Comprehension; Active Learning; Speaking.

Work Environment: Indoors; sitting.

Job Specialization: Recreation and Fitness Studies Teachers, Postsecondary

Teach courses pertaining to recreation, leisure, and fitness studies, including exercise physiology and facilities management. Evaluate and grade students' classwork, assignments, and papers. Maintain student attendance records, grades, and other required records. Prepare and deliver lectures to undergraduate and graduate students on topics such as anatomy, therapeutic recreation, and conditioning theory. Prepare course materials such as syllabi, homework assignments, and handouts. Maintain regularly scheduled office hours to advise and assist students. Compile, administer, and grade examinations or assign this work to others. Plan, evaluate, and revise curricula, course content, and course materials and methods of instruction. Initiate, facilitate, and moderate classroom discussions. Keep abreast of developments in their field by reading current literature, talking with colleagues, and participating in professional conferences. Advise students on academic and vocational curricula and on career issues. Participate in student recruitment, registration, and placement activities.

Education/Training Required: Doctoral degree. **Education and Training Programs:** Health and Physical Education, General; Parks, Recreation,

*C=Computer Systems Design, E=Educational Services, G=Government, H=Health Care, R=Repair and Maintenance, U=Utilities, *=All Fields*

and Leisure Studies; Sport and Fitness Administration/Management. **Knowledge/Courses:** Education and Training; Philosophy and Theology; Therapy and Counseling; Psychology; Medicine and Dentistry; Sociology and Anthropology.

Personality Type: Social. **Career Clusters:** 01 Agriculture, Food, and Natural Resources; 05 Education and Training. **Career Pathways:** 1.5 Natural Resources Systems; 5.1 Administration and Administrative Support; 5.3 Teaching/Training. **Other Jobs in These Pathways:** Adult Basic and Secondary Education and Literacy Teachers and Instructors; Career/Technical Education Teachers, Secondary School; Climate Change Analysts; Coaches and Scouts; Education Administrators, Elementary and Secondary School; Education Administrators, Postsecondary; Elementary School Teachers, Except Special Education; Environmental Restoration Planners; Environmental Scientists and Specialists, Including Health; Fitness Trainers and Aerobics Instructors; Industrial Ecologists; Industrial Truck and Tractor Operators; Instructional Coordinators; Instructional Designers and Technologists; Kindergarten Teachers, Except Special Education; Librarians; Middle School Teachers, Except Special and Career/Technical Education; Preschool Teachers, Except Special Education; Recreation Workers; Refuse and Recyclable Material Collectors; Secondary School Teachers, Except Special and Career/Technical Education; Self-Enrichment Education Teachers; Teacher Assistants; Tutors; 37 other postsecondary teaching occupations; others.

Skills: Learning Strategies; Operations Analysis; Active Learning; Instructing; Science; Speaking; Active Listening; Writing.

Work Environment: More often indoors than outdoors; standing.

Job Specialization: Social Sciences Teachers, Postsecondary, All Other

This occupation includes all postsecondary social sciences teachers not listed separately. No task data available.

Education/Training Required: Doctoral degree. **Education and Training Program:** Classics and Classical Languages, Literatures, and Linguistics, General. **Knowledge/Courses:** No data available.

Personality Type: No data available. **Career Cluster:** 15 Science, Technology, Engineering, and Mathematics. **Career Pathway:** 15.2 Science and Mathematics. **Other Jobs in This Pathway:** Architectural and Engineering Managers; Biochemists and Biophysicists; Biofuels/Biodiesel Technology and Product Development Managers; Bioinformatics Scientists; Biological Scientists, All Other; Biologists; Biostatisticians; Chemists; Clinical Data Managers; Clinical Research Coordinators; Community and Social Service Specialists, All Other; Dietitians and Nutritionists; Education, Training, and Library Workers, All Other; Geneticists; Geoscientists, Except Hydrologists and Geographers; Medical Scientists, Except Epidemiologists; Molecular and Cellular Biologists; Natural Sciences Managers; Operations Research Analysts; Physical Scientists, All Other; Social Scientists and Related Workers, All Other; Statisticians; Survey Researchers; Transportation Planners; Water Resource Specialists; 37 other postsecondary teaching occupations; others.

Skills: No data available.

Work Environment: No data available.

Job Specialization: Social Work Teachers, Postsecondary

Teach courses in social work. Initiate, facilitate, and moderate classroom discussions. Evaluate and grade students' classwork, assignments, and papers. Prepare and deliver lectures to undergraduate or graduate students on topics such as family behavior, child and adolescent mental health, and social intervention evaluation. Keep abreast of developments in their field by reading current literature, talking with colleagues, and participating in professional conferences. Supervise students' laboratory work and fieldwork. Conduct research in a particular field of knowledge and publish findings in professional journals, books, or electronic media. Prepare course materials such as syllabi, homework assignments, and handouts. Maintain regularly scheduled office hours to advise and assist students. Supervise undergraduate or graduate teaching, internship, and research work. Plan, evaluate, and revise curricula, course content, and course materials and methods of instruction.

Education/Training Required: Doctoral degree. **Education and Training Programs:** Clinical/Medical Social Work; Social Work; Teacher Education and Professional Development, Specific Subject Areas, Other. **Knowledge/Courses:** Therapy and Counseling; Sociology and Anthropology; Psychology; Philosophy and Theology; Education and Training; English Language.

Personality Type: Social-Investigative. **Career Clusters:** 05 Education and Training; 10 Human Services. **Career Pathways:** 5.3 Teaching/Training; 10.2 Counseling and Mental Health Services; 10.3 Family and Community Services. **Other Jobs in These Pathways:** Chief Executives; Child, Family, and School Social Workers; Childcare Workers; Clergy; Clinical Psychologists; Coaches and Scouts; Counseling Psychologists; Elementary School Teachers, Except Special Education; Fitness Trainers and Aerobics Instructors; Healthcare Social Workers; Kindergarten Teachers, Except Special Education; Librarians; Managers, All Other; Middle School Teachers, Except Special and Career/Technical Education; Nannies; Personal Care Aides; Preschool Teachers, Except

Special Education; Recreation Workers; School Psychologists; Secondary School Teachers, Except Special and Career/Technical Education; Self-Enrichment Education Teachers; Supply Chain Managers; Teacher Assistants; Tutors; 37 other postsecondary teaching occupations; others.

Skills: Instructing; Writing; Active Learning; Learning Strategies; Speaking; Reading Comprehension; Active Listening; Systems Evaluation.

Work Environment: Indoors; sitting.

Job Specialization: Sociology Teachers, Postsecondary

Teach courses in sociology. Evaluate and grade students' classwork, assignments, and papers. Prepare and deliver lectures to undergraduate and graduate students on topics such as race and ethnic relations, measurement and data collection, and workplace social relations. Initiate, facilitate, and moderate classroom discussions. Prepare course materials such as syllabi, homework assignments, and handouts. Compile, administer, and grade examinations or assign this work to others. Keep abreast of developments in their field by reading current literature, talking with colleagues, and participating in professional conferences. Maintain student attendance records, grades, and other required records. Maintain regularly scheduled office hours in order to advise and assist students. Plan, evaluate, and revise curricula, course content, and course materials and methods of instruction. Advise students on academic and vocational curricula and on career issues.

Education/Training Required: Doctoral degree. **Education and Training Programs:** Humanities/Humanistic Studies; Social Science Teacher Education; Sociology. **Knowledge/Courses:** Sociology and Anthropology; Philosophy and Theology; History and Archeology; Education and Training; English Language; Geography.

*C=Computer Systems Design, E=Educational Services, G=Government, H=Health Care, R=Repair and Maintenance, U=Utilities, *=All Fields*

Personality Type: Social-Investigative-Artistic. **Career Clusters:** 05 Education and Training; 15 Science, Technology, Engineering, and Mathematics. **Career Pathways:** 5.3 Teaching/Training; 15.2 Science and Mathematics. **Other Jobs in These Pathways:** Adult Basic and Secondary Education and Literacy Teachers and Instructors; Architectural and Engineering Managers; Biofuels/Biodiesel Technology and Product Development Managers; Biologists; Career/Technical Education Teachers, Secondary School; Chemists; Coaches and Scouts; Community and Social Service Specialists, All Other; Education, Training, and Library Workers, All Other; Elementary School Teachers, Except Special Education; Fitness Trainers and Aerobics Instructors; Instructional Coordinators; Instructional Designers and Technologists; Kindergarten Teachers, Except Special Education; Librarians; Medical Scientists, Except Epidemiologists; Middle School Teachers, Except Special and Career/Technical Education; Operations Research Analysts; Preschool Teachers, Except Special Education; Recreation Workers; Secondary School Teachers, Except Special and Career/Technical Education; Self-Enrichment Education Teachers; Teacher Assistants; Tutors; 37 other postsecondary teaching occupations; others.

Skills: Science; Learning Strategies; Writing; Instructing; Active Learning; Operations Analysis; Speaking; Reading Comprehension.

Work Environment: Indoors; sitting.

Job Specialization: Vocational Education Teachers, Postsecondary

Teach or instruct vocational or occupational subjects at the postsecondary level (but at less than the baccalaureate) to students who have graduated or left high school. Includes correspondence school instructors; industrial, commercial, and government training instructors; and adult education teachers and instructors who prepare persons to operate industrial machinery and equipment and transportation and communications equipment. Teaching may take place in public or private schools whose primary business is education or in a school associated with an organization whose primary business is other than education. Supervise and monitor students' use of tools and equipment. Observe and evaluate students' work to determine progress, provide feedback, and make suggestions for improvement. Present lectures and conduct discussions to increase students' knowledge and competence, using visual aids such as graphs, charts, videotapes, and slides. Administer oral, written, or performance tests to measure progress and to evaluate training effectiveness. Prepare reports and maintain records such as student grades, attendance rolls, and training activity details. Supervise independent or group projects, field placements, laboratory work, or other training. Determine training needs of students or workers. Provide individualized instruction and tutorial or remedial instruction. Conduct on-the-job training, classes, or training sessions to teach and demonstrate principles, techniques, procedures, and methods of designated subjects. Develop curricula and plan course content and methods of instruction.

Education/Training Required: Work experience in a related occupation. **Education and Training Programs:** Agricultural Teacher Education; Business Teacher Education; Health Occupations Teacher Education; Sales and Marketing Operations/Marketing and Distribution Teacher Education; Teacher Education and Professional Development, Specific Subject Areas, Other; Technical Teacher Education; Technology Teacher Education/Industrial Arts Teacher Education; Trade and Industrial Teacher Education. **Knowledge/Courses:** Education and Training; Therapy and

Counseling; Psychology; Computers and Electronics; Sales and Marketing; Design.

Personality Type: Social-Realistic. **Career Cluster:** 05 Education and Training. **Career Pathway:** 5.3 Teaching/Training. **Other Jobs in This Pathway:** Adult Basic and Secondary Education and Literacy Teachers and Instructors; Athletes and Sports Competitors; Audio-Visual and Multimedia Collections Specialists; Career/Technical Education Teachers, Middle School; Career/Technical Education Teachers, Secondary School; Chemists; Coaches and Scouts; Dietitians and Nutritionists; Elementary School Teachers, Except Special Education; Fitness Trainers and Aerobics Instructors; Historians; Instructional Coordinators; Instructional Designers and Technologists; Interpreters and Translators; Kindergarten Teachers, Except Special Education; Librarians; Middle School Teachers, Except Special and Career/Technical Education; Physicists; Preschool Teachers, Except Special Education; Recreation Workers; Secondary School Teachers, Except Special and Career/Technical Education; Self-Enrichment Education Teachers; Teacher Assistants; Tutors; 37 other postsecondary teaching occupations.

Skills: Instructing; Learning Strategies; Writing; Operations Analysis; Speaking; Active Learning; Monitoring; Reading Comprehension.

Work Environment: Indoors; standing; using hands.

Team Assemblers

- ❋ Annual Earnings: R $27,590, * $27,180
- ❋ Earnings Growth Potential: Low (34.0%)
- ❋ Growth: R 6.5%, * 0.0%
- ❋ Annual Job Openings: R 90, * 25,090
- ❋ Self-Employed: 1.4%

Detailed Fields with Greatest Employment: Fabricated Metal Product Manufacturing (7.7%); Miscellaneous Manufacturing (5.8%); Electrical Equipment, Appliance, and Component Manufacturing (5.4%); Computer and Electronic Product Manufacturing (5.2%); Plastics and Rubber Products Manufacturing (4.6%)

Detailed Fields with Highest Growth (Projected Growth for This Job): Educational Services, Public and Private (33.3%); Wholesale Electronic Markets and Agents and Brokers (31.0%); Social Assistance (27.2%); Professional, Scientific, and Technical Services (25.1%); Miscellaneous Manufacturing (22.9%)

Other Considerations for Job Outlook: Increased production and efficiency in manufacturing, where most of these workers are employed, should stabilize employment. Good job prospects are expected.

Work as part of a team having responsibility for assembling an entire product or component of a product. Team assemblers can perform all tasks conducted by the team in the assembly process and rotate through all or most of them rather than being assigned to a specific task on a permanent basis. May participate in making management decisions affecting the work. Team leaders who work as part of the team should be included. Rotate through all the tasks required in a particular production process. Determine work assignments and procedures. Shovel and sweep work areas. Operate heavy equipment such as forklifts. Provide assistance in the production of wiring assemblies.

Education/Training Required: Moderate-term on-the-job training. **Education and Training Program:** Precision Production, Other. **Knowledge/Courses:** Production and Processing; Mechanical.

---

*C=Computer Systems Design, E=Educational Services, G=Government, H=Health Care, R=Repair and Maintenance, U=Utilities, *=All Fields*

Personality Type: Realistic-Conventional-Enterprising. **Career Cluster:** 13 Manufacturing. **Career Pathway:** 13.1 Production. **Other Jobs in This Pathway:** Assemblers and Fabricators, All Other; Cabinetmakers and Bench Carpenters; Coating, Painting, and Spraying Machine Setters, Operators, and Tenders; Computer-Controlled Machine Tool Operators, Metal and Plastic; Cost Estimators; Cutting, Punching, and Press Machine Setters, Operators, and Tenders, Metal and Plastic; First-Line Supervisors of Mechanics, Installers, and Repairers; First-Line Supervisors of Production and Operating Workers; Geothermal Technicians; Grinding, Lapping, Polishing, and Buffing Machine Tool Setters, Operators, and Tenders, Metal and Plastic; Helpers—Production Workers; Machine Feeders and Offbearers; Machinists; Mixing and Blending Machine Setters, Operators, and Tenders; Molding, Coremaking, and Casting Machine Setters, Operators, and Tenders, Metal and Plastic; Packaging and Filling Machine Operators and Tenders; Packers and Packagers, Hand; Paper Goods Machine Setters, Operators, and Tenders; Production Workers, All Other; Recycling and Reclamation Workers; Recycling Coordinators; Sheet Metal Workers; Solderers and Brazers; Structural Metal Fabricators and Fitters; Welders, Cutters, and Welder Fitters; others.

Skills: Operation and Control; Operation Monitoring; Equipment Maintenance; Troubleshooting; Repairing; Coordination; Equipment Selection; Quality Control Analysis.

Work Environment: Indoors; standing; using hands; bending or twisting the body; repetitive motions; noise; contaminants.

Technical Writers

- Annual Earnings: C $66,860, * $63,280
- Earnings Growth Potential: High (41.3%)
- Growth: C 30.9%, * 18.2%
- Annual Job Openings: C 430, * 1,680
- Self-Employed: 2.0%

Detailed Fields with Greatest Employment: Computer and Electronic Product Manufacturing (8.4%); Administrative and Support Services (6.0%); Transportation Equipment Manufacturing (4.0%); Professional, Scientific, and Technical Services (38.9%); Machinery Manufacturing (2.9%)

Detailed Fields with Highest Growth (Projected Growth for This Job): Internet Service Providers, Web Search Portals, and Data Processing Services (63.3%); Ambulatory Health Care Services (50.0%); Support Activities for Transportation (45.5%); Waste Management and Remediation Services (45.5%); Performing Arts, Spectator Sports, and Related Industries (42.5%)

Other Considerations for Job Outlook: Fast growth is expected because of the need for technical writers to explain an increasing number of scientific and technical products. Prospects should be good, especially for workers with strong technical and communication skills. Competition will be keen for some jobs.

Write technical materials, such as equipment manuals, appendices, or operating and maintenance instructions. May assist in layout work. Organize material and complete writing assignment according to set standards regarding order, clarity, conciseness, style, and terminology. Maintain records and files of work and revisions. Edit, standardize, or make changes to material prepared by other writers or establishment personnel. Confer with customer representatives, vendors, plant executives, or publisher to establish technical specifications and to determine subject material to be developed for publication. Review published materials and recommend revisions or changes in scope, format, content, and methods of reproduction and binding. Select photographs, drawings, sketches, diagrams, and charts to illustrate material. Study drawings, specifications, mockups, and product samples to integrate and delineate technology, operating procedure, and production sequence and detail. Interview production and engineering personnel and read journals and other material to become familiar with product technologies and production methods.

Education/Training Required: Bachelor's degree. **Education and Training Programs:** Business/Corporate Communications; Speech Communication and Rhetoric. **Knowledge/Courses:** Communications and Media; Clerical Practices; English Language; Computers and Electronics; Education and Training; Engineering and Technology.

Personality Type: Artistic-Investigative-Conventional. **Career Clusters:** 03 Arts, Audio/Video Technology, and Communications; 04 Business, Management, and Administration. **Career Pathways:** 3.5 Journalism and Broadcasting; 4.5 Marketing. **Other Jobs in These Pathways:** Advertising Sales Agents; Audio and Video Equipment Technicians; Broadcast News Analysts; Broadcast Technicians; Camera Operators, Television, Video, and Motion Picture; Copy Writers; Directors—Stage, Motion Pictures, Television, and Radio; Editors; Film and Video Editors; Media and Communication Workers, All Other; Photographers; Producers; Program Directors; Public Address System and Other Announcers; Public Relations Specialists; Radio and Television Announcers; Reporters and Correspondents; Sound Engineering Technicians; Talent Directors; Technical Directors/Managers.

Skills: Writing; Reading Comprehension; Active Learning; Speaking; Critical Thinking; Operations Analysis; Complex Problem Solving; Active Listening.

Work Environment: Indoors; sitting; using hands; repetitive motions.

Telecommunications Equipment Installers and Repairers, Except Line Installers

- ❋ Annual Earnings: R $37,210, * $54,710
- ❋ Earnings Growth Potential: High (43.0%)
- ❋ Growth: R 6.7%, * –0.2%
- ❋ Annual Job Openings: R 110, * 3,560
- ❋ Self-Employed: 4.0%

Detailed Fields with Greatest Employment: Telecommunications (68.3%); Broadcasting (Except Internet) (3.5%); Repair and Maintenance (2.9%); Professional, Scientific, and Technical Services (2.7%); Merchant Wholesalers, Durable Goods (2.0%)

Detailed Fields with Highest Growth (Projected Growth for This Job): Internet Service Providers, Web Search Portals, and Data Processing Services (47.7%); Professional, Scientific, and Technical Services (42.9%); Specialty Trade Contractors (36.4%); Wholesale Electronic Markets and Agents and Brokers (29.2%); Broadcasting (Except Internet) (22.9%)

Other Considerations for Job Outlook: Telecommunications companies providing many new services, such as faster Internet connections and video on demand, are expected to result in employment growth for these workers. But better equipment will require less maintenance work, slowing employment

C=Computer Systems Design, E=Educational Services, G=Government, H=Health Care, R=Repair and Maintenance, U=Utilities, *=All Fields

150 Best Jobs for a Secure Future © JIST Works

379

growth. Prospects should be best for job seekers with computer skills and training in electronics.

Set up, rearrange, or remove switching and dialing equipment used in central offices. Service or repair telephones and other communication equipment on customers' properties. May install equipment in new locations or install wiring and telephone jacks in buildings under construction. Note differences in wire and cable colors so that work can be performed correctly. Test circuits and components of malfunctioning telecommunications equipment to isolate sources of malfunctions, using test meters, circuit diagrams, polarity probes, and other hand tools. Test repaired, newly installed, or updated equipment to ensure that it functions properly and conforms to specifications, using test equipment and observation. Drive crew trucks to and from work areas. Inspect equipment on a regular basis to ensure proper functioning. Repair or replace faulty equipment such as defective and damaged telephones, wires, switching system components, and associated equipment. Remove and remake connections to change circuit layouts, following work orders or diagrams. Demonstrate equipment to customers, explain how it is to be used, and respond to any inquiries or complaints.

Education/Training Required: Postsecondary vocational training. **Education and Training Program:** Communications Systems Installation and Repair Technology. **Knowledge/Courses:** Telecommunications; Mechanical Devices; Computers and Electronics; Engineering and Technology; Design; Public Safety and Security.

Personality Type: Realistic-Investigative-Conventional. **Career Cluster:** 03 Arts, Audio/Video Technology, and Communications. **Career Pathway:** 3.6 Telecommunications. **Other Jobs in This Pathway:** Broadcast Technicians; Communications Equipment Operators, All Other; Electronic Home Entertainment Equipment Installers and Repairers; Film and Video Editors; Media and Communication Workers, All Other; Radio Mechanics; Radio Operators; Radio, Cellular, and Tower Equipment Installers and Repairers; Sound Engineering Technicians.

Skills: Installation; Repairing; Equipment Maintenance; Troubleshooting; Equipment Selection; Quality Control Analysis; Operation and Control; Programming.

Work Environment: More often outdoors than indoors; standing; using hands; bending or twisting the body; repetitive motions; noise; very hot or cold; bright or inadequate lighting; contaminants; cramped work space; high places; hazardous conditions; hazardous equipment; minor burns, cuts, bites, or stings.

Training and Development Managers

- ❋ Annual Earnings: E $83,430, * $89,170
- ❋ Earnings Growth Potential: High (43.4%)
- ❋ Growth: E 27.3%, * 11.9%
- ❋ Annual Job Openings: E 60, * 1,010
- ❋ Self-Employed: 0.6%

Detailed Fields with Greatest Employment: Administrative and Support Services (9.6%); Professional, Scientific, and Technical Services (8.8%); Educational Services, Public and Private (8.7%); Insurance Carriers and Related Activities (6.6%); Credit Intermediation and Related Activities (6.5%)

Detailed Fields with Highest Growth (Projected Growth for This Job): Internet Service

Providers, Web Search Portals, and Data Processing Services (58.3%); Professional, Scientific, and Technical Services (50.4%); Lessors of Non-financial Intangible Assets (Except Copyrighted Works) (42.9%); Wholesale Electronic Markets and Agents and Brokers (36.4%); Educational Services, Public and Private (27.5%)

Other Considerations for Job Outlook: Efforts to recruit and retain employees, the growing importance of employee training, and new legal standards are expected to increase employment of these workers. College graduates and those with certification should have the best opportunities.

Plan, direct, or coordinate the training and development activities and staff of organizations. Conduct orientation sessions and arrange on-the-job training for new hires. Evaluate instructor performance and the effectiveness of training programs, providing recommendations for improvement. Develop testing and evaluation procedures. Conduct or arrange for ongoing technical training and personal development classes for staff members. Confer with management and conduct surveys to identify training needs based on projected production processes, changes, and other factors. Develop and organize training manuals, multimedia visual aids, and other educational materials. Plan, develop, and provide training and staff development programs, using knowledge of the effectiveness of methods such as classroom training, demonstrations, on-the-job training, meetings, conferences, and workshops. Analyze training needs to develop new training programs or modify and improve existing programs. Review and evaluate training and apprenticeship programs for compliance with government standards.

Education/Training Required: Work experience plus degree. **Education and Training Program:** Human Resources Development. **Knowledge/**

Courses: Education and Training; Personnel and Human Resources; Sociology and Anthropology; Sales and Marketing; Therapy and Counseling; English Language.

Personality Type: Enterprising-Social. **Career Clusters:** 04 Business, Management, and Administration; 05 Education and Training. **Career Pathway:** 4.3 Human Resources. **Other Jobs in This Pathway:** Human Resources Specialists.

Skills: Management of Financial Resources; Learning Strategies; Management of Personnel Resources; Instructing; Systems Evaluation; Management of Material Resources; Systems Analysis; Speaking.

Work Environment: Indoors; sitting.

Training and Development Specialists

- ❊ Annual Earnings: G $52,010, E $53,350, H $54,913, C $64,380, U $76,060, * $54,160
- ❊ Earnings Growth Potential: High (42.6%)
- ❊ Growth: U −7.9%, G 18.3%, H 25.6%, E 33.3%, C 54.3%, * 23.3%
- ❊ Annual Job Openings: U 120, C 490, E 600, G 680, H 1,400, * 10,710
- ❊ Self-Employed: 1.6%

Detailed Fields with Greatest Employment: State and Local Government (8.9%); Educational Services, Public and Private (7.7%); Administrative and Support Services (7.2%); Management of Companies and Enterprises (7.1%); Insurance Carriers and Related Activities (6.3%)

Detailed Fields with Highest Growth (Projected Growth for This Job): Internet Service

*C=Computer Systems Design, E=Educational Services, G=Government, H=Health Care, R=Repair and Maintenance, U=Utilities, *=All Fields*

Providers, Web Search Portals, and Data Processing Services (62.7%); Professional, Scientific, and Technical Services (60.4%); Lessors of Nonfinancial Intangible Assets (Except Copyrighted Works) (49.3%); Waste Management and Remediation Services (46.9%); Other Information Services (43.1%)

Other Considerations for Job Outlook: Efforts to recruit and retain employees, the growing importance of employee training, and new legal standards are expected to increase employment of these workers. College graduates and those with certification should have the best opportunities.

Conduct training and development programs for employees. Keep up with developments in area of expertise by reading current journals, books and magazine articles. Present information, using a variety of instructional techniques and formats such as role playing, simulations, team exercises, group discussions, videos, and lectures. Schedule classes based on availability of classrooms, equipment, and instructors. Organize and develop, or obtain, training procedure manuals and guides and course materials such as handouts and visual materials. Offer specific training programs to help workers maintain or improve job skills. Monitor, evaluate, and record training activities and program effectiveness. Attend meetings and seminars to obtain information for use in training programs, or to inform management of training program status. Coordinate recruitment and placement of training program participants. Evaluate training materials prepared by instructors, such as outlines, text, and handouts.

Education/Training Required: Work experience plus degree. **Education and Training Program:** Human Resources Development. **Knowledge/Courses:** Education and Training; Sociology and Anthropology; Sales and Marketing; Clerical Practices; Personnel and Human Resources; Psychology.

Personality Type: Social-Artistic-Conventional. **Career Clusters:** 04 Business, Management, and Administration; 05 Education and Training. **Career Pathway:** 4.3 Human Resources. **Other Jobs in This Pathway:** Human Resources Specialists.

Skills: Operations Analysis; Learning Strategies; Science; Instructing; Systems Evaluation; Management of Material Resources; Writing; Management of Financial Resources.

Work Environment: Indoors; sitting.

Transportation Inspectors

- ❀ Annual Earnings: R $29,390, G $63,000, * $57,640
- ❀ Earnings Growth Potential: High (46.3%)
- ❀ Growth: R 13.0%, G 18.7%, * 18.4%
- ❀ Annual Job Openings: R 50, G 340, * 1,130
- ❀ Self-Employed: 4.2%

Detailed Fields with Greatest Employment: Air Transportation (5.3%); Repair and Maintenance (4.5%); Truck Transportation (4.4%); Transportation Equipment Manufacturing (3.4%); State and Local Government (28.1%)

Detailed Fields with Highest Growth (Projected Growth for This Job): Wholesale Electronic Markets and Agents and Brokers (40.0%); Support Activities for Transportation (33.5%); Administrative and Support Services (33.3%); Warehousing and Storage (28.0%); Transit and Ground Passenger Transportation (21.4%)

Other Considerations for Job Outlook: Faster than average employment growth is projected.

Inspect equipment or goods in connection with the safe transport of cargo or people. Includes rail transport inspectors, such as freight inspectors, car inspectors, rail inspectors, and other nonprecision inspectors of other types of transportation vehicles. No task data available.

Education/Training Required: Work experience in a related occupation. **Education and Training Programs:** No related CIP programs; this job is learned through work experience in a related occupation. **Knowledge/Courses:** No data available.

Personality Type: No data available. **Career Cluster:** 16 Transportation, Distribution, and Logistics. **Career Pathway:** 16.1 Transportation Operations. **Other Jobs in This Pathway:** Airline Pilots, Copilots, and Flight Engineers; Automotive and Watercraft Service Attendants; Automotive Master Mechanics; Bus Drivers, School or Special Client; Bus Drivers, Transit and Intercity; Commercial Pilots; Crane and Tower Operators; First-Line Supervisors of Helpers, Laborers, and Material Movers, Hand; First-Line Supervisors of Transportation and Material-Moving Machine and Vehicle Operators; Freight and Cargo Inspectors; Heavy and Tractor-Trailer Truck Drivers; Laborers and Freight, Stock, and Material Movers, Hand; Light Truck or Delivery Services Drivers; Mates—Ship, Boat, and Barge; Motor Vehicle Operators, All Other; Operating Engineers and Other Construction Equipment Operators; Parking Lot Attendants; Pilots, Ship; Railroad Conductors and Yardmasters; Sailors and Marine Oilers; Ship and Boat Captains; Storage and Distribution Managers; Taxi Drivers and Chauffeurs; Transportation Managers; Transportation Workers, All Other; others.

Skills: No data available.

Work Environment: No data available.

Job Specialization: Aviation Inspectors

Inspect aircraft, maintenance procedures, air navigational aids, air traffic controls, and communications equipment to ensure conformance with federal safety regulations. Inspect work of aircraft mechanics performing maintenance, modification, or repair and overhaul of aircraft and aircraft mechanical systems to ensure adherence to standards and procedures. Start aircraft and observe gauges, meters, and other instruments to detect evidence of malfunctions. Examine aircraft access plates and doors for security. Examine landing gear, tires, and exteriors of fuselage, wings, and engines for evidence of damage or corrosion and to determine whether repairs are needed. Prepare and maintain detailed repair, inspection, investigation, and certification records and reports. Inspect new, repaired, or modified aircraft to identify damage or defects and to assess airworthiness and conformance to standards, using checklists, hand tools, and test instruments. Examine maintenance records and flight logs to determine if service and maintenance checks and overhauls were performed at prescribed intervals.

Education/Training Required: Work experience in a related occupation. **Education and Training Program:** Aircraft Powerplant Technology/Technician. **Knowledge/Courses:** Mechanical Devices; Physics; Transportation; Chemistry; Design; Law and Government.

Personality Type: Realistic-Conventional-Investigative. **Career Cluster:** 16 Transportation, Distribution, and Logistics. **Career Pathways:** 16.1 Transportation Operations; 16.5 Transportation Systems/Infrastructure Planning, Management, and Regulation. **Other Jobs in These Pathways:** Airline Pilots, Copilots, and Flight Engineers; Automotive and Watercraft Service Attendants; Automotive Master Mechanics; Bus Drivers, School

*C=Computer Systems Design, E=Educational Services, G=Government, H=Health Care, R=Repair and Maintenance, U=Utilities, *=All Fields*

150 Best Jobs for a Secure Future © JIST Works

383

or Special Client; Bus Drivers, Transit and Intercity; Commercial Pilots; Crane and Tower Operators; First-Line Supervisors of Helpers, Laborers, and Material Movers, Hand; First-Line Supervisors of Transportation and Material-Moving Machine and Vehicle Operators; Freight and Cargo Inspectors; Heavy and Tractor-Trailer Truck Drivers; Laborers and Freight, Stock, and Material Movers, Hand; Light Truck or Delivery Services Drivers; Mates—Ship, Boat, and Barge; Motor Vehicle Operators, All Other; Operating Engineers and Other Construction Equipment Operators; Parking Lot Attendants; Pilots, Ship; Railroad Conductors and Yardmasters; Sailors and Marine Oilers; Ship and Boat Captains; Storage and Distribution Managers; Taxi Drivers and Chauffeurs; Transportation Managers; Transportation Workers, All Other; others.

Skills: Science; Equipment Maintenance; Troubleshooting; Repairing; Operation and Control; Equipment Selection; Quality Control Analysis; Operation Monitoring.

Work Environment: More often indoors than outdoors; sitting; noise.

Job Specialization: Freight and Cargo Inspectors

Inspect the handling, storage, and stowing of freight and cargoes. Prepare and submit reports after completion of freight shipments. Inspect shipments to ensure that freight is securely braced and blocked. Record details about freight conditions, handling of freight, and any problems encountered. Advise crews in techniques of stowing dangerous and heavy cargo. Observe loading of freight to ensure that crews comply with procedures. Recommend remedial procedures to correct any violations found during inspections. Inspect loaded cargo, cargo lashed to decks or in storage facilities, and cargo handling devices to determine compliance with health and safety regulations and need for maintenance. Measure ships' holds and depths of fuel and water in tanks, using sounding lines and tape measures. Notify workers of any special treatment required for shipments. Direct crews to reload freight or to insert additional bracing or packing as necessary.

Education/Training Required: Work experience in a related occupation. **Education and Training Programs:** No related CIP programs; this job is learned through work experience in a related occupation. **Knowledge/Courses:** Transportation; Engineering and Technology; Public Safety and Security; Physics; Geography; Mechanical.

Personality Type: Realistic-Conventional. **Career Cluster:** 16 Transportation, Distribution, and Logistics. **Career Pathways:** 16.1 Transportation Operations; 16.5 Transportation Systems/Infrastructure Planning, Management, and Regulation. **Other Jobs in These Pathways:** Airline Pilots, Copilots, and Flight Engineers; Automotive and Watercraft Service Attendants; Automotive Master Mechanics; Bus Drivers, School or Special Client; Bus Drivers, Transit and Intercity; Commercial Pilots; Crane and Tower Operators; First-Line Supervisors of Helpers, Laborers, and Material Movers, Hand; First-Line Supervisors of Transportation and Material-Moving Machine and Vehicle Operators; Heavy and Tractor-Trailer Truck Drivers; Laborers and Freight, Stock, and Material Movers, Hand; Light Truck or Delivery Services Drivers; Mates—Ship, Boat, and Barge; Motor Vehicle Operators, All Other; Operating Engineers and Other Construction Equipment Operators; Parking Lot Attendants; Pilots, Ship; Railroad Conductors and Yardmasters; Sailors and Marine Oilers; Ship and Boat Captains; Storage and Distribution Managers; Taxi Drivers and Chauffeurs; Transportation Inspectors; Transportation Managers; Transportation Workers, All Other; others.

Skills: Operation and Control; Quality Control Analysis; Operation Monitoring; Science; Management of Personnel Resources; Troubleshooting; Writing; Judgment and Decision Making.

Work Environment: More often outdoors than indoors; standing; noise; very hot or cold; bright or inadequate lighting; contaminants; cramped work space; high places; hazardous equipment.

Job Specialization: Transportation Vehicle, Equipment and Systems Inspectors, Except Aviation

Inspect and monitor transportation equipment, vehicles, or systems to ensure compliance with regulations and safety standards. Conduct vehicle or transportation equipment tests, using diagnostic equipment. Investigate and make recommendations on carrier requests for waiver of federal standards. Prepare reports on investigations or inspections and actions taken. Issue notices and recommend corrective actions when infractions or problems are found. Investigate incidents or violations such as delays, accidents, and equipment failures. Investigate complaints regarding safety violations. Inspect repairs to transportation vehicles and equipment to ensure that repair work was performed properly. Examine transportation vehicles, equipment, or systems to detect damage, wear, or malfunction. Inspect vehicles and other equipment for evidence of abuse, damage, or mechanical malfunction. Examine carrier operating rules, employee qualification guidelines, and carrier training and testing programs for compliance with regulations or safety standards.

Education/Training Required: Work experience in a related occupation. **Education and Training Programs:** No related CIP programs; this job is learned through work experience in a related occupation. **Knowledge/Courses:** Mechanical Devices; Transportation; Public Safety and Security; Engineering and Technology; Administration and Management; Physics.

Personality Type: Realistic-Conventional-Investigative. **Career Cluster:** 16 Transportation, Distribution, and Logistics. **Career Pathways:** 16.1 Transportation Operations; 16.5 Transportation Systems/ Infrastructure Planning, Management, and Regulation. **Other Jobs in These Pathways:** Airline Pilots, Copilots, and Flight Engineers; Automotive and Watercraft Service Attendants; Automotive Master Mechanics; Bus Drivers, School or Special Client; Bus Drivers, Transit and Intercity; Commercial Pilots; Crane and Tower Operators; First-Line Supervisors of Helpers, Laborers, and Material Movers, Hand; First-Line Supervisors of Transportation and Material-Moving Machine and Vehicle Operators; Freight and Cargo Inspectors; Heavy and Tractor-Trailer Truck Drivers; Laborers and Freight, Stock, and Material Movers, Hand; Light Truck or Delivery Services Drivers; Mates—Ship, Boat, and Barge; Motor Vehicle Operators, All Other; Operating Engineers and Other Construction Equipment Operators; Parking Lot Attendants; Pilots, Ship; Railroad Conductors and Yardmasters; Sailors and Marine Oilers; Ship and Boat Captains; Storage and Distribution Managers; Taxi Drivers and Chauffeurs; Transportation Managers; Transportation Workers, All Other; others.

Skills: Equipment Maintenance; Repairing; Troubleshooting; Science; Operation and Control; Quality Control Analysis; Operation Monitoring; Equipment Selection.

*C=Computer Systems Design, E=Educational Services, G=Government, H=Health Care, R=Repair and Maintenance, U=Utilities, *=All Fields*

150 Best Jobs for a Secure Future © JIST Works 385

Work Environment: Outdoors; standing; walking and running; using hands; bending or twisting the body; repetitive motions; noise; very hot or cold; bright or inadequate lighting; contaminants; cramped work space; hazardous equipment; minor burns, cuts, bites, or stings.

Urban and Regional Planners

* ❋ Annual Earnings: G $61,920, * $63,040
* ❋ Earnings Growth Potential: Low (35.9%)
* ❋ Growth: G 14.0%, * 19.0%
* ❋ Annual Job Openings: G 790, * 1,470
* ❋ Self-Employed: 0.0%

Detailed Fields with Greatest Employment: Professional, Scientific, and Technical Services (19.9%); Religious, Grantmaking, Civic, Professional, and Similar Organizations (0.4%); Educational Services, Public and Private (0.3%); Management of Companies and Enterprises (0.2%); Utilities (0.2%)

Detailed Fields with Highest Growth (Projected Growth for This Job): Professional, Scientific, and Technical Services (39.7%); Management of Companies and Enterprises (16.7%); Educational Services, Public and Private (16.7%); Religious, Grantmaking, Civic, Professional, and Similar Organizations (14.3%); Utilities (–14.3%)

Other Considerations for Job Outlook: State and local governments are expected to hire urban and regional planners to help manage population growth and commercial development. Private businesses, mainly architecture and engineering firms, will also hire these workers to deal with storm water management, environmental regulation, and other concerns. Job prospects should be best for job seekers with a master's degree.

Develop comprehensive plans and programs for use of land and physical facilities of local jurisdictions such as towns, cities, counties, and metropolitan areas. Design, promote, and administer government plans and policies affecting land use, zoning, public utilities, community facilities, housing, and transportation. Hold public meetings and confer with government, social scientists, lawyers, developers, the public, and special interest groups to formulate and develop land use or community plans. Recommend approval, denial, or conditional approval of proposals. Determine the effects of regulatory limitations on projects. Assess the feasibility of proposals and identify necessary changes. Create, prepare, or requisition graphic and narrative reports on land use data, including land area maps overlaid with geographic variables such as population density. Conduct field investigations, surveys, impact studies, or other research to compile and analyze data on economic, social, regulatory, and physical factors affecting land use. Advise planning officials on project feasibility, cost-effectiveness, regulatory conformance, and possible alternatives.

Education/Training Required: Master's degree. **Education and Training Program:** City/Urban, Community and Regional Planning. **Knowledge/Courses:** Geography; History and Archeology; Transportation; Design; Law and Government; Building and Construction.

Personality Type: Investigative-Enterprising-Artistic. **Career Cluster:** 07 Government and Public Administration. **Career Pathway:** 7.4 Planning. **Other Jobs in This Pathway:** Political Science Teachers, Postsecondary.

Skills: Systems Analysis; Management of Financial Resources; Operations Analysis; Science;

Systems Evaluation; Judgment and Decision Making; Mathematics; Programming.

Work Environment: Indoors; sitting; noise.

Water and Wastewater Treatment Plant and System Operators

- ❋ Annual Earnings: G $40,820, * $40,770
- ❋ Earnings Growth Potential: Medium (39.0%)
- ❋ Growth: G 18.9%, * 19.8%
- ❋ Annual Job Openings: G 2,560, * 4,690
- ❋ Self-Employed: 0.0%

Detailed Fields with Greatest Employment: Waste Management and Remediation Services (2.4%); Utilities (11.0%); Food Manufacturing (1.1%); Professional, Scientific, and Technical Services (1.0%); Chemical Manufacturing (0.4%)

Detailed Fields with Highest Growth (Projected Growth for This Job): Professional, Scientific, and Technical Services (77.5%); Waste Management and Remediation Services (46.1%); Administrative and Support Services (34.2%); Educational Services, Public and Private (25.0%); Utilities (21.1%)

Other Considerations for Job Outlook: Growth in the population, especially in suburban areas, is expected to boost demand for water and wastewater-treatment services. Job opportunities should be excellent.

Operate or control an entire process or system of machines, often through the use of control boards, to transfer or treat water or liquid waste. Add chemicals such as ammonia, chlorine, or lime to disinfect and deodorize water and other liquids. Operate and adjust controls on equipment to purify and clarify water, process or dispose of sewage, and generate power. Inspect equipment or monitor operating conditions, meters, and gauges to determine load requirements and detect malfunctions. Collect and test water and sewage samples, using test equipment and color analysis standards. Record operational data, personnel attendance, or meter and gauge readings on specified forms. Maintain, repair, and lubricate equipment, using hand tools and power tools. Clean and maintain tanks and filter beds, using hand tools and power tools. Direct and coordinate plant workers engaged in routine operations and maintenance activities.

Education/Training Required: Long-term on-the-job training. **Education and Training Program:** Water Quality and Wastewater Treatment Management and Recycling Technology/Technician. **Knowledge/Courses:** Physics; Building and Construction; Mechanical Devices; Biology; Chemistry; Engineering and Technology.

Personality Type: Realistic-Conventional. **Career Cluster:** 01 Agriculture, Food, and Natural Resources. **Career Pathway:** 1.6 Environmental Service Systems. **Other Jobs in This Pathway:** Environmental Engineering Technicians; Hazardous Materials Removal Workers; Occupational Health and Safety Specialists.

Skills: Repairing; Equipment Maintenance; Troubleshooting; Operation and Control; Equipment Selection; Operation Monitoring; Quality Control Analysis; Systems Evaluation.

Work Environment: Outdoors; standing; climbing; walking and running; kneeling, crouching, stooping, or crawling; using hands; bending or twisting the body; repetitive motions; noise; very hot or cold; bright or inadequate lighting;

*C=Computer Systems Design, E=Educational Services, G=Government, H=Health Care, R=Repair and Maintenance, U=Utilities, *=All Fields*

150 Best Jobs for a Secure Future © JIST Works

387

contaminants; cramped work space; exposed to disease or infections; hazardous conditions; hazardous equipment; minor burns, cuts, bites, or stings.

Welders, Cutters, Solderers, and Brazers

- ❋ Annual Earnings: R $34,450, U $61,640, * $35,450
- ❋ Earnings Growth Potential: Low (32.5%)
- ❋ Growth: U –15.8%, R 2.6%, * –1.6%
- ❋ Annual Job Openings: U 70, R 670, * 12,630
- ❋ Self-Employed: 5.6%

Detailed Fields with Greatest Employment: Specialty Trade Contractors (6.5%); Repair and Maintenance (5.2%); Merchant Wholesalers, Durable Goods (4.7%); Heavy and Civil Engineering Construction (3.0%); Fabricated Metal Product Manufacturing (24.8%)

Detailed Fields with Highest Growth (Projected Growth for This Job): Professional, Scientific, and Technical Services (28.6%); Waste Management and Remediation Services (24.7%); Wholesale Electronic Markets and Agents and Brokers (24.5%); Administrative and Support Services (23.2%); Miscellaneous Manufacturing (20.5%)

Other Considerations for Job Outlook: An expected decline in the demand for welders due to automation should be offset somewhat by the need to visually inspect welds and operate welding machinery. Few people are training to enter this field, so good job prospects are expected.

Job Specialization: Solderers and Brazers

Braze or solder together components to assemble fabricated metal parts with soldering iron, torch, or welding machine and flux. Melt and apply solder along adjoining edges of workpieces to solder joints, using soldering irons, gas torches, or ultrasonic equipment. Heat soldering irons or workpieces to specified temperatures for soldering, using gas flames or electrical current. Examine seams for defects, and rework defective joints or broken parts. Melt and separate brazed or soldered joints to remove and straighten damaged or misaligned components, using hand torches, irons, or furnaces. Melt and apply solder to fill holes, indentations, and seams of fabricated metal products, using soldering equipment. Clean workpieces to remove dirt and excess acid, using chemical solutions, files, wire brushes, or grinders. Guide torches and rods along joints of workpieces to heat them to brazing temperature, melt braze alloys, and bond workpieces together. Adjust electrical current and timing cycles of resistance welding machines to heat metals to bonding temperature.

Education/Training Required: Postsecondary vocational training. **Education and Training Program:** Welding Technology/Welder. **Knowledge/Courses:** Production and Processing; Mechanical.

Personality Type: Realistic. **Career Cluster:** 13 Manufacturing. **Career Pathway:** 13.1 Production. **Other Jobs in This Pathway:** Assemblers and Fabricators, All Other; Cabinetmakers and Bench Carpenters; Coating, Painting, and Spraying Machine Setters, Operators, and Tenders; Computer-Controlled Machine Tool Operators, Metal and Plastic; Cost Estimators; Cutting, Punching, and Press Machine Setters, Operators, and Tenders, Metal and Plastic; First-Line Supervisors of Mechanics, Installers, and Repairers; First-Line Supervisors of Production and Operating Workers; Geothermal Technicians; Grinding, Lapping, Polishing, and Buffing Machine Tool Setters, Operators, and Tenders, Metal and Plastic;

Helpers—Production Workers; Machine Feeders and Offbearers; Machinists; Mixing and Blending Machine Setters, Operators, and Tenders; Molding, Coremaking, and Casting Machine Setters, Operators, and Tenders, Metal and Plastic; Packaging and Filling Machine Operators and Tenders; Packers and Packagers, Hand; Paper Goods Machine Setters, Operators, and Tenders; Production Workers, All Other; Recycling and Reclamation Workers; Recycling Coordinators; Sheet Metal Workers; Structural Metal Fabricators and Fitters; Team Assemblers; Welders, Cutters, and Welder Fitters; others.

Skills: Equipment Maintenance; Repairing; Equipment Selection; Troubleshooting; Quality Control Analysis; Operation Monitoring.

Work Environment: Indoors; more often sitting than standing; using hands; repetitive motions; noise; contaminants; minor burns, cuts, bites, or stings.

Job Specialization: Welders, Cutters, and Welder Fitters

Use hand-welding or flame-cutting equipment to weld or join metal components or to fill holes, indentations, or seams of fabricated metal products. Operate safety equipment and use safe work habits. Weld components in flat, vertical, or overhead positions. Ignite torches or start power supplies and strike arcs by touching electrodes to metals being welded, completing electrical circuits. Clamp, hold, tack-weld, heat-bend, grind, or bolt component parts to obtain required configurations and positions for welding. Detect faulty operation of equipment or defective materials and notify supervisors. Operate manual or semi-automatic welding equipment to fuse metal segments, using processes such as gas tungsten arc, gas metal arc, flux-cored arc, plasma arc, shielded metal arc, resistance welding, and submerged arc welding. Monitor the fitting, burning, and welding processes to avoid overheating of parts or warping, shrinking, distortion, or expansion of material. Examine workpieces for defects and measure workpieces with straightedges or templates to ensure conformance with specifications.

Education/Training Required: Postsecondary vocational training. **Education and Training Program:** Welding Technology/Welder. **Knowledge/Courses:** Building and Construction; Mechanical Devices; Design; Engineering and Technology.

Personality Type: Realistic-Conventional. **Career Cluster:** 13 Manufacturing. **Career Pathway:** 13.1 Production. **Other Jobs in This Pathway:** Assemblers and Fabricators, All Other; Cabinetmakers and Bench Carpenters; Coating, Painting, and Spraying Machine Setters, Operators, and Tenders; Computer-Controlled Machine Tool Operators, Metal and Plastic; Cost Estimators; Cutting, Punching, and Press Machine Setters, Operators, and Tenders, Metal and Plastic; First-Line Supervisors of Mechanics, Installers, and Repairers; First-Line Supervisors of Production and Operating Workers; Geothermal Technicians; Grinding, Lapping, Polishing, and Buffing Machine Tool Setters, Operators, and Tenders, Metal and Plastic; Helpers—Production Workers; Machine Feeders and Offbearers; Machinists; Mixing and Blending Machine Setters, Operators, and Tenders; Molding, Coremaking, and Casting Machine Setters, Operators, and Tenders, Metal and Plastic; Packaging and Filling Machine Operators and Tenders; Packers and Packagers, Hand; Paper Goods Machine Setters, Operators, and Tenders; Production Workers, All Other; Recycling and Reclamation Workers; Recycling Coordinators; Sheet Metal Workers; Solderers and Brazers; Structural Metal Fabricators and Fitters; Team Assemblers; others.

M

---

*C=Computer Systems Design, E=Educational Services, G=Government, H=Health Care, R=Repair and Maintenance, U=Utilities, *=All Fields*

Skills: Repairing; Operation and Control; Troubleshooting; Equipment Maintenance; Equipment Selection; Operation Monitoring; Quality Control Analysis; Installation.

Work Environment: Standing; using hands; bending or twisting the body; repetitive motions; noise; very hot or cold; bright or inadequate lighting; contaminants; hazardous equipment; minor burns, cuts, bites, or stings.

Writers and Authors

- ❊ Annual Earnings: G $70,020, * $55,420
- ❊ Earnings Growth Potential: High (48.4%)
- ❊ Growth: G 9.3%, * 14.8%
- ❊ Annual Job Openings: G 1,700, * 5,420
- ❊ Self-Employed: 69.4%

Detailed Fields with Greatest Employment: Broadcasting (Except Internet) (6.9%); Performing Arts, Spectator Sports, and Related Industries (5.8%); Motion Picture, Video, and Sound Recording Industries (5.3%); Educational Services, Public and Private (5.1%); Professional, Scientific, and Technical Services (23.7%)

Detailed Fields with Highest Growth (Projected Growth for This Job): Internet Service Providers, Web Search Portals, and Data Processing Services (52.9%); Performing Arts, Spectator Sports, and Related Industries (36.5%); Ambulatory Health Care Services (33.3%); Other Information Services (32.6%); Wholesale Electronic Markets and Agents and Brokers (30.0%)

Other Considerations for Job Outlook: Projected job growth for these workers stems from increased use of online media and growing demand for Web-based information. But print publishing is expected to continue weakening. Job competition should be keen.

Job Specialization: Copy Writers

Write advertising copy for use by publication or broadcast media to promote sale of goods and services. Write advertising copy for use by publication, broadcast, or Internet media to promote the sale of goods and services. Present drafts and ideas to clients. Discuss the product, advertising themes and methods, and any changes that should be made in advertising copy with the client. Consult with sales, media, and marketing representatives to obtain information on product or service and discuss style and length of advertising copy. Vary language and tone of messages based on product and medium. Edit or rewrite existing copy as necessary and submit copy for approval by supervisor. Write to customers in their terms and on their level so that the advertiser's sales message is more readily received. Write articles; bulletins; sales letters; speeches; and other related informative, marketing, and promotional material. Invent names for products and write the slogans that appear on packaging, brochures, and other promotional material.

Education/Training Required: Bachelor's degree. **Education and Training Programs:** Broadcast Journalism; Business/Corporate Communications; Communication, Journalism, and Related Programs, Other; Family and Consumer Sciences/Human Sciences Communication; Journalism; Mass Communication/Media Studies; Playwriting and Screenwriting; Speech Communication and Rhetoric. **Knowledge/Courses:**

Sales and Marketing; Communications and Media; English Language; Clerical Practices; Computers and Electronics; Administration and Management.

Personality Type: Enterprising-Artistic. **Career Cluster:** 03 Arts, Audio/Video Technology, and Communications. **Career Pathway:** 3.5 Journalism and Broadcasting. **Other Jobs in This Pathway:** Audio and Video Equipment Technicians; Broadcast News Analysts; Broadcast Technicians; Camera Operators, Television, Video, and Motion Picture; Directors—Stage, Motion Pictures, Television, and Radio; Editors; Film and Video Editors; Media and Communication Workers, All Other; Photographers; Producers; Program Directors; Public Address System and Other Announcers; Public Relations Specialists; Radio and Television Announcers; Reporters and Correspondents; Sound Engineering Technicians; Talent Directors; Technical Directors/Managers; Technical Writers.

Skills: Writing; Persuasion; Reading Comprehension; Negotiation; Operations Analysis; Active Listening; Management of Personnel Resources; Speaking.

Work Environment: Indoors; sitting.

Job Specialization: Poets, Lyricists, and Creative Writers

Create original written works, such as scripts, essays, prose, poetry, or song lyrics, for publication or performance. Revise written material to meet personal standards and to satisfy needs of clients, publishers, directors, or producers. Choose subject matter and suitable form to express personal feelings and experiences or ideas or to narrate stories or events. Plan project arrangements or outlines and organize material accordingly.

Prepare works in appropriate format for publication and send them to publishers or producers. Follow appropriate procedures to get copyrights for completed work. Write fiction or nonfiction prose such as short stories, novels, biographies, articles, descriptive or critical analyses, and essays. Develop factors such as themes, plots, characterizations, psychological analyses, historical environments, action, and dialogue to create material. Confer with clients, editors, publishers, or producers to discuss changes or revisions to written material.

Education/Training Required: Bachelor's degree. **Education and Training Programs:** Broadcast Journalism; Business/Corporate Communications; Communication, Journalism, and Related Programs, Other; Family and Consumer Sciences/Human Sciences Communication; Journalism; Mass Communication/Media Studies; Playwriting and Screenwriting; Speech Communication and Rhetoric. **Knowledge/Courses:** Fine Arts; Communications and Media; Philosophy and Theology; Sociology and Anthropology; Sales and Marketing; History and Archeology.

Personality Type: Artistic-Investigative. **Career Cluster:** 03 Arts, Audio/Video Technology, and Communications. **Career Pathway:** 3.4 Performing Arts. **Other Jobs in This Pathway:** Actors; Artists and Related Workers, All Other; Choreographers; Craft Artists; Dancers; Designers, All Other; Directors—Stage, Motion Pictures, Television, and Radio; Entertainers and Performers, Sports and Related Workers, All Other; Managers, All Other; Music Composers and Arrangers; Music Directors; Musicians, Instrumental; Producers; Program Directors; Set and Exhibit Designers; Singers; Talent Directors; Technical Directors/Managers.

M

C=Computer Systems Design, E=Educational Services, G=Government, H=Health Care, R=Repair and Maintenance, U=Utilities, *=All Fields

150 Best Jobs for a Secure Future © JIST Works   391

Skills: Writing; Reading Comprehension; Active Learning; Management of Financial Resources; Persuasion; Active Listening; Social Perceptiveness; Negotiation.

Work Environment: Indoors; sitting; using hands; repetitive motions.

APPENDIX

Definitions of Skills and Knowledge/Courses Referenced in This Book

Definitions of Skills	
Skill Name	Definition
Active Learning	Working with new material or information to grasp its implications.
Active Listening	Listening to what other people are saying and asking questions as appropriate.
Complex Problem Solving	Identifying complex problems, reviewing the options, and implementing solutions.
Coordination	Adjusting actions in relation to others' actions.
Critical Thinking	Using logic and analysis to identify the strengths and weaknesses of different approaches.
Equipment Maintenance	Performing routine maintenance and determining when and what kinds of maintenance are needed.
Equipment Selection	Determining the kinds of tools and equipment needed to do a job.
Installation	Installing equipment, machines, wiring, or programs to meet specifications.
Instructing	Teaching others how to do something.
Judgment and Decision Making	Weighing the relative costs and benefits of a potential action.

(continued)

(continued)

Definitions of Skills

Skill Name	Definition
Learning Strategies	Using multiple approaches when learning or teaching new things.
Management of Financial Resources	Determining how money will be spent to get the work done and accounting for these expenditures.
Management of Material Resources	Obtaining and seeing to the appropriate use of equipment, facilities, and materials needed to do certain work.
Management of Personnel Resources	Motivating, developing, and directing people as they work; identifying the best people for the job.
Mathematics	Using mathematics to solve problems.
Monitoring	Assessing how well one is doing when learning or doing something.
Negotiation	Bringing others together and trying to reconcile differences.
Operation and Control	Controlling operations of equipment or systems.
Operation Monitoring	Watching gauges, dials, or other indicators to make sure a machine is working properly.
Operations Analysis	Analyzing needs and product requirements to create a design.
Persuasion	Persuading others to approach things differently.
Programming	Writing computer programs for various purposes.
Quality Control Analysis	Evaluating the quality or performance of products, services, or processes.
Reading Comprehension	Understanding written sentences and paragraphs in work-related documents.
Repairing	Repairing machines or systems, using the needed tools.
Science	Using scientific methods to solve problems.
Service Orientation	Actively looking for ways to help people.
Social Perceptiveness	Being aware of others' reactions and understanding why they react the way they do.
Speaking	Talking to others to effectively convey information.
Systems Analysis	Determining how a system should work and how changes will affect outcomes.

Definitions of Skills

Skill Name	Definition
Systems Evaluation	Looking at many indicators of system performance and taking into account their accuracy.
Technology Design	Generating or adapting equipment and technology to serve user needs.
Time Management	Managing one's own time and the time of others.
Troubleshooting	Determining what is causing an operating error and deciding what to do about it.
Writing	Communicating effectively with others in writing as indicated by the needs of the audience.

Definitions of Knowledge/Courses

Knowledge/Course Name	Definition
Administration and Management	Knowledge of principles and processes involved in business and organizational planning, coordination, and execution. This includes strategic planning, resource allocation, manpower modeling, leadership techniques, and production methods.
Biology	Knowledge of plant and animal living tissue, cells, organisms, and entities, including their functions, interdependencies, and interactions with each other and the environment.
Building and Construction	Knowledge of materials, methods, and the appropriate tools to construct objects, structures, and buildings.
Chemistry	Knowledge of the composition, structure, and properties of substances and of the chemical processes and transformations that they undergo. This includes uses of chemicals and their interactions, danger signs, production techniques, and disposal methods.
Clerical Practices	Knowledge of administrative and clerical procedures and systems such as word-processing systems, filing and records management systems, stenography and transcription, forms, design principles, and other office procedures and terminology.

(continued)

(continued)

Definitions of Knowledge/Courses

Knowledge/Course Name	Definition
Communications and Media	Knowledge of media production, communication, and dissemination techniques and methods, including alternative ways to inform and entertain via written, oral, and visual media.
Computers and Electronics	Knowledge of electric circuit boards, processors, chips, and computer hardware and software, including applications and programming.
Customer and Personal Service	Knowledge of principles and processes for providing customer and personal services, including needs assessment techniques, quality service standards, alternative delivery systems, and customer satisfaction evaluation techniques.
Design	Knowledge of design techniques, principles, tools, and instruments involved in the production and use of precision technical plans, blueprints, drawings, and models.
Economics and Accounting	Knowledge of economic and accounting principles and practices, the financial markets, banking, and the analysis and reporting of financial data.
Education and Training	Knowledge of instructional methods and training techniques, including curriculum design principles, learning theory, group and individual teaching techniques, design of individual development plans, and test design principles.
Engineering and Technology	Knowledge of equipment, tools, and mechanical devices and their uses to produce motion, light, power, technology, and other applications.
English Language	Knowledge of the structure and content of the English language, including the meaning and spelling of words, rules of composition, and grammar.
Fine Arts	Knowledge of theory and techniques required to produce, compose, and perform works of music, dance, visual arts, drama, and sculpture.
Food Production	Knowledge of techniques and equipment for planting, growing, and harvesting of food for consumption, including crop rotation methods, animal husbandry, and food storage/handling techniques.

Definitions of Knowledge/Courses

Knowledge/Course Name	Definition
Foreign Language	Knowledge of the structure and content of a foreign (non-English) language, including the meaning and spelling of words, rules of composition and grammar, and pronunciation.
Geography	Knowledge of various methods for describing the location and distribution of land, sea, and air masses, including their physical locations, relationships, and characteristics.
History and Archeology	Knowledge of past historical events and their causes, indicators, and impact on particular civilizations and cultures.
Law and Government	Knowledge of laws, legal codes, court procedures, precedents, government regulations, executive orders, agency rules, and the democratic political process.
Mathematics	Knowledge of numbers and their operations and interrelationships, including arithmetic, algebra, geometry, calculus, and statistics and their applications.
Mechanical Devices	Knowledge of machines and tools, including their designs, uses, benefits, repair, and maintenance.
Medicine and Dentistry	Knowledge of the information and techniques needed to diagnose and treat injuries, diseases, and deformities. This includes symptoms, treatment alternatives, drug properties and interactions, and preventive health-care measures.
Personnel and Human Resources	Knowledge of policies and practices involved in personnel/human resource functions. This includes recruitment, selection, training, and promotion regulations and procedures; compensation and benefits packages; labor relations and negotiation strategies; and personnel information systems.
Philosophy and Theology	Knowledge of different philosophical systems and religions, including their basic principles, values, ethics, ways of thinking, customs, and practices and their impact on human culture.
Physics	Knowledge and prediction of physical principles, laws, and applications, including air, water, material dynamics, light, atomic principles, heat, electric theory, earth formations, and meteorological and related natural phenomena.

(continued)

(continued)

Definitions of Knowledge/Courses

Knowledge/Course Name	Definition
Production and Processing	Knowledge of inputs, outputs, raw materials, waste, quality control, costs, and techniques for maximizing the manufacture and distribution of goods.
Psychology	Knowledge of human behavior and performance, mental processes, psychological research methods, and the assessment and treatment of behavioral and affective disorders.
Public Safety and Security	Knowledge of weaponry; public safety; security operations, rules, regulations, precautions, and prevention; and the protection of people, data, and property.
Sales and Marketing	Knowledge of principles and methods involved in showing, promoting, and selling products or services. This includes marketing strategies and tactics, product demonstration and sales techniques, and sales control systems.
Sociology and Anthropology	Knowledge of group behavior and dynamics; societal trends and influences; and cultures and their history, migrations, ethnicity, and origins.
Telecommunications	Knowledge of transmission, broadcasting, switching, control, and operation of telecommunications systems.
Therapy and Counseling	Knowledge of information and techniques needed to rehabilitate physical and mental ailments and to provide career guidance, including alternative treatments, rehabilitation equipment and its proper use, and methods to evaluate treatment effects.
Transportation	Knowledge of principles and methods for moving people or goods by air, rail, sea, or road, including their relative costs, advantages, and limitations.

Index

F

G

K–L